CURRENT LAW STATUTES ANNOTATED
1986

VOLUME ONE

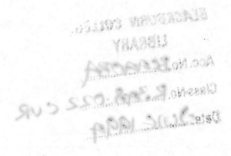

AUSTRALIA AND NEW ZEALAND
The Law Book Company Ltd.
Sydney : Melbourne : Perth

CANADA AND U.S.A.
The Carswell Company Ltd.
Agincourt, Ontario

INDIA
N. M. Tripathi Private Ltd.
Bombay
and
Eastern Law House Private Ltd.
Calcutta and Delhi

M.P.P. House
Bangalore

ISRAEL
Steimatzky's Agency Ltd.
Jerusalem : Tel Aviv : Haifa

MALAYSIA : SINGAPORE : BRUNEI
Malayan Law Journal (Pte.) Ltd.
Singapore and Kuala Lumpur

PAKISTAN
Pakistan Law House
Karachi

CURRENT LAW
STATUTES
ANNOTATED
1986

VOLUME ONE

EDITOR IN CHIEF

PETER ALLSOP, C.B.E., M.A.
Barrister

GENERAL EDITOR

KEVAN NORRIS, LL.B.
Solicitor

ASSISTANT GENERAL EDITOR

JULIE HARRIS, LL.B.

ADMINISTRATION

GILLIAN BRONZE, LL.B.

LONDON

SWEET & MAXWELL   STEVENS & SONS

EDINBURGH

W. GREEN & SON

1987

Published by
SWEET & MAXWELL LIMITED
and STEVENS & SONS LIMITED
of 11 New Fetter Lane, London,
and W. GREEN & SON LIMITED
of St. Giles Street, Edinburgh,
and printed in Scotland.

ISBN This Volume only : 421 38020 9
As a set   : 421 38060 8

CONTENTS

CHRONOLOGICAL TABLE

VOLUME ONE

STATUTES

c.1. Education (Amendment) Act 1986
  2. Australia Act 1986
  3. Atomic Energy Authority Act 1986
  4. Consolidated Fund Act 1986
  5. Agricultural Holdings Act 1986
  6. Prevention of Oil Pollution Act 1986
  7. Marriage (Wales) Act 1986
  8. Museum of London Act 1986
  9. Law Reform (Parent and Child) (Scotland) Act 1986
  10. Local Government Act 1986
  11. Gaming (Amendment) Act 1986
  12. Statute Law (Repeals) Act 1986
  13. Highways (Amendment) Act 1986
  14. Animals (Scientific Procedures) Act 1986
  15. Industrial Training Act 1986
  16. Marriage (Prohibited Degrees of Relationship) Act 1986
  17. Drainage Rates (Disabled Persons) Act 1986
  18. Corneal Tissue Act 1986
  19. British Shipbuilders (Borrowing Powers) Act 1986
  20. Horticultural Produce Act 1986
  21. Armed Forces Act 1986
  22. Civil Protection in Peacetime Act 1986
  23. Safety at Sea Act 1986
  24. Health Service Joint Consultative Committees (Access to Information) Act 1986
  25. Commonwealth Development Corporation Act 1986
  26. Land Registration Act 1986
  27. Road Traffic Regulation (Parking) Act 1986

INDEX OF SHORT TITLES

VOLUME ONE

References are to chapter numbers of 1986

EDUCATION (AMENDMENT) ACT 1986

(1986 c.1)

An Act to increase the limit in section 2(1) of the Education (Grants and Awards) Act 1984 on expenditure approved for education support grants purposes, and to exclude remuneration for midday supervision from the Remuneration of Teachers Act 1965.

[17th February 1986]

PARLIAMENTARY DEBATES
Hansard: H.C. Vol. 87, col. 276; Vol. 88, col. 459; Vol. 89, col. 107; H.L. Vol. 469, cols. 662, 965; Vol. 470, cols. 176, 544.

Increase of limit on expenditure approved for education support grant purposes

1. In section 2(1) of the Education (Grants and Awards) Act 1984 (which provides that the aggregate amount of the expenditure of local education authorities in England and Wales approved for any financial year for education support grant purposes shall not exceed 0·5 per cent. of the amount determined for that year in accordance with section 2 of that Act), for "0·5 per cent." there shall be substituted "1 per cent.".

Exclusion of certain remuneration from Remuneration of Teachers Act 1965

2. In section 8 (interpretation) of the Remuneration of Teachers Act 1965, after subsection (2) there shall be inserted—

"(2A) In this Act 'remuneration' does not include remuneration paid to teachers by local education authorities under contracts relating exclusively to the provision of midday supervision of pupils in schools.".

Short title and extent

3.—(1) This Act may be cited as the Education (Amendment) Act 1986.

(2) This Act extends to England and Wales only.

AUSTRALIA ACT 1986

(1986 c.2)

An Act to give effect to a request by the Parliament and Government of the Commonwealth of Australia.

[17th February 1986]

PARLIAMENTARY DEBATES
Hansard: H.L. Vol. 469, cols. 662, 1166; Vol. 470, cols. 346, 544; H.C. Vol. 91, cols. 81, 734.

Termination of power of Parliament of United Kingdom to legislate for Australia

1. No Act of the Parliament of the United Kingdom passed after the commencement of this Act shall extend, or be deemed to extend, to the Commonwealth, to a State or to a Territory as part of the law of the Commonwealth, of the State or of the Territory.

Legislative powers of Parliaments of States

2.—(1) It is hereby declared and enacted that the legislative powers of the Parliament of each State include full power to make laws for the peace, order and good government of that State that have extra-territorial operation.

(2) It is hereby further declared and enacted that the legislative powers of the Parliament of each State include all legislative powers that the Parliament of the United Kingdom might have exercised before the commencement of this Act for the peace, order and good government of that State but nothing in this subsection confers on a State any capacity that the State did not have immediately before the commencement of this Act to engage in relations with countries outside Australia.

Termination of restrictions on legislative powers of Parliaments of States

3.—(1) The Colonial Laws Validity Act 1865 shall not apply to any law made after the commencement of this Act by the Parliament of a State.

(2) No law and no provision of any law made after the commencement of this Act by the Parliament of a State shall be void or inoperative on the

ground that it is repugnant to the law of England, or to the provisions of any existing or future Act of the Parliament of the United Kingdom, or to any order, rule or regulation made under any such Act, and the powers of the Parliament of a State shall include the power to repeal or amend any such Act, order, rule or regulation in so far as it is part of the law of the State.

Powers of State Parliaments in relation to merchant shipping

4. Sections 735 and 736 of the Merchant Shipping Act 1894, in so far as they are part of the law of a State, are hereby repealed.

Commonwealth Constitution, Constitution Act and Statute of Westminster not affected

5. Sections 2 and 3(2) above—
   (*a*) are subject to the Commonwealth of Australia Constitution Act and to the Constitution of the Commonwealth; and
   (*b*) do not operate so as to give any force or effect to a provision of an Act of the Parliament of a State that would repeal, amend or be repugnant to this Act, the Commonwealth of Australia Constitution Act, the Constitution of the Commonwealth or the Statute of Westminster 1931 as amended and in force from time to time.

Manner and form of making certain State laws

6. Notwithstanding sections 2 and 3(2) above, a law made after the commencement of this Act by the Parliament of a State respecting the constitution, powers or procedure of the Parliament of the State shall be of no force or effect unless it is made in such manner and form as may from time to time be required by a law made by that Parliament, whether made before or after the commencement of this Act.

Powers and functions of Her Majesty and Governors in respect of States

7.—(1) Her Majesty's representative in each State shall be the Governor.
   (2) Subject to subsections (3) and (4) below, all powers and functions of Her Majesty in respect of a State are exercisable only by the Governor of the State.
   (3) Subsection (2) above does not apply in relation to the power to appoint, and the power to terminate the appointment of, the Governor of a State.
   (4) While Her Majesty is personally present in a State, Her Majesty is not precluded from exercising any of Her powers and functions in respect of the State that are the subject of subsection (2) above.
   (5) The advice to Her Majesty in relation to the exercise of the powers and functions of Her Majesty in respect of a State shall be tendered by the Premier of the State.

State laws not subject to disallowance or suspension of operation

8. An act of the Parliament of a State that has been assented to by the Governor of the State shall not, after the commencement of this Act, be subject to disallowance by Her Majesty, nor shall its operation be suspended pending the signification of Her Majesty's pleasure thereon.

State laws not subject to withholding of assent or reservation

9.—(1) No law or instrument shall be of any force or effect in so far as it purports to require the Governor of a State to withhold assent from any Bill for an Act of the State that has been passed in such manner and form as may from time to time be required by a law made by the Parliament of the State.

(2) No law or instrument shall be of any force or effect in so far as it purports to require the reservation of any Bill for an Act of a State for the signification of Her Majesty's pleasure thereon.

Termination of responsibility of United Kingdom Government in relation to State matters

10. After the commencement of this Act Her Majesty's Government in the United Kingdom shall have no responsibility for the government of any State.

Termination of appeals to Her Majesty in Council

11.—(1) Subject to subsection (4) below, no appeal to Her Majesty in Council lies or shall be brought, whether by leave or special leave of any court or of Her Majesty in Council or otherwise, and whether by virtue of any Act of the Parliament of the United Kingdom, the Royal Prerogative or otherwise, from or in respect of any decision of an Australian court.

(2) Subject to subsection (4) below—
  (*a*) the enactments specified in subsection (3) below and any orders, rules, regulations or other instruments made under, or for the purposes of, those enactments; and
  (*b*) any other provisions of Acts of the Parliament of the United Kingdom in force immediately before the commencement of this Act that make provision for or in relation to appeals to Her Majesty in Council from or in respect of decisions of courts, and any orders, rules, regulations or other instruments made under, or for the purposes of, any such provisions,
in so far as they are part of the law of the Commonwealth, of a State or of a Territory, are hereby repealed.

(3) The enactments referred to in subsection (2)(*a*) above are the following Acts of the Parliament of the United Kingdom or provisions of such Acts:
  The Australian Courts Act 1828, section 15
  The Judicial Committee Act 1833
  The Judicial Committee Act 1844
  The Australian Constitutions Act 1850, section 28
  The Colonial Courts of Admiralty Act 1890, section 6.

(4) Nothing in the foregoing provisions of this section—
  (*a*) affects an appeal instituted before the commencement of this Act to Her Majesty in Council from or in respect of a decision of an Australian court; or
  (*b*) precludes the institution after that commencement of an appeal to Her Majesty in Council from or in respect of such a decision where the appeal is instituted—
    (i) pursuant to leave granted by an Australian court on an application made before that commencement; or
    (ii) pursuant to special leave granted by Her Majesty in Council on a petition presented before that commencement,
but this subsection shall not be construed as permitting or enabling an appeal to Her Majesty in Council to be instituted or continued that could not have been instituted or continued if this section had not been enacted.

Amendment of Statute of Westminster

12. Sections 4, 9(2) and (3) and 10(2) of the Statute of Westminster 1931, in so far as they are part of the law of the Commonwealth, of a State or of a Territory, are hereby repealed.

Amendment of Constitution Act of Queensland

13.—(1) The Constitution Act 1867–1978 of the State of Queensland is in this section referred to as the Principal Act.

(2) Section 11A of the Principle Act is amended in subsection (3)—

(*a*) by omitting from paragraph (a)—
    (i) "and Signet"; and
    (ii) "constitued under Letters Patent under the Great Seal of the United Kingdom"; and

(*b*) by omitting from paragraph (b)—
    (i) "and Signet"; and
    (ii) "whenever and so long as the office of Governor is vacant or the Governor is incapable of discharging the duties of administration or has departed from Queensland".

(3) Section 11B of the Principal Act is amended—

(*a*) by omitting "Governor to conform to instructions" and substituting "Definition of Royal Sign Manual";

(*b*) by omitting subsection (1); and

(*c*) by omitting from subsection (2)—
    (i) "(2)";
    (ii) "this section and in"; and
    (iii) "and the expression 'Signet' means the seal commonly used for the sign manual of the Sovereign or the seal with which documents are sealed by the Secretary of State in the United Kingdom on behalf of the Sovereign".

(4) Section 14 of the Principle Act is amended in subsection (2) by omitting ", subject to his performing his duty prescribed by section 11B,".

Amendment of Constitution Act of Western Australia

14.—(1) The Constitution Act 1889 of the State of Western Australia is in this section referred to as the Principle Act.

(2) Section 50 of the Principle Act is amended in subsection (3)—

(*a*) by omitting from paragraph (a)—
    (i) "and Signet"; and
    (ii) "constituted under Letters Patent under the Great Seal of the United Kingdom";

(*b*) by omitting from paragraph (b)—
    (i) "and Signet"; and
    (ii) "whenever and so long as the office of Governor is vacant or the Governor is incapable of discharging the duties of administration or has departed from Western Australia"; and

(*c*) by omitting from paragraph (c)—
    (i) "under the Great Seal of the United Kingdom"; and
    (ii) "during a temporary absence of the Governor for a short period from the seat of Government or from the State."

(3) Section 51 of the Principle Act is amended—

(*a*) by omitting subsection (1); and

(*b*) by omitting from subsection (2)—
    (i) "(2)";
    (ii) "this section and in"; and

(iii) "and the expression 'Signet' means the seal commonly used for the sign manual of the Sovereign or the seal with which documents are sealed by the Secretary of State in the United Kingdom on behalf of the Sovereign".

Method of repeal or amendment of this Act or Statute of Westminster

15.—(1) This Act or the Statute of Westminster 1931, as amended and in force from time to time, in so far as it is part of the law of the Commonwealth, of a State or of a Territory, may be repealed or amended by an Act of the Parliament of the Commonwealth passed at the request or with the concurrence of the Parliaments of all the States and, subject to subsection (3) below, only in that manner.

(2) For the purposes of subsection (1) above, an Act of the Parliament of the Commonwealth that is repugnant to this Act or the Statute of Westminster 1931, as amended and in force from time to time, or to any provision of this Act or of that Statute as so amended and in force, shall, to the extent of the repugnancy, be deemed an Act to repeal or amend the Act, Statute or provision to which it is repugnant.

(3) Nothing in subsection (1) above limits or prevents the exercise by the Parliament of the Commonwealth of any powers that may be conferred upon that Parliament by any alteration to the Constitution of the Commonwealth made in accordance with section 128 of the Constitution of the Commonwealth after the commencement of this Act.

Interpretation

16.—(1) In this Act—

"appeal" includes a petition of appeal, and a complaint in the nature of an appeal;

"appeal to Her Majesty in Council" includes any appeal to Her Majesty;

"Australian court" means a court of a State or any other court of Australia or of a Territory other than the High Court of Australia;

"the Commonwealth" means the Commonwealth of Australia as established under the Commonwealth of Australia Constitution Act;

"the Constitution of the Commonwealth" means the Constitution of the Commonwealth set forth in section 9 of the Commonwealth of Australia Constitution Act, being that Constitution as altered and in force from time to time;

"court" includes a judge, judicial officer or other person acting judicially;

"decision" includes determination, judgment, decree, order or sentence;

"Governor", in relation to a State, includes any person for the time being administering the government of the State;

"State" means a State of the Commonwealth and includes a new State;

"Territory" means a territory referred to in section 122 of the Constitution of the Commonwealth.

(2) The expression "a law made by that Parliament" in section 6 above and the expression "a law made by the Parliament" in section 9 above include, in relation to the State of Western Australia, the Constitution Act 1889 of that State.

(3) A reference in this Act to the Parliament of a State includes, in relation to the State of New South Wales, a reference to the legislature of

that State as constituted from time to time in accordance with the Constitution Act, 1902, or any other Act of that State, whether or not, in relation to any particular legislative act, the consent of the Legislative Council of that State is necessary.

Citation and commencement

17.—(1) This Act may be cited as the Australia Act 1986.

(2) This Act shall come into force on such day and at such time as the Secretary of State may by order made by statutory instrument appoint.

ATOMIC ENERGY AUTHORITY ACT 1986

(1986 c.3)

An Act to put the finances of the United Kingdom Atomic Energy Authority on a trading fund basis; and for connected purposes.

[19th February 1986]

PARLIAMENTARY DEBATES
  Hansard: H.L. Vol. 468, cols. 21, 526; Vol. 469, cols. 119, 900; Vol. 471, col. 508; H.C. Vol. 90, col. 215; Vol. 91, col. 884.
  The Bill was considered by Standing Committee J on January 28 and 30, 1986.

The Authority's finances

Commencing capital debt

1.—(1) The United Kingdom Atomic Energy Authority shall, in respect of their net assets on 1st April 1986, assume a debt due to the Secretary of State (their "commencing capital debt") of such amount as the Secretary of State, after consulting the Authority, may with the approval of the Treasury specify by notice in writing.

(2) The commencing capital debt of the Authority shall be deemed to have been assumed by them on 1st April 1986 and a sum equal to the amount of that debt shall be deemed to have been issued to the Secretary of State out of the National Loans Fund on that date.

Borrowing powers

2.—(1) The Authority may borrow such sums as may be required for meeting the obligations and discharging the functions of the Authority or their subsidiaries—

(*a*) in sterling from the Secretary of State, or

(*b*) with the consent of the Secretary of State, or in accordance with a general authority given by him, in any currency from a person other than the Secretary of State.

(2) The Authority may borrow money from a wholly owned subsidiary of theirs without any consent or authority.

(3) The Authority shall exercise control over their subsidiaries so as to secure that no subsidiary borrows from a person other than the Authority

or another subsidiary except with the consent of the Secretary of State or in accordance with a general authority given by him.

(4) The Secretary of State may give general authority for—

(*a*) temporary borrowing, by way of overdraft or otherwise, and

(*b*) borrowing by subsidiaries of the Authority.

(5) The Secretary of State shall not give his consent or authority under this section except with the approval of the Treasury.

(6) The Authority may not borrow money except in accordance with this section; but a person lending to the Authority is not prejudiced by a failure to comply with the requirements of this Act as to borrowing by the Authority.

Limit on borrowing

3.—(1) The aggregate amount outstanding by way of principal in respect of—

(*a*) money borrowed by the Authority or a wholly owned subsidiary of theirs,

(*b*) money borrowed for the repayment of which the Authority or a wholly owned subsidiary of theirs is a guarantor or surety,

(*c*) the Authority's commencing capital debt, and

(*d*) sums issued by the Treasury in fulfilment of guarantees under section 5 (guarantees of borrowing by Authority or their subsidiaries),

shall not exceed £150 million or such greater sum, not exceeding £200 million, as the Secretary of State may specify by order.

(2) Borrowing between the Authority and a wholly owned subsidiary of theirs, or between two such subsidiaries, shall not be taken into account for the purposes of subsection (1).

(3) If a body corporate ceases to be a wholly owned subsidiary of the Authority, the Secretary of State may, having regard to the extent to which the amounts taken into account for the purposes of subsection (1) were attributable to—

(*a*) money borrowed by that body corporate, and

(*b*) money borrowed for the repayment of which that body corporate is a guarantor or surety,

by order provide that subsection (1) shall have effect with the substitution for the amounts specified in that subsection, or in an order in force under that subsection, of such lower amounts as he considers appropriate.

(4) Where the Authority or a wholly owned subsidiary of theirs enter into a transaction which involves credit or other financial services being made available to them, the Secretary of State may by order provide—

(*a*) that they shall be treated for the purposes of subsection (1) as having borrowed such amount as may be specified in the order, and

(*b*) for determining how much of that amount is to be treated for the purposes of that subsection as outstanding at any time.

(5) The Secretary of State may, when he consents to borrowing in a currency other than sterling, or later, give directions as to the method of calculation, and the date to be taken, in determining for the purposes of subsection (1) the value in sterling of the amount outstanding.

(6) The Secretary of State shall not make an order under subsection (1) or give directions under subsection (5) except with the approval of the Treasury; and before giving directions under subsection (5) he shall consult the Authority.

(7) Orders under this section shall be made by statutory instrument, and—

(*a*) an order shall not be made under subsection (1) unless a draft of it has been approved by a resolution of the House of Commons, and

(*b*) an order under subsection (3) or (4) shall be subject to annulment in pursuance of a resolution of that House.

Loans from the Secretary of State

4.—(1) The Secretary of State may lend to the Authority any sums which they have power to borrow from him.

(2) The Authority's commencing capital debt and any loans made to the Authority under this section shall be repaid to the Secretary of State—

(*a*) at such times and in such manner as he may direct, and

(*b*) with interest at such rates, and payable at such times, as he may direct.

(3) The Secretary of State shall not make such a loan or give such a direction except with the approval of the Treasury; and before giving a direction altering the terms for repayment, or for the payment of interest, he shall consult the Authority.

(4) The Treasury shall issue out of the National Loans Fund to the Secretary of State such sums as are necessary to enable him to make loans under this section.

(5) Sums received by the Secretary of State in respect of the Authority's commencing capital debt or a loan under this section shall be paid into the National Loans Fund.

(6) The Secretary of State shall—

(*a*) prepare in respect of each financial year an account, in such form and manner as the Treasury may direct, of sums issued to him for loans under this section, and of sums received by him under this section, and of the disposal by him of those sums, and

(*b*) send it to the Comptroller and Auditor General not later than the end of November in the following financial year;

and the Comptroller and Auditor General shall examine, certify and report on the account and lay copies of it, together with his report, before each House of Parliament.

Treasury guarantees

5.—(1) The Treasury may guarantee, in such manner and on such conditions as they think fit, the repayment of the principal of, and the payment of interest on, and any other financial obligation in connection with, any sums which the Authority or any of their subsidiaries borrow from a person other than the Secretary of State.

(2) Immediately after a guarantee is given the Treasury shall lay a statement of the guarantee before each House of Parliament.

(3) If any sums are issued in fulfilment of a guarantee, the Authority or, as the case may be, the subsidiary shall make to the Treasury, at such times and in such manner as the Treasury may direct—

(*a*) payments of such amounts as the Treasury may direct in or towards repayment of the sums issued, and

(*b*) payments of interest on what is outstanding in respect of sums issued, at such rate as the Treasury may direct.

(4) Before giving such a direction the Treasury shall consult the Authority.

(5) Where a sum is issued for fulfilling a guarantee, the Treasury shall, as soon as possible, lay before each House of Parliament a statement relating to that sum.

(6) Any sums required by the Treasury for fulfilling a guarantee shall be charged on and issued out of the Consolidated Fund; and sums received by the Treasury shall be paid into that Fund.

Other provisions relating to the Authority

Supervisory powers of Secretary of State

6.—(1) The Authority shall, in formulating and carrying out plans for the general conduct of their undertaking and the undertakings of their subsidiaries, act on lines settled from time to time by the Authority with the approval of the Secretary of State.

(2) The Authority shall as respects work involving an outlay on capital account—

 (*a*) from time to time settle a general programme of work, and

 (*b*) if the Secretary of State so requests, settle a programme of work in respect of a particular project or category of projects,

and submit the programme to the Secretary of State for his approval.

(3) The Authority shall not carry out a project involving substantial outlay on capital account, and shall exercise control over their subsidiaries so as to secure that they do not carry out such a project, except—

 (*a*) in accordance with a general programme approved by the Secretary of State, and

 (*b*) where the Secretary of State has requested the Authority to settle a programme relating wholly or partly to the project concerned, in accordance with a programme settled in pursuance of the request and approved by the Secretary of State.

(4) This section does not affect the power of the Secretary of State to give directions under section 3 of the Atomic Energy Authority Act 1954.

Remuneration and compensation of members of the Authority

7.—(1) Section 1 of the Atomic Energy Authority Act 1954 (constitution of the Authority) is amended as follows.

(2) Subsection (8) (duty to lay statements of remuneration, &c. of members before Parliament) is repealed.

(3) After that subsection insert—

 "(8A) The terms of appointment of a member of the Authority may, with the approval of the Treasury, entitle him to compensation to be paid by the Authority on his ceasing to be a member.

 (8B) Where a person ceases to be a member of the Authority otherwise than on the expiry of his term of office and is not entitled to compensation under the terms of his appointment, but it appears to the Secretary of State that there are special circumstances which make it right that he should receive compensation, the Secretary of State may, with the approval of the Treasury, require the Authority to make to that person a payment of such amount as may be determined by the Secretary of State with the approval of the Treasury.".

Powers of Authority with respect to exploitation of results of research

8.—(1) The Authority have power, and shall be deemed always to have had power, to exploit commercially by selling, licensing the use of or otherwise dealing with any intellectual property—

 (*a*) resulting from research and development carried out by the Authority or carried out by another person in pursuance of arrangements with the Authority, or (*b*) which is at the disposal of the Authority by virtue of arrangements for the exchange of results of research and development or the carrying out of research and development in collaboration with another person.

(2) For this purpose "intellectual property" includes patents, trade-marks, copyrights, registered designs and any other scientific or technical information of commercial value.

General

Interpretation

9. In this Act—

"the Authority" means the United Kingdom Atomic Energy Authority, and

"subsidiary" and "wholly owned subsidiary" have the same meaning
as in the Companies Act 1985.

Short title, commencement and extent

10.—(1) This Act may be cited as the Atomic Energy Authority Act 1986.

(2) This Act comes into force on 1st April 1986 or, if later, the day on which it is passed.

(3) This Act extends to England and Wales, Scotland and Northern Ireland.

CONSOLIDATED FUND ACT 1986

(1986 c.4)

An Act to apply certain sums out of the Consolidated Fund to the service of the years ending on 31st March 1985 and 1986.

[18th March 1986]

Parliamentary Debates
  Hansard: H.C. Vol. 93, cols. 899, 1093; H.L. Vol. 472, cols. 744, 796.

Issue out of the Consolidated Fund for the year ending 31st March 1985

1. The Treasury may issue out of the Consolidated Fund of the United Kingdom and apply towards making good the supply granted to Her Majesty for the service of the year ending on 31st March 1985 the sum of £155,484,146·89.

Issue out of the Consolidated Fund for the year ending 31st March 1986

2. The Treasury may issue out of the Consolidated Fund of the United Kingdom and apply towards making good the supply granted to Her Majesty for the service of the year ending on 31st March 1986 the sum of £1,032,019,000.

Short title

3. This Act may be cited as the Consolidated Fund Act 1986.

AGRICULTURAL HOLDINGS ACT 1986

(1986 c. 5)

Tables of derivations and destinations can be found at the end of the Act

ARRANGEMENT OF SECTIONS

PART I

INTRODUCTORY

PART V

COMPENSATION ON TERMINATION OF TENANCY

Compensation to tenant for disturbance

Compensation to tenant for improvements and tenant-right matters

Compensation to tenant for adoption of special system of farming

Compensation to landlord for deterioration of holding

Supplementary provisions with respect to compensation

PART VI

MARKET GARDENS AND SMALLHOLDINGS

PART VII

MISCELLANEOUS AND SUPPLEMENTAL

An Act to consolidate certain enactments relating to agricultural holdings, with amendments to give effect to recommendations of the Law Commission.

[18th March 1986]

PARLIAMENTARY DEBATES
Hansard: H.L. Vol. 468, col. 1190; Vol. 469, col. 662; Vol. 470, col. 1287; H.C. Vol. 92, col. 786.

GENERAL NOTE

This is a consolidation Act in which a daunting task of draftsmanship has been accomplished with a boldness and skill which compel admiration. The Act consolidates ten statutes covering nearly forty years and includes certain minor amendments allowed by Parliament in a consolidation Act in order to achieve a satisfactory consolidation. The integration with the basic structure of the 1948 Act of the 1977 Act and the amending 1984 Act, together with the succession provisions of the 1976 and 1984 Acts, has involved a substantial rearrangement of sections and Schedules in order to produce a logical whole.

As the Act consolidates pre-existing law it is not proposed to introduce each section with a note explaining its object but some explanations have been thought desirable, particularly in relation to substantial amendments made by the 1984 Act.

It is worth recalling that the 1984 Act would probably not have come into existence if it had not been for the "package agreement" reached in 1981 between the Country Landowners' Association and the National Farmers' Union relating mainly to a new rent arbitration formula and to the abolition (subject to far-reaching exceptions) of statutory succession to agricultural holdings. Apart from the main items of rent arbitration and succession, the 1984 Act contained a large number of extremely useful amendments to agricultural holdings legislation, the late fruit of many years of study and advice to government by interested bodies, which made consolidation possible.

It has been necessary to publish this annotated edition of the 1986 Act before the issue of a number of revised or amending statutory instruments. Under the transitional provisions in Schedule 13 it is possible for old instruments, made under the repealed Acts, to operate with perfect legality under the 1986 Act, but in some cases new matters are called for and in others the references to the old legislation are awkward or confusing. In the coming months a considerable number of new instruments are likely to appear. See note to Sched. 4, *post*. It seems likely that the amendment or replacement of statutory instruments will be a lengthy process and consequently the publication of this annotated edition of the Act cannot be held up in order to include them. Any which are issued in time will be included.

PART I

INTRODUCTORY

Principal definitions

1.—(1) In this Act "agricultural holding" means the aggregate of the land (whether agricultural land or not) comprised in a contract of tenancy which is a contract for an agricultural tenancy, not being a contract under which the land is let to the tenant during his continuance in any office, appointment or employment held under the landlord.

(2) For the purposes of this section, a contract of tenancy relating to land is a contract for an agricultural tenancy if, having regard to—

(*a*) the terms of the tenancy,

(*b*) the actual or contemplated use of the land at the time of the conclusion of the contract and subsequently, and

(*c*) any other relevant circumstances,

the whole of the land comprised in the contract, subject to such exceptions only as do not substantially affect the character of the tenancy, is let for use as agricultural land.

(3) A change in user of the land concerned subsequent to the conclusion of a contract of tenancy which involves any breach of the terms of the tenancy shall be disregarded for the purpose of determining whether a contract which was not originally a contract for an agricultural tenancy has subsequently become one unless it is effected with the landlord's permission, consent or acquiescence.

(4) In this Act "agricultural land" means—

(*a*) land used for agriculture which is so used for the purposes of a trade or business, and

(*b*) any other land which, by virtue of a designation under section 109(1) of the Agriculture Act 1947, is agricultural land within the meaning of that Act.

(5) In this Act "contract of tenancy" means a letting of land, or agreement for letting land, for a term of years or from year to year; and for the purposes of this definition a letting of land, or an agreement for letting land, which, by virtue of subsection (6) of section 149 of the Law of Property Act 1925, takes effect as such a letting of land or agreement for letting land as is mentioned in that subsection shall be deemed to be a letting of land or, as the case may be, an agreement for letting land, for a term of years.

DEFINITIONS

"Agriculture", "landlord", "tenant": s.96(1).

"Agricultural land" and "contract of tenancy" are defined in subss. (4) and (5) below.

Subs. (1)

Aggregate. This refers to the different kinds of land, agricultural or otherwise, comprised in the contract, but does not justify severance: tenancy may be mixed, but must be in substance agricultural: *Dunn* v. *Fidoe* [1950] 2 All E.R. 685; *Howkins* v. *Jardine* [1951] 1 All E.R. 320; *Monson* v. *Bound* [1954] 1 W.L.R. 1321; *Deith* v. *Brown* [1956] J.P.L. 736; *McClinton* v. *McFall* (1974) 232 E.G. 707; *Sykes* v. *Secretary of State for the Environment*

(1980) 257 E.G. 821; *cf. Re Lancaster and Macnamara* [1918] 2 K.B. 472 (under 1908 Act) and *Re Joel's Lease, Berwick* v. *Baird* [1930] 2 Ch. 359 (under the 1923 Act).

Whether agricultural land or not. The tenancy may comprise non-agricultural elements, but must be predominantly or substantially agricultural: see subs. (2).

Office, appointment or employment. For an arrangement held not to be an "appointment", see *Verrall* v. *Farnes* [1966] 1 W.L.R. 1254. The Rent (Agriculture) Act 1976 may apply.

Subs. (2)

Contract of tenancy. See notes below on definitions in subs. (5).

Land. There is no minimum size: *Stevens* v. *Sedgeman* [1951] 2 K.B. 434; *cf. Craddock* v. *Hampshire County Council* [1958] 1 W.L.R. 202 (0.229 acre to be relet as an agricultural holding). It must not be an allotment garden, but it can be a building without any land in popular sense: *Blackmore* v. *Butler* [1954] 2 Q.B. 171; *cf. Godfrey* v. *Waite* (1957) 157 E.G. 582; see also *Hasell* v. *McAulay* [1952] 2 All E.R. 825.

Contract for an agricultural tenancy. But the tenancy may be mixed, subject to the substantiality requirement: see notes to subs. (1).

Para. (b): and subsequently. A unilateral cessation of agricultural user can make the tenancy no longer a tenancy of an agricultural holding: *Hickson & Welch Ltd.* v. *Cann* (1977) 40 P. & C.R. 218; *Wetherall* v. *Smith* (1980) 256 E.G. 163; and *Russell* v. *Booker* (1982) 263 E.G. 513. But there can be no unilateral reverse change. See generally on change of user judgment of Slade L.J. in *Russell* v. *Booker.*

As do not substantially affect. A negative way of stating the principle in *Howkins* v. *Jardine* [1951] 1 All E.R. 320.

Subs. (3)

Any breach. This subs. gives statutory effect to previous better view: see *per* Lord Evershed M.R. in *Godfrey* v. *Waite* (1951) 157 E.G. 582 (referred to at p.175 of *Blackmore* v. *Butler, supra*) and judgment of Somervell L.J. in *Iredell* v. *Brocklehurst* (1950) 155 E.G. 268; also C.C. case of *Kempe* v. *Dillon-Trenchard* (1951) 101 L.J. 417.

Permission, consent or acquiescence. The range seems to be from written permission through oral consent to implied agreement: not sufficiently evidenced in *Russell* v. *Booker* (1982) 263 E.G. 513.

Subs. (4)

Para. (a): land used for agriculture. For definition of "agriculture" and subsidiary definition of "livestock", see s.96(1). For use "in connection with agriculture" (perhaps too liberal interpretation) see *Blackmore* v. *Butler, supra.* Breeding and keeping of horses, unless used for farming, is not "agriculture", but *grazing* of non-agricultural horses (*e.g.* riding horses) is, provided that the grazing is the predominant use: *Belmont Farm Ltd.* v. *Minister of Housing and Local Government* (1962) 13 P. & C.R. 417; *Rutherford* v. *Maurer* [1962] 1 Q.B. 16; *McClinton* v. *McFall* (1974) 232 E.G. 707; *Sykes* v. *Secretary of State for the Environment* (1981) 257 E.G. 821 (an occasional snack of grass by ponies waiting to be ridden not enough). Contrast a tenancy of "gallops", which may be a business use: *Bracey* v. *Read* [1963] Ch. 88; *cf. University of Reading* v. *Johnson-Houghton* [1985] 2 E.G.L.R. 113. Fish farming, but perhaps not mink farming, is within "agriculture": see *dicta* in *Belmont* case, *supra* and in *Minister of Agriculture, Fisheries and Food* v. *Appleton* [1970] 1 Q.B. 221; also, in regard to mink, *Jones (Valuation Officer)* v. *Davies* (1977) 244 E.G. 897 (L.T.). Lands Tribunal rating decisions, such as *Jones (Valuation Officer* v. *Bateman* (1974) 232 E.G. 1392 and *Gunter* v. *New Town Oyster Fishery Co. Ltd.* (1977) 244 E.G. 140, in favour of fish and oysters being livestock, are of interest, but not of authority; the C.A. decision in *Creswell (Valuation Officer)* v. *British Oxygen Co. Ltd.* [1980] 1 W.L.R. 1556; (1980) 255 E.G. 1101 is authoritative, but strictly only as to rating. The keeping of pheasants for sport is not "agriculture": *Glendyne (Lord)* v. *Rapley* [1978] 1 W.L.R. 61. *Reeve* v. *Atterby* [1978] C.L.Y. 73 and *Normanton (Earl)* v. *Giles* [1980] 1 W.L.R. 28 (H.L.).

trade or business. This need not be an agricultural trade or business: *Rutherford* v. *Maurer* [1962] 1 Q.B. 16 (grazing of riding school horses), rejecting dictum by Jenkins L.J. in *Howkins* v. *Jardine* [1951] 1 K.B. 614 at p.629. A use may be non-agricultural, although related to an ultimate use which is agricultural, *e.g.* the grazing of crops for testing weed-killer in the manufacturer of agricultural chemicals: *Dow Agrochemicals* v. *E. A. Lane (North Lynn) Ltd.* (1965) 115 L.J. 76 (C.C.).

Para. (b): designation. The Minister can designate land which would not otherwise be within the definition of agricultural land, *e.g.* land used non-commercially, as for research, or derelict land. Certain kinds of land are excluded from his powers: see s.109(1) of the 1947 Act.

Subs. (5)

Contract of tenancy. This is a most important definition. It means a single contract: *Darby* v. *Williams* (1974) 232 E.G. 579. But land may be added by a supplemental agreement: *Blackmore* v. *Butler* [1954] 2 Q.B. 171, 177, 180. The contract need not be in writing, but see s.6. As to contracting out, see generally *Johnson* v. *Moreton* [1980] A.C. 37. "Contract of tenancy" involves intention to create the legally binding relationship of landlord and tenant, not some other legal relationship or only a gentleman's agreement: see *Steyning and Littlehampton Building Society* v. *Wilson* [1951] Ch. 1018; *Goldsack* v. *Shore* [1950] 1 K.B. 708; *Bahamas International Trust Co. Ltd.* v. *Threadgold* [1974] 1 W.L.R. 1514; *Avon County Council* v. *Clothier* (1977) 242 E.G. 1048. It must be distinguished from a contractual licence, but see s.2 and notes thereon.

A term of years or from year to year. For some implications of these words, see note on s.2(2).

Section 149(6) of the Law of Property Act 1925. Agricultural leases falling within this subsection are now virtually, if not entirely, unknown.

Restriction on letting agricultural land for less than from year to year

2.—(1) An agreement to which this section applies shall take effect, with the necessary modifications, as if it were an agreement for the letting of land for a tenancy from year to year unless the agreement was approved by the Minister before it was entered into.

(2) Subject to subsection (3) below, this section applies to an agreement under which—

(*a*) any land is let to a person for use as agricultural land for an interest less than a tenancy from year to year, or

(*b*) a person is granted a licence to occupy land for use as agricultural land,

if the circumstances are such that if his interest were a tenancy from year to year he would in respect of that land be the tenant of an agricultural holding.

(3) This section does not apply to an agreement for the letting of land, or the granting of a licence to occupy land—

(*a*) made (whether or not it expressly so provides) in contemplation of the use of the land only for grazing or mowing (or both) during some specified period of the year, or

(*b*) by a person whose interest in the land is less than a tenancy from year to year and has not taken effect as such a tenancy by virtue of this section.

(4) Any dispute arising as to the operation of this section in relation to any agreement shall be determined by arbitration under this Act.

DEFINITIONS

"Agricultural holding" and "agricultural land", see s.1(1), (4).
"Agreement", "Minister", see s.96(1).

GENERAL NOTE

For some special provisions affecting opencast coal land, see Opencast Coal Act 1958, Sched. 6, paras. 20–25.

Subs. (1)

Agreement. This means an enforceable contract, *i.e.* an agreement supported by valuable consideration, although not necessarily a pecuniary rent; *Goldsack* v. *Shore* [1950] 1 K.B. 708; *King* v. *Turner* [1954] E.G.D. 7; *Harrison-Broadley* v. *Smith* [1964] 1 W.L.R. 456; *Verrall* v. *Farnes* [1966] 1 W.L.R. 1254; *Holder* v. *Holder* [1968] Ch. 353 (in part reversing Cross J., but not on this point); *Epps* v. *Ledger* (1972) 272 E.G. 1373; *Avon County Council* v. *Clothier* (1977) 75 L.G.R. 344; *Mitton* v. *Farrow* (1980) 255 E.G. 449; *Collier* v. *Hollinshead* (1984) 272 E.G. 941. Note that s.2 does not apply to agreements made before March 1, 1948: Sched. 12, para. 1.

With the necessary modifications. For view that this does not permit a radically different agreement, see *per* Lord Evershed M.R. in *Goldsack* v. *Shore, supra,* at p.713; *per* Pearson

L.J. in *Harrison-Broadley* v. *Smith, supra,* at p.467; and decision of Nourse J. in *Walter* v. *Roberts* (1980) 258 E.G. 965. For a word of caution, see *per* Cross J. in *Verrall* v. *Farnes* [1966] 1 W.L.R. 1254 at p.1268, and for mention of a possible "bold construction", see *per* Megaw L.J. in *Bahamas International Trust Co. Ltd.* v. *Threadgold* [1974] 1 W.L.R. 1514 at p.1521 and studious avoidance of comment by Lord Diplock in H.L. at p.1525.

Approved by the Minister. For the relevant considerations see the joint announcement by the agricultural departments, dated July 19, 1984. For cases, see *Finbow* v. *Air Ministry* [1963] 1 W.L.R. 697 ("blanket" approval); *Bedfordshire County Council* v. *Clarke* (1974) 230 E.G. 1587 (approval before agreement); *Secretary of State for Social Services* v. *Beavington* (1982) 262 E.G. 551 (approval must not have expired); *Epsom and Ewell Borough Council* v. *C. Bell (Tadworth) Ltd.* (1982) 266 E.G. 808 (tenancy by implication may be covered).

Subs. (2)

Para. (a): let . . . for an interest less than a tenancy from year to year. "Let" means that s.2(2)(*a*) is dealing with *tenancies* which are for less than from year to year (as distinct from the licences covered by s.2(2)(*b*)). This covers tenancies for less than one year, including *periodic* tenancies for *periods* of less than from year to year (such as the 364 day tenancy in *Land Settlement Association Ltd.* v. *Carr* [1944] K.B. 657). A tenancy for one year certain is also covered: *Bernays* v. *Prosser* [1963] 2 Q.B. 592; *Rutherford* v. *Maurer* [1962] 1 Q.B. 16; *Lower* v. *Sorrell* [1963] 1 W.L.R. 959 (particularly *per* Pearson L.J. at pp.977–978). But a tenancy for more than one year but less than two years is greater than a tenancy from year to year: *Gladstone* v. *Bower* [1960] 2 Q.B. 384. In favour of view that it is not a tenancy of an agricultural holding at all, because it is neither a letting for a term of years nor from year to year, see *Bishop of Bath's Case* (1605) 6 Co.Rep. 346, Bac-Ab. leases L.3; *Land Settlement Association Ltd.* v. *Carr, ante*; and *Esso Petroleum Co. Ltd.* v. *Secretary of State for the Environment* (1976) 23 P. & C.R. 55 (Lands Tribunal). Against this view is *Re Land and Premises at Liss, Hants* [1971] Ch. 986, *per* Goulding J., the wording of s.3(1) of the 1986 Act, and the assumption in s.36(2)(*b*) of the 1986 Act that it is a tenancy of an agricultural holding. If it is not, it may be within Part II of the Landlord and Tenant Act 1954. See also note 2 to s.36, *post*.

Para. (b): licence. A licence, to be within s.2(1), must confer exclusive occupation on the licensee. A non-exclusive licence is not within it; *Harrison-Broadley* v. *Smith* [1964] 1 W.L.R. 456 (C.A.); *Epps* v. *Ledger* (1972) 225 E.G. 1373; *Bahamas International Trust Co. Ltd.* v. *Threadgold* [1974] 1 W.L.R. 1514; and *Jones* v. *Lock* (1978) 246 E.G. 395. In *Midgley* v. *Scott* (1977) 244 E.G. 883 the non-exclusive point could not be taken for a technical reason. A mere right of access does not make a licence non-exclusive: *Harrison-Broadley* v. *Smith* and the *Bahamas* case, *ante*; see also *Lampard* v. *Barker* (1954) 272 E.G. 783. A licence only to go on land to take produce is not sufficient, as it does not confer occupation rights: *Wyatt* v. *King* (1951) 157 E.G. 124 (value of decision queried by Salmon J. in *Harrison-Broadley* v. *Smith* at first instance [1963] 1 W.L.R. 1262 at p.1270). It must be a licence for valuable consideration, not gratuitous; see cases cited on subs. (1) above (Agreement). The licence may be of any duration: there is no restriction on the length of term; *Snell* v. *Snell* (1964) 191 E.G. 361. See also generally *Finbow* v. *Air Ministry* [1963] 1 W.L.R. 697. See also the joint announcement of the agricultural departments on the approval of short term lettings and licences.

It would appear from the decision of the House of Lords in *Street* v. *Mountford* [1985] A.C. 809 that a licence for value conferring exclusive possession on the grantee and being for a term at a rent in fact creates a *tenancy.* "Term" in this context includes a periodic interest and "rent" need not be so called, but could be a licence fee. Thus some grants which were thought to create licences converted into tenancies by the operation of s.2 created tenancies without this operation. The effect of *Street* v. *Mountford* on agricultural interests has not yet been explored in case law.

If the circumstances are such. The agreement will not be transformed by s.2(1) if it would not, by becoming a tenancy from year to year, be a tenancy of an agricultural holding; this would be the case if the land was not used for a trade or business (s.1(4)) or if the occupant held office under the landlord (s.1(1)) or if the occupier was a purchaser in occupation pending completion: *Walters* v. *Roberts* (1980) 41 P. & C.R. 210.

Subs. (3)

Para. (a): contemplation. See for full discussion of the meaning *Scene Estate Ltd.* v. *Amos* [1957] 2 Q.B. 205, especially judgment of Denning L.J. See also curious case of *Stone* v. *Whitcombe* (1981) 257 E.G. 929 (contemplation of a specified period of the year within an agreement for a year certain). See also *Richardson* v. *Maurer* [1962] 1 Q.B. 16 ("grazing for

six months periods" contemplates at least one year); *Short Bros. (Plant) Ltd.* v. *Edwards*
(1978) 249 E.G. 539 ("several years" contemplated); *Chaloner* v. *Bower* (objective view of
consensus indicated grazing season in contemplation). As to place of extrinsic evidence, see
Scene Estate Ltd. v. *Amos, ante.*

Only. "Only" applies both to the use (grazing or mowing, or both) and to the period
("some specified period of the year"): *per* Parker L.J. in *Scene Estate Ltd.* v. *Amos, ante,*
at p.212. See next note for consequences of the restrictive "only".

Grazing or mowing (or both). "Or both" was added to avoid any misconstruction (see
Law Com. No. 153, Cmnd. 9665 (Dec. 1985)), but "or" was normally read conjunctively.
"Only" for grazing or mowing, or both, means that a use which includes some other purpose,
unless *de minimis*, is not within this exception. But purely ancillary or subsidiary activities,
such as maintaining fences or drains, providing shelter for grazing cattle, etc., are within the
main purpose: see *Avon County Council* v. *Clothier* (1977) 242 E.G. 1048 (stabling for
grazing ponies); *Boyce* v. *Rendells* (1983) 268 E.G. 268 (even some limited ploughing or
sowing), but there is a danger in allowing the grazier to plough, and certainly ploughing and
harrowing geared to improvement over the years take the case out of the exception: *Lory*
v. *London Borough of Brent* [1971] 1 All E.R. 1042. A grazing tenancy or licence is often
referred to "a sale of the grass keep". It must be distinguished from agistment, where
animals are taken in to feed and without allocation of a particular part of the farm. The
grantee of the grass keep may bring trespass against a third party: *Richards* v. *Davies* [1921]
1 Ch. 90 at p.94; *cf. Masters* v. *Green* (1888) 20 Q.B.D. 807; contrast *Thomas Fawcett &*
Sons Ltd. v. *Thompson* [1954] E.G.D. 5. Grazing is not confined to animals used in
agriculture: *Rutherford* v. *Maurer* [1962] 1 Q.B. 16; *McClinton* v. *McFall* (1974) 232 E.G.
707. Generally, see also Scottish decisions, *Mackenzie* v. *Laird* 1959 S.C. 266, *Sanson* v.
Chalmers 1965 S.L.C.R. App. 135 and the Sheriff Court case of *Duncan* v. *Shaw* 1944
S.L.T.(Sh.Ct.) 34.

Some specified period of the year. This could be anything short of a full year, *e.g.* 364
days: *Reid* v. *Dawson* [1955] 1 Q.B. 214. "Period" is simply "part": *Scene Estate Ltd.* v.
Amos [1957] 2 Q.B. 205 at p.212. The absence of an interval of time between one 364 day
tenancy and another is not in itself conclusive evidence that a yearly tenancy has been
created: *Reid* v. *Dawson, supra; Scene Estate Ltd.* v. *Amos, ante; Cox* v. *Hurst* (1976) 239
E.G. 123 at p.125; *Luton* v. *Tinsey* (1978) 249 E.G. 239; *South West Water Authority* v.
Palmer (1983) 268 E.G. 357, C.A.; *Epsom and Ewell Borough Council* v. *C. Bell (Tadworth)*
Ltd. (1982) 266 E.G. 808. But a clear break between terms is a counsel of prudence. Any
indication of an enduring interest of a year or more is to be avoided; but words of mere
reassurance as to probable continuance of grazing agreements should not be given contractual
force: *South West Water Authority* case, *supra*. A period may be "specified" although not
defined by actual dates, if intelligible to farmers, such as "the grazing season", "the summer
grasskeeping", even (in Scotland) "the growing season": see *Goldsack* v. *Shore* [1950] 1
K.B. 708 at pp.712–713; *Mackenzie* v. *Laird* 1959 S.C. 266, and the English C.C. case of
Butterfield v. *Burniston* (1961) 180 E.G. 597. See also *Luton* v. *Tinsey, supra; Stone* v.
Whitcombe (1980) 257 E.G. 929; *Chaloner* v. *Bower* (1983) 269 E.G. 725; *Boyce* v. *Rendells*
(1983) 268 E.G. 268; and, in the Scottish Land Court, *Gairneybridge Farm Ltd. and King*
1974 S.L.T. (Land Ct.) 8. As to extent to which extrinsic evidence is permissible to show
that the agreement is for more than a specified period of the year, see *per* Parker L.J. in
Scene Estate Ltd. v. *Amos* [1957] 2 Q.B. 205 at p.213, a statement approved in *Boyle* v.
Rendells, supra, and in *Chaloner* v. *Bower, supra.* In *Short Bros. (Plant) Ltd.* v. *Edwards*
(1979) 249 E.G. 539 an oral collateral agreement that grazing arrangements (for a specified
period of the year) were to last for "several years" resulted in a tenancy from year to year.
It should be noted that a letting from April 1 to March 31 is not for 364 days, but for a year
certain: *Cox* v. *Husk* (1976) 239 E.G. 123. It is possible for a full agricultural tenancy from
year to year to be surrendered by operation of law by the acceptance of a grazing licence,
but clear evidence of the genuineness of the transaction is necessary: see *Somerset County*
Council v. *Pearse* [1977] C.L.Y. 53 (C.C.). The onus of proof that the grazing or mowing
exception applies is on the landlord: *James* v. *Lock* (1978) 246 E.G. 395, following *Scene*
Estate Ltd. v. *Amos* [1957] 2 Q.B. 205 at p.212 (Parker L.J.).

Para. (b): whose interest in the land is less. This second limb does not appear to have
attracted case law. It relates to sub-tenancies or licences granted by a person whose own
interest is (and has remained) less than a tenancy from year to year. This would not cover
grants by a person who has no legal interest at all, *e.g.* a government department in
possession under requisitioning powers: *per* McNair J. in *Finbow* v. *Air Ministry* [1963] 1
W.L.R. 697 at p.711.

Subs. (4)

By arbitration. Questions as to the *applicability* of section 2, as distinct from its *operation,* are, however, matters for the courts: *Goldsack* v. *Shore* [1956] 1 K.B. 708. Thus a question as to whether a licence is supported by valuable consideration, and so within the section, would be a matter for the court. Disputes as to *details* of the "necessary modifications" mentioned in s.2(1) would be suitable for arbitration, but questions as to the scope and limits of the "necessary modifications" principle (see note to subs. (1)) would be for the courts. The county court decision in *Powell* v. *Stevens* (1951) 101 L.J. 109 (that disputes as to terms of a tenancy are referable to arbitration) is too briefly reported to determine its correctness.

Tenancies for two years or more to continue from year to year unless terminated by notice

3.—(1) Subject to section 5 below, a tenancy of an agricultural holding for a term of two years or more shall, instead of terminating on the term date, continue (as from that date) as a tenancy from year to year, but otherwise on the terms of the original tenancy so far as applicable, unless—

     (*a*) not less than one year nor more than two years before the term date a written notice has been given by either party to the other of his intention to terminate the tenancy, or

     (*b*) section 4 below applies.

     (2) A notice given under subsection (1) above shall be deemed, for the purposes of this Act, to be a notice to quit.

     (3) This section does not apply to a tenancy which, by virtue of subsection (6) of section 149 of the Law of Property Act 1925, takes effect as such a term of years as is mentioned in that subsection.

     (4) In this section "term date", in relation to a tenancy granted for a term of years, means the date fixed for the expiry of that term.

DEFINITIONS

"agricultural holding": see s.1(1).

"term date": see subs. (4).

Subs. (1)

Section 5 below. This refers to the exclusion in s.5 by joint agreement approved by the Minister.

A term of two years or more. A term of more than one year but less than two years is not caught by s.2 or s.3 of the 1986 Act and attracts no security of tenure: *Gladstone* v. *Bower* [1960] 2 Q.B. 384 (C.A.). It is not yet firmly settled whether it is outside the 1986 Act for all purposes, and in that case probably within Part II of the Landlord and Tenant Act 1954, or only outside the 1986 Act so far as security of tenure is concerned. The specific reference to a term "of two years or more" might suggest that a term of less than two years can be a term of years for the purpose of the definition in s.1(5); otherwise, why not say simply "for a term of years"? But this is not conclusive. See also note to s.2(2), *ante* and note to s.36(2) *post.*

Terminating. The definition of "termination" in s.96(1) must be read subject to the present section and sections 4 and 5.

As a tenancy from year to year. In which case it will require a notice to quit to terminate it, thus attracting s.26 and s.60 of the Act, but a tenancy from year to year will not arise if s.4 or s.5 applies.

Para (a): term date. See subs. (4). The break date or dates in a lease with options to break are not the "term date" within the meaning of the term, but a notice exercising such an option is a notice to quit: *Edell* v. *Dulieu* [1923] 2 K.B. 247 (C.A.), affirmed at [1924] A.C. 38.

Para. (b): section 4 below applies. S.3 has to be read subject to s.4 and s.5.

A notice to quit. This makes it clear that a notice of intention to terminate in subs. (1)(*a*) has the legal consequences of a notice to quit, including, *inter alia*, the attraction of s.26 and s.60. Subs. (2) may be drafted *ex abundante cautela*: see *per* Lord Sterndale M.R. in *Edell* v. *Dulieu, supra,* in C.A. at p.250, approving Bramwell L.J. in *Ahearn* v. *Bellman* (1879) 4 Ex.D. 201.

S.149(6) of the Law of Property Act 1925. Leases for a life or lives, converted by this provision into determinable leases for 90 years, are in practice never found in the agricultural world. There is some doubt as to the true effect of s.149(6): see *Woodfall* (28th ed., p.245).

Although perhaps not often relevant, it should be noted that s.3 does not apply to a tenancy granted or agreed to be granted before January 1, 1921 (Sched. 12, para. 2).

Death of tenant before term date

4.—(1) This section applies where—

(*a*) a tenancy such as is mentioned in subsection (1) of section 3 above is granted on or after 12th September 1984 to any person or persons,

(*b*) the person, or the survivor of the persons, dies before the term date, and

(*c*) no notice effective to terminate the tenancy on the term date has been given under that subsection.

(2) Where this section applies, the tenancy, instead of continuing as mentioned in section 3(1) above—

(*a*) shall, if the death is one year or more before the term date, terminate on that date, or

(*b*) shall, if the death is at any other time, continue (as from the term date) for a further period of twelve months, but otherwise on the terms of the tenancy so far as applicable, and shall accordingly terminate on the first anniversary of the term date.

(3) For the purposes of the provisions of this Act with respect to compensation any tenancy terminating in accordance with this section shall be deemed to terminate by reason of a notice to quit given by the landlord of the holding.

(4) In this section "term date" has the same meaning as in section 3 above.

DEFINITIONS
"term date": see s.3(4).

Subs. (1)
Para. (a): on or after September 12, 1984. The date of commencement of the 1984 Act. Note that s.4 came into operation on this date, not on July 12, 1984, the date of passing of that Act.
Para. (b): the person or the survivor of the persons. This means the original grantee or grantees, and excludes assignees. The assignee of an original grantee who dies before the term date may be surprised to find that his interest has ceased.

Subs. 2
Para (a): shall . . . terminate. This means what it says; the tenancy ceases and no security of tenure is attracted, but, of course, compensation for improvements and tenant-right, if appropriate, will be available, and, as a result of subs. (3), disturbance.

Subs. (3)
Deemed . . . notice to quit. This preserving the right to compensation for disturbance under s.60.

Restriction on agreements excluding effect of section 3

5.—(1) Except as provided in this section, section 3 above shall have effect notwithstanding any agreement to the contrary.

(2) Where before the grant of a tenancy of an agricultural holding for a term of not less than two, and not more than five, years—

(*a*) the persons who will be the landlord and the tenant in relation to the tenancy agree that section 3 above shall not apply to the tenancy, and (*b*) those persons make a joint application in writing to the Minister for his approval of that agreement, and

(*c*) the Minister notifies them of his approval,

section 3 shall not apply to the tenancy if it satisfies the requirements of subsection (3) below.

(3) A tenancy satisfies the requirements of this subsection if the contract of tenancy is in writing and it, or a statement endorsed upon it, indicates (in whatever terms) that section 3 does not apply to the tenancy.

DEFINITIONS
"agricultural holding": s.1(1).
"contract of tenancy": s.1(5).
"landlord" and "tenant" and "Minister": s.96(1).

Subs. (1)
Except as provided in this section. This section expressly authorises contracting-out of s.3 by an approved procedure and expressly prohibits it otherwise. See, however, *Johnson* v. *Moreton* [1980] A.C. 37 for an implied prohibition of contracting out on grounds of public policy.

Subs. (2)
Before the grant. The three conditions mentioned in subs. (2) must be satisfied *before* the grant. *Cf.* s.38(4) of the Landlord and Tenant Act 1954; possibly a lack of formality in the grant might be cured as in *Tottenham Hotspur Football & Athletic Co.* v. *Princegrove Publishers* [1974] 1 W.L.R. 113.
Not less than two, and not more than five, years. See statement of government policy as to approval of short-term lettings and licences, dated July 19, 1984.
Section 3 shall not apply to the tenancy. The term will in fact terminate on the expiry date and the possibility of further security under s.3 will be excluded. Compensation for disturbance will also be excluded, as there is no saving provision as in s.4(3), but compensation for improvements and tenant-right will be unaffected in principle, although less likely in practice owing to the shortness of the term.

Subs. (3)
Requirements of this subsection. The requirements of subs. (3), as regards an indication in the contract of tenancy or in an endorsed statement, must be observed as well as the conditions in subs. (2). If not, section 3 will operate.

PART II

PROVISIONS AFFECTING TENANCY DURING ITS CONTINUANCE

Written tenancy agreements

Right to written tenancy agreement

6.—(1) Where in respect of a tenancy of an agricultural holding—
(*a*) there is not in force an agreement in writing embodying all the terms of the tenancy (including any model clauses incorporated in the contract of tenancy by virtue of section 7 below), or
(*b*) such an agreement in writing is in force but the terms of the tenancy do not make provision for one or more of the matters specified in Schedule 1 to this Act,

the landlord or tenant of the holding may, if he has requested the other to enter into an agreement in writing embodying all the terms of the tenancy and containing provision for all of the said matters but no such agreement has been concluded, refer the terms of the tenancy to arbitration under this Act.

(2) On any such reference the arbitrator in his award—

(*a*) shall specify the existing terms of the tenancy, subject to any variations agreed between the landlord and the tenant,

(*b*) in so far as those terms as so varied neither make provision for, nor make provision inconsistent with, the matters specified in Schedule 1 to this Act, shall make provision for all of the said matters having such effect as may be agreed between the landlord and the tenant or, in default of agreement, as appears to the arbitrator to be reasonable and just between them, and

(*c*) may include any further provisions relating to the tenancy which may be agreed between the landlord and the tenant.

(3) Where it appears to the arbitrator on a reference under this section that, by reason of any provision which he is required to include in his award, it is equitable that the rent of the holding should be varied, he may vary the rent accordingly.

(4) The award of an arbitrator under this section shall have effect as if the terms and provisions specified and made in the award were contained in an agreement in writing entered into by the landlord and the tenant and having effect (by way of variation of the agreement previously in force in respect of the tenancy) as from the making of the award or, if the award so provides, from such later date as may be specified in it.

(5) Where in respect of a tenancy of an agricultural holding—

(*a*) the terms of the tenancy neither make provision for, nor make provision inconsistent with, the matter specified in paragraph 9 of Schedule 1 to this Act, and

(*b*) the landlord requests the tenant in writing to enter into such an agreement as is mentioned in subsection (1) above containing provision for all of the matters specified in that Schedule,

the tenant may not without the landlord's consent in writing assign, sub-let or part with possession of the holding or any part of it during the period while the determination of the terms of the tenancy is pending; and any transaction entered into in contravention of this subsection shall be void.

(6) The period mentioned in subsection (5) above is the period beginning with the date of service of the landlord's request on the tenant and ending with the date on which an agreement is concluded in accordance with that request or (as the case may be) with the date on which the award of an arbitrator on a reference under this section relating to the tenancy takes effect.

DEFINITIONS
"agricultural holding": s.1(1).
"agreement", "landlord", "tenant": s.96(1).
"arbitration under this Act": s.84.
"model clauses": s.7(1).

Subs. (1)
Para. (a): an agreement in writing. A purely oral agreement is perfectly legal. The agreement in writing need not be in a formal document; it may consist of letters, provided that they contain the terms of the tenancy: *Grieve and Sons* v. *Barr*, 1954 S.C. 414.

If he has requested. This (unsuccessful) request is a condition precedent to arbitration. It is advisable to make it in writing.

Refer. There is no time limit for a reference.

Subs. (2)
Para. (b): nor make provision inconsistent with. S.4(2) of the Agricultural Holdings (Scotland) Act 1949 enacts precisely the opposite, namely, that inconsistent provisions may be overridden.

As appears to the arbitrator to be reasonable and just between them. But paras. 6 and 7 of Sched. 1 set out covenants in the form in which the arbitrator *must* embody them in the absence of agreement between the parties.

Para. (c): any further provisions relating to the tenancy. Provided that they "relate to the tenancy", there is no restriction on the matters which may be agreed and included in the award.

Subs. (3)
Vary. It should be noted this variation is disregarded for the purpose of the frequency of rent arbitrations under Sched. 2, para. 4(1)(*b*): see para. 4(2)(*a*) of that Sched.

Subs. (4)
Award. The award is itself effective as an agreement and there is no need to draw up a formal agreement embodying the contents of the award; indeed it saves stamp duty to refrain from doing so.
By way of variation. This does away with the effect of the old decision in *Hollings* v. *Swindell* (1950) 155 E.G. 269, where it was held that the award as a notional agreement rendered null a notice to quit given before it.

Subs. (5)
Para. (a): paragraph 9 of Schedule 1. The covenant preventing assigning, sub-letting or parting with possession without the landlord's consent.
Para. (b): the landlord requests. The object of subss. (5) and (6) is to prevent an application to the arbitrator, with a view to the inclusion of a covenant in the terms of para. 9 of Sched. 1, from being frustrated by an assignment taking place pending the outcome of such an arbitration.
Void. This will defeat any argument, based on such cases as *Old Grovebury Manor Farm* v. *Seymour Plant Sales and Hire Ltd. (No. 2)* [1977] 1 W.L.R. 1397 and *Governors of Peabody Donation Fund* v. *Higgins* [1983] 1 W.L.R. 1091, that the assignment, although unlawful, would nevertheless actually vest the tenancy in the assignee.

Subs. (6)
Agreement. The tenant might fall in with the request and enter into an agreement on the lines of para. 9 of Sched. 1, but, if not, the period during which the landlord is protected against pre-emptive transactions will extend to the date when the award takes effect.

Fixed equipment

The model clauses

7.—(1) The Minister may, after consultation with such bodies of persons as appear to him to represent the interests of landlords and tenants of agricultural holdings, make regulations prescribing terms as to the maintenance, repair and insurance of fixed equipment (in this Act referred to as "the model clauses").

(2) Regulations under this section may make provision for any matter arising under them to be determined by arbitration under this Act.

(3) The model clauses shall be deemed to be incorporated in every contract of tenancy of an agricultural holding except in so far as they would impose on one of the parties to an agreement in writing a liability which under the agreement is imposed on the other.

DEFINITIONS
    "agricultural holding": s.1(1).
    "arbitration": s.84.
    "contract of tenancy": s.1(5).
    "Minister", "landlord" and "tenant": s.96(1).

Subs. (1)
Consultation. In practice the Minister has consulted not only the bodies representing landlords and tenants, such as the CLA and NFU, but also professional institutions concerned with agricultural land, such as the RICS, CAAV and ISVA.
Regulations. The regulations in force at the time of going to press are the Agriculture (Maintenance, Repair and Insurance of Fixed Equipment) Regulations 1973 (S.I. 1973 No. 1473). Cases in which the regulations (or the preceding ones (S.I. 1948 No. 184) were

discussed are *Burden* v. *Hannaford* [1956] 1 Q.B. 142, *Evans* v. *Jones* [1955] 2 Q.B. 58, *Barrow Green Estate Co.* v. *Exors. of Walker,* decd. [1954] 1 W.L.R. 231 and the county court case of *Robertson-Ackerman* v. *George* (1953) 103 L.J. 496.

Subs. (2)
Arbitration. See Sched. to the regulations mentioned in last note, paras. 4(3), 12(3), 13 and 15.

Subs. (3)
Except in so far as they would impose on one of the parties to an agreement in writing a liability which under the agreement is imposed on the other. The absence of a written contractual term positively imposing liability on the other party is thus a condition precedent to the incorporation of the relevant part of the model clauses, but once it has been incorporated it has still to be read with the contract and in case of inconsistency the contract prevails, *e.g.* a contractual provision expressly *excusing* the tenant from liability to repair hedges: see *Burden* v. *Hannaford* [1956] 1 Q.B. 142, an important but awkward decision on the regulations.

Arbitration where terms of written agreement are inconsistent with the model clauses

8.—(1) This section applies where an agreement in writing relating to a tenancy of an agricultural holding effects substantial modifications in the operation of regulations under section 7 above.

(2) Where this section applies, then, subject to subsection (6) below, the landlord or tenant of the holding may, if he has requested the other to vary the terms of the tenancy as to the maintenance, repair and insurance of fixed equipment so as to bring them into conformity with the model clauses but no agreement has been reached on the request, refer those terms of the tenancy to arbitration under this Act.

(3) On any reference under this section the arbitrator shall consider whether (disregarding the rent payable for the holding) the terms referred to arbitration are justifiable having regard to the circumstances of the holding and of the landlord and the tenant, and, if he determines that they are not so justifiable, he may by his award vary them in such manner as appears to him reasonable and just between the landlord and tenant.

(4) Where it appears to the arbitrator on any reference under this section that by reason of any provision included in his award it is equitable that the rent of the holding should be varied, he may vary the rent accordingly.

(5) The award of an arbitrator under this section shall have effect as if the terms and provisions specified and made in the award were contained in an agreement in writing entered into by the landlord and the tenant and having effect (by way of variation of the agreement previously in force in respect of the tenancy) as from the making of the award or, if the award so provides, from such later date as may be specified in it.

(6) Where there has been a reference under this section relating to a tenancy, no further such reference relating to that tenancy shall be made before the expiry of three years from the coming into effect of the award of the arbitrator on the previous reference.

DEFINITIONS
"agricultural holding": s.1(1).
"arbitration": s.84.
"landlord", "tenant": s.96(1).

Subs. (1)
Substantial modifications. As the question whether a departure from the model clauses is "substantial" goes to the root of the arbitrator's jurisdiction, it is suitable for a case stated where the decision is difficult. In the different context of the Rent Acts it has been held that "substantial" is not equivalent to "not insubstantial", or just enough to avoid the *de minimis*

principle, but means "considerable, solid or big": *Palser* v. *Grinling* [1948] A.C. 291 at
p.316.

Subs. (2)
    If he has requested. This request (which it would be wise to make in writing) and the
failure to reach agreement on it together constitute a conditon precedent to the reference to
arbitration.

Subs. (3)
    Circumstances. This seems to include personal circumstances, *e.g.* the absence of the
landlord abroad or the financial situation of the parties, but the rent is to be disregarded as
not a factor in deciding the justifiability of the terms but a matter to be adjusted when that
decision has been made: see subs. (4) below.

Subs. (4)
    Vary the rent accordingly. See previous note. The variation of rent under this subsection
is to be disregarded for the purpose of the frequency of rent arbitrations under section 12:
see Sched. 2, para. 4(1)(*b*) and 4(2)(*a*).

Subs. (5)
    Award. See note to s.6(4), *ante.*
    By way of variation. See note *ibid.*

Subs. (6)
    Three years. But there is nothing to prevent the first reference from taking place
immediately after the commencement of the tenancy: contrast the position in regard to rent
arbitrations under s.12: see Sched. 2, para. 4(1)(*a*).

Transitional arrangements where liability in respect of fixed equipment transferred

9.—(1) Where by virtue of section 6, 7 or 8 above the liability for the
maintenance or repair of any item of fixed equipment is transferred from
the tenant to the landlord, the landlord may within the prescribed period
beginning with the date on which the transfer takes effect require that
there shall be determined by arbitration under this Act and paid by the
tenant the amount of any relevant compensation.

(2) In subsection (1) above "relevant compensation" means compensation which would have been payable either under subsection (1) of
section 71 below or in accordance with subsection (3) of that section, in
respect of any previous failure by the tenant to discharge the liability
mentioned in subsection (1) above, if the tenant had quitted the holding
on the termination of his tenancy at the date on which the transfer takes
effect.

(3) Where by virtue of section 6, 7 or 8 above the liability for
maintenance or repair of any item of fixed equipment is transferred from
the landlord to the tenant, any claim by the tenant in respect of any
previous failure by the landlord to discharge the said liability shall, if the
tenant within the prescribed period beginning with the date on which the
transfer takes effect so requires, be determined by arbitration under this
Act.

(4) Where the terms of a tenancy of an agricultural holding as to the
maintenance, repair or insurance of fixed equipment (whether established
by the operation of regulations under section 7 above or by agreement)
are varied by new regulations made under that section, then, if a reference
is made under section 6 above within the prescribed period after the
coming into operation of the new regulations, the arbitrator shall, for the
purposes of subsection (2) of the said section 6, disregard the variation.

DEFINITIONS
"arbitration": s.84.
"landlord", "tenant, "fixed equipment", prescribed", "termination": s.96(1).

Subs. (1)
Transferred. This means the transfer of a previously existing liability. For difficulties of interpretation caused by *Burden* v. *Hannaford*, see article in [1956] J.P.L. 15.
Prescribed period. One month from the date when the transfer takes effect: see reg. 2(2) of the Agriculture (Miscellaneous Time-Limits) Regulations 1959 (S.I. 1959 No. 171).
And paid. I.e. paid immediately without waiting for the termination of the tenancy.

Subs. (2)
Section 71. Landlord's right to compensation for dilapidations, etc., which normally accrues on the tenant's quitting the holding on the termination of the tenancy but which is made available by s.9 on the transference of liability under ss.6, 7 or 8. This could result in a heavy bill for accrued dilapidations at an awkward time, possibly involving liability for putting the premises in repair: see *Payne* v. *Haine* (1847) 16 M. & W. 541; *Proudfoot* v. *Hart* (1890) 25 Q.B.D. 42; *Evans* v. *Jones* [1955] 2 Q.B. 58.

Subs. (3)
Transferred. See note on subs. (1) above.
Prescribed period. One month from the date when the transfer takes effect: see reg. 2(3) of the 1959 Regulations mentioned in note on subs. (1) above.

Subs. (4)
Prescribed period. The original prescribed period expired on March 1, 1949 and the second prescribed period on September 29, 1975: see the Agriculture (Time-Limit) Regulations 1973 (S.I. 1973 No. 1482). If the Agriculture (Maintenance, Repair and Insurance) Regulations 1973 (S.I. 1973 No. 1473) are replaced by new regulations it will be necessary to reactivate s.9(4). At the time of going to press s.9(4) is in suspense but could be revived.
Disregard the variation. Subs. (4) is a somewhat obscure and difficult provision. For an explanation and discussion of the difficulties, see note at [1956] J.P.L. 15–17.

Tenant's right to remove fixtures and buildings

10.—(1) Subject to the provisions of this section—
    (*a*) any engine, machinery, fencing or other fixture (of whatever description) affixed, whether for the purposes of agriculture or not, to an agricultural holding by the tenant, and
    (*b*) any building erected by him on the holding,
shall be removable by the tenant at any time during the continuance of the tenancy or before the expiry of two months from its termination, and shall remain his property so long as he may remove it by virtue of this subsection.
    (2) Subsection (1) above shall not apply—
    (*a*) to a fixture affixed or a building erected in pursuance of some obligation,
    (*b*) to a fixture affixed or a building erected instead of some fixture or building belonging to the landlord,
    (*c*) to a building in respect of which the tenant is entitled to compensation under this Act or otherwise, or
    (*d*) to a fixture affixed or a building erected before 1st January 1884.
    (3) The right conferred by subsection (1) above shall not be exercisable in relation to a fixture or building unless the tenant—
    (*a*) has paid all rent owing by him and has performed or satisfied all his other obligations to the landlord in respect of the holding, and
    (*b*) has, at least one month before both the exercise of the right and the termination of the tenancy, given to the landlord notice in writing of his intention to remove the fixture or building.
    (4) If, before the expiry of the notice mentioned in subsection (3) above, the landlord gives to the tenant a counter-notice in writing electing

to purchase a fixture or building comprised in the notice, subsection (1) above shall cease to apply to that fixture or building, but the landlord shall be liable to pay to the tenant the fair value of that fixture or building to an incoming tenant of the holding.

(5) In the removal of a fixture or building by virtue of subsection (1) above, the tenant shall not do any avoidable damage to any other building or other part of the holding, and immediately after the removal shall make good all damage so done that is occasioned by the removal.

(6) Any dispute between the landlord and the tenant with respect to the amount payable by the landlord under subsection (4) above in respect of any fixture or building shall be determined by arbitration under this Act.

(7) This section shall apply to a fixture or building acquired by a tenant as it applies to a fixture or building affixed or erected by him.

(8) This section shall not be taken as prejudicing any right to remove a fixture that subsists otherwise than by virtue of this section.

DEFINITIONS
"agriculture", "building", "fixture", "landlord", "tenant", "termination": s.96(1).
"agricultural holding": s.1(1).
"arbitration": s.84.

GENERAL NOTE
Elwes v. *Maw* (1802) 3 East 38 established that the common law exception to the maxim *"quicquid plantatur solo, solo cedit"* allowed in the case of trade fixtures (see *Poole's Case* (1703) 1 Salk. 368) did not extend to general agricultural fixtures, although it did apply to the fixtures of certain trades with a strongly agricultural flavour, such as the business of a market gardener or nurseryman, *e.g.* greenhouses, glass-houses, cider mills, even trees and shrubs planted by a nurseryman for sale: *Penton* v. *Robart* (1801) 2 East 88, 90; *Oakley* v. *Monck* (1866) L.R. 1 Exch. 159 at p.167; *Mears* v. *Callender* [1901] 2 Ch. 388; *Wardell* v. *Usher* (1841) 3 Scott N.R. 508. See also *Lawton* v. *Lawton* (1743) 3 Atk. 13, but *cf. Fisher* v. *Dixon* (1845) 12 Cl. & F. 312; *Walmsley* v. *Milne* (1859) 7 C.B.(N.S.) 115.

It has been generally held to be permissible to contract out of the predecessors of this section: see *Premier Dairies Ltd.* v. *Garlick* [1920] 2 Ch. 17, but some doubt was thrown on this view in *Johnson* v. *Moreton* [1980] A.C. 37 at p.58, where Lord Hailsham L.C. commented that the statutory scheme was different in some respects in 1920.

For the special position of market garden tenants, see ss.79–81.

Subs. (1)
Para. (a): other fixture. If an article is merely a loose chattel, *e.g.* a poultry ark which rests on the soil, or a barn or similar structure on staddles, as distinct from structures cemented or otherwise firmly fastened to the ground, it may, of course, be removed without the restrictions of s.10: *Wansborough* v. *Maton* (1836) 4 Ad. & El. 884; *Wiltshear* v. *Cottrell* (1853) 1 E. & B. 674.

Of whatever description. This appears to negate the application of the *ejusdem generis* rule to the previous words "engine, machinery, fencing or other fixture".

Affixed. This involves more than mere contact. The article must be let into or united with the land, or with some substance previously connected to it: *Palser* v. *Grinling* [1948] A.C. 291.

Whether for the purposes of agriculture or not. This extension to non-agricultural fixtures was made by the 1984 Act, Sched. 3, para. 6. The tenant may, however, be entitled to remove certain non-agricultural fixtures without any of the conditions in s.10, namely, trade or ornamental fixtures.

Before the expiry of two months. At common law the right of removal normally ceases when the tenancy expires except that if the lessor's own estate is uncertain, or if the tenancy is at will, the tenant seems to be given a reasonable time for removal after the termination of his interest: *Barff* v. *Probyn* (1895) 64 L.J.Q.B. 557; *Re Glasdir Copper Mines* [1904] 1 Ch. 819. (Consider in the light of *New Zealand Government Property Corporation* v. *H.M. & S. Ltd.* [1982] Q.B. 1145 what is the position of a tenant who remains in the holding during a succession of tenancies.)

Shall remain his property so long as he may remove it. This clears up doubts expressed in *Re Harvey and Mann's Arbitration* (1920) 89 L.J.K.B. 687, but there are still some obscurities: see note to subs. (3) below. While the property is vested in the tenant he would have a remedy in damages against the landlord if the latter prevented the severance and removal of the fixtures: *Thomas* v. *Jennings* (1896) 66 L.J.Q.B. 5; *Leschallas* v. *Woolf* [1908] 1 Ch. 641.

Subs. (2)
Para. (c): entitled to compensation. It is submitted that the tenant is not "entitled" to compensation (and thus may qualify to remove the building) if a period agreed between him and the landlord for "writing off" the building on the "years principle" has expired. It may thus be in the landlord's interest not to agree to a complete write-off, but to arrange for the tenant to retain a nominal entitlement to compensation. The tenant may, of course, not be entitled to compensation for the more obvious reason that he did not obtain consent or approval to the erection of the building: s.67.

Subs. (3)
Shall not be exercisable. It would appear that the effect of removing a fixture or building without satisfying either of the conditions in this subsection (although the removal takes place during the tenancy or within two months of its termination) is to revest the property in the landlord, so that he can sue the tenant (or a purchaser of the article) for conversion and is not confined to an action for damages against the tenant. The position would be the same if the tenant were to remove a fixture after the landlord had served a counter-notice electing to purchase it: see subs. (4). A practical difficulty seems to be that no machinery is provided to determine speedily, in the event of dispute, whether the tenant has performed or satisfied his obligations. The two-months period (subs. (1)) might have elapsed before the settlement of the dispute.
Para. (a): all rent . . . and . . . all his other obligations. This, strictly interpreted, is a formidable condition. As regards rent, particular care will be necessary where the last gale is payable in advance; but see county court decision of *Roberts* v. *Magor* [1953] E.G.D. 18 (C.C.). As regards other obligations, this would include, *inter alia*, all his repairing obligations, subject, no doubt, to the *de minimis* rule.
Para. (b): notice in writing of his intention to remove. Failure to give this notice will not only deprive the tenant of the legal right to remove and will have the effect mentioned above in this note, but as a consequence will deprive him of the right to claim compensation for disturbance for any loss sustained in connection with such removal if in fact it has taken place: *Re Harvey and Mann's Arbitration* (1920) 89 L.J.K.B. 687; 123 L.T. 242 (a better report), C.A.

Subs. (4)
Shall cease to apply. Although, unlike s.21(1), proviso (v), of the 1908 Act, it does not say so in terms, the fixture or building is the landlord's property from the time the counter-notice in subs. (3) is given.

Subs. (5)
Any avoidable damage. Presumably if damage is caused the tenant does not forfeit the property in the fixture (contrast subs. (3) and note *supra*) but, if he fails to make good, he is liable to an action for damages, or, if the matter arises at the end of the tenancy, to a claim for compensation in an arbitration.

Subs. (6)
Any dispute. Until the matter was clarified by the 1984 Act (Sched. 3, para. 6(3)) it did not appear that a dispute as to the fair value taking place *during* the tenancy could be referred to arbitration under the agricultural holdings code. It is now clear that the dispute is referable to arbitration under the 1986 Act, whether during or at the end of the tenancy. It was held in *Hassall* v. *Marquis of Cholmondeley* (1935) 79 S.J. 522; [1935] E.G.D. 82 that an arbitrator who exceeded his jurisdiction by including in his award articles not fixtures, within the section corresponding with section 10, was guilty of misconduct; but it is thought that if a landlord has agreed to take over certain articles of this kind at the end of the tenancy their value could be determined by arbitration under the Act.

Subs. (7)
Acquired. This does not appear to be confined to a purchase for value. But note that s.10(1) does not entitle a tenant to remove a fixture or building acquired by him before January 1, 1901: Sched. 12, para. 3.

Subs. (8)

Otherwise than by virtue of this section. This makes clear that the tenant's common law rights to remove trade or ornamental fixtures are not affected. (General agriculture is not a trade.)

See s.79(3) for special provisions affecting market gardens.

Provision of fixed equipment necessary to comply with statutory requirements

11.—(1) Where, on an application by the tenant of an agricultural holding, the Tribunal are satisfied that it is reasonable, having regard to the tenant's responsibilities to farm the holding in accordance with the rules of good husbandry, that he should carry on on the holding an agricultural activity specified in the application to the extent and in the manner so specified and—

(*a*) that, unless fixed equipment is provided on the holding, the tenant, in carrying on that activity to that extent and in that manner, will contravene requirements imposed by or under any enactment, or

(*b*) that it is reasonable that the tenant should use, for purposes connected with that activity, fixed equipment already provided on the holding, but that, unless that equipment is altered or repaired, the tenant, in using the equipment for those purposes, will contravene such requirements,

the Tribunal may direct the landlord to carry out, within a period specified in the direction, such work for the provision or, as the case may be, the alteration or repair of that fixed equipment as will enable the tenant to comply with the said requirements.

(2) Where it appears to the Tribunal that an agricultural activity specified in the tenant's application has not been carried on on the holding continuously for a period of at least three years immediately preceding the making of the application the Tribunal shall not direct the landlord to carry out work in connection with that activity unless they are satisfied that the starting of the activity did not or, where the activity has not yet been started, will not constitute or form part of a substantial alteration of the type of farming carried on on the holding.

(3) The Tribunal shall not direct the landlord to carry out work under this section unless they are satisfied—

(*a*) that it is reasonable to do so having regard to the landlord's responsibilities to manage the land comprised in the holding in accordance with the rules of good estate management and also to the period for which the holding may be expected to remain a separate holding and to any other material consideration, and

(*b*) that the landlord has refused to carry out that work on being requested in writing to do so by the tenant or has not agreed to carry it out within a reasonable time after being so requested.

(4) The Tribunal shall not direct the landlord to carry out that work under this section if he is under a duty to carry out the work in order to comply with a requirement imposed on him by or under any enactment or if provision is made by the contract of tenancy, or by any other agreement between the landlord and the tenant, for the carrying out of work by one of them.

(5) If the landlord fails to comply with a direction under this section the tenant shall have the same remedies as if the contract of tenancy had contained an undertaking by the landlord to carry out the work required by the direction within the period allowed by the Tribunal.

(6) Notwithstanding any term in the contract of tenancy restricting the carrying out by the tenant of alterations to the holding, the remedies referred to in subsection (5) above shall include the right of the tenant to

carry out the work himself and recover the reasonable cost of the work from the landlord.

(7) The Tribunal, on an application by the landlord, may extend or further extend the period specified in a direction under this section if it is shown to their satisfaction that the period so specified, or that period as previously extended under this subsection, as the case may be, will not allow sufficient time both for the completion of preliminary arrangements necessary or desirable in connection with the work required by the direction (including, in appropriate cases, the determination of an application by the landlord for a grant out of money provided by Parliament in respect of that work) and for the carrying out of the said work.

(8) The reference in subsection (6) above to the reasonable cost of work carried out by a tenant shall, where the tenant has received a grant in respect of the work out of money provided by Parliament, be construed as a reference to the reasonable cost reduced by the amount of the grant.

DEFINITIONS
  "agricultural holding": s.1(1).
  "contract of tenancy": s.1(5).
  "landlord", "tenant", "fixed equipment" and "tribunal": s.96(1).
  "rules of good estate management" and "rules of good husbandry": s.96(3).

Subs. (1)
  Application. For statutory form, see form 5 in the Appendix to Sched. 1 to the Agricultural Land Tribunals (Rules) Order 1978 (S.I. 1978 No. 259).
  Para. (a): by or under any enactment. For example, requirements under the Milk and Dairies (General) Regulations, under the Public Health Acts as to disposal of farm waste, and under the Agriculture (Safety, Health and Welfare Provisions) Act 1956.

Subs. (2)
  Continuously for a period of at least three years. The word "continuously" clarifies an ambiguity in s.4(1) of the 1958 Act, where the word "for" might have meant either "at any time within" or "continuously throughout": see 1984 Act, Sched. 3, para. 30.
  Substantial alteration. Examples are a change from arable to dairying or vice versa.

Subs. (3)
  Para. (a): a separate holding. This refers to a likelihood of amalgamation, which presumably must be more than a mere possibility.
  Any other material consideration. Whether this is to be interpreted narrowly as considerations having a direct relation to the individual holding or, more broadly, as matters such as the economic outlook for livestock, arable, or dairy farming in the light of government policy or EEC directives, is not clear.

Subs. (4)
  Contract of tenancy, or by any other agreement. The contract of tenancy will include any model clauses duly incorporated (s.7(3)) and "agreement" must mean an enforceable agreement as the object is to exclude a direction when other legal remedies are available.

Subs. (5)
  The same remedies. Thus the tenant can sue for damages for loss caused by the landlord's failure as if it were a breach of contract.
  Period allowed by the Tribunal. This may be the period specified in the direction or as extended under subs. (7).

Subs. (6)
  Reasonable cost. In the event of a dispute this would have to be determined by the courts, as there is no provision for arbitration on it under the 1986 Act.

Subs. (8)
  Reduced by the amount of the grant. See s.68(1) and (2) for complications where the tribunal give a direction on the sub-tenant's application, ordering his immediate landlord to

carry out work of repair or the provision of fixed equipment. For an explanation of s.68(2)(*b*) and the position in regard to a grant made to the sub-tenant, see the Law Commission's Report on the Agricultural Holdings Bill (Cmnd. 9665, Dec. 1985).

See also note 4 to 5, 68, *post.*

Increase of rent. An improvement carried out by the landlord in compliance with a direction given by the tribunal under s.11 will qualify for an increase of rent under s.13 (see s.13(2)(*b*)).

Variation of rent

Arbitration of rent

12.—(1) Subject to the provisions of Schedule 2 to this Act, the landlord or tenant of an agricultural holding may by notice in writing served on the other demand that the rent to be payable in respect of the holding as from the next termination date shall be referred to arbitration under this Act.

(2) On a reference under this section the arbitrator shall determine what rent should be properly payable in respect of the holding at the date of the reference and accordingly shall, with effect from the next termination date following the date of the demand for arbitration, increase or reduce the rent previously payable or direct that it shall continue unchanged.

(3) A demand for arbitration under this section shall cease to be effective for the purposes of this section on the next termination date following the date of the demand unless before the said termination date—

(*a*) an arbitrator has been appointed by agreement between the parties, or

(*b*) an application has been made to the President of the Royal Institution of Chartered Surveyors for the appointment of an arbitrator by him.

(4) References in this section (and in Schedule 2 to this Act) in relation to a demand for arbitration with respect to the rent of any holding, to the next termination date following the date of the demand are references to the next day following the date of the demand on which the tenancy of the holding could have been determined by notice to quit given at the date of the demand.

(5) Schedule 2 to this Act shall have effect for supplementing this section.

DEFINITIONS

"agricultural holding": s.1(1).
"arbitration": s.84.
"landlord", "tenant": s.96(1).
"termination date", see subs. (4) of s.12.

GENERAL NOTE

The main content of the rent arbitration provisions has been relegated to Sched. 2 in view of the amount of detail involved. This, however, seems the appropriate place for a few general observations. The fact that the interpretation of important parts of the formula is still controversial is not a reflection on the draftsmanship but on the failure of Parliament to make its intentions quite clear. Although the deliberate omission of any reference to an "open market" is probably not now regarded by many as significant, in view of the implications of such a market in the context, there are other matters where some doubt remains. There are still some who argue that the element of scarcity value is not required to be eliminated from the subject holding and there is a difference of opinion as to whether "marriage value" appertaining to the subject holding is to be disregarded or not. These matters are discussed in more detail in the notes on Sched. 2. It looks as if some litigation in inevitable. It is not clear whether tenant farmers received, in the new rent arbitration provisions, adequate consideration for surrendering (admittedly only over a prolonged period) their rights to family succession. The government of the day clearly considered (although their views are not evidence) that the Act required the scarcity element to be almost completely eliminated from the rent of the subject holding, but that this merely brought the law into line with the current practice of arbitrators (see Second Reading debate, *Hansard*, H.L., Vol. 444, cols. 714 and 782 (Nov. 8, 1983), H.C., Vol. 55, col. 861 (March 7, 1984)). The Act was a Toleration Act for arbitrators, not a Benefit Act for tenants.

Other provisions worth mentioning are a belated measure of justice for tenants who have carried out improvements during a previous tenancy of the holding and the abolition of the notorious and unworkable direction not to take into account the "relief from the payment of rates." See also tenant's right to give short notice to quit after rent increase: s.25(3).

It is important to read Part II of Sched. 2 in conjunction with Part I.

The detailed content of the rent arbitration provisions is in Sched. 2: see notes to the paras of that Sched.

Subs. (1)
Notice in writing. The notice must be carefully worded and in particular state accurately the date from which the proposed rent change is to take affect.

Demand. An attempt at agreement is not a condition precedent to a demand: Contrast s.6(1). For circumstances in which a demand may become ineffective, see subs. (3) of present section. It is submitted that a reference demanded by a landlord can be pursued by his successor in title: *cf. Morris Marks* v. *British Waterways Board* [1963] 1 W.L.R. 1008. It is considered that such a demand cannot be withdrawn without the consent of the other party.

Next termination date. This has the same meaning as, and is more self-explanatory than, "the next ensuing day" in the old s.8 of the 1948 Act. For definition, see subs. (4).

Subs. (3)
Unless before the said termination date. It will be noted that the effectiveness of a demand will be saved if an application has been made to (which should be taken to mean received by) the President before the next termination date. The President of the RICS was substituted for the Minister (in Wales the Secretary of State) as the appointing authority for arbitrators as from January 1, 1986 by s.8 of the Agricultural Holdings Act 1984 and the Agricultural Holdings Act 1984 (Commencement) Order 1985 (S.I. 1985 No. 1644 (C.39).

Subs. (4)
Rent of any holding. Rent as such is not defined, but it must be taken to have its ordinary meaning of the total annual amount payable in respect of the holding including any buildings and landlord's fixtures on it and services provided with it and also including any portion which may on analysis be attributable to the landlord's capital expenditure. "Sheep rents", *i.e.* annual payments made by the tenant of a hill farm to a landlord in respect of a stock of acclimatised sheep which are either let with the holding or under a separate agreement, are not as such subject to this section, but the value of the sheep stock and the terms of the letting agreement may be material factors to be considered in assessing the rent of the holding.

Subs. (5)
Schedule 2. This Act, unlike the 1948 Act as amended by the 1984 Act, has transferred to a schedule the substance of the law as to rent arbitration.

Increases of rent for landlord's improvements

13.—(1) Where the landlord of an agricultural holding has carried out on the holding any improvement to which this section applies he may by notice in writing served on the tenant within six months from the completion of the improvement increase the rent of the holding as from the completion of the improvement by an amount equal to the increase in the rental value of the holding attributable to the carrying out of the improvement.

(2) This section applies to—

(*a*) an improvement carried out at the request of, or in agreement with, the tenant,

(b) an improvement carried out in compliance with a direction given by the Tribunal under section 11 above,

(c) an improvement carried out in pursuance of a notice served by the landlord under section 67(5) below,

(d) an improvement carried out in compliance with a direction given by the Minister under powers conferred on him by or under any enactment,

(e) works executed on the holding for the purpose of complying with the requirements of a notice under section 3 of the Agriculture (Safety, Health and Welfare Provisions) Act 1956 (provision of sanitary conveniences and washing facilities),

(f) an improvement carried out in compliance with an improvement notice served, or an undertaking accepted, under Part VII of the Housing Act 1985 or Part VIII of the Housing Act 1974.

(3) No increase of rent shall be made under subsection (1) above in respect of an improvement within paragraph (a), (b) or (f) of subsection (2) above if within six months from its completion the landlord and tenant agree on any increase of rent or other benefit to the landlord in respect of the improvement.

(4) The increase in rent provided for by subsection (1) above shall be reduced proportionately—

(a) in the case of an improvement within paragraph (b) of subsection (2) above, where a grant has been made to the landlord in respect of the improvement out of money provided by Parliament,

(b) in the case of an improvement within any other paragraph of that subsection, where a grant has been made to the landlord in respect of the improvement out of money provided by Parliament or local government funds, and

(c) in the case of an improvement within paragraph (f) of that subsection, where the tenant has contributed to the cost incurred by his landlord in carrying out the improvement.

(5) Where, on the failure of a landlord to carry out an improvement specified in such a direction as is referred to in subsection (2)(b) above, the tenant has himself carried out the improvement, the provisions of this section shall apply as if the improvement had been carried out by the landlord and as if any grant made to the tenant in respect of the improvement out of money provided by Parliament had been made to the landlord.

(6) No increase in rent shall take effect by virtue of subsection (5) above until the tenant has recovered from the landlord the reasonable cost of the improvement reduced by the amount of any grant made to the tenant in respect of the improvement out of money provided by Parliament.

(7) Any dispute arising between the landlord and the tenant of the holding under this section shall be determined by arbitration under this Act.

(8) This section applies to an improvement whether or not it is one for the carrying out of which compensation is provided under Part V or VI of this Act.

DEFINITIONS
"agricultural holding": s.1(1).
"arbitration": s.84.
"landlord", "tenant", "Minister", "Tribunal", "local government funds": s.96(1).

Subs. (1)
Within six months. This is an absolute condition, but a landlord who does not satisfy it may be able to obtain an increase under s.12 by arbitration. If he does satisfy the condition,

an increase under s.13(1) or (3) is disregarded for the purpose of the frequency of arbitrations under s.12: see Sched. 2, para. 4(1)(*b*) and (2)(*b*).

Increase in the rental value. See s.14(8) of the Opencast Coal Act 1958 for a provision that any increase in rental value due to an improvement which has been affected by opencast coal operations is to be assessed as if they had not been carried out.

Subs. (2)

Para. (c): section 67(5) below. This is where the landlord proposes himself to carry out an improvement approved by the tribunal after originally refusing his consent to it.

Para. (d): by or under any enactment e.g. s.95 of the Agriculture Act 1947 as amended.

Para. (f): Part VII of the Housing Act 1985. See ss.214 and 215 and s.231.

Part VIII of the Housing Act 1974. Part VIII was repealed by the Housing (Consequential Provisions) Act 1985, s.3 and Sched. 1.

Subs. (3)

The landlord and tenant agree. An increase so agreed will be disregarded, in the same way as an increase in pursuance of subs. (1), for the purpose of the three-year restriction on the frequency of arbitrations: see Sched. 2, para. 4(2)(*b*).

Subs. (4)

Reduced proportionately. Presumably by the proportion which the grant or the contribution, as the case may be, bears to the capitalised increase of rental value.

Subs. (5)

As if the improvement had been carried out by the landlord. This and the next subs. allow a landlord, in the case of a direction under subs (2)(*b*), to recover an increase of rent, although he himself has failed to execute the improvement, if the tenant has done so and been duly reimbursed by the landlord. The subss. also ensure that any grant is taken into account in accordance with subs. (4)

Subs. (8)

Compensation. There may be a doubt as to whether works which are not identified as improvements under Part V or Part VI are in fact "improvements" for the purpose of this section. This is a matter which could be resolved by arbitration in accordance with subs. (7).

Cultivation of land and disposal of produce

Variation of terms of tenancies as to permanent pasture

14.—(1) This section applies where a contract for a tenancy of an agricultural holding provides for the maintenance of specified land, or a specified proportion of the holding, as permanent pasture.

(2) Where this section applies, the landlord or tenant may, by notice in writing served on the other, demand a reference to arbitration under this Act of the question whether it is expedient in order to secure the full and efficient farming of the holding that the area of land required to be maintained as permanent pasture should be reduced.

(3) On a reference under subsection (2) above the arbitrator may by his award direct that the provisions of the contract of tenancy as to land which is to be maintained as permanent pasture or is to be treated as arable land and as to cropping shall have effect subject to such modifications as may be specified in the direction.

(4) If, on a reference under subsection (2) above, the arbitrator gives a direction reducing the area of land which under the contract of tenancy is to be maintained as permanent pasture, he may order that the contract of tenancy shall have effect as if it provided that on quitting the holding on the termination of the tenancy the tenant should leave—

(*a*) as permanent pasture, or

(*b*) as temporary pasture sown with seeds mixture of such kind as may be specified in the order, such area of land (in addition to the area of land required by the contract of tenancy, as modified by the direction, to be maintained as permanent pasture) as may be so specified.

(5) The area of land specified in an order made under subsection (4) above shall not exceed the area by which the land required by the contract of tenancy to be maintained as permanent pasture has been reduced by virtue of the direction.

DEFINITIONS
"agricultural holding": s.1(1).
"arbitration": s.84.
"contract of tenancy": s.1(5).
"landlord", "pasture", "termination": s.96(1).

Subs. (1)
Provides for. Formerly, before grass was regarded as a crop, the scheduling of land as pasture, with covenants against ploughing up, and sometimes penal rent clauses (invalidated by s.24) were common.

Permanent pasture. The precise legal definition is not too clear and most of the cases are old. The criterion seems sometimes to be mere age (pasture laid down 20 or more years ago), sometimes the character of the seeds mixture (showing the intention to produce permanent grass and not a temporary ley), sometimes contractual (an obligation to maintain in the same condition throughout the tenancy); *cf.* s.15(7). The last is the most clear cut from a legal standpoint but does not always fit. For example, the 1923 Act regarded permanent pasture as an improvement which the tenant could make and for which, if laid down with the landlord's consent, he could obtain compensation. The essence of the meaning in the present section is contractual, but there is a physical flavour; otherwise the word "permanent" is really otiose. Among the old cases the following may be referred to: *Atkins* v. *Temple* (1625) 1 Rep. Ch. 13; *Fermier* v. *Maund* (1638) 1 Rep. Ch. 116; *Drury* v. *Molins* (1801) 6 Ves. 328; *Birch* v. *Stephenson* (1811) 3 Taunt. 469; *Morris* v. *Morris* (1825) 1 Hog. 238; *Martin* v. *Coggan* (1824) 1 Hog. 120; *Simmons* v. *Norton* (1831) 7 Bing. 640. At common law ploughing up "ancient meadow" was prime facie waste and could be restrained in equity by injunction, even in the absence of an express covenant not to plough up. Normally a tenant was not restrained from ploughing up pasture which he had laid down himself on land which was arable at the commencement of the tenancy: *Rush* v. *Lucas* [1910] 1 Ch. 437, but in the exceptional case of *Clarke-Jervoise* v. *Scutt* [1920] 1 Ch. 382, where the tenant had covenanted not to plough up "any" grassland, and there were other special circumstances, an injunction was granted to prevent him from ploughing up permanent grass over 20 years old laid down by himself during the tenancy. Today, apart from the machinery of section 14, ploughing up, if regarded as waste at all, would be more readily regarded as ameliorative or meliorating waste. Sched. 8 refers simply to "pasture" in Part II, para. 9, grass being treated as a crop and not as an improvement, in accordance with the modern outlook.

Subs. (2)
Arbitration. Originally under the 1948 Act this matter was decided by a direction by the Minister, but arbitration was substituted by the 1958 Act. Despite the generality of the word "modifications" in subs. (3), the arbitrator's jurisdiction is confined to considering the expediency of a *reduction*.

Subs. (3)
Shall have effect. The award will modify the contract as specified and the effect will be to enable pasture to be ploughed up without breach of contract. It should be noted that by s.78(2) the parties may agree in writing for such a variation as could be made by direction or order under the present section 14; and the agreement may exclude compensation in the same manner as it is excluded by s.76(1)(*a*) in respect of anything done in pursuance of an order under s.14(4).

Note on compensation. The tenant will not be entitled to any compensation when he leaves for pasture laid down to restore the pasture area: s.76(1)(*a*). Further, there is a provision, as will be seen later, to prevent him from treating his inferior pieces of pasture as laid down in compliance with the order and claiming compensation on his superior pieces, when he leaves: s.76(1)(*b*).

Disposal of produce and cropping

15.—(1) Subject to the provisions of this section and to section 82 below, the tenant of an agricultural holding shall (notwithstanding any custom of the country or the provisions of the contract of tenancy or of any agreement respecting the disposal of crops or the method of cropping of arable land) have, without incurring any penalty, forfeiture or liability, the following rights, namely—

(a) to dispose of the produce of the holding, other than manure produced on the holding, and

(b) to practise any system of cropping of the arable land on the holding.

(2) Subsection (1) above shall not apply—

(a) in the case of a tenancy from year to year, as respects the year before the tenant quits the holding or any period after he has given or received notice to quit which results in his quitting the holding, or

(b) in the case of any other tenancy, as respects the year before its termination.

(3) Subject to any agreement in writing to the contrary, the tenant of an agricultural holding shall not at any time after he has given or received notice to quit the holding sell or remove from the holding any manure or compost or any hay or straw or roots grown in the last year of the tenancy unless the landlord's written consent has been obtained before the sale or removal.

(4) Before, or as soon as possible after, exercising his rights under subsection (1) above, a tenant shall make suitable and adequate provision—

(a) in the case of an exercise of the right to dispose of produce, to return to the holding the full equivalent manurial value of all crops sold off or removed from the holding in contravention of the custom, contract or agreement, and

(b) in the case of an exercise of the right to practise any system of cropping, to protect the holding from injury or deterioration.

(5) If the tenant of an agricultural holding exercises his rights under subsection (1) above in such manner as to, or to be likely to, injure or deteriorate the holding, the landlord shall have the following remedies, but no other, namely—

(a) the right to obtain, if the case so requires, an injunction to restrain the exercise of those rights in that manner, and

(b) the right in any case, on the tenant's quitting the holding on the termination of the tenancy, to recover damages for any injury to or deterioration of the holding attributable to the exercise by the tenant of those rights.

(6) For the purposes of any proceedings for an injunction brought under paragraph (a) of subsection (5) above, the question whether the tenant is exercising, or has exercised, his rights under subsection (1) above in such a manner as to, or to be likely to, injure or deteriorate his holding shall be determined by arbitration under this Act; and the award of the arbitrator shall, for the purposes of any proceedings brought under subsection (5) (including an arbitration under paragraph (b)) be conclusive proof of the facts stated in the award.

(7) In this section—

"arable land" does not include land in grass which, by the terms of a contract of tenancy, is to be retained in the same condition throughout the tenancy; and

"roots" means the produce of any root crop of a kind normally grown for consumption on the holding.

DEFINITIONS

"agreement", "landlord", "tenant", "termination": s.96(1).
"agricultural holding": s.1(1).
"arbitration": s.84.
"contract of tenancy": s.1(5).

Subs. (1)

Subject to the provisions of this section. The freedom given by s.15(1) is qualified by subss. (4) and (5) which require provision to safeguard the holding against injury or deterioration, and is subject to the prohibitions in subss. (2) and (3). See also s.82 excluding application of s.15(1) to smallholdings.

Notwithstanding. Section 15(1) presupposes a contractual or customary restriction on disposal or cropping: contrast *Gough* v. *Howard* (1801) Peake's Add.Cas. 197.

Custom of the country. This need not be immemorial or universal, but must be more than an individual or estate practice and must be reasonable: *Tucker* v. *Linger* (1883) 8 App.Cas. 508; *Womersley* v. *Dally* (1857) 29 L.J.Ex. 219; *Bradburn* v. *Foley* (1878) 3 C.P.D. 129.

Contract of tenancy. For examples of covenants in the contract of tenancy restricting selling-off and cropping, see *Legh* v. *Lillie* (1860) 6 H. & N. 165; *Willson* v. *Love* [1896] 1 Q.B. 626; *Chapman* v. *Smith* [1907] 2 Ch. 97; *Bowers* v. *Nixon* (1848) 12 Q.B. 558; *Fleming* v. *Snook* (1842) 5 Beav. 250; *Doe* v. *Broad* (1841) 10 L.J.C.P. 80. Covenants prohibiting selling-off in the last year of the tenancy cover the produce of previous years as well as the produce of the last year; *Gale* v. *Bates* (1864) 33 L.J.Ex. 235; *Meggeson* v. *Groves* [1917] 1 Ch. 158. For the effect on a covenant to conserve hay and straw of their destruction by fire, see *Re Hull and Meux (Lady)* [1905] 1 K.B. 588.

Para. (a): produce. This includes hay from permanent pasture, although the freedom of cropping does not apply to the latter: see s.15(1)(*b*) and (7).

Manure produced on the holding. This removed a doubt which existed under s.30 of the 1923 Act.

Para. (b): arable land. See subs. (7). In *Taylor* v. *Steel-Maitland,* 1913 S.C. 562 it was held that market garden ground was not arable land within a corresponding Scottish provision.

Subs. (2)

Shall not apply. Although the meaning of subs. (2) has caused doubts in the past, it seems to be accepted that s.15(1) is excluded in any case during the last year of the tenancy even if a shorter notice than twelve months is legitimately given, but that if a longer notice than twelve months is in fact given s.15(1) is excluded during that longer period. It may seem odd that a tenant's freedom should be withdrawn for a period which antedates the notice, but *cf.* *Wilmot* v. *Rose* (1854) 23 L.J.Q.B. 281 and *Eldon (Lord)* v. *Hedley Bros.* [1935] 2 K.B. 1. As to the sale during the material period of the produce of an earlier period, see note on subs. (1). As to the effect of s.11 of the Sale of Farming Stock Act 1816 and the possible liability of a purchaser of produce sold off in breach of covenant, see *Eldon* v. *Hedley Bros., ante.* Clearly in order to restore the prescribed rotation in the last year earlier action may well be essential. This may put the tenant in a difficulty where the landlord gives a bare twelve months' notice and in an almost impossible position where less than twelve months notice is properly given under s.25(2). But parties may agree specially as to cropping in the last year.

Subs. (3)

To the contrary. This means an agreement (in writing) *enabling* a tenant to sell or remove the produce mentioned after the giving or receipt of a notice to quit. Most agreements, however, are *restrictive* of disposal of the manure and other produce in question. It would appear that the effective field of operation of subs. (3) is where there is no agreement or custom restricting disposal and no "contrary" written agreement permitting it.

Grown in the last year of the tenancy. These words qualify only "any hay or straw or roots". This is so grammatically; apart from the inaptness of saying that manure or compost is "grown".

Subs. (4)

Suitable and adequate provision. It is still important to include disposal and cropping clauses in agricultural tenancy agreements, since they will operate fully in the last year (s.15(2)) and will, in addition, ensure that in earlier years "suitable and adequate provision" can be required to return the manurial equivalent or prevent deterioration. See s.76(3) for an express exclusion of compensation for doing so.

Subs. (5)

Remedies. The landlord is to have "the following remedies but no other". He cannot, therefore, in this context bring an action for damages on the *Kent* v. *Conniff* [1953] 1 Q.B. 361 principle.

Para. (a): injunction. The landlord may seek an injunction if the tenant exercises his rights in such a way as to injure the holding. The landlord's other remedy is to recover compensation on the tenant's quitting the holding on the termination of the tenancy. (See next note as to "damages".) See subs. (6) and note below as to the necessity for an arbitrator's award as a prerequisite for injunction proceedings. It seems doubtful whether damages could be obtained in lieu of an injunction. For a case where an injunction was granted under a corresponding earlier provision, see *Heap* v. *Wilkes* (1910), reported only in *The Times,* October 29, 1910.

Para. (b): damages. The word "damages" suggests an action in the courts, but it would seem from s.15(5) and s.83(1) that the landlord's remedy (apart from the possibility of an injunction during the tenancy) is compensation to be determined by arbitration at the end of the tenancy. Singleton L.J. in *Kent* v. *Conniff* [1953] 1 Q.B. 361 at p. 370 referred to a "right to recover damages" on the tenant's quitting the holding, suggesting a postponed action for damages in the courts. This would seem contrary to the scheme of the Act, but in that case one would have expected the matter to have been clarified on consolidation. A doubt remains.

Subs. (6)

Shall be determined by arbitration under this Act. This refers to an arbitration during the tenancy in aid of an injunction, as distinct from an arbitration to determine compensation at the end of the tenancy. Arbitration under subs. (6) is a condition precedent to proceedings for an injunction to restrain the tenant from injuring the holding and the award is conclusive proof of the facts stated in it for the purpose of such proceedings, It is also conclusive proof of such facts for the purpose of a subsequent arbitration to determine compensation at the end of the tenancy.

Subs. (7)

Land in grass. Since "arable land" would not normally include old meadow or recognised permanent pasture, it appears that this provision is intended to make it clear that freedom of cropping does not apply to any grass, however recently laid down, which the contract has impressed with the character of permanent pasture for the purpose of the tenancy.

Smallholdings. Attention is drawn to s.82(1), which excludes the operation of s.15(1) in the case of smallholdings let in pursuance of a scheme which fulfils the conditions set out in s.82. For a case in which the exclusion applied, but which turned on a tenancy agreement between the Minister and tenants, see *Williams* v. *Minister of Agriculture, Fisheries and Food* (1985) (unreported but mentioned at (1985) 275 E.G. 1080).

Distress

No distress for rent due more than a year previously

16.—(1) Subject to subsection (2) below, the landlord of an agricultural holding shall not be entitled to distrain for rent which became due in respect of that holding more than one year before the making of the distress.

(2) Where it appears that, according to the ordinary course of dealing between the landlord and the tenant of the holding, the payment of rent has been deferred until the expiry of a quarter or half-year after the date at which the rent legally became due, the rent shall, for the purposes of subsection (1) above, be deemed to have become due at the expiry of that quarter or half-year and not at the date at which it became legally due.

DEFINITIONS
"agricultural holding": s.1(1).
"landlord", "tenant": s.96(1).

More than one year. In contrast with the normal six-year period; but actions for recovery of rent are not affected.

Subs. (2)
Be deemed to have become due. This may enable the landlord in certain cases to distrain for more than one year's rent: *Re Bew, ex p. Ball* (1887) 18 Q.B.D. 642. Read strictly the provision seems to apply only where payment is deferred for *precisely* a quarter or half-year, neither more nor less, but the contrary appears to be assumed in *Re Bew.*

Became legally due. Rent is due on the morning of the day appointed for payment, but is not in arrear until after midnight: *Cutting* v. *Derby* (1776) 2 W.Bl. 1075; *Dibble* v. *Bowater* (1853) 2 E. & B. 564; *Re Aspinall, Aspinall* v. *Aspinall* [1961] Ch. 526. On the limitation in cases of bankruptcy to six months' rent prior to adjudication, see s.35(1) of the Bankruptcy Act 1914, now s.180 of the Insolvency Act 1985. The balance is provable in the bankruptcy. The balance of the arrears of rent which the landlord is prevented from recovering by distress is recoverable in an action at law, subject to the normal maximum of six years' arrears.

Compensation to be set off against rent for purposes of distress

17. Where the amount of any compensation due to the tenant of an agricultural holding, whether under this Act or under custom or agreement, has been ascertained before the landlord distrains for rent, that amount may be set off against the rent and the landlord shall not be entitled to distrain for more than the balance.

DEFINITIONS
"agreement", "landlord", "tenant": s.96(1).
"agricultural holding": s.1(1).

GENERAL NOTE
Although this provision applies to *any* compensation due to the tenant of a holding, it would be unlikely to apply to compensation for disturbance or improvements. It could apply, say, to game damage compensation (s.20). At common law set off is not allowed: *Absolem* v. *Knight* (1742) Bull.N.P. 181; *Willson* v. *Davenport* (1833) 5 C. & P. 531; *Pratt* v. *Keith* (1864) 33 L.J.Ch. 528.

Restrictions on distraining on property of third party

18.—(1) Property belonging to a person other than the tenant of an agricultural holding shall not be distrained for rent if—
  (*a*) the property is agricultural or other machinery and is on the holding under an agreement with the tenant for its hire or use in the conduct of his business, or
  (*b*) the property is livestock and is on the holding solely for breeding purposes.
  (2) Agisted livestock shall not be distrained by the landlord of an agricultural holding for rent where there is other sufficient distress to be found; and if such livestock is distrained by him by reason of other sufficient distress not being found, there shall not be recovered by that distress a sum exceeding the amount of the price agreed to be paid for the feeding, or any part of the price which remains unpaid.
  (3) The owner of the agisted livestock may, at any time before it is sold, redeem it by paying to the distrainer a sum equal to the amount mentioned in subsection (2) above, and payment of that sum to the distrainer shall be in full discharge as against the tenant of any sum of that amount which would otherwise be due from the owner of the livestock to the tenant in respect of the price of feeding.
  (4) Any portion of the agisted livestock shall, so long as it remains on the holding, continue liable to be distrained for the amount for which the whole of the livestock is distrainable.

(5) In this section "livestock" includes any animal capable of being distrained; and "agisted livestock" means livestock belonging to another person which has been taken in by the tenant of an agricultural holding to be fed at a fair price.

DEFINITIONS
"agisted livestock": see subs. (5).
"agreement", "landlord", "tenant": s.96(1).
"agricultural holding": s.1(1).
"livestock": subs. (5) of this section, *not* the definition in s.96(1).

Subs. (1)
Shall not be distrained. The two types of property mentioned in subs. (1) are *absolutely* privileged from distress, as distinct from the qualified privilege given to agisted livestock by subss. (2), (3) and (4).
Para. (a): hire. Although the matter is not free from doubt, some forms of hire-purchase agreement appear to be included.
Para. (b). breeding purposes. This protects not only female stock but also, *e.g.*, bulls and rams brought on to the holding to serve female stock. Livestock within this section are excluded from the protection of the Law of Distress Amendment Act 1908: see s.4(1) of that Act.

Subs. (2)
Agisted livestock. See definitions in subs. (5). Contrast arrangements, whether lettings or licences, which give exclusive possession of land for feeding: *Masters* v. *Green* (1888) 20 Q.B.D. 807. Making an agistment contract is not a breach of a covenant against assignment and subletting: *cf. Richards* v. *Davies* [1921] 1 Ch. 90. Gratuitous arrangements are clearly outside this section, but the consideration may be in kind and not monetary (*e.g.* "milk for meat"): *London and Yorkshire Bank* v. *Belton* (1885) 15 Q.B.D. 457. Agisted *sheep* were probably conditionally privileged apart from this section: *Keen* v. *Priest* (1859) 28 L.J. Ex. 157. Agisted *cattle* were probably distrainable at common law, but not perhaps where a *trade* of agisting was carried on: *Miles* v. *Furber* (1873) L.R. 8 Q.B. 77. For an agister's liability for safe custody, see *Coldman* v. *Hill* [1919] 1 K.B. 443. Note that the contract of agistment is not normally such as to enable the bailee of the stock to claim either a general or a particular lien against the stock owner: see *Re Southern Livestock Producers Ltd.* [1964] 1 W.L.R. 24, where it was held that a contract to care for pigs did not involve the element of "improvement" which the cases have established as a necessary ingredient of entitlement to a particular lien.
Other sufficient distress. Presumably not itself conditionally privileged. An owner of stock will be able to recover their value from the distrainer if he sells them contrary to this section: see, *e.g. Keen* v. *Priest, supra.*

Subs. (3)
The amount mentioned in subs. (2) above. This means the price agreed without the addition of costs.

Settlement of disputes as to distress

19.—(1) Where a dispute arises—
  (*a*) in respect of any distress having been levied on an agricultural holding contrary to the provisions of this Act,
  (*b*) as to the ownership of any livestock distrained or as to the price to be paid for the feeding of that stock, or
  (*c*) as to any other matter or thing relating to a distress on an agricultural holding,
the dispute may be determined by the county court or on complaint by a magistrates' court, and the court may make an order for restoration of any livestock or things unlawfully distrained, may declare the price agreed to be paid for feeding or may make any other order that justice requires.
  (2) Any person aggrieved by a decision of a magistrates' court under this section may appeal to the Crown Court.

(3) In this section "livestock" includes any animal capable of being distrained.

"agricultural holding": s.1(1).
"County Court": s.96(1).
"livestock": subs. (3).

Subs. (1)
May be determined. This provides a summary procedure, but does not take away any existing remedy.
Any other order that justice requires. Despite their width, it is doubtful whether these words confer on a magistrates' court a power to award damages for illegal distress: *Lowe* v. *Dorling* [1905] 2 K.B. 501 at p.504.

Subs. (2)
Appeal to the Crown Court. See Courts Act 1971, s.56(2) and Sched. 9. An appeal from the county court is to the Court of Appeal: County Courts Act 1984, s.77. See *Hanmer* v. *King* (1887) 57 L.T. 367.

Miscellaneous

Compensation for damage by game

20.—(1) Where the tenant of an agricultural holding has sustained damage to his crops from any wild animals or birds the right to kill and take which is vested in the landlord or anyone (other than the tenant himself) claiming under the landlord, being animals or birds which the tenant has not permission in writing to kill, he shall, if he complies with the requirements of subsection (2) below, be entitled to compensation from his landlord for the damage.

(2) The requirements of this subsection are that the tenant shall give his landlord—

    (*a*) notice in writing within one month after the tenant first became, or ought reasonably to have become, aware of the occurrence of the damage,

    (*b*) a reasonable opportunity to inspect the damage—

        (i) in the case of damage to a growing crop, before the crop is begun to be reaped, raised or consumed, and

        (ii) in the case of damage to a crop which has been reaped or raised, before the crop is begun to be removed from the land, and

    (*c*) notice in writing of the claim, together with particulars of it, within one month after the expiry of the year in respect of which the claim is made.

(3) For the purposes of subsection (2) above—

    (*a*) seed once sown shall be treated as a growing crop whether or not it has germinated, and

    (*b*) "year" means any period of twelve months ending, in any year, with 29th September or with such other date as may by agreement between the landlord and tenant be substituted for that date.

(4) The amount of compensation under this section shall, in default of agreement made after the damage has been suffered, be determined by arbitration under this Act.

(5) Where the right to kill and take the wild animals or birds that did the damage is vested in some person other than the landlord, the landlord shall be entitled to be indemnified by that other person against all claims for compensation under this section; and any question arising under this subsection shall be determined by arbitration under this Act.

"agreement", "landlord", "tenant": s.96(1).
"agricultural holding": s.1(1).
"arbitration": s.84.

GENERAL NOTE
For the common law position, see *Woodfall* (28th ed.), pp.724–736 and see *Moore* v. *Plymouth (Lord)* (1819) 3 B. & Ald. 66; *Pochin* v. *Smith* (1887) 52 J.P. 4; *Farrer* v. *Nelson* (1885) 15 Q.B.D. 258; *Hilton* v. *Green* (1862) 2 F. & F 821; *Birkbeck* v. *Paget* (1862) 31 Beav. 403; *Seligman* v. *Docker* [1949] Ch. 53. On the position of the sporting tenant, see *Cope* v. *Sharpe* [1912] 1 K.B. 496; *Mason* v. *Clarke* [1955] A.C. 778. See also the Game Act 1831, for protection for express reservations of game, and the Ground Game Act 1880, as amended by the Ground Game (Amendment) Act 1906, for tenant's concurrent right to kill ground game (hares and rabbits).

Subs. (1)
Damage. It was held (on a corresponding Scottish provision) that this includes damage by game from a neighbouring estate, as well as from the landlord's own coverts, and even during the close season: *Thomson* v. *Galloway (Earl)*, 1919 S.C. 611.
Wild animals or birds. It will be noted that s.20, unlike its predecessors from 1909 onwards, does not use the word "game" and then define it by enumerating a number of species (in the 1948 Act, "deer, pheasants, partridges, grouse and black game"). At common law "game" was a word of undefined meaning: per Erle J. in *Jeffryes* v. *Evans* (1865) 19 C.B.(N.S.) 246 at p.264 and it has been used in statutes in a variety of meanings: see, *e.g.* the Game Acts mentioned above. Certain wild birds listed in Sched. 1 to the Wildlife and Countryside Act 1981 are protected under Part I of that Act and are not treated as "game". See also the Protection of Birds Act 1954.
Claiming under the landlord. This is an improvement on the 1948 wording, which appeared to make the landlord's title derivative from the tenant. At the same time it safeguards the tenant's rights if the landlord, instead of reserving sporting rights in the tenancy, arranges for the tenant to sublet them to the landlord.
Permission in writing to kill. If the permission is to kill one particular species of wild animals or birds, *e.g.* pheasants, the permission will exclude compensation for damage from that kind, but not other kinds: *cf. Ross* v. *Watson*, 1943 S.C. 406. Presumably a permission which the tenant has not asked for and does not want will exclude compensation, but probably not a purported permission to kill in the close season.
Shall . . . be entitled to compensation. The agricultural tenant's rights to compensation under this section cannot be cut down by contract: s.78(1). There seems, however, to be nothing to prevent the *sporting* tenant from contracting out of liability to indemnify the landlord under subs. (5). A tenant can obtain a charge on the holding for game damage compensation: s.85(2).

Subs. (2)
Para. (a): notice in writing. Two notices in writing are essential conditions, the preliminary notice of the occurrence of the damage under para. (a) and the particularised notice of claim under para. (b).
Para. (b): reasonable opportunity. This will depend on circumstances. The tenant should warn the landlord if there is urgency, *e.g.* a reaped crop exposed to bad weather or where delay will magnify the damage, as in the case of damage from grouse to oats in stooks. On the question generally what is a reasonable opportunity, see *Dale* v. *Hatfield Chase Corporation* [1922] 2 K.B. 282; *Barbour* v. *McDouall*, 1914 S.C. 844.
growing crop. Subs. 3(*a*) removes a doubt as to whether a "growing crop" covers grain duly sown which has not yet had time to germinate (amendment made by 1984 Act, Sched. 3, para. 7).
Para. (c): particulars. There is no prescribed form or other guidance as to the detail required. It is suggested that the particulars should be fairly full and indicate the period during which the damage continued.

Subs. (3)
Para. (b): such other date. The parties might, for example, agree on February 1 as the end of the pheasant and partridge shooting season.

Subs. (4)
The amount of compensation. Under the 1948 Act before amendment by the 1984 Act (Sched. 3, para. 7) there was a condition that compensation would not be paid unless the

damage exceeded 12p per hectare (originally 1s. per acre). This obsolete condition was abolished in 1984.

Arbitration. The arbitrator's task is not easy as he will have to exclude damage not due to wild animals or birds which fulfil the requirements in subs. (1) and he will have to decide *e.g.* whether a crop would have grown satisfactorily apart from the damage. The measure of compensation seems to be the full amount of the damage.

Subs. (5)

Indemnified. As mentioned in note to subs. (1) on entitlement to compensation above, the sporting tenant can probably contract out of this liability to indemnify. A landlord has no statutory right of indemnity against a neighbouring owner, although game from the latter's property may cause damage for which the agricultural tenant can claim against the landlord under this section; but there may be a common law right of indemnity: *Thomson* v. *Galloway (Earl),* 1919 S.C. 911; *Farrer* v. *Nelson* (1885) 15 Q.B.D. 258. The agricultural tenant has no direct remedy under the Act against the sporting tenant; *cf. Inglis* v. *Moir's Tutors* (1871) 10 M. 204. For the sporting tenant's power to protect his rights against interference by the agricultural tenant, see *Mason* v. *Clarke* [1955] A.C. 778.

Extension of tenancies in lieu of claims to emblements

21.—(1) Where the tenancy of an agricultural holding held by a tenant at a rackrent determines by the death or cesser of the estate of any landlord entitled for his life, or for any other uncertain interest, instead of claims to emblements the tenant shall continue to hold and occupy the holding until the occupation is determined by a twelve months' notice to quit expiring at the end of a year of the tenancy, and shall then quit upon the terms of his tenancy in the same manner as if the tenancy were then determined by effluxion of time or other lawful means during the continuance of his landlord's estate.

(2) The succeeding landlord shall be entitled to recover from the tenant, in the same manner as his predecessor could have done, a fair proportion of the rent for the period which may have elapsed from the date of the death or cesser of the estate of his predecessor to the time of the tenant so quitting.

(3) The succeeding landlord and the tenant respectively shall as between themselves and as against each other be entitled to all the benefits and advantages and be subject to the terms, conditions and restrictions to which the preceding landlord and the tenant respectively would have been entitled and subject if the tenancy had determined in manner aforesaid at the expiry of the said twelve months' notice.

DEFINITIONS
"agricultural holding": s.1(1).
"landlord", "tenant": s.96(1).

GENERAL NOTE
This section has a history going back to the Landlord and Tenant Act 1851, s.1.

Subs. (1)

Rackrent. This means a rent of the full annual value or near it: *Re Sawyer and Withall* [1919] 2 Ch. 333 at p.338.

Landlord entitled for his life. When, as is now normal, a tenant for life of settled land grants tenancies under his Settled Land Act powers, the farm tenant will not be affected by the death of the tenant for life or the cesser of his beneficial interest. In practice, therefore, the present section is not likely to be of much importance. It is not clear whether a tenancy granted *by* a landlord entitled for his life is necessarily a tenancy "for life or lives or for any term of years determinable with life or lives" so as to bring into play s.149(6) of the Law of Property Act 1925. Is it an estate *pur autre vie?* See Challis's *Law of Real Property* (3rd ed.), p.357.

Any other uncertain interest. It was considered by Judge Carey Evans in *Stephens* v. *Balls* (1957) 107 L.J. 764, C.C. (see also [1957] E.G.D. 237) that s.21 would apply to a tenancy granted to an incumbent.

Emblements. For a discussion of emblements, see *Woodfall* (28th ed.), Vol. 2, 2–0064. The word includes not only corn sown, but also roots, potatoes, hemp, flax, hops and other "growing crops of those vegetable productions of the soil which are annually produced by the labour of the cultivator". It does not include such things as fruit trees, or oak, elm, ash or other trees or crops such as clover which remain productive beyond the first year. As the rights given by s.21 are "instead of claims to emblements", they can only be exercised by persons who would have been entitled to emblements at common law: *Stradbrooke* v. *Mulcahy* (1852) 2 Ir.C.L.R. 406. But to claim under s.21 a tenant must also be a tenant of an agricultural holding under s.1(1): contrast *Haines* v. *Welch* (1868) L.R. 4 C.P. 91.

And shall then quit. Although these words might be cited to the contrary, it is submitted that the notice to quit will have the normal consequences of, *inter alia,* attracting s.26 and s.60. See also *Woodfall* (28th ed.), Vol. 2, 2–0065.

Subs. (2)
A fair proportion. Presumably, the apportioned amount ascertained under the Apportionment Act 1870.

Rights to require certain records to be made

22.—(1) At any time during the tenancy of an agricultural holding—

  (*a*) the landlord or the tenant may require the making of a record of the condition of the fixed equipment on the holding and of the general condition of the holding itself (including any parts not under cultivation), and

  (*b*) the tenant may require the making of a record of any fixtures or buildings which, under section 10 above, he is entitled to remove and of existing improvements executed by him or in respect of the execution of which he, with the written consent of the landlord, paid compensation to an outgoing tenant.

(2) Any such record shall be made by a person appointed, in default of agreement between the landlord and tenant, by the President of the Royal Institution of Chartered Surveyors (referred to in this section as "the President"); and any person so appointed may, on production of evidence of his appointment, enter the holding at all reasonable times for the purpose of making any such record.

(3) The cost of making any such record shall, in default of agreement between the landlord and tenant, be borne by them in equal shares.

(4) No application may be made to the President for a person to be appointed by him under subsection (2) above unless the application is accompanied by such fee as may be prescribed as the fee for such an application.

(5) Any instrument of appointment purporting to be made by the President by virtue of subsection (2) above and to be signed by or on behalf of the President shall be taken to be such an instrument unless the contrary is shown.

DEFINITIONS
"agreement", "building", "fixed equipment", "landlord", "tenant": s.96(1).
"agricultural holding": s.1(1).

Subs. (1)
Para. (a): fixed equipment. By amendments made by the 1984 Act (Sched. 3, para. 8) the scope of the record was extended to cover all fixed equipment and the general condition of the holding.

Subs. (2)
Enter the holding. One of the amendments made in 1984 (see last note) was to give the appointed person a power of entry. At the same time the more general power of entry by a person authorised by the Minister was abolished by the repeal of s.91 of the 1948 Act (1984 Act, Sched. 4).

Subs. (3)
Cost. It appears that any dispute as to the cost would have to be determined, in the last resort, by an action at law.

Subs. (4)
Prescribed. The fee at present prescribed is £70. The same amount is charged for the application to the President to appoint an arbitrator; Agricultural Holdings (Fee) Regulations 1985 (S.I. 1985 No. 1967). It is quite likely that the President would appoint a member of the panel of arbitrators constituted under para. 1 of Sched. 11, but he is not obliged to do so and the person so appointed would not be acting *as* an arbitrator.

Landlord's power of entry

23. The landlord of an agricultural holding or any person authorised by him may at all reasonable times enter on the holding for any of the following purposes, namely—
(*a*) viewing the state of the holding,
(*b*) fulfilling the landlord's responsibilities to manage the holding in accordance with the rules of good estate management,
(*c*) providing or improving fixed equipment on the holding otherwise than in fulfilment of those responsibilities.

DEFINITIONS
"agricultural holding": s.1(1).
"landlord": s.96(1).
"rules of good estate management": s.96(3).

GENERAL NOTE
Purposes. The purposes mentioned in paras. (*b*) and (*c*) were added to (*a*) (which was in s.28 of the 1923 Act) by s.43 of the 1947 Act. For a strong case showing that the landlord commits a trespass if he enters his tenant's premises without contractual or statutory authority, see *Stocker* v. *Planet Building Society* (1879) 27 W.R. 877. The contractual authority may be implied: *Saner* v. *Bilton* (1878) 7 Ch.D. 815; *Mint* v. *Good* [1951] 1 K.B. 517; *McGreal* v. *Wake* (1984) 269 E.G. 1254. A right of entry to execute repairs is given to the landlord by the Agriculture (Maintenance, Repair and Insurance of Fixed Equipment) Regulations 1973 (S.I. 1973 No. 1473), para. 4(2) of Sched. For a saving of rights of entry, see Opencast Coal Act 1958, Sched. 7, para. 6(2).

Restriction of landlord's remedies for breach of contract of tenancy

24. Notwithstanding any provision in a contract of tenancy of an agricultural holding making the tenant liable to pay a higher rent or other liquidated damages in the event of a breach or non-fulfilment of a term or condition of the contract, the landlord shall not be entitled to recover in consequence of any such breach or non-fulfilment, by distress or otherwise, any sum in excess of the damage actually suffered by him in consequence of the breach or non-fulfilment.

DEFINITIONS
"agricultural holding": s.1(1).
"contract of tenancy": s.1(5).
"landlord", "tenant": s.96(1).

GENERAL NOTE
The 1947 Act (Sched. 7, para. 7) removed certain exceptions to the restriction which had remained since s.6 of the 1900 Act, namely, the breaking up of permanent pasture, the grubbing of underwoods, the felling, cutting, lopping or injuring of trees, or regulating the burning of heather. Thus only the amount of actual damage can now be recovered in any case, and clauses providing for increased rents if, say, permanent pasture is broken up, are no longer included in tenancy agreements. Formerly, a liquidated sum was recoverable provided that it was not in substance a penalty, and the general rule was that if the stipulated amount was proportioned to the extent of the breach of covenant it was treated as liquidated

damages, but if the same amount was payable on the breach of any one of various stipulations of different degrees of importance it was a penalty. (For cases, see p.268 of the 12th edition of this work.) For the old learning, see *Woodfall* (28th ed.), vol. I, pp.291–295. It may be noted that covenants restricting the burning of heather (one of the old exceptions mentioned above) may be relaxed by the agricultural land tribunal on the tenant's application: see the Agricultural Land Tribunals (Rules) Order 1978 (S.I. 1978 No. 259), Sched. 1, rule 9 and forms 9 and 9R. S.71(5) of the present Act and s.18(1) of the Landlord and Tenant Act 1927 are also relevant on the question of the measure of damages for dilapidations.

PART III

NOTICES TO QUIT

GENERAL NOTE

Part III picks up most of the provisions which were in sections 1 to 10 of the 1977 Act, but with some matters now consigned to schedules. Part of the detail of s.1 of the 1977 Act (as to land required for naval, military or air force purposes and land of statutory undertakers) will now be found in para. 4 of Sched. 12 instead of being in s.25. The details of the Cases A, B, C, D, E, F, G and H are transferred to Parts I and II of Sched. 3 instead of cluttering up s.26, which is the successor to s.2 of the 1977 Act. Case A is now the Case I introduced by s.6(6) of the 1984 Act (notice to quit given to a smallholdings tenant who has attained the age of 65). (The original Case A (consent by tribunal to a notice to quit before it was served) was abolished by the 1984 Act, s.6(2)). S.27 corresponds with s.3 and s.28 with s.4 of the 1977 Act. The old s.7 (notice to quit during currency of a contract of sale) has disappeared, having been repealed by the 1984 Act (Sched. 4). S.11 of the 1977 Act (notice to quit where tenant is a serviceman) is now in Sched. 5. The old ss.8 to 10 of the 1977 Act are now in ss.31 to 33.

Notices to quit whole or part of agricultural holding

Length of notice to quit

25.—(1) A notice to quit an agricultural holding or part of an agricultural holding shall (notwithstanding any provision to the contrary in the contract of tenancy of the holding) be invalid if it purports to terminate the tenancy before the expiry of twelve months from the end of the then current year of tenancy.

(2) Subsection (1) above shall not apply—

(*a*) where the tenant is insolvent,

(*b*) to a notice given in pursuance of a provision in the contract of tenancy authorising the resumption of possession of the holding or some part of it for some specified purpose other than the use of the land for agriculture,

(*c*) to a notice given by a tenant to a sub-tenant,

(*d*) where the tenancy is one which, by virtue of subsection (6) of section 149 of the Law of Property Act 1925, has taken effect as such a term of years as is mentioned in that subsection.

(3) Where on a reference under section 12 above with respect to an agricultural holding the arbitrator determines that the rent payable in respect of the holding shall be increased, a notice to quit the holding given by the tenant at least six months before it purports to take effect shall not be invalid by virtue of subsection (1) above if it purports to terminate the tenancy at the end of the year of the tenancy beginning with the date as from which the increase of rent is effective.

(4) On an application made to the Tribunal with respect to an agricultural holding under paragraph 9 of Part II of Schedule 3 to this Act, the Tribunal may, if they grant a certificate in accordance with the application—

(a) specify in the certificate a minimum period of notice for termination of the tenancy (not being a period of less than two months), and

(b) direct that the period shall apply instead of the period of notice required in accordance with subsection (1) above;

and in any such case a notice to quit the holding which states that the Tribunal have given a direction under this subsection shall not be invalid by virtue of subsection (1) above if the notice given is not less than the minimum notice specified in the certificate.

(5) A notice to quit within subsection (3) or (4) above shall not be invalid by virtue of any term of the contract of tenancy requiring a longer period of notice to terminate the tenancy, and a notice to quit within subsection (4) above shall not be invalid by reason of its terminating at a date other than the end of a year of the tenancy.

DEFINITIONS

"agricultural holding" and "contract of tenancy": s.1(1) and (5).
"insolvent": s.96(2).
"tenant", "termination", "tribunal": s.96(1).
"use of land for agriculture": s.96(5).

GENERAL NOTE

For the general law governing notices to quit, see *Woodfall* (28th ed.), Vol. I, 1–1967 to 1–2032.

Subs. (1)

Notice to quit. This applies to a notice exercising an option to determine a fixed term before its normal expiry: *Edell* v. *Dulieu* [1924] A.C. 38; and to a notice given *by* as well as *to* a tenant: *Flather* v. *Hood* (1928) 44 T.L.R. 698. If tenant responds to an *Edell* v. *Dulieu* notice by a counter-notice under s.26(1) the result seems to be to break the fixed term, but to preserve tenant's security as a tenant from year to year (so held in unreported county court case in 1968 (*Young* v. *Hopkins* at Cheltenham County Court, by Judge A. C. Bulger)).

Invalid. A notice which is invalid under this section may still be effective if the tenant actually quits in pursuance of it: *Thomas* v. *N.F.U. Mutual Insurance Society Ltd.* [1961] 1 W.L.R. 386. There is nothing to prevent a person served with a notice to quit of less than the statutory length from waiving his rights: *Elsdon* v. *Pick* [1980] 1 W.L.R. 898. A notice to quit of the correct length is nevertheless invalid if served before the commencement of the tenancy: *Lower* v. *Sorrell* [1963] 1 Q.B. 959, especially judgment of Pearson L.J. There is nothing invalid in the *addition* of a fetter to the statutory length: *Re Midland Railway Co.'s Agreement, Charles Clay & Sons Ltd.* v. *British Railways Board* [1971] Ch. 725.

Subs. (2)

Shall not apply. In addition to the four exceptions specified here and in subsections (3) and (4), note the following exceptions also: (1) Sched. 12, para. 4, for certain agreements before March 25, 1947. (2) Arts. 7(4) and 14(4) of the Agricultural Holdings (Arbitration on Notices) Order 1978 (S.I. 1978 No. 257). Note also that the rule applies only to agricultural holdings, not to every tenancy with an agricultural flavour: *Steyning and Littlehampton Building Society* v. *Wilson* [1951] Ch. 1018.

Para. (a): insolvent. The definition of "insolvent" in s.96(2) now covers the insolvency of tenants which are bodies corporate.

Para. (b): resumption of possession. Note the need for the contract of tenancy to provide for a length of notice sufficient to enable the tenant to claim under s.60(3)(b) and (6) or s.70(2)(a) or the landlord to claim under s.72(4): see *Re Disraeli Agreement* [1939] Ch. 382; *Coates* v. *Diment* [1951] 1 All E.R. 890; *Parry* v. *Million Pigs Ltd.* (1980) 260 E.G. 281. Otherwise, s.78(1) applies and the invalidity is not cured by actually *giving* a notice of the requisite length. Note importance of precise wording of resumption clause: *Rugby Joint Water Board* v. *Foottit* [1973] A.C. 208 (not affected by s.48 of Land Compensation Act 1973) and note s.62 (additional compensation to tenant in case of early resumption).

other than the use of the land for agriculture. A clause authorising resumption for "any non-agricultural purpose" is within this para.: *Paddock Investments Ltd.* v. *Lory* (1975) 236 E.G. 803, C.A., approving C.C. decision in *Dow Agrochemicals Ltd.* v. *E. A. Lane (North*

Lynn) Ltd. (1964) 192 E.G. 737, "specified" not being the same as "specific": *cf. McMorran v. A. E. Marrison (Contractors) Ltd.* [1944] 2 All E.R. 448.

Para. (c): sub-tenant. The exception is not confined to cases where the tenant has been given notice by his own landlord. It does not apply to a notice to quit given *by* a sub-tenant to the tenant. Although relieved of the 12 months' requirement, the common law rules apply as to length and otherwise.

Subs. (3)
Shall not be invalid. This is derived from an amendment made by s.5 of the 1984 Act. It enables a tenant, dissatisfied with the arbitrator's rent increase, to get out at the end of the first year in which the rise is effective, provided that he gives not less than six months notice ending on the correct term date.

Subs. (4)
Minimum notice specified in the certificate. Also derived from s.5 of 1984 Act. The minimum period of two months means *any* period of two months, not necessarily two months ending at the end of a year of the tenancy: contrast note to subs. (3) above; see subs. (5) below. The holding in this case may be deteriorating rapidly.

Subs. (5)
Contract of tenancy. This subsection preserves the validity of the shortened notice against challenge under contract or at common law as well as under s.25(1).

Note the provisions of Sched. 12, para. 4 in regard to notices to quit given by the Secretary of State and by statutory undertakers in the case of certain agreements made before March 25, 1947.

Restriction on operation of notices to quit

26.—(1) Where—

(*a*) notice to quit an agricultural holding or part of an agricultural holding is given to the tenant, and

(*b*) not later than one month from the giving of the notice to quit the tenant serves on the landlord a counter-notice in writing requiring that this subsection shall apply to the notice to quit,

then, subject to subsection (2) below, the notice to quit shall not have effect unless, on an application by the landlord, the Tribunal consent to its operation.

(2) Subsection (1) above shall not apply in any of the Cases set out in Part I of Schedule 3 to this Act; and in this Act "Case A", "Case B" (and so on) refer severally to the Cases set out and so named in that Part of that Schedule.

(3) Part II of that Schedule shall have effect in relation to the Cases there specified.

DEFINITIONS
"agricultural holding": s.1(1).
"landlord", "tenant", "tribunal": s.96(1).

Subs. (1)
Para. (a): notice to quit. A notice under s.3(1) is deemed by s.3(2) to be a notice to quit, and a notice exercising an option to break is a notice to quit: *Edell* v. *Dulieu* [1924] A.C. 38; *Gladstone* v. *Bower* [1960] 2 Q.B. 385 at p.394. Apart from statute, a notice to quit must be clear and unambiguous, so that the recipient would be reasonably safe in acting on it: *Norfolk County Council* v. *Child* [1918] 2 K.B. 351; *Gardner* v. *Ingram* (1889) 61 L.T. 729; *Harmond Properties Ltd.* v. *Gajdzis* [1968] 1 W.L.R. 1858. A minor misdescription may not be fatal if the meaning is plain: *Mountford* v. *Hodgkinson* [1956] 1 W.L.R. 422; *Frankland* v. *Capstick* [1959] 1 W.L.R. 204; *Att.-Gen. (Duchy of Lancaster)* v. *Simcock* [1966] Ch. 1 at p.3.

Para. (b): not later than one month. This is rigid: there is no power to extend. In reckoning time "from" a particular date the general rule is that the day of that date is excluded: *Goldsmith's Co.* v. *West Metropolitan Railway Co.* [1904] 1 K.B. 1; *Trow* v. *Ind Coope*

(West Midlands) Ltd. [1967] 2 Q.B. 899. And see generally *Dodds* v. *Walker* [1981] 1 W.L.R. 1027 (H.L.) and *E. J. Riley Investments Ltd.* v. *Eurostile Holdings Ltd.* [1985] 2 E.G.L.R. 124.

counter-notice in writing. No form is prescribed, but the notice must unambiguously invoke the provision in s.26(1)(*b*), although a merely technical, non-misleading defect will not invalidate it: *Mountford* v. *Hodkinson* [1956] 1 W.L.R. 422; *cf. Frankland* v. *Capstick* [1959] 1 W.L.R. 204. As to ineffectiveness of an agreement not to serve a counter-notice, see *Johnson* v. *Moreton* [1980] A.C. 37. In *Featherstone* v. *Staples* [1975] 1 E.G.L.R. 1 in very special circumstances counter-notices by two out of three joint tenants were held effective. For another special case affecting counter-notices by joint tenants, see *Sykes* v. *Land* (1981) 271 E.G. 1265. For the strict view, see *Newman* v. *Keedwell* (1977) 244 E.G. 469; *cf. Jacobs* v. *Chaudhuri* [1968] 2 Q.B. 470. A more liberal doctrine of joint proprietorship is found in other contexts, such as *Howson* v. *Buxton* (1928) 97 L.J.K.B. 749, *Lloyd* v. *Sadler* [1978] Q.B. 774 and *Tilling* v. *Whiteman* [1980] A.C. 1, as well as in *Featherstone*.

Unless, on an application by the landlord, the tribunal consent. See s.27 for the provisions as to consents. The landlord must apply for consent on the prescribed form within one month of the service upon him of the tenant's counter-notice, otherwise the notice to quit is of no effect: see the Agricultural Land Tribunals (Rules) Order 1978 (S.I. 1978 No. 259) Sched. 1, rule 2(2) and Form I in Appendix. But "no effect" must be qualified if a notice in the alternative or two separate notices are served.

Subs. (2)

Subsection (1) above shall not apply. This most important exclusion introduces the Cases A, B, C, D, E, F, G and H set out in Part I, with supplementary provisions in Part II, of Sched. 3. In respect of Case D the exclusion of the counter-notice procedure is qualified in certain cases: see s.28. Arbitration is provided with respect to contests affecting Cases A, B, D and E: see the Agricultural Holdings (Arbitration on Notices) Order 1978 (S.I. 1978 No. 257), art. 9, as amended by the Agricultural Holdings (Arbitration on Notices) (Variation) Order 1984 (S.I. 1984 No. 1300), art. 4. (Case I mentioned in the latter order is Case A in the 1986 Act).

See annotations to Sched. 3 for notes on Cases A to H.

Tribunal's consent to operation of notice to quit

27.—(1) Subject to subsection (2) below, the Tribunal shall consent under section 26 above to the operation of a notice to quit an agricultural holding or part of an agricultural holding if, but only if, they are satisfied as to one or more of the matters mentioned in subsection (3) below, being a matter or matters specified by the landlord in his application for their consent.

(2) Even if they are satisfied as mentioned in subsection (1) above, the Tribunal shall withhold consent under section 26 above to the operation of the notice to quit if in all the circumstances it appears to them that a fair and reasonable landlord would not insist on possession.

(3) The matters referred to in subsection (1) above are—

(*a*) that the carrying out of the purpose for which the landlord proposes to terminate the tenancy is desirable in the interests of good husbandry as respects the land to which the notice relates, treated as a separate unit;

(*b*) that the carrying out of the purpose is desirable in the interests of sound management of the estate of which the land to which the notice relates forms part or which that land constitutes;

(*c*) that the carrying out of the purpose is desirable for the purposes of agricultural research, education, experiment or demonstration, or for the purposes of the enactments relating to smallholdings;

(*d*) that the carrying out of the purpose is desirable for the purposes of the enactments relating to allotments;

(*e*) that greater hardship would be caused by withholding than by giving consent to the operation of the notice;

(*f*) that the landlord proposes to terminate the tenancy for the purpose of the land's being used for a use, other than for agriculture, not falling within Case B.

(4) Where the Tribunal consent under section 26 above to the operation of a notice to quit, they may impose such conditions as appear to them requisite for securing that the land to which the notice relates will be used for the purpose for which the landlord proposes to terminate the tenancy.

(5) Where, on an application by the landlord, the Tribunal are satisfied that, by reason of any change of circumstances or otherwise, any condition imposed under subsection (4) above ought to be varied or revoked, they shall vary or revoke the condition accordingly.

(6) Where—

> (*a*) on giving consent under section 26 above to the operation of a notice to quit the Tribunal imposed a condition under subsection (4) above, and
>
> (*b*) it is proved on an application to the Tribunal on behalf of the Crown that the landlord has acted in contravention of the condition or has failed within the time allowed by the condition to comply with it,

the Tribunal may by order impose on the landlord a penalty of an amount not exceeding two years' rent of the holding at the rate at which rent was payable immediately before the termination of the tenancy, or, where the notice to quit related to a part only of the holding, of an amount not exceeding the proportion of the said two years' rent which it appears to the Tribunal is attributable to that part.

(7) The Tribunal may, in proceedings under this section, by order provide for the payment by any party of such sum as the Tribunal consider a reasonable contribution towards costs.

(8) A penalty imposed under subsection (6) above shall be a debt due to the Crown and shall, when recovered, be paid into the Consolidated Fund.

(9) An order under subsection (6) or (7) above shall be enforceable in the same manner as a judgment or order of the county court to the like effect.

DEFINITIONS

> "agricultural holding": s.1(1).
> "agriculture", "landlord", "termination", "tribunal": s.96(1).
> "good husbandry": s.96(3).

Subs. (1)

Shall consent. But see the overriding provision in subs. (2). To avoid confusion, and a possible legal challenge, tribunals should consider as separate issues (1) whether they are satisfied as to one or more of the matters in subs. (3)(*a*) to (*f*), (2) whether, notwithstanding this satisfaction, consent should be withheld under subs. (2): *cf. R.* v. *ALT for the Eastern Province, ex p. Grant* [1956] 1 W.L.R. 1240 and *Evans* v. *Roper* [1960] 1 W.L.R. 814.

If they are satisfied. The onus is on the landlord to satisfy the tribunal. "Satisfied" has a subjective or discretionary flavour, but the decision could be upset if it could be shown that no reasonable tribunal could have been so satisfied: *cf. Ross-Clunis* v. *Papadopoullos* [1958] 1 W.L.R. 546 at p.560.

Specified by the landlord in his application. The landlord must specify in his application the ground or grounds (being those set out in subs. (3)) on which he relies. See Form I in the Appendix to Sched. 1 to the Agricultural Land Tribunals (Rules) Order 1978 (S.I. 1978 No. 259) and see rule 2(2) in Sched. 1. Failure to comply with the statutory form in all respects is not necessarily fatal (see rule 38) but is risky: *cf. Ward* v. *Scott* [1950] W.N. 76.

Subs. (2)

Even if they are satisfied. See note to subs. (1) on consent above, as to the separate issues to which the tribunal should apply their minds. See also *Cowane's Hospital* v. *Rennie* 1966 S.C.L.R. App. 147.

A fair and reasonable landlord would not insist on possession. For cases, see *Evans* v. *Roper* [1960] 1 W.L.R. 814; *Carnegie* v. *Davidson,* 1966 S.L.T. (Land Ct.) 3; *Jones* v. *Burgoyne* (1963) 188 E.G. 497; [1963] E.G.D. 435; *Collins* v. *Spurway* (1967) 204 E.G. 801;

Altyre Estate Trustees v. *McLay,* 1972 S.L.T. (Land Ct.) 12; *Cooke* v. *Talbot* (1977) 243 E.G. 831; *Clegg* v. *Fraser* (1982) 264 E.G. 144 (under what is now s.28(5)).

Subs. (3)
Para. (a): good husbandry. For responsibilities, see s.96(3). This para. envisages a comparison between present and proposed regime with reference to subject holding "treated as a separate unit": see *Davies* v. *Price* [1958] 1 W.L.R. 434. This is more restrictive than the position as it was at the time of the decisions in *R.* v. *ALT for Wales and Monmouth Area, ex. p. Davies* [1953] 1 W.L.R. 722 and *R.* v. *ALT for the Eastern Province, ex p. Grant* [1956] 1 W.L.R. 1240, when advantage to the holding by amalgamation could be relied on under the corresponding para. For the comparison now envisaged, see *Davies* v. *Price* [1958] 1 W.L.R. 434. See also ALT decision in *Lewis* v. *Moss* (1962) 181 E.G. 685. This head must be kept distinct from the next (sound management) in principle, although the same facts may manifest both aspects: *Greaves* v. *Mitchell* (1971) 222 E.G. 1395.
Para. (b): sound management. Under this head the tribunal may look beyond the land to which the notice relates to other land being part of the landlord's estate. For cases, see *Evans* v. *Roper* [1960] 1 W.L.R. 814; *Lewis* v. *Moss* (1962) 181 E.G. 685 (ALT); *Greaves* v. *Mitchell* (1972) 222 E.G. 1395; *National Coal Board* v. *Naylor* [1972] 1 W.L.R. 908; *Purser* v. *Bailey* [1967] 2 Q.B. 500 (landlord's personal financial position not relevant under this head); *Wickington* v. *Bonney* (1982) 266 E.G. 434 (*res judicata* not applicable to a changing situation). Note that "sound management" has a wider connotation than "good estate management" in s.96(3).
Para. (c): agricultural research, etc. "Agricultural" qualifies all the four nouns which follow. "Research" could cover private research. See tribunal cases of *Wilts County Council* v. *Habershon* (1952) 159 E.G. 157 (Trib.) and *Wood* v. *E. Sussex County Council* [1954–55] A.L.R. 159 (Trib.). The obvious case is where a research body wishes to obtain possession for purposes of extension. As to smallholdings, this para. would enable an authority to end a tenancy where a smallholder had taken on land which brought him out of the class of a smallholder.
Para. (d): allotments. The enactments relating to allotments comprise the Smallholdings and Allotments Act 1908 as amended, the Allotments Act 1922 as amended and the Allotments Act 1950. Distinguish an "allotment garden", which is cultivated by the occupier for the purpose of consumption by himself and his family: Allotments Act 1922, s.22(1).
Para. (e): greater hardship. This is not restricted to hardship in the possession or use of the holding, but is entirely at large, and the analogy is with the provisions of the Rent Act 1977, Sched. 15, Case 9: see *Purser* v. *Bailey* [1967] 2 Q.B. 500 and the Rent Act case of *Harte* v. *Frampton* [1948] K.B. 73 at p.79. For other cases, see Rent Act decisions on greater hardship and the following: *Addington* v. *Sims* [1952] E.G.D. 1 (ALT); *Kinson* v. *Swinnerton* (1961) 179 E.G. 691; *R.* v. *ALT for the S.E. Area, ex p. Bracey* [1960] 1 W.L.R. 911; *Jones* v. *Burgoyne* [1963] E.G.D. 435; *Gordon-Lennox Estate Co. Ltd.* v. *Christie,* 1963 S.L.C.R. App. 84; *Cowane's Hospital* v. *Rennie* 1966 S.L.C.R. App. 147; *Chelwynd (Viscountess)* v. *Edwards* (1967) 204 E.G. 822 (ALT); *Graham* v. *Lamont,* 1971 S.C. 170; *Copeland* v. *McQuaker,* 1973 S.L.T. 186; *Cooke* v. *Talbot* (1977) 243 E.G. 831; *R.* v. *ALT for S.E. Area, ex p. Parslow* (1979) 251 E.G. 667; *Wickington* v. *Bonney* (1983) 266 E.G. 436.
Para. (f): not falling within Case B. The present para. therefore, covers cases where, *by virtue* of a provision in the town and country planning legislation, planning permission is not required, *e.g.* private forestry: see Town and Country Planning Act 1971, s.22(2)(*e*), and see *Minister of Agriculture* v. *Jenkins* [1963] 2 Q.B. 317. Planning permission derived from a special development order is not permission "granted on an application" within the meaning of Case B in Sched. 3, so that a development corporation would be correct in applying for consent under the present s.27(3)(*f*) to a notice to quit in respect of land required for industrial development. This was correctly decided by the agricultural land tribunal for the Eastern Area in the unreported case (in 1960) of *Stevenage Development Corporation* v. *Ivory.* See s.14(6) of the Opencast Coal Act 1958 as amended by the present Act (Sched. 14, para. 25) for a provision that the use of land for opencast coal production by virtue of an operation under the 1958 Act shall be treated as not being such a use as is referred to in the present para. (*f*).

Subs. (4)
Conditions. The condition must relate to the purpose mentioned: see *R.* v. *ALT (S.E. Area), ex p. Boucher* (1952) E.G. 192; *National Coal Board* v. *Naylor* [1972] 1 W.L.R. 908 at p.913. The condition in *Shaw-Mackenzie* v. *Forbes,* 1957 S.L.C.R. 34 was probably invalid.

Subs. (5)

Application by the landlord. For form, see Form 4 in Appendix to Sched. 1 to the Agricultural Land Tribunals (Rules) Order 1978 (S.I. 1978 No. 259). For an unsuccessful application, see *Jones* v. *West Midlands ALT* (1962) 184 E.G. 78 (ALT); the variation would have split the holding.

Subs. (6)

Penalty. The penalty is paid to the Exchequer, not to the tenant (subs. 8) and the landlord's default does not affect the operation of the notice to quit: *cf. Martin-Smith* v. *Smale* [1954] 1 W.L.R. 247.

Subs. (7)

Costs. But there is no provision for compensation to tenant.

Additional restrictions on operation of notice to quit given under Case D

28.—(1) This section applies where—

   (*a*) notice to quit an agricultural holding or part of an agricultural holding is given to the tenant, and

   (*b*) the notice includes a statement in accordance with Case D to the effect that it is given by reason of the tenant's failure to comply with a notice to do work.

(2) If the tenant serves on the landlord a counter-notice in writing in accordance with subsection (3) or (4) below requiring that this subsection shall apply to the notice to quit, the notice to quit shall not have effect (whether as a notice to which section 26(1) above does or does not apply) unless, on an application by the landlord, the Tribunal consent to its operation.

(3) Subject to subsection (4) below, a counter-notice under subsection (2) above shall be served not later than one month from the giving of the notice to quit.

(4) Where the tenant not later than one month from the giving of the notice to quit serves on the landlord an effective notice requiring the validity of the reason stated in the notice to quit to be determined by arbitration under this Act—

   (*a*) any counter-notice already served under subsection (2) above shall be of no effect, but

   (*b*) if the notice to quit would, apart from this subsection, have effect in consequence of the arbitration, the tenant may serve a counter-notice under subsection (2) not later than one month from the date on which the arbitrator's award is delivered to him.

(5) The Tribunal shall consent under subsection (2) above to the operation of the notice to quit unless it appears to them, having regard—

   (*a*) to the extent to which the tenant has failed to comply with the notice to do work,

   (*b*) to the consequences of his failure to comply with it in any respect, and

   (*c*) to the circumstances surrounding any such failure,

that a fair and reasonable landlord would not insist on possession.

(6) In this section "notice to work" means a notice served on a tenant of an agricultural holding for the purposes of paragraph (*b*) of Case D, being a notice requiring the doing of any work of repair, maintenance or replacement.

DEFINITIONS

  "agricultural holding": s.1(1).

  "arbitration": s.84.

  "notice to do work": subs. (6).

  "tenant", "landlord," "tribunal": s.96(1).

Subs. (1)

Para. (b): the notice includes a statement. This seems to mean that the additional remedy given to the tenant by this section depends on the landlord's notice to quit containing a specific reference to a failure *to do work* rather than the more general wording in Case D itself in Sched. 3, Part I.

Subs. (2)

Counter-notice. This section gives the tenant a choice of remedies, a counter-notice or a notice requiring arbitration and also allows him, if arbitration fails, to try again by means of a counter-notice. But he cannot first *complete* proceedings by way of counter-notice and then, having failed before the tribunal, fall back on arbitration; though he can abort proceedings by counter-notice, then proceed by arbitration, then on failing by arbitration, resort to the complete counter-notice procedure: see subs. (4). This provides the tenant with a remarkably flexible armoury.

Subs. (3)

Not later than one month. This time-limit is rigid and incapable of extension except where the tenant has failed in recourse to arbitration and is given the new time-limit in subs. (4)(*b*).

Subs. (4)

Para. (a) shall be of no effect, but. See note 2 above for the striking package of remedies contained in these provisions.

Subs. (5)

The tribunal shall consent . . . unless. Consent is mandatory unless, having regard *only* to the three factors mentioned in (*a*), (*b*) and (*c*), a fair and reasonable landlord would not insist. Contrast present wording with s.4(4) of the 1977 Act—"unless in all the circumstances." It was clearly intended to cut down the latter expression, no doubt to prevent the repetition of issues raised at the notice to do work stage of arbitration or the raising of general issues of hardship. The present subsection in effect overrules *Clegg* v. *Fraser* (1982) 264 E.G. 144.

Subs. (6)

"Notices to do work." For the statutory form of notice, see the Agricultural Holdings (Forms of Notice to Pay Rent or to Remedy) Regulations 1984 (S.I. 1984 No. 1308), Form 2 in Sched.

Power to make supplementary provision

29. The Lord Chancellor may by order provide for any of the matters specified in Schedule 4 to this Act.

GENERAL NOTE

The matters specified in Sched. 4 were covered by statutory instruments made under earlier legislation, such as the 1947 Act, the 1948 Act and the 1977 Act. As a result of the saving provision in Sched. 13, para. 1(2) such statutory instruments remain operative until superseded by new instruments made by the Lord Chancellor under s.29 and Sched. 4. See further comments in the note to Sched. 4.

Notices to quit where tenant is a service man

30. Schedule 5 to this Act, which makes provision as to notices to quit in cases where the tenant of an agricultural holding is a service man, shall have effect.

GENERAL NOTE

The relevant regulations for the purpose of s.30 and Sched. 5 in regard to service men are at present the Reserve and Auxiliary Forces (Agricultural Tenants) Regulations 1959 (S.I. 1959 No. 84) and, in the Agricultural Holdings (Arbitration on Notices) Order 1978 (S.I. 1978 No. 257), art. 16. See notes on Sched. 5 *post*.

Notices to quit part of agricultural holding

Notice to quit part of holding valid in certain cases

31.—(1) A notice to quit part of an agricultural holding held on a tenancy from year to year given by the landlord of the holding shall not be invalid on the ground that it relates to part only of the holding if it is given—

(*a*) for the purpose of adjusting the boundaries between agricultural units or amalgamating agricultural units or parts of such units, or

(*b*) with a view to the use of the land to which the notice relates for any of the objects mentioned in subsection (2) below,

and the notice states that it is given for that purpose or with a view to any such use, as the case may be.

(2) The objects referred to in subsection (1) above are—

(*a*) the erection of cottages or other houses for farm labourers, whether with or without gardens;

(*b*) the provision of gardens for cottages or other houses for farm labourers;

(*c*) the provision of allotments;

(*d*) the letting of land (with or without other land) as a smallholding under Part III of the Agriculture Act 1970;

(*e*) the planting of trees;

(*f*) the opening or working of a deposit of coal, ironstone, limestone, brick-earth or other mineral, or a stone quarry or a clay, sand or gravel pit, or the construction of any works or buildings to be used in connection therewith;

(*g*) the making of a watercourse or reservoir;

(*h*) the making of a road, railway, tramroad, siding, canal or basin, or a wharf, pier, or other work connected therewith.

DEFINITIONS

"agricultural holding": s.1(1).

"agricultural unit", "building", "landlord": s.96(1).

Subs. (1)

Tenancy from year to year. Thus s.31 does not apply to a "break" clause in a lease for a fixed term.

Shall not be invalid. As it would be at common law in the absence of a contractual provision: see *Right d. Fisher* v. *Cuthell* (1804) 5 East 491; *Doe d. Rodd* v. *Archer* (1811) 14 East 244; *Price* v. *Evans* (1872) 29 L.T. 835; *Re Bebington's Tenancy, Bebington* v. *Wildman* [1921] 1 Ch. 559; *Woodward* v. *Earl of Dudley* [1954] Ch. 283. Under s.140 of the Law of Property Act 1925 a notice to quit part may, however, be given by a person entitled to a severed part of the reversion: see curious decision in *Persey* v. *Bazley* (1984) 47 P. & C.R. 37 and non-agricultural cases such as *Jelley* v. *Buckman* [1974] 1 Q.B. 488; *William Skelton & Son* v. *Harrison and Pinder* [1975] 1 Q.B. 361; *Dodson Bull Carpet Co.* v. *City of London Corpn.* [1975] 1 W.L.R. 781 and *Nevill Long & Co. (Boards)* v. *Firmenich* (1984) 47 P. & C.R. 59.

The notice states. This statement in the notice, which must be a notice in writing, is essential. If it is desired to take advantage of Case B as well as the present section, *e.g.* where planning permission has been given to build farm labourers' cottages, the notice must contain the statements made by both provisions.

Subs. (2)

Para. (a): cottages or other houses for farm labourers. Replacing the ambiguous phrase "farm labourers' cottages or other houses": 1984 Act, Sched. 3, para. 39, thus giving statutory effect to the better view taken by *Paddock Investments Ltd.* v. *Lory* (1975) 236 E.G. 803.

Para. (b): gardens for cottages or other houses for farm labourers. Replacing "gardens for farm labourers' cottages or other houses": see last note.

Para. (e): the planting of trees. See *Secretary of State for Wales* v. *Pugh* (1970) 120 L.J. 357 (C.C.)

Right to treat notice to quit part of holding as notice to quit entire holding

32.—(1) Where there is given to the tenant of an agricultural holding a notice to quit part of the holding, being either—

   (*a*) such a notice as is rendered valid by section 31 above, or

   (*b*) a notice given by a person entitled to a severed part of the reversionary estate in the holding.

subsection (2) below shall apply.

   (2) If—

   (*a*) within twenty-eight days after the giving of the notice, or

   (*b*) where the operation of the notice depends on any proceedings under this Part of this Act, within twenty-eight days after the time at which it is determined that the notice has effect,

the tenant gives to the landlord or (as the case may be) to the persons severally entitled to the severed parts of the reversion a counter-notice in writing to the effect that he accepts the notice to quit as a notice to quit the entire holding given by the landlord or (as the case may be) those persons, to take effect at the same time as the original notice, the notice to quit shall have effect accordingly.

DEFINITIONS

   "agricultural holding": s.1(1).

   "landlord", "tenant": s.96(1).

Subs. (1)

   Part. For position at common law, see note 2 to s.31 above. For compensation for disturbance, see s.60(1)(*b*). For position in regard to notice to quit to a sub-tenant (so far as the exclusion of the counter-notice procedure is concerned), see art. 15(3) of the Agricultural Holdings (Arbitration on Notices) Order 1978 (S.I. 1978 No. 257).

   Para. (b): severed part of the reversionary estate. S.32 and s.63(3) together include the substance of the proviso to s.140(2) of the Law of Property Act 1925 which was added by s.2 of the Law of Property (Amendment) Act 1926 (repealed by the 1948 Act, s.98 and Sched. 8). S.140(1) and (2) made it clear that a notice to quit can be given by the owner of a severed part of the reversion which would be effective in respect of the corresponding part of the land despite the fact that the tenancy of the entirety remains undivided and there is no legal apportionment of the rent: See *Re Bebington's Tenancy, Bebington* v. *Wildman* [1921] 1 Ch. 559 for the position before 1926 and *Smith* v. *Kinsey* (1936) 53 T.L.R. 45 for the position after 1925. For the position generally on the severance of the reversion, see ss.140, 141 and 142 of the Law of Property Act 1925. For cases, see *Jelly* v. *Buckman* [1974] Q.B. 488; *Stiles* v. *Farrow* (1977) 241 E.G. 623 (C.C.) and the questionable case of *Persey* v. *Bazley* (1984) 47 P. & C.R. 37.

Subs. (2)

   Para. (b): any proceedings. This would include an arbitration in respect of the relevant Cases A, B, D, E, in Sched. 3 or an application to the tribunal for consent to the notice to quit.

   Counter-notice in writing. There is no prescribed form. Instead of giving this counter-notice, which involves a willingness to quit the entire holding, the tenant may, of course, decide to resist the notice to quit part, and for this purpose to serve a counter-notice under s.26(1) in respect of that part.

   Shall have effect accordingly. Compensation for disturbance is then payable in respect of the whole: see s.60(1)(*b*), but note also s.63(3) for a possible limitation on the amount.

Reduction of rent where notice is given to quit part of holding

33.—(1) Where the landlord of an agricultural holding resumes pos-session of part of the holding either—

   (*a*) by virtue of section 31(1) above, or

(b) in pursuance of a provision in that behalf contained in the contract of tenancy,

the tenant shall be entitled to a reduction of rent proportionate to that part of the holding and in respect of any depreciation of the value to him of the residue of the holding caused by the severance or by the use to be made of the part severed.

(2) The amount of any reduction of rent under this section shall, in default of agreement made after the landlord resumes possession of the part of the holding concerned, be determined by arbitration under this Act.

(3) In a case falling within subsection (1)(b) above that falls to be determined by arbitration under this Act the arbitrator, in assessing the amount of the reduction, shall take into consideration any benefit or relief allowed to the tenant under the contract of tenancy in respect of the land possession of which is resumed by the landlord.

DEFINITIONS
"agricultural holding": s.1(1).
"arbitration": s.84.
"contract of tenancy": s.1(5).
"landlord", "tenant": s.96(1).

GENERAL NOTE
For provisions as to compensations when part of the holding is reserved, see s.74.

Subs. (1)
Resumes possession of part. No mention is made of a notice to quit, but s.31 requires a notice to quit and, in the case of a resumption under a contractual provision, *Re Disraeli Agreement* [1939] Ch. 382, *Coates* v. *Diment* [1951] 1 All E.R. 890 and *Parry* v. *Million Pigs Ltd.* (1980) 260 E.G. 281 establish not only that notice to quit must be given but that it must be of sufficient length to permit the tenant, if he wishes, to serve in reply the minimum of one month's notice required by s.60(6)(a) or s.70(2)(a). If the clause in the contract does not provide for such length of notice, or if it does not provide for any notice, it is void (and the invalidity is not cured by actually *giving* a notice of the required length). It will be noted that the present section makes no reference to a resumption of part by a person entitled to a severed part of the reversion; this involves an apportionment which is not between landlord and tenant only but also between the several owners of the reversion.

Subs. (2)
In default of agreement. Until an amendment was made by the 1984 Act (Sched. 3, para. 40, referring to s.10 of the 1977 Act, which replaced s.33 of the 1948 Act) the wording suggested that arbitration was mandatory in *all* cases in order to determine the reduction.

Subs. (3)
Benefit or relief. Cf. the Scottish cases of *McQuater* v. *Fergusson,* 1911 S.C. 640; *Galloway (Earl)* v. *McClelland,* 1915 S.C. 1062; *Findlay* v. *Munro,* 1917 S.C. 419; *Mackenzie* v. *Macgillivray,* 1921 S.C. 722.

PART IV

SUCCESSION ON DEATH OR RETIREMENT OF TENANT

GENERAL NOTE
Part II of the 1976 Act introduced a family succession scheme by which a tenancy granted to a farmer might not only endure for his life but also generate two further successions, the three tenancies lasting for perhaps a hundred years or more. There were increasing complaints that this legislation, together with fiscal disadvantages, was leading to a marked decline in the traditional landlord and tenant system. S.2 of the 1984 Act brought the

succession scheme to an end, but with a meticulous care to avoid unfair retrospection, so much so that the legacy of successions will be carried well into the 21st century. The 1984 Act also added the fresh complication of provisions for succession on a tenant's retirement at 65 or over, without the consent of the landlord. Part IV of the present Act comprises both the death and the retirement schemes, with the difficult topic of eligibility, and in particular the fulfilment of "the occupancy condition", consigned to Sched. 6. The apparently simple and sensible idea of denying succession to a close relative who was already in occupation of a commercial unit has proved, when translated into legislation, to necessitate abstruse refinements in order to defeat avoidance. One of the deemed occupation provisions (in para. 10 of Sched. 6) seems to reveal a mistrust of close relatives which borders on the paranoic, but land-hunger is a powerful motive. A surprising provision is a right for a landlord and tenant to "contract-in" to the succession scheme (s.34(1)(*b*)(iii)). What landlord would be prepared to do so? Perhaps a benevolent institutional landlord might be willing as part of the arrangements for a sale to the institution with a lease back.

Note: References in this Part to *Hamilton* are to *Agricultural Land Tribunals Succession Decisions, Abstracts and Commentaries,* by R. N. D. Hamilton, published by the Royal Institution of Chartered Surveyors.

Tenancies to which Part IV applies

Tenancies to which Part IV applies

34.—(1) The provisions of this Part of this Act shall have effect with respect to—

(*a*) any tenancy of an agricultural holding granted before 12th July 1984, and

(*b*) a tenancy granted on or after that date if (but only if)—

(i) the tenancy was obtained by virtue of a direction of the Tribunal under section 39 or 53 below,

(ii) the tenancy was granted (following a direction under section 39 below) in circumstances within section 45(6) below,

(iii) the tenancy was granted by a written contract of tenancy indicating (in whatever terms) that this Part of this Act is to apply in relation to the tenancy, or

(iv) the tenancy was granted otherwise than as mentioned in the preceding provisions of this subsection to a person who, immediately before that date, was a tenant of the holding or of any agricultural holding which comprised the whole or a substantial part of the land comprised in the holding.

(2) In this section "tenant" does not include an executor, administrator, trustee in bankruptcy or other person deriving title from a tenant by operation of law.

DEFINITIONS
"agricultural holding": s.1(1).
"contract of tenancy": s.1(5).
See also exclusions in subs. (2) from definition of "tenant" in this section.

Subs. (1)
Para. (a) before 12th July 1984. The date when s.2 of the 1984 Act, the section which abolished statutory succession for new tenancies granted on or after that date, came into force (see s.11 of 1984 Act). July 12, 1984, was the date of the passing of the 1984 Act, but for certain purposes it did not come into operation until September 12, 1984. Full succession rights are preserved for any tenancy granted (in the ordinary sense of the word) before that July 12, but the rights as set out in Part II of the Agriculture (Miscellaneous Provisions) Act 1976 are amended in certain respects (the amendments having been made by the 1984 Act and consolidated in the present Act).
Para. (b): any tenancy granted on or after that date if (but only if). Para. (*b*)(i) and (ii) safeguard rights of succession taking effect on or after July 12, 1984, where the original tenancy from which these rights flow was itself granted by the landlord before July 12, 1984. This is the effect where para. (*b*)(i) and (ii) is read with para. (*a*). In some cases a first succession under the 1976 Act provisions will have taken place before July 12, 1984; in such

cases a second succession on or after that date is safeguarded. In other cases both a first and second succession may take place on or after that date and will be safeguarded by para. (b)(i).

or 53 below. This refers to a successful application *inter vivos* by a nominated successor on the tenant's retirement. The two-succession rule, whether on death or retirement, is preserved by s.37(1) and s.51.

the tenancy was granted. Sub-para. (ii) covers the case of a tenant who, having been given a direction by the tribunal under s.39, in fact obtains his tenancy by a direct grant from the landlord under s.45(6) before the time when it would have vested in him by a statutory deemed grant under s.45(1). "Grant" in relation to sub-para. (ii) is a grant in the ordinary sense; in relation to sub-para. (i), it refers to a deemed grant.

by a written contract of tenancy. This allows parties to "contract in" to the succession scheme in its full dimension, *i.e.* as if the tenancy had been granted before July 12, 1984. This facility might conceivably be used in the case of a lease back on a sale to an institutional landlord. There is a question as to whether the "indication" mentioned in sub-para. (iii) is a term which might affect rental value.

a person who, immediately before that date, was a tenant of the holding. This would safeguard the succession rights attached to a tenancy granted before July 12, 1984 if, after that date, there has been a surrender and regrant, thereby producing a new tenancy which, but for this sub-para., would attract no succession rights.

Subs. (2)
Does not include. An obviously necessary exclusion to prevent succession rights attaching to tenancies held by persons in trustee-like capacities.

Succession on death of tenant

Application of sections 36 to 48

35.—(1) Sections 36 to 48 below (except sections 40(5), 42 and 45(8) which are of general application) shall apply where—
    (a) an agricultural holding is held under a tenancy which falls within paragraph (a) or (b) of section 34(1) above, and
    (b) the sole (or sole surviving) tenant (within the meaning of that section) dies and is survived by a close relative of his.
  (2) In sections 36 to 48 below (and in Part I of Schedule 6 to this Act)—
    "close relative" of a deceased tenant means—
        (a) the wife or husband of the deceased;
        (b) a brother or sister of the deceased;
        (c) a child of the deceased;
        (d) any person (not within (b) or (c) above) who, in the case of any marriage to which the deceased was at any time a party, was treated by the deceased as a child of the family in relation to that marriage;
    "the date of death" means the date of the death of the deceased;
    "the deceased" means the deceased tenant of the holding;
    "the holding" (except where the context otherwise requires) means the agricultural holding mentioned in subsection (1) above;
    "related holding" means, in relation to the holding, any agricultural holding comprising the whole or a substantial part of the land comprised in the holding;
    "the tenancy" means the tenancy of the holding.

GENERAL NOTE
  S.35 applies the corpus of detailed provisions set out in ss.36 to 38, which constitute an amended version of the 1976 succession on death scheme, to the tenancies mentioned in s.34, *i.e.* to the tenancies which survive the humanely non-retrospective phasing-out of the 1976 Act provisions. The definitions in subs. (2) should be noted: see also s.59(1). Part I of

Sched. 6 contains supplementary provisions on the complex subject of eligibility. Sections 49 to 58 together with s.59(2) and Part II of Sched. 6 cover succession *inter vivos* on retirement.

Subs. (1)

Treated. The requirement of treatment in relation to a marriage of which the deceased was then a party gave rise to some difficult cases: see *Berridge* case (1979); *Hamilton* No. 10, p. 168; *Williams* v. *Douglas* (1980); *Hamilton* No. 115, p. 185; *Thomas* v. *Electricity Supply Nominees Ltd.* (1979); *Hamilton* No. 84 p. 121.

Right of any eligible person to apply for new tenancy on death of tenant

36.—(1) Any eligible person may apply under section 39 below to the Tribunal for a direction entitling him to a tenancy of the holding unless excluded by subsection (2) or section 37 or 38 below.

(2) Subsection (1) above (and section 41 below) shall not apply if on the date of death the holding was held by the deceased under—

(*a*) a tenancy for a fixed term of years of which more than twenty-seven months remained unexpired, or

(*b*) a tenancy for a fixed term of more than one but less than two years.

(3) For the purposes of this section and sections 37 to 48 below, "eligible person" means (subject to the provisions of Part I of Schedule 6 to this Act and without prejudice to section 41 below) any surviving close relative of the deceased in whose case the following conditions are satisfied—

(*a*) in the seven years ending with the date of death his only or principal source of livelihood throughout a continuous period of not less than five years, or two or more discontinuous periods together amounting to not less than five years, derived from his agricultural work on the holding or on an agricultural unit of which the holding forms part, and

(*b*) he is not the occupier of a commercial unit of agricultural land.

(4) In the case of the deceased's wife the reference in subsection (3)(*a*) above to the relative's agricultural work shall be read as a reference to agricultural work carried out by either the wife or the deceased (or both of them).

(5) Part I of Schedule 6 to this Act, which supplements subsection (3) above and makes provision with respect to the assessment of the productive capacity of agricultural land for the purposes of paragraph (*b*) of that subsection, shall have effect.

DEFINITIONS

"agricultural land": s.1.

"close relative": s.35(2).

"commercial unit": see paras. 3 and 4 of Sched. 6.

"eligible person": see subs. (3) and Sched. 6.

Subs. (2)

Para. (a): more than twenty-seven months remained unexpired. It is at first sight difficult to see why this exclusion, which appeared in s.18(4)(*d*)(i) of the 1976 Act, is still relevant in view of s.4 of the present Act. The explanation may be connected with the fact that s.4 applies only to tenancies granted on or after September 12, 1984, whereas s.36(2)(*a*) covers tenancies granted on or after July 12, 1984, which fall within the categories covered by s.34(1)(*b*).

Para. (b): more than one, but less than two years. This refers to *Gladstone* v. *Bower* [1960] 2 Q.B. 384 tenancies. This exclusion is clearly correct on the assumption that these are tenancies of agricultural holdings and may no doubt be used in support of the view that they are: see note to s.2(2)(*a*), *ante,* and note on "terminating" to s.3(1).

Subs. (3)

Para. (a): only or principal source of livelihood. See Sched. 6, para. 2, for provision that attendance at a full-time course of further education can count (to the limit of three years) towards this livelihood condition. "Livelihood" cannot be confined to earned income or to income in the form of cash. It would seem that all kinds of income, earned and unearned, including a retirement pension, but apparently not undrawn profits from a partnership, can be taken into account: see *Trinity College, Cambridge* v. *Caines* (1983) 272 E.G. 1287 on the latter point. Tribunal decisions which are of some help are: *Melli* v. *Executors of Brooks* (1978); *Hamilton* No. 54, p. 72; *Colson* v. *Midwood Trustees* (1979); *Hamilton* No. 81, p. 112; *Mercer* v. *Waddington* (1979); *Hamilton* No. 98, p. 141; *Hughes* v. *Owen* (1980); *Hamilton* No. 131, p. 212; *Jones* v. *Midland Bank Trust Co. Ltd.* (1981); *Hamilton* No. 158, p. 228; *Goodwin* v. *The Iscoyd Estate* (1980) and *Mollett* v. *County Estates (Yorkshire) Ltd., Hamilton* Nos. 108 and 109, pp. 171–179; *Dewsbury* v. *Drusilla Roberts Trust* (1981); *Hamilton* No. 159, p. 228; *Rigby* v. *Helm* (1978); *Hamilton* No. 36, p. 42; see also *Wilson* v. *Earl Spencers Settlement Trusteees* (1984) 274 E.G. 1254, *per* Hodgson J.

agricultural work. See concession for widows in subs. (4), derived from an amendment by the 1984 Act (s.3(2)) following hard cases before tribunals: *e.g. Hulme* v. *Earl of Aylesford* (1978); *Hamilton* No. 22, p. 23, (1978) 245 E.G. 851. Other cases were *Firth* v. *Barraclough* (1977); *Hamilton* No. 12, p. 16; *Heal* v. *Sidcot School* (1978); *Hamilton* No. 34, p. 40. The concession was partly anticipated by *Littlewood* v. *Rolfe* (1981) 258 E.G. 168. "Agricultural Work" must include not only manual labour, but also managerial or supervisory functions and necessary record-keeping: see the tribunal's decision in *Dagg* v. *Lovett* (1979) 251 E.G. 75, a decision restored by the Court of Appeal (1980) 256 E.G. 491, after being quashed at first instance (1980) 254 E.G. 993. See also *Colson* v. *Midland Trustees* (1979); *Hamilton* No. 81, p. 112.

agricultural unit of which the holding forms part. The unit at the date of the deceased's death must be precisely the same as that from which the applicant's livelihood was derived during the relevant five years: *Trinity College, Cambridge* v. *Caines* (1983) 272 E.G. 1287 at p. 1284 (a narrow interpretation). It seems that the different parcels of land said to be comprised in a unit must be occupied by the same person: the definition in s.109 of the Agriculture Act 1967 (applied by s.96(1) of the present Act) is not entirely conclusive, as the word "including" is somewhat ambiguous. Tribunals have been at variance on the point: see *Evans* v. *Trustees of Rudge Settlement* (1977); *Hamilton* No. 15, p. 18 and *Heal* v. *Sidcot School* (1978); *Hamilton* No. 34, p. 40 (both considering single occupation essential) and *Scott* v. *Durham County Council* (1979); *Hamilton* No. 99, p. 155; *Yardley* v. *Evans* (1980); *Hamilton* No. 108, p. 164 and *Jerrett* v. *Hutchings* (1980); *Hamilton* No. 128, p. 210 (all taking the opposite view).

Para. (b): not the occupier of a commercial unit of agricultural land. The complex and difficult details of this "occupancy condition" are set out in Sched. 6, to which the reader is referred for the text and explanatory notes.

Subs. (4)
   In the case of deceased's wife. This provision eliminated the old disputes as to whether the widow's livelihood was derived from agricultural work or from her marital relationship; see note to subs. (3) on agricultural work above.

Subs. (5)
   Productive capacity. See Sched. 6, paras. 3, 4 and 5 and see the Agriculture (Miscellaneous Provisions) Act 1976 (Units of Production) Order 1985 (S.I. 1985 No. 997), revoking the 1984 Order of the same title (S.I. 1984 No. 1309). This will be an annual order.

Exclusion of statutory succession where two successions have already occurred

37.—(1) Section 36(1) above (and section 41 below) shall not apply if on each of the last two occasions when there died a sole (or sole surviving) tenant of the holding or of a related holding there occurred one or other of the following things, namely—

(*a*) a tenancy of the holding or of a related holding was obtained by virtue of a direction of the Tribunal under section 39 below, or such a tenancy was granted (following such a direction) in circumstances within section 45(6) below, or

(*b*) a tenancy of the holding or of a related holding was granted by the landlord to a person who, being a close relative of the tenant who died on that occasion, was or had become the sole or sole remaining applicant for such a direction.

(2) If on any occasion prior to the date of death, as a result of an agreement between the landlord and the tenant for the time being of the holding or of a related holding, the holding or a related holding became let—

(*a*) under a tenancy granted by the landlord, or

(*b*) by virtue of an assignment of the current tenancy,

to a person who, if the said tenant had died immediately before the grant or assignment would have been his close relative, that occasion shall for the purposes of subsection (1) above be deemed to be an occasion such as is mentioned in that subsection on which a tenancy of the holding or a related holding was obtained by virtue of a direction of the Tribunal under section 39 below.

(3) If any such tenancy was granted as mentioned in subsection (2) above for a term commencing later than the date of the grant, the holding under that tenancy shall for the purposes of that subsection not be taken to have become let under that tenancy until the commencement of the term.

(4) Subsections (1) and (2) above—

(*a*) shall apply whether or not any tenancy granted or obtained (otherwise than by virtue of an assignment) as mentioned in those provisions related to the whole of the land held by the tenant on the occasion of whose death, or with whose agreement, the tenancy was so granted or obtained, as the case may be, and

(*b*) shall apply where a joint tenancy is granted by the landlord to persons one of whom is a person such as is mentioned in either of those subsections as they apply where a tenancy is granted by the landlord to any such person alone.

(5) Subsection (2) above shall apply where a tenancy is assigned to joint tenants one of whom is a person such as is mentioned in that subsection as it applies where a tenancy is assigned to any such person alone.

(6) Where a tenancy of the holding or of a related holding was obtained by virtue of a direction of the Tribunal under section 53(7) below, that occasion shall for the purposes of subsection (1) above be deemed to be an occasion such as is mentioned in that subsection on which a tenancy of the holding or a related holding was obtained by virtue of a direction of the Tribunal under section 39 below.

(7) Subsection (2) above shall, in relation to any time before 12th September 1984, have effect with the substitution for the words from "as a result" to "grant or assignment" of the words "the holding or a related holding became let under a new tenancy granted by the landlord, with the agreement of the outgoing tenant, to a person who, if the outgoing tenant had died immediately before the grant".

(8) Subsections (4) and (5) above shall not apply in relation to any tenancy if—

(*a*) it was granted before 12th September 1984,

(*b*) it was obtained by virtue of any direction given in any proceedings arising out of an application made under Part II of the Agriculture (Miscellaneous Provisions) Act 1976 before 12th September 1984, or

(*c*) it was granted (following such a direction) in circumstances within section 23(6) of the said Act of 1976.

(9) In this section "tenant" has the same meaning as in section 34 above.

DEFINITIONS
Note restricted definition of "tenant": see subs. (9) and s.34(2).
"related holding", "close relative" and other definitions, see s.35(2).

Subs. (1)
Each of the last two occasions. This is the important two-succession rule, which is activated
by a number of occurrences mentioned in the section.
Para. (a): by virtue of a direction. In this case the direction has been followed by a
statutory deemed grant under s.45, not by an actual grant, as in para. (*b*) below.
or such a tenancy was granted. Here there has been a direction, but there has been a
subsequent actual grant by the landlord, eliminating the need for a deemed grant under
s.45, to the person entitled under the direction.
Para. (b): granted by the landlord to . . . the sole or sole remaining applicant. Here there
has been no direction following the death, but there has been an application (or applications)
for one and the landlord has granted a tenancy to the close relative who was the sole or sole
remaining applicant. Note that, although this grant activates the two-succession rule, the
resulting tenancy is not one which under s.34(1)(*b*) attracts any further succession rights.

Subs. (2)
Any occasion prior to the date of death. In contrast with the occurrences above mentioned,
this is an agreement *inter vivos*, not a consequence of the tenant's death. It is an entirely
voluntary arrangement and must be distinguished from the succession on retirement
provisions in ss.49 to 58, which also takes place *inter vivos* but which can operate *in invitum,*
i.e. without agreement with, and against the wishes of, the landlord. The present transaction
can take the form of the grant of a new tenancy or the assignment of the existing tenancy.
The grantee or assignee must be a "close relative" of the tenant at the date of the transaction.
The transaction, in whatever form, activates the two-succession rule.

Subs. (4)
Subsections (1) and (2) above. The provisions in s.37(1) and (2) are applied where what
is granted is a tenancy of a *part* only of the land held by the deceased or outgoing tenant,
but this concession does not apply to an assignment. It is also provided that where a joint
tenancy is granted or assigned (subs. (5) only one of the joint tenants need be a close
relative.

Subs. (6)
Under section 53(7) below. Here, no doubt for convenience and completeness, although
its context is within ss.49 to 58, it is stated that when a tenancy is obtained by a nominated
successor as a result of a tribunal direction under s.53(7) it will be deemed an occasion for
the application of the two-succession restriction.

Subs. (7)
Substitution. Subs. (7) restores wording which was amended by the 1984 Act (Sched. 1,
para. 2(7)) to what it was before that amendment, which came into effect on September 12,
1984.

Subs. (8)
Subsections (4) and (5) above shall not apply. Subs. (8) has the same basic anti-
retrospective purpose as subs. (7), namely, to ensure that amended provisions which came
into operation on September 12, 1984, shall not be taken to affect occurrences which took
place before that date.

Other excluded cases

38.—(1) Section 36(1) above (and section 41 below) shall not apply if
on the date of death the tenancy is the subject of a valid notice to quit to
which subsection (1) of section 26 above applies, being a notice given
before that date in the case of which—

(*a*) the month allowed by that subsection for serving a counter-notice
under that subsection expired before that date without such a
counter-notice having been served, or

(*b*) the Tribunal consented before that date to its operation.

(2) Section 36(1) (and section 41) shall not apply if on the date of death the tenancy is the subject of a valid notice to quit given before that date and falling within Case C or F.

(3) Those sections shall not apply if on the date of death the tenancy is the subject of a valid notice to quit given before that date and falling within Case B, D or E, and

  (a) the time within which the tenant could have required any question arising in connection with the notice to be determined by arbitration under this Act expired before that date without such a requirement having been made by the tenant, and the month allowed for serving any counter-notice in respect of the notice expired before that date without any such counter-notice having been served, or

  (b) questions arising in connection with the notice were referred to arbitration under this Act before that date and were determined before that date in such a way as to uphold the operation of the notice and (where applicable) the month allowed for serving any counter-notice in respect of the notice expired before that date without a counter-notice having been served, or

  (c) the Tribunal consented before that date to the operation of the notice.

(4) Those sections shall not apply if the holding consists of land held by a smallholding authority or the Minister for the purposes of smallholdings within the meaning of Part III of the Agriculture Act 1970 (whether the tenancy was granted before or after the commencement of the said Part III).

(5) Those sections shall not apply if the tenancy was granted by trustees in whom the land is vested on charitable trusts the sole or principal object of which is the settlement or employment of agriculture of persons who have served in any of Her Majesty's naval, military or air forces.

DEFINITIONS
  Cases B, C, D, E, F: see Sched. 3.
  "date of death", "tenancy", "holding": s.35(2).

Subss. (1), (2), (3)
  Shall not apply. Subss. (1), (2) and (3) are all concerned with applications of the same principle. Tenancies are excluded from the succession scheme if on the date of death they are subject to valid notices to quit which, for one reason or another under the Act, cannot be effectively challenged. It may be that no counter-notice had been served in time or that the tribunal have consented (subs. (1)); or that there is no procedure under the Act for challenging them (subs. (2)); or that the time for arbitration or serving a counter-notice has lapsed or that the landlord has succeeded in the arbitration or that the tribunal have consented to the notice under s.28 (subs. (3)).

Subs. (2)
  For the purpose of smallholdings. This provision, consolidating para. 2(6) of Sched. 1 to the 1984 Act, overrules the Court of Appeal decision in *Saul* v. *Norfolk County Council* [1984] Q.B. 559 that a smallholdings tenancy granted before the 1970 Act was not excluded from succession.

Applications for tenancy of holding

39.—(1) An application under this section by an eligible person to the Tribunal for a direction entitling him to a tenancy of the holding shall be made within the period of three months beginning with the day after the date of death.

(2) Where only one application is made under this section the Tribunal, if satisfied—

  (a) that the applicant was an eligible person at the date of death, and
  (b) that he has not subsequently ceased to be such a person,

shall determine whether he is in their opinion a suitable person to become the tenant of the holding.

(3) Where two or more applications are made under this section, then, subject to subsection (4) below, subsection (2) above shall apply to each of the applicants as if he were the only applicant.

(4) If the applicants under this section include a person validly designated by the deceased in his will as the person he wished to succeed him as tenant of the holding, the Tribunal shall first make a determination under subsection (2) above as regards that person, and shall do so as regards the other applicant or each of the other applicants only if the Tribunal determine that the person so designated is not in their opinion a suitable person to become the tenant of the holding.

(5) If under the preceding provisions of this section only one applicant is determined by the Tribunal to be in their opinion a suitable person to become the tenant of the holding, the Tribunal shall, subject to subsection (10) and section 44 below, give a direction entitling him to a tenancy of the holding.

(6) If under the preceding provisions of this section each of two or more applicants is determined by the Tribunal to be in their opinion a suitable person to become the tenant of the holding, the Tribunal—

(a) shall, subject to subsection (9) below, determine which of those applicants is in their opinion the more or most suitable person to become the tenant of the holding, and

(b) shall, subject to subsection (10) and section 44 below, give a direction entitling that applicant to a tenancy of the holding.

(7) Before making a determination under subsection (2) above in the case of any applicant the Tribunal shall afford the landlord an opportunity of stating his views on the suitability of that applicant.

(8) In making a determination under subsection (2) above in the case of a particular applicant, or a determination under subsection (6) above as between two or more applicants, the Tribunal shall have regard to all relevant matters including—

(a) the extent to which the applicant or each of those applicants has been trained in, or has had practical experience of, agriculture,

(b) the age, physical health and financial standing of the applicant or each of those applicants, and

(c) the views (if any) stated by the landlord on the suitability of the applicant or any of those applicants.

(9) Where subsection (6) above would apply apart from this subsection, the Tribunal may, with the consent of the landlord, give instead a direction specifying any two, any three or any four of the applicants within that subsection, and entitling the specified applicants to a joint tenancy of the holding.

(10) Where the person or persons who would, subject to section 44 below, be entitled to a direction under this section entitling him or them to a tenancy or (as the case may be) to a joint tenancy of the holding agree to accept instead a tenancy or joint tenancy of a part of the holding, any direction given by the Tribunal under subsection (5), (6) or (9) above shall relate to that part of the holding only.

DEFINITIONS
"a person validly designated by the deceased in his will": s.40(1).
"eligible person": s.36(3).
"tribunal": s.96(1).

Subs. (1)
Within the period of three months. This time-limit is inflexible and failure to observe it renders the application invalid: Kellett v. Alexander (1980) 257 E.G. 494 at p.497. Note that

an application under s.41 by a person not fully eligible is subject to the same time-limit and the application is made on the same form: form 1 in Appendix to Sched. 1 to the Agricultural Land Tribunals (Rules) Order 1978 (S.I. 1978 No. 259).

Subs. (2)
Para. (b): that he has not subsequently ceased to be such a person. This re-states in statutory form the effect of the decisions in *Jackson* v. *Hall* and *Williamson* v. *Thompson* [1980] A.C. 854.

Subs. (4)
A person validly designated by the deceased in his will. If the tribunal find a person so designated to be suitable they are directed to look no further. He has already been found eligible (subs. (2)) and under subs. (5) he will be given a direction entitling him to a tenancy: for supplementary provisions, see s.40. In this one respect the desires of the deceased tenant are effective, but only if expressed in a will or codicil. An informally expressed intention, even one which would give rise to a trust in equity, will not suffice.

Subs. (5)
Subject to subsection (10) and section 44 below. I.e. subject to applicant's agreement to accept a tenancy of a *part* only of the holding, and subject to the landlord's right to apply for consent to a notice to quit.

Subs. (6)
Para. (a): subject to subsection (9) below. I.e. to the possibility of the landlord's agreeing to grant a joint tenancy.

Subs. (7)
His views on the suitablility of the applicant. The landlord can (1) dispute the eligibility of the applicant (see Form 1R in the Appendix to the Agricultural Land Tribunals (Succession to Agricultural Tenancies) Order 1984 (S.I. 1984 No. 1301); (2) question the applicant's suitability; (3) apply for consent to a notice to quit served on the deceased's personal representatives (Form 2, *ibid.*). All these matters will come before the tribunal in the same proceedings.

Subs. (8)
Regard to all relevant matters. Tribunals generally have shown humanity and balance in their consideration of suitability: see, for example, *Dagg* v. *Lovett* (1979) *Hamilton* No. 72, p.88, praised by Lord Denning M.R. at (1980) 256 E.G. 491.

Subs. (9)
Or any four. Even with consent of the landlord the tribunal cannot specify more than four joint tenants. It is not provided that the *most* suitable are to be specified.

Subs. (10)
Agree to accept. The tribunal cannot, except with the *consent* of the applicant or applicants give a direction which entitles to a tenancy of part only of the holding.

Provisions supplementary to section 39

40.—(1) In section 39 above "will" includes codicil, and for the purposes of that section a person shall be taken to be validly designated by the deceased in his will as the person he wishes to succeed him as tenant of the holding if, but only if, a will of the deceased which is the subject of a grant of probate or administration—

(*a*) contains an effective specific bequest to that person of the deceased's tenancy of the holding, or

(*b*) does not contain an effective specific bequest of that tenancy, but does contain a statement specifically mentioning the holding or the deceased's tenancy of the holding and exclusively designating that person (in whatever words, and whether by name or description) as the person whom the deceased wishes to succeed him as tenant of the holding.

(2) For the purposes of subsection (1) above a statement which is framed so as to designate as mentioned in paragraph (*b*) of that subsection different persons in different circumstances shall be taken to satisfy that paragraph if, in the events which have happened, the statement exclusively designates a particular person.

(3) A direction under section 39 above given in favour of a person by reason of his being a person validly designated by the deceased as mentioned in subsection (4) of that section shall be valid even if the probate or administration by virtue of which he was such a person at the giving of the direction is subsequently revoked or varied.

(4) For the purposes of this Part of this Act an application under section 39 above which is withdrawn or abandoned shall be treated as if it had never been made.

(5) Provision shall be made by order under section 73(3) of the Agriculture Act 1947 (procedure of Agricultural Land Tribunals) for requiring any person making an application to the Tribunal under section 39 above or section 41 below to give notice of the application to the landlord of the agricultural holding to which the application relates and to take such steps as the order may require for bringing the application to the notice of other persons interested in the outcome of the application.

DEFINITIONS
  "the deceased", "the holding": s.35(2)

Subs. (1)
  A person. The deceased cannot make a valid designation of two or more persons to succeed as joint tenants; such a purported designation would be void: see also s.39(4).
  Para. (b): exclusively designating that person. A testator might be better advised to make a specific bequest of the tenancy in order to avoid possible confusion or doubt, especially if the designation is contingent on events under subs. (2). The well established phrasing for bequests might be safer.

Subs. (3)
  Subsequently revoked or varied. There must have been a grant of probate or administration, but it is immaterial if it was subsquently revoked or varied.

Subs. (4)
  As if it had never been made. If after an application the tenant enters into direct negotiations with his landlord he should be careful to avoid giving any evidence of withdrawal or abandonment which would defeat his statutory rights if the negotiations should fail.

Subs. (5)
  Provision shall be made by order: see the Agricultural Land Tribunals (Succession to Agricultural Tenancies) Order 1984 (S.I. 1984 No. 1301), Sched, rule 5; and see *Kellett* v. *Alexander* (1980) 257 E.G. 494 for effect of non-compliance.

Application by not fully eligible person to be treated as eligible

41.—(1) This section applies to any surviving close relative of the deceased who for some part of the seven years ending with the date of death engaged (whether full-time or part-time) in agricultural work on the holding, being a person in whose case—

(*a*) the condition specified in paragraph (*b*) of the definition of "eligible person" in section 36(3) above is satisfied, and

(*b*) the condition specified in paragraph (*a*) of that definition, though not fully satisfied, is satisfied to a material extent.

(2) A person to whom this section applies may within the period of three months beginning with the day after the date of death apply to the Tribunal for a determination that he is to be treated as an eligible person for the purposes of sections 36 to 48 of this Act.

(3) If on an application under this section—
  (a) the Tribunal are satisfied that the applicant is a person to whom this section applies, and
  (b) it appears to the Tribunal that in all the circumstances it would be fair and reasonable for the applicant to be able to apply under section 39 above for a direction entitling him to a tenancy of the holding,
the Tribunal shall determine that he is to be treated as an eligible person for the purposes of sections 36 to 48 of this Act, but shall otherwise dismiss the application.

(4) In relation to a person in respect of whom the Tribunal have determined as mentioned in subsection (3) above sections 36 to 48 of this Act shall apply as if he were an eligible person.

(5) A person to whom this section applies may make an application under section 39 above as well as an application under this section; and if the Tribunal determine as mentioned in subsection (3) above in respect of a person who has made an application under that section, the application under that section shall (without prejudice to subsection (4) above) be treated as made by an eligible person.

(6) Without prejudice to the generality of paragraph (b) of subsection (1) above, cases where the condition mentioned in that paragraph might be less than fully satisfied include cases where the close relative's agricultural work on the holding fell short of providing him with his principal source of livelihood because the holding was too small.

DEFINITIONS
"close relative", "date of death", "holding": s.35(2).
"eligible person": s.36(3).
"tribunal": s.96(1).

Subs. (1)
  Para. (a): the condition specified in paragraph (b) . . . is satisfied. The "occupancy condition" must be fully satisfied: there is no power to relax this condition, which is spelt out in Sched. 6. The "close relative" connection must also be fully satisfied.
  Para. (b): satisfied to a material extent. The only or principal source of livelihood condition (s.36(3)(a), though not fully satisfied, must be satisfied "to a material extent". Full satisfaction of the condition would occur if the applicant's livelihood from the holding represented more than 50 per cent. of his total livelihood: see *Wilson* v. *Earl Spencer's Settlement Trustees* (1985) 274 E.G. 1254. Something less would therefore constitute satisfaction "to a material extent". An "almost but not quite" interpretation suggested by Lord Russell in *Jackson* v. *Hall* [1980] A.C. 854 at p.888 has not found favour either in relation to the five-year period or the amount of the livelihood. The tribunal formulation in *Dagg* v. *Lovett* (1979) 251 E.G. 75, "substantial in point of time and important in terms of value" has been approved in *Littlewood* v. *Rolfe* [1981] 2 All E.R. 51, *Wilson* v. *Earl Spencer's Settlement Trustees* (1984) 274 E.G. 1254 and *Trustees of James Raine (Senior)* v. *Raine* (1985) 275 E.G. 374. "Important" means not important to the applicant but an important satisfaction of the over 50 per cent. requirement: *Wilson* v. *Earl Spencer's Settlement Trustees, supra,* at p.1258.

Subs. (2)
  May within the period of three months. The wording here is slightly misleading, since in fact the application must be made at the same time, and on the same form, as the application under s.39(1). There is no power to apply under s.41 after dismissal under s.39(1): see Part B of Form 1 in Appendix to the Sched. to the Agricultural Land Tribunals (Succession to Agricultural Tenancies) Order 1984 (S.I. 1984 No. 1301).

Subs. (3)
  Para. (b): fair and reasonable. "A further hurdle" for the applicant: *Littlewood* v. *Rolfe* [1981] 2 All E.R. 51 at p.58. See *Trustees of James Raine (Senior)* v. *Raine* (1985) 275 E.G. 374 at p.378 for a restriction on the meaning of this phrase.

Subs. (5)

May make an application under section 39 above as well. In fact an applicant to whom s.41 applies *has* to complete Part A as well as Part B of the form mentioned in note to subs. (2) above, so that in practice an applicant applies *under both s.39(1) and s.41(2)* in all cases where there are any grounds for applying under s.41(2)

Subs. (6)

Too small. This seems a simple and straightforward example; the only query is why it was thought necessary to include it. Another simple case would be where a father dies before a son or daughter had put in five years' work on the holding.

Procedure where deceased held more than one holding

42.—(1) Subsections (2) and (3) below shall have effect where at the expiry of the period of three months beginning with the day after the date of death of a tenant there are pending before the Tribunal separate applications made under section 39 above by any person, or (as the case may be) by each one of a number of persons, in respect of more than one agricultural holding held by the tenant at that date.

(2) The applications referred to in subsection (1) above (together with, in each case, any associated application made under section 41 above) shall, subject to and in accordance with the provisions of any such order as is referred to in section 40(5) above, be heard and determined by the Tribunal in such order as may be decided—

(*a*) where the applications were made by one person, by that person,

(*b*) where the applications were made by two or more persons, by agreement between those persons or, in default of agreement, by the chairman of the Tribunal.

(3) Any decision made by the chairman under subsection (2)(*b*) above shall be made according to the respective sizes of the holdings concerned so that any application in respect of any holding which is larger than any other of those holdings shall be heard and determined by the Tribunal before any application in respect of that other holding.

DEFINITIONS
"date of death": s.35(2)
"tenant": s.34(2).
"tribunal": s.96(1)

Subs. (2)

Any such order as is referred to in section 40(5). The relevant order is at present the Agricultural Land Tribunals (Succession to Agricultural Tenancies) Order 1984 (S.I. 1984 No. 1301). There are no provisions in this order affecting the rules laid down in s.42.

Restriction on operation of notice to quit given by reason of death of tenant

43.—(1) A notice to quit the holding given to the tenant of the holding by reason of the death of the deceased and falling within Case G shall not have effect unless—

(*a*) no application to become the tenant of the holding is made (or has already at the time of the notice to quit been made) under section 39 above within the period mentioned in subsection (1) of that section, or

(*b*) one or more such applications having been made within that period—

(i) none of the applicants is determined by the Tribunal to be in their opinion a suitable person to become the tenant of the holding, or

(ii) the Tribunal consent under section 44 below to the operation of the notice to quit in relation to the whole or part of the holding.

(2) Where the Tribunal consent under section 44 below to the operation of a notice to quit to which subsection (1) above applies in relation to part only of the holding, the notice shall have effect accordingly as a notice to quit that part and shall not be invalid by reason that it relates only to part of the holding.

DEFINITIONS
"tenant": both s.96(1) and s.34(2) according to the context.
"deceased" and "holding": s.35(1).
"tribunal": s.96(1).

Subs. (1)
Given to the tenant of the holding. This would be a notice to quit normally given to the personal representatives in whom the deceased's tenancy will have vested on his death. Although the landlord's rights have been curtailed by the succession scheme it is essential from his point of view to serve notice to quit in accordance with Case G in order to safeguard his limited chances of obtaining possession. S.43 sets out these possibilities. The landlord will have to follow up his notice to quit, where there is an application for succession, by applying to the tribunal for consent to the notice to quit as mentioned in the notes below to s.44.
Para. (a): or has already . . . been made. It is quite possible that an application from a hopeful successor will have been made before the landlord serves his notice to quit.

Subs. (2)
Shall not be invalid. The common law rule is that a notice to quit part only of the land demised is invalid. The present subsection adds a new statutory exception to this rule. Other exceptions are under s.31 of the present Act; s.140 of the Law of Property Act 1925 in respect of a notice given by a person entitled to a severed part of the reversion (see also s.32(1)(*b*) of the present Act); and under an express provision in the contract of tenancy.

Opportunity for landlord to obtain Tribunal's consent to operation of notice to quit

44.—(1) Before giving a direction under section 39(5) or (6) above in a case where a notice to quit to which section 43(1) above applies has been given the Tribunal shall afford the landlord an opportunity of applying for their consent under this section to the operation of the notice.

(2) Subject to subsection (5) below, section 27 above shall apply in relation to an application for, or the giving of, the Tribunal's consent under this section as it applies in relation to an application for, or the giving of, their consent under section 26 above.

(3) The Tribunal shall not entertain an application for their consent to the operation of a notice to quit to which section 43(1) above applies unless it is made in pursuance of subsection (1) above.

(4) Subject to subsection (5) below, if the Tribunal give their consent on an application made in pursuance of subsection (1) above, they shall dismiss the application or each of the applications made under section 39 above.

(5) Where in any case—
   (*a*) a notice to quit to which section 43(1) above applies has been given, and
   (*b*) section 39(10) above applies,
the Tribunal shall give their consent to the operation of the notice to quit in relation to the part of the holding which would, in accordance with section 39(10), be excluded from any direction given by the Tribunal with respect to the holding under section 39; and subsections (2) and (4) above shall not apply.

(6) If on an application made in pursuance of subsection (1) above the Tribunal give their consent to the operation of a notice to quit—
   (*a*) within the period of three months ending with the date on which

the notice purports to terminate the tenancy ("the original operative date"), or

(*b*) at any time after that date,

the Tribunal may, on the application of the tenant, direct that the notice shall have effect from a later date ("the new operative date").

(7) The new operative date, in the case of a notice to quit, must be a date not later than the end of the period of three months beginning with—

(*a*) the original operative date, or

(*b*) the date on which the Tribunal give their consent to the operation of the notice,

whichever last occurs.

DEFINITIONS
"holding": s.35(2)
"tribunal": s.96(1)

Subs. (1)

Applying for their consent. See, for form of application and time-limit, rule 4 of the rules in the Sched. to the Agricultural Land Tribunals (Succession to Agricultural Tenancies) Order 1984 (S.I. 1984 No. 1301). The landlord's application must be on Form 2 and the reply from the applicant for succession on Form 2R.

Subs. (2)

Section 27 above shall apply. This means that the landlord must establish one of the six grounds for consent set out in s.27(3), as in a case where there are no succession complications, and that the "fair and reasonable landlord" provision applies.

Subs. (3)

Shall not entertain. The purpose of this subsection is not self-evident. It may be to prevent the landlord from making an application for consent, when there are applications for succession, otherwise than in the course of, and subject to the rules of, the succession proceedings governed by the order referred to in note to subs. (1) above, *i.e.* to obviate two different sets of proceedings taking place.

Subs. (4)

Dismiss the application. If the tribunal consent to the notice to quit it follows that the application or applications for succession will be dismissed. This is subject to the complication mentioned in subs. (5) where the consent is given in relation to part of the holding only: see next note.

Subs. (5)

In relation to the part of the holding. If, with the agreement of the person entitled, the tribunal give a direction relating to a part only of the holding, then they are *bound* to consent to the operation of the notice to quit in relation to the *remainder* of the holding; no question of establishing grounds for consent under s.27 arises in regard to that remainder.

Subs. (6)

Have effect from a later date. Subss. (6) and (7) empower the tribunal, on the tenant's application, to defer the effective date of the notice to quit to which they have consented where there is too little time left between the date of giving consent and the date of expiry of the notice. The deferment may be to a date not later than the end of three months beginning with the original expiry date or with the date of consent, whichever is later.

Effect of direction under section 39

45.—(1) A direction by the Tribunal—

(*a*) under section 39(5) or (6) above entitling an applicant to a tenancy of the holding, or

(*b*) under section 39(9) above entitling two or more applicants to a joint tenancy of the holding, shall entitle him or them to a tenancy or joint tenancy of the holding as from the relevant time on the terms provided by sections 47 and 48 below; and accordingly such a tenancy or joint tenancy shall be deemed to be at that time granted by the landlord to, and accepted by, the person or persons so entitled.

(2) Where the deceased's tenancy was not derived from the interest held by the landlord at the relevant time, the tenancy or joint tenancy deemed by virtue of subsection (1) above to be granted to, and accepted by, the person or persons so entitled shall be deemed to be granted by the person for the time being entitled to the interest from which the deceased's tenancy was derived, instead of by the landlord, with like effect as if the landlord's interest and any other supervening interest were not subsisting at the relevant time.

(3) The reference in subsection (2) above to a supervening interest is a reference to any interest in the land comprised in the deceased's tenancy, being an interest created subsequently to that tenancy and derived (whether immediately or otherwise) from the interest from which that tenancy was derived and still subsisting at the relevant time.

(4) Subsection (2) above shall not be read as affecting the rights and liabilities of the landlord under this Part of this Act.

(5) Any tenancy of the holding inconsistent with the tenancy to which a direction such as is mentioned in subsection (1) above entitles the person or persons concerned shall, if it would not cease at the relevant time apart from this subsection, cease at that time as if terminated at that time by a valid notice to quit given by the tenant.

(6) If the person or persons whom such a direction entitles to a tenancy or joint tenancy of the holding as from the relevant time becomes or become the tenant or joint tenants of the holding before that time under a tenancy granted by the landlord to, and accepted by, the person or persons concerned, the direction shall cease to have effect and section 48 below shall not apply.

(7) The rights conferred on any person by such a direction (as distinct from his rights under his tenancy of the holding after he has become the tenant or joint tenant of the holding) shall not be capable of assignment.

(8) The Lord Chancellor may by regulations provide for all or any of the provisions of sections 36 to 48 of this Act (except this subsection) to apply, with such exceptions, additions or other modifications as may be specified in the regulations, in cases where the person or any of the persons whom such a direction entitles to a tenancy or joint tenancy of the holding dies before the relevant time.

DEFINITIONS
"agricultural holding": s.1(1).
"deceased": s.35(2).
"holding": s.35(2).
"landlord", "tribunal": s.96(1).
"relevant time": s.46.

Subs. (1)
As from the relevant time. For "relevant time" and deferment of such time, see s.46. Section 45 assumes that the applicant or applicants have been found eligible and suitable; the section deals with the mechanism and effect of a direction.
Shall be deemed to be at that time granted. This is important as providing for the vesting of title to the tenancy by means of a deemed grant and acceptance at the relevant time. At that point of time a *new* tenancy vests in the applicant or joint applicants; the deceased's tenancy is not assigned by this mechanism. (Contrast the possibility of assignment of the current tenancy in the *inter vivos* arrangement mentioned in s.37(2)(*b*).)

Subs. (2)

From which the deceased's tenancy was derived. Subss. (2) to (4) are designed to protect the successor against being turned into the weak position of a subtenant by the interposition of a tenancy of the reversion between him and the freeholder. Subs. (2) achieves this by deeming the new tenancy resulting from the tribunal's direction to be derived from the original landlord and not from the concurrent lessee. By this elegant hypothesis the successor's security of tenure is safeguarded.

Subs. (3)

Whether immediately or otherwise. These words are intended to close a loophole which might otherwise have remained, which could have allowed a reversioner to defeat the intention of these subsections by creating a series of tenancies of the reversion. It has been questioned whether subs. (3) is effective for this purpose, but it is thought that the words "or otherwise" do achieve the object.

Subs. (4)

Rights and liabilities of the landlord. During the subsistence of the concurrent lease the lessee of the reversion is the successor's *landlord* for the purpose of all the ordinary rights and liabilities of landlord and tenant. He is *pro tanto* and *pro tempore* an assignee of the reversion. The fiction invented in subs. (2) for the particular object explained above is not to be taken to interfere with these rights and duties.

Subs. (5)

If it would not cease at the relevant time. This subsection removes any doubt as to whether any tenancy inconsistent with the new tenancy which vests in the successor under s.45(1) automatically ceases to exist when the new tenancy is deemed to be granted. If it would not so cease subs. (5) provides that it shall then cease as if terminated at that time by a valid notice to quit given by the tenant. The tenancy held by the deceased tenant's personal representatives is obviously covered by this subsection.

Subs. (6)

Under a tenancy granted by the landlord. In some cases the person or persons entitled under a direction may, before the new tenancy has vested in him or them by deemed grant under s.45(1) at the relevant time, negotiate the terms of a tenancy with the landlord and accept a direct grant from him. In that case the new tenancy is created by the grant and the direction ceases to have effect. Arbitration under s.48 does not apply as the terms have been settled by agreement. See s.37(1)(*a*) for the application of the two-succession rule in these circumstances and the reference in s.34(1)(*b*)(ii).

Subs. (7)

Rights conferred on any person by such a direction. This absolute prohibition of assignment of such rights, which have not yet evolved into a tenancy, must be distinguished from the qualified restriction on assignment, etc., which is written into the new tenancy when it vests: see s.47(3).

Subs. (8)

The Lord Chancellor may by regulations. See the Agriculture (Miscellaneous Provisions) Act 1976 (Application of Provisions) Regulations 1977 (S.I. 1977 No. 1215).

Interpretation of section 45

46.—(1) Subject to subsection (2) below, in sections 45 above and 48 below "the relevant time"—

    (*a*) except where the following paragraph applies, means the end of the twelve months immediately following the end of the year of tenancy in which the deceased died,

    (*b*) if a notice to quit the holding was given to the tenant by reason of the death of the deceased, being a notice falling within Case G which, apart from section 43 above, would have terminated the tenancy at a time after the end of those twelve months, means that time.

(2) Where the Tribunal give a direction under section 39(5), (6) or (9) above in relation to the holding at any time after the beginning of the period of three months ending with the relevant time apart from this subsection ("the original relevant time"), then—

   (*a*) if the direction is given within that period, the Tribunal may, on the application of the tenant, specify in the direction, as the relevant time for the purposes of this section and section 48 below, such a time falling within the period of three months immediately following the original relevant time as they think fit,

   (*b*) if the direction is given at any time after the original relevant time the Tribunal shall specify in the direction, as the relevant time for those purposes, such a time falling within the period of three months immediately following the date of the giving of the direction as they think fit,

and any time so specified shall be the relevant time for those purposes accordingly.

(3) Where in accordance with section 39(10) above, the tenancy to which a direction under that section entitles the person or persons concerned is a tenancy of part of the deceased's holding, references in sections 45 above and 48 below to the holding shall be read as references to the whole of the deceased's holding or to the part of that holding to which the direction relates, as the context requires.

DEFINITIONS
   "deceased", "holding": s.35(2)
   "tribunal: s.96(1).

Subs. (1)
   The relevant time. The definition is important as the new tenancy vests by deemed grant at the relevant time: s.45(1). Also the relevant time is involved in the definition of "the prescribed period" for the purpose of the arbitration provisions in s. 48: see s.48(2).

Subs. (2)
   At any time after. Normally the time provisions in subs. (1) will allow for necessary arrangements, but sometimes the direction may be given near the relevant time or even after it, *e.g.* if a point of law has had to be referred to the High Court.
   Para. (a): the Tribunal may. If the direction is given *within* the three months ending with the relevant time it is in the tribunal's discretion, on the tenant's application, to specify a new relevant time, falling within three months after the original relevant time.
   Para. (b): the Tribunal shall. If the direction is not given until *after* the original relevant time no application by the tenant is necessary. The tribunal *must* then specify as the relevant time a time falling within the three months after the date of giving their direction, their only discretion being to fix such date within this period as they think fit.

Terms of new tenancy unless varied by arbitration

47.—(1) Subject to the provisions of this section and section 48 below, the terms of the tenancy or joint tenancy to which a direction under section 39(5), (6) or (9) above entitles the person or persons concerned shall be the same as the terms on which the holding was let immediately before it ceased to be let under the contract of tenancy under which it was let at the date of death.

(2) If on the date of death the holding was held by the deceased under a tenancy for a fixed term of years, subsection (1) above shall have effect as if the tenancy under which the holding was let at the date of death had before that date become a tenancy from year to year on (with that exception) the terms of the actual tenancy as far as applicable.

(3) If the terms of the tenancy to which such a direction entitles the person or persons concerned would not, apart from this subsection, include a covenant by the tenant or each of the tenants not to assign,

sub-let or part with possession of the holding or any part of it without the landlord's consent in writing, subsection (1) above shall have effect as if those terms included such a covenant.

DEFINITIONS
"contract of tenancy": s.1(5).
"the holding", "the tenancy": s.35(2).

Subs. (1)
Immediately before it ceased to be let. After the deceased's death the tenancy will normally vest in the personal representatives until the deemed statutory grant under s.45(1) at "the relevant time" or an earlier direct grant by the landlord to the applicant under s.45(6).

Subs. (2)
Shall have effect as if. The transformation by statutory alchemy of the fixed term vested in the deceased into a tenancy from year to year taking effect immediately before his death is essential for the tenancy to fit into the pattern of the succession scheme.

Subs. (3)
Include a covenant. This qualified covenant written in to the tenancy, if not otherwise there, has to be distinguished from the absolute prohibition taking effect from the date of the direction until the new tenancy vests under s.45(1): see s.45(7).

Note that the terms may be varied by arbitration under s.48: s.47(1).

Arbitration on terms of new tenancy

48.—(1) Where the Tribunal give a direction such as is mentioned in subsection (1) of section 45 above, the provisions of this section shall apply unless excluded by subsection (6) of that section.

(2) In the following provisions of this section—
"the landlord" means the landlord of the holding;
"the prescribed period" means the period between the giving of the direction and—
> (*a*) the end of the three months immediately following the relevant time, or
> (*b*) the end of the three months immediately following the date of the giving of the direction,
> whichever last occurs;
"the relevant time" has the meaning given by subsection (1) or (as the case may require) subsection (2) of section 46 above;
"the tenant" means the person or persons entitled to a tenancy or joint tenancy of the holding by virtue of the direction;
and references to the holding shall be read in accordance with section 46(3) above.

(3) At any time within the prescribed period the landlord or the tenant may by notice in writing served on the other demand a reference to arbitration under this Act of one or both of the questions specified in subsection (4) below.

(4) Those questions (referred to in the following provisions of this section as "question (*a*)" and "question (*b*)" respectively) are—
> (*a*) what variations in the terms of the tenancy which the tenant is entitled to or has obtained by virtue of the direction are justifiable having regard to the circumstances of the holding and the length of time since the holding was first let on those terms;
> (*b*) what rent should be or should have been properly payable in respect of the holding at the relevant time.

(5) Where question (*a*) is referred to arbitration under subsection (3) above (with or without question (*b*)), the arbitrator—

    (*a*) shall determine what variations, if any, in the terms mentioned in that question are justifiable as there mentioned, and

    (*b*) without prejudice to the preceding paragraph, shall include in his award such provisions, if any, as are necessary—

        (i) for entitling the landlord to recover from the tenant under those terms a sum equal to so much as is in all the circumstances fair and reasonable of the aggregate amount of the compensation mentioned in subsection (8)(*a*) below, and

        (ii) for entitling the tenant to recover from the landlord under those terms a sum equal to so much as is in all the circumstances fair and reasonable of the aggregate amount of the compensation mentioned in subsection (8)(*b*) below,

and shall accordingly, with effect from the relevant time, vary those terms in accordance with his determination or direct that they are to remain unchanged.

(6) Where question (*a*) but not question (*b*) is referred to arbitration under subsection (3) above and it appears to the arbitrator that by reason of any provision included in his award under subsection (5) above (not being a provision of a kind mentioned in paragraph (*b*) of that subsection) it is equitable that the rent of the holding should be varied, he may vary the rent accordingly with effect from the relevant time.

(7) Where question (*b*) is referred to arbitration under subsection (3) above (with or without question (*a*)), the arbitrator shall determine what rent should be or should have been properly payable in respect of the holding at the relevant time and accordingly shall, with effect from that time, increase or reduce the rent which would otherwise be or have been payable or direct that it shall remain unchanged.

(8) The compensation referred to in subsection (5)(*b*) above is—

    (*a*) the compensation paid or payable by the landlord, whether under this Act or under agreement or custom, on the termination of the deceased's tenancy of the holding,

    (*b*) the compensation paid or payable to the landlord, whether under this Act or under agreement. on that termination in respect of any such dilapidation or deterioration of, or damage to, any part of the holding or anything in or on the holding as the tenant is or will be liable to make good under the terms of his tenancy.

(9) For the purposes of this section the rent properly payable in respect of the holding shall be the rent at which the holding might reasonably be expected to be let by a prudent and willing landlord to a prudent and willing tenant, taking into account all relevant factors, including (in every case) the terms of the tenancy or prospective tenancy (including those relating to rent) and any such other matters as are specifically mentioned in sub-paragraph (1) of paragraph 1 of Schedule 2 to this Act (read with sub-paragraphs (2) and (3) of that paragraph).

(10) On any reference under subsection (3) above the arbitrator may include in his award such further provisions, if any, relating to the tenancy which the tenant is entitled to or has obtained by virtue of the direction as may be agreed between the landlord and the tenant.

(11) If the award of an arbitrator under this section is made before the relevant time, section 47(1) above shall have effect subject to, and in accordance with, the award.

(12) If the award of an arbitrator under this section is made after the relevant time, it shall have effect as if the terms of the award were contained in an agreement in writing entered into by the landlord and the tenant and having effect as from the relevant time.

Arbitration under this Act, see s.84.
"holding": s.35(2) and s.1(1).
"landlord, "tenant", "termination": s.96(1).
"relevant time": s.46(1), (2).
See definitions in subs. (2). See also for "rent properly payable", subs. (9).

Subs. (1)
Unless excluded by subsection (6). S.45(6) excludes arbitration, for which there is no need, where the tenancy has been granted, after negotiation between the parties, before the deemed statutory grant under s.45(1).

Subs. (2)
The prescribed period. This period needs some care in calculating as it can be somewhat complex.

Subs. (4)
Para. (a): what variations in the terms of the tenancy. where question (a) alone is referred, a restricted adjustment of rent consequential on the variation of terms, as distinct from the full review of the rent when question (b) is referred, may be made by the arbitrator: see subs. (6).
Para. (b): properly payable. If question (b) is referred, whether with or without question (a), a full review of the rent properly payable, as defined by subs. (9) is to be undertaken.

Subs. (5)
Para. (a): are justifiable. The terms of the new tenancy are, subject to s.47 and to the present provisions for arbitration, the same as those of the deceased's tenancy and may date back for a very long time.
Para. (b): such provisions, if any, as are necessary. Subs. 5(b) has to be read with subs. (8). Briefly, the position is as follows. As between the landlord and the deceased tenant's personal representatives compensation (for improvements and tenant-right and for dilapidations) will be settled according to the contract of tenancy and the statute. But there is no contract between the landlord and the successor (except in a s.45(6) case), so that special statutory provisions are required. These statutory provisions are modelled on the normal ingoing payment made by a new tenant and the payment made by the landlord to the incoming tenant, related to the dilapidation monies received by the landlord from the outgoing tenant: see subs. 5(b) and subs. (8). The arbitrator has a good deal of discretion in deciding what is fair and reasonable, but as an experienced valuer he will be familiar with the practice on changes of tenancy, which is reproduced in principle in these subsections.

Subs. (6)
He may vary the rent. The variation is to the extent to which it appears to the arbitrator to be equitable in view of the variations in the terms of the old tenancy which he has considered justifiable. This falls short of a general review of the rent to determine the rent properly payable and if the arbitrator's remit is so limited he must be careful not to go beyond it and assume the larger jurisdiction. If he does his award could be challenged.

Subs. (7)
Properly payable. See subs. (9).

Subs. (8)
Compensation. This subsection must be read closely with subs. (5)(b) and bearing in mind what normally happens on a change of tenancy. The payment by the new tenant to the landlord referred to in subs. (5)(b)(i) is based on the analogy of the payment made by an ingoer, which is related to what the landlord has paid to the outgoer (*i.e.* the deceased tenant's personal representatives) as mentioned in subs. (8)(a). The payment by the landlord to the new tenant referred to in subs. (5)(b)(ii) is based on the analogy of the payment some times made by the landlord related to what the landlord receives from the outgoer (*i.e.* in this case the deceased tenant's personal representatives) in respect of dilapidations, as mentioned in subs. (8)(b).

Subs. (9)

Taking into account. This subsection embodies the central part of the rent formula as set out in s.12 and Sched. 2, paras. 1, 2 and 3. It necessarily omits those provisions in Sched. 2, such as the disregard of improvements, which relate to the previous history of a tenancy. In the case of future rent arbitrations Sched. 2 as a whole will apply in the normal way.

Subs. (10)

As may be agreed. The arbitrator is given specific authority to include in his award matters which have been agreed between the parties but which fall outside the questions covered by section 48. This may well be a convenient facility. The matters must, of course, "relate" to the tenancy.

Subs. (11)

Before the relevant time. For "relevant time" see s.46(1) and (2). If the award is made before the relevant time the new tenancy will not yet have vested and s.47(1), which continues the terms of the old tenancy, will take effect subject to the award.

Subs. (12)

After the relevant time. By that time the new tenancy will have vested and the award will then have effect as if made in an agreement in writing entered into by the landlord and tenant having effect as from that time.

Succession on retirement of tenant

Application of sections 50 to 58

49.—(1) Sections 50 to 58 below (except sections 53(11) and 55(7) which are of general application) shall apply where—

(a) an agricultural holding is held under a tenancy from year to year, being a tenancy which falls within paragraph (a) or (b) of section 34(1) above, and

(b) a notice is given to the landlord by the tenant, or (in the case of a joint tenancy) by all the tenants, of the holding indicating (in whatever terms) that he or they wish a single eligible person named in the notice to succeed him or them as tenant of the holding as from a date specified in the notice, being a date on which the tenancy of the holding could have been determined by notice to quit given at the date of the notice and which falls not less than one year, but not more than two years, after the date of the notice.

(2) In subsection (1) above "tenant" has the same meaning as in section 34 above.

(3) In this section and sections 50 to 58 below (and in Part I of Schedule 6 to this Act as applied by section 50(4))—

"close relative" of the retiring tenant means—

(a) the wife or husband of the retiring tenant;

(b) a brother or sister of the retiring tenant;

(c) a child of the retiring tenant;

(d) any person (not within (b) or (c) above) who, in the case of any marriage to which the retiring tenant has been at any time a party, has been treated by the latter as a child of the family in relation to that marriage;

"eligible person" has the meaning given by section 50 below;

"the holding" means the holding in respect of which the retirement notice is given;

"the nominated successor" means the eligible person named in the retirement notice;

"related holding" means, in relation to the holding, any agricultural holding comprising the whole or a substantial part of the land comprised in the holding;

"the retirement date" means the date specified in the retirement notice as the date as from which the proposed succession is to take place;

"the retirement notice" means the notice mentioned in subsection (1) above;

"the retiring tenant" means the tenant by whom the retirement notice was given, or, where it was given by joint tenants (and the context so permits), any one of those tenants, and "the retiring tenants" accordingly means those tenants;

"the tenancy" means the tenancy of the holding.

GENERAL NOTE: SECTIONS 49–59

The retirement provisions consolidated in sections 49–50 are derived from Sched. 2 to the 1984 Act, which gave legislative force to a recommendation of the Northfield Committee (Report of the Committee of Inquiry into the Acquisition and Occupancy of Agricultural Land, Cmnd. 7599, 1979). The committee recommended (para. 634):

"that there should be encouragement for transfer earlier than death. We are agreed that this could be achieved by providing that the tenant might, at or after age sixty five, with his nominated successor, apply for the transfer of the tenancy. The landlord could contest the application both to oppose the succession and to put his own case for possession (as though a notice to quit on death had been served). If the ALT . . . found for the landlord, or that the successor was not suitable, the existing tenancy would continue until the tenant's death again brought the 1976 . . . Act into play".

This is in substance, although not entirely accurate as to the mechanics, what Parliament enacted. It will be noted that, in accordance with the unanimous conclusion of the Northfield Committee, there is no provision for the compulsory retirement of the tenant. The arrangements require his voluntary cooperation. (There is, however, a provision for the compulsory retirement of tenants of statutory smallholdings: see *post*, note on Case A in Sched. 3 and paras. 559–563 of the Northfield Report, *supra*).]

In its details the retirement scheme follows *mutatis mutandis* the provisions of the scheme for succession on death.

DEFINITIONS

"agricultural holding": s.1(1).
"landlord": s.96(1).
"tenant": s.34(2).
And see subs. (3) for definitions applicable in ss.49 to 58 and Part I of Sched. 6.

Subs. (1)

Para. (a): being a tenancy which falls within paragraph (a) or (b) of section 34(1) above. The 1984 Act limited the duration of succession but at the same time created a new variety of it, the succession on retirement now set out in sections 49 to 58. However, succession on retirement is constrained by the same general restriction as succession on death—the tenancy of the tenant whose retirement is sought must be a tenancy granted before July 12, 1984 or a tenancy within section 34(1)(*b*).

Para. (b): a single eligible person. The "nominated successor" (see subs. (3)) must be an individual (there is no provision here for joint successors) and must be an eligible person, *i.e.* a close relative of the retiring tenant, satisfying the livelihood condition, and not being the occupier of a commercial unit (see s.50(2)).

named in the notice. This is the "retirement notice" (subs. (3)). There is no prescribed form.

a date specified in the notice. The date specified must be a date at which the tenancy could have been lawfully terminated *by a notice to quit* given at the date of the notice. The retirement notice must therefore specify a normal term date for expiry. It would have required at least 12 months' notice and the subs. goes on to say that the date specified must in any case be not less than one year and not more than two years after the date of the retirement notice.

Subs. (3)

"Close relative". Mutatis mutandis this is the same as the definition in s.35(2). The tests of eligibility as a whole reproduce with necessary variations those which apply to succession on death.

Right to apply for new tenancy on retirement of tenant

50.—(1) The eligible person named in the retirement notice may (subject to section 57(2) below) apply under section 53 below to the Tribunal for a direction entitling him to a tenancy of the holding unless excluded by section 51 below.

(2) For the purposes of sections 49 to 58 of this Act, "eligible person" means (subject to the provisions of Part I of Schedule 6 to this Act as applied by subsection (4) below) a close relative of the retiring tenant in whose case the following conditions are satisfied—

(a) in the last seven years his only or principal source of livelihood throughout a continuous period of not less than five years, or two or more discontinuous periods together amounting to not less than five years, derived from his agricultural work on the holding or on an agricultural unit of which the holding forms part, and

(b) he is not the occupier of a commercial unit of agricultural land.

(3) In the case of the wife of the retiring tenant the reference in subsection (2)(a) above to the relative's agricultural work shall be read as a reference to agricultural work carried out by either the wife or the retiring tenant (or both of them).

(4) Part I of Schedule 6 to this Act shall apply for the purposes of supplementing subsection (2) above and making provision with respect to the assessment of the productive capacity of agricultural land for the purposes of paragraph (b) of that subsection, but subject to the modifications set out in Part II of that Schedule.

DEFINITIONS
"close relative", "holding" and "retiring tenant": s.49(3).
"eligible person": subss. 2 and 3.
"tribunal": s.96(1).

Subs. (1)
The *"eligible person"*. There must be strict eligibility; there is no place here for the benevolent concession to the not fully eligible in s.41.

Subs. (2)
The following conditions are satisfied. These conditions, apart from the introductory words of para. (*a*), are identical with those in s.36(3)(*a*) and (*b*) in the case of succession on death.
Para. (*a*): *only or principal source of livelihood*. See notes to s.36(3) *ante*.
agricultural work. See notes to s.36(4) *ante*.
Para. (*b*): *occupier of a commercial unit of agricultural land*. Sched. 6, paras. 3 to 10 deals with this complicated subject. See notes thereto.

Subs. (3)
Wife of the retiring tenant. See notes to s.36(3) and (4).

Excluded cases

51.—(1) Sections 37 and 38 above shall apply for the purpose of excluding the application of section 50(1) above, but subject to the following modifications—

(a) references to sections 36(1) and 41 above shall be read as references to section 50(1),

(b) references to the holding, a related holding and the tenancy shall be read in accordance with section 49(3) above, and

(c) references to the date of death shall be read as references to the date of the giving of the retirement notice.

(2) Section 50(1) shall not apply if the retiring tenant has at any time given any other notice under section 49(1) above in respect of the holding

or a related holding and an application to become the tenant of the holding or a related holding has been duly made by any person under section 53 below in respect of that notice.

(3) Section 50(1) shall not apply if at the retirement date the retiring tenant will be under sixty-five, unless the retirement notice is given on the grounds that—

(*a*) the retiring tenant or (where the notice is given by joint tenants) each of the retiring tenants is or will at the retirement date be incapable, by reason of bodily or mental infirmity, of conducting the farming of the holding in such a way as to secure the fulfilment of the responsibilities of the tenant to farm in accordance with the rules of good husbandry, and

(*b*) any such incapacity is likely to be permanent,

and that fact is stated in the notice.

(4) If on the date of the giving of the retirement notice the tenancy is the subject of a valid notice to quit given before that date and including a statement that it is given for any such reason as is referred to in Case B, D or E (not being a notice to quit falling within section 38(3) above as applied by subsection (1) above), section 50(1) shall not apply unless one of the events mentioned in subsection (5) below occurs.

(5) Those events are as follows—

(*a*) it is determined by arbitration under this Act that the notice to quit is ineffective for the purposes of section 26(2) above on account of the invalidity of any such reason as aforesaid, or

(*b*) where a counter-notice is duly served under section 28(2) above—

(i) the Tribunal withhold consent to the operation of the notice to quit, or

(ii) the period for making an application to the Tribunal for such consent expires without such an application having been made.

(6) Where one of the events mentioned in subsection (5) above occurs the relevant period shall for the purposes of sections 53(1) and 54(2) below be the period of one month beginning with the date on which the arbitrator's award is delivered to the tenant, with the date of the Tribunal's decision to withhold consent, or with the expiry of the said period for making an application (as the case may be).

DEFINITIONS

Arbitration under this Act, see s.84.

"retirement date", "retirement notice" and "retiring tenant": s.49(3).

Subs. (1)

Following modifications. These modifications are merely the essential changes to substitute applications for a direction on the tenant's retirement for applications on the death of the tenant, and to make any consequential modifications. See annotations to ss.37 and 38 *ante*.

Subs. (2)

And an application . . . has been duly made. If a retirement notice has been followed by an application by the nominated successor to the tribunal, no further retirement notice can be served by the retiring tenant in respect of that holding. It is a once for all exercise, subject to the withdrawal or abandonment of the application by the nominated successor: s.53(10) and to s.52(5). In these cases a new retirement notice can be served. Some clear evidence or record of the abandonment is desirable. If the application is processed and the nominee found unsuitable, the retiring tenant will be unable to put up another candidate.

Subs. (3)

The retiring tenant. If there are joint tenants both or all must have attained 65 at the retirement date; if retiring under that age on the ground of infirmity both or all must be able to establish incapacity at the retirement date. The facts, including the likelihood of permanent incapacity, must be stated in the retirement notice.

Subs. (4)

Section 50(1) shall not apply unless. The effect of this subsection is as follows. If a valid notice to quit, based on Case B, D or E has been served before the retirement notice has been given (and the notice is not one of those (identified in the parenthesis) where the retirement provisions are wholly excluded because procedures to impeach the notice to quit have either not been taken in time or have wholly failed) the retirement notice will be held in suspense pending the outcome of the events mentioned in subs. (5) below. See note to that subs.

Subs. (5)

Those events are as follows. The events are the decisions of the arbitrator or the tribunal, as the case may be, under the procedures of the Act upon which the fate of the notice to quit depends. If the notice to quit is upheld, by arbitration award or by the tribunal's consent, the retirement notice will lapse. If, on the other hand, the notice to quit fails to take effect, the retirement notice and the subsequent succession process will operate.

Subs. (6)

The relevant period. If the notice to quit fails to take effect for one of the reasons mentioned in subs. (5), the relevant period within which the nominated successor has to make his application to the tribunal is extended. The normal period is the period of one month beginning with the day after the date of the giving of the retirement notice: s.53(1). The extended period is one month from the date of the event which has settled the fate of the notice to quit, *i.e.* the delivery of the arbitrator's award to the tenant, the tribunal's decision to withhold consent, or the expiry of the time for applying for consent, as the case may be.

Notices to quit restricting operation of section 53

52.—(1) If the tenancy becomes the subject of a valid notice to quit given on or after the date of the giving of the retirement notice (but before the Tribunal have begun to hear any application by the nominated successor under section 53 below in respect of the retirement notice) and the notice to quit—

    (*a*) falls within Case C and is founded on a certificate granted under paragraph 9 of Part II of Schedule 3 to this Act in accordance with an application made before that date, or

    (*b*) falls within Case F,

the retirement notice shall be of no effect and no proceedings, or (as the case may be) no further proceedings, shall be taken under this Part of this Act in respect of it.

(2) If the tenancy becomes the subject of a valid notice to quit given on or after the date of the giving of the retirement notice (but before the Tribunal have begun to hear any application by the nominated successor under section 53 below in respect of the retirement notice) and the notice to quit—

    (*a*) includes a statement that it is given for any such reason as is referred to in Case B, or

    (*b*) includes a statement that it is given for any such reason as is referred to in Case D and is founded on a notice given for the purposes of that Case before that date,

the retirement notice shall be of no effect and no proceedings, or (as the case may be) no further proceedings, shall be taken under this Part of this Act in respect of it unless one of the events mentioned in subsection (3) below occurs.

(3) Those events are as follows—

    (*a*) it is determined by arbitration under this Act that the notice to quit is ineffective for the purposes of section 26(2) above on account of the invalidity of any such reason as aforesaid, or (*b*) where a counter-notice is duly served under section 28(2) above—

(i) the Tribunal withhold consent to the operation of the notice to quit, or

(ii) the period for making an application to the Tribunal for such consent expires without such an application having been made.

(4) Where—

(*a*) one of the events mentioned in subsection (3) above occurs, and

(*b*) the notice to quit was given before the time when the relevant period for the purposes of sections 53(1) and 54(2) would expire apart from this subsection,

that period shall for those purposes expire at the end of the period of one month beginning with the date on which the arbitrator's award is delivered to the tenant, with the date of the Tribunal's decision to withhold consent, or with the expiry of the said period for making an application (as the case may be).

(5) For the purposes of this Part of this Act an application by the nominated successor under section 53 below which is invalidated by subsection (1) or (2) above shall be treated as if it had never been made.

DEFINITIONS

Arbitration under this Act, see s.84 and for "tribunal": s.96(1).
"nominated successor", "retirement notice" and "tenancy": s.49(3).

Subs. (1)

The retirement notice shall be of no effect and no proceedings. This subsection sets out rules applicable where a valid notice to quit is given *on or after* the date of the giving of the retirement notice, but before the tribunal have begun to hear any application by the nominated successor. The effect of subs. (1) is briefly as follows. If the notice to quit is served, on or after the giving of the retirement notice, in accordance with Case C (a certificate of bad husbandry having already been given in response to an application made before the above date), or if the notice to quit is given under Case F (insolvency), the retirement notice is immediately, and without more, of no effect.

Subs. (2)

The retirement notice shall be of no effect . . . unless. If on or after the date of the giving of the retirement notice a notice to quit is given under Case B (non-agricultural use), or under Case D (founded on a notice to pay rent or to remedy given before the date of the giving of the retirement notice), the notice to quit is held for the time being in suspense pending the outcome of the events mentioned in the next subsection. Unlike the position in subs. (1), where the retirement notice becomes of no effect at once, in the present case its ineffectiveness depends on a contingency.

Subs. (3)

Those events are as follows. The events upon which the fate of the retirement notice depends are the decisions of the arbitrator or the tribunal in accordance with the procedures laid down in the Act and subordinate legislation. If the notice to quit is upheld, the retirement notice is of no effect. If the notice to quit fails, the retirement notice and the subsequent succession processes operate.

Subs. (4)

That period shall for those purposes expire. If the notice to quit does fail as a result of one of the events mentioned in the last subsection, the relevant period for the nominated successor to apply to the tribunal f >r a direction is extended if necessary under the present subsection for one month beginning with the date of the decisive event.

Subs. (5)

Treated as if it had never been made. The result being that the tenant can give another retirement notice, despite the general prohibition of a second attempt in s.51(2).

STATS.—4

Application for tenancy of holding by nominated successor

53.—(1) An application under this section by the nominated successor to the Tribunal for a direction entitling him to a tenancy of the holding shall be made within the relevant period.

(2) In subsection (1) above "the relevant period" means (subject to sections 51(6) and 52(4) above) the period of one month beginning with the day after the date of the giving of the retirement notice.

(3) Any such application—

(*a*) must be accompanied by a copy of the retirement notice, and

(*b*) must be signed by both the nominated successor and the retiring tenant or, where the notice was given by joint tenants, by each of the retiring tenants.

(4) If the retirement notice includes a statement in accordance with section 51(3) above that it is given on the grounds mentioned in that provision, then, before the nominated successor's application is further proceeded with under this section, the Tribunal must be satisfied—

(*a*) that the retiring tenant or (as the case may be) each of the retiring tenants either is or will at the retirement date be incapable, by reason of bodily or mental infirmity, of conducting the farming of the holding in such a way as to secure the fulfilment of the responsibilities of the tenant to farm in accordance with the rules of good husbandry, and

(*b*) that any such incapacity is likely to be permanent.

(5) If the Tribunal are satisfied—

(*a*) that the nominated successor was an eligible person at the date of the giving of the retirement notice, and

(*b*) that he has not subsequently ceased to be such a person,

the Tribunal shall determine whether he is in their opinion a suitable person to become the tenant of the holding.

(6) Before making a determination under subsection (5) above the Tribunal shall afford the landlord an opportunity of stating his views on the suitability of the nominated successor; and in making any such determination the Tribunal shall have regard to all relevant matters, including—

(*a*) the extent to which the nominated successor has been trained in, or has had practical experience of, agriculture,

(*b*) his age, physical health and financial standing,

(*c*) the views (if any) stated by the landlord on his suitability.

(7) If the nominated successor is determined under that subsection to be in their opinion a suitable person to become the tenant of the holding, the Tribunal shall, subject to subsection (8) below, give a direction entitling him to a tenancy of the holding.

(8) The Tribunal shall not give such a direction if, on an application made by the landlord, it appears to the Tribunal that greater hardship would be caused by giving the direction than by refusing the nominated successor's application under this section.

(9) If the Tribunal dispose of the nominated successor's application otherwise than by the giving of a direction under subsection (7) above the retirement notice shall be of no effect (but without prejudice to section 51(2) above).

(10) For the purposes of this Part of this Act, an application by the nominated successor under this section which is withdrawn or abandoned shall be treated as if it had never been made.

(11) Provision shall be made by order under section 73(3) of the Agriculture Act 1947 (procedure of Agricultural Land Tribunals) for requiring any person making an application to the Tribunal for a direction

under this section to give notice of the application to the landlord of the agricultural holding to which the application relates.

<small>DEFINITIONS</small>
"eligible person": s.50(2).
"holding", "nominated successor", "retirement notice", "retiring tenant": s.49(3).
"landlord" and "tribunal": s.96(1).

Subs. (1)
Shall be made within the relevant period. This time limit, defined in subs. (2), is inflexible, subject to the statutory extension allowed under ss.51(6) and 52(4) when there are proceedings to determine the effectiveness of the notice to quit.

Subs. (4)
The tribunal must be satisfied. The allegation of the retiring tenant's incapacity, by reason of bodily or mental infirmity, goes to the tribunal's jurisdiction and should be decided as a preliminary issue. The Act does not give any guidance to the tribunal as to how they are to satisfy themselves; no doubt they will require suitable medical evidence. If the tribunal are not so satisfied and dismiss the application, the particular successor nominated in the application cannot try his fortune again on the tenant's death: see s.57(4).

Subs. (5)
Para. (b): that he has not subsequently ceased to be such a person. Cf. 39(2)(*b*). This provision gives statutory effect to one of the points in *Jackson* v. *Hall* and *Williamson* v. *Thompson* [1980] A.C. 854. Note that there is no provision similar to that in s.41, for succession on death, enabling a not fully eligible person to be treated as eligible.

Subs. (6)
All relevant matters, including. The matters specifically mentioned are the same as in s.39(8). Note that subs. (6), like s.39(7), obliges the tribunal to give the landlord an opportunity to express his views on suitability.

Subs. (7)
Give a direction entitling him to a tenancy. See s.55(1) and (8) for the time when the tenancy vests in the nominated successor. There is a deemed grant and acceptance, as in s.45(1).

Subs. (8)
Greater hardship. There is no provision like this in the scheme for succession on death, but it is in a sense comparable with, or analogous to, the opportunity given to the landlord by s.44 to obtain the tribunal's consent to a notice to quit given under Case G in consequence of the death. In both cases, but necessarily by different procedures, the landlord is given a chance to put his case against the direction. It is submitted that the onus of proof of greater hardship is on the landlord. It will be noted that under this provision the landlord can rely only on greater hardship, whereas under s.44 he can rely on any of the grounds in s.27.

Subs. (9)
But without prejudice to s.51(2) above. Rejection of the nominated successor's application leaves the tenancy vested in the retiring tenant (who will not now be retiring). Unfortunately for him, s.51(2) will apply, so that the service of the retirement notice, although non-productive so far as the application by the nominated successor was concerned, will have excluded any other application in pursuance of a retirement notice given by that retiring tenant. See, however, s.52(5) and s.53(10).

Subs. (10)
Shall be treated as if it had never been made. If the application is withdrawn or abandoned, instead of being pursued to a rejection, the consequences mentioned in the last note will be avoided, as the application will be a nullity. In that case a fresh retirement notice can be served. But it is important that there should be clear evidence of withdrawal or abandonment before the tribunal make a decision. Unambiguous documentary evidence of withdrawal or abandonment is desirable.

Subs. (11)

Order under section 73(3) of the Agriculture Act 1947. See the Agricultural Land Tribunals (succession to Agricultural Tenancies) Order 1984 (S.I. 1984 No. 1301), Part III, para. 24, and see Form 5, para. 16.

Restriction on operation of certain notices to quit

54.—(1) This section applies to any notice to quit the holding or part of it given to the tenant of the holding (whether before or on or after the date of the giving of the retirement notice), not being a notice to quit falling within any provision of section 38 above (as applied by section 51(1) above) or section 51 or 52 above.

(2) A notice to quit to which this section applies shall not, if it would otherwise be capable of so having effect, have effect—

(*a*) at any time during the relevant period, or

(*b*) where an application to become the tenant of the holding is made by the nominated successor under section 53 above within that period, at any time before the application has been finally disposed of by the Tribunal or withdrawn or abandoned,

and shall in any event not have effect if any such application is disposed of by the Tribunal by the giving of a direction under section 53(7) above.

(3) In subsection (2) above "the relevant period" means (subject to sections 51(6) and 52(4) above) the period of one month beginning with the day after the date of the giving of the retirement notice.

DEFINITIONS

"holding", "nominated successor", "retirement notice": s.49(3).
"relevant period": subs. (3) below.
"tribunal": s.96(1).

Subs. (1)

Not being a notice to quit. This is a residual category of notices to quit not falling within those mentioned in the subsection and its object appears to be to ensure that notices in this residual category do not prevent an application for a tenancy being made by a nominated successor under s.53. The effect of s.54 is to suspend the operation of the notice to quit pending the outcome of the nominated successor's application to the tribunal. If the tribunal give a direction entitling him to a tenancy, the notice to quit will lapse.

Effect of direction under section 53

55.—(1) A direction by the Tribunal under section 53(7) above entitling the nominated successor to a tenancy of the holding shall entitle him to a tenancy of the holding as from the relevant time on the terms provided by section 56 below; and accordingly such a tenancy shall be deemed to be at that time granted by the landlord to, and accepted by, the nominated successor.

(2) Where the tenancy of the retiring tenant or (as the case may be) of the retiring tenants was not derived from the interest held by the landlord at the relevant time, the tenancy deemed by virtue of subsection (1) above to be granted to, and accepted by, the nominated successor shall be deemed to be granted by the person for the time being entitled to the interest from which the tenancy of the retiring tenant or tenants was derived, instead of by the landlord, with like effect as if the landlord's interest and any other supervening interest were not subsisting at the relevant time.

(3) The reference in subsection (2) above to a supervening interest is a reference to any interest in the land comprised in the tenancy of the retiring tenant or tenants, being an interest created subsequently to that tenancy and derived (whether immediately or otherwise) from the interest

from which that tenancy was derived and still subsisting at the relevant time.

(4) Subsection (2) above shall not be read as affecting the rights and liabilities of the landlord under this Part of this Act.

(5) Any tenancy of the holding inconsistent with the tenancy to which the nominated successor is entitled by virtue of a direction under section 53(7) above shall, if it would not cease at the relevant time apart from this subsection, cease at that time as if terminated at that time by a valid notice to quit given by the tenant.

(6) The rights conferred on any person by such a direction (as distinct from his rights under his tenancy of the holding after he has become the tenant) shall not be capable of assignment.

(7) The Lord Chancellor may by regulations provide for all or any of the provisions of sections 37(6) and 50 to 58 of this Act (except this subsection) to apply, with such exceptions, additions or other modifications as may be specified in the regulations, in cases where the nominated successor, being entitled to a tenancy of the holding by virtue of such a direction, dies before the relevant time.

(8) In this section "the relevant time" means the retirement date, except that—

(*a*) where such a direction is given within the period of three months ending with the retirement date, the Tribunal may, on the application of the tenant, specify in the direction, as the relevant time for the purposes of this section, such a time falling within the period of three months immediately following the retirement date as they think fit,

(*b*) where such a direction is given at any time after the retirement date, the Tribunal shall specify in the direction, as the relevant time for those purposes, such a time falling within the period of three months immediately following the date of the giving of the direction as they think fit,

and any time so specified shall be the relevant time for those purposes accordingly.

DEFINITIONS
"holding", "nominated successor", "retiring tenant": s.49(3).
"relevant time": subs. (8).
"tribunal": s.96(1).

Subs. (1)
Such a tenancy shall be deemed. This section closely mirrors s.45, the corresponding section in the case of succession on death. The statutory vesting of the new tenancy in the nominated successor takes effect by a deemed grant and acceptance at the relevant time, as to which see subs. (8).

Subs. (2)
From which the tenancy of the retiring tenant or tenants was derived. See note 3 to s.45 *ante.* Subss. (2), (3) and (4) have the same object as the corresponding subss. of s.45, namely, to protect (in the present case) the nominated successor against the possible adverse effect on his interest of the interposition of a concurrent lease, or lease of the reversion, between him and the freeholder. "The landlord at the relevant time" is the concurrent lessee, who is *pro tanto* the assignee of the reversion.

Subs. (3)
Whether immediately or otherwise. See note to s.45(3) *ante.*

Subs. (4)
Rights and liabilities of the landlord. See note to s.45(4) *ante.*

Subs. (5)

If it would not cease at the relevant time. It seems probable that there would in any case be an implied surrender of the retiring tenant's tenancy, but this subsection removes any doubt.

Subs. (6)

Rights conferred on any person by such a direction. This absolute prohibition of the assignment of the rights, which are still inchoate, must be distinguished from the qualified restriction which is embodied in the new tenancy once it has vested: see s.56(2).

Subs. (7)

The Lord Chancellor may by regulations. No such regulations have been made. The Agriculture (Miscellaneous Provisions) Act 1976 (Application of Provisions) Regulations 1977 (S.I. 1977 No. 1215) make the necessary provisions for a similar contingency in the case of a person entitled to a tenancy under a direction following the deceased tenant's death himself dying before the relevant time; but the regulations have not been added to or amended to cover nominated successors dying before the relevant time set out in subs. (8).

Subs. (8)

The retirement date. The new tenancy will thus vest in the nominated successor at the retirement date as specified in the retirement notice, except where there has been delay in giving the direction and the "relevant time" is deferred as mentioned in subs. (8)(*a*) and (*b*).

Terms of new tenancy

56.—(1) Subject to subsections (2) and (3) below, the terms of the tenancy to which a direction under section 53(7) above entitles the nominated successor shall be the same as the terms on which the holding was let immediately before it ceased to be let under the contract of tenancy under which it was let at the date of the giving of the retirement notice.

(2) If the terms of the tenancy to which the nominated successor is entitled as mentioned in subsection (1) above would not, apart from this subsection, include a covenant by the tenant not to assign, sub-let or part with possession of the holding or any part of it without the landlord's consent in writing, subsection (1) above shall have effect as if those terms included that covenant.

(3) Where the Tribunal give a direction under section 53(7) above, subsections (3) to (12) of section 48 above shall have effect in relation to the tenancy which the nominated successor is entitled to or has obtained by virtue of the direction, but with the substitution—

(*a*) in subsection (8)(*a*) of a reference to the tenancy of the retiring tenant or (as the case may be) tenants for the reference to the deceased's tenancy,

(*b*) in subsection (11) of a reference to subsection (1) above for the reference to section 47(1).

(4) In those provisions, as extended by subsection (3) above—

"the landlord" means the landlord of the holding;

"the prescribed period" means the period between the giving of the direction and—

(*a*) the end of the three months immediately following the relevant time, or

(*b*) the end of the three months immediately following the date of the giving of the direction,

whichever last occurs;

"the relevant time" has the meaning given by section 55(8) above;

"the tenant" means the nominated successor.

<small>DEFINITIONS</small>

"the holding", "nominated successor", "retirement notice", "retiring tenant": s.49(3).

"contract of tenancy": s.1(5).

"prescribed period", "landlord", "the tenant" (in provisions as extended by subs. (3)): subs. (4).

"relevant time": s.55(8).

Subs. (1)

At the date of the giving of the retirement notice. Unless varied by arbitration (see subs. (3)), the terms of the new tenancy will be the same as those under which the retiring tenant held immediately before the date of the giving of the retirement notice.

Subs. (2)

Included that covenant. See note to s.47(3) *ante.*

Subs. (3)

Subsections (3) to (12) of section 48 above shall have effect. Subs. (3) applies the arbitration provisions in the case of succession on death to the new tenancy which arises on the retirement, subject merely to the necessary minor modifications in paras. (*a*) and (*b*). See notes to s.48 *ante.*

Subs. (4)

As extended by subsection (3) above. The position then is that the nominated successor will have become the tenant (see revised definition of "the tenant") and the arbitration provisions in s.48 as applied by s.56(3) will be in operation.

Effect of death of retiring tenant on succession to the holding

57.—(1) Subsections (2) to (4) below apply where the retiring tenant, being the sole (or sole surviving) tenant of the holding, dies after giving the retirement notice.

(2) If the tenant's death occurs at a time when no application by the nominated successor has been made under section 53 above or such an application has not been finally disposed of by the Tribunal, the retirement notice shall be of no effect and no proceedings, or (as the case may be) no further proceedings, shall be taken under section 53 above in respect of it; and accordingly sections 36 to 48 above shall apply on the tenant's death in relation to the holding.

(3) If the tenant's death occurs at a time when any such application has been so disposed of by the giving of a direction such as is mentioned in subsection (1) of section 55 above, but before the relevant time (within the meaning of that section), that section and section 56 above shall continue to have effect in relation to the holding; and accordingly sections 36 to 48 above shall not apply on the tenant's death in relation to the holding.

(4) If the tenant's death occurs at a time when any such application has been so disposed of otherwise than by the giving of any such direction, sections 36 to 48 above shall apply on the tenant's death in relation to the holding, but no application under section 39 (or 41) above may be made on that occasion by the nominated successor in relation to the holding.

(5) Where the retirement notice was given by joint tenants and one of those tenants, not being the sole surviving tenant of the holding, dies, his death shall not affect any rights of the nominated successor under sections 50 to 56 above.

Definitions

"the holding", "nominated successor", "retirement notice", "retiring tenant": s.49(3).

"tribunal": s.96(1).

Subs. (2)

Such an application has not been finally disposed of. If the retiring tenant dies before any application has been finally disposed of, proceedings under the retirement notice lapse and the succession on death procedure comes into operation. In some cases "finally disposed of" might involve completion of legal proceedings.

Subs. (3)

Disposed of by the giving of a direction. If the retiring tenant's death occurs after a direction entitling the nominated successor to a tenancy (although before the "relevant time" (s.55(8)) when the new tenancy would have vested in him), the matter proceeds as a retirement succession, not as a succession on death. S.56 will apply.

Subs. (4)

Otherwise than by the giving of any such direction. In this case the nominated successor's application has failed and the succession on death provisions in sections 36 to 48 will come into operation. Note, however, that the nominated successor who has failed is prohibited from applying under s.39 or 41 on the death, perhaps because he has already been involved in contests with the landlord, once if he approached the latter under s.37(2), and once on his application as a nominated successor.

Subs. (5)

His death shall not affect any rights. If the retirement notice was given by joint retiring tenants (s.49(1)(*b*)), the death of one of them (provided at least one is left) will not prevent the nominated successor from pursuing his application.

Effect of direction under section 53 on succession to other holdings

58. Where—

(*a*) the retiring tenant, being the sole (or sole surviving) tenant of the holding, dies, and

(*b*) the nominated successor is for the time being entitled to a tenancy of the holding by virtue of a direction under section 53(7) above,

then for the purpose of determining whether, in relation to any other agricultural holding held by the retiring tenant at the date of his death, the nominated successor is a person in whose case the condition specified in paragraph (*b*) of section 36(3) above is satisfied, the nominated successor shall be deemed to be in occupation of the holding.

DEFINITIONS

"the holding", "nominated successor" and "retiring tenant": s.49(3).
"tribunal": s.91(6).

GENERAL NOTE

Shall be deemed to be in occupation of the holding. This provision is designed as a check on multiple succession. Where the nominated successor is entitled to a tenancy of *the holding,* by virtue of a direction then, for the purpose of determining his eligibility under the commercial unit test in relation to *any other holding,* he shall be deemed to be in occupation of *the holding* although a tenancy has not yet vested in him. If the holding is a "commercial unit" within Sched. 6, he would fail the "occupancy condition" in s.36(3) in the event of his applying for a tenancy of any other holding held by the retiring tenant. See also para. 16 of Part II of Sched. 6.

Interpretation

Interpretation of Part IV

59.—(1) In sections 36 to 48 above (and in Part I of Schedule 6 to this Act)—

"close relative" of a deceased tenant,
"the date of death",
"the deceased",
"the holding",
"related holding", and
"the tenancy",

have the meanings given by section 35(2) above; and in those sections "eligible person" has the meaning given by section 36(3) above.

(2) In sections 49 to 58 above (and in Part I of Schedule 6 to this Act as applied by section 50(4) above)—

"close relative" of the retiring tenant,
"the holding",
"the nominated successor",
"related holding",
"the retirement date",
"the retirement notice",
"the retiring tenant",
"the retiring tenants", and
"the tenancy",

have the meanings given by section 49(3) above; and in those sections "eligible person" has the meaning given by section 50(2) above.

Part V

Compensation on Termination of Tenancy

General Note

Part V covers compensation payable on the termination of the tenancy, whether to the tenant for disturbance, improvements and tenant-right or to the landlord for dilapidations. Market garden tenancies are dealt with separately in Part VI. Compensation for old improvements, *i.e.* improvements begun before March 1, 1948, is dealt with in Sched. 9.

Compensation for disturbance is now divided into "basic" and "additional" compensation (s.60), the former being what was previously called compensation for disturbance (under s.34 of the 1948 Act) and the latter being the "sum to assist in the reorganisation of the tenant's affairs" (ss.9 and 10 of the 1968 Act). This is a neat piece of consolidation drafting. Two matters in regard to which s.34 of the 1948 Act was defective, namely, the position of the sub-tenant (partially covered by s.34(3)) and the application of s.34(4) to a notice to quit given by a person entitled to a severed part of the reversion, have been tidied up in s.63 of the present Act. The old s.61 of the 1948 Act, the drafting of which left much to be desired, appears now in an improved form in s.75.

Compensation to tenant for disturbance

Right to, and measure of, compensation for disturbance

60.—(1) This section applies where the tenancy of an agricultural holding terminates by reason—

(*a*) of a notice to quit the holding given by the landlord, or

(*b*) of a counter-notice given by the tenant under section 32 above after the giving to him of such a notice to quit part of the holding as is mentioned in that section,

and the tenant quits the holding in consequence of the notice or counter-notice.

(2) Subject to section 61 below, where this section applies there shall be payable by the landlord to the tenant by way of compensation for disturbance—

(*a*) a sum computed under subsection (3) below (in this section referred to as "basic compensation"), and

(*b*) a sum computed under subsection (4) below (in this section referred to as "additional compensation").

(3) The amount of basic compensation shall be—

(*a*) an amount equal to one year's rent of the holding at the rate at which rent was payable immediately before the termination of the tenancy, or

(*b*) where the tenant has complied with the requirements of sub-section (6) below, a greater amount equal to either the amount of the tenant's actual loss or two years' rent of the holding whichever is the smaller.

(4) The amount of additional compensation shall be an amount equal to four years' rent of the holding at the rate at which rent was payable immediately before the termination of the tenancy of the holding.

(5) In subsection (3) above "the amount of the tenant's actual loss" means the amount of the loss or expense directly attributable to the quitting of the holding which is unavoidably incurred by the tenant upon or in connection with the sale or removal of his household goods, implements of husbandry, fixtures, farm produce or farm stock on or used in connection with the holding, and includes any expenses reasonably incurred by him in the preparation of his claim for basic compensation (not being costs of an arbitration to determine any question arising under this section or section 61 below).

(6) The requirements of this subsection are—

    (*a*) that the tenant has not less than one month before the termination of the tenancy given to the landlord notice in writing of his intention to make a claim for an amount under subsection (3)(*b*) above, and

    (*b*) that the tenant has, before their sale, given to the landlord a reasonable opportunity of making a valuation of any such goods, implements, fixtures, produce or stock as are mentioned in subsection (5) above.

(7) Compensation payable under this section shall be in addition to any compensation to which the tenant may be entitled apart from this section.

DEFINITIONS
    "agricultural holding": s.1(1).
    "landlord", "tenant", "termination": s.96(1).

Subs. (1)
    Para. (a): landlord. The landlord when the notice to quit is given may not be the same as when the compensation is payable: see *Dale* v. *Hatfield Chase Corporation* [1922] 2 K.B. 282; and see *Bradshaw* v. *Bird* [1920] 3 K.B. 144; *Tombs* v. *Turvey* (1923) 93 L.J.K.B. 785; *Waddell* v. *Howat*, 1925 S.C. 484; *Richards* v. *Pryse* [1927] 2 K.B. 76; *Farrow* v. *Orttewell* [1933] Ch. 480. An equitable owner, such as a purchaser under an uncompleted contract of sale, may be a "landlord" within the definition in s.96(1), but only a legal owner can give a valid notice to quit: *Bradshaw* v. *Bird, Farrow* v. *Orttewell, supra.*
    In consequence of the notice or counter-notice. As to the need for an unbroken causal sequence, and its existence despite an intervening court order, see *Preston* v. *Norfolk County Council* [1947] K.B. 775; *Gulliver* v. *Catt* [1952] 2 K.B. 308. *Preston* v. *Norfolk County Council* followed *Mills* v. *Rose* (1923) 68 S.J. 420, distinguishing *Cave* v. *Page* (1923) 67 S.J. 659 and dissenting from *Hendry* v. *Walker*, 1927 S.L.T. 333. For position of a tenant who quits in consequence of an invalid notice, see *Westlake* v. *Page* [1926] 1 K.B. 298 at p.304 (Bankes L.J.); *Kestell* v. *Langmaid* [1950] 1 K.B. 233; see also *Farrow* v. *Orttewell, supra*; *Street* v. *Cottey* [1947] E.G.D. 136; *cf. Johnston* v. *Malcolm*, 1923 S.L.T. (Sh.Ct.) 81 and *Thomas* v. *N.F.U. Mutual Insurance Society Ltd.* [1961] 1 W.L.R. 386. But the quitting must be in consequence of a notice to quit even if invalid, not, *e.g.* forfeiture. Despite a possible implication by Lord Evershed M.R. in *Kestell* v. *Langmaid, supra,* at p.239, it would seem that if the tenant accepts a notice to quit as good, and quits in consequence of it, the precise reason for its invalidity is immaterial. Note s.3(2) and s.4(3) of the present Act, which safeguard the tenant's right to compensation for disturbance in the case of the expiry of certain fixed terms.

Subs. (2)
    Para. (a): basic compensation. This is the name now given to compensation for disturbance as previously understood since the 1906 Act.
    Para. (b): additional compensation. This is the name now given to the "sum to assist in the reorganisation of the tenant's affairs" which was provided by s.9 of the 1968 Act and which was payable only if compensation for disturbance in the traditional sense was payable (but was not always payable then).

Subs. (3)

Para. (a): an amount equal to one year's rent of the holding. This is the minimum amount of basic compensation, payable without proof of any actual loss.

Para. (b): a greater amount. Subject to compliance with the conditions in subs. (6), the tenant may, on proof of actual loss, obtain more than the minimum basic compensation of one year's rent but not, under the head of basic compensation, more than the amount of two year's rent of the holding.

Subs. (4)

An amount equal to four years' rent of the holding. This in substance reproduces s.9(2) of the 1968 Act. In the case of part of a holding the amount will be four times the appropriate portion of that rent: s.74. Thus the maximum total compensation for disturbance which a tenant could obtain would equal six years' rent of the holding.

Subs. (5)

The amount of the tenant's actual loss. The loss or expense must be both "directly attributable" to the quitting and "unavoidably incurred" in relation to the sale or removal of the articles mentioned in subs. (5). As to loss or expense directly attributable, see *Re Evans and Glamorgan County Council* (1912) 76 J.P. 468; *Barbour* v. *McDouall*, 1914 S.C. 844; *Keswick* v. *Wright*, 1924 S.C. 766; *Macgregor* v. *Board of Agriculture for Scotland*, 1925 S.C. 613; *Evans* v. *Lloyd* [1912] E.G.D. 392. See also the county court case of *Re Sampson and Horsfall* (1921) 10 L.J.C.C.R. 90. As to professional fees, see *Dunstan* v. *Benney* [1938] 2 K.B. 1.

In the preparation of his claim for basic compensation. This wording removes a slight doubt as to whether the "claim" in this context included claims other than for disturbance. The costs of the arbitration, which are expressly excluded here, will be dealt with in the award.

Subs. (6)

Para. (a): notice in writing of his intention. The decision in *Howson* v. *Buxton* (1928) 97 L.J.K.B. 749 that notice by one only of joint tenants, being the one who in fact suffered loss, was sufficient has subsequently been regarded with doubt in view of the remarks of Greer L.J. in that case (p.755) and comments in *Jacobs* v. *Chaudhuri* [1968] 2 Q.B. 470. *Howson* v. *Buxton* was distinguished in *Newman* v. *Keedwell* (1977) 244 E.G. 469, where a strict view was taken on an analogous point. Subsequent decisions in other contexts which have taken a more flexible view of joint proprietorship, *Lloyd* v. *Sadler* [1978] Q.B. 774, *Tilling* v. *Whiteman* [1980] A.C. 1 and *Featherstone* v. *Staples* (1986) 83 L.S.Gaz. 1226, C.A.; (1984) 49 P. & C.R. 273; 273 E.G. 193, have somewhat restored the authority of *Howson* v. *Buxton,* but for safety all joint tenants should join in the notice. A resumption clause in a contract of tenancy is void if it does not allow the tenant to give the one month's notice required by the present provision: *Re Disraeli Agreement* [1939] Ch. 382; *Coates* v. *Diment* [1951] 1 All E.R. 890; and *Parry* v. *Million Pigs Ltd.* (1980) 260 E.G. 281. On the question whether one notice would satisfy both s.60(6)(*a*) and s.83(2), *cf. Hallinan (Lady)* v. *Jones* (1984) 272 E.G. 1081 (C.C.), but it is wise to serve two. On the words "not less than one month", consider recent cases on such time provisions: *Dodds* v. *Walker* [1981] 1 W.L.R. 1027; *E. J. Riley Investments Ltd.* v. *Eurostile Holdings Ltd.* [1985] 1 W.L.R. 119; *Manorlike Ltd.* v. *Le Vitas Travel Agency & Consultancy Services Ltd.* (1986) 278 E.G. 412.

Para. (b): a reasonable opportunity. This is a question of fact: see *Dale* v. *Hatfield Chase Corporation* [1922] 2 K.B. 282; *Barbour* v. *McDouall*, 1914 S.C. 844.

Subs. (7)

Apart from this section. E.g. compensation for improvements and tenant-right.

Cases where compensation under section 60 is not payable

61.—(1) Neither basic compensation nor additional compensation shall be payable under section 60 above where the operation of section 26(1) above in relation to the relevant notice is excluded by virtue of Case C, D, E, F or G.

(2) Additional compensation shall not be so payable where the operation of section 26(1) above in relation to the relevant notice is excluded by virtue of Case A or H.

(3) Except as provided by subsection (4) below, additional compensation shall not be payable under section 60 above where—

(a) the relevant notice contains a statement either that the carrying out of the purpose for which the landlord proposes to terminate the tenancy is desirable on any of the grounds mentioned in paragraphs (a) to (c) of section 27(3) above or that the landlord will suffer hardship unless the notice has effect, and

(b) if an application for consent in respect of the notice is made to the Tribunal in pursuance of section 26(1) above, the Tribunal consent to its operation and state in the reasons for their decision that they are satisfied as to any of the matters mentioned in paragraphs (a), (b), (c) and (e) of section 27(3).

(4) Additional compensation shall be payable in a case falling within subsection (3) above where such an application as is mentioned in paragraph (b) of that subsection is made and—

(a) the reasons given by the Tribunal also include the reason that they are satisfied as to the matter mentioned in paragraph (f) of section 27(3) above, or

(b) the Tribunal include in their decision a statement under subsection (5) below.

(5) Where such an application as is mentioned in subsection (3)(b) above is made in respect of the relevant notice and the application specifies the matter mentioned in paragraph (b) of section 27(3) above (but not that mentioned in paragraph (f) of that subsection), the Tribunal shall if they are satisfied as to the matter mentioned in paragraph (b) but would, if it had been specified in the application, have been satisfied also as to the matter mentioned in paragraph (f) include a statement to that effect in their decision.

(6) In this section—

"basic compensation" and "additional compensation" have the same meanings as in section 60 above;

"the relevant notice" means the notice to quit the holding or part of the holding, as the case may be, mentioned in section 60(1) above.

DEFINITION
"tribunal": s.96(1).

Subs. (1)
By virtue of Case C, D, E, F or G. Both basic and additional compensation are excluded when any of these Cases applies. The remaining Cases in Sched. 3 are A, B and H. Basic compensation but not additional compensation is payable in respect of Cases A and H (subs. (2) below). Where Case B applies, both basic and additional compensation are payable (subject of course to the statutory conditions, including those in subss. (3), (4) and (5)).

Subs. (2)
Case A or H. Case A relates to notices to quit to smallholding tenants on attaining age 65 and Case H to notices to quit by the Minister for the purpose of amalgamations or the reshaping of agricultural units.

Subs. (3)
Except as provided by subsection (4) below. See note on subs. (4) for the rationale of this important exception.
Para. (a): the relevant notice contains a statement. Expressed very broadly the object is to deprive the tenant of the additional compensation if the landlord can show either a good agricultural reason for the notice to quit (s.27(3)(a) to (c)) or hardship. However, even if there is a good agricultural reason or hardship the landlord will have to pay the additional compensation *unless his notice to quit contains the appropriate statement.* Thus the absence of a few words on a piece of paper may cost the landlord many thousands of pounds. On the

other hand the mere *statement* may exclude this liability if the tenant does not serve a counter-notice under s.26(1)(*b*).

Para. (b): the tribunal consent to its operation and state in the reasons for their decision. If, as will normally happen, the tenant serves a counter-notice and the landlord applies to the tribunal for consent to the notice to quit, the landlord will have to satisfy the tribunal as to the ground relied on under s.27(3)(*a*), (*b*), (*c*) or (*e*). The tribunal will then have to state their satisfaction in the reasons for their decision. It will be noted that para. (*d*) of s.27(3) (purposes of enactments relating to allotments) is not mentioned as a ground which excludes additional compensation; this means that the additional payment is not excluded where the tribunal have consented to the notice for the allotment reason.

Subs. (4)

Also include . . . the matter mentioned in paragraph (f) of section 27(3) above. The additional compensation *becomes* payable if the tribunal's reasoning shows that a good agricultural ground for dispossession (or hardship) is, as it were, tainted by association with the non-agricultural purpose in para. (*f*) of s.27(3). This is a curious application of the *noscitur a sociis* doctrine. An example would be consent on the dual ground of greater hardship to the landlord and the landlord's afforestation projects.

Subs. (5)

Would, if it had been specified in the application, have been satisfied. Here the taint by association is even hypothetical. The good agricultural reason (sound management) for denying additional compensation is cancelled if the tribunal *would* have been satisfied as to the contaminating presence of the non-agricultural s.27(3)(*f*) matter, *if* the latter *had* been specified in the landlord's application for consent. The tribunal, if they would have been so satisfied, must include a statement to that effect in their decision. The result is that the additional compensation becomes payable. This amounts to a doctrine of *noscitur a sociis fictis* or guilt by hypothetical association.

Compensation on termination in pursuance of early resumption clause

62.—(1) Where—

    (*a*) the tenancy of an agricultural holding terminates by reason of a notice to quit the holding given in pursuance of a provision in the contract of tenancy authorising the resumption of possession of the holding for some specified purpose other than the use of the land for agriculture, and

    (*b*) the tenant quits the holding in consequence of the notice,

compensation shall be payable by the landlord to the tenant, in addition to any other compensation so payable apart from this section in respect of the holding.

(2) The amount of compensation payable under this section shall be equal to the value of the additional benefit (if any) which would have accrued to the tenant if the tenancy had, instead of being terminated as provided by the notice, been terminated by it on the expiration of twelve months from the end of the year of tenancy current when the notice was given.

(3) For the purposes of subsection (2) above, the current year of a tenancy for a term of two years or more is the year beginning with such day in the period of twelve months ending with the date on which the notice is served as corresponds to the day on which the term would expire by the effluxion of time.

DEFINITIONS

    "agricultural holding": s.1(1).
    "agriculture" and "tenant": s.96(1).
    "contract of tenancy": s.1(5).

Subs. (1)

Para. (a): for some specified purpose other than the use of the land for agriculture. See s.25(2)(*b*) for power to give a notice to quit of less than 12 months for this purpose. This power is not affected by the present provision, which merely cancels the disadvantageous effect on compensation which such short notice could produce.

Subs. (2)
Value of the additional benefit. The tenant is to be put, by compensation, in the same position as he would have been in if the tenancy had been terminated by a normal 12 months notice. This is put in a more elaborate manner in subs. (3).

Compensation for disturbance: supplementary provisions

63.—(1) Where—
> (*a*) the tenant of an agricultural holding has sub-let the holding, and
> (*b*) the sub-tenancy terminates by operation of law in consequence of the termination of the tenancy by reason of any such notice or counter-notice as is referred to in section 60(1)(*a*) or (*b*) above,

section 60 shall apply if the sub-tenant quits the holding in consequence of the termination of the sub-tenancy as mentioned in paragraph (*b*) above as it applies where a tenant quits a holding in consequence of any such notice or counter-notice.

(2) Where the tenant of an agricultural holding has sub-let the holding and in consequence of a notice to quit given by his landlord becomes liable to pay compensation under section 60 or 62 above to the sub-tenant, the tenant shall not be debarred from recovering compensation under that section by reason only that, owing to not being in occupation of the holding, on the termination of his tenancy he does not quit the holding.

(3) Where the tenancy of an agricultural holding terminates by virtue of such a counter-notice as is mentioned in section 60(1)(*b*) above, and—
> (*a*) the part of the holding affected by the notice to quit together with any part of the holding affected by any relevant previous notice rendered valid by section 31 above is less than one-fourth of the original holding, and
> (*b*) the holding as proposed to be diminished is reasonably capable of being farmed as a separate holding,

compensation shall not be payable under section 60 above except in respect of the part of the holding to which the notice to quit relates.

(4) In subsection (3) above "relevant previous notice" means any notice to quit given by the same person who gave the current notice to quit or, where that person is a person entitled to a severed part of the reversionary estate in the holding, by that person or by any other person so entitled.

DEFINITIONS
   "agricultural holding": s.1(1).
   "landlord", "tenant", "termination": s.96(1).

Subs. (1)
   As it applies where a tenant quits a holding. The provision in this subsection, which should be read with subs. (2), was introduced by the 1984 Act (see Sched. 3, para. 9 of the latter) and solved a mystery in the 1948 Act, s.34(3) of which (now subs. (2) of the present section) implied that a sub-tenant in occupation was entitled to claim compensation for disturbance although there was no provision for the tenant to give a notice to quit to the sub-tenant. The mystery is now solved by the provision that if the sub-tenant quits, because his interest perishes at common law by reason of the termination of the superior interest by notice to quit or counter-notice, the sub-tenant is entitled to compensation *as if* he were a tenant quitting in consequence of such a notice or counter-notice.

Subs. (2)
   Owing to not being in occupation of the holding. This subsection overcomes the technical difficulty that the superior tenant who has paid compensation to his sub-tenant would be

debarred from himself claiming compensation because (not being in occupation) he did not "quit" the holding.

Subs. (3)
Except in respect of the part of the holding. Normally the result of a counter-notice by the tenant in reply to a notice to quit part is that the tenant will be entitled to compensation for disturbance in respect of the whole holding. However, if the two conditions mentioned in this section are present the tenant, although quitting the whole holding, will receive compensation only in respect of that part of the holding to which the notice to quit relates. One condition concerns the fraction of the holding affected while the other concerns the effect of the loss on the farming capabilities of the remainder. For the reduced compensation to apply, the part affected by the notice to quit, together with any part affected by any "relevant previous notice" rendered valid by s.31, must be less than one-fourth of the original holding. The remainder must be reasonably capable of being farmed as a separate holding.

Subs. (4)
Relevant previous notice. Subs. (4) is the result of redrafting by the 1984 Act of s.34(4) of the 1948 Act, which appeared to use the word "landlord" to mean two different things in the same sentence (see 1984 Act, Sched. 3, para. 9(3)). The redrafted provisions cover notices given by persons entitled to severed parts of the reversion as well as by the landlord of the entirety.

Compensation to tenant for improvements and tenant-right matters

Tenant's right to compensation for improvements

64.—(1) The tenant of an agricultural holding shall, subject to the provisions of this Act, be entitled on the termination of the tenancy, on quitting the holding, to obtain from his landlord compensation for an improvement specified in Schedule 7 or Part I of Schedule 8 to this Act carried out on the holding by the tenant, being an improvement begun on or after 1st March 1948.

(2) In this Act "relevant improvement" means an improvement falling within subsection (1) above.

(3) Subsection (1) above shall have effect as well where the tenant entered into occupation of the holding before 1st March 1948 as where he entered into occupation on or after that date.

(4) The provisions of Part I of Schedule 9 to this Act shall have effect with respect to the rights of the tenant of an agricultural holding with respect to compensation for improvements specified in Part II of that Schedule carried out on the holding, being improvements begun before 1st March 1948.

DEFINITIONS
"agricultural holding": s.1(1).
"landlord", "tenant", "termination": s.96(1).

Subs. (1)
On the termination of the tenancy, on quitting the holding. See s.69 for the position where there has been a series of tenancies and the quitting takes place only on the termination of the last. For special provisions relating to land subject to opencast coal operations, see ss.24 and 25 of the Opencast Coal Act 1958 as amended by Sched. 14 of the present Act, paras. 26 and 27.
Specified in Schedule 7 or Part I of Schedule 8. These comprise long-term and short-term improvements, being in each case improvements begun on or after March 1, 1948. These are now called "relevant improvements" instead of, as under the 1948 Act (s.46(2)), "new improvements" (see subs. (2) of present section). See Housing Act 1985, s.231(2) for inclusion of works carried out in compliance with an improvement notice or undertaking. See also Sched. 9 of the present Act for improvements begun before March 1, 1948.

Subs. (3)

As well where. The date of entry into *occupation* is immaterial as long as the improvement was *begun* on or after March 1, 1948. In the case of tenant-right matters, however, see s.65(3) and Sched. 12, paras. 6 to 9.

Subs. (4)

Begun before March 1, 1948. Part I of Sched. 9 contains the code, and Part II the list of items, relating to what were called "old improvements" in Sched. 2 to the 1948 Act. Some of the items which were in the old Sched. 2 have now for obvious reasons disappeared— "laying down of permanent pasture", "protecting young fruit trees", "the removal of bracken, gorse, tree roots, boulders or other like obstructions to cultivation", and the old short-term improvements in Part III of Sched. 2, such as liming and consumption of feeding stuff not produced on the holding. It is unlikely that many of the old items which still remain claimable in theory will in fact be found in practice.

Note: Although perhaps of small relevance, it may be noted that a tenant cannot claim compensation under s.64(1) for an improvement which he was required to carry out by the terms of a contract of tenancy made before January 1, 1921. See Sched. 12, para. 5.

Tenant's right to compensation for tenant-right matters

65.—(1) The tenant of an agricultural holding shall, subject to the provisions of this Act, be entitled on the termination of the tenancy, on quitting the holding, to obtain from his landlord compensation for any such matter as is specified in Part II of Schedule 8 to this Act.

(2) The tenant shall not be entitled to compensation under subsection (1) above for crops or produce grown, seeds sown, cultivations, fallows or acts of husbandry performed, or pasture laid down, in contravention of the terms of a written contract of tenancy unless—

   (*a*) the growing of the crops or produce, the sowing of the seeds, the performance of the cultivations, fallows or acts of husbandry, or the laying down of the pasture was reasonably necessary in consequence of the giving of a direction under the Agriculture Act 1947, or

   (*b*) the tenant shows that the term of the contract contravened was inconsistent with the fulfilment of his responsibilities to farm the holding in accordance with the rules of good husbandry.

(3) Subject to paragraphs 6 and 7 of Schedule 12 to this Act, subsection (1) above shall apply to a tenant on whatever date he entered into occupation of the holding.

DEFINITIONS

"agricultural holding": s.1(1).
"landlord", "tenant", "termination": s.96(1).
"rules of good husbandry": s.96(3).

Subs. (1)

Any such matter. These are the tenant-right matters for which a *statutory* right to compensation was given for the first time by the 1947 Act.

Subs. (2)

In contravention. See, for the application of this principle in practice, reg. 4(3) of the Agriculture (Calculation of Value for Compensation) Regulations 1978 (S.I. 1978 No. 809).

Para. (a): direction under the Agriculture Act 1947. This refers to the Minister's power under s.95 of the Agriculture Act 1947 to give special directions to secure production.

Para. (b): inconsistent with the fulfilment of his responsibilities. The burden of proof would be on the tenant to show that the term contravened was one which he was entitled to ignore because it conflicted with his responsibilities under the rules of good husbandry. For the latter see s.11 of the 1947 Act (applied by s.96(3) of the present Act). Such a contention could present an arbitrator with a difficult point to determine.

Subject to paragraphs 6 and 7 of Schedule 12. These paras. require a tenant who entered into occupation before certain dates to *elect* that the statutory basis of compensation should apply to him. The relevant date in regard to tenant-right matters generally is March 1, 1948. The relevant date in regard to the item of acclimatisation, hefting or settlement of hill sheep is December 1, 1951, but in the case of those entering before March 1, 1948 who had already made an election in regard to tenant-right generally another, specific, election is required. See further, annotations to Sched. 12, *post.*

Measure of compensation

66.—(1) The amount of any compensation under this Act for a relevant improvement specified in Schedule 7 to this Act shall be an amount equal to the increase attributable to the improvement in the value of the agricultural holding as a holding, having regard to the character and situation of the holding and the average requirements of tenants reasonably skilled in husbandry.

(2) The amount of any compensation under this Act for a relevant improvement specified in Part I of Schedule 8 to this Act, or for any matter falling within Part II of that Schedule, shall be the value of the improvement or matter to an incoming tenant calculated in accordance with such method, if any, as may be prescribed.

(3) Where the landlord and the tenant of an agricultural holding have entered into an agreement in writing whereby any benefit is given or allowed to the tenant in consideration of his carrying out an improvement specified in Part I of Schedule 8 to this Act, the benefit shall be taken into account in assessing compensation under this Act for the improvement.

(4) Nothing in this Act shall prevent the substitution, in the case of matters falling within Part II of Schedule 8 to this Act, for the measure of compensation specified in subsection (2) above, of such measure of compensation, to be calculated according to such method, if any, as may be specified in a written contract of tenancy.

(5) Where a grant out of money provided by Parliament or local government funds has been or will be made to the tenant of an agricultural holding in respect of a relevant improvement, the grant shall be taken into account in assessing compensation under this Act for the improvement.

DEFINITIONS
"agricultural holding": s.1(1).
"landlord," "tenant," "local government funds": s.96(1).
"relevant improvement": s.64(2).

Subs. (1)
Value of the agricultural holding as a holding. The actual method of calculation for improvements included in Sched. 7 is not prescribed, in contrast with those in Sched. 8. It is left entirely to the skill of the valuer. The usual method is to capitalise the increase in the rental value of the holding attributable to the improvement. Note that works carried out in compliance with an improvement notice or an undertaking accepted under Part VII of the Housing Act 1985 will be treated as included under improvements specified in para. 9 of Sched. 7 to the present Act (compensation for the erection, alteration or enlargement of buildings): see Housing Act 1985, s.231(2). See also s.231(4) of that Act for proportionate reduction of compensation where a person other than the tenant has contributed to the cost. As to subsidence damage, see s.10 of the Coal-Mining Subsidence Act 1957, as amended by Sched. 14, para. 24, of the present Act, which contains a provision for the protection of a tenant.

Subs. (2)
Calculated in accordance with such method, if any, as may be prescribed. The present regulations prescribing the method are the Agriculture (Calculation of Value for Compensation) Regulations 1978 (S.I. 1978 No. 809), the Agriculture (Calculation of Value for

Compensation) (Amendment) Regulations 1981 (S.I. 1981 No. 822) and the Agriculture (Calculation of Value for Compensation (Amendment) Regulations 1983 (S.I. 1983 No. 1475). (Regulations made in 1980 (S.I. 1980 No. 751) were superseded by S.I. 1981 No. 822.)

Subs. (3)
The benefit shall be taken into account. The parties cannot contract out of the statutory prescribed measure for the improvements in Part I of Sched. 8 (in contrast with the position in regard to the "matters" in Part II of Sched. 8) but benefits given or allowed to the tenant under an agreement in writing are to be "taken into account" in assessing the compensation. As to "benefit", there are some useful Scottish decisions on corresponding provisions: see *McQuater* v. *Fergusson*, 1911 S.C. 640; *Galloway (Earl)* v. *McClelland*, 1915 S.C. 1062; *Buchanan* v. *Taylor*, 1916 S.C. 129; *Mackenzie* v. *Macgillivray*, 1921 S.C. 722; *Findlay* v. *Munro*, 1917 S.C. 419.

Subs. (4)
Substitution. It is thus open to the parties in the case of Sched. 8, Part II, matters, but not Sched. 8, Part I, improvements, to contract out, in a written contract of tenancy, both of the measure of compensation laid down in s.66(2) and of the method of calculation prescribed by statutory instruments thereunder. By this means the scale of customary compensation formerly applicable in a particular district may be embodied in a written contract and continue to operate, albeit by force of contract and not of custom. There seems, however, to have been a tendency to accept the statutory basis as satisfactory.

Subs. (5)
A grant. This section, which applies to all "relevant improvements" (s.64(2)), but not to tenant-right matters, is of very wide importance in practice, and by an amendment introduced by the 1984 Act (Sched. 3, para. 11) now extends to grants from local government funds (s.96(1)) as well as to Exchequer grants.
Shall be taken into account. This is not quite as definite a direction as in s.13(4) where (in the case of a grant to a landlord) the increase in rent is to be "reduced proportionately". It would, however, seem correct to scale down the deduction for grant in proportion to the diminishing value of the improvement. Besides being justifiable in law, this would be sensible in reducing the disincentive effect of the section.

Compensation for long-term improvements: consent required

67.—(1) The tenant of an agricultural holding shall not be entitled to compensation for a relevant improvement specified in Schedule 7 to this Act unless the landlord has given his consent in writing to the carrying out of the improvement.

(2) Any such consent may be given by the landlord unconditionally or upon such terms as to compensation or otherwise as may be agreed upon in writing between the landlord and the tenant; and the provisions of section 66(1) above shall have effect subject to the provisions of any such agreement as is made.

(3) Where, in the case of an improvement specified in Part II of Schedule 7 to this Act, a tenant is aggrieved by the refusal of his landlord to give his consent under subsection (1) above, or is unwilling to agree to any terms subject to which the landlord is prepared to give his consent, the tenant may apply to the Tribunal for approval of the carrying out of the improvement, and the following provisions of this section shall have effect with respect to the application.

(4) The Tribunal may approve the carrying out of the improvement, either unconditionally or upon such terms, whether as to reduction of the compensation which would be payable if the Tribunal approved unconditionally or as to other matters, as appear to them to be just, or may withhold their approval.

(5) If the Tribunal grant their approval, the landlord may, within the prescribed period from receiving notification of the Tribunal's decision,

serve notice in writing on the Tribunal and the tenant that the landlord proposes himself to carry out the improvement.

(6) Where the Tribunal grant their approval, then if—

    (*a*) no notice is duly served by the landlord under subsection (5) above, or

    (*b*) such a notice is duly served, but on an application made by the tenant the Tribunal determines that the landlord has failed to carry out the improvement within a reasonable time,

the approval of the Tribunal shall have effect for the purposes of subsection (1) above as if it were the consent of the landlord, and any terms subject to which the approval was given shall have effect as if they were contained in an agreement in writing between the landlord and the tenant.

(7) In subsection (5) above, "the prescribed period" means the period prescribed by the Lord Chancellor by order.

DEFINITIONS

    "agricultural holding": s.1(1).
    "landlord", "tenant", "tribunal": s.96(1).
    "prescribed period": subs. (7) of this section.
    "relevant improvement": 64(2).

Subs. (1)

Unless the landlord has given his consent in writing. In the case of the improvements specified in Part I of Sched. 7 the consent of the landlord himself (with no recourse to the agricultural land tribunal) is an absolute condition of compensation. In contrast with old improvements (see Sched. 9, para. 3(1)) it is not stated that this consent must be obtained *before* the execution of the improvement, but it would be wise for the tenant to do so. See s.231(3) of Housing Act 1985 for exclusion of the need to obtain the landlord's consent in the case of works carried out in compliance with an improvement notice or an accepted undertaking under Part VII of that Act. The consent may be given in the contract of tenancy itself: *cf. Mears* v. *Callender* [1901] 2 Ch. 388; *Gardner* v. *Beck* [1947] E.G.D. 169. It must be clear, not hypothetical or ambiguous: *Re Morse and Dixon* (1917) 87 L.J.K.B. 1. Probably a land agent charged with the general management of an estate can give it: *Re Pearson and I'Anson* [1899] 2 Q.B. 618. It is advisable for a tenant to obtain the landlord's personal consent and preserve it like a document of title. See as to the position of a purchaser from the landlord, *Re Derby (Earl) and Fergusson's Contract* [1912] 1 Ch. 479. These Part I improvements either alter the character of the holding or otherwise are of a type such as to make it reasonable to give the landlord an absolute veto.

Subs. (2)

Upon such terms as to compensation or otherwise. The better view, contrary to the opinion of Cozens-Hardy J. in *Mears* v. *Callender, supra,* at p.399, is that the landlord may stipulate that there should be *no* compensation: see *Turnbull* v. *Miller*, 1942 S.C. 521 (although Lord Jamieson dissented), a view strengthened by the observations of Lord Hailsham L.C. in *Johnson* v. *Morton* [1980] A.C. 37 at p.58.

Subs. (3)

A tenant is aggrieved. The tenant must first seek the landlord's consent and then be "aggrieved" by refusal or unacceptable conditions; he cannot apply to the tribunal without approaching the landlord.

Apply to the tribunal for approval. For form of application, see Form 6 in the Appendix to the Rules in the Agricultural Land Tribunals (Rules) Order 1978 (S.I. 1978 No. 259) and see rule 7.

Subs. (4)

As to reduction of the compensation. If the tribunal approve unconditionally the compensation will be calculated in accordance with s.66(1). The tribunal may, however, *reduce* the compensation, *e.g.* by deducting a percentage if there is an element of doubt about the improvement's success, but, it is submitted, they cannot decide that there should be *no* compensation. They cannot increase the compensation beyond the s.66(1) basis.

Subs. (5)

Within the prescribed period. This is one month from the date on which he receives notice in writing of the tribunal's approval of the carrying out of the improvement: see rule 7(2) of the rules mentioned in note to subs. (3) on application to tribunal above. It would be prudent for the tenant not to start carrying out the improvement until this prescribed period is past. If the landlord does proceed to exercise his option to carry out the improvement, see s.13(2)(*c*) as to his power to increase the rent and s.86(1)(*b*) as to his power to obtain an order charging the holding.

Subs. (6)

Para. (b): on an application made by the tenant. See rule 7(3) in the rules mentioned in note to subs. (3) on application to tribunal above and Form 7 in the appendix to the rules.

Subs. (7)

By order. see S.I. mentioned in note to subs. (3).

Improvements: special cases

68.—(1) The tenant of an agricultural holding shall not be entitled to compensation for a relevant improvement specified in paragraph 1 of Schedule 8 to this Act unless, not later than one month before the improvement was begun, he gave notice in writing to the landlord of his intention to carry out the improvement.

(2) Where, on an application of the sub-tenant of an agricultural holding, the Tribunal have directed the immediate landlord of the sub-tenant to carry out work under section 11 above being work which constitutes an improvement specified in Schedule 7 to this Act—

  (*a*) section 67 above shall not apply as respects a claim by the immediate landlord against his superior landlord for compensation in respect of that work, and

  (*b*) if, on the failure of the immediate landlord to comply with the direction of the Tribunal, the sub-tenant has himself carried out the work, sections 64 and 66 above shall have effect for the purposes of a claim for compensation by the immediate landlord against his superior landlord as if the work had been carried out by the immediate landlord and as if any grant made to the sub-tenant in respect of the work out of money provided by Parliament had been made to the immediate landlord.

(3) Where the tenant of an agricultural holding has carried out on the holding an improvement specified in Schedule 7 to this Act in accordance with provision for the making of the improvement and for the tenant's being responsible for doing the work in a hill farming land improvement scheme approved under section 1 of the Hill Farming Act 1946, being provision included in the scheme at the instance or with the consent of the landlord—

  (*a*) the landlord shall be deemed to have consented as mentioned in subsection (1) of section 67 above,

  (*b*) any agreement as to compensation or otherwise made between the landlord and the tenant in relation to the improvement shall have effect as if it had been such an agreement on terms as is mentioned in subsection (2) of that section, and

  (*c*) the provisions of subsections (5) and (6) of that section as to the carrying out of improvements by the landlord shall not apply.

(4) In assessing the amount of any compensation payable under custom or agreement to the tenant of an agricultural holding, if it is shown to the satisfaction of the person assessing the compensation that the cultivations in respect of which the compensation is claimed were wholly or in part the result of or incidental to work in respect of the cost of which an improvement grant has been paid under section 1 of the Hill Farming Act

1946, the amount of the grant shall be taken into account as if it had been a benefit allowed to the tenant in consideration of his executing the cultivations and the compensation shall be reduced to such extent as that person considers appropriate.

(5) Where the tenant of an agricultural holding claims compensation in respect of works carried out in compliance with an improvement notice served, or an undertaking accepted, under Part VII of the Housing Act 1985 or Part VIII of the Housing Act 1974—

(*a*) section 67 above shall not apply as respects the works, and

(*b*) if a person other than the tenant has contributed to the cost of carrying out the works, compensation in respect of the works as assessed under section 66 above shall be reduced proportionately.

DEFINITIONS
    "agricultural holding": s.1(1)
    "landlord", "tenant", "tribunal": s.96(1)
    "relevant improvement": s.64(2)

Subs. (1)

Paragraph 1 of Schedule 8 to this Act. The item in question is mole drainage. Notice to the landlord of the tenant's intention to carry out mole draining is required, but the landlord's consent is not necessary. Such consent (or approval by the tribunal) is, however, necessary to the carrying out of land drainage other than mole drainage (para. 23 of Sched. 7). Although consent to mole drainage is not required, the notice will allow time for the landlord, if he wishes, to seek the tenant's agreement to the landlord's carrying out the works. There are cases where it would be more appropriate for the landlord to do so. For the calculation of compenastion for mole drainage, see the Agriculture (Calculation of Value for Compensation) Regulations 1978 (S.I. 1978 No. 809), Sched. 1, para. 1.

Subs. (2)

Application of the subtenant. The provisions of s.11 enabling a tenant to apply to the tribunal for a direction requiring his landlord to carry out work for the provision, alteration or repair of fixed equipment can apply as between a subtenant and his immediate landlord. This can in turn result in certain events in complications between the immediate and the superior landlords, which are reflected in paras. (*a*) and (*b*) of this subsection: see notes below.

Para (a): section 67 above shall not apply as respects a claim by the immediate landlord. If on the application of the subtenant the immediate landlord has carried out the works required, the immediate landlord will have a claim for compensation against his superior landlord at the termination of the tenancy if the required works constituted a relevant improvement within Sched. 7. The present subsection provides that s.67 will not apply in respect of such a claim; in other words, the actual consent of the superior landlord to the works will not be a condition of compensation: para. (*a*) of subs. (2). This is clearly necessary.

Para. (b): as if the work had been carried out by the immediate landlord. The immediate landlord may not carry out the work as required by the direction, in which case the subtenant, under the general powers of s.11, is entitled to carry out the work himself and recover the reasonable cost thereof from the immediate landlord. If the subtenant has received a grant he will be able to recover only the reasonable cost reduced by the amount of the grant: s.11(8). At the termination of the immediate landlord's tenancy he will be entitled to compensation from his superior landlord in respect of the work, in so far as it constitutes a relevant improvement. It would, however, be anomalous if the immediate landlord, who has repaid to the subtenant the costs less the grant, should be able to recover from the superior landlord compensation which did not take the grant into account: this would be an undeserved windfall for the immediate landlord. In fact such a windfall arose under s.4(6)(*b*) of the 1958 Act, but it is eliminated by the draftsman of the present Act by virtue of the words "and as if any grant made to the subtenant in respect of the work out of money provided by Parliament had been made to the immediate landlord". See also *Law Com.*: No. 153 and Minutes and Report of Joint Committee on Consolidation Bills, H.L. 56–1 and H.C. 178–1, where the point is discussed.

Subs. (3)
Hill farming land improvement scheme. The provisions in this subsection are evidently intended to safeguard accrued rights under previous enactments. The actual schemes referred to are obsolete.

Subs. (4)
Hill Farming Act 1946. See preceding note.

Subs. (5)
Improvement notice served, or an undertaking accepted. See s.231 of the Housing Act 1985. This section replaced s.98 of the Housing Act 1974, which was repealed for consolidation purposes by the Housing (Consequential Provisions) Act 1985, s.3 and Sched. 1. The present subs. applies where a tenant of a holding claims compensation on the termination of the tenancy for an improvement which consists of works carried out in compliance with an improvement notice or an undertaking under Part VII of the Housing Act 1985, or under Part VIII of the Housing Act 1974 when the latter was in force. S.67 of the present Act is excluded, so that the consent of the landlord is not a condition of compensation; and if a person other than the tenant (*e.g.* the landlord) has contributed to the cost of the works, compensation will be scaled down proportionately.

Improvements: successive tenancies

69.—(1) Where the tenant of an agricultural holding has remained in the holding during two or more tenancies, he shall not be deprived of his right to compensation under this Act in respect of relevant improvements by reason only that the improvements were made during a tenancy other than the one at the termination of which he quits the holding.

(2) Where, on entering into occupation of an agricultural holding, the tenant—

(*a*) with the consent in writing of his landlord paid to an outgoing tenant any compensation payable by the landlord under or in pursuance of this Act (or the Agricultural Holdings Act 1948 or Part III of the Agriculture Act 1947) in respect of the whole or part of a relevant improvement, or

(*b*) has paid to the landlord the amount of any such compensation payable to an outgoing tenant,

the tenant shall be entitled, on quitting the holding, to claim compensation in respect of the improvement or part in the same manner, if at all, as the outgoing tenant would have been entitled if the outgoing tenant had remained tenant of the holding and quitted it at the time at which the tenant quits it.

(3) Where, in a case not falling within subsection (2) above, the tenant, on entering into occupation of an agricultural holding, paid to his landlord any amount in respect of the whole or part of a relevant improvement, he shall, subject to any agreement in writing between the landlord and the tenant, be entitled on quitting the holding to claim compensation in respect of the improvement or part in the same manner, if at all, as he would have been entitled if he had been tenant of the holding at the time when the improvement was carried out and the improvement or part had been carried out by him.

<small>Definitions</small>
"agricultural holding": s.1(1).
"relevant improvement": s.64(2).
"tenant" and "termination": s.96(1).

Subs. (1)
Where the tenant of an agricultural holding has remained. It is implicit in this subsection that both the *tenant* and the *holding* maintain their identities during the successive tenancies. Any significant change in the identity of either could invalidate a claim made under this provision. The change of tenancy could have been the result of an express or implied

surrender and regrant. It could come about without the awareness of the tenant. It would be most unfair if the tenant were to lose his right to compensation for improvements by remaining in occupation under more than one tenancy. Of course, the value of the improvement remaining after more than one tenancy may be small.

Subs. (2)

Para (a): with the consent in writing of his landlord. Such a consent should be preserved like a document of title. Note that it is not required in the case of a market garden tenant: s.79(5). This subs. covers both compensation paid direct to an outgoing tenant and compensation paid to the landlord which is payable to an outgoing tenant. An alleged custom that the outgoer should look to the incomer rather than the landlord for compensation has, however, been held bad: *Bradburn* v. *Foley* (1878) 3 C.P.D. 129.

In the same manner, if at all. He has such rights only as his predecessor would have had if he had remained tenant. The value of the improvement may have become exhausted by the time the incomer quits. He is thus not entitled as of right to claim the amount he paid his predecessor, but he should keep receipts and vouchers to show that he did pay. As to the enforcement of an agreement by the incomer to pay compensation to the outgoer and the application of the Statutes of Limitations, see *Cheshire County Council* v. *Hopley* (1923) 130 L.T. 123.

Subs. (3)

In a case not falling within subsection (2) above. This subsection covers cases where an amount is paid to the landlord in respect of a relevant improvement where there is no outgoing tenant, or because, for some reason, the outgoing tenant is not eligible to receive compensation.

In the same manner, if at all. See note to subs. (2) above. Here again the value of the improvement may have become exhausted by the time the incomer quits.

Compensation to tenant for adoption of special system of farming

Compensation for special system of farming

70.—(1) Where the tenant of an agricultural holding shows that, by the continuous adoption of a system of farming which has been more beneficial to the holding—

    (*a*) than the system of farming required by the contract of tenancy, or

    (*b*) in so far as no system of farming is so required, than the system of farming normally practised on comparable agricultural holdings,

the value of the holding as a holding has been increased during the tenancy, having regard to the character and situation of the holding and the average requirements of tenants reasonably skilled in husbandry, the tenant shall be entitled, on quitting the holding on the termination of the tenancy, to obtain from the landlord compensation of an amount equal to the increase.

(2) Compensation shall not be recoverable under this section unless—

    (*a*) the tenant has, not later than one month before the termination of the tenancy, given to the landlord notice in writing of his intention to claim compensation under this section, and

    (*b*) a record has been made under section 22 above of the condition of the fixed equipment on the holding and of the general condition of the holding.

(3) Compensation shall not be recoverable under this section in respect of any matter arising before the date of the making of the record referred to in subsection (2) above or, if more than one such record has been made, the first of them.

(4) In assessing the value of an agricultural holding for the purposes of this section due allowance shall be made for any compensation agreed or awarded to be paid to the tenant for an improvement falling within section 64(1) or (4) above or (subject to paragraph 8 of Schedule 12 to this Act) for any such matter as is specified in Part II of Schedule 8 to this Act,

being an improvement or matter which has caused, or contributed to, the benefit.

(5) Nothing in this section shall entitle a tenant to recover for an improvement falling within section 64(1) or (4) above or an improvement to which the provisions of this Act relating to market gardens apply or (subject to the said paragraph 8) for any such matter as is specified in Part II of Schedule 8 to this Act, any compensation which he is not entitled to recover apart from this section.

DEFINITIONS
    "agricultural holding": s.1(1).
    "landlord", "tenant", "termination": s.96(1).

Subs. (1)
    System of farming. The word "system" implies a plan and the methodical pursuit of it. The name "high farming" has been given to it, but the present section, like its predecessors (s.16 of the 1920 Act, s.9 of the 1923 Act and s.56 of the 1948 Act) is likely to be a dead letter owing to the difficulty of establishing a case. Note that Sched. 2, para. 2(4), requires an arbitrator to disregard an increase of rental value due to the adoption by the tenant of a s.70 "system" as if it were an improvement executed at the tenant's expense.
    The value of the holding as a holding. This is the same measure as for a relevant improvement specified in Sched. 7 (see s.66(1)).
    During the tenancy. There is no provision in s.70, similar to that in s.69(1), for the benefit of a tenant who has occupied during a succession of tenancies. The enhancement of value for the purpose of s.70 must have taken place during the tenancy at the end of which compensation is claimed. A contrary view in *Connell's Agricultural Holdings (Scotland) Acts* (6th ed.), p.170 is not supported by Gill's *Law of Agricultural Holdings in Scotland* (1982) para. 258.
    On the termination of the tenancy. For a special provision enabling a tenant to claim compensation *during* the tenancy where, owing to opencast coal production, the benefit of the adoption of a system of farming which would have qualified for compensation under s.70 is lost, see s.24 of the Opencast Coal Act 1958, as amended by para. 26 of Sched. 14 to the present Act.

Subs. (2)
    Para. (a): notice in writing of his intention. This preliminary notice is a condition precedent to a claim. The safe course is undoubtedly to assume that a *separate* notice under s.83(2) is also required, although it has been held in the county court, in a persuasive judgment on a cognate provision, that this is not essential: see *Hallinan (Lady)* v. *Jones* (1984) 272 E.G. 1081. See *Re Disraeli Agreement* [1939] Ch. 382, *Coates* v. *Diment* [1951] 1 All E.R. 890, and *Parry* v. *Million Pigs Ltd.* (1980) 260 E.G. 281, on the need for any resumption clause in a tenancy agreement to permit of the tenant's giving a preliminary notice of the present kind, if desired, a point apparently overlooked in the Scottish case of *Pigott* v. *Robson*, 1958 S.L.T. 49. The need to give this notice is excluded in the cases to which s.25(2) of the Open-cast Coal Act 1958, as amended by Sched. 14, para. 27 of the present Act, applies.
    Para. (b): a record. This is also a condition precedent, and is, incidentally, the only case where the record under s.22 is given a *statutory* effect (see subs. (3)). The effect of a record in Scotland is very different: see Gill's *Law of Agricultural Holdings in Scotland* (1982), pp.52–54.

Subs. (3)
    Before the date of the making of the record. The need for a record as a condition of a claim for "high farming", and the importance of the date of the record, become more obvious where the unspecific and ambulatory nature of the claim is considered in comparison with that for an identifiable improvement. But the whole matter is somewhat academic.

Subs. (4)
    Due allowance shall be made. The practical difficulty of doing this reduces the likelihood of establishing a claim.
    Subject to paragraph 8 of Schedule 12 to this Act. This refers to the fact that a tenant may not have elected for the statutory basis of compensation (under Part II of Sched. 8) in accordance with para. 6 or 7 of Sched. 12. See para. 8 of that Sched.

Subs. (5)

Nothing in this section shall entitle. This would, *e.g.* exclude an attempt to obtain compensation under this section for a Sched. 7 improvement to which the landlord had not consented.

Compensation to landlord for deterioration of holding

Compensation for deterioration of particular parts of holding

71.—(1) The landlord of an agricultural holding shall be entitled to recover from a tenant of the holding, on the tenant's quitting the holding on the termination of the tenancy, compensation in respect of the dilapidation or deterioration of, or damage to, any part of the holding or anything in or on the holding caused by non-fulfilment by the tenant of his responsibilities to farm in accordance with the rules of good husbandry.

(2) Subject to subsection (5) below, the amount of the compensation payable under subsection (1) above shall be the cost, as at the date of the tenant's quitting the holding, of making good the dilapidation, deterioration or damage.

(3) Notwithstanding anything in this Act, the landlord may, in lieu of claiming compensation under subsection (1) above, claim compensation in respect of matters specified in that subsection under and in accordance with a written contract of tenancy.

(4) Where the landlord claims compensation in accordance with subsection (3) above—

 (a) compensation shall be so claimed only on the tenant's quitting the holding on the termination of the tenancy, and

 (b) compensation shall not be claimed in respect of any one holding both under such a contract as is mentioned in that subsection and under subsection (1) above;

and for the purposes of paragraph (b) above any claim under section 9(1) above shall be disregarded.

(5) The amount of the compensation payable under subsection (1) above, or in accordance with subsection (3) above, shall in no case exceed the amount (if any) by which the value of the landlord's reversion in the holding is diminished owing to the dilapidation, deterioration or damage in question.

DEFINITIONS

 "agricultural holding": s.1(1) and for "contract of tenancy", s.1(5).
 "Landlord", "tenant", "termination": s.96(1).
 "rules of good husbandry", s.96(3).

Subs. (1)

On the tenant's quitting the holding on the termination of the tenancy. Apart from special provisions (see s.9 of present Act and s.25 of the Opencast Coal Act 1958 as amended by the present Act, Sched. 14, para 27), the *statutory* dilapidations claim cannot be pursued during the tenancy. The procedure at the end of the tenancy is by arbitration under the Act: s.83(1) and s.84. But see note to subs. (3) below as to an action at *common law* during the tenancy.

Any part of the holding or anything in or on the holding. The statutory dilapidations claim under s.71(1) relates to specific dilapidations or deterioration affecting particular parts of the holding or anything in or on the holding. For examples, see *Evans* v. *Jones* [1955] 2 Q.B. 58. In determining the statutory claim the contract of tenancy, any other agreement, and the "model clauses" (see s.7 *ante*) are relevant: *Barrow Green Estate Co.* v. *Exors. of Walker, decd.* [1954] 1 W.L.R. 231. "Dilapidations" in the wide sense used by valuers cover not only disrepair of buildings but also neglect of fences, gates, roads, ditches and drains, foul land, irregularity of cropping, and even selling off of produce contrary to custom or agreement. On the "incorporation" of the "model clauses", see *Burden* v. *Hannaford* [1956] 1 Q.B. 142.

Responsibilities to farm in accordance with the rules of good husbandry. These responsibilities are still *defined* by s.11 of the Agriculture Act 1947 (see s.96(3) of present Act) although the sanctions by which they were originally enforced in the 1947 Act have long since disappeared. As far as the 1947 Act is concerned, s.11 provides only a definition, but it is given a statutory effect in the present s.71(1) and it is frequently given contractual effect by being incorporated in tenancy agreements.

Subs. (2)
Subject to subsection (5) below. Note the "ceiling" imposed by subs. (5) on the cost of making good.
Cost . . . of making good. The measure of compensation for the statutory claim under s.71(1) is the actual cost, at the date of quitting, of making good the dilapidation or damage, but, since 1984, this measure must not be allowed to *exceed* the diminution in the value of the reversion (subs. (5); it may in many cases be less. There is no rule that a tenant is either bound or entitled to leave the land as he found it; he must leave it in the condition required to discharge his good husbandry responsibilities: see *Williams* v. *Lewis* [1915] 3 K.B. 493; *Evans* v. *Jones* [1955] 2 Q.B. 58; *cf. Proudfoot* v. *Hart* (1890) 25 Q.B.D. 42.

Subs. (3)
In accordance with a written contract of tenancy. Subject to the transitional exception in s.9(1) and (2), the contractual claim can only be pursued at the end of the tenancy, on the tenant's quitting the holding, and only by means of arbitration proceedings under the Act: see subs. (4)(*a*) below and s.83(1). But note the decision in *Kent* v. *Conniff* [1953] 1 Q.B. 361, following dicta in *Gulliver* v. *Catt* [1952] 2 Q.B. 308, that a landlord who wishes to rely on a breach of the contract of tenancy may bring a *common law* action for damages in the courts *during* the tenancy. (Note also the possibility of injunction proceedings during the tenancy under s.15(5)(*a*)). For some contemporary comments on the *Kent* v. *Conniff* decision, which was unexpected at the time, see (1952) 16 Conv. (N.S.) 372. The words "in respect of matters specified in that subsection" may mean the dilapidation or deterioration of, or damage to, any part of the holding, or anything in or on it, without the requirement that this must be caused by non-fulfilment by the tenant of his good husbandry responsibilities, or they may mean to add this qualification. Morris L. J. in *Kent* v. *Conniff, supra,* at pp.377–378 gave the words the former interpretation, but the narrower interpretation is possible and is consistent with some of the wording of s.72. S.71(3) seems intended to meet the difficulty that a contractual claim covering the same ground as s.71(1) would otherwise be invalidated by s.78(1). The "written contract of tenancy" will incorporate, as appropriate, the "model clauses" of s.7, but for effect of incorporation see *Burden* v. *Hannaford* [1956] 1 Q.B. 142. So far as the claim under s.71(3) is for the breach of a repairing covenant, s.18(1) of the Landlord and Tenant Act 1927 will apply. On the measure of compensation at common law, see *Joyner* v. *Weeks* [1891] 2 Q.B. 31; *Hanson* v. *Newman* [1934] Ch. 298; *Jones* v. *Herxheimer* [1950] 2 K.B. 106, disagreeing with dictum of Lynskey J. in *Landeau* v. *Marchbank* [1949] 2 All E.R. 172; *Smiley* v. *Townshend* [1950] 2 K.B. 311; *Maddox Properties* v. *Davis* (1950) 155 E.G. 155; *Havilland* v. *Long* [1952] 2 Q.B. 80; *Jaquin* v. *Holland* [1960] 1 W.L.R. 258; *Family Management* v. *Gray* (1979) 253 E.G. 369. As to implied obligations, see *Wedd* v. *Porter* [1916] 2 K.B. 91; *Williams* v. *Lewis* [1915] 3 K.B. 493; *Warren* v. *Keen* [1954] 1 Q.B. 15; *Regis Property Ltd.* v. *Dudley* [1959] A.C. 370 at p.407.

Subs, (4)
Para. (a): only. See Morris L.J.'s observations on this provision in *Kent* v. *Conniff* [1953] 1 Q.B. 361 at p.378. A minor exception to the rule is the transitional one in s.9(1), (2).
Para. (b) shall not be claimed. The predecessor of s.71(4)(*b*) was considered in *Boyd* v. *Wilton* [1957] 2 Q.B. 277, where it was held not to invalidate a notice under what is now s.83, setting out claims framed in the alternative under the statutory and the contractual basis, the landlord at the hearing before the arbitrator electing to rely solely on the claim under the contract. Probably, even if the claims are in form cumulative and not alternative, the landlord would not be disqualified from recovering, provided he made his decision clear in time, since s.71(4)(3) is concerned with rights or enforceable claims, not with the procedure or formality of claiming; *per* Jenkins L.J., *loc cit*, at p.287. The cumulative formulation of claims is not, however, recommended.

Subs. (5)
Shall in no case exceed. This "ceiling" on the *cost* basis of the statutory claim, as stated in subs. (2), was introduced by the 1984 Act (Sched. 3, para. 13). Before that the compensation

under subs. (1) could have exceeded the amount by which the value of the landlord's reversion had been diminished; the position under the contractual claim in subs. (3) was different, but now both kinds of claim are subject to the ceiling.

Compensation for general deterioration of holding

72.—(1) This section applies where, on the quitting of an agricultural holding by the tenant on the termination of the tenancy, the landlord shows that the value of the holding generally has been reduced by reason of any such dilapidation, deterioration or damage as is mentioned in section 71(1) above or otherwise by non-fulfilment by the tenant of his responsibilities to farm in accordance with the rules of good husbandry.

(2) Where this section applies, the landlord shall be entitled to recover from the tenant compensation for the matter in question, in so far as the landlord is not compensated for it under subsection (1), or in accordance with subsection (3), of section 71 above.

(3) The amount of the compensation payable under this section shall be equal to the decrease attributable to the matter in question in the value of the holding as a holding, having regard to the character and situation of the holding and the average requirements of tenants reasonably skilled in husbandry.

(4) Compensation shall not be recoverable under this section unless the landlord has, not later than one month before the termination of the tenancy, given notice in writing to the tenant of his intention to claim such compensation.

DEFINITIONS
"agricultural holding": s.1(1)
"landlord"
"rules of good husbandry": s.96(3).
"tenant", "termination": s.96(1).

Subs. (1)
Value of the holding generally. See Evershed M.R.'s explanation of the relation between the sections which are now ss.71 and 72 in *Evans* v. *Jones* [1955] 2 Q.B. 58 at p.64. It is clear from that case that a claim under s.72 may be made in conjunction with one under s.71 or as an independent claim. Whether in conjunction or independently, it is obviously designed to identify and compensate for the loss of a slice of value not met by s.71, but there is some theoretical, and a good deal of practical difficulty in isolating it. A record of the "general condition of the holding" under s.22, made before deterioration set in, might be useful for purposes of comparison later. In Scotland, such a record is a *condition* of recovery: Agricultural Holdings (Scotland) Act 1949, s.59(2)(*a*). The general deterioration must have been caused by one or more of the specific dilapidations which come within s.71(1) but it must be something more than the sum of the individual items of damage.

Subs. (2)
Insofar as the landlord is not compensated. The landlord can recover, under s.72, compensation which he cannot obtain under s.71, but he must "bring into account anything he recovers under [s.71], so that he does not in any case recover twice over": *per* Evershed M.R. in *Evans* v. *Jones*, *supra*, at p.64.

Subs. (3)
The value of the holding as a holding. This is the same measure of compensation as for a relevant improvement under s.66(1).

Subs. (4)
Not later than one month before the termination of the tenancy. This prior notice is an essential condition of a s.72 claim. The safe course is to assume that this notice does not dispense with the need for a notice under s.83(2) before the expiry of two months from the termination of the tenancy, although there is an important county court decision to the contrary: *Hallinan (Lady)* v. *Jones* (1984) 272 E.G. 1081, where this contrary view is well set out. *Woodfall* (28th ed.), vol. 2, para. 2–0159, expresses the opinion that two notices are

necessary. No preliminary notice is required for the s.71 claim, although the position in Scotland is otherwise (Agricultural Holdings (Scotland) Act 1949, s.59(1)). On the expression "not later than one month", see recent cases on time expressions cited in note to s.60(6)(*a*) *ante*.

Deterioration of holding: successive tenancies

73.—Where the tenant of an agricultural holding has remained on the holding during two or more tenancies his landlord shall not be deprived of his right to compensation under section 71 or 72 above in respect of any dilapidation, deterioration or damage by reason only that the tenancy during which an act or omission occurred which in whole or in part caused the dilapidation, deterioration or damage was a tenancy other than the tenancy at the termination of which the tenant quits the holding.

DEFINITIONS
   "agricultural holding": s.1(1).
   "landlord", "tenant", "termination": s.96(1).

GENERAL NOTE
   Shall not be deprived of his right to compensation. This section safeguards the landlord in the same way as s.69(1) safeguards the tenant against losing rights to compensation by reason of a succession of tenancies, where the material event did not occur in the last of the tenancies. A new tenancy may arise as a result of a surrender and regrant, the significance of which may at the time escape the notice of the parties: see *Jenkin R. Lewis & Son Ltd.* v. *Kerman* [1971] Ch. 477, 487 for various circumstances which may give rise to a new tenancy. Note, however, that s.73 will apply only if both "the tenant" and "the holding" preserve a substantial identity throughout the succession of tenancies. A substantial increase in the size of the holding, for example, might cause it to be regarded as no longer "the holding". This could present an arbitrator, and perhaps the court, with a difficult problem.

Supplementary provisions with respect to compensation

Termination of tenancy of part of holding

74.—(1) Where the landlord of an agricultural holding resumes possession of part of the holding by virtue of section 31 or 43(2) above, the provisions of this Act with respect to compensation shall apply to that part of the holding as if it were a separate holding which the tenant had quitted in consequence of a notice to quit.

(2) Where the landlord of an agricultural holding resumes possession of part of the holding in pursuance of a provision in that behalf contained in the contract of tenancy—

   (*a*) the provisions of this Act with respect to compensation shall apply to that part of the holding as if it were a separate holding which the tenant had quitted in consequence of a notice to quit, but

   (*b*) the arbitrator in assessing the amount of compensation payable to the tenant, except the amount of compensation under section 60(2)(*b*) above, shall take into consideration any benefit or relief allowed to the tenant under the contract of tenancy in respect of the land possession of which is resumed by the landlord.

(3) Where a person entitled to a severed part of the reversionary estate in an agricultural holding resumes possession of part of the holding by virtue of a notice to quit that part given to the tenant by virtue of section 140 of the Law of Property Act 1925 the provisions of this Act with respect to compensation shall apply to that part of the holding as if—

   (*a*) it were a separate holding which the tenant had quitted in consequence of the notice to quit, and

   (*b*) the person resuming possession were the landlord of that separate holding.

(4) References in this Act to the termination of the tenancy of, or (as the case may be) of part of, an agricultural holding include references to the resumption of possession of part of an agricultural holding in circumstances within subsection (1), (2) or (3) above

DEFINITIONS
"agricultural holding,": s.1(1).
"contract of tenancy": s.1(5).
"landlord", "tenant", "termination": s.96(1).
"termination": subs. (4) of present section.

Subs. (1)
Resumes possession of part. This section covers four cases of resumption of part of a holding and provides in each case, but with some differences in detail, that compensation shall apply to the part in question as if it were a separate holding. Subs. (1) covers two cases. The first is under s.31 which validates a notice to quit given for one of the nine purposes or objects detailed in that section. The second is under s.43(2) where, on a notice to quit in pursuance of Case G, the tribunal consent to a notice to quit part only. "Compensation" in this section includes compensation for improvements, tenant-right and disturbance.

Subs. (2)
A provision in that behalf contained in the contract of tenancy. Contracts of tenancy which contain a clause enabling the landlord to resume a portion of the land, usually on short notice (see s.25(2)(*b*), for various purposes sometimes provide a benefit or relief to the tenant in respect of the land resumed. It is only fair that, in general, such a benefit or relief should be taken into consideration by the arbitrator in assessing compensation in respect of the part. It is, however, specifically provided that the amount of compensation under s.60(2)(*b*), *i.e.* the old 1968 Act sum for the reorganisation of the tenant's affairs, now called "additional compensation" for disturbance, is not so to be taken into account. In other words, the "additional compensation" is to be left intact. As to "benefit", some Scottish decisions are helpful, *McQuater* v. *Fergusson*, 1911 S.C. 640; *Galloway (Earl)* v. *McClelland*, 1915 S.C. 1062; *Findlay* v. *Munro*, 1917 S.C. 419; *Mackenzie* v. *Macgillivray*, 1921 S.C. 722. Note also as to minimum length of notice to quit the cases of *Re Disraeli Agreement* [1939] Ch. 382; *Coates* v. *Diment* [1951] 1 All E.R. 890 and *Parry* v. *Million Pigs Ltd.* (1980) 260 E.G. 281.

Subs. (3)
A person entitled to a severed part of the reversionary estate. This subs. results from an amendment made by the 1984 Act (Sched. 3, para. 14), before which a tenant of the entirety served with a notice to quit part under s.140 of the Law of Property Act 1925 could not obtain compensation *in respect of that part only*, although he could by counternotice served on all the reversioners obtain compensation against them as together landlord of the whole. The mere severance of the reversion does not result in the creation of separate tenancies, although s.140 of the 1925 Act grants important separate rights: see generally *Jelley* v. *Buchman* [1974] Q.B. 488 and the odd decision in *Persey* v. *Bazeley* (1984) 47 P. & C.R. 37 as to the conveyance of part of the reversion to "bare trustees".

Compensation where reversionary estate in holding is severed

75.—(1) Where the reversionary estate in an agricultural holding is for the time being vested in more than one person in several parts, the tenant shall be entitled, on quitting the entire holding, to require that any compensation payable to him under this Act shall be determined as if the reversionary estate were not so severed.

(2) Where subsection (1) above applies, the arbitrator shall, where necessary, apportion the amount awarded between the persons who for the purposes of this Act together constitute the landlord of the holding, and any additional costs of the award caused by the apportionment shall be directed by the arbitrator to be paid by those persons in such proportions as he shall determine.

Subs. (1)
As if the reversionary estate were not so severed. This is an improved version of s.61 of the 1948 Act (amended by 1984 Act, Sched. 3, para. 15). It *enables*, but does not compel, the tenant of the entirety, where the reversion has become vested in a plurality or reversioners, to require that any compensation payable to him should be determined *as if* the reversion were not severed. It may be to the tenant's financial advantage to require this. There seems, however, nothing to prevent the tenant from pursuing the several reversioners separately, by virtue of s.74, if he thinks fit, and this may avoid some procedural difficulties which seem to attend the operation of s.75. There is no superior court authority on it and the county court case of *Weston* v. *Devonshire (Duke)* (1923) 12 L.J.C.C.R. 74 is based on the old confusing wording of the provision. There may be complications where some, but not all, the reversioners have counterclaims for dilapidations against the tenant.

Subs. (2)
Apportion the amount awarded. It appears that, although the compensation is to be calculated as if the reversion had not been severed, when the arbitrator has apportioned the amount so calculated between the reversioners the resulting sums will be the *several* liability of each reversioner, not the joint, or joint and several, liability of them all: this was the view of Judge Moore Cann in *Weston* v. *Devonshire (Duke), supra.*

Restrictions on compensation for things done in compliance with this Act

76.—(1) Notwithstanding anything in this Act or any custom or agreement—

(*a*) no compensation shall be payable to the tenant of an agricultural holding in respect of anything done in pursuance of an order under section 14(4) above,

(*b*) in assessing compensation to an outgoing tenant of an agricultural holding where land has been ploughed up in pursuance of a direction under that section, the value per hectare of any tenant's pasture comprised in the holding shall be taken not to exceed the average value per hectare of the whole of the tenant's pasture comprised in the holding on the termination of the tenancy.

(2) In subsection (1) above "tenant's pasture" means pasture laid down at the expense of the tenant or paid for by the tenant on entering on the holding.

(3) The tenant of an agricultural holding shall not be entitled to any compensation for a relevant improvement specified in Part I of Schedule 8 to this Act or (subject to paragraph 8 of Schedule 12 to this Act) for any such matter as is specified in Part II of Schedule 8 if it is an improvement or matter made or effected for the purposes of section 15(4) above.

Subs. (1)
Agreement. This is one of the provisions where contracting out is *specifically* forbidden, as distinct from those where the prohibition has to be inferred from public policy considerations: see *Johnson* v. *Moreton* [1980] A.C. 37. Note s.78(2) as to an agreement for variation, instead of a direction under s.14, providing for the exclusion of compensation in the same manner as under s.76(1).
Para. (a): order under s.14(4) above. Clearly the tenant ought not to be compensated for restoring the pasture area which he had been given the privilege of reducing during the tenancy.

Para. (b): not to exceed the average value . . . of the whole. Otherwise the tenant might treat his inferior pieces of pasture as laid down in compliance with the order and claim compensation on his superior pieces.

Subs. (2)
Tenant's pasture. Cf. Sched. 8, para. 9.

Subs. (3)
For the purposes of section 15(4) above. Again, it is obvious that the tenant should not be entitled to claim compensation for protecting the land against injury caused in the exercise of his rights of cropping and disposal of produce. The words "(subject to paragraph 8 of Schedule 12 to this Act)" are required because the reference to Part II of Sched. 8 would be inappropriate where a tenant had not elected for the statutory basis in Part II.

No compensation under custom for improvement or tenant-right matter

77.—(1) A landlord or tenant of an agricultural holding shall not be entitled under custom to any compensation from the other for any improvement, whether or not one in respect of the carrying out of which compensation is provided under this Act, or (subject to paragraph 8 of Schedule 12 to this Act) for any matter specified in Part II of Schedule 8 to this Act or otherwise.

(2) Subsection (1) above shall not apply to compensation for an improvement of a kind specified in Schedule 7 or Part I of Schedule 8 to this Act begun before 1st March 1948.

DEFINITIONS
"agricultural holding": s.1(1).
"landlord", "tenant": s.96(1).

Subs. (1)
Shall not be entitled under custom. This is a total abolition of customary *compensation* (subject to the savings mentioned in the section) but not of custom otherwise than in relation to compensation: see express saving for custom in s.97. For a full discussion, see *Muir Watt's Agricultural Holdings* (12th ed.), pp.148 to 153. And see Sched. 12, para. 8(1)(*b*).

Extent to which compensation recoverable under agreements

78.—(1) Save as expressly provided in this Act, in any case for which apart from this section the provisions of this Act provide for compensation, a tenant or landlord shall be entitled to compensation in accordance with those provisions and not otherwise, and shall be so entitled notwithstanding any agreement to the contrary.

(2) Where the landlord and tenant of an agricultural holding enter into an agreement in writing for any such variation of the terms of the contract of tenancy as could be made by direction or order under section 14 above, the agreement may provide for the exclusion of compensation in the same manner as under section 76(1) above.

(3) Nothing in the provisions of this Act, apart from this section, shall be construed as disentitling a tenant or landlord to compensation in any case for which the said provisions do not provide for compensation, but (subject to paragraph 8 of Schedule 12 to this Act) a claim for compensation in any such case shall not be enforceable except under an agreement in writing.

DEFINITIONS
"agreement", "landlord", "tenant": 96(1).
"agricultural holding": s.1(1).
"contract of tenancy": s.1(5).

Subs. (1)

Save as expressly provided in this Act. There are a number of such express provisions, in addition to those mentioned in s.78 itself, *e.g.* s.66(4), s.67(2), s.71(3), s.81(1), Sched. 9, para. 1(4), para. 3(2).

Not otherwise. For cases where agreements which purported to exclude or modify, or which would have had the effect of impairing or frustrating, the statutory compensation provisions were held void, see *Cathcart* v. *Chalmers* [1911] A.C. 246; *Mears* v. *Callender* [1901] 2 Ch. 388 (but see *Turnbull* v. *Millar*, 1942 S.C. 521): *Gardner* v. *Beck* [1947] E.G.D. 169; *Re Disraeli Agreement* [1939] Ch. 382; *Coates* v. *Diment* [1951] 1 All E.R. 890; *Parry* v. *Million Pigs Ltd.* (1980) 260 E.G. 281 (forfeiture clause). Contrast *Re Masters and Duveen* [1923] 2 K.B. 729 and *Re Smith and Duke of Devonshire* (1906) 22 T.L.R. 619. See also *Kent* v. *Conniff* [1953] 1 Q.B. 361 at pp.370, 371, 374 and 378–379. An agreement that the outgoer should look only to the incomer, to the exclusion of the landlord, for compensation would probably offend against s.78, but not, of course, an agreement by the incomer to take over responsibility for the landlord's admitted liability.

Subs. (2)

The agreement may provide for the exclusion of compensation. The parties may by agreement in writing do what may be done by an arbitrator's award under s.14, and so may exclude compensation as s.76(1) does in the case of an award.

Subs. (3)

For which the said provisions do not provide for compensation. The first part of this subsection may be *ex abundante cautela*; *cf. Dean* v. *Secretary of State for War* [1950] W.N. 71.

(Subject to paragraph 8 of Schedule 12 to this Act). It is perfectly in order for a landlord and tenant to agree that there shall be compensation in cases where the Act does not provide for it, but the general rule is that such an agreement must be in writing. This general rule is subject to the exception that if the tenant has not elected for the statutory basis of tenant-right compensation, either as a whole or in relation to the "acclimatisation, hefting or settlement of hill sheep on hill land," he may rest his claim to compensation for the matters or matter in question on custom: customary rights are thus preserved in such cases.

PART VI

MARKET GARDENS AND SMALLHOLDINGS

Additional rights with respect to improvements for tenants of market gardens

79. —(1) Subsections (2) to (5) below apply in the case of an agricultural holding in respect of which it is agreed by an agreement in writing that the holding shall be let or treated as a market garden; and where the land to which such agreement relates consists of part of an agricultural holding only, those subsections shall apply as if that part were a separate holding.

(2) The provisions of this Act shall apply as if improvements of a kind specified in Schedule 10 to this Act begun on or after 1st March 1948 were included amongst the improvements specified in Part I of Schedule 8 to this Act and as if improvements begun before that day consisting of the erection or enlargement of buildings for the purpose of the trade or business of a market gardener were included amongst the improvements specified in Part II of Schedule 9 to this Act.

(3) In section 10 above—

(a) subsection (2)(c) shall not exclude that section from applying to any building erected by the tenant on the holding or acquired by him for the purposes of his trade or business as a market gardener, and

(b) subsection (2)(d) shall not exclude that section from applying to any building acquired by him for those purposes (whenever erected).

(4) It shall be lawful for the tenant to remove all fruit trees and fruit bushes planted by him on the holding and not permanently set out, but if the tenant does not remove them before the termination of his tenancy they shall remain the property of the landlord and the tenant shall not be entitled to any compensation in respect of them.

(5) The right of an incoming tenant to claim compensation in respect of the whole or part of an improvement which he has purchased may be exercised although his landlord has not consented in writing to the purchase.

DEFINITIONS
"agreement", "landlord", "tenant": s.96(1).
"agricultural holding": s.1.

GENERAL NOTE
For provisions relating to market gardens and opencast coal operations on the land, see s.28 of the Opencast Coal Act 1958 as amended by Sched. 14, para. 30, to present Act.

Subs. (1)
Agreement in writing. This may be, but need not be, the contract of tenancy. The managing agent of an estate normally had power to make such an agreement with the tenant: *Re Pearson and I'Anson* [1899] 2 Q.B. 618.
Shall be let or treated as a market garden. It need not relate to the entire holding: see second limb of this subs. and see s.80(7) in relation to a *direction as to part.* Cf. *Callander* v. *Smith* (1900) 2 F. 1140, 1147. As to "let or treated", see *Saunders-Jacobs* v. *Yates* [1933] 2 K.B. 240 (covenant excluding user *except* for market gardening sufficient); *Re Morse and Dixon* (1917) 87 L.J.K.B. 1 (mere right to remove fruit trees, bushes or plants insufficient); *Re Masters and Duveen* [1923] 2 K.B. 729 (express provision negating market garden rights effective although tenant described as "market gardener"). As to onus of proof on tenant, see *Bickerdike* v. *Lucy* [1920] 1 K.B. 707. On effect of conversion to market garden without agreement, see *Meux* v. *Cobley* [1892] 2 Ch. 253. On meaning of "market garden", see s.96(1) ("agriculture"), read in conjunction with s.1, and the following cases: *Watters* v. *Hunter*, 1927 S.C. 310 (land let for experimental bulb growing not a market garden: useful description by the Lord President); *Re Hammond* (1844) 14 L.J.Q.B. 14 (occasional sale of market garden produce insufficient); also *Bickerdike* v. *Lucy* [1920] 1 K.B. 707 and *Re Wallis* (1885) 14 Q.B.D. 950; *Purser* v. *Worthing Local Board* (1887) 18 Q.B.D. 818 (land practically covered with greenhouses a market garden), but see *Smith* v. *Richmond* [1899] A.C. 448; *Lowther* v. *Clifford* [1927] 1 K.B. 130 (orchard with rhubarb and other crops growing underneath the trees a market garden); *Grewar* v. *Moncur's Curator Bonis* 1916 S.C. 764 (ground used for growing raspberries used for jam-making a market garden: *Hood Barrs* v.*Howard* (1967) 201 E.G. 765 (apiary).

Subs. (2)
As if improvements. The effect of this subsection is a little complex. The market garden improvements set out in Sched. 10, including No. 5 (erection, alteration or enlargement of buildings), begun *on or after* March 1, 1948, do not require the consent of the landlord as a condition of qualifying for compensation. Compensation for the market garden improvements set out in Sched. 10 other than No. 5 begun *before* that date has lapsed, both in practice and legal entitlement (see 1984 Act, Sched. 3, para. 27(*b*). Improvement No. 5 begun before that date still qualifies, provided that it had the landlord's consent, but only in respect of the erection or enlargement of buildings, not their alteration. (The reason for the exception of alteration is that "alteration" was added by the 1947 Act, taking effect on March 1, 1948.)

Subs. (3)
Para. (a): subsection (2)(c) shall not exclude. This means that if a market garden tenant is otherwise entitled to remove a building he does not lose that right, because he is entitled to compensation in respect of it, whereas a non-market garden tenant does forfeit the right of removal if he has a right to compensation.
Para. (b): subsection (2)(d) shall not exclude. This means that the tenant's right to remove a building acquired by him applies no matter when the building was erected (even if it was before January 1, 1884).

Subs. (4)

Not permanently set out. This seems to mean kept for sale or transplanting and not too aged for the latter; this puts the market garden tenant in virtually the same position as a nurseryman was at common law: *cf. Wardell* v.*Usher* (1841) 3 Scott N.R. 508 and *Wyndham* v. *Way* (1812) 4 Taunt. 316. Removal must take place before the termination of the tenancy: see *Barff* v. *Probyn* (1895) 64 L.J.Q.B. 557.

Subs. (5)

Not consented. An ordinary agricultural tenant must obtain such consent: see s.69(2).

Note that subss. (2) to (5) of this section do not apply unless the agreement in writing mentioned in subs. (1) was made on or after January 1, 1896. This, however, is subject to para. 10 of Sched. 12, under which a holding qualifies as a market garden if it fulfilled certain conditions on January 1, 1896, obviously a diminishing category. Briefly, the holding must have been at that date in use or cultivation as a market garden with knowledge of the landlord and the tenant must by then have executed an improvement without having received before execution a written notice of dissent from the landlord. The improvement must have been of the kind specified in Sched. 10 (other than one consisting of such alteration of a building as did not constitute an enlargement of it).

Power of Tribunal to direct holding to be treated as market garden

80.—(1) Where the tenant of an agricultural holding desires to make on the holding or any part of it an improvement specified in Schedule 10 to this Act and the landlord refuses, or fails within a reasonable time, to agree in writing that the holding or that part of it, as the case may be, shall be treated as a market garden, the tenant may apply to the Tribunal for a direction under subsection (2) below.

(2) On such an application, the Tribunal may, after being satisfied that the holding or part is suitable for the purposes of market gardening, direct that subsections (2) to (5) of section 79 above shall, either in respect of all the improvements specified in the said Schedule 10 or in respect of some only of those improvements, apply to the holding or to that part of it; and the said subsections shall apply accordingly as respects any improvements executed after the date on which the direction is given.

(3) Where a direction is given under subsection (2) above, then, if the tenancy is terminated by notice to quit given by the tenant or by reason of the tenant becoming insolvent, the tenant shall not be entitled to compensation in respect of improvements specified in the direction unless the conditions mentioned in subsection (4) below are satisfied.

(4) Those conditions are that—

(*a*) the tenant not later than one month after the date on which the notice to quit is given or the date of the insolvency, as the case may be, or such later date as may be agreed, produces to the landlord an offer in writing by a substantial and otherwise suitable person (being an offer which is to hold good for a period of three months from the date on which it is produced)—

(i) to accept a tenancy of the holding from the termination of the existing tenancy, and on the terms and conditions of that tenancy so far as applicable, and

(ii) subject as hereinafter provided, to pay to the outgoing tenant all compensation payable under this Act or under the contract of tenancy, and

(*b*) the landlord fails to accept the offer within three months after it has been produced.

(5) If the landlord accepts any such offer as is mentioned in subsection (4) above, the incoming tenant shall pay to the landlord on demand all sums payable to him by the outgoing tenant on the termination of the tenancy in respect of rent or breach of contract or otherwise in respect of

the holding, and any amount so paid may, subject to any agreement between the outgoing tenant and incoming tenant, be deducted by the incoming tenant from any compensation payable by him to the outgoing tenant.

(6) A direction under subsection (2) above may be given subject to such conditions (if any) for the protection of the landlord as the Tribunal think fit.

(7) Without prejudice to the generality of subsection (6) above, where a direction relates to part only of an agricultural holding, it may, on the application of the landlord, be given subject to the condition that it shall become operative only in the event of the tenant's consenting to the division of the holding into two parts, of which one shall be that to which the direction relates, to be held at rents settled, in default of agreement, by arbitration under this Act, but otherwise on the same terms and conditions (so far as applicable) as those on which the holding is held.

(8) A new tenancy created by the acceptance of a tenant in accordance with the provisions of this section on the terms and conditions of the existing tenancy shall be deemed for the purposes of Schedule 2 to this Act not to be a new tenancy.

(9) For the purposes of subsection (3) above a person has become insolvent if any of the events mentioned in section 96(2)(*a*) or (*b*) below has occurred; and the reference in subsection (4) above to the date of the insolvency is a reference to the date of the occurrence of the event in question.

DEFINITIONS
"agreement," "landlord", "tenant", "tribunal", "termination": s.96(1).
"agricultural holding": s.(1).

"insolvent": s.96(2) and subs. (9) of present section.

Subs. (1)
Refuses, or fails within a reasonable time, to agree. This refusal or failure is a condition precedent of the tribunal's jurisdiction. The tenant should, therefore, make a formal request to the landland, invoking this section. In fact the section, like its predecessors, may well be a dead letter. The tenant may apply, and the tribunal may direct, even if the contract of tenancy excludes use as a market garden. For provisions in relation to opencast coal production, see Opencast Coal Act 1958, s.28, as amended by Sched. 14, para. 30, to the present Act.

Subs. (2)
Suitable for the purposes of market gardening. Owing to the rare use of these provisions there is an absence of guidance as to the factors which tribunals are likely to take into account in deciding whether the holding or part is suitable.

Subs. (3)
Terminated by notice to quit given by the tenant or by reason of the tenant becoming insolvent. Subs. (3), (4) and (5) set out the "Evesham custom", which is applied following a tribunal direction if the tenancy is terminated in either of these two ways. (It may be noted that the Evesham custom may be applied simply by the agreement of the parties, without reference to a tribunal direction: see s.81(2). In this case the source of the compensation rights is neither statute nor custom, but written contract). This statutory embodiment of the Evesham custom has appeared in all Agricultural Holdings Acts since the Agriculture Act 1920, s.15(3), introduced it.

Shall not be entitled to compensation. The tenant will not be entitled to any compensation in respect of the market garden improvements specified in the direction unless he introduces a successor in accordance with the conditions in subs. (4). It must be remembered that the peculiar compensation conditions in subs. (4) and (5) have no application if the notice to quit is given by the landlord.

Para. (a) offer in writing by a substantial and otherwise suitable person. Presumably in case of doubt the arbitrator would have to decide whether the person put forward answered this description. It will be appreciated that the compensation at the end of a market garden tenancy could be extremely large. The essential elements in subs. (4) are the introduction by the tenant of a suitable successor and the failure of the landlord to accept the successor, resulting in the landlord's liability for the market garden compensation (plus any other compensation to which the tenant is entitled.)

Subs. (5)
If the landlord accepts any such offer. The tenant will then look to the "substantial" incomer for all the compensation due to the tenant (including his market garden compensation); the incomer will be liable to pay to the landlord any sums due from the outgoing tenant, *e.g.* for dilapidations; and, subject to agreement between them, the incomer may deduct such sums from the compensation due to the outgoing tenant. It should be noted that a new tenancy created by the acceptance of the incomer on the terms and conditions of the existing tenancy is deemed not to be a new tenancy for the purpose of the rent provisions in Sched. 2, *i.e.* it will not trigger off a three-year bar on rent changes: see subs. (8).

Subs. (7)
Division of the holding into two parts. The special compensation provisions in subs. (3), (4) and (5) will apply only to that part which the tribunal designate as a market garden.

Agreements as to compensation relating to market gardens

81.—(1) Where an agreement in writing secures to the tenant of an agricultural holding, for an improvement for which compensation is payable by virtue of section 79 or section 80 above, fair and reasonable compensation having regard to the circumstances existing when the agreement was made, the compensation so secured shall, as respects that improvement, be substituted for compensation under this Act.

(2) The landlord and tenant of an agricultural holding who have agreed that the holding shall be let or treated as a market garden may by agreement in writing substitute, for the provisions as to compensation which would otherwise be applicable to the holding, the provisions as to compensation known as the "Evesham custom", and set out in subsections (3) to (5) of section 80 above.

DEFINITIONS
"agreement", "landlord", "tenant": s.96(1).
"agricultural holding": s.1(1).

Subs. (1)
Fair and reasonable compensation. This is a question which the arbitrator may be called upon to decide. In a Scottish case where the phrase had to be considered, *Bell* v. *Graham* 1908 S.C. 1060, the Lord President said "if parties of full age sign an agreement the presumption of fact is very strong that it is fair and reasonable."

Subs. (2)
The provisions as to compensation known as the "Evesham custom". The "Evesham Custom" as a *custom* relating to compensation has been abolished ever since the 1947 Act (s.27) and the abolition is continued by the present Act in s.77. It survives in two ways, by its statutory application in s.79 and by the possibility of its terms being embodied in an agreement between the parties in writing, as mentioned in the present section. The Committee on Agricultural Valuation were told in 1950 "that in the Evesham District written tenancy agreements are usual, and that the basis of compensation is specified": Committee's Second Report (1950), p.5. Banished as a custom, the Evesham formula maintains a somewhat shadowy existence in an infrequently invoked statutory form and perhaps in localised agreements.

Application of section 15 to smallholdings

82.—(1) Section 15(1) above shall not apply to a tenancy of land let as a smallholding by a smallholdings authority or by the Minister in pursuance of a scheme, approved by the Minister for the purposes of this section, which—

  (*a*) provides for the farming of such holdings on a co-operative basis,
  (*b*) provides for the disposal of the produce of such holdings, or
  (*c*) provides other centralised services for the use of the tenants of such holdings.

(2) Where it appears to the Minister that the provisions of any scheme approved by him for the purposes of this section are not being satisfactorily carried out, he may, in accordance with subsection (3) below, withdraw his approval to the scheme.

(3) Before withdrawing his approval to a scheme the Minister shall—

  (*a*) serve a notice on the persons responsible for the management of the scheme specifying a date (not being earlier than one month after the service of the notice) and stating that on that date his approval to the scheme will cease to have effect and that, accordingly, section 15(1) will then apply to the tenancies granted in pursuance of the scheme,
  (*b*) give to those persons an opportunity of making representations to him;

and, if the said notice is not withdrawn by the Minister before the said date, section 15(1) shall as from that date apply to the said tenancies.

DEFINITIONS
    For "the Minister": s.96(1).

Subs. (1)
    Section 15(1) above shall not apply. The freedom of cropping and disposal of produce provisions in s.15(1) do not apply to a smallholdings tenancy let in pursuance of a scheme which fulfils the conditions in s.82(1). Co-operative schemes for farming and centralised provisions for disposal of produce are inconsistent with the freedom given by s.15(1).

Subs. (2)
    Withdraw his approval to the scheme. Subss. (2) and (3) provide for withdrawal of the Minister's approval where it appears to him that the scheme is not being satisfactorily carried out. For a case where a scheme was terminated by the Minister, not because of any defects in the carrying out of the scheme, but because he considered that the arrangements were no longer necessary or expedient, see *Williams* v. *Minister of Agriculture, Fisheries and Food* (1985), reported only in *The Times* of July 11, 1985, but mentioned in a note in (1985) 275 E.G. 1082.

PART VII

MISCELLANEOUS AND SUPPLEMENTAL

Settlement of claims on termination of tenancy

  83.—(1) Without prejudice to any other provision of this Act, any claim of whatever nature by the tenant or landlord of an agricultural holding against the other, being a claim which arises—

  (*a*) under this Act or any custom or agreement, and
  (*b*) on or out of the termination of the tenancy of the holding or part of it,

shall, subject to the provisions of this section, be determined by arbitration under this Act.

(2) No such claim as is mentioned in subsection (1) above shall be enforceable unless before the expiry of two months from the termination of the tenancy the claimant has served notice in writing on his landlord or tenant, as the case may be, of his intention to make the claim.

(3) A notice under subsection (2) above shall specify the nature of the claim; but it shall be sufficient if the notice refers to the statutory provision, custom or term of an agreement under which the claim is made.

(4) The landlord and tenant may, within the period of eight months from the termination of the tenancy, by agreement in writing settle any such claim as is mentioned in subsection (1) above.

(5) Where by the expiry of the said period any such claim as is mentioned in subsection (1) above has not been settled, it shall be determined by arbitration under this Act.

(6) Where a tenant lawfully remains in occupation of part of an agricultural holding after the termination of a tenancy, references in subsections (2) and (4) above to the termination of the tenancy shall, in the case of a claim relating to that part of the holding, be construed as references to the termination of the occupation.

DEFINITIONS
"agreement", "landlord", "tenant", "termination": s.96(1).
"agricultural holding": s.1(1).
arbitration under this Act, see s.84 and Sched. 11.

Subs. (1)
Without prejudice to any other provision. There are a number of other specific matters referred to arbitration under the Act in other sections. See, *e.g.,* ss.2(4), 6(1), 8(2), 9(3), 10(6), 12(1), 13(7), 14(2), 15(6), 20(4),(5), 28(4), 29 and Sched. 4, s.33(2), s.48, s.56(3). There are also some matters so referred under subordinate legislation, such as the Agricultural Holdings (Arbitration on Notices) Order 1978 (S.I. 1978 No. 257) and the Agricultural Holdings (Arbitration on Notices) (Variation) Order 1984 (S.I. 1984 No. 1300).

Para (a): custom. This has to be read subject to s.77, which (with certain savings) abolishes customary *compensation.*

agreement. Claims based on tort, such as trespass or nuisance, are clearly not within this formula. The 1923 Act (s.16(1)) included the tort of waste, which overlaps with a breach of contract to repair, etc., but the 1948 Act and the present Act make no reference to it except in the general saving for other rights or remedies (s.97 of present Act).

Para (b): on or out of the termination of the tenancy. Claims which do not so arise, and which are not otherwise specifically referred to arbitration under the Act, may be pursued in the courts. For example, a landlord may bring an action against a tenant during the tenancy for breach of contract: *Kent* v. *Conniff* [1953] 1 Q.B. 361. Also tenants may bring actions against landlords during the tenancy for breaches of contract or to raise matters not within the jurisdiction of an arbitrator: *cf. R.* v. *Powell, ex p. Camden (Marquis)* [1925] 1 K.B. 641; *Harrison* v. *Ridgeway* (1925) 135 L.T. 238.

Shall. If the claim does fall within s.83(1) it is compulsorily referred to arbitration and the jurisdiction of the court is excluded. Such a claim cannot even be made the subject of a set-off or counterclaim in an action properly brought by the other party in the court, *e.g.* for rent or breach of covenant: *Gaslight Coke Co.* v. *Holloway* (1885) 52 L.T. 434; *Schofield* v. *Hincks* (1888) 58 L.J.Q.B. 147. But the compulsory reference of a claim to arbitration does not mean that more fundamental questions, upon which the existence of the claim, or the jurisdiction of the arbitrator, depends, are excluded from the purview of the courts: *cf. Farrow* v. *Orttewell* [1933] Ch. 480; *R.* v. *Powell, ex p. Camden (Marquis), supra; Simpson* v. *Batey* [1924] 2 K.B. 666; *Donaldson's Hospital Trustees* v. *Esslemont* 1926 SLT 526; *Goldsack* v. *Shore* [1950] 1 K.B. 708. Note also the interesting case of *Paddock Investments Ltd.* v. *Lory* (1975) 236 E.G. 863, where the High Court accepted jurisdiction to grant declaratory relief as to the validity of notices to quit; the Court of Appeal refused the declarations sought by the landlords, but did not question the legitimacy of the procedure, despite the arbitration machinery under the Act. It must also be remembered that the formidable administrative law remedy of judicial review may on occasion be available to a party to the contract. A tenant may defend an action for possession in the court on the ground that a notice to quit is bad at common law. And s.83(1) refers only to claims between landlord and tenant. It does not cover claims between incoming and outgoing tenants: *cf. Greenshields* v. *Rodger* 1922 S.C.(H.L.) 140; *Cameron* v. *Nicol* 1930 SC 1. Nor does it cover a question between a landlord and a bank which has taken an assignment of farming stock and other assets: *Ecclesiastical Commissioners for England* v. *National Provincial Bank Ltd.* [1935] 1 K.B. 566. It seems that certain matters preliminary to the determination of a claim, such as a question whether a tenancy has terminated, may be decided either as a separate issue by the courts or by an arbitrator (subject to the possibility of a case being stated) as incidental to the claim.

Subs. (2)

No such claim . . . shall be enforceable. This is unqualified, but a claim unenforceable as such may be met as part of an agreement for a settlement for which there is consideration. A valuer has no implied authority to concede a claim which is unenforceable under this provision, but his express authority may cover the compromise of doubtful claims. Subs (2) is, however, excluded in the cases to which s.25(2) of the Opencast Coal Act 1958, as amended by Sched. 14, para. 27, of the present Act applies. It is submitted that a notice under this section should be served even in the case of an agreement to surrender.

Before the expiry of two months from the termination of the tenancy. Two points arise in regard to this most important condition of an enforceable compensation claim. The first is whether the words "before the expiration of two months from the termination of the tenancy" imply that the notice must be served after the termination but before the expiry of two months after, or whether a notice served before the termination (which is necessarily before the expiration of two months from the termination) satisfies the requirement. The second is whether, if the latter is sufficient, a notice served not less than one month before the termination of the tenancy under s.60(6)(*a*), s.70(2)(*a*) or s.72(4) could do duty also, if properly drafted, as a notice under s.83(2); or are two separate notices required? It was decided in the county court case of *Hallinan (Lady)* v. *Jones* (1984) 272 E.G. 1081 that a notice under what is now s.72(4), served not later than a month before the termination of the tenancy, satisfied the requirements both of that section and of what is now section 83(2). The logic of this decision is impeccable, but in the absence of a High Court ruling it may be that the prudent, if pusillanimous, course is to assume that two notices are necessary and that the s.83(2) notice should be served after the termination of the tenancy. A notice of intention to serve a notice of intention to claim is not itself a notice of intention: *Hallinan (Lady)* v. *Jones, supra.* On "before the expiry of two months", see recent cases on such time expressions: *Dodds* v. *Walker* [1981] 1 W.L.R. 1027; *E. J. Riley Investments Ltd.* v. *Eurostile Holdings Ltd.* [1985] 1 W.L.R. 1139; *Manorlike Ltd.* v. *LeVitas Travel Agency & Consultancy Services Ltd.* (1986) 278 E.G. 412.

Subs. (3)

Specify the nature of the claim. The object is to give the other party fair and reasonable notice of the claim he has to meet in order to enable him to decide whether to agree, compromise or resist, but not at this stage to particularise the items of claim in minute detail. A notice so vague and general as to give no real assistance to the other party in deciding his course of action, however, is, it is submitted, insufficient. See next note and *cf.* the reasoning in the following Scottish cases, although decided under the 1923 Scottish Act: *McLaren* v. *Turnbull* 1942 S.C. 179 at p.195; *Simpson* v. *Henderson* 1944 S.C. 365, especially at p.379; *Adam* v. *Smythe* 1948 S.C. 445; *Edinburgh Corporation* v. *Gray* 1948 S.C. 538. Full "particulars" are not required at this stage: contrast *Spreckley* v. *Leicestershire County Council* [1934] 1 K.B. 366 and *Re O'Connor and Brewin's Arbitration* [1933] 1 K.B. 20 under the 1923 Act. But full particulars must be delivered to the arbitrator in due course: see para. 7 of Sched. 11. Presumably the submission of a fully particularised claim under s.83(2) instead of a notice of intention to claim, although not necessary, would in fact comply with the subsection, assuming that it referred to the statutory provision, custom or term of the agreement in question: *cf. Jones* v. *Evans* [1923] 1 K.B. 12. For a case where a county court judge upheld a minimum specification, not to be taken as a model, see *Hewetson* v. *Pennington-Ramsden* (1966) 116 L.J. 613 ("My claim will be for tenant-right improvements, painting and under clause quiet enjoyment"). Also, see *Lord Newborough* v. *Davies* (1966) 116 L.J. 1291.

Statutory provision, custom or term of an agreement. Despite the *Hewetson* v. *Pennington-Ramsden* decision cited in the last note, it would be unsafe to regard as a sufficient specification a general description such as "improvements" or "tenant-right" or a bare reference to a Schedule to an Act (there are 28 items in Sched. 7). It is also submitted that a bare reference to the number of a clause (*e.g.* "clause 5") in a contract of tenancy is not enough if the clause covers a number of distinct matters. A schedule of works was held good in *Lord Newborough* v. *Davies, supra.* For a discussion of the difference between the notice of intention to claim, under s.83(2) and the statement of claim with necessary particulars, and a comparison with the 1923 Act procedure, see *EA & AD Cooke Bourne (Farms) Ltd.* v. *Mellows* [1983] Q.B. 104, (1981) 262 E.G. 229.

Subs. (5)

It shall be determined by arbitration under this Act. By an amendment made by the 1984 Act (Sched. 3, para. 18) the provisions for extension contained in s.70(3) and (4) of the 1948 Act were abolished and a *definite* period of eight months only from the termination allowed for the settlement of claims by agreement, failing which they have to be determined by arbitration. But it is submitted that, on the analogy of the views expressed by the House of Lords in *Kammins Ballroom Co. Ltd.* v. *Zenith Investments (Torquay) Ltd.* [1971] A.C. 850 (dealing with procedures under the Landlord and Tenant Act 1954), the parties could by agreement waive the eight months' time-limit.

Subs. (6)

Lawfully remains in occupation of part. This seems to refer, not to cases where under the contract of tenancy possession of a part is given up at a different time from the rest, but where the tenant is allowed to remain, usually for a short period, after the original contract has ended: see *Swinburne* v. *Andrews* [1923] 2 K.B. 483 (particularly *per* Bankes L.J. at p.489) and *Re Arden and Rutter* [1923] 2 K.B. 65. Limited rights of access to safeguard an away-going crop neither prolong the tenancy nor attract s.83(6): see *Coutts* v. *Barclay-Harvey* 1956 S.L.T.(Sh.Ct.) 54.

Arbitrations

84.—(1) Any matter which by or by virtue of this Act or regulations made under this Act is required to be determined by arbitration under this Act shall, notwithstanding any agreement (under a contract of tenancy or otherwise) providing for a different method of arbitration, be determined by the arbitration of a single arbitrator in accordance with the provisions of any order under this section, together with the provisions of Schedule 11 to this Act (as for the time being in force); and the Arbitration Act 1950 shall not apply to any such arbitration.

(2) The Lord Chancellor may by order make provision as to the procedure to be followed in, or in connection with, proceedings on arbitrations under this Act.

(3) An order under this section may in particular—

(a) provide for the provisions of Schedule 11 to this Act, exclusive of those mentioned in subsection (4) below, to have effect subject to such modifications as may be specified in the order;

(b) prescribe forms for proceedings on arbitrations under this Act which, if used, shall be sufficient;

(c) prescribe the form in which awards in such proceedings are to be made.

(4) An order under this section shall not make provision inconsistent with the following provisions of Schedule 11 to this Act, namely paragraphs 1 to 6, 11 to 13, 14(2), 17, 19, 21, 22, 26 to 29 and 32.

(5) In this section "modifications" includes additions, omissions and amendments.

DEFINITIONS

"agreement": s.96(1).

"contract of tenancy", s.1(5).

GENERAL NOTE

Sched. 11 contains the details of the arbitration code, reproducing Sched. 6 to the 1948 Act with a number of improvements which are referred to in the annotations to Sched. 11. The main constitutional change is the substitution of the President of the Royal Institution of Chartered Surveyors for the Minister as the authority for the appointment of arbitrators and for some consequential matters, such as the fixing of remuneration and the enlargement of the time for making the award.

The agricultural arbitration code has approached nearer to the commercial code in the Arbitration Act 1950 as a result of amendments made by the 1984 Act, such as the power given to the county court to remit an award for the reconsideration of the arbitrator. The Lord Chancellor's power to modify (subject to certain restrictions) the provisions of Sched.

11 introduces a welcome element of flexibility into a code which over the years has seemed resistant to change. Although the agricultural code remains distinctively separate from the commercial, much of the case law which has arisen on the latter in respect of matters of principle is applicable to the former.

Subs. (1)

Arbitration of a single arbitrator. The mandatory requirement of arbitration by a single arbitrator dates from the Agricultural Holdings Act 1906 (which in fact only came into operation when consolidated as the Agricultural Holdings Act 1908). It put an end to the confusion reigning at the end of the nineteenth century between arbitration and valuation, when it was possible to find two "arbitrators" and an "umpire" performing a purely valuation function and, on the other hand, "referees" or "valuers", with an "umpire", engaged strictly on arbitration. The present provision has appeared in all agricultural holdings legislation since 1908 and since then the Arbitration Acts (1889, 1934 and 1950) have always been excluded from agricultural arbitration.

Schedule 11 to this Act. See annotations to this Sched., *post.*

Subs. (2)

The Lord Chancellor may by order. Apart from an order making minor amendments to "the principal rules" (*i.e.* the Agricultural Holdings (England and Wales) Rules 1948 (S.R. & O. 1948 No. 1943)), the Lord Chancellor has made no order so far in respect of arbitration procedure. The minor amendments, which relate mainly to the substitution of the President of the RICS for the Minister as the authority for the appointment of arbitrators, were made by the Agricultural Holdings (England and Wales) Rules (Variation) Order 1985 (S.I. 1985 No. 1829) under s.77 of the 1948 Act as amended by the 1984 Act (Sched. 3, para. 19 and Sched. 5, para. 14). Further orders are expected.

Subs. (3)

Para (a): such modifications as may be specified in the order. This could introduce a welcome flexibility into provisions hitherto alterable only by legislation, *e.g.* as to statements of case.

Para (b): forms for proceedings. Without making the procedure too legalistic, some guidance as to proper pleadings could be an improvement.

Para (c): awards. See note to subs. (2) above as to minor amendments so far made.

Subs. (4)

Shall not make provision inconsistent with. The Lord Chancellor is forbidden to tamper with provisions for the appointment and remuneration of arbitrators, witnesses, enlargement of time for award, compensation in accordance with valid agreements, binding nature of award, duty to give reasons, interest, special case, setting aside award, remission. It is perhaps a pity that he is prevented from substituting a simple appeal for the special case procedure.

Enforcement

85.—(1) Subject to subsection (3) below, where a sum agreed or awarded under this Act to be paid for compensation, costs or otherwise by a landlord or tenant of an agricultural holding is not paid within fourteen days after the time when the payment becomes due, it shall be recoverable, if the county court so orders, as if it were payable under an order of that court.

(2) Where a sum becomes due to a tenant of an agricultural holding in respect of compensation from the landlord, and the landlord fails to discharge his liability within the period of one month from the date on which the sum becomes due, the tenant shall be entitled to obtain from the Minister an order charging the holding with payment of the amount due.

(3) Where the landlord of an agricultural holding is entitled to receive the rents and profits of the holding otherwise than for his own benefit (whether as trustee or in any other character)—

　　(*a*) he shall not be under any liability to pay any sum agreed or awarded under this Act to be paid to the tenant or awarded under this Act to be paid by the landlord, and it shall not be recoverable against him personally, but

(*b*) if he fails to pay any such sum to the tenant for one month after it becomes due, the tenant shall be entitled to obtain from the Minister an order charging the holding with payment of the sum.

DEFINITIONS
"agricultural holding": s.1(1).
"county court", "landlord", "Minister", "tenant": s.96(1).

Subs. (1)
A sum agreed or awarded under this Act. These very general words would cover, *inter alia,* the "additional compensation" payable under s.60(2), and the "early resumption clause" compensation under s.62, as well as the ordinary compensation for improvements and tenant-right. It would also cover the sums payable, following death or retirement, under s.48(5)(*b*) and s.56(3). See *Law Com*: No. 153, p.6 and Minutes and Report of Joint Committee on Consolidation Bills (H.L. 56, H.C. 178) for interesting history of present section.
Compensation, costs or otherwise. This includes rent increased as a result of a rental arbitration. The *ejusdem generis* rule does not apply. See *Grundy* v. *Hewson* [1933] 1 K.B. 787.
Becomes due. If the sum is agreed, it becomes due on the date, if any, specified in the agreement, or, if no date is specified, on the date of the agreement. In the case of an award the arbitrator must, by para. 18 of Sched. 11, fix a day not later than one month after delivery thereof for payment.
Order of that court. This subs. gives the county court jurisdiction whatever the amount. The view taken by Talbot J. in *Horrell* v. *St. John of Bletso (Lord)* [1928] 2 K.B. 616 that the jurisdiction of the High Court was not ousted was doubted by Megaw J. in *Jones* v. *Pembrokeshire County Council* [1967] 1 Q.B. 181 as inconsistent with the principle of *Re Jones and Carter* [1922] 2 Ch. 599 that where the county court is expressly given jurisdiction the jurisdiction of the High Court is *pro tanto* abrogated.

Subs. (2)
In respect of compensation. This is a narrower expression than "compensation, costs or otherwise" in subs. (1) or "any sum agreed or awarded under this Act" in subs. (3). But see s.87(1) as to costs. See s.87 for general provisions in regard to charges and Sched. 14, para. 51 for registration of land charges.

Subs. (3)
Otherwise than for his own benefit. There is some doubt whether a tenant for life of settled land can be regarded as entitled to receive the rents and profits thereof "otherwise than for his own benefit". See article by E. H. Scamell on "The Special Position of Limited Owners of Agricultural Land" in (1951) 15 Conv. (N.S.) 415, 418–419. Ordinary trustees are, however, within s.85(3).
Para. (a): he shall not be under any liability. But he may pay and obtain a charge under s.86(1). A personal action cannot be brought by the tenant against the personal representatives of a deceased landlord who is within the words of s.85(3), the tenant being restricted to the charge: *Edwardson* v. *Townend* (1929) 73 S.J. 109.
Para. (b): an order charging the holding. See s.87(6) as to priority of such a charge. See also first note to subs. (1) above as to sums covered.

Power of landlord to obtain charge on holding

86.—(1) Where the landlord of an agricultural holding—

(*a*) has paid to the tenant of the holding an amount due to him under this Act, or under custom or agreement, or otherwise, in respect of compensation for an improvement falling within section 64(1) or (4) above, for any such matter as is specified in Part II of Schedule 8 to this Act or for disturbance, or

(*b*) has defrayed the cost of the execution by him, in pursuance of a notice served under section 67(5) above, of an improvement specified in Part II of Schedule 7 to this Act, he shall be entitled to obtain from the Minister an order charging the holding or any part of it with repayment of the amount of the compensation or the amount of the cost, as the case may be.

(2) Where there falls to be determined by arbitration under this Act the amount of compensation for an improvement falling within 64(1) or (4) above or for any such matter as is specified in Part II of Schedule 8 to this Act payment of which entitles the landlord to obtain a charge under subsection (1) above, the arbitrator shall, at the request and cost of the landlord, certify—

(*a*) the amount of the compensation, and

(*b*) the term for which the charge may properly be made having regard to the time at which each improvement or matter in respect of which compensation is awarded is to be deemed to be exhausted.

(3) Where the landlord of an agricultural holding is entitled to receive the rents and profits of the holding otherwise than for his own benefit (whether as trustee or in any other character) he shall, either before or after paying to the tenant of the holding any sum agreed or awarded under this Act to be paid to the tenant for compensation or awarded under this Act to be paid by the landlord, be entitled to obtain from the Minister an order charging the holding with repayment of that sum.

(4) The rights conferred by this section on a landlord of an agricultural holding to obtain an order charging land shall not be exercised by trustees for ecclesiastical or charitable purposes except with the approval in writing of the Charity Commissioners.

DEFINITIONS

"agreement", "landlord", "Minister", "tenant": s.96(1).
"agricultural holding": s.1(1).
arbitration under this Act, see s.84 and Sched. 11.

Subs. (1)

The landlord. This will include the executors of a deceased landlord: *cf. Gough* v. *Gough* [1891] 2 Q.B. 665.

Para (a): has paid. Contrast subs. (3) where the charge is obtainable before payment. Note that s.86(1)(*a*) does not cover compensation paid in respect of damage from game, but covers disturbance.

Para. (b): has defrayed. See last note.

Charging the holding. See s.87 for general provisions in regard to charges and Sched. 14, para. 15 for registration of land charges.

Subs. (2)

The term for which the charge may properly be made. See s.87(4), which refers only to the exhaustion of improvements, not tenant-right.

Subs. (3)

Otherwise than for his own benefit. See note to s.85(3) above.

(Whether as trustee or in any other character). cf. *Bennet* v. *Stone* [1902] 1 Ch. 226, where the vendor was in the position of a trustee for the purchaser; in such a case a vendor who paid compensation to the tenant would presumably be able to obtain such a charge.

Either before of after paying. Contrast subs. (1).

General provisions as to charges under this Act on holdings

87.—(1) An order of the Minister under this Act charging an agricultural holding or any part of an agricultural holding with payment or repayment of a sum shall charge it, in addition, with payment of all costs properly incurred in obtaining the charge.

(2) Any such order shall be made in favour of the person obtaining the charge and of his executors, administrators and assigns, and the order shall make such provision as to the payment of interest and the payment

of the sum charged by instalments, and shall contain such directions for giving effect to the charge, as the Minister thinks fit.

(3) In the case of a charge under section 86 above the sum charged shall be a charge on the holding or the part of the holding charged, as the case may be, for the landlord's interest in the holding and for all interests in the holding subsequent to that of the landlord, but so that in any case where the landlord's interest is an interest in a leasehold, the charge shall not extend beyond the interest of the landlord, his executors, administrators and assigns.

(4) In the case of a charge under section 86 above where the landlord is not absolute owner of the holding for his own benefit, no instalment or interest shall be made payable after the time when the improvement in respect of which compensation is paid will, in the opinion of the Minister, have become exhausted.

(5) Notwithstanding anything in any deed, will or other instrument to the contrary, where the estate or interest in an agricultural holding of the landlord is determinable or liable to forfeiture by reason of his creating or suffering any charge on it, that estate or interest shall not be determined or forfeited by reason that the tenant obtains a charge on the holding under section 85(2) above or that the landlord obtains a charge on the holding under section 86 above.

(6) A charge created under section 85 above or section 74 of the Agricultural Holdings Act 1948 shall rank in priority to any other charge, however and whenever created or arising; and charges created under those sections shall, as between themselves, rank in the order of their creation.

(7) Any company now or hereafter incorporated by Parliament, and having power to advance money for the improvement of land, may take an assignment of any charge created under section 85(2) or 86(1) above upon such terms and conditions as may be agreed upon between the company and the person entitled to the charge, and may assign any charge of which they have taken an assignment under this subsection.

(8) Subsection (6) above shall bind the Crown.

DEFINITIONS
"agricultural holding": s.1(1).
"landlord", "Minister": s.96(1).

Subs. (3)
All interests in the holding subsequent to that of the landlord. Thus a life tenant of settled land can obtain a charge which is binding on the remaindermen, but a lessee cannot obtain a charge which will bind the reversioner.

Subs. (4)
Where the landlord is not absolute owner. In practice the Ministry requires an applicant for a charge, who is not absolutely entitled for his own benefit, to give notice of the application to other persons likely to be affected. Such notice has to be served personally or by recorded delivery. There is no official form of charge or form of application for a charge.

Subs. (6)
In priority to any other charge. This would include the Crown's charge for tax: see subs. (8). Charges created under s.85 are land charges registrable under the Land Charges Act 1972, but charges under s.85 rank in the order of creation, not registration.

Subs. (7)
For the improvement of land. The Agricultural Mortgage Corporation and the Lands Improvement Company are within this category.

Power of limited owners to give consents etc.

88. The landlord of an agricultural holding, whatever his estate or interest in it, may, for the purposes of this Act, give any consent, make any agreement or do or have done to him any other act which he might give, make, do or have done to him if he were owner in fee simple or, if his interest is an interest in a leasehold, were absolutely entitled to that leasehold.

DEFINITIONS
    "agreement", "landlord": s.96(1).
    "agricultural holding": s.1(1).

GENERAL NOTE
    For the purposes of this Act. As this is a consolidation Act, the power given by s.88 covers matters arising not only under the 1948 Act as originally enacted but also under the 1968 Act, Part II of the 1976 Act and Sched. 2 to the 1984 Act, so far as consolidated in the present Act. See on this *Law Com:* No. 153 and the Minutes and Report of the Joint Committee on Consolidation Bills (H.L. 56-II and H.C. 178-II).

Power of limited owners to apply capital for improvements

89.—(1) Where under powers conferred by the Settled Land Act 1925 or the Law of Property Act 1925 capital money is applied in or about the execution of any improvement specified in Schedule 7 to this Act no provision shall be made for requiring the money or any part of it to be replaced out of income, and accordingly any such improvement shall be deemed to be an improvement authorised by Part I of Schedule 3 to the Settled Land Act 1925.

    (2) Where under powers conferred by the Universities and College Estates Act 1925 capital money is applied in payment for any improvement specified in Schedule 7 to this Act no provision shall be made for replacing the money out of income unless the Minister requires such provison to be made under section 26(5) of that Act or, in the case of a university or college to which section 2 of the Universities and College Estates Act 1964 applies, it appears to the university or college to be necessary to make such provision under the said section 26(5) as modified by Schedule I to the said Act of 1964.

DEFINITION
    "Minister": s.96(1).

Subs. (1)
    In or about the execution of any improvement. S.89, an apparently simple and straightforward section, in fact conceals some complex and difficult law. The position is briefly as follows. (1) Contrary to a dictum by Joyce J. in *Re De La Warr's Cooden Beach Estate* [1913] 1 Ch. 142, it is now clear from *Re Duke of Wellington's Parliamentary Estates* [1972] Ch. 374 that if a tenant for life pays compensation to farm tenants in respect of improvements at the end of their tenancies he cannot be reimbursed directly by the trustees of the settlement out of capital money which is subject to the trusts of the settlement; *a fortiori* this is so in respect of tenant-right and disturbance. (2) Despite a somewhat wide dictum by Plowman J. in *Re Duke of Wellington* above, even if a tenant for life can obtain a charge under s.86(1), it is not entirely clear that he can require the trustees of the settlement to redeem such a charge out of capital money by virtue of s.73(1)(ii) of the Settled Land Act 1925. (3) Even if a tenant for life could require the trustees to do so, that would by no means close the account between tenant for life and remainderman: see *Re Duke of Manchester's Settlement* [1910] 1 Ch. 106. All that s.89(1) says in fact is that "if capital is spent on such improvements, it cannot be recouped out of income": *per* Harman J. in *Re Wynn* [1955] 1 W.L.R. 940, at p.947. On the question of the payment for repairs out of capital money, see *Re Duke of Northumberland, decd.* [1951] Ch. 203, *Re Lord Brougham and Vaux's Settled Estates* [1954] Ch. 24, *Re Sutherland Settlement Trusts* [1953] Ch. 792, Re

Wynn, *supra, Re Boston's Will Trusts* [1956] Ch. 395 and *Re Pelly's Will Trusts* [1957] Ch. 1, *per* Lord Evershed M.R. at p.12.

Subs. (2)
Unless. This subsection contains a provision in respect of improvements within the Universities and College Estates Acts similar to the above in subs. (1), but with the proviso that the Minister, or (where applicable) the university or college itself, may decide that the money should be replaced out of income.

Estimation of best rent for purposes of Acts and other instruments

90. In estimating the best rent or reservation in the nature of rent of an agricultural holding for the purposes of any Act of Parliament, deed or other instrument, authorising a lease to be made provided that the best rent, or reservation in the nature of rent, is reserved, it shall not be necessary to take into account against the tenant any increase in the value of the holding arising from any improvements made or paid for by him.

DEFINITIONS
"agricultural holding": s.1(1).
"tenant": s.96(1).

GENERAL NOTE
Authorising a lease to be made. S.42(1)(ii) of the Settled Land Act 1925 and s.99 of the Law of Property Act 1925 provide that one of the conditions of the exercise of the leasing powers thereby given is that the lease "shall reserve the best rent that can reasonably be obtained". S.90 seems to have in mind negotiations for a fresh tenancy to the sitting tenant. In the case of rent arbitrations during a tenancy, increases of rental value due to the tenant's improvements are excluded by Sched. 2, para. 2.

Power of Minister to vary Schedules 7, 8 and 10

91.—(1) The Minister may, after consultation with such bodies of persons as appear to him to represent the interests of landlords and tenants of agricultural holdings, by order vary the provisions of Schedules 7, 8 and 10 to this Act.

(2) An order under this section may make such provision as to the operation of this Act in relation to tenancies current when the order takes effect as appears to the Minister to be just having regard to the variation of the said Schedules effected by the order.

DEFINITIONS
"agricultural holding": s.1(1).
"landlord", "Minister", "tenant": s.96(1).

Subs. (1)
Schedules 7, 8 and 10. Under a similar power in the 1948 Act, in relation to Scheds. 3, 4 and 5 to that Act, the Minister varied Sched. 4 three times, by S.I. 1951 No. 2168, S.I. 1978 No. 742 and S.I. 1985 No. 1947. These instruments were revoked by Sched. 15, Part II, to the present Act. Note that the present power of variation extends to the works mentioned in s.231(2) of the Housing Act 1985. The Minister usually consults professional bodies concerned with agricultural land as well as the bodies representing landowners and tenant farmers.

Advisory committee on valuation of improvements and tenant-right matters

92.—(1) The Minister shall appoint a committee to advise him as to the provisions to be included in regulations under section 66(2) above, consisting of such number of persons, having such qualifications, as the Minister thinks expedient, including persons appointed by the Minister as having experience in land agency, farming, estate management and the valuation of tenant-right.

(2) The Minister may pay to the members of the committee such travelling and other allowances as he may with the consent of the Treasury determine.

DEFINITIONS
"Minister": s.96(1).

GENERAL NOTE
Committee
This is the Committee on Agricultural Valuation. The Committee have published four reports, in 1948, 1950, 1969 and 1977 respectively. The reports have been followed by changes based on their recommendations in regard to improvements and tenant-right matters. The reports are of particular interest to professional people concerned with land agency and valuation.

Service of notices

93.—(1) Any notice, request, demand or other instrument under this Act shall be duly given to or served on the person to or on whom it is to be given or served if it is delivered to him, or left at his proper address, or sent to him by post in a registered letter or by the recorded delivery service.

(2) Any such instrument shall be duly given to or served on an incorporated company or body if it is given or served on the secretary or clerk of the company or body.

(3) Any such instrument to be given to or served on a landlord or tenant shall, where an agent or servant is responsible for the control of the management or farming, as the case may be, of the agricultural holding, be duly given or served if given to or served on that agent or servant.

(4) For the purposes of this section and of section 7 of the Interpretation Act 1978 (service by post), the proper address of any person to or on whom any such instrument is to be given or served shall, in the case of the secretary or clerk of an incorporated company or body, be that of the registered or principal office of the company or body, and in any other case be the last known address of the person in question.

(5) Unless or until the tenant of an agricultural holding has received—
    (*a*) notice that the person who before that time was entitled to receive the rents and profits of the holding ("the original landlord") has ceased to be so entitled, and
    (*b*) notice of the name and address of the person who has become entitled to receive the rents and profits,
any notice or other document served upon or delivered to the original landlord by the tenant shall be deemed for the purposes of this Act to have been served upon or delivered to the landlord of the holding.

DEFINITIONS
"agricultural holding": s.1(1).
"landlord", "tenant": s.96(1).

Subs. (1)
Any notice. This, of course, includes a notice to quit. See subs. (5) as to change of landlord without tenant's knowledge. If there is a change of ownership between the giving of the notice and the commencement of arbitration proceedings, the notice will still be operative and enure for the benefit of, or be valid against, the new owner: *Dale* v. *Hatfield Chase Corporation* [1922] 2 K.B. 282. "Any notice" covers notices served under all the provisions consolidated in the Act. See *Law Com.* No. 153, pp.7–8 and Minutes and Report of the Joint Committee on Consolidation Bills (H.L. 56–II; H.C. 178–II).
Left at his proper address. Service by leaving at the proper address must be in a manner which a reasonable person would adopt to bring the document to the notice of the addressee:

Newborough (Lord) v. *Jones* [1975] Ch. (C.A.) (notice slipped under side door normally used held to be well served although it went under linoleum and was not found for many months): *Datnow* v. *Jones* [1985] 2 E.G.L.R. 1, (1985) 275 E.G. 145 (notice put through letter-box in a door in back porch of farmhouse and not actually received by the tenant held left at proper address and well served, but case decided on another issue). Leaving at the proper address would be satisfied by placing it in the letter-box at the place for service, but it would not be satisfied by leaving it with the porter of a block of flats. It must be remembered that at common law a notice is not properly served unless it is received by the person to whom it is addressed. S.93 modifies the law in certain ways.

By post in a registered letter or by the recorded delivery service. A notice sent by *ordinary* post is, however, properly served if it can be shown to have been duly delivered and received: see *per* Megaw J. in *Re Poyser and Mills' Arbitration* [1964] 2 Q.B. 467 at p.479; see also *Sharpley* v. *Manby* [1942] 1 K.B. 217 (decided on the somewhat different wording of s.53 of the Agricultural Holdings Act 1923); *Stylo Shoes Ltd.* v. *Prices Tailors Ltd.* [1960] Ch. 396 (on s.23(1) of the Landlord and Tenant Act 1927, as applied by s.66(4) of the Landlord and Tenant Act 1954). In considering s.93 of the present Act, s.7 of the Interpretation Act 1978 should be kept in mind:

> "Where an Act authorises or requires any document to be served by post (whether the expression 'serve' or the expression 'give' or 'send' or any other expression is used) then, unless the contrary intention appears, the service is deemed to be effected by properly addressing, pre-paying and posting a letter containing the document and, unless the contrary is proved, to have been effected at the time at which the letter would be delivered in the ordinary course of post".

See also R.S.C., Ord. 65, r.5 and the notes thereto. See as to the prima facie rule that, if the notice is properly addressed, prepaid and posted to the proper address of the person to be served, service is deemed to have been effected and also the precise effect of the second limb of s.7 of the 1978 Act, "unless the contrary is proved", etc., the case of *R.* v. *County of London Quarter Sessions Appeals Committee, ex p. Rossi* [1956] 1 Q.B. 682; *Beer* v. *Davies* [1958] 2 Q.B. 187; *Moody* v. *Godstone Rural District Council* [1966] 1 W.L.R. 1085 (somewhat doubtful); *Hewitt* v. *Leicester Corporation* [1969] 1 W.L.R. 855; *White* v. *Weston* [1968] 2 Q.B. 647; *Cooper* v. *Scott-Farnell* [1968] 1 W.L.R. 120; *B. B. Estates Ltd.* v. *Antoniou* (1968) 207 E.G. 245; *Re Berkeley Road (88) London, N.W.9, Rickwood* v. *Turnsek* [1971] Ch. 648; *Hosier* v. *Goodall* [1962] 2 Q.B. 401; *Price* v. *West London Investment Building Society* [1964] 1 W.L.R. 616; *Chiswell* v. *Griffon Land and Estates Ltd.* [1975] 1 W.L.R. 1181 at p.1188 (*per* Megaw J.); *Hallinan (Lady)* v. *Jones* (1984) 272 E.G. 1081 (a county court decision of unusual importance). But note old agricultural holdings case under differently worded legislation, *Van Grutten* v. *Trevenen* [1902] 2 K.B. 82 (in which it was held that a notice to quit was duly served where it was proved that the addressee *refused to sign* for the registered packet containing the notice and it was returned to the post office and never in fact delivered). *Jones* v. *Lewis* (1973) 25 P. & C.R. 375 (C.A.) was not a case on the service of notices but on the need to comply with a prescribed form of notice. *Thorlby* v. *Olivant* [1960] E.G.D. 257 should be noted as a warning (notice served on President of the Family Division when tenancy is not in fact vested in him).

The following cases, although not concerning agricultural holdings, could be helpful: *Bishop (Thomas) Ltd.* v. *Helmville Ltd.* [1972] 1 Q.B. 464; *A/S Cathrineholm* v. *Norequipment Trading Ltd.* [1972] 2 Q.B. 314; *Maltglade Ltd.* v. *St. Albans Rural District Council* [1972] 1 W.L.R. 1230; *Nicholson* v. *Tapp* [1972] 1 W.L.R. 1044; *Yates Building Co. Ltd.* v. *R. J. Pulleyn & Sons (York) Ltd.* (1975) 119 S.J. 370; 237 E.G. 183; *Italica Holdings S.A.* v. *Bayadea* [1985] 1 E.G.L.R. 70, (1983) 273 E.G. 888.

Subs. (3)

Where an agent or servant is responsible. This subsection is useful where, on a tenant's death, there is a doubt about the vesting of the tenancy. Thus where it has been held that a tenant died intestate and his tenancy in fact vested in the President of the Family Division, by virtue of s.9 of the Administration of Estates Act 1925, service on the tenant's relatives who were in occupation and farming the land was effective, as they were regarded as in the position of agents of the President. See *Egerton* v. *Rutter* [1951] 1 K.B. 472; *Harrowby* v. *Snelson* [1951] W.N. 11; *Wilbraham* v. *Colclough* [1952] 1 All E.R. 979. *Cf.* the position at common law: *Jones d. Griffiths* v. *Marsh* (1791) 4 Term Rep. 464; *Doe d. Neville* v. *Dunbar* (1826) Mood. & M. 10. But note *Thorlby* v. *Olivant* [1960] E.G.D. 257, where the notice was served on the President of the Family Division, but, unfortunately, the tenancy was not vested in him. Service on a *duly authorised* agent, although not responsible for the control of the management or farming, is presumably valid; *cf. Hemington* v. *Walter* (1950) 100 L.J. 51 (C.C.). Where there are joint tenants the only safe course is to serve notices on them all.

See *Practice Direction (Central Office: First and Second Class Mail)* [1968] 1 W.L.R. 1489, based on the assumption that first class mail will usually be delivered on the day after posting and second class on the next day but one after posting.

Orders and regulations

94.—(1) Any power to make an order or regulations conferred on the Minister or the Lord Chancellor by any provision of this Act (except section 85 or 86) shall be exercisable by statutory instrument.

(2) Any statutory instrument containing an order or regulations made under any provision of this Act (except section 22(4) or 91 or paragraph 1(2) of Schedule 11) shall be subject to annulment in pursuance of a resolution of either House of Parliament.

(3) No regulations shall be made under section 22(4) above or paragraph 1(2) of Schedule 11 to this Act unless a draft of the regulations has been laid before and approved by a resolution of each House of Parliament.

(4) An order made under section 91 above shall be of no effect unless approved by a resolution of each House of Parliament.

DEFINITIONS
"the Minister": s.96(1).

Subs. (1)
(Except section 85 or 86). The reason for the exception is that the orders mentioned in these sections are orders charging individual holdings with payments, not subordinate legislation of a general import. It would be inappropriate for these orders to be made by statutory instrument. This seems to explain why s.93 of the 1948 Act is absent from the consolidation. The orders corresponding to those mentioned in s.93 (after the amendment made by the 1984 Act, Sched. 3, para. 22) are orders under ss.85 and 86 of the present Act.

Subs. (2)
(Except section 22(4) or 91 or paragraph 1(2) of Schedule 11.) The general mass of statutory instruments are subject to negative resolution in Parliament, *i.e.* they become effective *unless* either House goes to the trouble of resolving that they be annulled. In the cases here excepted, regs. under s.22(4) and para. 1(2) of Sched. 11 relate to prescribed fees payable on applications to the President of the R.I.C.S. in connection with the making of a record and the appointment of an arbitrator, while orders under s.91 vary provisions in an Act of Parliament, Scheds. 7, 8 or 10 of the present Act. In these exceptional cases it is considered that the *affirmative* approval of each House is necessary. See subss. (3) and (4).

Subs. (3)
Unless a draft of the regulations. For different forms of the affirmative resolution procedure, see *Erskine May's Parliamentary Practice* (20th ed.), pp.616–617. In some cases, of which those mentioned in subs. (3) are examples, a draft of the regulations has to be laid before Parliament for approval by resolution.

Subs. (4)
An order. Here the order has to be approved by affirmative resolution, but the procedure does not require a *draft* to be laid before Parliament. According to *Erskine May, supra,* there is no substantial difference between these two affirmative resolution procedures. The main difference is between the affirmative and the negative resolution procedures.

Crown land

95.—(1) The provisions of this Act, except section 11 above, shall apply to land belonging to Her Majesty in right of the Crown or the Duchy of Lancaster and to land belonging to the Duchy of Cornwall, subject in either case to such modifications as may be prescribed.

(2) For the purposes of this Act—

    (*a*) as respects land belonging to Her Majesty in right of the Crown, the Crown Estate Commissioners or other the proper officer or body having charge of the land for the time being, or, if there is no such officer or body, such person as Her Majesty may appoint in writing under the Royal Sign Manual, shall represent Her Majesty and shall be deemed to be the landlord,

(b) as respects land belonging to Her Majesty in right of the Duchy of Lancaster, the Chancellor of the Duchy shall represent Her Majesty and shall be deemed to be the landlord,

(c) as respects land belonging to the Duchy of Cornwall, such person as the Duke of Cornwall or other the possessor for the time being of the Duchy of Cornwall appoints shall represent the Duke of Cornwall or other the possessor aforesaid, and shall be deemed to be the landlord and may do any act or thing which a landlord is authorised or required to do under this Act.

(3) Without prejudice to subsection (1) above it is hereby declared that the provisions of this Act, except section 11 above, apply to land notwithstanding that the interest of the landlord or tenant is held on behalf of Her Majesty for the purposes of any government department; but those provisions shall, in their application to any land in which an interest is so held, have effect subject to such modifications as may be prescribed.

(4) Any compensation payable under this Act by the Chancellor of the Duchy of Lancaster for long-term improvements shall, and any compensation so payable under section 60(2)(b) or 62 above may, be raised and paid as an expense incurred in improvement of land belonging to Her Majesty in right of the Duchy within section 25 of the Duchy of Lancaster Act 1817; and any compensation so payable under this Act for short-term improvements and tenant-right matters shall be paid out of the annual revenues of the Duchy.

(5) Any compensation payable under this Act by the Duke of Cornwall or other the possessor for the time being of the Duchy of Cornwall for long-term improvements shall, and any compensation so payable under section 60(2)(b) or 62 above may, be paid and advances therefor made in the manner and subject to the provisions of section 8 of the Duchy of Cornwall Management Act 1863 with respect to improvements of land mentioned in that section.

(6) Nothing in subsection (5) above shall be taken as prejudicing the operation of the Duchy of Cornwall Management Act 1982.

(7) In this section—

"long-term improvements" means relevant improvements specified in Schedule 7 to this Act, improvements falling within section 64(4) above and improvements specified in Schedule 10 to this Act;

"short-term improvements and tenant-right matters" means relevant improvements specified in Part I of Schedule 8 to this Act and such matters as are specified in Part II of that Schedule.

DEFINITIONS
"landlord", "prescribed", "tenant": s.96(1).

Subss. (1), (3)
Except section 11 above. Neither the Crown estate nor land held for the purposes of government departments is subject to directions by an agricultural land tribunal for the provision, alteration or repair of fixed equipment under s.11.
As may be prescribed. No regulations have been made at date of going to press.

Subs. (5)
With respect to improvements. There are differences between the provisions affecting the two royal duchies which can only be explained historically by the development of different parts of the royal demesne.

Interpretation

96.—(1) In this Act, unless the context otherwise requires—

"agreement" includes an agreement arrived at by means of valuation or otherwise, and "agreed" has a corresponding meaning;

"agricultural holding" has the meaning given by section 1 above;

"agricultural land" has the meaning given by section 1 above;

"agricultural unit" means land which is an agricultural unit for the purposes of the Agriculture Act 1947;

"agriculture" includes horticulture, fruit growing, seed growing, dairy farming and livestock breeding and keeping, the use of land as grazing land, meadow land, osier land, market gardens and nursery grounds, and the use of land for woodlands where that use is ancillary to the farming of land for other agricultural purposes, and "agricultural" shall be construed accordingly;

"building" includes any part of a building;

"Case A", "Case B" (and so on) refer severally to the Cases set out and so named in Part I of Schedule 3 to this Act;

"contract of tenancy" has the meaning given by section 1 above;

"county court", in relation to an agricultural holding, means the county court within the district in which the holding or the larger part of the holding is situated;

"fixed equipment" includes any building or structure affixed to land and any works on, in, over or under land, and also includes anything grown on land for a purpose other than use after severance from the land, consumption of the thing grown or of its produce, or amenity, and any reference to fixed equipment on land shall be construed accordingly;

"landlord" means any person for the time being entitled to receive the rents and profits of any land;

"livestock" includes any creature kept for the production of food, wool, skins, or fur or for the purpose of its use in the farming of land or the carrying on in relation to land of any agricultural activity;

"local government funds" means, in relation to any grant in respect of an improvement executed by the landlord or tenant of an agricultural holding, the funds of any body which, under or by virtue of any enactment, has power to make grants in respect of improvements of the description in question within any particular area (whether or not it is a local authority for that area);

"the Minister" means—

(*a*) in relation to England, the Minister of Agriculture, Fisheries and Food, and

(*b*) in relation to Wales, the Secretary of State;

"the model clauses" has the meaning given by section 7 above;

"pasture" includes meadow;

"prescribed" means prescribed by the Minister by regulations;

"relevant improvement" has the meaning given by section 64(2) above;

"tenant" means the holder of land under a contract of tenancy, and includes the executors, administrators, assigns, or trustee in bankruptcy of a tenant, or other person deriving title from a tenant;

"termination", in relation to a tenancy, means the cesser of the contract of tenancy by reason of effluxion of time or from any other cause;

"the Tribunal" means an Agricultural Land Tribunal established under Part V of the Agriculture Act 1947.

(2) For the purposes of this Act, a tenant is insolvent if—

(a) he has been adjudged bankrupt or has made a composition or arrangement with his creditors, or

(b) where the tenant is a body corporate, a winding-up order has been made with respect to it or a resolution for voluntary winding-up has been passed with respect to it (other than a resolution passed solely for the purposes of its reconstruction or of its amalgamation with another body corporate).

(3) Sections 10 and 11 of the Agriculture Act 1947 (which specify the circumstances in which an owner of agricultural land is deemed for the purposes of that Act to fulfil his responsibilities to manage the land in accordance with the rules of good estate management and an occupier of such land is deemed for those purposes to fulfil his responsibilities to farm it in accordance with the rules of good husbandry) shall apply for the purposes of this Act.

(4) References in this Act to the farming of land include references to the carrying on in relation to the land of any agricultural activity.

(5) References in this Act to the use of land for agriculture include, in relation to land forming part of an agricultural unit, references to any use of the land in connection with the farming of the unit.

(6) The designations of landlord and tenant shall continue to apply to the parties until the conclusion of any proceedings taken under or in pursuance of this Act in respect of compensation.

GENERAL NOTE

For reasons of space and to avoid duplication it is not proposed to annotate the interpretation section in detail. Most of the definitions have been mentioned or discussed in the preceding pages. A note on the definition of "agriculture" may, however, be helpful in view of its importance.

"Agriculture". "Agriculture" is defined extensively. The expression "includes" indicates that "agriculture" means what it would ordinarily mean and also means all the things which are mentioned after the word "includes" although they, or some of them, are not what "agriculture" would normally mean. Thus arable farming is not specifically mentioned, but it is clearly part of the ordinary meaning of "agriculture". The use of the word "other" before "agricultural purposes" may be technically superfluous: see *Secretary of State for Wales* v. *Pugh* (1970) 120 L.J. 357 (C.C.). The reference in the definition to "livestock breeding and keeping" incorporates the definition of "livestock", which is also extensively defined lower down in s.96. In *Minister of Agriculture* v. *Appleton* [1970] 1 Q.B. 221, under similar definitions in a different statute, it was held that the breeding of cats and dogs for research was not within the words "livestock breeding and keeping", although the definitions of both "agriculture" and "livestock" are extensive. "Livestock breeding and keeping" must be confined to activities which can be brought within the general meaning of "agriculture". It is now well established that, although the keeping of horses used for recreation does not come within the definition of "agriculture", the use of land as grazing land for such "non-agricultural" horses does satisfy the definition: *Rutherford* v. *Maurer* [1962] 1 Q.B. 16; *McClinton* v. *McFall* (1974) 232 E.G. 707. The grazing must, however, be the predominant or substantial use: *cf. Sykes* v. *Secretary of State for the Environment* (1981) 257 E.G. 821 (*incidental* grazing in paddocks used for schooling horses, training young riders, or awaiting gymkhana events not sufficient). And, although the grazing of stud horses is within the definition, the running of the stud farm itself is not: *McClinton* v. *McFall, supra, Re Joel's Lease, Berwick* v. *Baird* [1930] 2 Ch. 359; nor is the use of land for gallops, *i.e.* for the exercise of racehorses over it; *Bracey* v. *Read* [1963] Ch. 88. The keeping of pheasants for sport is not "agriculture": *Glendyne (Lord)* v. *Rapley* [1978] 1 W.L.R. 661; *Reeve* v. *Atterby* [1978] C.L.Y. 73; *Normanton (Earl)* v. *Giles* [1980] 1 W.L.R. 28. Fish farming has given rise to divergent views according to whether the subject-matter is the law of rating or the law of agricultural holdings. For *rating* purposes, whether in England and Wales or Scotland, fish are not livestock, a divergence from Scottish law having been removed by the decision of the Court of Appeal in *Creswell (Valuation Officer)* v. *British Oxygen Co. Ltd.* [1930] 1 W.L.R. 1556. So far as agricultural holdings are concerned, dicta by Lord Parker C.J. in

Belmont Farm Ltd. v. *Minister of Housing and Local Government* (1962) 13 P. & C.R. 47 and *Minister of Agriculture, Fisheries and Food* v. *Appleton* [1970] 1 Q.B. 221 are in favour of the view that fish are "livestock". They appear to come within the extensive part of the definition in s.96(1) which covers "any creature kept for the production of food, wool, skins, or fur or for the purpose of its use in the farming of land or the carrying on in relation to land of any agricultural activity". Mink may also be "livestock" within this definition, although not so for rating purposes: *Jones (Valuation Officer)* v. *Davies* (1977) 244 E.G. 897 (Lands Trib.).

Saving for other rights etc.

97. Subject to sections 15(5) and 83(1) above in particular, and to any other provision of this Act which otherwise expressly provides, nothing in this Act shall prejudicially affect any power, right or remedy of a landlord, tenant or other person vested in or exercisable by him by virtue of any other Act or law or under any custom of the country or otherwise, in respect of a contract of tenancy or other contract, or of any improvements, deteriorations, waste, emblements, tillages, away-going crops, fixtures, tax, rate, tithe rentcharge, rent or other thing.

DEFINITIONS
  "contract of tenancy": s.1(5).
  "landlord", "tenant": s.96(1).

GENERAL NOTE
  The scope of this section is not so wide as might appear at first sight. It is one of those sections which are frequently invoked, but with infrequent success. For successful invocations of its predecessor (s.101 of the 1948 Act), see *Goldsack* v. *Shore* [1950] 1 K.B. 708; *Kent* v. *Conniff* [1953] 1 Q.B. 361.

Subs. (1)
  Subject to sections 15(5) and 83(1). S.15(5) cuts down the landlord's remedies to those mentioned in the subsection where the tenant has exercised his freedom of cropping or disposal in such a manner as to injure or deteriorate, or to be likely to injure or deteriorate the holding. S.83(1) restricts the remedy available for claims on the termination of a tenancy to arbitration.
  Any custom of the country. This must be read subject to s.77, which abolishes customary rights to *compensation,* subject to certain exceptions. Customary rights, not being rights to compensation, are preserved. These would include, *e.g.* customs of holdover or pre-entry.
  Waste. Waste, as a tort, is unaffected by the Act's restrictions on contractual claims.
  Away-going crops. A customary right to take an away-going crop, in the sense of physical removal, would remain exercisable, subject to any agreement to the contrary. A customary right to *compensation* on an away-going crop basis is, however, abolished by s.77, this being a "provision of this Act which otherwise expressly provides".
  Fixtures. A customary right to remove fixtures free from the statutory restrictions contained in s.10 is thus preserved.

Application of Act to old tenancies etc.

98.—(1) Subject to sections 4 and 34 above, to the provisions of Schedule 12 to this Act and to any other provision to the contrary, this Act applies in relation to tenancies of agricultural holdings whenever created, agreements whenever made and other things whenever done.

(2) The provisions of this Act shall apply in relation to tenancies of agricultural holdings granted or agreed to be granted, agreements made and things done before the dates specified in paragraphs 1 to 5 and 10 of Schedule 12 to this Act (being dates no later than 1st March 1948) subject to the modifications there specified.

(3) Paragraphs 6 to 9 of Schedule 12 to this Act, which make provision with respect to compensation for tenant-right matters in relation to tenants of agricultural holdings who entered into occupation before the dates

specified in those paragraphs (being dates no later than 31st December 1951), shall have effect.

Subs. (1)
    This Act applies. The general rule that the Act applies irrespective of the time when acts take place or events occur is subject to certain exceptions. The main provisions where time is a relevant factor are set out in Sched. 12.

Transitional provisions and savings

99.—(1) Schedule 13 to this Act, which excepts from the operation of this Act certain cases current at the commencement of this Act and contains other transitional provisions and savings, shall have effect.

(2) The re-enactment in paragraphs 6 to 8 of Schedule 12 to this Act of provisions contained in the Agricultural Holdings Act (Variation of Fourth Schedule) Order 1951 shall be without prejudice to the validity of those provisions; and any question as to the validity of any of those provisions shall be determined as if the re-enacting provisions of this Act were contained in a statutory instrument made under the powers under which the original provision was made.

(3) Nothing in this Act (except paragraph 8 of Schedule 13) shall be taken as prejudicing the operation of sections 16 and 17 of the Interpretation Act 1978 (which relate to the effect of repeals).

GENERAL NOTE
    Sched. 13, to which this section gives effect, is likely to be for a time of considerable importance in practice and should be consulted in conjunction with the section which is to form the basis of any proposed action in case a transitional provision is applicable.

Subs. (2)
    Agricultural Holdings Act (Variation of Fourth Schedule) Order 1951. This Order (S.I. 1951 No. 2168) is formally revoked by Part II of Sched. 15. The order added to tenant-right, matters "the acclimatisation, hefting or settlement of hill sheep on hill land", which is now in para. 10 of Sched. 8. The special rules for election are set out in paras. 6 to 8 of Sched. 12. The basis of compensation has been amended from time to time.

Consequential amendments

100. Schedule 14 to this Act shall have effect.

Repeals and revocations

101.—(1) The enactments specified in Part I of Schedule 15 to this Act are hereby repealed to the extent specified in the third column of that Schedule.

(2) The instruments specified in Part II of Schedule 15 to this Act are hereby revoked to the extent specified in the third column of that Schedule.

Citation, commencement and extent

102.—(1) This Act may be cited as the Agricultural Holdings Act 1986.

(2) This Act shall come into force at the end of the period of three months beginning with the day on which it is passed.

(3) Subject to subsection (4) below, this Act extends to England and Wales only.

(4) Subject to subsection (5) below and to paragraph 26(6) of Schedule 14 to this Act, the amendment or repeal by this Act of an enactment which extends to Scotland or Northern Ireland shall also extend there.

(5) Subsection (4) above does not apply to the amendment or repeal by this Act of section 9 of the Hill Farming Act 1946, section 48(4) of the Agriculture Act 1967 or an enactment contained in the Agriculture (Miscellaneous Provisions) Act 1968.

GENERAL NOTE
Subs. (2)
Three months. The Act was passed on March 18, 1986 and comes into force on June 18, 1986.

SCHEDULES

Section 6   SCHEDULE 1

MATTERS FOR WHICH PROVISION IS TO BE MADE IN WRITTEN TENANCY AGREEMENTS

1. The names of the parties.
2. Particulars of the holding with sufficient description, by reference to a map or plan, of the fields and other parcels of land comprised in the holding to identify its extent.
3. The term or terms for which the holding or different parts of it is or are agreed to be let.
4. The rent reserved and the dates on which it is payable.
5. The incidence of the liability for rates (including drainage rates).
6. A covenant by the tenant in the event of the destruction by fire of harvested crops grown on the holding for consumption on it to return to the holding the full equivalent manurial value of the crops destroyed, in so far as the return of that value is required for the fulfilment of his responsibilities to farm in accordance with the rules of good husbandry.
7. A covenant by the tenant (except where the interest of the tenant is held for the purposes of a government department or where the tenant has made provision approved by the Minister in lieu of such insurance) to insure against damage by fire all dead stock on the holding and all harvested crops grown on the holding for consumption on it.
8. A power for the landlord to re-enter on the holding in the event of the tenant not performing his obligations under the agreement.
9. A covenant by the tenant not to assign, sub-let or part with possession of the holding or any part of it without the landlord's consent in writing.

DEFINITIONS
"landlord", "the Minister", "tenant": s.96(1).

GENERAL NOTE
The old paras. 6 and 7 in this Schedule (maintenance and repair of fixed equipment and landlord's covenant to reinstate or replace buildings damaged by fire and to insure against such damage) were deleted by the 1984 Act (See Sched. 3, para. 24 and Sched. 4). These paras were largely covered by provisions in the Sched. to the Agriculture (Maintenance, Repair and Insurance of Fixed Equipment) Regulations 1973 (S.I. 1973 No. 1473). It was in any case preferable to leave these matters to be dealt with in regulations, which can be amended without legislation.

Para. 6
Destruction by fire of harvested crops. As a result of the decision in *Re Hull and Meux (Lady)* [1905] 1 K.B. 588, it became a common practice to require a tenant to covenant to insure his hay and straw against fire and to replace the manurial value of any hay or straw destroyed by fire. In that case the tenant had covenanted to stack and consume on the holding all hay and straw produced thereon, and to carry out and spread on the fields the manure arising therefrom. Some stacks were accidentally destroyed by fire during the tenancy and it was held that the landlord was not entitled to compensation for the resulting loss of manurial value, the covenant applying only to things in existence and there being no breach on the tenant's part. See, however, reg. 4(2) of the Agriculture (Calculation of Value

for Compensation) Regulations 1978 (S.I. 1978 No. 809), which requires a deduction to be made from the tenant's compensation when hay, fodder crops, straw, roots, manure or compost are, *inter alia,* destroyed by fire.

Para. 8

A power for the landlord to re-enter. This refers to the ordinary type of forfeiture clause, although it does not specify as a cause of forfeiture the tenant's insolvency. It should be remembered that a forfeiture clause should provide for a notice of re-entry of sufficient length to enable a tenant to exercise a possible right under s.60(6)(*a*) or s.70(2)(*a*). Otherwise the clause will be void: *Parry* v. *Million Pigs Ltd.* (1980) 260 E.G. 281, following the principle of *Re Disraeli Agreement* [1939] Ch. 382 and *Coates* v. *Diment* [1951] 1 All E.R. 890.

Para. 9

Not to assign, sublet or part with possession. This important matter was for a long time lacking from Sched. 1, but was added first by s.17 of the Agriculture (Miscellaneous Provisions) Act 1976. See also s.6(5) of the present Act for machinery designed to prevent an assignment from taking place pending the outcome of an arbitration under s.6.

Section 12   SCHEDULE 2

ARBITRATION OF RENT: PROVISIONS SUPPLEMENTARY TO SECTION 12

Amount of rent

1.—(1) For the purposes of section 12 of this Act, the rent properly payable in respect of a holding shall be the rent at which the holding might reasonably be expected to be let by a prudent and willing landlord to a prudent and willing tenant, taking into account (subject to sub-paragraph (3) and paragraphs 2 and 3 below) all relevant factors, including (in every case) the terms of the tenancy (including those relating to rent), the character and situation of the holding (including the locality in which it is situated), the productive capacity of the holding and its related earning capacity, and the current level of rents for comparable lettings, as determined in accordance with sub-paragraph (3) below.

(2) In sub-paragraph (1) above, in relation to the holding—

    (*a*) "productive capacity" means the productive capacity of the holding (taking into account fixed equipment and any other available facilities on the holding) on the assumption that it is in the occupation of a competent tenant practising a system of farming suitable to the holding, and

    (*b*) "related earning capacity" means the extent to which, in the light of that productive capacity, a competent tenant practising such a system of farming could reasonably be expected to profit from farming the holding.

(3) In determining for the purposes of that sub-paragraph the current level of rents for comparable lettings, the arbitrator shall take into account any available evidence with respect to the rents (whether fixed by agreement between the parties or by arbitration under this Act) which are, or (in view of rents currently being tendered) are likely to become, payable in respect of tenancies of comparable agricultural holdings on terms (other than terms fixing the rent payable) similar to those of the tenancy under consideration, but shall disregard—

    (*a*) any element of the rents in question which is due to an appreciable scarcity of comparable holdings available for letting on such terms compared with the number of persons seeking to become tenants of such holdings on such terms,

    (*b*) any element of those rents which is due to the fact that the tenant of, or a person tendering for, any comparable holding is in occupation of other land in the vicinity of that holding that may conveniently be occupied together with that holding, and

    (*c*) any effect on those rents which is due to any allowances or reductions made in consideration of the charging of premiums.

2.—(1) On a reference under section 12 of this Act, the arbitrator shall disregard any increase in the rental value of the holding which is due to—

    (*a*) tenant's improvements or fixed equipment other than improvements executed or equipment provided under an obligation imposed on the tenant by the terms of his contract of tenancy, and

    (*b*) landlord's improvements, in so far as the landlord has received or will receive grants out of money provided by Parliament or local government funds in respect of the execution of those improvements.

(2) In this paragraph—

(*a*) "tenant's improvements" means any improvements which have been executed on the holding, in so far as they were executed wholly or partly at the expense of the tenant (whether or not that expense has been or will be reimbursed by a grant out of money provided by Parliament or local government funds) without any equivalent allowance or benefit made or given by the landlord in consideration of their execution,

(*b*) "tenant's fixed equipment" means fixed equipment provided by the tenant, and

(*c*) "landlord's improvements" means improvements executed on the holding by the landlord.

(3) Where the tenant has held a previous tenancy of the holding, then—

(*a*) in the definition of "tenant's improvements" in sub-paragraph (2)(*a*) above, the reference to any such improvements as are there mentioned shall extend to improvements executed during that tenancy, and

(*b*) in the definition of "tenant's fixed equipment" in sub-paragraph (2)(*b*), the reference to such equipment as is there mentioned shall extend to equipment provided during that tenancy,

excluding, however, any improvement or fixed equipment so executed or provided, in respect of which the tenant received any compensation on the termination of that (or any other) tenancy.

(4) For the purposes of sub-paragraph (2)(*a*) above, the continuous adoption by the tenant of a system of farming more beneficial to the holding—

(*a*) than the system of farming required by the contract of tenancy, or

(*b*) in so far as no system is so required, than the system of farming normally practised on comparable agricultural holdings,

shall be treated as an improvement executed at his expense.

3. On a reference under section 12 of this Act the arbitrator—

(*a*) shall disregard any effect on the rent of the fact that the tenant who is a party to the arbitration is in occupation of the holding, and

(*b*) shall not fix the rent at a lower amount by reason of any dilapidation or deterioration of, or damage to, buildings or land caused or permitted by the tenant.

Frequency of arbitrations under section 12

4.—(1) Subject to the following provisions of this Schedule, a demand for arbitration shall not be effective for the purposes of section 12 of this Act if the next termination date following the date of the demand falls earlier than the end of three years from any of the following dates, that is to say—

(*a*) the commencement of the tenancy, or

(*b*) the date as from which there took effect a previous increase or reduction of rent (whether made under that section or otherwise), or

(*c*) the date as from which there took effect a previous direction of an arbitrator under that section that the rent should continue unchanged.

(2) The following shall be disregarded for the purposes of sub-paragraph (1)(*b*) above—

(*a*) an increase or reduction of rent under section 6(3) or 8(4) of this Act;

(*b*) an increase of rent under subsection (1) of section 13 of this Act or such an increase as is referred to in subsection (3) of that section, or any reduction of rent agreed between the landlord and the tenant of the holding in consequence of any change in the fixed equipment provided on the holding by the landlord;

(*c*) a reduction of rent under section 33 of this Act.

5.—(1) This paragraph applies in any case where a tenancy of an agricultural holding ("the new holding") commences under a contract of tenancy between—

(*a*) a person who immediately before the date of the commencement of the tenancy was entitled to a severed part of the reversionary estate in an agricultural holding ("the original holding") in which the new holding was then comprised, and

(*b*) the person who immediately before that date was the tenant of the original holding.

and where the rent payable in respect of the new holding at the commencement of the tenancy of that holding represents merely the appropriate portion of the rent payable in respect of the original holding immediately before the commencement of that tenancy.

(2) In any case to which this paragraph applies—

(*a*) paragraph (*a*) of sub-paragraph (1) of paragraph 4 above shall be read as referring to the commencement of the tenancy of the original holding, and

(*b*) references to rent in paragraphs (*b*) and (*c*) of that sub-paragraph shall be read as references to the rent payable in respect of the original holding, until the first occasion following the commencement of the tenancy of the new holding on which any such increase or reduction of, or direction with respect to, the rent of the new holding as is mentioned in paragraph (*b*) or (*c*) takes effect.

6. Where under an agreement between the landlord and the tenant of the holding (not being an agreement expressed to take effect as a new contract of tenancy between the parties) provision is made for adjustment of the boundaries of the holding or for any other variation of the terms of the tenancy, exclusive of those relating to rent, then, unless the agreement otherwise provides—

(*a*) that provision shall for the purposes of sub-paragraph (1) of paragraph 4 above be treated as not operating to terminate the tenancy, and accordingly as not resulting in the commencement of a new contract of tenancy between the parties, and

(*b*) any increase or reduction of rent solely attributable to any such adjustment or variation as aforesaid shall be disregarded for the purposes of paragraph (*b*) of that sub-paragraph.

GENERAL NOTE
Sched. 2 contains the details of the rent formula which is introduced by s.12. It embodies the substantial amendments made by the 1984 Act.

Para. 1(1)
The rent properly payable. It is clear from s.12 that there are two dates of importance; the "date of the reference", which is the valuation date, and the "next termination date", which is the date as from which the rent determined becomes payable. The "date of the reference" (the same expression as used in the 1948 Act) is the date when the arbitrator is effectively appointed. An arbitrator appointed by the President is effectively appointed when the President executes the instrument of appointment (Sched. 11, para. 31). An arbitrator appointed by agreement of the parties is not effectively appointed until the parties are notified of the acceptance. Sched. 11, para. 31 gives statutory effect to the view taken in *University College, Oxford* v. *Durdy* [1982] Ch 413, (1981) 262 E.G. 338 (CA) as to the time of effective appointment by the Minister (now by the President) but the suggested "benevolent construction that time should not run against the parties until they receive notice is not adopted in the statute.

Might reasonably be expected to be let. It should be noted that it is the expectations which are to be reasonable, not the rent.

By a prudent and willing landlord to a prudent and willing tenant. The word "prudent" was added by the 1984 Act (s.1) to "willing". It is doubtful whether it adds anything of substance as the "willing" landlord or tenant was reasonably expected to be prudent rather than reckless or irresponsible. The 1948 Act assumed the holding to be let by a willing landlord to a willing tenant "in the open market". There is no reference to the open market in Sched. 2, but it is submitted that the conception of the open market is necessarily implied, for three reasons, (1) the reasonable expectations of informed people are based on some market knowledge or experience, even if slight and second-hand, (2) the use of rents of comparable holdings as persuasive evidence points to the idea of a market, and (3) the instruction to disregard scarcity in the rents of "comparables" assumes an ability to perceive an actual market distorted by the vice of scarcity and an ability to make appropriate deductions therefrom so as to arrive at a hypothetical market from which scarcity has been eliminated.

All relevant factors including. Thus "all relevant factors" has its normal meaning and, without prejudice to that, covers the specific factors enumerated. Some at least of the latter would ordinarily be taken into account by a competent arbitrator without any express direction to do so.

The productive capacity of the holding and its related earning capacity. See note on productive capacity below.

The current level of rents for comparable lettings. This is developed in subpara. (3) by reference to evidence and matters to be disregarded. The existence of a "level of rents for comparable lettings" seems inevitably to imply a market, as judgments based on price comparison are of the essence of a market.

Para. 1(2)
Productive capacity. Note the assumption as to a competent tenant practising a suitable system. The tenant and the system are hypothetical for the purpose of the formula, but the fixed equipment is actual. The actual tenant may not be competent and he may not be practising a suitable system.

Related earning capacity. Productive capacity by itself is not a direct guide to profit, but "related earning capacity" suggests the profit which a competent tenant, doing his best with the fixed equipment at his disposal (which may not be sufficient or sufficiently up to date) and devising a system of farming which is at least suitable for the holding (even if not the ideal system), may be reasonably expected to make. This is only one factor in the determination of the rent; there is no short cut to the rent by some conclusive division of profit. Earnings from some non-agricultural activity practised by farmers, such as provision for caravan sites or catering for tourism, are not within "related earning capacity" as defined, but are within the broader category of "relevant factors" in sub-para. (1). There are difficulties about relating rent to profitability which go beyond legal analysis. For example, does rent enter into cost of production at all? Ricardo in his *Principles of Political Economy,* Chap. II said:

"Corn is not high because a rent is paid, but a rent is paid because corn is high . . .

rent does not and cannot enter in the least degree as a component part of its price."
But it is perhaps unlikely that an arbitrator will receive a submission based on the marginal theory of value.

Para. 1(3)

Any available evidence. It is clear from sub-para. (1) that a most important factor in judging the rent properly payable is comparison with the rents of other holdings. Sub-para. (3) mentions different species of evidence of such rents which are to be taken into account and also certain of the matters to be disregarded. Evidence may be of rents fixed by agreement, rents fixed by arbitration and rents not fixed but currently being tendered. Sub-para. (1) has already mentioned as relevant (what is obvious) the terms of the subject tenancy and the character and situation of the subject holding. Sub-para. (3) indicates that the holdings to be compared must be held on terms broadly similar (clearly it does not mean identical) to those of the subject holding. Terms *fixing* the rent payable are excluded as these may be related to idiosyncratic features of the particular contract of tenancy. It is part of the valuer's art to know when another holding is "comparable" and to make such allowance as is necessary for differences from the subject holding in physical character and situation and in the terms of the tenancy. In this part of Sched. 2 Parliament appears to be verging on an attempt to teach valuers and arbitrators their jobs.

But shall disregard. The "disregards" in this sub-para. are in relation to the rents of comparable holdings. There are further disregards in paras 2 and 3 of Sched. 2 for different reasons, *e.g.* an increase in the rental value of the subject holding itself which is due to tenant's improvements.

An appreciable scarcity of comparable holdings. This is in terms an instruction to the arbitrator to disregard the element of scarcity in the rents of comparable holdings and it is immediately evident (and has not escaped comment) that there is no express instruction to disregard scarcity in the rent of the subject holding itself. Does this mean, as literal interpretations have suggested, that in the case of the subject holding scarcity should be accepted as an element in rental value? It is submitted that the answer is no, for the following reasons. (1) It would be contrary to the decision of the House of Lords in *Western Heritable Investment Co. Ltd.* v. *Husband* [1983] 2 A.C. 849 on s.42(2) of the Rent (Scotland) Act 1971, which is similar to s.70(2) of the Rent Act 1977, and in principle the same as the present para. (3)(*a*), although the formula in the Rent Acts is perhaps more scientifically expressed. (2) The literal interpretation fails to appreciate that scarcity in the subject holding can only be *defined* in terms of the demand and supply for similar holdings; scarcity is not a characteristic inherent in the subject holding in itself, but is an attribute which it derives from the relationship between such demand and supply. (3) It is difficult to see what conceivable point there could be in eliminating scarcity from the rents of comparables other than to arrive at a rent for the subject holding from which scarcity was likewise eliminated: *cf. per* Lloyd J. in *99 Bishopsgate Ltd.* v. *Prudential Assurance Co. Ltd.* (1984) 270 E.G. 950 at p.952 in relation to comparables and vacant possession (decision affirmed by CA, (1985) 273 E.G. 984. It will be noted that any "appreciable" scarcity is to be eliminated, which is stronger than the Rent Acts' "substantial" scarcity. Scarcity value should be distinguished from special amenity value, which is not to be eliminated: *cf. Metropolitan Property Holdings* v. *Finegold* [1975] 1 W.L.R. 349 at p. 352.

Occupation of other land in the vicinity. This refers to what valuers know as "marriage value" and the arbitrator is directed to disregard one kind of marriage value, namely, the enhancement of the rent of a comparable holding due to the fact that the tenant thereof occupies other land in the vicinity which might conveniently be occupied with that holding. The direction even extends to a person tendering for the holding as well as to the tenant of it, but the significance of this is doubtful. A question of some difficulty, and one which might lead to litigation, arises here. Does the direction to eliminate marriage value, which in terms applies only to the rents of comparable holdings, apply also to the rent of the subject holding? There is obviously a fairly strong argument, based on consistency with the interpretation given above to the disregard of scarcity, that marriage value should be disregarded in the case of the subject holding also. It might be said, what conceivable point would there be in disregarding marriage value in the case of the comparables if it is not to arrive at a rent which is free from this element in the case of the subject holding? Against this view it could be argued that in the case of marriage value a literal interpretation of sub-para. (3)(*b*) produces a sensible result, namely, the avoidance of confusion which the use of rents of comparables reflecting a wide diversity of "marriages", with pieces of land of varying sizes and values, would produce. In other words, the object is simply to ensure that "comparables" are truly comparable. Besides, the elimination of scarcity from the rent of the subject holding has a public policy justification which the elimination of marriage value does not appear to have. Again, the argument based on the need to define scarcity by reference to the relationship between the demand and supply of similar holdings does not apply. Only a court can decide between the possible constructions.

Premiums. The meaning of a premium here seems to be a pecuniary consideration in addition to the rent: *cf.* Rent Act 1977, s.128(2). The object of disregarding the effect on the rents of comparable holdings of premiums charged is clearly to enable a true judgment to be made of these rents for the purpose of comparison.

Para. 2(1)
    Tenant's improvements or fixed equipment. "Fixed equipment" was added in the amendments made by the 1984 Act, s.1. Presumably it refers to equipment which has become part of the premises. See sub-para. (3) as to improvements executed and equipment provided during a *previous* tenancy. "Increase in the rental value" can include latent value released or realized by the improvement: see analysis in *Tummon* v. *Barclay's Bank Trust Co. Ltd.* (1979) 250 E.G. 980 (C.C.) "High farming" is treated as a tenant's improvement: sub-para. (4).
    Landlord's improvements. A landlord is not entitled to the rental benefit of his improvement in so far as it has been paid for out of public money. Apart from this, he reaps the benefit.

Para. 2(2)
    Whether or not that expense has been or will be reimbursed. It would be unfair to require a tenant to pay a higher rent because of his own expenditure, even if it has been subsidised by government or local authority.

Para. 2(3)
    Where the tenant has held a previous tenancy of the holding. This measure of justice to tenants who had been in occupation during more than one tenancy was granted by the 1984 Act (s.1). Before that the harsh principle of *East Coast Amusement Co. Ltd.* v. *British Transport Board (Re "Wonderland," Cleethorpes)* [1965] A.C. 58 probably applied.

Para. 2(4)
    System of farming. The arbitrator is unlikely to be troubled frequently with a claim in respect of "high farming" either in this context or under s.70.

Para. 3
    In occupation of the holding. For the construction of similar words in s.34 of the Landlord and Tenant Act 1954, see *Harewood Hotels Ltd.* v. *Harris* [1958] 1 W.L.R. 108 at p.111. See also *Woodfall* (28th ed.), vol. 2, p.2441, n.94, for passage approved by Lord Evershed M.R. in above case.
    Caused or permitted by the tenant. The arbitrator must treat the holding as if the dilapidation, etc., did not exist. *Cf. per* Lord Parker C.J. in *Metropolitan Properties Ltd.* v. *Wooldridge* (1968) 20 P. & C.R. 64, 66: "there is only one course open under the statute: that is, to value the premises as they are, assuming that the tenant had performed the covenants, whatever they are and however severe they are". Para. 3(*b*) would in fact cover dilapidations caused by the tenant's tort, *e.g.* waste, but such would probably also be a breach of contract.

Para. 4(1)
    Three years from any of the following dates. These rules are subject to modifications in sub-para (2) and in paras. 5 and 6 below.

A previous increase or reduction of rent. An agreed reduction of rent following the compulsory acquisition of part of the holding thus sets off the three-year bar and does not come within one of the exceptions: it is unlikely that it could be regarded as "an adjustment of boundaries" within para. 6, as this seems to be aimed at comparatively small alterations. In cases where a part of a holding is resumed, or taken by compulsory acquisition, and *no* reduction of rent is made, there is in fact an increase of rent *per hectare*, but it is submitted that this is not an increase within the meaning of para. 4(1)(*b*), which must refer to the actual *amount* of rent for the holding as a whole. It was held by a county court judge in *Bolesworth Estate Co. Ltd.* v. *Cook* (1966) 116 New L.J. 1318 (note in (1966) 116 L.J. 739) that a "built-in" formula for the calculation of rent (*e.g.* by reference to the gallonage of milk sold) which in fact produces a variable money rent does not result in an "increase or reduction" within (what is now) para. 4(1)(*b*), so as to create a continuing bar to arbitration. There is much to be said for this view in principle, as the *basis* of rent agreed by the parties has remained unchanged, but the point is open to doubt in the absence of a superior court decision. Is an increase pursuant to a progressive rent formula in the agreement an "increase" within the provision? It is difficult to argue that it is not. It is not entirely clear why para. 4(2) refers only to the present sub-para. (*b*) of para. 4(1) and not to sub-paras. (*a*) and (*c*) also.

Para. 4(2)
   Under section 6(3) or 8(4). The former relates to a variation consequential on an award specifying terms of a written tenancy agreement and the latter to a variation consequential on an award where the terms of a written agreement were inconsistent with the "model clauses".
   Subsection (1) of section 13 . . . subsection (3) of that section. Increases of rent for landlord's improvements, notified under s.13(1) or agreed under s.13(3).
   Change in the fixed equipment. A reduction of rent on this account was added to the "disregards" by the 1984 Act (s.1).
   Under section 33. Reductions consequent on a resumption of part of the holding by virtue of s.31(1) or under a provision in the contract of tenancy.

Para. 5(1)
   A contract of tenancy between. Such a contract between a person entitled to a severed part of the reversion and the tenant of the entirety results in the creation of a new tenancy and a new holding. In this it differs from the effect of a notice to quit given by such a reversioner to the tenant of the entirety: See *Jelley* v. *Buckman* [1974] Q.B. 488.

Para. 5(2)
   The original holding. Sub-para. (2) prevents a new three year cycle from starting to run when all that has happened is the creation of a new contract of tenancy of part of the original holding at a proportionate rent. But in due course para. 4 will apply to increases, reductions or directions in respect of the new holding.

Para. 6
   Adjustment of the boundaries of the holding or for any other variation of the terms of the tenancy. Such minor variations and consequential adjustments of rent are not to be taken to create a new tenancy or otherwise to trigger off a new three-year cycle. Reference should be made to *Jenkin R. Lewis & Son* v. *Kerman* [1971] Ch. 477, C.A. for the general law as to the kind of variations which result in a new tenancy.

Section 26   SCHEDULE 3

CASES WHERE CONSENT OF TRIBUNAL TO OPERATION OF NOTICE TO QUIT IS NOT
REQUIRED

PART I

THE CASES

CASE A

   The holding is let as a smallholding by a smallholdings authority or the Minister in pursuance of Part III of the Agriculture Act 1970 and was so let on or after 12th September 1984, and (*a*) the tenant has attained the age of sixty-five, and

(*b*) if the result of the notice to quit taking effect would be to deprive the tenant of living accommodation occupied by him under the tenancy, suitable alternative accommodation is available for him, or will be available for him when the notice takes effect, and

(*c*) the instrument under which the tenancy was granted contains an acknowledgment signed by the tenant that the tenancy is subject to the provisions of this Case (or to those of Case I in section 2(3) of the Agricultural Holdings (Notices to Quit) Act 1977),

and it is stated in the notice to quit that it is given by reason of the said matter.

GENERAL NOTE

The tenant has attained the age of sixty-five. This Case, added by the 1984 Act (s.6(6), then called Case I) enables a smallholdings authority or the Minister to give a notice to quit to a smallholdings tenant who has attained the age of 65, subject to the availability of suitable alternative accommodation, as set out in paras. 1 to 7 of Part II of Sched. 3. See Part III of the Agriculture Act 1970 for the law in regard to smallholdings. Case A is, therefore, a provision for the *compulsory* retirement of smallholders, as recommended by the Northfield Committee: see Report of the Committee of Inquiry into the Acquisition and Occupancy of Agricultural Land, Cmnd. 7599, July 1979, paras. 559 to 563. The succession provisions do not apply to smallholdings. A decision to the contrary, *Saul* v. *Norfolk County Council* [1984] Q.B. 559, C.A. was annulled by the 1984 Act (Sched. 1, para. 2(6)): see now 1986 Act, s.38(4). Note that the appropriate statement must be contained in the notice to quit. Arbitration is the procedure for contesting reasons stated: art. 9 of the Agricultural Holdings (Arbitration on Notices) Order 1978 (S.I. 1978 No. 257 as amended by art. 4 of the Agricultural Holdings (Arbitration on Notices) (Variation) Order 1984 (S.I. 1984 No. 1300). Basic, but not additional, compensation is payable for disturbance: s.61(2). See for supplementary provisions, Part II of Sched. 3, paras. 1 to 7.

CASE B

The notice to quit is given on the ground that the land is required for a use, other than for agriculture—

(*a*) for which permission has been granted on an application made under the enactments relating to town and country planning, or

(*b*) for which, otherwise than by virtue of any provision of those enactments, such permission is not required,

and that fact is stated in the notice.

GENERAL NOTE

Required for a use. A use may be non-agricultural although the ultimate purpose is agricultural: *Dow Agrochemicals* v. *E. A. Lane (North Lynn) Ltd.* (1964) 192 E.G. 737, (1965) L.J. 76, (C.C.) "Required" involves both a firm bona fide intention to carry out development and a reasonable prospect that it will be carried out: *Paddock Investments Ltd.* v. *Lory* (1975) 236 E.G. 803, approving *Jones* v. *Gates* [1954] 1 W.L.R. 222 on this point only. "Required" does not imply a requirement by the landlord himself exclusively: *Rugby Joint Water Board* v. *Foottit* [1973] A.C. 202 (but the compulsory purchase position is different: see s.48 of Land Compensation Act 1973).

Permission has been granted on an application. A general permission under a General Development Order would not suffice: *Ministry of Agriculture* v. *Jenkins* [1963] 2 Q.B. 317 at p.324, but an outline permission will: *Paddock Investments Ltd.* v. *Lory, supra, Dow Agrochemicals* v. *E. A. Lane (North Lynn Ltd, supra.* But see below as to certain permissions on applications by the National Coal Board: Sched. 3, Part II, para. 8.

Otherwise than by virtue of any provision of those enactments. This would cover the Crown exemption, *e.g.* in afforestation cases. See *Ministry of Agriculture* v. *Jenkins, supra;* also *Secretary of State for Wales* v. *Pugh* (1970) 120 L.J. 357, C.C.

Note that arbitration is the procedure for contesting reasons under Case B: see reference to orders in note to Case A above. Note also that the notice to quit must contain the appropriate statement, but cannot exclude either basic or additional compensation for disturbance: see s.61(1) for Cases which do exclude them. See also Part II of Sched. 3, para. 8.

CASE C

Not more than six months before the giving of the notice to quit, the Tribunal granted a certificate under paragraph 9 of Part II of this Schedule that the tenant of the holding was not fulfilling his responsibilities to farm in accordance with the rules of good husbandry, and that fact is stated in the notice.

GENERAL NOTE

The Tribunal granted a certificate. The six months run from the grant of, not the application for, the certificate as a result of an amendment by the 1984 Act (s.6(3)). The old provision was anomalous and created difficulties: see *Cooke* v. *Talbot* (1977) 243 E.G. 831.

Rules of good husbandry. See s.96(3) and ss.10 and 11 of 1947 Act.

Stated in the notice. See s.25(4) as to specification of a minimum length of notice by the tribunal. The notice will not then be invalid under s.25(1) or at common law because of shortness of length and need not terminate at the end of a year of the tenancy: s.25(5). See as to opencast coal working, Opencast Coal Act 1958, s.14(3) and (4), as amended by present Act, Sched. 14, para. 25.

It may be noted that arbitration is not available to contest the landlord's application for a certificate. The whole matter is in the hands of the tribunal. Neither basic nor additional compensation for disturbance is payable where s.26(1) is excluded by Case C: s.61(1). See also Part II of Sched. 3, para. 9.

CASE D

At the date of the giving of the notice to quit the tenant had failed to comply with a notice in writing served on him by the landlord, being either—

(*a*) a notice requiring him within two months from the service of the notice to pay any rent due in respect of the agricultural holding to which the notice to quit relates, or

(*b*) a notice requiring him within a reasonable period specified in the notice to remedy any breach by the tenant that was capable of being remedied of any term or condition of his tenancy which was not inconsistent with his responsibilities to farm in accordance with the rules of good husbandry,

and it is stated in the notice to quit that it is given by reason of the said matter.

GENERAL NOTE

Notice in writing. A preliminary written notice in a prescribed form is an essential requirement of each limb of Case D: see Agricultural Holdings (Forms of Notice to Pay Rent or to Remedy) Regulations 1984 (S.I. 1984 No. 1308). Courts have taken a very strict view of preliminary notices: see *Macnab of Macnab* v. *Anderson* 1957 S.C. 213, 1958 S.L.T. 8; *Pickard* v. *Bishop* (1975) 31 P. & C.R. 108, 235 E.G. 133; *Jones* v. *Lewis* (1973) 25 P. & C.R. 375; *Dickinson* v. *Boucher* (1983) 269 E.G. 1159; *Magdalen College, Oxford* v. *Heritage* [1974] 1 W.L.R. 441, (1974) 230 E.G. 219. It must, however, be remembered that defects, even serious ones, in a preliminary notice may not avail a tenant if he neglects to protect his rights by requiring arbitration on the notice to quit: see *Magdalen College, Oxford* v. *Heritage, supra*; *Ladd's Radio and Television Ltd.* v. *Docker* (1973) 226 E.G. 1565; *Crown Estate Commissioners* v. *Allingham* (1973) 226 E.G. 2153; *Att.-Gen. for Duchy of Lancaster* v. *Simcock* [1966] Ch. 1; *Harding* v. *Marshall* (1983) 267 E.G. 161; *Parrish* v. *Kinsey* (1983) 268 E.G. 1113. Note that the tenant's attention is now drawn to his danger: see notes to forms in the Agricultural Holdings (Forms of Notice to Pay Rent or to Remedy) Regulations 1984 (S.I. 1984 No. 1308), thus meeting a criticism made by Ackner L.J. in *Harding* v. *Marshall, supra*, at pp.161 and 162. The notice to pay rent due is Form 1 in the Sched. to these regs.

To pay any rent due. Rent must actually be due at date of the preliminary notice: *Magdalen College, Oxford* v. *Heritage, supra*; *Pickard* v. *Bishop, supra*; contrast *Urwick* v. *Taylor* [1969] E.G.D. 1106. A settled practice of payment and acceptance may substitute a date other than that mentioned in the contract as the "due" date: see *Crown Estate Commissioners* v. *Allingham, supra*, where, however, the point was not actually decided. The notice to quit must not be served prematurely, but in one case where the two-months' time-limit expired at midnight a notice to quit posted before, but not delivered until after, that midnight was held not premature: *French* v. *Elliott* [1960] 1 W.L.R. 40; see also *Macnabb* v. *A. J. Anderson* 1955 S.C. 38. A cheque posted before the expiry date, but not received until two days after, was held to be in time as the accepted mode of payment over the years was by cheque posted by the tenant: *Beevers* v. *Mason* (1978) 248 E.G. 781 (but it is not authority for a general rule that posting is service). It is not compliance if a cheque given within the time-limit is dishonoured, even if honoured on re-presentation after the time-limit: *Oakley* v. *Young* (1970), unreported decision of Judge A. C. Bulger at Cheltenham County Court. A post-dated cheque received before, but not payable until after, the time-limit is not a compliance: *Att.-Gen. for Duchy of Lancaster* v. *Simcock* [1966] Ch. 1. A cheque sent to and received by the landlord before the time-limit, but not presented because landlord had reasons for not accepting payment of rent at that time, did not constitute compliance: *Official Solicitor* v. *Thomas, The Times*, March 3, 1986. It is not compliance if rent is paid after the time-limit of two months but before the service of a notice to quit; there is no *locus poenitentiae* between the expiry of the time-limit and the service: *cf. Price* v. *Romilly* [1960] 1 W.L.R. 1360. Full payment is required; a substantial but not full payment is insufficient as is substantial compliance with a notice to remedy: *ibid.* Payment must be made in the recognised and proper manner: *Flint* v. *Fox* (1956) 106 L.J. 828. Naming the wrong landlord or stating the wrong amount of rent may be fatal: *Pickard* v. *Bishop* (1975) 235 E.G. 133; *Dickinson* v. *Boucher* (1983) 269 E.G. 1159. Omitting to specify the time-limit of two months cannot now be a defect if the statutory form is used but was so formerly: *Magdalen College, Oxford* v. *Heritage* [1974] 1 W.L.R. 441, (1974) 230 E.G. 219. It must be repeated that in some of the above cases of defective preliminary notices the tenant made the fatal mistake of failing to challenge the subsequent notice to quit by arbitration. By contrast with the strict line taken on these statutory notices, the courts have been more benevolent in regard to non-statutory ones: see *Carradine Properties Ltd.* v. *Aslam* [1976] 1 W.L.R. 442, and even in respect of a notice under the 1954 Act in *Germax Securities Ltd.* v. *Spiegal* (1978) 37 P. & C.R. 204, (1978) 250 E.G. 449: see also *Sunrose* v. *Gould* [1962] 1 W.L.R. 20 and *Frankland* v. *Capstick* [1959] 1 W.L.R. 205.

To remedy any breach. Two forms of notice to remedy are prescribed, Forms 2 and 3 in the Sched. to the regs. mentioned in notes above, Form 2 being the notice to do work of repair, maintenance or replacement, Form 3 being the notice to remedy breaches of other kinds. In the case of notices to do work there is an important procedure for intermediate arbitration at the notice to do work stage (see Part II of the Agricultural Holdings (Arbitration on Notices) Order 1978 (S.I. 1978 No. 257) which does not exist at the other kind of notice to remedy stage. Any notice to remedy must specify a definite time for compliance, which must be a reasonable period. A notice to remedy which complied with the prescribed form so far as its layout was concerned might still be defective if it was ambiguous, confused or obscure as to the breaches alleged or the remedial action required: *cf. Morris* v. *Muirhead* 1969 S.L.T. 70. Subject to the *de minimis* rule, the failure to remedy any of the breaches alleged will be a basis for a notice to quit under Case D: *Price* v. *Romilly* [1960] 1 W.L.R. 1360. A notice to remedy which relates to several breaches must specify a time for compliance reasonable for *all* the breaches included in the notice: *Wykes* v. *Davis* [1975] Q.B. 843. But if the time specified is reasonable for all the breaches, the fact that it subsequently *becomes unreasonable* for some does not deprive the notice of validity for the others for which the time remains reasonable: *Shepherd* v. *Lomas* [1963] 1 W.L.R. 962. Whether the risk of a notice to remedy being held invalid can be avoided by specifying different time-limits in the notice or by serving at the same time a number of notices each specifying a different time-limit was left undecided in *Wykes* v. *Davis*. As in the cases on notices to pay rent due, the notice to quit must not be served before the time for compliance has expired: *Cowan* v. *Wrayford* [1953] 1 W.L.R. 1340 at p.1343; *Hughes* v. *Taylor* (1950) 156 E.G. 141 (C.C.); and *cf. French* v. *Elliott* [1960] 1 W.L.R. 40 where the notice to quit, based on alleged failure to pay rent due, narrowly missed being premature. There is no compliance if the breach is remedied after the date set for completion, but before the service of the notice to quit: *Price* v. *Romilly* [1960] 1 W.L.R. 1360; *Stoneman* v. *Brown* [1973] 1 W.L.R. 459. The point arose in *Att.-Gen. for Duchy of Lancaster* v. *Simcock* [1966] Ch. 1, but did not require decision owing to the jurisdiction issue. There is some risk, however, that the service of the notice to quit might be construed as a waiver of the landlord's rights: a point apparently overlooked by Pennycuick J. in *Simcock's* case, at p.7: *cf. Segal Securities* v. *Thoseby* [1963] 1 Q.B. 887. The notice to quit must make it clear that the intention is to rely on Case D, not Case E, although the risk of ambiguity or confusion is probably less than it was: *Budge* v. *Hicks* [1951] 2 K.B. 335. The words "a calculated obscurity" in *Macnab of Macnab* v. *Anderson* 1958 S.L.T. 8 were actually used of a preliminary notice, but could apply to a notice to quit. A notice to quit might be based on both the limbs of Case D, (*a*) and (*b*), and be effective if, say, (*a*) is established and (*b*) is not, perhaps because arbitration proceedings were in process: see *French* v. *Elliott* [1960] 1 W.L.R. 40; but it may be preferable to serve two independent notices so that one can take effect if the other fails or is suspended. Despite an obvious analogy with notices under s.146 of the Law of Property Act 1925, decisions on the latter are not necessarily applicable to Case D. For example, contrary to a reservation expressed in *Wykes* v. *Davis*]1975] Q.B. 843, a notice under s.146

in respect of a number of breaches is capable of operating as a separate notice in respect of each breach. (But see *per* Purchas L.J. in *Troop* v. *Gibson* (1985) 277 E.G. 1134 at p.1143 as to the construction of s.146 and Case E being indistinguishable.) A landlord's breach of a tenancy obligation does not by itself prevent him from invoking Case D, but it is otherwise if some act, such as the provision of materials, is a *condition precedent* to the tenant's obligation: *Shepherd* v. *Lomas* [1963] 1 W.L.R. 962, especially at p.974. A tenant must carry out items of work which he is not challenging in the landlord's notice to do work, even if he is contesting other items: *Ladd's Radio and Television Ltd.* v. *Docker* (1973) 226 E.G. 1565. "Capable of being remedied" is not susceptible of exact interpretation. Clearly an assignment contrary to covenant is incapable of being remedied, since it vests the tenancy in the assignee: *Old Grovebury Manor Farm Ltd.* v. *W. Seymour Plant Sales and Hire Ltd. (No. 2)* [1979] 1 W.L.R. 1397. It was at one time thought that a subletting in breach of covenant was capable of remedied: *Thomas Fawcett & Sons Ltd.* v. *Thompson* [1954] E.G.D. 5. But this view is no longer held: *Scala House and District Property Co. Ltd.* v. *Forbes* [1974] Q.B. 575 (not agricultural); and see *Troop* v. *Gibson* (1985) 277 E.G. 1134, at p.1139, *per* Purchas L.J. See Part II of Sched. 3, para. 10(1)(*d*) as to the effect of a conservation covenant. Arbitration is, of course, available to contest reasons in a notice to quit based on Case D. Neither basic nor additional compensation for disturbance is payable where s.26(1) is excluded by virtue of Case D: s.61(1).

CASE E

At the date of the giving of the notice to quit the interest of the landlord in the agricultural holding had been materially prejudiced by the commission by the tenant of a breach, which was not capable of being remedied, of any term or condition of the tenancy that was not inconsistent with the tenant's responsibilities to farm in accordance with the rules of good husbandry, and it is stated in the notice that it is given by reason of the said matter.

GENERAL NOTE

A breach, which was not capable of being remedied. This is usually indicated by evidence of a substantial reduction in the value of the landlord's reversion, but in some cases it might be a case of *res ipsa loquitur.* There is a special provision as to material prejudice in the case of a smallholdings tenancy: see Part II of Sched. 3, para. 11(1). The correct view is now that a subletting in breach of covenant falls within Case E: see *Scala House and District Property Co. Ltd.* v. *Forbes* [1974] Q.B. 575 (a non-agricultural case) and see *Troop* v. *Gibson* (1985) 277 E.G. 1134 at p.1143. An assignment in breach of covenant seems to be clearly within Case E; in *Troop* v. *Gibson, supra,* the landlords failed on the principle of "estoppel by convention", as explained in *Amalgamated Investment and Property Co. Ltd.* v. *Texas Commerce International Bank Ltd.* [1982] Q.B. 84. Breaches of negative user covenants are more likely to be non-remediable than breaches of continuing positive covenants: see (although in the context of s.146 of the Law of Property Act 1925) *Expert Clothing Service and Sales Ltd.* v. *Hillgate House Ltd.* [1985] 3 W.L.R. 359. Really bad husbandry, causing lasting deterioration, with gross neglect of repair of buildings, might qualify for Case E. For an unusual argument based on Case E see *Johnson* v. *Moreton* in Court of Appeal (not House of Lords) (1977) 35 P. & C.R. 378.

Rules of good husbandry. For a provision safeguarding the effectiveness of conservation covenants in relation to a possible conflict with the rules of good husbandry, see Sched. 3, Part II, para. 11(2).

Stated in the notice. The notice should make it clear beyond doubt that the landlord is intending to proceed under Case E and not under Case D: see *Budge* v. *Hicks* [1951] 2 K.B. 335. No preliminary notice is required for the purpose of Case E. The notice to quit should not attempt to combine the invocation of Cases D and E, as a "calculated obscurity" is not likely to succeed (a phrase in fact used in connection with a preliminary notice to pay rent in *Macnab of Macnab* v. *Anderson* 1958 S.L.T. 8).

It should be noted that Case E is one of the four Cases (A, B, D and E) for which resort to arbitration is provided for the purpose of contesting any reason stated in the notice to quit and is the only procedure for that purpose: art. 9 of the Agricultural Holdings (Arbitration on Notices) Order 1978 (S.I. 1978 No. 257) as amended by the Agricultural Holdings (Arbitration on Notices) (Variation) Order 1984 (S.I. 1984 No. 1300). Case E is one of the five Cases (C, D, E, F and G) where both basic and additional compensation for disturbance are excluded: s.61(1).

CASE F

At the date of the giving of the notice to quit the tenant was a person who had become insolvent, and it is stated in the notice that it is given by reason of the said matter.

GENERAL NOTE

Insolvent. For a definition of the tenant's insolvency, see s.96(2). See s.25(2)(*a*) for exception in the case of the tenant's insolvency from the requirement of a 12 months' length of notice to quit. The contract of tenancy, if properly drawn, will probably contain a forfeiture clause providing for re-entry in the case of insolvency, so that the landlord will be able to choose between Case E and forfeiture proceedings. A forfeiture clause will be void if it does not provide for notice to the tenant of sufficient length to allow him to serve notice of claim under s.60(6)(*a*) or s.70(2)(*a*): see *Parry* v. *Million Pigs Ltd.* (1980) 260 E.G. 281. Arbitration is not provided to resolve any dispute as to the tenant's insolvency. Such a dispute, if it arises, must be settled by the courts. Neither basic nor additional compensation for disturbance is payable where s.26(1) is excluded by Case F.

CASE G

The notice to quit is given—
(*a*) following the death of a person who immediately before his death was the sole (or sole surviving) tenant under the contract of tenancy, and
(*b*) not later than the end of the period of three months beginning with the date of any relevant notice,
and it is stated in the notice to quit that it is given by reason of that person's death.

GENERAL NOTE

Notice to quit. The effectiveness of a notice to quit following the death of a tenant has, of course, been fundamentally restricted by the family succession scheme, but may still operate in the event of (1) no application being made for a tenancy by a potential successor, or (2) no application being successful, or (3) the tribunal giving consent to the notice as to the whole or part of the holding: s.43(1), s.44. Also, a landlord can express his views as to an applicant's eligibility and suitability in the course of the proceedings: s.39(2), (7). It is therefore in the landlord's interest to serve a notice to quit in accordance with Case G.

The sole (or sole surviving) tenant under the contract of tenancy. Case G as at present worded embodies amendments made by the 1984 Act (s.6(5)) to the wording in the 1977 Act, which itself embodied amendments made by the 1976 Act to the original formula in s.24(2)(*g*) of the 1948 Act. S.24(2)(*g*) had been interpreted in *Clarke* v. *Hall* [1961] 2 Q.B. 331 to produce the anomalous result that the landlord could serve a notice to quit on an assignee of the tenancy in consequence of the death of a person who had then no interest in the tenancy, namely, the person with whom the contract of tenancy had originally been made, the original grantee of the tenancy. Such a person might have assigned many years before and there might have been intermediate assignees. The present wording, despite doubts which have been expressed by some purists, seems to obviate this anomaly. See para. 12(*a*) of Part II of Sched. 3 below for a restriction in the definition of "tenant" for the purposes of Case G. If there has been a joint tenancy of the holding Case G and the succession scheme apply on the death of the surviving joint tenant: Case G(*a*), s.35(1)(*b*).

Three months beginning with the date of any relevant notice. For the meaning of "the date of any relevant notice", see para. 12(*b*) of Part II of Sched. 3 below. This formula replaced the reference to the date of the tenant's death, which had given rise to difficulties and criticism in practice: the landlord did not always receive timely notification of the tenant's death. The amendment now embodied in the present Act was made by the 1984 Act (s.6(5)). For cases on the service of notices to quit following the death, see *Egerton* v. *Rutter* [1951] 1 K.B. 472; *Harrowby* v. *Snelson* [1951] 1 All E.R. 140; *Wilbraham* v. *Colclough* [1952] 1 All E.R. 979 and, for service on the President of the Family Division, s.9 of the Administration of Estates Act 1925, in the case of an intestacy; but note *Thorlby* v. *Olivant* [1960] E.G.D. 257.

It should be noted that arbitration is not available to resolve disputes in regard to the application of Case G. Neither basic nor additional compensation for disturbance is payable where s.26(1) is excluded by Case G: s.61(1).

CASE H

The notice to quit is given by the Minister and—
(*a*) the Minister certifies in writing that the notice to quit is given in order to enable him

to use or dispose of the land for the purpose of effecting any amalgamation (within the meaning of section 26(1) of the Agriculture Act 1967) or the reshaping of any agricultural unit, and

(*b*) the instrument under which the tenancy was granted contains an acknowledgement signed by the tenant that the tenancy is subject to the provisions of this Case (or to those of Case H in section 2(3) of the Agricultural Holdings (Notices to Quit) Act 1977 or of section 29 of the Agriculture Act 1967).

GENERAL NOTE

The Minister certifies in writing. If this certificate is given and the instrument granting the tenancy has contained the acknowledgment mentioned in (*b*), the notice to quit will be excluded from s.26(1) of the Act. It is not provided that the certificate is to be contained in the notice to quit; it appears to be effective whether contained in the notice to quit or in a separate document, provided that the latter clearly refers to and identifies the notice.

Contains an acknowledgment. Case H in s.2(3) of the 1977 Act was the predecessor of the present Case H. The original provisions were in s.29(4) of the Agriculture Act 1967.

PART II

SUPPLEMENTARY PROVISIONS APPLICABLE TO CASES A, B, C, D, E AND G

Provisions applicable to Case A

1. Paragraphs 2 to 7 below have effect for determining whether, for the purposes of paragraph (*b*) of Case A, suitable alternative accommodation is or will be available for the tenant.

2. For the purposes of paragraph (*b*) of Case A, a certificate of the housing authority for the district in which the living accommodation in question is situated, certifying that the authority will provide suitable alternative accommodation for the tenant by a date specified in the certificate, shall be conclusive evidence that suitable alternative accommodation will be available for him by that date.

3. Where no such certificate as is mentioned in paragraph 2 above has been issued, accommodation shall be deemed to be suitable for the purposes of paragraph (*b*) of Case A if it consists of either—

(*a*) premises which are to be let as a separate dwelling such that they will then be let on a protected tenancy (within the meaning of the Rent Act 1977), or

(*b*) premises to be let as a separate dwelling on terms which will afford to the tenant security of tenure reasonably equivalent to the security afforded by Part VII of that Act in the case of a protected tenancy,

and the accommodation fulfils the conditions in paragraph 4 below.

4.—(1) The accommodation must be reasonably suitable to the needs of the tenant's family as regards proximity to place of work and either—

(*a*) similar as regards rental and extent to the accommodation afforded by dwelling-houses provided in the neighbourhood by any housing authority for persons whose needs as regards extent are similar to those of the tenant and his family, or

(*b*) reasonably suitable to the means of the tenant and to the needs of the tenant and his family as regards extent and character.

(2) For the purposes of sub-paragraph (1)(*a*) above, a certificate of a housing authority stating—

(*a*) the extent of the accommodation afforded by dwelling-houses provided by the authority to meet the needs of tenants with families of such number as may be specified in the certificate, and

(*b*) the amount of the rent charged by the authority for dwelling-houses affording accommodation of that extent,

shall be conclusive evidence of the facts so stated.

(3) If any furniture was provided by the landlord for use under the tenancy in question, furniture must be provided for use in the alternative accommodation which is either—

(*a*) similar to that so provided, or

(*b*) reasonably suitable to the needs of the tenant and his family.

5. Accommodation shall not be deemed to be suitable to the needs of the tenant and his family if the result of their occupation of the accommodation would be that it would be an overcrowded dwelling-house for the purposes of Part X of the Housing Act 1985.

6. Any document purporting—

(*a*) to be a certificate of a housing authority named in it issued for the purposes of this Schedule, and

(*b*) to be signed by the proper officer of the authority,

shall be received in evidence and, unless the contrary is shown, shall be deemed to be such a certificate without further proof.

7.—(1) In paragraphs 2, 4 and 6 above "housing authority", and "district" in relation to such an authority, mean a local housing authority and their district within the meaning of the Housing Act 1985.

(2) For the purposes of paragraphs 4 and 5 a dwelling-house may be a house or part of a house.

Provisions applicable to Case B

8.—(1) For the purposes of Case B no account shall be taken of any permission granted as mentioned in paragraph (*a*) of that Case if the permission—

(*a*) was granted on an application made by the National Coal Board, and

(*b*) relates to the working of coal by opencast operations, and

(*c*) was granted subject to a restoration condition and to an aftercare condition in which the use specified is use for agriculture or use for forestry.

(2) In this paragraph "restoration condition" and "aftercare condition" have the meaning given by section 30A(2) of the Town and Country Planning Act 1971.

Provisions applicable to Case C

9.—(1) For the purposes of Case C the landlord of an agricultural holding may apply to the Tribunal for a certificate that the tenant is not fulfilling his responsibilities to farm in accordance with the rules of good husbandry; and the Tribunal, if satisfied that the tenant is not fulfilling his said responsibilities, shall grant such a certificate.

(2) In determining whether to grant a certificate under this paragraph the Tribunal shall disregard any practice adopted by the tenant in pursuance of any provision of the contract of tenancy, or of any other agreement with the landlord, which indicates (in whatever terms) that its object is the furtherance of one or more of the following purposes, namely—

(*a*) the conservation of flora or fauna or of geological or physiographical features of special interest;

(*b*) the protection of buildings or other objects of archaeological, architectural or historic interest;

(*c*) the conservation or enhancement of the natural beauty or amenity of the countryside or the promotion of its enjoyment by the public.

Provisions applicable to Case D

10.—(1) For the purposes of Case D—

(*a*) a notice such as that mentioned in paragraph (*a*) or (*b*) of that Case must be in the prescribed form,

(*b*) where such a notice in the prescribed form requires the doing of any work of repair, maintenance or replacement, any further notice requiring the doing of any such work which is served on the tenant less than twelve months after the earlier notice shall be disregarded unless the earlier notice was withdrawn with his agreement in writing.

(*c*) a period of less than six months shall not be treated as a reasonable period within which to do any such work, and

(*d*) any provision such as is mentioned in paragraph 9(2) above shall (if it would not otherwise be so regarded) be regarded as a term or condition of the tenancy which is not inconsistent with the tenant's responsibilities to farm in accordance with the rules of good husbandry.

(2) Different forms may be prescribed for the purpose of paragraph (*b*) of Case D in relation to different circumstances.

Provisions applicable to Case E

11.—(1) Where—

(*a*) the landlord is a smallholdings authority, or

(*b*) the landlord is the Minister and the holding is on land held by him for the purposes of smallholdings, then, in considering whether the interest of the landlord has been materially prejudiced as mentioned in Case E, regard shall be had to the effect of the breach in question not only on the holding itself but also on the carrying out of the arrangements made by the smallholdings authority or the Minister (as the case may be) for the letting and conduct of smallholdings.

(2) For the purposes of Case E any provision such as is mentioned in paragraph 9(2) above shall (if it would not otherwise be so regarded) be regarded as a term or condition of the tenancy which is not inconsistent with the tenant's responsibilities to farm in accordance with the rules of good husbandry.

Provisions applicable to Case G

12. For the purposes of Case G—
   (*a*) "tenant" does not include an executor, administrator, trustee in bankruptcy or other person deriving title from a tenant by operation of law, and
   (*b*) the reference to the date of any relevant notice shall be construed as a reference—
      (i) to the date on which a notice in writing was served on the landlord by or on behalf of an executor or administrator of the tenant's estate informing the landlord of the tenant's death or the date on which the landlord was given notice by virtue of section 40(5) of this Act of any application with respect to the holding under section 39 or 41, or
      (ii) where both of those events occur, to the date of whichever of them occurs first.

GENERAL NOTE
Para. 1
Paragraphs 2 to 7 below. These paras., dealing with the provision of suitable alternative accommodation for dispossessed smallholders, are closely modelled on paras. 3 to 8 of Part IV of Sched. 15 to the Rent Act 1977. Case law on the alternative accommodation provisions of that Act and earlier Rent Acts will be of help on the present provisions.

Para. 8(1)
National Coal Board. Opencast planning applications are now dealt with by the normal minerals planning machinery. The present provision safeguards the tenant against being served with an "incontestable" notice to quit under Case B following a planning permission if the permission relates to opencast coal operations and was granted subject to the usual restoration and aftercare conditions. The permission must be granted on an *application* by the N.C.B., but will enure for the benefit of the land and any other persons interested in it. Note definitions of "restoration condition" and "aftercare condition" in the 1971 Act.

Para. 9(2)
Shall disregard any practice. The tribunal is in effect directed, when considering whether to grant a certificate of bad husbandry under Case C, not to treat as bad husbandry any practice adopted by the tenant in pursuance of any conservation provisions in the tenancy or other agreement (such as a management agreement) with the landlord. This is a remarkably wide concession; it will be noted that the tribunals are required to accept an "indication" that a provision is for the benefit of conservation.

Para. 10(1)
Prescribed form. The forms are at present prescribed by the Agricultural Holdings (Forms of Notice to Pay Rent or to Remedy) Regulations 1984 (S.I. 1984 No. 1308).
Withdrawn with his agreement in writing. See *Mercantile and General Reinsurance Co. Ltd.* v. *Groves* [1974] Q.B. 43; it is sufficient if the earlier notice is withdrawn by the date of service of the notice to quit, it does not have to be withdrawn before the further notice to do work is served.
Any provision such as is mentioned in paragraph 9(2) above. See note to para. 9(2) above. In the present context conservation provisions in the tenancy or other agreement are *required to be regarded* as terms not inconsistent with the rules of good husbandry.

Para. 11(1)
Materially prejudiced. Normally "material prejudice" is sought in the diminution of the value of the landlord's reversion as a result of the breach. For breaches by smallholdings

tenants an additional test is required for the purpose of Case E, namely, the effect of the breach on the carrying out of the smallholdings administration.

Para. 11(2)
Any provision such as is mentioned in paragraph 9(2) above. See notes to paras. 9(2) and 10(1) above.

Para. 12
"Tenant". This cuts down, for the purpose of Case G, the definition of a "tenant" in s.96(1). The death of an executor or other person deriving title by operation of law is not an event which enables a notice to quit to be served under Case G or an application to be made for a tenancy by succession under Part IV. See also s.34(2) and the old decision in *Costagliola* v. *Bunting* [1958] 1 W.L.R. 580.
Relevant notice. The notice to quit for the purpose of Case G must be served not later than the end of the three months beginning with the date of any relevant notice: Part I of Sched. 3. This date covers the date of service of a notice containing the information by a personal representative of the deceased or the date of receipt by the landlord of notice of an application by a survivor under Part IV of the Act. Presumably notice by the applicant or (see *Kellett* v. *Alexander* (1980) 257 E.G. 494) by the secretary of the tribunal would suffice. This provision as to a "relevant notice" is the result of an amendment by the 1984 Act (see s.6(5) of that Act) to meet criticism that the landlord did not always receive timely notification of the tenant's death.

Section 29   SCHEDULE 4

MATTERS FOR WHICH PROVISION MAY BE MADE BY ORDER UNDER SECTION 29

1. Requiring any question arising under the provisions of section 26(2) of, and Schedule 3 to, this Act to be determined by arbitration under this Act.
2. Limiting the time within which any such arbitration may be required or within which an arbitrator may be appointed by agreement between the parties, or (in default of such agreement) an application may be made under paragraph 1 of Schedule 11 to this Act for the appointment of an arbitrator, for the purposes of any such arbitration.
3. Extending the period within which a counter-notice may be given by the tenant under section 26(1) of this Act where any such arbitration is required.
4. Suspending the operation of notices to quit until the expiry of any time fixed in pursuance of paragraph 2 above for the making of any such appointment by agreement or application as is there mentioned or, where any such appointment or application has been duly made, until the termination of any such arbitration.
5. Postponing the date at which a tenancy is to be terminated by a notice to quit which has effect in consequence of any such arbitration or of an application under section 26(1) or 28(2) of this Act or under provisions made by virtue of paragraph 12 below.
6. Excluding the application of section 26(1) of this Act in relation to sub-tenancies in such cases as may be specified in the order.
7. Making such provision as appears to the Lord Chancellor expedient for the purpose of safeguarding the interests of sub-tenants including provision enabling the Tribunal, where the interest of a tenant is terminated by notice to quit, to secure that a sub-tenant will hold from the landlord on the like terms as he held from the tenant.
8. The determination by arbitration under this Act of any question arising under such a notice as is mentioned in paragraph (*b*) of Case D, being a notice requiring the doing of any work of repair, maintenance or replacement (including the question whether the notice is capable of having effect for the purposes of that Case).
9. Enabling the arbitrator, on an arbitration under this Act relating to such a notice as is mentioned in paragraph 8 above, to modify the notice—
   (*a*) by deleting any item or part of an item of work specified in the notice as to which, having due regard to the interests of good husbandry as respects the agricultural holding to which the notice relates and of sound management of the estate of which that holding forms part or which that holding constitutes, the arbitrator is satisfied that it is unnecessary or unjustified, or
   (*b*) by substituting, in the case of any item or part of an item of work so specified, a different method or material for the method or material which the notice would otherwise require to be followed or used where, having regard to the purpose which that item or part is intended to achieve, the arbitrator is satisfied that—

(i) the last-mentioned method or material would involve undue difficulty or expense,

(ii) the first-mentioned method or material would be substantially as effective for the purpose, and

(iii) in all the circumstances the substitution is justified.

10. Enabling the time within which anything is to be done in pursuance of such a notice as is mentioned in paragraph (*b*) of Case D to be extended or to be treated as having been extended.

11. Enabling a tenancy, in a case where that time is extended, to be terminated either by a notice to quit served less than twelve months before the date on which it is to be terminated, or at a date other than the end of a year of the tenancy, or both by such a notice and at such a date.

12. Securing that, where a subsequent notice to quit is given in accordance with provisions made by virtue of paragraph 11 above in a case where the original notice to quit fell within section 28(1) of this Act, then, if the tenant serves on the landlord a counter-notice in writing within one month after the giving of the subsequent notice to quit (or, if the date specified in that notice for the termination of the tenancy is earlier, before that date), the subsequent notice to quit shall not have effect unless the Tribunal consent to its operation, and applying section 28(5) of this Act as regards the giving of that consent.

13. The recovery by a tenant of the cost of any work which is done by him in compliance with a notice requiring him to do it, but which is found by arbitration under this Act to be work which he was not under an obligation to do.

GENERAL NOTE

At the time of going to press the matters mentioned in Sched. 4 are covered by the Agricultural Holdings (Arbitration on Notices) Order 1978 (S.I. 1978 No. 257) as amended by the Agricultural Holdings (Arbitration on Notices) (Variation) Order 1984 (S.I. 1984 No. 1300). It seems likely that these orders will before long be superseded by a new statutory instrument. Although made under repealed provisions (s.5(1) of the 1977 Act as amended by Sched. 3, para. 38, to the 1984 Act), they remain effective for the purposes of the 1986 Act by virtue of Sched. 13 to the latter. But there is a certain awkwardness in references to "Case I" which has now to be read as Case A, and to Sched. 1A to the 1977 Act, which is now embodied in paras. 1 to 7 of Part II of Sched. 3 to the 1986 Act, as well as in having to read S.I. 1978 No. 257 and S.I. 1984 No. 1300 together to pick up the amendments to the former. It is also possible that a new S.I. may include substantive changes as well as changes purely consequential on consolidation.

Section 30   SCHEDULE 5

NOTICE TO QUIT WHERE TENANT IS A SERVICE MAN

1. In this Schedule—

"the 1951 Act" means the Reserve and Auxiliary Forces (Protection of Civil Interests) Act 1951;

"period of residence protection" in the case of a service man who performs a period of relevant service, other than a short period of training, means the period comprising that period of service and the four months immediately following the date on which it ends;

"relevant service" means service (as defined in section 64(1) of the 1951 Act) of a description specified in Schedule 1 to that Act;

"service man" means a man or woman who performs a period of relevant service;

"short period of training" has the meaning given by section 64(1) of the 1951 Act.

2.—(1) Paragraph 3 below shall have effect where—

(*a*) the tenant of an agricultural holding to which this Schedule applies performs a period of relevant service, other than a short period of training, and

(*b*) during his period of residence protection there is given to him—

(i) notice to quit the holding, or

(ii) notice to quit a part of it to which this Schedule applies.

(2) This Schedule applies to—

(*a*) any agricultural holding which comprises such a dwelling-house as is mentioned in section 10 of the Rent Act 1977, that is to say a dwelling-house occupied by the person responsible for the control (whether as tenant or as servant or agent of the tenant) of the farming of the holding, and (*b*) any part of an agricultural holding, being a part which consists of or comprises such a dwelling-house.

3.—(1) Section 26(1) of this Act shall apply notwithstanding the existence of any such circumstances as are mentioned in Cases B to G; but where the Tribunal are satisfied that such circumstances exist, then, subject to sub-paragraph (2) below, the Tribunal shall not be required to withhold their consent to the operation of the notice to quit by reason only that they are not satisfied that circumstances exist such as are mentioned in paragraphs (*a*) to (*f*) of section 27(3) of this Act.

(2) In determining whether to give or withhold their consent under section 26 of this Act the Tribunal—

(*a*) if satisfied that circumstances exist such as are mentioned in Cases B to G or in section 27(3) of this Act, shall consider to what extent (if at all) the existence of those circumstances is directly or indirectly attributable to the service man's performing or having performed the period of service in question, and

(*b*) in any case, shall consider to what extent (if at all) the giving of such consent at a time during the period of protection would cause special hardship in view of circumstances directly or indirectly attributable to the service man's performing or having performed that period of service,

and the Tribunal shall withhold their consent to the operation of the notice to quit unless in all the circumstances they consider it reasonable to give their consent.

4. Where the tenant of an agricultural holding to which this Schedule applies performs a period of relevant service, other than a short period of training, and—

(*a*) a notice to quit the holding, or a part of it to which this Schedule applies, is given to him before the beginning of his period of residence protection, and

(*b*) the tenant duly serves a counter-notice under section 26(1) of this Act, and

(*c*) the Tribunal have not before the beginning of his period of residence protection decided whether to give or withhold consent to the operation of the notice to quit,

paragraph 3(2) above shall (with the necessary modifications) apply in relation to the giving or withholding of consent to the operation of the notice to quit as it applies in relation to the giving or withholding of consent to the operation of a notice to quit given in the circumstances mentioned in paragraph 2(1) above.

5. The Lord Chancellor's power under section 29 of this Act to provide for the matters specified in paragraphs 1 to 7 of Schedule 4 to this Act shall apply in relation to the provisions of sections 26 and 27 of this Act as modified by the preceding provisions of this Schedule as they apply in relation to the provisions of those sections apart from this Schedule.

6.—(1) The Lord Chancellor may make regulations—

(*a*) for enabling a counter-notice under section 26(1) of this Act to be served on behalf of a service man at a time when he is serving abroad, in a case where a notice to quit is given to him as mentioned in paragraph 2(1) above, and

(*b*) for enabling an act or proceedings consequential upon the service of a counter-notice under section 26(1) to be performed or conducted on behalf of a service man at a time when he is serving abroad, either in such a case as is mentioned in paragraph (*a*) above or in a case where paragraph 4 above applies in relation to him.

(2) References in sub-paragraph (1) above to a time when a service man is serving abroad are references to a time when he is performing a period of relevant service and is outside the United Kingdom.

(3) Regulations under this paragraph may contain such incidental and consequential provisions as appear to the Lord Chancellor to be necessary or expedient for the purposes of the regulations.

GENERAL NOTE

During the period which has elapsed since the end of the 1939–45 war the scope for the application of Schedule 5 and the associated statutory instruments has been greatly reduced. The Schedule does not apply to members of the regular armed forces and a number of the kinds of "relevant service" in a non-regular capacity listed in Sched. 1 to the Reserve and Auxiliary Forces (Protection of Civil Interests) Act 1951 no longer exist. The 1951 Act, however, is still law and is operative to a restricted extent. It applies only to an agricultural holding which comprises a dwelling-house occupied by the person responsible for the control (whether as tenant or as servant or agent of the tenant) of the farming of the holding. A tenancy of such a dwelling-house is not a protected tenancy under the Rent Act 1977 (see s.10 thereof. A serviceman who has a protected tenancy of a dwelling-house is safeguarded by the Rent Act). The main concession which a serviceman who qualifies under the present

Schedule enjoys is that his right to serve a counter-notice in reply to a notice to quit is enlarged by the exclusion of the bar in s.26(2) and that the range of matters which the tribunal can consider in deciding whether to give or withhold consent to the notice to quit is extended. In the case of a serviceman who is serving abroad there are regulations which enable a counter-notice to be served on his behalf and other necessary steps to be taken in his interest, although he has given no authorisation for these actions.

Para. 5

Matters specified in paragraphs 1 to 7 of Schedule 4 to this Act. See art. 16 of the Agricultural Holdings (Arbitration on Notices) Order 1978 (S.I. 1978 No. 257), as amended by the Agricultural Holdings (Arbitration on Notices) (Variation) Order 1984 (S.I. 1984 No. 1300).

Para 6

Regulations. These are still the Reserve and Auxiliary Forces (Agricultural Tenants) Regulations 1959 (S.I. 1959 No. 84).

Sections 36 and 50   SCHEDULE 6

ELIGIBILITY TO APPLY FOR NEW TENANCY UNDER PART IV OF THIS ACT

PART I

"ELIGIBLE PERSON": SUPPLEMENTARY PROVISIONS

Preliminary

1.—(1) In this Schedule—

"the livelihood condition" means paragraph (*a*) of the definition of "eligible person" in section 36(3) of this Act;

"the occupancy condition" means paragraph (*b*) of that definition.

(2) For the purposes of this Schedule a body corporate is controlled by a close relative of the deceased if he or his spouse, or he and his spouse together, have the power to secure—

(*a*) by means of the holding of shares or the possession of voting power in or in relation to that or any other body corporate, or

(*b*) by virtue of any powers conferred by the articles of association or other document regulating that or any other body corporate,

that the affairs of that body corporate are conducted in accordance with his, her or their wishes, respectively.

(3) Any reference in this Schedule to the spouse of a close relative of the deceased does not apply in relation to any time when the relative's marriage is the subject of a decree of judicial separation or a decree nisi of divorce or of nullity of marriage.

The livelihood condition

2. For the purposes of the livelihood condition, any period during which a close relative of the deceased was, in the period of seven years mentioned in that condition, attending a full-time course at a university, college or other establishment of further education shall be treated as a period throughout which his only or principal source of livelihood derived from his agricultural work on the holding; but not more than three years in all shall be so treated by virtue of this paragraph.

Commercial unit of agricultural land

3.—(1) In the occupancy condition "commercial unit of agricultural land" means a unit of agricultural land which is capable, when farmed under competent management, of producing a net annual income of an amount not less than the aggregate of the average annual earnings of two full-time, male agricultural workers aged twenty or over.

(2) In so far as any units of production for the time being prescribed by an order under paragraph 4 below are relevant to the assessment of the productive capacity of a unit of agricultural land when farmed as aforesaid, the net annual income which that unit is capable

of producing for the purposes of this paragraph shall be ascertained by reference to the provisions of that order.

4. The Minister shall by order—

   (a) prescribe such units of production relating to agricultural land as he considers appropriate, being units framed by reference to any circumstances whatever and designed for the assessment of the productive capacity of such land, and

   (b) for any period of twelve months specified in the order, determine in relation to any unit of production so prescribed the amount which is to be regarded for the purposes of paragraph 3 above as the net annual income from that unit in that period.

Ministerial statements as to net annual income of land

5.—(1) For the purposes of any proceedings under sections 36 to 48 of this Act in relation to the holding, the Minister shall—

   (a) at the request of any of the following persons, namely any close relative of the deceased, the landlord or the secretary of the Tribunal, and

   (b) in relation to any relevant land,

determine by reference to the provisions of any order for the time being in force under paragraph 4 above the net annual income which, in his view, the land is capable of producing for the purposes of paragraph 3 above, and shall issue a written statement of his view and the grounds for it to the person making the request.

(2) In sub-paragraph (1) above "relevant land" means agricultural land which is—

   (a) occupied (or, by virtue of section 58 of this Act or this Part of this Schedule, deemed to be occupied) by any close relative of the deceased (whether he is, where the request is made by such a relative, the person making the request or not), or

   (b) the subject of an application made under section 39 of this Act by any such relative.

(3) Where—

   (a) for the purposes of any proceedings under sections 36 to 48 of this Act the Minister has issued a statement to any person containing a determination under sub-paragraph (1) above made by reference to the provisions of an order under paragraph 4 above; and

   (b) before any hearing by the Tribunal in those proceedings is due to begin it appears to him that any subsequent order under that paragraph has affected any matter on which that determination was based,

he shall make a revised determination under sub-paragraph (1) above and shall issue a written statement of his view and the grounds for it to the person in question.

(4) Any statement issued by the Minister in pursuance of this paragraph shall be evidence of any facts stated in it as facts on which his view is based.

(5) Any document purporting to be a statement issued by the Minister in pursuance of this paragraph and to be signed for or on behalf of the Minister shall be taken to be such a statement unless the contrary is shown.

Occupation to be disregarded for purposes of occupancy condition

6.—(1) Occupation by a close relative of the deceased of any agricultural land shall be disregarded for the purposes of the occupancy condition if he occupies it only—

   (a) under a tenancy approved by the Minister under subsection (1) of section 2 of this Act or under a tenancy falling within subsection (3)(a) of that section,

   (b) under a tenancy for more than one year but less than two years,

   (c) under a tenancy not falling within paragraph (a) or (b) above and not having effect as a contract of tenancy,

   (d) under a tenancy to which section 3 of this Act does not apply by virtue of section 5 of this Act,

   (e) as a licensee, or

   (f) as an executor, administrator, trustee in bankruptcy or person otherwise deriving title from another person by operation of law.

(2) Paragraphs (a) to (e) of sub-paragraph (1) above do not apply in the case of a tenancy or licence granted to a close relative of the deceased by his spouse or by a body corporate controlled by him.

(3) References in the following provisions of this Schedule to the occupation of land by any person do not include occupation under a tenancy, or in a capacity, falling within paragraphs (*a*) to (*f*) of that sub-paragraph.

Joint occupation

7.—(1) Where any agricultural land is jointly occupied by a close relative of the deceased and one or more other persons as—

(*a*) beneficial joint tenants,

(*b*) tenants in common,

(*c*) joint tenants under a tenancy, or

(*d*) joint licensees,

the relative shall be treated for the purposes of the occupancy condition as occupying the whole of the land.

(2) If, however, the Tribunal in proceedings under section 39 of this Act determine on the application of the close relative that his appropriate share of the net annual income which the land is, or was at any time, capable of producing for the purposes of paragraph 3 above is or was then less than the aggregate of the earnings referred to in that paragraph, then, for the purpose of determining whether the occupancy condition is or was then satisfied in his case, the net annual income which the land is, or (as the case may be) was, capable of so producing shall be treated as limited to his appropriate share.

(3) For the purposes of sub-paragraph (2) above the appropriate share of the close relative shall be ascertained—

(*a*) where he is a beneficial or other joint tenant or a joint licensee, by dividing the net annual income which the land is or was at the time in question capable of producing for the purposes of paragraph 3 above by the total number of joint tenants or joint licensees for the time being,

(*b*) where he is a tenant in common, by dividing the said net annual income in such a way as to attribute to him and to the other tenant or tenants in common shares of the income proportionate to the extent for the time being of their respective undivided shares in the land.

Deemed occupation in case of Tribunal direction

8.—(1) Where a close relative of the deceased is, by virtue of a direction of the Tribunal under section 39 of this Act, for the time being entitled (whether or not with any other person) to a tenancy of the whole or part of any agricultural holding held by the deceased at the date of death other than the holding, he shall, for the purposes of the occupancy condition, be deemed to be in occupation of the land comprised in that holding or (as the case may be) in that part of that holding.

(2) Where by virtue of sub-paragraph (1) above any land is deemed to be occupied by each of two or more close relatives of the deceased as a result of a direction entitling them to a joint tenancy of the land, the provisions of paragraph 7 above shall apply to each of the relatives as if the land were jointly occupied by him and the other relative or relatives as joint tenants under that tenancy.

Occupation by spouse or controlled company

9.—(1) For the purposes of the occupancy condition and of paragraph 7 above, occupation—

(*a*) by the spouse of a close relative of the deceased, or

(*b*) by a body corporate controlled by a close relative of the deceased,

shall be treated as occupation by the relative.

(2) Where, in accordance with sub-paragraph (1) above, paragraph 7 above applies to a close relative of the deceased in relation to any time by virtue of the joint occupation of land by his spouse or a body corporate and any other person or persons, sub-paragraphs (2) and (3) of that paragraph shall apply to the relative as if he were the holder of the interest in the land for the time being held by his spouse or the body corporate, as the case may be.

Deemed occupation in case of tenancy or licence granted by close relative, spouse or controlled company

10.—(1) Where—

(*a*) any agricultural land is occupied by any person under such a tenancy as is mentioned in paragraphs (*a*) to (*d*) of paragraph 6(1) above or as a licensee, and

(b) that tenancy or licence was granted by a close relative of the deceased or a connected person (or both), being at the time it was granted a person or persons entitled to occupy the land otherwise than under a tenancy, or in a capacity, falling within paragraphs (*a*) to (*f*) of paragraph 6(1),

then, unless sub-paragraph (2) below applies, the close relative shall, for the purposes of the occupancy condition, be deemed to be in occupation of the whole of the land.

(2) Where the tenancy or licence referred to in sub-paragraph (1) above was granted by the person or persons there referred to and one or more other persons who were at the time it was granted entitled to occupy the land as mentioned in paragraph (*b*) of that sub-paragraph, sub-paragraphs (2) and (3) of paragraph 7 above shall apply to the close relative as if the land were jointly occupied by him and the said other person or persons as holders of their respective interests for the time being in the land.

(3) In this paragraph "connected person", in relation to a close relative of the deceased, means—

(*a*) the relative's spouse, or

(*b*) a body corporate controlled by the relative;

and for the purposes of sub-paragraph (2) above and the provisions of paragraph 7 there mentioned any interest in the land for the time being held by a connected person by whom the tenancy or licence was granted shall be attributed to the relative.

PART II

MODIFICATIONS OF PART I OF THIS SCHEDULE IN ITS APPLICATION TO SUCCESSION ON RETIREMENT

11. The modifications of Part I of this Schedule referred to in section 50(4) of this Act are as follows.

12. The reference in paragraph 1(1) to section 36(3) of this Act shall be read as a reference to section 50(2) of this Act.

13. References to a close relative of the deceased shall be read as references to the nominated successor.

14. In paragraph 5—

(*a*) references to sections 36 to 48 of this Act shall be read as references to sections 50 to 58 of this Act,

(*b*) the reference in sub-paragraph (1) to any close relative of the deceased shall be read as a reference to the nominated successor, and

(*c*) for sub-paragraph (2) there shall be substituted—

"(2) In sub-paragraph (1) above 'relevant land' means agricultural land which is occupied (or, by virtue of this Part of this Schedule, is deemed to be occupied) by the nominated successor."

15. The reference in paragraph 7(2) to section 39 of this Act shall be read as a reference to section 53 of this Act.

16. For paragraph 8 there shall be substituted—

"8. Where the nominated successor is, by virtue of a direction of the Tribunal under section 53(7) of this Act, for the time being entitled to a tenancy of any agricultural holding held by the retiring tenant other than the holding he shall, for the purposes of the occupancy condition, be deemed to be in occupation of that holding."

GENERAL NOTE

Para 1

A body corporate is controlled. In order to prevent obvious devices to avoid the occupancy condition the close relative's spouse, a company controlled by the close relative, and a company controlled by the close relative and his spouse, are deemed to be the *alter egos* of the close relative, so that their occupation is his occupation: see also para. 9.

Para. 2

A full-time course. This need not have any agricultural content: it could be on Chinese literature.

Para. 3(1)

Occupancy condition. That "*he is not the occupier of a commercial unit of agricultural land*": s.36(3)(b). The underlying idea of the occupancy condition is the simple one that a person already sufficiently provided for by farming an adequate area should not be allowed to become the deceased tenant's statutory successor: see Report of the (Northfield) Committee of Inquiry into the Acquisition and Occupancy of Agricultural Land (Cmnd. 7599, July 1979), para. 630. As Sched. 6 shows, however, the translation of this idea into legislation has not proved simple or easy.

Para. 3(2)
Shall be ascertained. The method of assessing income for the purpose of the definition of a commercial unit is not left to private valuation judgment, but is prescribed by order: see below.

Para. 4
The Minister shall by order. These orders will be annual. At the time of writing the current order is the Agriculture (Miscellaneous Provisions) Act 1976 (Units of Production) Order 1985 (S.I. 1985 No. 997).

Para. 5
A written statement. Parties will not be able to question the content of the units in the statutory instrument, but they can question the choice of the units applied to the holding, *e.g.* whether beef, dairy or cereal is the appropriate unit. And the statement will be evidence of facts stated in it as facts on which the Minister's view is based, but the statement is not said to be conclusive evidence; it may be questioned before the tribunal (see para. 5(4)).

Para. 6
Shall be disregarded. The kind of occupancies to be disregarded for the purpose of the occupancy condition seem to be either precarious, short-term or non-beneficial; as such they do not justify the exclusion of the close relative from the succession to the subject holding. But a transfer of even such minor interests to the close relative by a spouse or controlled company is not to be disregarded.

Para. 7
Jointly occupied. In the case of these four common types of joint occupation the close relative is to be treated as occupying the whole of the land for the purpose of the occupancy condition. This is modified by sub-para. (2), which allows him to show that his share of income from the land is less than the qualifying income for a commercial unit. It seems that in the case of types of joint occupation other than the four mentioned the tribunal must decide, in the light of s.36(3)(*b*) and the guidance in *Williamson* v. *Thompson* [1980] A.C. 854, whether the close relative is in fact the occupier of a commercial unit.

Para. 8
Deemed to be in occupation. A close relative who is *entitled* under a tribunal direction to a tenancy of an agricultural holding held by the deceased, other than the holding which is under consideration, is to be deemed to be in occupation of the land comprised in that other holding, although the tenancy of it has not yet vested in him. If the entitlement under the direction is a joint one the deeming provision applies as if the land were jointly occupied. This is part of the policy of preventing multiple succession, a policy recommended by the Northfield Committee. See ref. in note to para. 3(1) above.

Para. 10
Deemed to be in occupation of the whole of the land. It appears that this para. is intended to frustrate the following device where the death of the tenant is anticipated by his loving close relatives in the not too distant future. The potential successor is the owner-occupier of a commercial unit which would render him ineligible. He grants one of the short interests listed in para. 6(1) to another person, presumably another member of the family, thus making himself eligible to succeed, as he will no longer be the occupier (although he remains the owner) of a commercial unit. He could then establish his eligibility when the tenant's anticipated death occurs. Later, he could resume occupation of the commercial unit, the short-term interest having expired. There are provisions to meet attempts at avoidance by the use of connected persons; and there is also an "appropriate share" limitation on the lines of para. 7(2) and (3) (showing scrupulous fairness by Parliament even in framing measures to counteract a distasteful scheme).

Para. 11

Modifications. These are purely consequential on the application of the Schedule to succession on retirement.

Sections 64, 66, etc.   SCHEDULE 7

Long-Term Improvements begun on or after 1st March 1948 for which Compensation is Payable

Part I

Improvements to which Consent of Landlord Required

1. Making or planting of osier beds.
2. Making of water meadows.
3. Making of watercress beds.
4. Planting of hops.
5. Planting of orchards or fruit bushes.
6. Warping or weiring of land.
7. Making of gardens.
8. Provision of underground tanks.

Part II

Improvements to which Consent of Landlord or Approval of Tribunal Required

9. Erection, alteration or enlargement of buildings, and making or improvement of permanent yards.
10. Carrying out works in compliance with an improvement notice served, or an undertaking accepted, under Part VII of the Housing Act 1985 or Part VIII of the Housing Act 1974.
11. Erection or construction of loading platforms, ramps, hard standings for vehicles or other similar facilities.
12. Construction of silos.
13. Claying of land.
14. Marling of land.
15. Making or improvement of roads or bridges.
16. Making or improvement of water courses, culverts, ponds, wells or reservoirs, or of works for the application of water power for agricultural or domestic purposes or of works for the supply, distribution or use of water for such purposes (including the erection or installation of any structures or equipment which form part of or are to be used for or in connection with operating any such works).
17. Making or removal of permanent fences.
18. Reclaiming of waste land.
19. Making or improvement of embankments or sluices.
20. Erection of wirework for hop gardens.
21. Provision of permanent sheep-dipping accommodation.
22. Removal of bracken, gorse, tree roots, boulders or other like obstructions to cultivation.
23. Land drainage (other than improvements falling within paragraph 1 of Schedule 8 to this Act).
24. Provision or laying-on of electric light or power.
25. Provision of facilities for the storage or disposal of sewage or farm waste.
26. Repairs to fixed equipment, being equipment reasonably required for the proper farming of the holding, other than repairs which the tenant is under an obligation to carry out.
27. The grubbing up of orchards or fruit bushes.
28. Planting trees otherwise than as an orchard and bushes other than fruit bushes.

General Note

This schedule replaces Sched. 3 to the 1948 Act with a few amendments made by the 1984 Act (Sched. 3, para. 25). The changes are as follows:

Part I
> *Item 2 :* omission of "works of irrigation." Neither this nor the "making of water
> meadows", which remains, is normally a tenant's improvement.
> *Item 8 :* "provision of underground tanks", a modern improvement, is added.

Part II
> *Item 10*: These are derived from s.98(3) of the Housing Act 1974 and s.231(2) of the
> Housing Act 1985.
> *Item 11*: This, another essential modern improvement, was added by the 1984 Act.
> *Item 16*: This item is the old No. 13 replaced by a more elaborate formula for water
> installations including, *e.g.*, equipment for spray irrigation.
> *Item 25*: This is extended from "provision of means of sewage disposal."
> *Items 27 and 28*: These are new since 1984. The old final item, "the growing of herbage
> crops for commercial seed production" has been transferred to Sched.
> 8, item 8, where it requires neither landlord's consent nor tribunal's
> approval.

Sections 64, 65, etc.   SCHEDULE 8

Short-Term Improvements Begun on or After 1st March 1948, and other Matters, for
which Compensation is Payable

Part I

Improvements (to which no Consent Required)

1. Mole drainage and works carried out to secure its efficient functioning.
2. Protection of fruit trees against animals.
3. Clay burning.
4. Liming (including chalking) of land.
5. Application to land of purchased manure and fertiliser, whether organic or inorganic.
6. Consumption on the holding of corn (whether produced on the holding or not), or of cake or other feeding stuff not produced on the holding, by horses, cattle, sheep, pigs or poultry.

Part II

Tenant-Right Matters

7. Growing crops and severed or harvested crops and produce, being in either case crops or produce grown on the holding in the last year of tenancy, but not including crops or produce which the tenant has a right to sell or remove from the holding.
8. Seeds sown and cultivations, fallows and acts of husbandry performed on the holding at the expense of the tenant (including the growing of herbage crops for commercial seed production).
9. Pasture laid down with clover, grass, lucerne, sainfoin or other seeds, being either—
> (*a*) pasture laid down at the expense of the tenant otherwise than in compliance
> with an obligation imposed on him by an agreement in writing to lay it down to
> replace temporary pasture comprised in the holding when the tenant entered on
> the holding which was not paid for by him, or
> (*b*) pasture paid for by the tenant on entering on the holding.
10.—(1) Acclimatisation, hefting or settlement of hill sheep on hill land.
(2) In this paragraph —
> "hill sheep" means sheep which—
>> (*a*) have been reared and managed on a particular hill or mountain,
>> (*b*) have developed an instinct not to stray from the hill or mountain,
>> (*c*) are able to withstand the climatic conditions typical of the hill or mountain,
>> and
>> (*d*) have developed resistance to diseases which are likely to occur in the area
>> in which the hill or mountain is situated;
> "hill land" means any hill or mountain where only hill sheep are likely to thrive
> throughout the year.
11.—(1) In areas of the country where arable crops can be grown in an unbroken series of not less than six years and it is reasonable that they should be grown on the holding or

part of it, the residual fertility value of the sod of the excess qualifying leys on the holding, if any.

(2) For the purposes of this paragraph—

(*a*) the growing of an arable crop includes the growing of clover, grass, lucerne, sainfoin or other seeds grown for a period of less than one year but does not include the laying down of a ley continuously maintained as such for more than one year,

(*b*) the qualifying leys comprising the excess qualifying leys shall be those indicated to be such by the tenant, and

(*c*) qualifying leys laid down at the expense of the landlord without reimbursement by the tenant or any previous tenant of the holding or laid down by and at the expense of the tenant pursuant to agreement by him with the landlord for the establishment of a specified area of leys on the holding as a condition of the landlord giving consent to the ploughing or other destruction of permanent pasture or pursuant to a direction given by an arbitrator on a reference under section 14(2) of this Act, shall not be included in the excess qualifying leys.

(3) In this paragraph —

"leys" means land laid down with clover, grass, lucerne, sainfoin or other seeds, but does not include permanent pasture;

"qualifying leys" means—

(*a*) leys continuously maintained as such for a period of three or more growing seasons since being laid down excluding, if the leys were undersown or autumn-sown, the calendar year in which the sowing took place, and

(*b*) arable land which within the three growing seasons immediately preceding the termination of the tenancy was ley continuously maintained as aforesaid before being destroyed by ploughing or some other means for the production of a tillage crop or crops;

and for the purpose of paragraph (*a*) above the destruction of a ley (by ploughing or some other means) followed as soon as practicable by re-seeding to a ley without sowing a crop in the interval between such destruction and such re-seeding shall be treated as not constituting a break in the continuity of the maintenance of the ley;

"the excess qualifying leys" means the area of qualifying leys on the holding at the termination of the tenancy which is equal to the area (if any) by which one-third of the aggregate of the areas of leys on the holding on the following dates, namely,

(*a*) at the termination of the tenancy,

(*b*) on the date one year prior to such termination, and

(*c*) on the date two years prior to such termination,

exceeds the accepted proportion at the termination of the tenancy;

"the accepted proportion" means the area which represents the proportion which the total area of the leys on the holding would, taking into account the capability of the holding, be expected to bear to the area of the holding, excluding the permanent pasture on the holding, or, if a greater proportion is provided for by or under the terms of the tenancy, that proportion.

GENERAL NOTE

Schedule 8 includes amendments made to its predecessor (Sched. 4 to the 1948 Act) as a result of recommendations of the Committee on Agricultural Valuation in their Third and Fourth Reports (1969 and 1977). The amendments to Sched. 4 to the 1948 Act were made by the Agricultural Holdings Act 1948 (Variation of Fourth Schedule) Orders of 1978 and 1985 (S.I. 1978 No. 742 and S.I. 1985 No. 1947). Both of these orders were revoked by the present Act (see Sched. 15, part II).

The changes, embodied in the present Sched. 8, some of which are minor, are the following:

Item 4 : Liming now includes chalking, which does not now appear as a separate item.

Item 5 : The present wording replaces the rather out of date "purchased manure (including artificial manure)."

Item 6 : The reference to the "folding" of poultry is omitted. The old wording did not include poultry fed in intensive poultry units.

Item 10 : A new definition of "hill sheep" and "hill land."

Item 11 : This was a more important change, introduced in 1978 but developed later, the new claim for "sod fertility." This is intended to compensate a tenant for increased fertility resulting from having left more arable land in pasture, with increased inherent fertility, than he is obliged to do, by the contract of tenancy or accepted local practice. (This is a rough description of a somewhat complex formula.)

SCHEDULE 9

COMPENSATION TO TENANT FOR IMPROVEMENTS BEGUN BEFORE 1ST MARCH 1948

PART I

TENANT'S RIGHT TO COMPENSATION FOR OLD IMPROVEMENTS

1.—(1) The tenant of an agricultural holding shall, subject to the provisions of this Act, be entitled on the termination of the tenancy, on quitting the holding, to obtain from his landlord compensation for an improvement specified in Part II of this Schedule carried out on the holding by the tenant, being an improvement begun before 1st March 1948.

(2) Improvements falling within sub-paragraph (1) above are in this Schedule referred to as "old improvements".

(3) The tenant of an agricultural holding shall not be entitled to compensation under this Schedule for an improvement which he was required to carry out by the terms of his tenancy where the contract of tenancy was made before 1st January 1921.

(4) Nothing in this Schedule shall prejudice the right of a tenant to claim any compensation to which he may be entitled under custom or agreement, or otherwise, in lieu of any compensation provided by this Schedule.

(5) The tenant of an agricultural holding shall not be entitled to compensation under this Schedule for an old improvement made on land which, at the time when the improvement was begun, was not a holding within the meaning of the Agricultural Holdings Act 1923, as originally enacted, and would not have fallen to be treated as such a holding by virtue of section 33 of that Act.

2.—(1) The amount of any compensation under this Schedule for an old improvement shall be an amount equal to the increase attributable to the improvement in the value of the agricultural holding as a holding, having regard to the character and situation of the holding and the average requirements of tenants reasonably skilled in husbandry.

(2) In the ascertainment of the amount of the compensation payable under this Schedule to the tenant of an agricultural holding in respect of an old improvement, there shall be taken into account any benefit which the landlord has given or allowed to the tenant in consideration of the tenant's executing the improvement, whether expressly stated in the contract of tenancy to be so given or allowed or not.

3.—(1) Compensation under this Schedule shall not be payable for an old improvement specified in any of paragraphs 1 to 15 of Part II of this Schedule unless, before the execution of the improvement, the landlord consented in writing (whether unconditionally or upon terms as to compensation or otherwise agreed between him and the tenant) to the execution of the improvement.

(2) Where the consent was given upon agreed terms as to compensation, compensation payable under the agreement shall be substituted for compensation under this Schedule.

4.—(1) Compensation under this Schedule shall not be payable for an old improvement consisting of that specified in paragraph 16 of Part II of this Schedule unless the tenant gave to the landlord, not more than three nor less than two months before beginning to execute the improvement, notice in writing under section 3 of the Agricultural Holdings Act 1923 of his intention to execute the improvement and of the manner in which he proposed to execute it, and—

(*a*) the landlord and tenant agreed on the terms on which the improvement was to be executed, or

(*b*) in a case where no agreement was reached and the tenant did not withdraw the notice, the landlord failed to exercise the right conferred on him by that section to execute the improvement himself within a reasonable time.

(2) Subsection (1) above shall not have effect if the landlord and tenant agreed, by the contract of tenancy or otherwise, to dispense with notice under the said section 3.

(3) If the landlord and tenant agreed (whether after notice was given under the said section 3 or by an agreement to dispense with notice under that section) upon terms as to compensation upon which the improvement was to be executed, compensation payable under the agreement shall be substituted for compensation under this Schedule.

5.—(1) Where the tenant of an agricultural holding has remained in the holding during two or more tenancies, he shall not be deprived of his right to compensation under this

Schedule in respect of old improvements by reason only that the improvements were made during a tenancy other than the one at the termination of which he quits the holding.

(2) Where, on entering into occupation of an agricultural holding, the tenant, with the consent in writing of his landlord, paid to an outgoing tenant any compensation payable under or in pursuance of this Schedule (or the Agricultural Holdings Act 1948 or the Agricultural Holdings Act 1923) in respect of the whole or part of an old improvement, he shall be entitled, on quitting the holding, to claim compensation for the improvement or part in the same manner, if at all, as the outgoing tenant would have been entitled if the outgoing tenant had remained tenant of the holding and quitted it at the time at which the tenant quits it.

PART II

OLD IMPROVEMENTS FOR WHICH COMPENSATION IS PAYABLE

1. Erection, alteration or enlargement of buildings.
2. Formation of silos.
3. Making and planting of osier beds.
4. Making of water meadows or works of irrigation.
5. Making of gardens.
6. Making or improvement of roads or bridges.
7. Making or improvement of watercourses, ponds, wells or reservoirs or of works for the application of water power or for supply of water for agricultural or domestic purposes.
8. Making or removal of permanent fences.
9. Planting of hops.
10. Planting of orchards or fruit bushes.
11. Reclaiming of waste land.
12. Warping or weiring of land.
13. Embankments and sluices against floods.
14. Erection of wirework in hop gardens.
15. Provision of permanent sheep-dipping accommodation.
16. Drainage.

GENERAL NOTE

Sched. 9 deals with old improvements, begun before March 1, 1948, some of which may still have a value the right to compensation for which must be preserved. Sched. 9, Part I, reproduces in substance ss.35 to 45 of the 1948 Act. Part II of Sched. 9 reproduces in the main the items in Parts I and II of Sched. 2 to the 1948 Act. The explanation of the few omissions is the passage of time since 1948. The short-term improvements which were in Part III of Sched. 2 to the 1948 Act are omitted: clearly any possible claims in respect of them have long since lapsed. A somewhat surprising change was an amendment of the measure of compensation for old improvements from that in s.37 of the 1948 Act to the measure now stated in para. 2(1) of Sched. 9. This amendment, which brought the measure into line with s.66(1) of the present Act, was made by the 1984 Act, Sched. 3, para. 10.

Sections 79 and 80   SCHEDULE 10

MARKET GARDEN IMPROVEMENTS

1. Planting of standard or other fruit trees permanently set out.
2. Planting of fruit bushes permanently set out.
3. Planting of strawberry plants.
4. Planting of asparagus, rhubarb and other vegetable crops which continue productive for two or more years.
5. Erection, alteration or enlargement of buildings for the purpose of the trade or business of a market gardener.

GENERAL NOTE

Sched. 10 reproduces the market garden improvements in Sched. 5 to the 1948 Act. An improvement consisting of the erection or enlargement (but not the alteration) of buildings begun before March 1, 1948 is still compensatable (see s.79(2)).

        SCHEDULE 11

ARBITRATIONS

Appointment and remuneration of arbitrator

1.—(1) The arbitrator shall be a person appointed by agreement between the parties or, in default of agreement, a person appointed on the application of either of the parties by the President of the Royal Institution of Chartered Surveyors (referred to in this Schedule as "the President") from among the members of the panel constituted for the purposes of this paragraph.

(2) No application may be made to the President for an arbitrator to be appointed by him under this paragraph unless the application is accompanied by such fee as may be prescribed as the fee for such an application; but once the fee has been paid in connection with any such application no further fee shall be payable in connection with any subsequent application for the President to exercise any function exercisable by him in relation to the arbitration by virtue of this Schedule (including an application for the appointment by him in an appropriate case of a new arbitrator).

(3) Any such appointment by the President shall be made by him as soon as possible after receiving the application; but where the application is referable to a demand for arbitration made under section 12 of this Act any such appointment shall in any event not be made by him earlier than four months before the next termination date following the date of the demand (as defined by subsection (4) of that section).

(4) A person appointed by the President as arbitrator shall, where the arbitration relates to an agricultural holding in Wales, be a person who possesses a knowledge of Welsh agricultural conditions, and, if either party to the arbitration so requires, a knowledge also of the Welsh language.

(5) For the purposes of this Schedule there shall be constituted a panel consisting of such number of persons as the Lord Chancellor may determine, to be appointed by him.

2. If the arbitrator dies, or is incapable of acting, or for seven days after notice from either party requiring him to act fails to act, a new arbitrator may be appointed as if no arbitrator had been appointed.

3. In relation to an arbitrator who is appointed in place of another arbitrator (whether under paragraph 2 above or otherwise) the reference in section 12(2) of this Act to the date of the reference shall be construed as a reference to the date when the original arbitrator was appointed.

4. Neither party shall have power to revoke the appointment of the arbitrator without the consent of the other party; and his appointment shall not be revoked by the death of either party.

5. Every appointment, application, notice, revocation and consent under the foregoing paragraphs must be in writing.

6. The remuneration of the arbitrator shall be—

  (*a*) where he is appointed by agreement between the parties, such amount as may be agreed upon by him and the parties or, in default of agreement, fixed by the registrar of the county court (subject to an appeal to the judge of the court) on an application made by the arbitrator or either of the parties,

  (*b*) where he is appointed by the President, such amount as may be agreed upon by the arbitrator and the parties or, in default of agreement, fixed by the President,

and shall be recoverable by the arbitrator as a debt due from either of the parties to the arbitration.

Conduct of proceedings and witnesses

7. The parties to the arbitration shall, within thirty-five days from the appointment of the arbitrator, deliver to him a statement of their respective cases with all necessary particulars and—

  (*a*) no amendment or addition to the statement or particulars delivered shall be allowed after the expiry of the said thirty-five days except with the consent of the arbitrator,

  (*b*) a party to the arbitration shall be confined at the hearing to the matters alleged in the statement and particulars delivered by him and any amendment or addition duly made.

8. The parties to the arbitration and all persons claiming through them respectively shall, subject to any legal objection, submit to be examined by the arbitrator, on oath or affirmation, in relation to the matters in dispute and shall, subject to any such objection,

produce before the arbitrator all samples and documents within their possession or power respectively which may be required or called for, and do all other things which during the proceedings the arbitrator may require.

9. Witnesses appearing at the arbitration shall, if the arbitrator thinks fit, be examined on oath or affirmation, and the arbitrator shall have power to administer oaths to, or to take the affirmation of, the parties and witnesses appearing.

10. The provisions of county court rules as to the issuing of witness summonses shall, subject to such modifications as may be prescribed by such rules, apply for the purposes of the arbitration as if it were an action or matter in the county court.

11.—(1) Subject to sub-paragraphs (2) and (3) below, any person who—

  (a) having been summoned in pursuance of county court rules as a witness in the arbitration refuses or neglects, without sufficient cause, to appear or to produce any documents required by the summons to be produced, or

  (b) having been so summoned or being present at the arbitration and being required to give evidence, refuses to be sworn or give evidence,

shall forfeit such fine as the judge of the county court may direct.

(2) A judge shall not have power under sub-paragraph (1) above to direct that a person shall forfeit a fine of an amount exceeding £10.

(3) No person summoned in pursuance of county court rules as a witness in the arbitration shall forfeit a fine under this paragraph unless there has been paid or tendered to him at the time of the service of the summons such sum in respect of his expenses (including, in such cases as may be prescribed by county court rules, compensation for loss of time) as may be so prescribed for the purposes of section 55 of the County Courts Act 1984.

(4) The judge of the county court may at his discretion direct that the whole or any part of any such fine, after deducting costs, shall be applicable towards indemnifying the party injured by the refusal or neglect.

12.—(1) Subject to sub-paragraph (2) below, the judge of the county court may, if he thinks fit, upon application on affidavit by either party to the arbitration, issue an order under his hand for bringing up before the arbitrator any person (in this paragraph referred to as a "prisoner") confined in any place under any sentence or under committal for trial or otherwise, to be examined as a witness in the arbitration.

(2) No such order shall be made with respect to a person confined under process in any civil action or matter.

(3) Subject to sub-paragraph (4) below, the prisoner mentioned in any such order shall be brought before the arbitrator under the same custody, and shall be dealt with in the same manner in all respects, as a prisoner required by a writ of habeas corpus to be brought before the High Court and examined there as a witness.

(4) The person having the custody of the prisoner shall not be bound to obey the order unless there is tendered to him a reasonable sum for the conveyance and maintenance of a proper officer or officers and of the prisoner in going to, remaining at, and returning from, the place where the arbitration is held.

13. The High Court may order that a writ of habeas corpus ad testificandum shall issue to bring up a prisoner for examination before the arbitrator, if the prisoner is confined in any prison under process in any civil action or matter.

Award

14.—(1) Subject to sub-paragraph (2) below, the arbitrator shall make and sign his award within fifty-six days of his appointment.

(2) The President may from time to time enlarge the time limited for making the award, whether that time has expired or not.

15. The arbitrator may if he thinks fit make an interim award for the payment of any sum on account of the sum to be finally awarded.

16. The arbitrator shall—

  (a) state separately in the award the amounts awarded in respect of the several claims referred to him, and

  (b) on the application of either party, specify the amount awarded in respect of any particular improvement or any particular matter the subject of the award.

17. Where by virtue of this Act compensation under an agreement is to be substituted for compensation under this Act for improvements or for any such matters as are specified in Part II of Schedule 8 to this Act, the arbitrator shall award compensation in accordance with the agreement instead of in accordance with this Act.

18. The award shall fix a day not later than one month after the delivery of the award for the payment of the money awarded as compensation, costs or otherwise.

19. The award shall be final and binding on the parties and the persons claiming under them respectively.

20. The arbitrator shall have power to correct in the award any clerical mistake or error arising from any accidental slip or omission.

Reasons for award

21. Section 12 of the Tribunals and Inquiries Act 1971 (reasons to be given for decisions of tribunals etc.) shall apply in relation to the award of an arbitrator appointed under this Schedule by agreement between the parties as it applies in relation to the award of an arbitrator appointed under this Schedule otherwise than by such agreement.

Interest on awards

22. Any sum directed to be paid by the award shall, unless the award otherwise directs, carry interest as from the date of the award and at the same rate as a judgment debt.

Costs

23. The costs of, and incidental to, the arbitration and award shall be in the discretion of the arbitrator who may direct to and by whom and in what manner the costs, or any part of the costs, are to be paid.

24. On the application of either party, any such costs shall be taxable in the county court according to such of the scales prescribed by county court rules for proceedings in the county court as may be directed by the arbitrator under paragraph 23 above, or, in the absence of any such direction, by the county court.

25.—(1) The arbitrator shall, in awarding costs, take into consideration—

(*a*) the reasonableness or unreasonableness of the claim of either party, whether in respect of amount or otherwise,

(*b*) any unreasonable demand for particulars or refusal to supply particulars, and

(*c*) generally all the circumstances of the case.

(2) The arbitrator may disallow the costs of any witness whom he considers to have been called unnecessarily and any other costs which he considers to have been unnecessarily incurred.

Special case, setting aside award and remission

26. The arbitrator may, at any stage of the proceedings, and shall, upon a direction in that behalf given by the judge of the county court upon an application made by either party, state in the form of a special case for the opinion of the county court any question of law arising in the course of the arbitration and any question as to the jurisdiction of the arbitrator.

27.—(1) Where the arbitrator has misconducted himself, the county court may remove him.

(2) Where the arbitrator has misconducted himself, or an arbitration or award has been improperly procured, or there is an error of law on the face of the award, the county court may set the award aside.

28.—(1) The county court may from time to time remit the award, or any part of the award, to the reconsideration of the arbitrator.

(2) In any case where it appears to the county court that there is an error of law on the face of the award, the court may, instead of exercising its power of remission under sub-paragraph (1) above, vary the award by substituting for so much of it as is affected by the error such award as the court considers that it would have been proper for the arbitrator to make in the circumstances; and the award shall thereupon have effect as so varied.

(3) Where remission is ordered under that sub-paragraph, the arbitrator shall, unless the order otherwise directs, make and sign his award within thirty days after the date of the order.

(4) If the county court is satisfied that the time limited for making the said award is for any good reason insufficient, the court may extend or further extend that time for such period as it thinks proper.

Miscellaneous

29. Any amount paid, in respect of the remuneration of the arbitrator by either party to the arbitration, in excess of the amount, if any, directed by the award to be paid by him in respect of the costs of the award shall be recoverable from the other party.

30. The provisions of this Schedule relating to the fixing and recovery of the remuneration of an arbitrator and the making and enforcement of an award as to costs, together with any other provision in this Schedule applicable for the purposes of or in connection with those provisions, shall apply where the arbitrator has no jurisdiction to decide the question referred to him as they apply where the arbitrator has jurisdiction to decide that question.

31. For the purposes of this Schedule, an arbitrator appointed by the President shall be taken to have been so appointed at the time when the President executed the instrument of appointment; and in the case of any such arbitrator the periods mentioned in paragraphs 7 and 14 above shall accordingly run from that time.

32. Any instrument of appointment or other document purporting to be made in the exercise of any function exercisable by the President under paragraph 1, 6 or 14 above and to be signed by or on behalf of the President shall be taken to be such an instrument or document unless the contrary is shown.

GENERAL NOTE

The annotations to Sched. 11 are the minimum necessary for explanation of changes made by the 1984 Act and now consolidated in the present Act, but they are the maximum that space allows. Agricultural arbitrations will be treated fully in the forthcoming new edition of *Muir Watt's Agricultural Holdings.*

Para. 1(1)

The President. The transfer of the appointing function from the Minister (see s.96(1)) to the President of the RICS was made by s.8 of the 1984 Act and the Agricultural Holdings Act 1984 (Commencement) Order 1985 (S.I. 1985 No. 1644 (C.39)) and took effect on January 1, 1986.

Para. 1(2)

Such fee as may be prescribed. See the Agricultural Holdings (Fee) Regulations 1985 (S.I. 1985 No. 1967) prescribing a fee of £70. Forms of application are available from the offices of the RICS, 12 Great George Street, Parliament Square, London, SWIP 3AD (Tel. 01-222 7000, ext. 229). Attention is drawn to the need, in the case of a rent arbitration, for the application to the President to be made before "the next termination date" as defined in s.12(4); otherwise the demand for arbitration ceases to be effective.

Para. 1 (3)

Not . . . earlier than four months before the next termination date. The idea is to ensure that the circumstances at the "date of the reference" (the date when the arbitrator's appointment is completed), which is the date of the valuation, do not differ markedly from the circumstances when the new rent begins to be payable.

Para. 3

The date when the original arbitrator was appointed. This para, resulting from an amendment made by the 1984 Act (Sched. 3, para. 28(3)) embodies the principle of the Scottish decision in *Dundee Corporation* v. *Guthrie* 1969 S.L.T. 93 and resolved a doubt as to the position in England and Wales.

Para. 4

Shall not be revoked by the death of either party. A 1984 Act amendment (Sched. 3, para. 28(4)) resolving a previous doubt.

Para. 6

Fixed by the President. Note that the arbitrator and the parties should try to agree the arbitrator's remuneration. It is only in default of agreement that it is to be fixed by the President.

Para. 7

Amendment. See *ED & AD Cook-Bourne (Farms) Ltd.* v. *Mellows* (1981) 262 E.G. 229 for guidance by C.A. as to the attitude which arbitrators should adopt towards amendments (assuming, of course, that a statement had been delivered before the expiry of the 35-day time-limit). The express power given to allow amendments or additions appears clearly to negate the existence of any implied power for the arbitrator to extend the time for delivery of the statement of case itself; there is no High Court authority on this, but see *Church Commissioners for England* v. *Mathews* (1979) 251 E.G. 1074 (C.C.) and *Richards* v. *Allinson* (1978) 249 E.G. 59 (C.C.).

Para. 21

Appointed under this Schedule by agreement. By a 1984 Act amendment (Sched. 3, para. 28(7)) an arbitrator appointed by agreement must (as was already the case where the arbitrator was appointed by the Minister, now by the President) give reasons for his award on request under the Tribunals and Inquiries Act 1971.

Para. 22

Interest. This provision results from another 1984 Act amendment (Sched. 3, para. 28(7)). There is no provision for interest before the date of the award.

Para. 24

By the county court. This reworded paragraph, substituted for the previous one by the 1984 Act (Sched. 3, para. 28(8)) closes a previous gap by providing that the county court can fix the scale if the arbitrator does not.

Para. 28

Remit the award. In 1984 for the first time the power to remit an agricultural arbitrator's award was given to the county court (1984 Act, Sched. 3, para. 28(9)) and is now embodied in para. 28. The court is also given a new power to vary an award by correcting an error on its face. A time-limit is set for making the award on remission, but the court may extend the time. These were long overdue modernisations of the agricultural code.

Para. 30

Where the arbitrator has no jurisdiction. This para. is derived from the Agriculture Act 1958, before which an arbitrator who had no jurisdiction could not make an order as to costs.

Para. 31

When the President exercised the instrument of appointment. This was an important amendment made by the 1984 Act (Sched. 3, para. 28(10)). An arbitrator is appointed by the President at the precise time when he executes the instrument of appointment. The time for delivery of statements of case by the parties and for the making of an award by the arbitrator run strictly from that time. This negates the "benevolent construction" (that the time runs only from the *receipt* of the appointment) suggested in *University College, Oxford* v. *Durdy* [1982] Ch. 413.

Sections 65, 70, 76, 77, 78, 98   SCHEDULE 12

MODIFICATIONS APPLICABLE TO OLD TENANCIES AND OTHER SIMILAR CASES

General

1. Section 2 of this Act shall not apply to an agreement made before 1st March 1948.
2. Section 3 of this Act shall not apply to a tenancy granted or agreed to be granted before 1st January 1921.

Right to remove fixtures

3. A tenant shall not be entitled by virtue of section 10(1) or 79 of this Act (or the said section 79 as applied by paragraph 10 below) to remove a fixture or building acquired by him before 1st January 1901.

Notices to quit

4.—(1) Where a tenancy of an agricultural holding subsists under an agreement entered into before 25th March 1947, section 25(1) of this Act does not apply—

(*a*) to a notice given by or on behalf of the Secretary of State under the provisions of any agreement of tenancy, where possession of the land is required for naval, military or air force purposes, or

(*b*) to a notice given by a corporation carrying on a railway, dock, canal, water or other undertaking in respect of land acquired by the corporation for the purposes of their undertaking or by a government department or local authority, where possession of the land is required by the corporation, government department or authority for the purpose (not being the use of the land for agriculture) for which it was acquired by the corporation, department or authority or appropriated under any statutory provision.

(2) In the application of sub-paragraph (1)(*b*) above to a Board, the reference to land acquired by the corporation for the purposes of their undertaking shall be construed as including a reference to land transferred to that Board by section 31 of the Transport Act 1962 or, in the case of London Regional Transport, by section 16 of the Transport (London) Act 1969, being land—

(*a*) acquired, for the purpose of an undertaking vested in the British Transport Commission by Part II of the Transport Act 1947, by the body carrying on that undertaking, or

(*b*) acquired by a body carrying on an undertaking vested in any such undertaking as is mentioned in paragraph (*a*) above by virtue of an amalgamation or absorption scheme under the Railways Act 1921, being a scheme that came into operation on or after 7th July 1923,

and the reference to the purpose for which the land was acquired or appropriated by the corporation shall be construed accordingly.

(3) In sub-paragraph (2) above "a Board" means any of the following, namely—

Associated British Ports,
the British Railways Board,
the British Waterways Board, and
London Regional Transport.

(4) Sub-paragraph (2) above shall have effect in relation to a subsidiary of London Regional Transport (within the meaning of the London Regional Transport Act 1984) as it has effect in relation to London Regional Transport, so far as relates to land transferred to London Regional Transport as there mentioned and subsequently transferred to that subsidiary by a scheme made under section 4 or 5 of that Act.

(5) Where by a scheme under section 7 of the Transport Act 1968 relevant land has been transferred by the British Railways Board to another body, sub-paragraph (2) above shall (so far as relates to relevant land so transferred) have effect in relation to that body as it has effect in relation to the British Railways Board; and in this sub-paragraph "relevant land" means land falling within paragraph (*a*) or (*b*) of sub-paragraph (2) above and transferred to the British Railways Board as there mentioned.

(6) Where, by virtue of an Act (whether public, general or local) passed, or an instrument having effect under an Act made, after 7th July 1923 and before 30th July 1948, any right of a corporation carrying on a water undertaking or of a local authority to avail itself of the benefit conferred by section 25(2)(*b*) of the Agricultural Holdings Act 1923 was transferred to some other person, that other person shall have the same right to avail himself of the benefit conferred by sub-paragraph (1)(*b*) above as the corporation or authority would have had if the Act or instrument by virtue of which the transfer was effected had not been passed or made.

Compensation for improvements

5. The tenant of an agricultural holding shall not be entitled to compensation under section 64(1) of this Act for an improvement which he was required to carry out by the terms of his tenancy where the contract of tenancy was made before 1st January 1921.

Compensation for tenant-right matters

6.—(1) Where the tenant of an agricultural holding entered into occupation of the holding before 1st March 1948, section 65(1) of this Act shall not apply to him as regards the matters specified in paragraphs 7 to 10 of Part II of Schedule 8 to this Act, unless, before the termination of the tenancy, he gives notice in writing to the landlord stating that he elects that it is to apply to him as regards those matters.

(2) Where the tenancy terminates by reason of a notice to quit and at any time while the notice to quit is current the landlord gives notice in writing to the tenant requiring him to

elect whether section 65(1) of this Act is to apply to him as regards the matters specified in paragraphs 7 to 10 of Part II of Schedule 8 to this Act, the tenant shall not be entitled to give a notice under sub-paragraph (1) above after the expiry of—

(*a*) one month from the giving of the notice under this sub-paragraph, or

(*b*) if the operation of the notice to quit depends upon any proceedings under section 26 or 27 of this Act (including any proceedings under Schedule 3 to this Act), one month from the termination of those proceedings.

7.—(1) This paragraph applies where the tenant of an agricultural holding entered into occupation of the holding before 31st December 1951 and immediately before that date subsection (1) of section 47 of the Agricultural Holdings Act 1948 applied to him as regards the matters now specified in paragraphs 7 to 9 of Part II of Schedule 8 to this Act (whether by virtue of his having entered into occupation of the holding on or after 1st March 1948 or by virtue of a notice having been given under paragraph (*c*) of the proviso to subsection (1) of the said section 47).

(2) Where this paragraph applies, section 65(1) of this Act shall not apply to the tenant as regards the matters specified in paragraph 10 of Part II of Schedule 8 to this Act unless, before the termination of the tenancy, he gives notice in writing to the landlord that it is to apply to him as regards those matters.

(3) Paragraph 6(2) above shall have effect in relation to a notice under this paragraph as if in that provision there were substituted—

(*a*) for the reference to the matters specified in paragraphs 7 to 10 of Part II of Schedule 8 to this Act a reference to the matters specified in paragraph 10 of Part II of that Schedule, and

(*b*) for the reference to a notice under paragraph 6(1) above, a reference to a notice under this paragraph.

8.—(1) In a case where, by virtue of paragraph 6 or 7 above, section 65(1) above does not apply to a tenant as regards all or any of the matters specified in paragraphs 7 to 10 of Part II of Schedule 8 to this Act—

(*a*) sections 70(4) and (5) and 76(3) of this Act shall have effect with the omission of references to the excluded matters,

(*b*) section 77(1) of this Act shall not apply to compensation to the tenant for the excluded matters, and

(*c*) section 78(3) of this Act, in so far as it provides that a claim for compensation in a case for which the provisions of this Act do not provide for compensation shall not be enforceable except under an agreement in writing, shall not apply to a claim by a tenant for compensation for the excluded matters.

(2) In this paragraph "the excluded matters" means, in relation to a case to which this paragraph applies, the matters as regards which section 65(1) does not apply to the tenant.

9. The Minister may revoke or vary the provisions of paragraphs 6 to 8 above so far as they relate to the matters specified in paragraph 10 of Part II of Schedule 8 to this Act as if those provisions were contained in an order made under section 91 of this Act.

Market gardens

10.—(1) Except as provided by this paragraph, subsections (2) to (5) of section 79 of this Act shall not apply unless the agreement in writing mentioned in subsection (1) of that section was made on or after 1st January 1896.

(2) Where—

(*a*) under a contract of tenancy current on 1st January 1896 an agricultural holding was at that date in use or cultivation as a market garden with the knowledge of the landlord, and

(*b*) the tenant had then executed on the holding, without having received before the execution a written notice of dissent by the landlord, an improvement of a kind specified in Schedule 10 to this Act (other than one consisting of such an alteration of a building as did not constitute an enlargement of it),

subsections (2) to (5) of section 79 (and section 81) of this Act shall apply in respect of the holding as if it had been agreed in writing after that date that the holding should be let or treated as a market garden.

(3) The improvements in respect of which compensation is payable under subsections (2) to (5) of section 79 of this Act as applied by this paragraph shall include improvements executed before, as well as improvements executed after, 1st January 1896.

(4) Where the land used and cultivated as mentioned in sub-paragraph (2) above consists of part of an agricultural holding only, this paragraph shall apply as if that part were a separate holding.

GENERAL NOTE

Most of the modifications mentioned in this Schedule have been noted in the annotations to the sections affected. The paras. concerning tenant-right matters and market gardens, however, need a few more words of explanation.

Tenant-right matters

A tenant who entered into occupation of his holding before March 1, 1948 is required to make a written election, in a notice to his landlord, in favour of the statutory basis of compensation for tenant-right matters. Although to a large extent now a matter of history, there may still be tenants who have not elected for the general statutory basis for tenant-right; any customary rights which such tenants may have for tenant-right compensation are preserved: see s.77. Special provisions for election were required when in 1951 the acclimatisation, hefting or settlement of hill sheep on hill land was recognised as a statutory tenant-right matter by the Agricultural Holdings Act (Variation of Fourth Schedule) Order 1951 (S.I. 1951 No. 2168). A tenant in occupation before March 1, 1948 who had already made an election in favour of the general statutory basis had to make a new, specific, election in favour of the new statutory item. A tenant who entered on or after March 1, 1948 but before December 31, 1951 has to make an election that the new statutory item should apply. Such a tenant who does not elect will be entitled to claim customary compensation, despite its general abolition by s.77, for acclimatisation if such a customary right exists in his district. As regards the latest statutory addition to tenant-right, residual soil fertility, there was an interesting change of policy. At first it was provided that tenants entering into occupation on or after March 1, 1948 but before July 1, 1978 had to elect for this item (Agricultural Holdings Act 1948 (Variation of Fourth Schedule) Order 1978 (S.I. 1978 No. 742)). But this requirement was revoked in 1985 by the Agricultural Holdings Act 1948 (Variation of Fourth Schedule) Order 1985 (S.I. 1985 No. 1947). Accordingly compensation for sod fertility became available to such tenants automatically. No reference is, therefore, needed to it in Sched. 12. Para. 8 of Sched. 12 makes a number of purely consequential amendments to provisions in the Act in cases where the tenant has not elected for the statutory basis of tenant-right compensation.

Market gardens

Attention has already been drawn in the annotations to s.79 to a vanishing method by which a holding may qualify for market garden privileges, namely, by having fulfilled certain conditions on January 1, 1896. It is not known how many holdings today are in this category, but there may be a few and it is still necessary to preserve in legislative form the qualifying conditions. This is done in para. 10 of Sched. 12. The explanation of the odd-looking exception in para. 10(2)(*b*), "(other than one consisting of such an alteration of a building as did not constitute an enlargement of it)" is that the "alteration", as distinct from the "enlargement", of a building was only added to the list of market garden improvements by the 1947 Act (s.45 and para. 22(1) of Sched. 7) with effect from March 1, 1948.

Section 99   SCHEDULE 13

TRANSITIONAL PROVISIONS AND SAVINGS

Construction of references to old and new law

1.—(1) Any reference, whether express or implied, in any enactment, instrument or document (including this Act and any enactment amended by Schedule 14 to this Act) to, or to things done or falling to be done under or for the purposes of, any provision of this Act shall, if and so far as the nature of the reference permits, be construed as including, in relation to the times, circumstances or purposes in relation to which the corresponding provision repealed by this Act has or had effect, a reference to, or as the case may be, to things done or falling to be done under or for the purposes of, that corresponding provision.

(2) Any reference, whether express or implied, in any enactment, instrument or document (including the enactments repealed by this Act and enactments, instruments and documents passed or made after the passing of this Act) to, or to things done or falling to be done under or for the purposes of, any provision repealed by this Act shall, if and so far as the nature of the reference permits, be construed as including, in relation to the times, circumstances or purposes in relation to which the corresponding provision of this Act has effect, a reference to, or as the case may be, to things done or falling to be done under or for the purposes of, that corresponding provision.

(3) In this paragraph references to any provision repealed by this Act include references to any earlier provision, corresponding to a provision so repealed, which was repealed by the Agricultural Holdings (Notices to Quit) Act 1977, the Agricultural Holdings Act 1948, the Agricultural Holdings Act 1923 or the Agricultural Holdings Act 1908.

2. References, in whatever terms, in any enactment to a holding within the meaning of the Agricultural Holdings Act 1923 shall be construed as references to an agricultural holding within the meaning of this Act.

Continuation of old law for certain pending cases

3.—(1) Nothing in this Act shall apply in relation to—

(*a*) a notice to quit an agricultural holding or part of an agricultural holding—
> (i) given before the commencement of this Act, or
> (ii) in the case of a notice to quit given after that time which includes a statement that it is given by reason of the death of a former tenant, where the date of death was before that time,

(*b*) an agricultural holding—
> (i) the tenancy of which terminated before the commencement of this Act, or
> (ii) the tenant of which quitted the holding before the commencement of this Act or quitted after that time in consequence of a notice to quit falling within paragraph (*a*) above,

(*c*) an arbitration where the arbitrator was appointed under the Agricultural Holdings Act 1948 before the commencement of this Act,

(*d*) an application made before the commencement of this Act to the Tribunal under any of the enactments repealed by this Act, or

(*e*) an application made after the commencement of this Act to the Tribunal for a direction entitling the applicant to a tenancy of an agricultural holding on the death or retirement of the tenant where the date of death or the date of the giving of the retirement notice was before that time;

and accordingly the enactments repealed or amended by this Act shall in relation to any such notice to quit, agricultural holding, arbitration (including an award made in such an arbitration) or application (including any proceedings arising out of any such application or any direction given in any such proceedings) continue to have effect as if this Act had not been passed.

(2) This paragraph shall have effect subject to paragraph 1 above and paragraph 11 below.

Periods of time

4. Where a period of time specified in any enactment repealed by this Act is current at the commencement of this Act, this Act shall have effect as if the corresponding provision of this Act had been in force when the period began to run.

Transfer of functions

5. Any reference, whether express or implied, in this Act (or any enactment amended by Schedule 14 to this Act) to, or to anything done by, the Minister, the Tribunal, an arbitrator or the President of the Royal Institution of Chartered Surveyors shall where the relevant function has been transferred to that person be construed, in relation to any time before the transfer, as including a reference to, or to the corresponding thing done by, the person by whom the function was then exercisable.

6. Section 22 of this Act shall have effect in relation to the appointment of a person in pursuance of an application made before 1st January 1986 under section 16(2) of the Agricultural Holdings Act 1948 as if for references to the President of the Royal Institution of Chartered Surveyors there were substituted references to the Minister and as if subsections (4) and (5) were omitted.

7.—(1) Schedule 11 to this Act shall have effect in relation to the appointment of an arbitrator in pursuance of an application made before 1st January 1986 under Schedule 6 to the Agricultural Holdings Act 1948 and in relation to an arbitrator appointed in pursuance of such an application as if—

(*a*) for references to the President of the Royal Institution of Chartered Surveyors there were substituted references to the Minister,

(*b*) paragraphs 1(2) and 32 were omitted, and

(*c*) at the end there were inserted—

"33. Where the Minister or any other person acting on behalf of Her Majesty is a party to the arbitration, anything which under this Schedule is to be done by the Minister in relation to the appointment or remuneration of the arbitrator or the extension of time for making and signing his award shall be done instead by the President of the Royal Institution of Chartered Surveyors."

(2) An order under section 84 of this Act shall not make provision inconsistent with the modifications of Schedule 11 effected by sub-paragraph (1) above.

Compensation

8. Notwithstanding section 16 of the Interpretation Act 1978, rights to compensation conferred by this Act shall be in lieu of rights to compensation conferred by any enactment repealed by this Act.

Right to remove fixtures

9. Sections 13 and 67 of the Agricultural Holdings Act 1948 shall continue to have effect (to the exclusion of sections 10 and 79 of this Act) in relation to an agricultural holding in a case where the tenant gave notice under subsection (2)(*b*) of the said section 13 before 12th September 1984 as the said sections 13 and 67 had effect before that date.

Compensation for damage by game

10. Section 14 of the Agricultural Holdings Act 1948 shall continue to have effect (to the exclusion of section 20 of this Act) in relation to an agricultural holding in a case where a notice was given to the landlord under paragraph (*a*) of the proviso to subsection (1) of the said section 14 before 12th September 1984 as the said section 14 had effect before that date.

Succession on death or retirement

11.—(1) Where Part IV of this Act has effect in relation to an application under that Part, references in that Part to notices to quit shall include references to notices to quit given before the commencement of this Act and, in particular, section 54 of this Act shall apply (to the exclusion of paragraph 4 of Schedule 2 to the Agricultural Holdings Act 1984) in relation to a notice to quit given before the commencement of this Act as it applies in relation to a notice to quit given after that time.

(2) Where, by virtue of paragraph 3(1) above, Part II of the Agriculture (Miscellaneous Provisions) Act 1976 or Schedule 2 to the Agricultural Holdings Act 1984 has effect in relation to an application under the said Part II or, as the case may be, under the said Schedule 2, references in the said Part II or the said Schedule 2 to notices to quit shall include references to notices to quit given after the commencement of this Act and, in particular, paragraph 4 of the said Schedule 2 shall apply (to the exclusion of section 54 of this Act) in relation to a notice to quit given after the commencement of this Act as it applies in relation to a notice to quit given before that time.

(3) This paragraph is without prejudice to the generality of paragraph 1 above.

12. Without prejudice to the generality of section 34(1)(*b*)(iii) of this Act, a written contract of tenancy which grants the tenancy of an agricultural holding and indicates (in whatever terms) that section 2(1) of the Agricultural Holdings Act 1984 is not to apply in relation to the tenancy shall be taken to be such a contract of tenancy as is mentioned in that section.

Record of condition of holding

13.—(1) In section 70(2)(*b*) of this Act the reference to a record made under section 22 of this Act shall include a reference to a record made before 12th September 1984 under section 16 of the Agricultural Holdings Act 1948 as it had effect before that date.

(2) Sub-paragraph (1) above is without prejudice to the generality of paragraph 1 above.

Insolvency

14. Sections 80(9) and 96(2) of this Act shall have effect—

(*a*) until the date on which Part III of the Insolvency Act 1985 comes into force, and (*b*) on or after that date, in any case in which a petition of bankruptcy was presented, or a receiving order or adjudication in bankruptcy was made, before that date,

as if for paragraph (*a*) of section 96(2) there were substituted—

"(*a*) he has become bankrupt or has made a composition or arrangement with his creditors or a receiving order is made against him".

Forms for arbitration

15. Any form specified in pursuance of paragraph 15 or 27 of Schedule 6 to the Agricultural Holdings Act 1948 and in force immediately before 12th September 1984 shall have effect as if prescribed by an order under section 84 of this Act, and may be varied or revoked accordingly.

Notices to quit

16. Paragraphs 10(1)(*d*) and 11(2) of Part II of Schedule 3 to this Act shall not apply in relation to any act or omission by a tenant which occurred before 12th September 1984.

GENERAL NOTE

This Schedule brings together a number of fairly self-explanatory cases where transitional provisions are required. It is necessary only to draw attention to a few of them.

Construction of references to old and new law

It is under the provisions of para. 1 that statutory instruments made under earlier Acts, such as the 1948 Act, continue to be operative until new orders or regulations are made under section 94.

Continuation of old law for certain pending cases

Attention is drawn to para. 3 for the position where a notice to quit has been given, or a death has taken place, before the commencement of the present Act, *i.e.* before June 18, 1986. It will also be noted that the Act does not apply, *i.e.* that the old law will still apply, to an arbitration where the arbitrator was appointed under the 1948 Act before that date, and where an application to the agricultural land tribunal was made before that date. Again, the previous enactments will apply even where an application was made after that date for a direction entitling the applicant to a tenancy on the death or retirement of the tenant, where the date of death or the date of the giving of the retirement notice took place before that date. But the provisions of para. 3 are subject in certain respects to para. 11, below.

Succession on death or retirement: notices to quit

Para. 11 clarifies the position where, owing to the date of application, the succession provisions as enacted in the consolidation Act apply, but notices to quit are given before its commencement, and (the converse case) where, owing to the date of application, the succession provisions as amended by the 1984 Act apply, but notices to quit are given after the commencement of the consolidation Act. The solution is that in the former case the consolidation Act will apply to notices to quit given before the commencement as well as to those given after; and in the latter case Sched. 2 to the 1984 Act will apply to those given after the commencement as well as to those given before. These provisions apply in particular to s.54 of the present Act and para. 4 of Sched. 2 to the 1984 Act.

Section 100   SCHEDULE 14

CONSEQUENTIAL AMENDMENTS

The Small Holdings and Allotments Act 1908

1.—(1) Section 47 of the Small Holdings and Allotments Act 1908 shall be amended as follows.

(2) In subsection (1) for the words "section forty-two of the Agricultural Holdings Act 1908" there shall be substituted the words "subsections (2) to (5) of section 79 of the Agricultural Holdings Act 1986".

(3) In subsection (2)—

(*a*) for the words "Agricultural Holdings Act 1908", in the first place where they occur, there shall be substituted the words "Agricultural Holdings Act 1986", (*b*) for the words "section forty-two of the Agricultural Holdings Act 1908" there shall be substituted the words "subsections (2) to (5) of section 79 of the Agricultural Holdings Act 1986", and

(*c*) for the words "Part III of the First Schedule to the Agricultural Holdings Act 1908" there shall be substituted the words "Schedule 8 to the Agricultural Holdings Act 1986".

(4) In subsection (3) for the words "Agricultural Holdings Act 1908" there shall be substituted the words "Agricultural Holdings Act 1986".

2. In section 58 of that Act for the words "Agricultural Holdings Act 1908" there shall be substituted the words "Agricultural Holdings Act 1986".

3. In paragraph (3) of Part II of Schedule 1 to that Act for the words "Agricultural Holdings Act 1908" there shall be substituted the words "Agricultural Holdings Act 1986".

The Law of Distress Amendment Act 1908

4. In section 4(1) of the Law of Distress Amendment Act 1908 for the words from "live stock" to "Act 1908" there shall be substituted the words "agisted livestock within the meaning of section 18 of the Agricultural Holdings Act 1986 to which that section".

The Chequers Estate Act 1917

5. In clauses 6B(*b*) and 8D of the Deed set out in the Schedule to the Chequers Estate Act 1917 for the words "Agricultural Holdings Act 1948" there shall be substituted the words "Agricultural Holdings Act 1986, except section 60(2)(*b*) or 62 of that Act".

The Land Settlement (Facilities) Act 1919

6. In section 2(3) of the Land Settlement (Facilities Act) 1919 for the words "Second Schedule of the Agricultural Holdings Act 1908" there shall be substituted the words "Agricultural Holdings Act 1986".

7. In section 11(4) of that Act for the words "Second Schedule to the Agricultural Holdings Act 1908" there shall be substituted the words "Agricultural Holdings Act 1986".

8. In section 27(7) of that Act—

(*a*) for the words "Second Schedule to the Agricultural Holdings Act 1923" there shall be substituted the words "Agricultural Holdings Act 1986", and

(*b*) for the words "the said Second Schedule" there shall be substituted the words "Schedule 11 to the said Act of 1986".

The Allotments Act 1922

9. In section 3(5) of the Allotments Act 1922—

(*a*) for the words "Agricultural Holdings Acts 1908 to 1925" there shall be substituted the words "Agricultural Holdings Act 1986",

(*b*) for the words "to which those Acts apply" there shall be substituted the words "which is an agricultural holding within the meaning of that Act", and

(*c*) for the words "those Acts", in the second and third places where they occur, there shall be substituted the words "that Act".

10. In section 11(2) of that Act for the words "Second Schedule to the Agricultural Holdings Act 1908" there shall be substituted the words "Agricultural Holdings Act 1986".

The Settled Land Act 1925

11. In section 73(1) of the Settled Land Act 1925—

(*a*) for the words "Agricultural Holdings Act 1923", in both places where they occur, there shall be substituted the words "Agricultural Holdings Act 1986", and

(*b*) for the words "Part I or Part II of the First Schedule" there shall be substituted the words "Schedule 7".

The Law of Property Act 1925

12.—(1) In section 99 of the Law of Property Act 1925 (which provides for the making by a mortgagee or mortgagor of such leases as are authorised by that section, which shall be binding on the mortgagor or mortgagee), subsection (13), which provides that the section applies only if and so far as the contrary intention is not expressed in the mortgage deed or otherwise in writing and that the section has effect subject to the terms of the mortgage deed or of any such writing, shall continue not to have effect in relation to a mortgage made after 1st March 1948 of agricultural land within the meaning of the Agriculture Act 1947.

(2) This paragraph shall be construed as one with the said section 99.

The Universities and College Estates Act 1925

13. In section 26(1) of the Universities and College Estates Act 1925—
   (*a*) for the words "Agricultural Holdings Act 1923", in both places where they occur, there shall be substituted the words "Agricultural Holdings Act 1986", and
   (*b*) for the words "Part I and Part II of the First Schedule" there shall be substituted the words "Schedule 7".

The Landlord and Tenant Act 1927

14. In section 17(1) of the Landlord and Tenant Act 1927 for the words "Agricultural Holdings Act 1923" there shall be substituted the words "Agricultural Holdings Act 1986".

15. In section 19(4) of that Act for the words "Agricultural Holdings Act 1923" there shall be substituted the words "Agricultural Holdings Act 1986".

The Agricultural Credits Act 1928

16. In section 5(7) of the Agricultural Credits Act 1928 for the words "Agricultural Holdings Act 1923" there shall be substituted the words "Agricultural Holdings Act 1986, except under section 60(2)(*b*) or 62,".

The Leasehold Property (Repairs) Act 1938

17. In section 7(1) of the Leasehold Property (Repairs) Act 1938 for the words "Agricultural Holdings Act 1948" there shall be substituted the words "Agricultural Holdings Act 1986".

The Agriculture Act 1947

18. In section 73(3)(*a*) of the Agriculture Act 1947 for the words "Agricultural Holdings Act 1923" there shall be substituted the words "Agricultural Holdings Act 1986".

19. In Schedule 2 to that Act—
   (*a*) in paragraph 1 for the words "any provision of Part III of this Act" there shall be substituted the words "section 14 of the Agricultural Holdings Act 1986", and
   (*b*) in paragraph 3 for the words "Part III of this Act" there shall be substituted the words "the Agricultural Holdings Act 1986" and for the words "a holding (as defined in the Agricultural Holdings Act 1923)" there shall be substituted the words "an agricultural holding within the meaning of the Agricultural Holdings Act 1986".

The Reserve and Auxiliary Forces (Protection of Civil Interests) Act 1951

20. In section 27(1) of the Reserve and Auxiliary Forces (Protection of Civil Interests) Act 1951 for the words "Agricultural Holdings Act 1948" there shall be substituted the words "Agricultural Holdings Act 1986".

The Landlord and Tenant Act 1954

21. In section 43(1)(*a*) of the Landlord and Tenant Act 1954 for the words from "the proviso" to "the said subsection (1)" there shall be substituted the words "subsection (3) of section 2 of the Agricultural Holdings Act 1986 did not have effect or, in a case where approval was given under subsection (1) of that section".

22. In section 69(1) of that Act for the words "Agricultural Holdings Act 1948" there shall be substituted the words "Agricultural Holdings Act 1986".

The Agriculture (Safety, Health and Welfare Provisions) Act 1956

23. In section 24(1) of the Agriculture (Safety, Health and Welfare Provisions) Act 1956 for the words "Agricultural Holdings Act 1948" there shall be substituted the words "Agricultural Holdings Act 1986".

The Coal-Mining (Subsidence) Act 1957

24.—(1) Section 10 of the Coal-Mining (Subsidence) Act 1957 shall be amended as follows.

(2) In subsection (1)(*a*) for the words "Agricultural Holdings Act 1948" there shall be substituted the words "Agricultural Holdings Act 1986".

(3) In subsection (2)(*b*) for the words "section thirty-seven or section forty-eight of the said Act of 1948" there shall be substituted the words "section 66(1) of, or paragraph 2(1) of Part I of Schedule 9 to, the said Act of 1986".

(4) In subsection (6)—

(*a*) for the words "Act of 1948" there shall be substituted the words "Act of 1986", and

(*b*) for the words "Minister of Agriculture, Fisheries and Food" there shall be substituted the words "President of the Royal Institution of Chartered Surveyors".

The Opencast Coal Act 1958

25.—(1) Section 14 of the Opencast Coal Act 1958 shall be amended as follows.

(2) In subsection (2)—

(*a*) for the words "Agricultural Holdings Act 1948" there shall be substituted the words "Agricultural Holdings Act 1986", and

(*b*) for the words "Act of 1948" there shall be substituted the words "Act of 1986".

(3) In subsections (3) and (4) for the words "Act of 1948" there shall be substituted the words "Act of 1986".

(4) In subsection (5) for the words "Case B in section 2(3) of the Agricultural Holdings (Notices to Quit) Act 1977" there shall be substituted the words "Case B in Part I of Schedule 3 to the Agricultural Holdings Act 1986"; and that subsection shall continue to have effect with the substitution of the words "that Case" for the words "that paragraph" made by paragraph 3(3) of Schedule I to the Agricultural Holdings (Notices to Quit) Act 1977.

(5) In subsection (6)—

(*a*) for the words from "section 3" to "section 2" there shall be substituted the words "section 27 of the Agricultural Holdings Act 1986 (in which subsections (1) to (3) specify conditions for the giving of consent under section 26", and

(*b*) for the words "paragraph (*e*) of the said subsection (3)" there shall be substituted the words "paragraph (*f*) of the said subsection (3)".

(6) In subsection (7) for the words "section eight of the Act of 1948" there shall be substituted the words "section 12 of the Act of 1986".

(7) In subsection (8) for the words "section nine of the Act of 1948" there shall be substituted the words "section 13 of the Act of 1986".

(8) In subsection (9) for paragraph (*a*) there shall be substituted—

"(*a*) for the references—

(i) to the Act of 1986 and sections 12, 13 and 26 of that Act there shall be substituted respectively references to the Agricultural Holdings (Scotland) Act 1949 (in this Act referred to as "the Scottish Act of 1949") and sections 7, 8 and 25 of that Act,

(ii) to section 27 of the Act of 1986, subsections (1) to (3) of that section and paragraph (*f*) of the said subsection (3) there shall be substituted respectively references to section 26 of the Scottish Act of 1949, subsection (1) of that section and paragraph (*e*) of the said subsection (1), and

(iii) to Case B in Part I of Schedule 3 to the Act of 1986 there shall be substituted references to paragraph (*c*) of subsection (2) of section 25 of that Act."

26.—(1) Section 24 of that Act shall be amended as follows.

(2) In subsection (1) for the words "Act of 1948" there shall be substituted the words "Act of 1986".

(3) In subsection (2) for the words "Act of 1948" there shall be substituted the words "Act of 1986".

(4) In subsection (3) for the words "Act of 1948", in each place where they occur, there shall be substituted the words "Act of 1986".

(5) In subsection (5)—

(*a*) for the words "section forty-four or section fifty-four of the Act of 1948" there shall be substituted the words "section 69(1) of the Act of 1986 or paragraph 5(1) of Part I of Schedule 9 to that Act", and

(*b*) for the words "section forty-five or section fifty-five of the Act of 1948" there shall be substituted the words "section 69(2) or (3) of the Act of 1986 or paragraph 5(2) of Part I of Schedule 9 to that Act".

(6) In subsection (6)—

(*a*) for the words "Act of 1948", in both places where they occur, there shall be substituted the words "Act of 1986", and

(*b*) for the words "subsection (3) of section seventy" there shall be substituted the words "section 83(4)";

and that subsection in its application to England and Wales shall continue to have effect with the substitution for each of the words "four" and "five" of the word "eight" made by paragraph 29 of Schedule 3 to the Agricultural Holdings Act 1984.

(7) In subsection (7)—

(*a*) for the words "Act of 1948", in both places where they occur, there shall be substituted the words "Act of 1986" and

(*b*) for the words "section fifty-six" there shall be substituted the words "section 70".

(8) In subsection (8) for the words "Act of 1948" there shall be substituted the words "Act of 1986".

(9) In subsection (9) for the words "the Third Schedule to the Act of 1948" there shall be substituted the words "Schedule 7 to the Act of 1986".

(10) After subsection (9) there shall be inserted—

"(9A) In this section the references to the Act of 1986 in subsections (1)(*b*), (7) and (8) and the second and fourth references to that Act in subsection (3) include references to the Agricultural Holdings Act 1948 (in this Act called the Act of 1948) and the reference to section 70 of the Act of 1986 in subsection (7)(*b*) includes a reference to section 56 of the Act of 1948."

(11) For subsection (10) there shall be substituted—

"(10) In the application of this section to Scotland, for references—

(*a*) to the Act of 1986 and to sections 70 and 83(4) of that Act there shall be substituted respectively references to the Scottish Act of 1949 and to sections 56 and 68(3) of that Act,

(*b*) to subsections (1), (2) and (3) of section 69 of the Act of 1986 there shall be substituted respectively references to sections 54, and subsections (1) and (2) of section 55 of the Scottish Act of 1949,

(*c*) to Parts I and II of Schedule 7 to the Act of 1986 and to the first day of March 1948 there shall be substituted references to Parts I and II of Schedule 1 to the Scottish Act of 1949 and to the first day of November 1948, and

(*d*) to sub-paragraphs (1) and (2) of paragraph 5 of Part I of Schedule 9 to the 1986 Act there shall be substituted respectively references to sections 45 and 46 of the Scottish Act of 1949."

27.—(1) Section 25 of that Act shall be amended as follows.

(2) In subsection (1)—

(*a*) for the words "section fifty-seven of the Act of 1948" there shall be substituted the words "section 71 of the Act of 1986", and

(*b*) for the words "section fifty-eight" there shall be substituted the words "section 72".

(3) In subsection (2) for the words "Act of 1948" there shall be substituted the words "Act of 1986".

(4) After subsection (2) there shall be inserted—

"(2A) In this section references to the Act of 1986 and to sections 71 and 72 of that Act include respectively references to the Act of 1948 and to sections 57 and 58 of that Act".

(5) In subsection (3) for the words from "Act of 1948" to "fifty-eight" there shall be substituted the words "Act of 1986 and to sections 71 and 72".

28.—(1) Section 26 of that Act shall be amended as follows.

(2) In subsection (3) for the words "Act of 1948" there shall be substituted the words "Act of 1986".

(3) In subsection (5) for the words "section seventy-eight of the Act of 1948, the provisions of the Fourth Schedule" there shall be substituted the words "section 91 of the Act of 1986, the provisions of Schedule 8".

(4) After subsection (5) there shall be inserted—

"(5A) the reference in subsection (3) of this section to the 1986 Act includes a reference to the 1948 Act".

(5) In subsection (6)—

(*a*) for the words "Act of 1948", in the first place where they occur, there shall be substituted the words "Act of 1986", and

(*b*) for the words "section seventy-eight of the Act of 1948 and to the Fourth Schedule" there shall be substituted the words "section 91 of the Act of 1986 and to Schedule 8".

29.—(1) Section 27 of that Act shall be amended as follows.

(2) In subsection (1)(*b*) for the words "section thirteen of the Act of 1948" there shall be substituted the words "section 10 of the Act of 1986".

(3) In subsection (4) for the words "section thirteen of the Act of 1948" there shall be substituted the words "section 10 of the Act of 1986".

30.—(1) Section 28 of that Act shall be amended as follows.

(2) In subsection (3)—

(*a*) for the words "section sixty-seven of the Act of 1948" there shall be substituted the words "subsections (2) to (5) of section 79 of the Act of 1986", and

(*b*) for the words "subsection (1) of section sixty-eight" there shall be substituted the words "subsection (2) of section 80".

(3) In subsection (4)—

(*a*) for the words "section thirteen of the Act of 1948" there shall be substituted the words "section 10 of the Act of 1986", and

(*b*) for the words "paragraph (*b*) of subsection (1) of section sixty-seven of the Act of 1948" there shall be substituted the words "subsection (3) of section 79 of the Act of 1986".

(4) In subsection (5) for the words from "section seventy-eight" to "Fifth Schedule" there shall be substituted the words "section 91 of the Act of 1986 the provisions of Schedule 10".

(5) In subsection (6)—

(*a*) for the words "section sixty-seven of the Act of 1948 and to paragraph (*b*) of subsection (1)" there shall be substituted the words "subsections (2) to (5) of section 79 of the Act of 1986 and subsection (3) of that section",

(*b*) for the words "subsection (1) of section sixty-eight of the Act of 1948 and to section thirteen" there shall be substituted the words "subsection (2) of section 80 of the Act of 1986 and to section 10", and

(*c*) for the words "section seventy-eight of the Act of 1948 and to the Fifth Schedule" there shall be substituted the words "section 91 of the Act of 1986 and to Schedule 10".

31. In section 51(1) of that Act—

(*a*) after the definition of "the Acquisition of Land Act" there shall be inserted—
" 'the Act of 1986' means the Agricultural Holdings Act 1986;", and

(*b*) in the definition of "agricultural holding" for the words "Act of 1948" there shall be substituted the words "Act of 1986".

32.—(1) Schedule 6 to that Act shall be amended as follows.

(2) In paragraph 20(*a*) for the words from "made" to "year" there shall be substituted the words "falling within section 2(3)(*a*) of the 1986 Act".

(3) In paragraph 24—

(*a*) for the words from "by the Minister" to "1948 ("" there shall be substituted the words "under section 2 of the Act of 1986 or of the Act of 1948 (each of", and

(*b*) for the words from "by the said Minister" to "of the section)" there shall be substituted the words "under that section from the operation of that section)".

(4) In paragraph 25 for the words from "by the Minister" to "section two" there shall be substituted the words "under section 2 of the Act of 1986 or".

(5) In paragraph 31 for the words from "for the letting" to "Secretary of State" there shall be substituted the words "falling within section 2(3)(*a*) of the 1986 Act, to an agreement for the letting of land and to section 2 of the Act of 1986 there shall be substituted respectively references to a lease of land entered into in contemplation of the use of the land only for grazing or mowing falling within the proviso to section 2(1) of the Scottish Act of 1949, to a lease".

33.—(1) Schedule 7 to that Act shall be amended as follows.

(2) In paragraph 1(2) for the words "Act of 1948" there shall be substituted the words "Act of 1986".

(3) In paragraph 2—

(*a*) for the words "Act of 1948", in each place where they occur, there shall be substituted the words "Act of 1986", and

(b) after sub-paragraph (3) there shall be inserted—

   "(3A) The references in sub-paragraph (1)(a) of this paragraph to the Act of 1986 include references to the Act of 1948".

(4) In paragraph 3—

(a) in sub-paragraph (1) for the words "Act of 1948" there shall be substituted the words "Act of 1986", and

(b) in sub-paragraph (2) for the words "section nine of the Act of 1948 in so far as the said section nine" there shall be substituted the words "section 13 of the Act of 1986 in so far as the said section 13".

(5) In paragraph 4—

(a) in sub-paragraph (2) for the words "Act of 1948" there shall be substituted the words "Act of 1986",

(b) in sub-paragraph (4) for the words "Section seventy-seven of the Act of 1948" there shall be substituted the words "Section 84 of the Act of 1986" and for the words "Act of 1948", in the second place where they occur, there shall be substituted the words "Act of 1986".

(c) in sub-paragraph (5) for the words "section eight or section nine of the Act of 1948" there shall be substituted the words "section 12 or section 13 of the Act of 1986", and

(d) in sub-paragraph (6) for the words "section nine of the Act of 1948" there shall be substituted the words "section 13 of the Act of 1986".

(6) In paragraph 5—

(a) in sub-paragraph (1) for the words "section thirteen of the Act of 1948" there shall be substituted the words "section 10 of the Act of 1986".

(b) in sub-paragraph (2) for the words "subsection (2)" there shall be substituted the words "subsection (3)",

(c) in sub-paragraph (3) for the words "subsection (2)" there shall be substituted the words "subsection (3)" and for the words "subsection (3)" there shall be substituted the words "subsection (4)", and

(d) in sub-paragraph (5) for the words "section thirteen of the Act of 1948" there shall be substituted the words "section 10 of the Act of 1986" and for the words "paragraph (b) of subsection (1) of section sixty-seven" there shall be substituted the words "subsection (3) of section 79".

(7) In paragraph 6(2) for the words "section seventeen of the Act of 1948" there shall be substituted the words "section 23 of the Act of 1986".

(8) In paragraph 25, for sub-paragraph (a) there shall be substituted—

   "(a) for references—

      (i) to the Act of 1986 and to sections 12, 13, 23 and 84 of that Act there shall be substituted respectively references to the Scottish Act of 1949 and to sections 7, 8, 18 and 75 of that Act,

      (ii) to section 10 of the Act of 1986 and to subsections (3) and (4) of that section there shall be substituted respectively references to section 14 of the Scottish Act of 1949 and to subsections (2) and (3) of that section, and

      (ii) to subsection (3) of section 79 of the Act of 1986 there shall be substituted references to paragraph (b) of subsection (1) of section 65 of the Scottish Act of 1949."

The Chevening Estate Act 1959

34. In clauses 15(i) and 23(b) of the Trust Instrument set out in the Schedule to the Chevening Estate Act 1959 for the words "Agricultural Holdings Act 1948" there shall be substituted the words "Agricultural Holdings Act 1986, except section 60(2)(b) or 62 of that Act,".

The Horticulture Act 1960

35. In section 1(1)(b) of the Horticulture Act 1960 for the words "Agricultural Holdings Act 1948" there shall be substituted the words "Agricultural Holdings Act 1986".

The Agriculture (Miscellaneous Provisions) Act 1963

36. In subsections (1)(a) and (6)(c) of section 22 of the Agriculture (Miscellaneous Provisions) Act 1963 for the words "Agricultural Holdings Act 1948" there shall be substituted the words "Agricultural Holdings Act 1986".

The Agriculture Act 1967

37. In section 26(1) of the Agriculture Act 1967 for the words "Agricultural Holdings Act 1948", in both places where they occur, there shall be substituted the words "Agricultural Holdings Act 1986".

38. In section 27(5B)(*a*) of that Act for the words "Agricultural Holdings Act 1948" there shall be substituted the words "Agricultural Holdings Act 1986".

39. In section 28(1)(*a*) of that Act for the words "section 34 of the Agricultural Holdings Act 1948" there shall be substituted the words "section 60(2)(*a*) of the Agricultural Holdings Act 1986".

40. In section 29(3)(*a*) of that Act for the words "section 34 of the Agricultural Holdings Act 1948" there shall be substituted the words "section 60(2)(*a*) of the Agricultural Holdings Act 1986".

41.—(1) Section 48 of that Act shall be amended as follows.

(2) In subsection (2)(*a*) for the words "section 34 of the Agricultural Holdings Act 1948" there shall be substituted the words "section 60(2)(*a*) of the Agricultural Holdings Act 1986".

(3) For subsection (4) there shall be substituted—

"(4) Case H in Part I of Schedule 3 to the Agricultural Holdings Act 1986 shall apply in relation to a Rural Development Board as it applies in relation to the Minister within the meaning of that Act."

42. In paragraph 7(4) of Schedule 3 to that Act for the words "Section 77 of the Agricultural Holdings Act 1948" there shall be substituted the words "Section 84 of the Agricultural Holdings Act 1986".

The Leasehold Reform Act 1967

43. In section 1(3)(*b*) of the Leasehold Reform Act 1967 for the words "Agricultural Holdings Act 1948" there shall be substituted the words "Agricultural Holdings Act 1986".

The Agriculture (Miscellaneous Provisions) Act 1968

44. In section 12(1) of the Agriculture (Miscellaneous Provisions) Act 1968 for the words from "section 9" to the end there shall be substituted the words "subsection (2)(*b*) of section 60 of the Agricultural Holdings Act 1986 (additional compensation to tenant for disturbance) shall apply as if the acquiring authority were the landlord of the holding and on the date of the acquisition or taking of possession the tenancy of the holding or part of it had terminated, and the tenant had quitted the holding or part of it, in consequence of such a notice or counter-notice as is mentioned in subsection (1) of that section; and section 61 of that Act (exceptions to section 60) shall not apply in such a case".

45. In section 13(1) of that Act for the words "section 2(1) of the principal Act" there shall be substituted the words "section 2(2) of the Agricultural Holdings Act 1986".

46.—(1) Section 17 of that Act shall be amended as follows.

(2) In subsection (1) for the words "principal Act", in the second place where they occur, there shall be substituted the words "Agricultural Holdings Act 1986".

(3) In subsection (3) for the words "Section 87(1) and (2) of the principal Act" there shall be substituted the words "Section 95(1), (2) and (3) of the Agricultural Holdings Act 1986".

47. In section 42(2) of that Act, as it has effect for the purposes of section 48(6) of the Land Compensation Act 1973, for the words "section 24 of the principal Act" there shall be substituted the words "section 26 of the Agricultural Holdings Act 1986" and for the words "principal Act", in the second place where they occur, there shall be substituted the words "Agricultural Holdings Act 1986".

48.—(1) Schedule 3 to that Act shall be amended as follows.

(2) In paragraph 2—

(*a*) for the words "section 9(2) of this Act" there shall be substituted the words "section 60(4) of the Agricultural Holdings Act 1986", and

(*b*) for the words "section 8 or section 9 of the principal Act" there shall be substituted the words "section 12 or section 13 of the Agricultural Holdings Act 1986".

(3) In paragraph 3—

(*a*) for the words "section 8 of the principal Act" there shall be substituted the words "section 12 of the Agricultural Holdings Act 1986", and

(*b*) for the words "section 9(2)" there shall be substituted the words "section 60(4)".

The Tribunals and Inquiries Act 1971

49. In paragraph 1(*b*) of Part I of Schedule 1 to the Tribunals and Inquiries Act 1971 for the words "Schedule 6 to the Agricultural Holdings Act 1948 (c.63)" there shall be substituted the words "Schedule 11 to the Agricultural Holdings Act 1986".

The Town and Country Planning Act 1971

50. In section 27(7) of the Town and Country Planning Act 1971 for the words "Agricultural Holdings Act 1948" there shall be substituted the words "Agricultural Holdings Act 1986".

The Land Charges Act 1972

51.—(1) Schedule 2 to the Land Charges Act 1972 shall be amended as follows.
(2) In paragraph 1(*g*) for the words from "Sections" to "tenant or" there shall be substituted the words "Section 74 (charge in respect of sums due to" and the words from "Section 82" to "improvements)" shall be omitted.
(3) After paragraph 1(*h*) there shall be inserted—

"(i) The Agricultural Holdings   Section 85 (charges in respect of sums due
Act 1986   to tenant of agricultural holding).
                                 Section 86 (charges in favour of landlord of
                                 agricultural holding in respect of compen-
                                 sation for or cost of certain
                                 improvements)."

(4) In paragraph 3 for the words from the beginning to "Act 1948" there shall be substituted the words "The reference in paragraph 1(*g*) above to section 74 of the Agricultural Holdings Act 1948 and the references in paragraph 1 (i) above to section 85 and 86 of the Agricultural Holdings Act 1986".

The Land Compensation Act 1973

52. In section 34(3)(*c*) of the Land Compensation Act 1973 for the words "Agricultural Holdings Act 1948" there shall be substituted the words "Agricultural Holdings Act 1986".
53.—(1) Section 48 of that Act shall be amended as follows.
(2) In subsection (2)—
(*a*) for the words "Case B in section 2(3) of the Agricultural Holdings (Notices to Quit) Act 1977" there shall be substituted the words "Case B in Part I of Schedule 3 to the Agricultural Holdings Act 1986",
(*b*) for the words "section 3(3)(*e*)" there shall be substituted the words "section 27(3)(*f*)"; and that subsection shall continue to have effect with the substitution of the words "the said Case B" for the words "section 24(2)(*b*)" made by paragraph 6 of Schedule 1 to the Agricultural Holdings (Notices to Quit) Act 1977.
(3) In subsection (3) for the words "Case B and section 3(3)(*e*)" there shall be substituted the words "Case B and section 27(3)(*f*)".
(4) After subsection (6) there shall be inserted—
"(6A) In assessing the tenant's compensation no account shall be taken of any benefit which might accrue to the tenant by virtue of section 60(2)(*b*) of the Agricultural Holdings Act 1986 (additional payments by landlord for disturbance); and in this subsection the reference to the said section 60(2)(*b*) does not include a reference to it as applied by section 12 of the Agriculture (Miscellaneous Provisions) Act 1968."
54.—(1) Section 56 of that Act shall be amended as follows.
(2) In subsection (3)(*d*) for the words "Agricultural Holdings Act 1948" there shall be substituted the words "Agricultural Holdings Act 1986".
(3) In subsection (4) for the words "section 58 of the Agricultural Holdings Act 1948" there shall be substituted the words "section 72 of the Agricultural Holdings Act 1986" and for the words "the proviso" there shall be substituted the words "subsection (4) of that section".
55.—(1) Section 59 of that Act shall be amended as follows.
(2) In subsection (1)(*b*)—
(*a*) in paragraph (i) for the words "subsection (1) of section 2 of the Agricultural Holdings (Notices to Quit) Act 1977" there shall be substituted the words "section 26(1) of the Agricultural Holdings Act 1986" and for the words "Case B in subsection (3) of that

section" there shall be substituted the words "Case B in Part I of Schedule 3 to that Act", and

(*b*) in paragraph (ii) for the words "section 3(3)(*e*)" there shall be substituted the words "section 27(3)(*f*)";

and that subsection shall continue to have effect with the substitution of the words "the said Case B" for the words "section 24(2)(*b*)" made by paragraph 6 of Schedule 1 to the Agricultural Holdings (Notices to Quit) Act 1977.

(3) In subsection (2)(*b*) for the words from "Agricultural Holdings Act 1948" to "notice to quit)" there shall be substituted the words "Agricultural Holdings Act 1986 relating to compensation to a tenant on the termination of his tenancy".

(4) In subsection (6) for the words "section 9 of the Agricultural Holdings (Notices to Quit) Act 1977" there shall be substituted the words "section 32 of the Agricultural Holdings Act 1986".

56. In section 87(1) for the words "Agricultural Holdings Act 1948" there shall be substituted the words "Agricultural Holdings Act 1986".

The Rent (Agriculture) Act 1976

57. In section 9(3) and (4)(*c*) of the Rent (Agriculture) Act 1976 for the words "Agricultural Holdings Act 1948" there shall be substituted the words "Agricultural Holdings Act 1986".

58. In paragraph 2 of Schedule 2 to that Act for the words "Agricultural Holdings Act 1948" there shall be substituted the words "Agricultural Holdings Act 1986".

The Rent Act 1977

59. In section 10 of the Rent Act 1977 for the words "Agricultural Holdings Act 1948" there shall be substituted the words "Agricultural Holdings Act 1986".

60. In section 137(3) and (4)(*c*) of that Act for the words "Agricultural Holdings Act 1948" there shall be substituted the words "Agricultural Holdings Act 1986".

The Protection from Eviction Act 1977

61. In section 8(1)(*d*) of the Protection from Eviction Act 1977 for the words "Agricultural Holdings Act 1948" there shall be substituted the words "Agricultural Holdings Act 1986".

The Cycle Tracks Act 1984

62. In section 3(2) of the Cycle Tracks Act 1984 for the words "section 1(2) of the Agricultural Holdings Act 1948" there shall be substituted the words "section 1(4) of the Agricultural Holdings Act 1986".

The Housing Act 1985

63. In paragraph 8 of Schedule 1 to the Housing Act 1985 for the words "Agricultural Holdings Act 1948" there shall be substituted the words "Agricultural Holdings Act 1986".

The Landlord and Tenant Act 1985

64. In section 14(3) of the Landlord and Tenant Act 1985 for the words "Agricultural Holdings Act 1948" there shall be substituted the words "Agricultural Holdings Act 1986".

Section 101   SCHEDULE 15

REPEALS AND REVOCATIONS

PART I

REPEALS

Chapter	Short title	Extent of repeal
9 & 10 Geo. 6. c.73.	The Hill Farming Act 1946.	Section 9.
11 & 12 Geo. 6. c.63.	The Agricultural Holdings Act 1948.	The whole Act.
12 & 13 Geo. 6. c.37.	The Agriculture (Miscellaneous Provisions) Act 1949.	Section 10. In the Schedule, Part II.
6 & 7 Eliz. 2. c.71.	The Agriculture Act 1958.	Section 4. In section 9(1), in the definition of "agricultural holding" the words from "as respects England" to "1948 and", the definitions of "contract of tenancy" and "fixed equipment" and in the definition of "landlord and tenant" the words from "as respects England" to "1948 and". In Schedule 1, in Part I, paragraphs 6, 7, 14 to 18, 20 and 21. In Schedule 4, paragraphs 5, 9 and 11.
1963 c.11.	The Agriculture (Miscellaneous Provisions) Act 1963.	In section 20, paragraph (*b*), the words "and the period within which the arbitrator is to make his award", the words "the said paragraph 6 or" and paragraph (ii).
1964 c.51.	The Universities and College Estates Act 1964.	In Schedule 3, in Part I, the entry relating to the Agricultural Holdings Act 1948.
1968 c.34.	The Agriculture (Miscellaneous Provisions) Act 1968.	Sections 9 and 10. In section 15, subsection (2), in subsection (4) the words from the beginning to "section and", the words "subsection (2) or" and the words "as the case may be" and in subsection (5)(*a*) the words "or subsection (2)". In section 17, in subsection (1) the definition of "the principal Act" and in subsection (2) the words from "references to the termination" to "holding and".
1970 c.40.	The Agriculture Act 1970.	In Schedule 4, the entry relating to the Agricultural Holdings Act 1948.
1971 c.23.	The Courts Act 1971.	In Schedule 9, in Part I, the entry relating to the Agricultural Holdings Act 1948.
1972 c.61.	The Land Charges Act 1972.	In Schedule 2, in paragraph 1(*g*), the words from "Section 82" to "improvements)".
1972 c.62.	The Agriculture (Miscellaneous Provisions) Act 1972.	Section 15.
1976 c.55.	The Agriculture (Miscellaneous Provisions) Act 1976.	Sections 17 to 24. In section 27(5), the words "and Part II". In Schedule 3, the entries relating to the Agricultural Holdings Act 1948. Schedule 3A.
1977 c.12.	The Agricultural Holdings (Notices to Quit) Act 1977.	The whole Act.

Chapter	Short title	Extent of repeal
1984 c.32.	The London Regional Transport Act 1984.	In Schedule 6, paragraph 13.
1984 c.41.	The Agricultural Holdings Act 1984.	The whole Act.
1985 c.65.	The Insolvency Act 1985.	In Schedule 8, paragraphs 9 and 30.
1985 c.68.	The Housing Act 1985.	Section 231.
1985 c.71.	The Housing (Consequential Provisions) Act 1985.	In Schedule 2, paragraph 34.

PART II

REVOCATIONS

Number	Title	Extent of Revocation
S.I. 1951/2168.	The Agricultural Holdings Act (Variation of Fourth Schedule) Order 1951.	The whole order.
S.I. 1978/447.	The Agricultural Holdings Act 1948 (Amendment) Regulations 1978.	The whole instrument.
S.I. 1978/742.	The Agricultural Holdings Act 1948 (Variation of Fourth Schedule) Order 1978.	The whole order.
S.I. 1985/1947.	The Agricultural Holdings Act 1948 (Variation of Fourth Schedule) Order 1985.	The whole order.

TABLE OF DERIVATIONS

Note: The following abbreviations are used in this Table:—

1948	=	The Agricultural Holdings Act 1948 (11 & 12 Geo. 6. c.63)
1949	=	The Agriculture (Miscellaneous Provisions) Act 1949 (12 & 13 Geo. 6. c.37)
1958	=	The Agriculture Act 1958 (6 & 7 Eliz. 2. c.71)
1963	=	The Agriculture (Miscellaneous Provisions) Act 1963 (c.11)
1968	=	The Agriculture (Miscellaneous Provisions) Act 1968 (c.34)
1970	=	The Agriculture Act 1970 (c.40)
1972	=	The Agriculture (Miscellaneous Provisions) Act 1972 (c.62)
1976	=	The Agriculture (Miscellaneous Provisions) Act 1976 (c.55)
1977	=	The Agricultural Holdings (Notices to Quit) Act 1977 (c.12)
1984	=	The Agricultural Holdings Act 1984 (c.41)
S.I. 1951/2168	=	The Agricultural Holdings Act (Variation of Fourth Schedule) Order 1951 (S.I. 1951/2168)
S.I. 1955/554	=	The Transfer of Functions (Ministry of Food) Order 1955 (S.I. 1955/554)
S.I. 1978/272	=	The Transfer of Functions (Wales) (No. 1) Order 1978 (S.I. 1978/272)
S.I. 1978/447	=	The Agricultural Holdings Act 1948 (Amendment) Regulations 1978 (S.I. 1978/447)
S.I. 1978/742	=	The Agricultural Holdings Act 1948 (Variation of Fourth Schedule) Order 1978 (S.I. 1978/742)
S.I. 1985/1947	=	The Agricultural Holdings Act 1948 (Variation of Fourth Schedule) Order 1985 (S.I. 1985/1947)
R (followed by a number)	=	The recommendation set out in the paragraph of that number in the Appendix to the Report of the Law Commission on this Act (Cmnd. 9665).

Provision	Derivation
1(1)	1948 s.1(1); 1984 Sch. 3 para. 1(2).
(2)(3)	1948 s.1(1A) (1B); 1984 Sch. 3 para. 1(3).
(4)	1948 s.1(2); 1976 s.18(2); 1984 Sch. 1 para. 1, Sch. 2 para. 1(2).
(5)	1948 s.94(1).
2	1984 s.2; R.1.
3(1)	1948 s.3(1); 1984 Sch. 3 para. 2(1)(*a*).
(2)	1948 s.3(2).
(3)	1948 s.3(3).
(4)	1948 s.3(1).
4(1)	1948 s.3A(1) (2) (3); 1984 Sch. 3 para. 2(2).
(2)	1948 s.3A(2) (3); 1984 Sch. 3 para. 2(2).
(3)	1948 s.3A(4); 1984 Sch. 3 para. 2(2).
(4)	1948 s.3A(2) (3); 1984 Sch. 3 para. 2(2).
5(1)	1948 s.3(4); 1984 Sch. 3 para. 2(1)(*b*).
(2)(3)	1948 s.3B; 1984 Sch. 3 para. 2(2).
6(1)	1948 s.5(1); 1984 Sch. 3 para. 3(2).
(2)	1948 s.5(2) (3).
(3)	1948 s.7(3).
(4)	1948 s.7(5); 1984 Sch. 3 para. 4.
(5)	1948 s.5(4) (6); 1984 Sch. 3 para. 3(3).
(6)	1948 s.5(5); 1984 Sch. 3 para. 3(3).
7(1)	1948 s.6(1).
(2)	1972 s.15(2).
(3)	1948 s.6(1).
8(1)(2)	1948 s.6(2).
(3)	1948 s.6(3).
(4)	1948 s.7(3).
(5)	1948 s.7(5); 1984 Sch. 3 para. 4.
(6)	1948 s.6(2).

Provision	Derivation
9(1)(2)	1948 s.7(1).
(3)	1948 s.7(2).
(4)	1948 s.7(4).
10(1)	1948 s.13(1) (4A); 1984 Sch. 3 para. 6(2) (3).
(2)	1948 s.13(1) (5)(*b*).
(3) to (5)	1948 s.13(2) to (4).
(6)	1948 s.13(4B); 1984 Sch. 3 para. 6(3).
(7)	1948 s.13(5)(*a*).
(8)	1948 s.13(4A); 1984 Sch. 3 para. 6(3).
11(1)	1958 s.4(1).
(2)	1958 s.4(1); 1984 Sch. 3 para. 30.
(3) to (7)	1958 s.4(2) to (4).
(8)	1958 s.4(7).
12(1)(2)	1948 s.8(1) (2); 1984 s.1.
(3)	1948 s.8(13); 1984 ss.1, 8(2).
(4)	1948 s.8A(2); 1984 s.1.
(5)	Introduces Schedule 2.
13(1)	1948 s.9(1).
(2)	1948 s.9(1); 1958 s.4(5); 1984 Sch. 3 para. 5(2)(*b*); Housing Act 1985 (c.68) s.231(1).
(3)	1948 s.9(2); 1958 s.4(5); 1984 Sch. 3 para. 5(3); Housing Act 1985 (c.68) s.231(1).
(4)	1948 s.9(1); 1958 s.4(5); 1984 Sch. 3 para. 5(2)(*c*); Housing Act 1985 (c.68) s.231(1)(2).
(5)(6)	1958 s.4(5)(7).
(7)	1948 s.9(4).
(8)	1948 s.9(1).
14(1)(2)	1948 s.10(1); 1958 Sch. 1 Pt. I para. 6.
(3)	1948 s.10(2)(*a*); 1958 Sch. 1 Pt. I para. 6.
(4)(5)	1948 s.10(2)(*b*); 1958 Sch. 1 Pt. I para. 6.
15(1)	1948 s.11(1).
(2)	1948 s.11(4)(*a*) (*b*).
(3)	1948 s.12(1).
(4)(5)	1948 s.11(1) (2).
(6)	1948 s.11(3); 1958 Sch. 1 Pt. I para. 7.
(7)	1948 ss.11(5), 12(2).
16	1948 s.18.
17	1948 s.22.
18(1)	1948 s.20(1).
(2)(3)(4)	1948 s.19(1)(2)(3).
(5)	1948 ss.19(1)(4), 20(2).
19(1)	1948 s.21(1)(2).
(2)	1948 s.21(3); Courts Act 1971 (c.23) Sch. 9 Pt. I.
(3)	1948 s.21(4).
20(1)(2)(3)	1948 s.14(1); 1984 Sch. 3 para. 7(2).
(4)	1948 s.14(2).
(5)	1948 s.14(3); 1984 Sch. 3 para. 7(3).
21(1)(2)(3)	1948 s.4(1)(2)(3).
22(1)	1948 s.16(1); 1984 Sch. 3 para. 8(*a*).
(2)	1948 s.16(2); 1984 s.8(1)(2), Sch. 3 para. 8(*b*).
(3)	1948 s.16(3).
(4)	1948 s.8(3)(4).
(5)	1984 s.8(5).
23	1948 s.17.
24	1948 s.15.
25(1)	1977 s.1(1).
(2)	1977 s.1(2); 1984 Sch. 3 para. 36.
(3) to (5)	1977 s.1(5) to (7); 1984 s.5.
26(1)	1977 s.2(1).
(2)	1977 ss.2(2), 12(1).
(3)	Introduces Schedule 3.

Provision	Derivation
27(1) to (5).	1977 s.3.
(6)	1977 s.6(1).
(7)	1977 s.6(3).
(8)	1977 s.6(2).
(9)	1977 s.6(4).
28(1)	1977 s.4(1).
(2)	1977 s.4(2)(3).
(3)	1977 s.4(2).
(4)	1977 s.4(2)(3).
(5)	1977 s.4(4), 1984 s.7.
(6)	1977 s.4(5).
29	Introduces Schedule 4.
30	Introduces Schedule 5.
31(1)	1977 s.8(1).
(2)	1977 s.8(2); 1984 Sch. 3 para. 39.
32	1977 s.9.
33(1)	1977 s.10(1); 1984 Sch. 3 para. 40(*a*).
(2)	1977 s.10(1A); 1984 Sch. 3 para. 40(*b*).
(3)	1977 s.10(2); 1984 Sch. 3 para. 40(*c*).
34(1)	1984 s.2(1)(2), Sch. 2 paras. 1(1)(*a*), 10(1)(*a*).
(2)	1984 s.2(3).
35(1)	1976 s.18(1); 1984 s.2(1)(2), Sch. 1 para. 5(1).
(2)	1976 s.18(1)(2); 1984 Sch. 1 para. 1.
36(1)	1976 ss.18(1), 20(1).
(2)	1976 s.18(4)(*d*).
(3)	1976 s.18(2).
(4)	1976 s.18(2); 1984 s.3(2)(*b*).
(5)	Introduces Schedule 6.
37(1)	1976 s.18(4)(*e*); 1984 Sch. 1 para. 2(5).
(2)(3)	1976 s.18(5); 1984 Sch. 1 para. 2(7).
(4)(5)	1976 s.18(5A); 1984 Sch. 1 para. 2(7).
(6)	1984 Sch. 2 para. 10(1)(*b*), (2).
(7)	1984 Sch. 5 para. 2(2)(*a*).
(8)	1984 Sch. 5 para. 2(2)(*b*).
(9)	1976 s.18(4)(*e*), (5); 1984 Sch. 1 para. 2(5), (7).
38(1)	1976 s.18(4)(*a*); 1977 Sch. 1 para. 7(2)(*b*); 1984 Sch. 1 para. 2(2).
(2)	1976 s.18(4)(*b*); 1977 Sch. 1 para. 7(2)(*c*); 1984 Sch. 3 para. 34.
(3)	1976 s.18(4)(*c*); 1977 Sch. 1 para. 7(2)(*d*); 1984 Sch. 1 para. 2(3).
(4)	1976 s.18(4)(*f*); 1984 Sch. 1 para. 2(6).
(5)	1976 s.18(4)(*g*).
39(1)	1976 ss.18(2), 20(1).
(2)	1976 s.20(2); 1984 Sch. 1 para. 4.
(3)	1976 s.20(3).
(4)	1976 s.20(4).
(5)	1976 s.20(5); 1984 Sch. 1 para. 3(3)(*a*).
(6)	1976 s.20(6); 1984 Sch. 1 para. 3(3)(*a*).
(7) to (9)	1976 s.20(7) to (9).
(10)	1976 s.20(9A); 1984 Sch. 1 para. 3(3)(*b*).
40(1) to (5)	1976 s.20(10) to (14).
41	1976 ss.18(2), 21.
42	1976 s.20(15); 1984 Sch. 1 para. 5(2).
43	1976 s.19; 1977 Sch. 1 para. 7(3); 1984 s.6(9), Sch. 1 para. 3(2).
44(1)	1976 s.22(1).
(2)	1976 s.22(2); 1977 Sch. 1 para. 7(4); 1984 Sch. 1 para. 3(4)(*a*).
(3)	1976 s.22(3).
(4)	1976 s.22(4); 1984 Sch. 1 para. 3(4)(*a*).
(5)	1976 s.22(5); 1984 Sch. 1 para. 3(4)(*b*).
(6)	1976 s.22(6); 1984 Sch. 1 para. 6.
(7)	1976 s.22(7); 1984 Sch. 1 para. 6.

Provision	Derivation
45(1)	1976 s.23(1).
(2) to (4)	1976 s.23(1A); 1984 s.3(1).
(5) to (8)	1976 s.23(5) to (8).
46(1)	1976 s.23(2); 1977 Sch. 1 para. 7(5); 1984 Sch. 1 para. 7(1).
(2)	1976 s.23(2A); 1984 Sch. 1 para. 7(2).
(3)	1976 s.23(9); 1984 Sch. 1 para. 3(5).
47(1)	1976 s.23(1).
(2)	1976 s.23(3).
(3)	1976 s.23(4).
48(1)	1976 s.24(1).
(2)	1976 s.24(2); 1984 Sch. 1 paras. 3(6), 7(3).
(3)(4)	1976 s.24(3).
(5)	1976 s.24(4)(*a*).
(6)	1976 s.24(4)(*b*).
(7)	1976 s.24(4)(*c*).
(8)	1976 s.24(5).
(9)	1976 s.24(6); 1984 Sch. 3 para. 35.
(10)	1976 s.24(7).
(11)	1976 s.24(4).
(12)	1976 s.24(8).
49(1)(2)	1984 Sch. 2 para. 1(1)(2).
(3)	1984 Sch. 2 para. 1(2), 2(2).
50(1)	1984 Sch. 2 paras. 1(1), 5(1).
(2)(3)	1984 Sch. 2 para. 1(2).
(4)	Introduces Schedule 6.
51(1)	1984 Sch. 2 para. 2(1)(*a*)(*b*)(*c*)(*f*)(*g*), (4).
(2)	1984 Sch. 2 para. 2(1)(*d*).
(3)	1984 Sch. 2 para. 2(1)(*e*), (3).
(4)	1984 Sch. 2 para. 2(5).
(5)(6)	1984 Sch. 2 para. 2(6).
52(1)(2)	1984 Sch. 2 para. 3(1)(2).
(3)(4)	1984 Sch. 2 para. 3(3).
(5)	1984 Sch. 2 para. 3(4).
53(1)	1984 Sch. 2 para. 5(1).
(2)	1984 Sch. 2 para. 1(2).
(3) to (11)	1984 Sch. 2 para. 5(2) to (10).
54(1)(2)	1984 Sch. 2 para. 4.
(3)	1984 Sch. 2 para. 1(2).
55(1)	1984 Sch. 2 para. 6(1).
(2) to (4)	1984 Sch. 2 para. 6(2).
(5) to (8)	1984 Sch. 2 para. 6(4) to (7).
56(1)	1984 Sch. 2 para. 6(1).
(2)	1984 Sch. 2 para. 6(3).
(3)(4)	1984 Sch. 2 para. 7(1)(2).
57	1984 Sch. 2 para. 8.
58	1984 Sch. 2 para. 9.
59	Index of definitions.
60(1)(2)	1948 s.34(1); 1968 s.9(1); 1977 Sch. 1 para. 1(3)(*a*).
(3)	1948 s.34(2)(*a*)(*d*).
(4)	1968 s.9(2).
(5)	1948 s.34(2).
(6)	1948 s.34(2)(*b*)(*c*).
(7)	1948 s.34(5); 1968 s.9(1).
61(1)	1948 s.34(1); 1968 s.9(1); 1977 Sch. 1 para. 1(3)(*b*).
(2)	1968 s.10(1)(*d*)(*e*); 1977 Sch. 1 para. 5; 1984 Sch. 3 para. 32(*b*).
(3)(4)	1968 s.10(1)(*b*)(*c*); (2), (8); 1977 Sch. 1 para. 5; 1984 Sch. 3 para. 32(1)(*a*).
(5)	1968 s.10(2); 1977 Sch. 1 para. 5.
(6)	1948 s.34(1); 1968 s.10(8).
62(1)(2)	1968 s.15(2).
(3)	1968 s.15(5).

Provision	Derivation
63(1)	1948 s.34(2A); 1968 s.9(1); 1984 Sch. 3 para. 9(2).
(2)	1948 s.34(3); 1968 ss.10(5), 15(4).
(3)	1948 s.34(4); 1968 s.9(1); 1977 Sch. 1 para. 1(3)(*c*); 1984 Sch. 3 para. 9(3)(*a*)(*b*).
(4)	1948 s.34(4); 1984 Sch. 3 para. 9(3)(*c*).
64(1)	1948 ss.46(1), 47(1).
(2)	1948 s.46(2).
(3)	1948 s.46(1).
(4)	1948 s.35(1).
65(1)	1948 ss.46(1), 47(1).
(2)	1948 s.47(1)(*b*).
(3)	1948 s.46(1).
66(1)	1948 s.48.
(2)	1948 s.51(1).
(3)	1948 s.51(3).
(4)	1948 s.51(2).
(5)	1948 s.53; 1984 Sch. 3 para. 11.
67(1)	1948 s.49(1).
(2)	1948 s.49(1)(2).
(3) to (6)	1948 s.50(1) to (4); 1958 Sch. 1 Pt. I para. 14.
(7)	1948 s.50(3); 1958 Sch. 1 Pt. I para. 15.
68(1)	1948 s.52.
(2)	1958 s.4(6); R.2.
(3)(4)	Hill Farming Act 1946 (c.73) s.9(2)(4); 1948 Sch. 7 para. 4.
(5)	Housing Act 1985 (c.68) s.231(3)(4).
69(1)	1948 s.54.
(2)(3)	1948 s.55(1)(2).
70(1)	1948 s.56(1).
(2)(3)	1948 s.56(1); 1984 Sch. 3 para. 12.
(4)(5)	1948 s.56(2)(3).
71(1)	1948 s.57(1).
(2)	1948 s.57(2); 1984 Sch. 3 para. 13(*a*).
(3)(4)	1948 s.57(3).
(5)	1948 s.57(4); 1984 Sch. 3 para. 13(*b*).
72	1948 s.58.
73	1958 s.59.
74(1)	1948 s.60(1); 1968 s.9(1)(2); 1977 Sch. 1 para. 1(5); 1984 Sch. 3 para. 14(*a*).
(2)	1948 s.60(1); 1968 ss.9(1)(2), 15(2).
(3)	1948 s.60(2); 1968 s.9(1A); 1984 Sch. 3 paras. 14(*b*), 31.
(4)	1948 s.60(3); 1968 s.17(2); 1984 Sch. 3 paras. 14(*b*), 33.
75	1948 s.61; 1968 ss.10(5); 15(4); 1984 Sch. 3 para. 15.
76(1)	1948 s.63(1); 1958 Sch. 1 Pt. I para. 16; S.I. 1978/447 reg. 2(2).
(2)	1948 s.63(1).
(3)	1948 s.63(2).
77	1948 s.64.
78(1)(2)	1948 s.65(1); 1968 ss.10(4), 15(4).
(3)	1948 s.65(2).
79	1948 s.67(1)(3)(4); 1984 Sch. 3 paras. 16 and 27(*b*).
80(1)(2)	1948 s.68(1); 1958 Sch. 1 Pt. I para. 17.
(3)(4)	1948 s.68(2); 1984 Sch. 3 para. 17(*a*).
(5)	1948 s.68(3).
(6)	1948 s.68(4); 1958 Sch. 1 Pt. I para. 17.
(7)	1948 s.68(4).
(8)	1948 s.68(5).
(9)	1948 s.68(6); 1984 Sch. 3 para. 17(*b*).
81	1948 s.69
82(1)	1948 s.11(4)(*c*); 1949 s.10(1); 1970 Sch. 4.
(2)(3)	1949 s.10(2); S.I. 1955/554 art. 3; S.I. 1978/272 art. 2(1), Sch. 1.

Provision	Derivation
83(1) to (3)	1948 s.70(1)(2); 1968 ss.10(5), 15(4).
(4)	1948 s.70(3); 1984 Sch. 3 para. 18(*a*).
(5)	1948 s.70(4); 1984 Sch. 3 para. 18(*b*).
(6)	1948 s.70(5).
84(1)	1948 s.77(1); Arbitration Act 1950 (c.27), s.44(3); 1968 ss.10(5), 15(4); 1976 s.24(9); 1984 Sch. 2 para. 7(3), Sch. 3 para. 19(2).
(2) to (5)	1948 s.77(2) to (4), (6); 1984 Sch. 3 para. 19(3).
85(1)	1948 s.71; 1968 ss.10(5), 15(4); R.3.
(2)	1948 s.72; 1968 ss.10(5), 15(4).
(3)	1948 s.73; 1968 ss.10(5), 15(4); R.3.
86(1) to (3)	1948 s.82(1)(2); 1968 ss.10(5), 15(4).
(4)	1948 s.89; 1968 ss.10(5), 15(4).
87	1948 s.83; 1968 ss.10(5), 15(4).
88	1948 s.80; 1968 ss.10(5), 15(4); R.4.
89(1)	1948 s.81(1).
(2)	1948 s.81(2); Universities and College Estates Act 1964 (c.51) Sch. 3 Pt. I.
90	1948 s.86.
91	1948 s.78; Housing Act 1985 (c.68) s.231(2).
92	1948 s.79.
93(1)	1948 s.92(1); 1968 ss.10(5), 15(4); 1977 s.12(2)(*a*); 1984 Sch. 2 para. 1(7), Sch. 3 para. 21; R.5.
(2)(3)	1948 s.92(2)(3).
(4)	1948 s.92(4); Interpretation Act 1978 (c.30) s.25(2).
(5)	1948 s.92(5); 1968 ss.10(5), 15(4); 1977 s.12(2)(*a*); 1984 Sch. 2 para. 1(7); R.5.
94(1)(2)	1948 ss.6(4), 50(3), 77(5), 78(1), 94(1); 1958 Sch. 1 Pt. I para. 15; 1976 ss.18(3B), 23(8); 1977 ss.5(2), 11(9); 1984 ss.3(3), 8(4), Sch. 2 para. 6(6), Sch. 3 para. 19(3).
(3)	1984 s.8(4).
(4)	1978 s.78(3).
95	1948 s.87; Crown Estate Act 1956 (c.73); Crown Estate Act 1961 (c.55); 1968 ss.10(5), 15(4), 17(3); 1976 s.18(8); 1977 s.12(2)(*a*); 1984 s.9(3).
96(1)	1948 s.94(1); 1958 s.9(1); 1968 s.17(1); 1976 s.18(2)(7); 1977 ss.2(3); Case H, 12(1)(2)(*a*); 1984 ss.8(4), 9(2), Sch. 1 para. 1(*a*), Sch. 2 para. 1(2), Sch. 3 para. 23.
(2)	1948 s.68(6); 1977 s.12(1A); 1984 Sch. 3 paras. 17(*b*), 42(*b*); Insolvency Act 1985 (c.65) Sch. 8 paras. 9 and 30.
(3)	1948 s.94(2); 1958 s.4(8); 1977 s.12(2)(*a*); 1984 s.9(2).
(4)(5)	1948 s.94(3)(4).
(6)	1948 s.94(5), 1968 ss.10(5), 15(4).
97	1948 s.101; 1968 ss.10(5), 15(4).
98	1948 ss.5(1), 6(1)(2), 8A(1), 9(1), 10(1); 1984 s.1.
99–102	—
Sch. 1	
paras. 1 to 5	1948 Sch. 1 paras. 1 to 5.
6 and 7	1948 Sch. 1 para. 8.
8	1948 Sch. 1 para. 9.
9	1948 Sch. 1 para. 10; 1976 s.17.
Sch. 2	
para. 1(1) to (3)	1948 s.8(3) to (5); 1984 s.1.
2(1)	1948 s.8(6); 1984 s.1.
(2) to (4)	1948 s.8A(3) to (5); 1984 s.1.
3	1948 s.8(7); 1984 s.1.
4(1)	1948 s.8(8); 1984 s.1.
(2)	1948 s.8(12); 1984 s.1.
5(1)	1948 s.8(9); 1984 s.1.
(2)	1948 s.8(10); 1984 s.1.
6	1948 s.8(11); 1984 s.1.

Provision	Derivation
Sch. 3	
Pt. I	
Case A	1977 s.2(3) Case I; 1984 ss.6(6), 11(2).
Case B	1977 s.2(3) Case B.
Case C	1977 s.2(3) Case C; 1984 s.6(3).
Case D	1977 s.2(3) Case D.
Case E	1977 s.2(3) Case E.
Case F	1977 s.2(3) Case F; 1984 Sch. 3 para. 37.
Case G	1977 s.2(3) Case G; 1984 s.6(5)(*a*).
Case H	1977 s.2(3) Case H.
Pt. II	
para. 1	1977 s.2(3) Case I; 1984 s.6(6).
2 to 7	1977 Sch. 1A paras. 1 to 6; 1984 Sch. 3 para. 43; Housing (Consequential Provisions) Act 1985 (c.71) Sch. 2 para. 34.
8	1977 s.2(3A); 1984 s.6(7).
9(1)	1977 s.2(4).
(2)	1977 s.2(4A); 1984 s.6(8).
10(1)	1977 s.2(3) Case D, (4B); 1984 s.6(4)(8).
(2)	1977 s.2(6).
11(1)	1977 s.2(5).
(2)	1977 s.2(4B); 1984 s.6(8).
12	1977 s.2(3) Case G; 1984 s.6(5)(*b*).
Sch. 4	1977 s.5(1); 1984 Sch. 3 para. 38.
Sch. 5.	
para. 1	1977 s.11(10).
2	1977 s.11(1), (2).
3	1977 s.11(3), (4); 1984 Sch. 3 para. 41.
4	1977 s.11(5).
5	1977 s.11(6).
6	1977 s.11(7), (8).
Sch. 6	
Pt. I	
para. 1	1976 Sch. 3A para. 1; 1984 Sch. 1 para. 3, Sch. 2 para. 1(4).
2	1976 s.18(3); 1984 Sch. 2 para. 1(3).
3	1976 s.18(3A); 1984 s.3(3), Sch. 2 para. 1(4).
4	1976 s.18(3B); 1984 s.3(3); Sch. 2 para. 1(4).
5(1)	1976 s.18(6); 1984 s.3(4); Sch. 2 para. 1(5).
(2)	1976 s.18(6); Sch. 3A para. 7; 1984 s.3(4); Sch. 1 para. 8, Sch. 2 paras. 1(5), 9.
(3)	1976 s.18(6A); 1984 s.3(4), Sch. 2 para. 1(5).
(4)(5)	1976 s.18(6B); 1984 s.3(4), Sch. 2 para. 1(5).
6	1976 Sch. 3A para. 2; 1984 Sch. 1 para. 8; Sch. 2 para. 1(4).
7	1976 Sch. 3A para. 4(1) to (3); 1984 Sch. 1 para. 8; Sch. 2 para. 1(4).
8(1)	1976 Sch. 3A para. 3; 1984 Sch. 1 para. 8.
(2)	1976 Sch. 3A para. 4(4); 1984 Sch. 1 para. 8.
9	1976 Sch. 3A para. 5; 1984 Sch. 1 para. 8; Sch. 2 para. 1(4).
10	1976 Sch. 3A para. 6; 1984 Sch. 1 para. 8; Sch. 2 para. 1(4).
Pt. II	1984 Sch. 2 para. 1(3) to (6).
Sch. 7	
Pt. I	
para. 1	1948 Sch. 3 Pt. I para. 1.
2	1948 Sch. 3 Pt. I para. 2.
3 to 7	1948 Sch. 3 Pt. I paras. 3 to 7.
8	1948 Sch. 3 Pt. I para. 7A; 1984 Sch. 3 para. 25(1)(*b*).
Pt. II	
para. 9	1948 Sch. 3 Pt. II para. 8.
10	Housing Act 1985 (c.68) s.231(2).
11	1948 Sch. 3 Pt. II para. 8A; 1984 Sch. 3 para. 25(2)(*a*).
12 to 15	1948 Sch. 3 Pt. II paras. 9 to 12.
16	1948 Sch. 3 Pt. II para. 13; 1984 Sch. 3 para. 25(2)(*b*).

Provision	Derivation
Sch. 7	
Pt. II	
paras. 17 to 24	1948 Sch. 3 Pt. II paras. 14 to 21.
25	1948 Sch. 3 Pt. II para. 22; 1984 Sch. 3 para. 25(2)(*c*).
26	1948 Sch. 3 Pt. II para. 23.
27 and 28	1948 Sch. 3 Pt. II paras. 24, 25; 1984 Sch. 3 para. 25(2)(*d*).
Sch. 8	
Pt. I	
para. 1 to 3	1948 Sch. 4 Pt. I paras. 1, 2, 4.
4 to 6	1948 Sch. 4 Pt. I paras. 5 to 7; S.I. 1978/742 Sch. para. 1.
Pt. II	
para. 7	1948 Sch. 4 Pt. II para. 8.
8	1948 Sch. 4 Pt. II para. 9; 1984 Sch. 3 para. 26.
9	1948 Sch. 4 Pt. II para. 10.
10	1948 Sch. 4 Pt. II para. 11; S.I. 1951/2168 art. 3(1); S.I. 1985/1947 art. 3(2).
11	1948 Sch. 4 Pt. II para. 12; S.I. 1978/742 Sch. para. 2; S.I. 1985/1947 art. 3(3).
Sch. 9	
Pt. I	
para. 1(1)	1948 s.36(1).
(2)	1948 s.35(2).
(3)	1948 s.36(1).
(4)	1948 s.36(2).
(5)	1948 s.43(3).
2(1)	1948 s.37; 1984 Sch. 3 para. 10.
(2)	1948 s.43(1).
3	1948 s.38.
4(1)(2)	1948 s.39(1).
(3)	1948 s.39(2).
5(1)	1948 s.44.
(2)	1948 s.45.
Pt. II	
paras. 1 to 15	1948 Sch. 2 Pt. I paras. 1, 2, 4 to 11, 13 to 17.
16	1948 Sch. 2 Pt. II.
Sch. 10	
paras. 1 to 5	1948 Sch. 5 paras. 1 to 5.
Sch. 11	
para. 1(1)	1948 Sch. 6 para. 1(1); 1984 s.8(1)(2).
(2)	1984 s.8(3)(4).
(3)	1948 Sch. 6 para. 1(1A); 1984 s.8(2), Sch. 3 para. 28(2).
(4)	1948 Sch. 6 para. 1(2); 1984 s.8(2).
(5)	1948 Sch. 6 para. 1(3); 1958 Sch. 1 Pt. I para. 20.
2	1948 Sch. 6 para. 2.
3	1948 Sch. 6 para. 2A; 1984 Sch. 3 para. 28(3).
4	1948 Sch. 6 para. 3; 1984 Sch. 3 para. 28(4).
5	1948 Sch. 6 para. 4.
6	1948 Sch. 6 para. 5; 1984 s.8(2), Sch. 3 para. 28(5).
7	1948 Sch. 6 para. 6; 1984 Sch. 3 para. 28(6).
8	1948 Sch. 6 para. 7.
9	1948 Sch. 6 para. 8.
10	1948 Sch. 6 para. 9.
11(1)	1948 Sch. 6 para. 10(1)(2).
(2)(3)	1948 Sch. 6 para. 10(1).
(4)	1948 Sch. 6 para. 10(3).
12(1)(2)	1948 Sch. 6 para. 11(1).
(3)(4)	1948 Sch. 6 para. 11(2).
13	1948 Sch. 6 para. 12.
14(1)	1948 Sch. 6 para. 13; 1963 s.20.
(2)	1948 Sch. 6 para. 13; 1984 s.8(2).
15	1948 Sch. 6 para. 14.

Provision	Derivation
Sch. 11	
para. 16	1948 Sch. 6 para. 16.
17	1948 Sch. 6 para. 17.
18	1948 Sch. 6 para. 18.
19	1948 Sch. 6 para. 19.
20	1948 Sch. 6 para. 20.
21	1948 Sch. 6 para. 20A; 1984 Sch. 3 para. 28(7).
22	1948 Sch. 6 para. 20B; 1984 Sch. 3 para. 28(7).
23	1948 Sch. 6 para. 21.
24	1948 Sch. 6 para. 22; 1984 Sch. 3 para. 28(8).
25	1948 Sch. 6 para. 23.
26	1948 Sch. 6 para. 24; 1958 Sch. 1 Pt. I para. 21(1).
27(1)	1948 Sch. 6 para. 25(1).
(2)	1948 Sch. 6 para. 25(2); 1972 s.15(1).
28(1) to (4)	1948 Sch. 6 para. 25A(1) to (4); 1984 Sch. 3 para. 28(9).
29	1948 Sch. 6 para. 26.
30	1958 Sch. I Pt. I para. 21(2).
31	1948 Sch. 6 para. 29; 1984 s.8(2), Sch. 3 para. 28(10).
32	1984 s.8(5).
Sch. 12	
para. 1	1948 s.2(1).
2	1948 s.3(3).
3	1948 ss.13(5)(*a*), 67(1)(*b*); 1984 Sch. 3 para. 16.
4	1977 s.1(2)(*d*), (3), (3A), (4); Transport Act 1981 (c.56) s.5; London Regional Transport Act 1984 (c.32) Sch. 6 para. 13.
5	1948 s.47(1)(*a*).
6	1948 s.47(1)(*c*), (2); 1977 Sch. 1 para. 1.
7	S.I. 1951/2168 art. 4.
8	1948 ss.56(4), 63(2), 64, 65(2); S.I. 1951/2168 art. 4.
9	Saving.
10	1948 s.67(1)(2)(3).
Sch. 13	
para. 1	—
2	1948 s.96(2).
3–5	—
6, 7	1984 Sch. 5 para. 5.
8	—
9	1984 Sch. 5 para. 7.
10	1984 Sch. 5 para. 8.
11, 12	—
13	1984 Sch. 5 para. 10.
14	Insolvency Act 1985 (c.65) Sch. 9 para. 11.
15	1984 Sch. 5 para. 14.
16	1984 Sch. 5 para. 4(*d*).
Sch. 14	
para. 12	1948 Sch. 7 para. 2.
44	1968 s.10(8).
53(4)	1968 s.10(3)(8).
remainder	—
Sch. 15	—

TABLE OF DESTINATIONS

HILL FARMING ACT 1946

1946	1986
s.9(2)(4)	.......s.68(3)(4)

THE AGRICULTURAL HOLDINGS ACT 1948

THE AGRICULTURAL HOLDINGS ACT 1948—*continued*

1948	1986
ss.70(1), (2)	...ss.83(1)–(3)
(3)	83(4)
(4)	83(5)
(5)	83(6)
71	85(1)
72	85(2)
73	85(3)
77(1)	84(1)
(2)–(4), (6)	84(2)–(5)
(5)	94(1), (2)
78	91
(1)	94(1), (2)
79	92
80	88
81(1)	89(1)
(2)	89(2)
82(1), (2)	86(1)–(3)
83	87
86	90
87	95
89	86(4)
92(1)	93(1)
(2), (3)	93(2), (3)
(4)	93(4)
(5)	93(5)
(2)	96(3)
94(1)	ss.1(5), 94(1), (2), 96(1)
(3), (4)	s.96(4), (5)
(5)	94(6)
96(2)	Sch. 13, para. 1
Sch. 1,	
paras. 1–5	Sch. 1, paras. 1–5
8	Sch. 1, paras. 6 and 7
9	Sch. 1, para. 8
10	Sch. 1, para. 9
Sch. 2, Pt. I,	
paras. 1, 2, 4–11, 13–17	Sch. 9, Pt. I, paras. 1–15
Pt. II	Sch. 9, Pt. II, para. 16
Sch. 3, Pt. I,	
para. 1	Sch. 7, Pt. I, para. I
2	Sch. 7, Pt. 1, para. 2
3–7	Sch. 7, Pt. I, paras. 3–7
7A	Sch. 7, Pt. I, para. 8
Pt. II,	
para. 8	Sch. 7, Pt. II, para. 9

1948	1986
Sch. 3, Pt. II,	
paras. 8A	Sch. 7, Pt. II, para. 11
9–12	Sch. 7, Pt. II, paras. 12–15
13	Sch. 7, Pt. II, para. 16
14–21	Sch. 7, Pt. II, paras. 17–24
22	Sch. 7, Pt. II, para. 25
23	Sch. 7, Pt. II, para. 26
24, 25	Sch. 7, Pt. II, paras. 27, 28
Sch. 4, Pt. I,	
paras. 1, 2,	
4	Sch. 8, Pt. I, paras. 1–3
5–7	Sch. 8, Pt. I, paras. 4–6
Pt. II,	
para. 8	Sch. 8, Pt. II, para. 7
9	Sch. 8, Pt. II, para. 8
10	Sch. 8, Pt. II, para. 9
11	Sch. 8, Pt. II, para. 10
12	Sch. 8, Pt. II, para. 11
Sch. 5,	
paras. 1–5	Sch. 10, paras. 1–5
Sch. 6,	
para. 1(1)	Sch. 11, para. 1(1)
(1A)	Sch. 11, para. 1(3)
(2)	Sch. 11, para. 1(4)
(3)	Sch. 11, para. 1(5)
2	Sch. 11, para. 2
2A	Sch. 11, para. 3
3	Sch. 11, para. 4
4	Sch. 11, para. 5
5	Sch. 11, para. 6
6	Sch. 11, para. 7
7	Sch. 11, para. 8
8	Sch. 11, para. 9
9	Sch. 11, para. 10

1948	1986
Sch. 6,	
para. 10(1)	Sch. 11, para. 11(2), (3)
(1),	
(2)	Sch. 11, para. 11(1)
(3)	Sch. 11, para. 11(4)
11(1)	Sch. 11, para. 12(1), (2)
(2)	Sch. 11, para. 12(3), (4)
12	Sch. 11, para. 13
13	Sch. 11, para. 14(1), (2)
14	Sch. 11, para. 15
16	Sch. 11, para. 16
17	Sch. 11, para. 17
18	Sch. 11, para. 18
19	Sch. 11, para. 19
20	Sch. 11, para. 20
20A	Sch. 11, para. 21
20B	Sch. 11, para. 22
21	Sch. 11, para. 23
22	Sch. 11, para. 24
23	Sch. 11, para. 25
24	Sch. 11, para. 26
25(1)	Sch. 11, para. 27(1)
(2)	Sch. 11, para. 27(2)
25A (1)–(4)	Sch. 11, para. 28(1)–(4)
26	Sch. 11, para. 29
28(7)	Sch. 11, para. 21
29	Sch. 11, para. 31
Sch. 7,	
para. 2	Sch. 14, para. 12
4	s.68(3), (4)

THE AGRICULTURE (MISCELLANEOUS PROVISIONS) ACT 1949

1949	1986
s.10(1)	s.82(1)
10(2)	82(2), (3)

ARBITRATION ACT 1950

1950	1986
s.44(3)	.... s.84(1)

CROWN ESTATE ACT 1956

1956	1986
Crown Estate Act 1956	.... s.95

THE AGRICULTURE ACT 1958

1958	1986	1958	1986	1958	1986
s.4(1)	s.11(1), (2)	Sch. 1, Pt. I		Sch. 1, Pt. I	
4(2)–(4)	11(3)–(7)	para. 6	14(1)–(5)	para. 20	Sch. 11, para. 1(5)
(5)	13(2)–(6)	7	15(4), (5)		
(6)	68(2)	14	62(3)–(6)	21(1)	Sch. 11, para. 26
(7)	ss.11(8), 13(5),(6)	15	ss.67(7), 94(1), (2)	(2)	Sch. 11, para. 30
(8)	s.96(3)				
9(1)	96(1)	16	s.76(1)		
59	73	17	80(1), (2),(6)		

CROWN ESTATE ACT 1961

1961	1986
Crown Estate Act 1961	.... s.95

THE AGRICULTURE (MISCELLANEOUS PROVISIONS) ACT 1963

1963	1986
s.20	............Sch. 11, para. 14(1)

UNIVERSITIES AND COLLEGE ESTATES ACT 1964

1964	1986
Sch. 3, Pt. I	.. s.89(2)

THE AGRICULTURE (MISCELLANEOUS PROVISIONS) ACT 1968

1968	1986	1968	1986	1968	1986
s.9(1)	ss.60(1), (2), (7), 61(1), 63(1), (3), 74(1), (2)	s.10(4)	s.78(1), (2)	s.15(2)	ss.62(1), (2), 74(2)
(1A)	s.74(3)	(5)	ss.63(2), 75, 83(1)–(3), 85(1)–(3), 86(1)–(4), 87, 88, 93(1), (4), 95, 96(6), 97	(4)	63(2), 75, 83(1)–(3), 85(1)–(3), 86(1)–(4), 87, 88, 93(1), (4), 95, 96(6), 97
(2)	ss.60(4), 74(1), (2)	(8)	s.61(3), (4), Sch. 14, paras. 44(4), 53(4), 61(6)	(5)	s.62(3)
10(1)(*b*), (*c*)	s.61(3), (4)			17(1)	96(1)
(1)(*d*), (*e*)	61(2)			(2)	74(4)
(2)	61(3)–(5)				
(3)	Sch. 14, para. 53(4)				

THE AGRICULTURE ACT 1970

1970	1986
Sch. 4	.... s.82(1)

COURTS ACT 1971

1971	1986
Sch. 9, Pt. I	.. s.19(2)

THE AGRICULTURE (MISCELLANEOUS PROVISIONS) ACT 1972

1972	1986
s.15(1)	........Sch. 11, para. 27(2)
(2)	.... s.7(2)

THE AGRICULTURE (MISCELLANEOUS PROVISIONS) ACT 1976

1976	1986	1976	1986	1976	1986
s.17 ....Sch. 1,		s.18(7) .... s.96(1)		s.24(1) .... s.48(1)	
	para. 9	(8) 95		(2) .... 48(2)	
18(1) ....ss.35(1), (2),		19 43		(3) .... 48(3), (4)	
	36(1)	20(1) ....ss.36(1), 39(1)		(4) .... 48(11)	
(2) .... 1(4), 35(2),		(2) .... s.39(2)		(a) .... 48(5)	
	36(3), (4),	(3) .... 39(3)		(b) .... 48(6)	
	39(1), 41,	(4) .... 39(4)		(c) .... 48(7)	
	96(1)	(5) .... 39(5)		(5) .... 48(8)	
(3) ....Sch. 6, Pt. I,		(6) .... 39(6)		(6) .... 48(9)	
	para. 2	(7)–(9) ... 39(7)–(9)		(7) .... 48(10)	
(3A) ......Sch. 6, Pt. I,		(9A) .... 39(10)		(8) .... 48(12)	
	para. 3	(10)–(14) .. 40(1)–(5)		(9) .... 84(1)	
(3B) ...... s.94(1), (2),		(15) 42		Sch. 3A,	
	Sch. 6, Pt. I,	21 41		para. 1 ......Sch. 6, Pt. I,	
	para. 4	22(1) .... 44(1)			para. 1
(4)(a) ..... 38(1)		(2) .... 44(2)		2 ......Sch. 6, Pt. I,	
(b) .... 38(2)		(3) .... 44(3)			para. 6
(c) ..... 38(3)		(4) .... 44(4)		3 ......Sch. 6, Pt. I,	
(d) .... 36(2)		(5) .... 44(5)			para. 8(1)
(e) .... 37(1), (9)		(6) .... 44(6)		4(1)–	
(f) ..... 38(4)		(7) .... 44(7)		(3) ....Sch. 6, Pt. I,	
(g) ..... 38(5)		23(1) .... 45(1)			para. 7
(5) .... 37(2), (3),		(1) .... 47(1)		5 ......Sch. 6, Pt. I,	
	(9)	(1A) ...... 45(2)–(4)			para. 9
(5A) ...... 37(4), (5)		(2) .... 46(1)		6 ......Sch. 6, Pt. I,	
(6) ....Sch. 6, Pt. I,		(2A) ...... 46(2)			para. 10
	para. 5(1),	(3) .... 47(2)		7 ......Sch. 6, Pt. I,	
	(2)	(4) .... 47(3)			para. 5(2)
(6A) ......Sch. 6, Pt. I,		(5)–(7) ... 45(5)–(8)			
	para. 5(3)	(8) ....ss.45(5)–(8),			
(6B) ......Sch. 6, Pt. I,			94(1), (2)		
	para. 5(4)(5)	(9) .... s.46(3)			

THE AGRICULTURAL HOLDINGS (NOTICES TO QUIT) ACT 1977

1977	1986	1977	1986	1977	1986
s.1(1) .... s.25(1)		s.2(3A) ......Sch. 3, Pt. II,		s.10(1) .... s.33(1)	
(2) .... 25(2)			para. 8	(1A) ...... 33(2)	
(2)(d), (3),		(4) ....Sch. 3, Pt. II,		(2) .... 33(2), (3)	
(3A), (4) ..Sch. 12,			para. 9(1)	11(1), (2) ...Sch. 5, para. 2	
	para. 4	(4A) ......Sch. 3, Pt. II,		(3), (4) ...Sch. 5, para. 3	
(5)–(7) ..... s.25(3)–(5)			para. 9(2)	(5) ....Sch. 5, para. 4	
2(1) .... 26(1)		(4B) ....Sch. 3, Pt. II,		(6) ....Sch. 5, para. 5	
(2) .... 26(2)			paras. 10(1),	(7), (8) ...Sch. 5, para. 6	
(3) Case B Sch. 3, Pt. I,			11(2)	(9) .... s.94(1), (2)	
	Case B	(5) ....Sch. 3, Pt. II,		(10) ....Sch. 5, para. 1	
Case C Sch. 3, Pt. I,			para. 11(1)	12(1) ....ss.26(2), 96(1)	
	Case C	(6) ....Sch. 3, Pt. II,		(1A) ...... s.96(2)	
Case D Sch. 3, Pt. I,			para. 10(2)	(2)(a) .....ss.93(1), (5),	
	Case D,	3 .... s.27(1)–(5)			95, 96(1), (3)
	Pt. II,	4(1) .... 28(1)		Sch. 1,	
	para. 10(1)	(2) .... 28(2)–(4)		para. 1 ......Sch. 12,	
Case E Sch. 3, Pt. I,		(3) .... 28(2), (4)			para. 6
	Case E	(4) .... 28(5)		(3)(a) s.60(1), (2)	
Case F Sch. 3, Pt. I,		(5) .... 28(6)		(3)(b) 61(1)	
	Case F	5(1) ....Sch. 4		(3)(c) 63(3)	
Case G Sch. 3, Pt. I,		(2) .... s.94(1), (2)		(5) .. 74(1)	
	Case G,	6(1) .... 27(6)		5 ...... 61(2)–(5)	
	Pt. II,	(2) .... 27(8)		7(2)(b) 38(1)	
	para. 12	(3) .... 27(7)		(c) 38(2)	
Case H s.96, Sch. 3,		(4) .... 27(9)		(d) 38(3)	
	Pt. I, Case H	8(1) .... 31(1)		(3) .. 43	
Case I Sch. 3, Pt. I,		(2) .... 31(2)		(4) .. 44(2)	
	Case A,	9 32		(5) .. 46(1)	
	Pt. II,			Sch. 1A	
	para. 1			paras. 1–6 ..Sch. 3, Pt. II,	
					paras. 2–7

INTERPRETATION ACT 1978

1978	1986
s.25(2)	.... s.93(4)
78(3)	.... 94(4)

TRANSPORT ACT 1981

1981	1986
s.5	..............Sch. 12, para. 4

LONDON REGIONAL TRANSPORT ACT 1984

1984	1986
Sch. 6, para. 13	...............Sch. 12, para. 4

THE AGRICULTURAL HOLDINGS ACT 1984

1984	1986
s.1	...............ss.12(1)–(4), 98, Sch. 2, paras. 1(1)–(3), 2(1)–(4), 3, 4(1), (2), 5(1), (2), 6
2(1), (2)	.... 34(1), 35(1)
(3)	.... s.34(2)
3(1)	.... 45(2)–(4)
(2)(*b*)	...... 36(4)
(3)	.... 94(1), (2), Sch. 6, Pt. I, paras. 3, 4
(4)	.........Sch. 6, Pt. I, para. 5(1)–(5)
5	.... s.25(3)–(5)
6(3)	..........Sch. 3, Pt. I, Case C
(4), (8)	....Sch. 3, Pt. II, para. 10(1)
(5)(*a*)	......Sch. 3, Pt. I, Case G
(*b*)	......Sch. 3, Pt. II, para. 12
(6)	..........Sch. 3, Pt. I, Case A, Pt. II, paras. 2–7
(7)	..........Sch. 3, Pt. I, para. 8
(8)	..........Sch. 3, Pt. II, paras. 9(2), 11(2)
(9)	.... s.43
7	.... 28(5)
8(1)	.... 22(2), Sch. 11, para. 1(1)
(2)	.........ss.12(3), 22(2), Sch. 11, paras. 1(1), (3), (4), 6, 14(2), 31
(3)	..........Sch. 11, para. 1(2)
(4)	..........ss.94(1)–(3), 96(1), Sch. 11, para. 1(2)
(5)	.... s.22(5), Sch. 11, para. 32

1984	1986
s.9(2)	.... s.96(1), (3)
(3)	 95
11(2)	........Sch. 3, Pt. I, Case A
Sch. 1, para. 1	......ss.1(4), 35(2)
(*a*)	.. 96(1)
2(2)	.. 38(1)
(3)	.. 38(3)
(5)	.. 37(1), (9)
(6)	.. 38(4)
(7)	.. 37(2)–(5), (9)
3	......Sch. 6, Pt. I, para. 1
(2)	.. s.43
(3)(*a*)	39(5), (6)
(*b*)	39(10)
(4)(*a*)	44(2), (4)
(*b*)	44(5)
(5)	.. 46(3)
(6)	.. 48(2)
4	...... 39(2)
5(1)	.. 35(1)
(2)	.. 42
6	...... 44(6), (7)
7(3)	.. 48(2)
8	......Sch. 6, Pt. I, paras. 1(4), 5(2), 6, 8(2), 9, 10
Sch. 2, para. 1(1)	..ss.49(1), (2), 50(1)
(1)(*a*)	s.34(1)
(2)	..ss.1(4), 49(1)– (3), 50(2)(3), 53(2), 54(3), 96(1)
(3)	..Sch. 6, Pt. I, para. 2, Pt. II
(4)	..Sch. 6, Pt. I, paras. 1(4), 3, 4, 5(1), 6, 9, 10, Pt. II
(5)	..Sch. 6, Pt. I, para. 5(2)–(5), Pt. II

1984	1986
Sch. 2, para. 1(6)	..Sch. 6, Pt. II
(7)	.. s.93(1), (5)
2(1)	
(*a*)–(*c*)	
(*f*), (*g*)	51(1)
(*d*)	.... 51(2)
(*e*), (3)	.... 51(3)
(2)	.. 49(3)
(4)	.. 51(1)
(5)	.. 51(4)
(6)	.. 51(5), (6)
3(1),	
(2)	.... 52(1), (2)
(3)	.. 52(3), (4)
(4)	.. 52(5)
4	...... 54(1), (2)
5(1)	...ss.50(1), 53(1)
(2)–	
(10)	. s.53(3)–(11)
6(1)	...ss.55(1), 56(1)
(2)	.. s.55(2)–(4)
(3)	.. 56(2)
(4)–	
(7)	.. 55(5)–(8)
(6)	.. 94(1), (2)
7(1)	...ss.46(1), 56(3), (4)
(2)	.. 46(2), 56(3), (4)
(3)	.. s.84(1)
8	 57
9	...... 58, Sch. 6, Pt. I, para. 5(2)
10(1)	
(*a*)	. 34(1)
(1)(*b*),	
(2)	.... 37(6)
Sch. 3, para. 1(2)	.. 1(1)
(3)	.. 1(2), (3)
2(1)(*a*)	3(1)
(*b*)	5(1)
(2)	...ss.4(1)–(4), 5(2), (3)
3(2)	.. s.6(1)
(3)	.. 6(5), (6)

Destinations for Statutory Instruments

THE TRANSFER OF FUNCTIONS (WALES) (NO. 1) ORDER 1978

1978   **1986**

S.I. 1978 No. 272

art. 2(1), Sch. 1 .... s.82(2), (3)

THE AGRICULTURAL HOLDINGS ACT 1948 (AMENDMENT) REGULATIONS 1978

1978   **1986**

S.I. 1978 No. 447,

reg. 2(2) .... s.76(1)

THE AGRICULTURAL HOLDINGS ACT 1948 (VARIATION OF FOURTH SCHEDULE) ORDER 1978

S.I. 1978 No. 742 Sch.,

para. 1   Sch. 8, Pt. I,

para. 4–6

2   ....Sch. 8, Pt. II, para. 11

THE AGRICULTURAL HOLDINGS ACT 1948 (VARIATION OF FOURTH SCHEDULE) ORDER 1985

1985   **1986**

S.I. 1985 No. 1947 art.

3(2) ....Sch. 8, Pt. II, para. 10

(3)   ....Sch. 8, Pt. II, para. 11

REPORT OF THE LAW COMMISSION ON THIS ACT (Cmnd. 9665) RECOMMENDATIONS

R.1   .... s.2

R.2   ....   68(3), (4)

R.3   ....   85(1), (3)

R.4   88

R.5   ....   93(1), (5)

PREVENTION OF OIL POLLUTION ACT 1986

(1986 c.6)

An Act to prohibit the discharge from vessels of oil or mixtures containing oil into certain United Kingdom waters; and for connected purposes.

[18th March 1986]

PARLIAMENTARY DEBATES
Hansard: H.L. Vol. 468, col. 978; Vol. 469, col. 598; Vol. 470, cols. 544, 1013; Vol. 471, col. 104; H.C. Vol. 92, cols. 646, 1234.

Discharge of oil from vessels into certain United Kingdom waters

1.—(1) In section 2 of the Prevention of Oil Pollution Act 1971 (discharge of oil into United Kingdom waters) after subsection (2) there shall be inserted the following subsections—

"(2A) If any oil or mixture containing oil is discharged as mentioned in paragraph (i) or (ii) below into waters (including inland waters) which—

(*a*) are landward of the line which for the time being is the baseline for measuring the breadth of the territorial waters of the United Kingdom; and

(*b*) are navigable by sea-going ships,

then, subject to the provisions of this Act, the following shall be guilty of an offence, that is to say—

(i) if the discharge is from a vessel, the owner or master of the vessel, unless the proves that the discharge took place and was caused as mentioned in paragraph (ii) below;

(ii) if the discharge is from a vessel but takes place in the course of a transfer of oil to or from another vessel or a place on land and is caused by the act or omission of any person in charge of any apparatus in that other vessel or that place, the owner or master of that other vessel or, as the case may be, the occupier of that place.

(2B) Subsection (2A) above shall not apply to any discharge which—

(*a*) is made into the sea; and

(*b*) is of a kind or is made in circumstances for the time being prescribed by regulations made by the Secretary of State."

(2) Subject to subsection (3) below, regulations 12 and 13 of the Merchant Shipping (Prevention of Oil Pollution) Regulations 1983 (control of discharge of oil by ships) shall accordingly cease to have effect in relation to any discharge within the meaning of those regulations which occurs landward of the line referred to in section 2(2A)(*a*) of the said Act of 1971.

(3) Nothing in subsection (2) above shall affect the operation of so much of regulations 12(4) and 13(4) as prohibits the discharge into the sea of chemicals or other substances in quantities or concentrations which are hazardous to the marine environment.

Short title, commencement and extent

2.—(1) This Act may be cited as the Prevention of Oil Pollution Act 1986.

(2) This Act shall come into force at the end of the period of two months beginning with the date on which it is passed.

(3) This Act extends to Northern Ireland.

MARRIAGE (WALES) ACT 1986

(1986 c.7)

An Act to extend section 23 of the Marriage Act 1949 to Wales.

[18th March 1986]

PARLIAMENTARY DEBATES
Hansard: H.C. Vol. 88, col. 531; Vol. 89, 1413; H.L. Vol. 470, col. 44; Vol. 471, col. 576; Vol. 472, col. 869.

Benefices held in plurality

1. Section 23 of the Marriage Act 1949 (benefices held in plurality) shall extend to Wales with the omission of the words "under the Pastoral Reorganisation Measure, 1949," and accordingly Schedule 6 to that Act (which specifies provisions of the Act which do not extend to Wales) shall be amended by the omission of the reference to that section.

Short title and citation

2.—(1) This Act may be cited as the Marriage (Wales) Act 1986.

(2) This Act and the Marriage Acts 1949 to 1983 may be cited together as the Marriage Acts 1949 to 1986.

MUSEUM OF LONDON ACT 1986

(1986 c.8)

An Act to make provision with respect to the composition and functions of the Board of Governors of the Museum of London and the funding of the Museum.

[26th March 1986]

PARLIAMENTARY DEBATES
Hansard: H.C. Vol. 86, col. 119; Vol. 87, col. 469; Vol. 91, col. 93; Vol. 94, col. 736; H.L. Vol. 470, col. 1096; Vol. 471, col. 792; Vol. 472, cols. 12, 402, 797.
The Bill was considered by Standing Committee E on December 10, 1985 to January 23, 1986.

Composition of Board of Governors

1.—(1) The persons who immediately before 1st April 1986 are members of the Board of Governors of the Museum of London by virtue of appointments made by the Greater London Council under paragraph (*c*) of subsection (2) of section 1 of the Museum of London Act 1965 shall cease to be members on that date; and as from that date the number of members to be appointed by the Prime Minister under paragraph (*a*) of that sub-section and by the Corporation of the City of London under paragraph (*b*) of that subsection shall be increased in each case from six to nine.

(2) Of the three additional members first appointed by the Prime Minister ("Ministerial appointees") and of the three additional members first appointed by the Corporation of the City of London ("City appointees") one Ministerial and one City appointee shall be appointed to hold office for the period beginning with 1st April 1986 and ending on the first occasion on which other members of the Board are due to retire after that date, one Ministerial and one City appointee shall be appointed to hold office for the period beginning with 1st April 1986 and ending on the second such occasion and one Ministerial and one City appointee shall be appointed to hold office for the period beginning with 1st April 1986 and ending on the third such occasion.

(3) Section 43(1) and (2) of the Local Government Act 1985 (which makes provision concerning the membership of the Board of Governors of the Museum and is superseded by this section) shall not have effect.

Functions of Board of Governors

2.—(1) For section 3 of the Museum of London Act 1965 (general powers of the Board of Governors of the Museum) there shall be substituted—

"General functions of Board
    3.—(1) So far as practicable and subject to the following provisions of this Act, it shall be the duty of the Board—
    (*a*) to care for, preserve and add to the objects in their collections;
    (*b*) to secure that those objects are exhibited to the public and made available to persons seeking to inspect them in connection with study or research; and
    (*c*) generally to promote understanding and appreciation of historic and contemporary London and of its society and culture, both by means of their collections and by such other means as they consider appropriate.

(2) The Board may, subject to the provisions of this Act, do all such things as they think necessary or expedient for those purposes and their functions under this Act.

(3) Without prejudice to the generality of sub-section (2) above, for the purposes mentioned in sub-section (1) above the Board may—

(*a*) provide archaeological services and undertake archaeological investigations and research in connection with land in London, publish information concerning such investigations and research and promote the provision of such services and the undertaking of such investigations and research and the publishing of such information;

(*b*) subject to subsection (4) below, acquire or dispose of any land or any estate or interest in land.

(4) The Board shall not acquire or dispose of any land or any estate or interest in land without the consent of the Secretary of State and the Corporation and such consent may be given subject to such conditions as the Secretary of State and the Corporation consider appropriate.

(5) In this section 'London' includes all Greater London and the surrounding region."

(2) For section 8 of that Act there shall be substituted—

"Use of premises occupied or managed by the Board

8.—(1) The Board may use the premises known as the Museum of London for any educational or cultural purpose whether or not connected with the Board's functions under this Act.

(2) The Board may allow any premises occupied or managed by them to be used by other persons (for payment or otherwise) for purposes not connected with the Board's functions under this Act if the Board are satisfied that to do so would not conflict with those functions.".

(3) At the end of section 9(1) of that Act (which provides for the appointment of a Director of the Museum and for his functions) there shall be added "and for the administration of any services provided by the Board in the exercise of their functions".

Funding of general expenses in respect of Museum

3.—(1) In section 15(3) of the Museum of London Act 1965 (payment of the expenses of the Corporation of the City of London in respect of the Museum as to one-third out of moneys provided by Parliament and one-third by the Greater London Council)—

(*a*) for the words "the Secretary of State out of moneys provided by Parliament, and the Greater London Council shall each pay to the Corporation a sum equal to one-third" there shall be substituted the words "the Secretary of State shall pay to the Corporation out of moneys provided by Parliament a sum equal to one-half"; and

(*b*) for the words "the Corporation, the Secretary of State and the Greater London Council" there shall be substituted the words "the Corporation and the Secretary of State".

(2) Section 43(4) of the Local Government Act 1985 (which makes provision concerning the funding of expenses in respect of the Museum and is superseded by this section) shall not have effect.

Funding of Greater London archaeological service

4.—(1) The Historic Buildings and Monuments Commission for England may make grants to the Board of Governors of the Museum of

London for the purpose of assisting the Board in providing archaeological services and undertaking archaeological investigations and research in connection with land in London and publishing information concerning such investigations and research or in promoting the provision of such services or the undertaking of such investigations and research or the publishing of such information by another body or person.

(2) A grant under this section may be made subject to such conditions as the Commission think fit to impose.

(3) In this section "London" includes all Greater London and the surrounding region.

(4) In section 14(1) of the Museum of London Act 1965 (general obligation on Board to apply moneys received by them otherwise than as mentioned in paragraphs (*a*) to (*c*) to defray general administrative expenses) after paragraph (*c*) there shall be inserted the words "or

(*d*) under section 4 of the Museum of London Act 1986".

Reports

5. Not later than 31st March 1989 and subsequently at intervals not exceeding three years the Secretary of State shall lay before each House of Parliament a report on the exercise of the functions of the Board of Governors of the Museum of London since the commencement of this Act or, in the case of the second and subsequent reports, since the end of the period to which the previous report related.

Expenses

6. There shall be paid out of money provided by Parliament any increase attributable to this Act in the sums payable out of money so provided under any other Act.

Short title, commencement and repeals

7.—(1) This Act may be cited as the Museum of London Act 1986.

(2) This Act shall come into force on 1st April 1986.

(3) The enactments mentioned in the Schedule to this Act (which include spent provisions) are hereby repealed to the extent specified in the third column of that Schedule.

Section 7(3)   SCHEDULE

REPEALS

Chapter	Short title	Extent of repeal
1965 c.17.	The Museum of London Act 1965.	Section 1(2)(*c*) and the word "and" immediately preceding it. Section 13. In section 14(1)(*a*), the words "section 13 or".
1973 c.2.	The National Theatre and Museum of London Act 1973.	The whole Act.
1985 c.51.	The Local Government Act 1985.	In section 43, subsections (1), (2) and (4). In Schedule 17, in column 3, the entry relating to section 1(2)(*c*) of the Museum of London Act 1965.

8–3

LAW REFORM (PARENT AND CHILD) (SCOTLAND) ACT 1986*

(1986 c. 9)

ARRANGEMENT OF SECTIONS

An Act to make fresh provision in the law of Scotland with respect to the consequences of birth out of wedlock, the rights and duties of parents, the determination of parentage and the taking of blood samples in relation to the determination of parentage; to amend the law as to guardianship; and for connected purposes.

[26th March 1986]

GENERAL NOTE

This Act implements the Scottish Law Commission's Report on Illegitimacy (Scot.Law Com. No. 82) published in January 1984. Apart from some minor drafting amendments the Act is identical to the draft Bill annexed to the Report. The Law Reform (Parent and Child) (Scotland) Bill was introduced in the Commons as a Private Member's Bill by Lord James Douglas-Hamilton. Its sponsor in the Lords was his kinsman the Earl of Selkirk making the Act in the words of the Lord Advocate "very much a family Act."

The brevity of the Act, 11 sections and 2 schedules, belies its scope. It makes sweeping changes to many areas of the law where previously distinctions had been made between children born within marriage and children born outwith marriage. These changes will affect a great number of people. According to figures produced by the Earl of Selkirk about 17 per cent. of all children born in Scotland in the last year or so were born to unmarried parents.

Previous attempts to effect a general reform of the law of illegitimacy had not met with much success. The last attempt was a Bill introduced by Mr. James White MP in 1979. It failed to get a second reading because it was thought that the subject was more complex than it seemed and that legislation should be delayed until the reports of the Law Commissions became available.

The scheme of the reform adopted by the Act is elegant in its simplicity. Instead of piecemeal reform of the law in all the many areas where differences between legitimate and illegitimate children existed, or mere label changing replacing "illegitimate" by "non-marital" for example, the Act contains a general provision granting equality of status to all persons whatever the marital status of their parents. One of the main criticisms of the concept of illegitimacy was that it penalised children for something they were not responsible for. The equality provision meets this criticism exactly.

Equality for children would have the undesirable consequence of making all fathers equal. While the majority of children born outwith marriage nowadays are the product of parents who live together in a stable relationship, many are not, so that it would be inappropriate to confer by law on every father who was not married to the child's mother, all the legal rights enjoyed by a married father. The Act provides that such rights may be granted by the court on application, thus filtering out fathers whose claims are without merit, but enabling an unmarried father living in family with the mother and child to acquire the same legal

---

* Annotations by D. I. Nichols, M.A., Ph.D., W.S. (The opinions expressed are those of the annotator alone and should not be taken to represent the views of any Government department or body).

relationship towards the child as if the couple were married. In short the concept of disadvantaged children has been replaced by one of disadvantaged fathers.

In the process of reforming the law relating to children born outwith marriage the opportunity was taken to tidy up the legislation relating to custody and guardianship of children generally. The Guardianship of Infants Acts 1886 to 1925 are repealed (so far as Scotland is concerned) and the provisions of these and other Acts replaced by the more general provisions contained in ss.2 to 4 of the Act.

Other topics dealt with by the Act are presumptions of paternity (s.5), consents to taking of blood samples for testing in order to determine parentage (s.6), and court proceedings for determination of the parentage or status of a person (s.7). The Act does not make any change in the legal status of children born as a result of artificial insemination by a donor or surrogacy.

COMMENCEMENT

The Act received the Royal Assent on March 26, 1986. It will come into force on such date as the Secretary of State may appoint (s.11(2)).

EXTENT

The Act applies to Scotland only (s.11(4)).

PARLIAMENTARY DEBATES

Hansard: H.C. Vol. 88, col. 928; Vol. 89, col. 1413; Vol. 91, col. 611; H.L. Vol. 471, col. 73; Vol. 472, cols. 127, 869, 1284.

The Bill was considered by the Second Scottish Standing Committee January 29, 1986.

Legal equality of children

1.—(1) The fact that a person's parents are not or have not been married to one another shall be left out of account in establishing the legal relationship between the person and any other person; and accordingly any such relationship shall have effect as if the parents were or had been married to one another.

(2) Subject to subsection (4) below, any reference (however expressed) in any enactment or deed to any relative shall, unless the contrary intention appears in the enactment or deed, be construed in accordance with subsection (1) above.

(3) Subsection (1) above is subject to the following provisions of this Act—

　　(*a*) subsection (4) below;
　　(*b*) section 2(1)(*b*); and
　　(*c*) section 9(1).

(4) Nothing in this section shall apply to the construction or effect of—

　　(*a*) any enactment passed or made before the commencement of this Act unless the enactment is amended by Schedule 1 to this Act and, as so amended, otherwise provides;
　　(*b*) any deed executed before such commencement;
　　(*c*) any reference (however expressed) in any deed executed after such commencement to a legitimate or illegitimate person or relationship.

DEFINITIONS

"deed": s.8.
"parent": s.8.

GENERAL NOTE

This is the key section of the Act. It enunciates the general principle of legal equality of children irrespective of their parents' marriage or lack of marriage to each other, and sets out or refers to various exceptions to this general principle.

Subs. (1)
The position of a child born to parents who were not or are not married to each other is equated to that of a child born to married parents. The principle of equality applies not only to the parent-child relationship but also to all other relationships. Thus, a person's nephew includes the son of an unmarried sister, the son of a sister who was born outwith marriage and the son of an unmarried sister who was herself born outwith marriage, as well as the cases where the person was born outwith marriage.

Subss. (2) and (4)
These subsections set out the effect of the general equality principle set out in subs. (1) above on deeds executed and enactments passed before and after commencement of the Act.

Future enactments (which by virtue of the words "made or passed" means both statutes and subordinate legislation) mentioning a person's children, parents or other relationships are to be construed without regard to whether the children, parents or other relatives were born within or outwith marriage, unless the enactment clearly draws a distinction (subs. (2)).

Future deeds are to be construed in accordance with the principle of equality unless the deed by using expressions such as legitimate, illegitimate or similar terms shows a contrary intention (subss. (2) and (4)(c)). Thus it will remain competent for parents to make bequests only to their children born within marriage and to exclude those born outwith marriage (although the latter could claim legitim). But future grants of titles of honour are an exception (s.9(1)(c)). They will not have to be drawn in terms that expressly exclude succession by illegitimate relatives to achieve that effect.

Deeds executed prior to commencement are not affected because of the need to avoid retrospective variation of previous arrangements. They will continue to be construed according to the law in force prior to commencement. With the exception of wills and testamentary writings executed after 1968 (Law Reform (Miscellaneous Provisions) (Scotland) Act 1968, s.5) the expressions, "children," "descendants," "issue" and "relatives" are presumed to refer to legitimate relationships only (subss. (2) and (4)(b)).

Pre-commencement enactments, meaning both statutes and subordinate legislation, are unaffected unless amended in Sched. 1 in accordance with the principle of equality. The previous rule of construction, that references to a relationship meant (unless the context otherwise required) a legitimate relationship, only continues to apply to unamended statutes.

The main areas of law where differences remain depending on whether or not a person's parents are or were married to each other are:

Nationality
The British Nationality Act 1981, s.50(9) provides that for the purposes of that Act the relationship of father and child exists only between a man and his legitimate or legitimated children. As a result children born outwith marriage cannot acquire British citizenship through their father, although they are British citizens if they were born in the United Kingdom and their mother was settled here (s.1(1)(b)). Otherwise they can become British citizens by registration (s.1(3) and (4)).

Registration of Birth
Where the parents of a child are married to each other the father is a qualified informant. He can have himself registered as father without any supporting document being needed from the mother as his paternity is presumed from the fact of marriage. Where the child's parents are not married to each other, the father although he is now a qualified informant, must in order to be registered as such acknowledge his paternity in prescribed form and produce a statutory declaration by the mother declaring him to be the father (Sched. 1, para. 8(2) amending the Registration of Births, Deaths and Marriages (Scotland) Act 1965 s.18(1)).

A father who is not married to the child's mother has no duty to give information about the child's birth unlike a married father (Sched. 1, para. 8(1)).

Recording a change of name of a child under 16 requires an application under s.43 of the 1965 Act. If the child was born within marriage the application must be made by both parents, if alive. In the case of a child born outwith marriage the father is only required to join in the application if he is the child's tutor or curator or has custody of the child (Sched. 1, para. 8(8) amending s.43).

See Notes on Sched. 1 for further details.

Mental Health
The relatives and nearest relatives of a person suffering from mental disorder have various rights and obligations under the Mental Health (Scotland) Act 1984. S. 53 defines "relative" as a spouse, child, father or mother, brother or sister, grandparent, grandchild, uncle or aunt, nephew or niece. In deducing a relationship an illegitimate person is treated as the legitimate child of his or her mother. Even though a person is not the patient's "relative" because a link in of the relationship involves an unmarried father the person may qualify if the patient has been ordinarily resident with him or her for not less than five years (s.53(6)).

Adoption
Where married parents are concerned the father must agree to the child's adoption or freeing for adoption unless his agreement is dispensed with by the court (Adoption (Scotland) Act 1978, ss.16 and 18).
An unmarried father's agreement is required only if he has been awarded tutory, curatory, custody, access or any other parental right in relation to the child or is the child's guardian. He is not counted as a parent of the child (*A.* v. *B,* 1955 S.C. 378 construing similar provisions in the Adoption Act 1950). Similarly such a father's agreement is not required to freeing for adoption unless he is the guardian or he has been awarded tutory, curatory, custody, access or any other parental right in relation to the child, or the court is satisfied that he has no intention of applying for any parental right or if he did that his application would be likely to be refused: see Sched. 1, para. 18 amending the Adoption (Scotland) Act 1978.

Incest
Sexual intercourse between an illegitimate person and any of the relatives by blood or affinity of his or her parents is not incestuous (*H.M. Advocate* v. *R.M.,* 1969 J.C. 52). It is not clear whether incest is committed by intercourse between a mother and her illegitimate son or a father and his illegitimate daughter. The Incest and Related Offences (Scotland) Bill currently before Parliament reforms the law of incest and removes the present distinction between legitimate and illegitimate relationships.

Protection of trustees and executors
S. 7 of the Law Reform (Miscellaneous Provisions) (Scotland) Act 1968 protects trustees and executors distributing the estate from the later emergence of persons born outwith marriage either as claimants or as persons whose existence results in a different distribution (see also Sched. 1, para. 10 of the present Act). There is no express statutory protection in relation to the emergence of persons born within marriage.

Child care
The father of a child born within marriage has certain statutory rights and duties under the Social Work (Scotland) Act 1968. For example he is entitled to object to the making of a resolution assuming parental rights (s.16), he has a duty to attend a children's hearing involving his child unless excused (s.41), and he is entitled to appeal against the hearing's decision and to require a review of it (ss.49 and 48). A local authority is not authorised to keep a child in care under s.15 by virtue of that section if the father wishes to take care of the child.
An unmarried father has these rights and duties only if he is the child's tutor, curator or guardian or if he is considered to have custody or charge of or control over the child (Sched. 1, para. 9(6) amending s.94(1) of the 1968 Act).

Other statutory references to illegitimate persons
Despite the elimination of many existing references to illegitimate persons or bastards in Scottish legislation or provisions applicable to Scotland some such references remain. They include:—
> Court of Session Act 1850, s.16—declaration of bastardy.
> Legitimacy Declaration Act 1858, s.9—procedure to be same as in declaration of bastardy.
> Succession (Scotland) Act 1964, s.24(1A)—adoption of illegitimate child by one parent.
> Social Security Act 1975, s.23(2)(*b*)—maternity benefit not to be taken into account in awarding inlying expenses to mother of an illegitimate child.
> Adoption (Scotland) Act 1978, s.65(1)—"relative" includes the father and paternal relatives of an illegitimate child.
> Foster Children (Scotland) Act 1984, s.21(1)—definition of relative includes illegitimate child.

There are also references in a number of United Kingdom statutes such as the Army Act 1955, s.150—enforcement of maintenance for illegitimate children by deductions from pay; Consumer Credit Act 1975, s.184(5)—relative includes illegitimate child. These could not have been readily altered for Scotland alone.

Subs. (3)
   This subsection contains the major exceptions to the principle of equality set out in subs. (1). S. 2(1)(*b*) precludes an unmarried father from having parental rights unless he has been awarded them by court decree or he has been nominated as a testamentary tutor or curator. S. 9(1) saves certain common law rules. These relate to domicile of orgin or dependence, adoption, titles of honour, and legitim in connection with pre-commencement deaths.

Parental rights and their exercise

   2.—(1) Subject to sections 3 and 4 of this Act—
      (*a*) a child's mother shall have parental rights whether or not she is or has been married to the child's father;
      (*b*) a child's father shall have parental rights only if he is married to the child's mother or was married to her at the time of the child's conception or subsequently.
   (2) For the purposes of subsection (1)(*b*) above, the father shall be regarded as having been married to the mother at any time when he was a party to a purported marriage with her which was—
      (*a*) voidable, or
      (*b*) void, but believed by him in good faith at that time to be valid, whether that belief was due to an error of fact or an error of law.
   (3) Nothing in this section shall affect any enactment or rule of law by virtue of which a parent may be granted or deprived of parental rights.
   (4) Where two or more persons have any parental right, each of them may exercise that right without the consent of the other person or, as the case may be, any of the other persons unless any decree or deed conferring the right otherwise provides.

DEFINITIONS
   "child": s.8.
   "deed": s.8.
   "parent": s.8.
   "parental rights": s.8.

GENERAL NOTE
Subs. (1)
   This subsection sets out the parental rights which the law confers on parents of children. It is however subject to subs. (3) and ss.3 and 4, in terms of which a court may grant some or all parental rights to a person, or deprive a person of all or any parental rights, or a parent may appoint a person to act as a testamentary tutor or curator.

Para. (a)
   This paragraph preserves the previous law in relation to children born within marriage. The mother continues to be a tutor or curator of the child, has custody of the child and has other parental rights such as the right to consent to medical treatment of the child and to direct the child's education. It changes the law, however, with regard to a mother who is not married to the child's father. Formerly she was not the child's tutor or curator (*Jones* v. *Somervell's Tr.*, 1907 S.C. 545), but she had a *prima facie* right to custody (*A* v. *B*, 1955 S.C. 378; *McCormack* v. *McCormack*, 1963 S.L.T.(Notes) 3). Her position regarding other parental rights was not clear. Now such a mother has parental rights which, by virtue of the definition in s.8, means tutory, curatory, custody, access and all the other rights of a parent.

Para. (b)
   This paragraph restates the previous law as regards both married and unmarried fathers. Where the father was married to the child's mother at the time of conception or any time up to the date of birth, the child is presumed legitimate, while marriage after birth legitimates

the child. In both cases the father had and has full parental rights. Where the father is not and never has been married to the mother he had no rights, either as a tutor, curator or custodier (*Corrie* v. *Adair* (1860) 22 D. 897).

Subs. (2)

This subsection is necessary because of the word "only" in subs. (1)(*b*) above. It also extends the previous law slightly. Para. (*a*) equiparates the parental rights enjoyed by a father whose marriage to the child's mother is voidable with those of fathers whose marriage is valid, thus restating in a somewhat different fashion s.4 of the Law Reform (Miscellaneous Provisions) Act 1949 (child of voidable marriage legitimate notwithstanding its annulment).

The children of a void marriage were legitimate if at least one of the parties believed the marriage to be valid and the mistaken belief arose out of an error of fact, rather than an error of law (*Purves' Trs.* v. *Purves* (1895) 22 R. 513; *Philp's Trs.* v. *Beaton*, 1938 S.C. 733). Now errors of law are to be treated in the same way as errors of fact. The father has no automatic parental rights in relation to a child conceived after the marriage was known to be void as there would be no belief in good faith in the marriage's validity at "the time of the child's conception or subsequently." Previously the status of such a child was thought to be illegitimate (Fraser, *Parent and Child* (3rd ed.), p. 34).

It should be noted that these changes only affect the position of fathers in relation to parental rights ("for the purposes of subs. (1)(*b*) above"). The previous law still applies for the determination of the status of the children involved.

Subs. (3)

A parent who has none or some of the parental rights (tutory, curatory, custody, access or other parental right) continues to be entitled to apply to a Scottish court for a grant of a parental right. The subsection also preserves the rights granted by an order of a foreign court which is recognised in Scotland or a deed appointing him or her as testamentary tutor or curator.

Parents remain liable to be deprived of their parental rights. Power to deprive persons other than parents is conferred by s.3(1).

Subs. (4)

As far as married parents were concerned s.10(1) of the Guardianship Act 1973 entitled either to act without the other. The surviving parent and a tutor appointed by the deceased parent or tutors appointed by each parent acted jointly (Guardianship of Infants Act 1925, ss.4 and 5). New provisions would have been necessary to regulate the position where an unmarried father was granted some or all parental rights. Rather than continue the piecemeal and not entirely consistent approach of the existing legislation subs. (4) makes new provision applicable to any parental rights.

The phrase "any parental right" must mean that each of the persons concerned has the same parental right (such as custody), for if one has one right (say tutory) and the other another right (such as access) it is obvious that each can exercise his or her right without the consent of the other.

The deed or decree may provide otherwise. For example in appointing a testamentary tutor a parent may wish to give the surviving parent a veto, or the court in awarding an unmarried father joint custody might direct that the child should remain in the mother's care and control.

Orders as to parental rights

3.—(1) Any person claiming interest may make an application to the court for an order relating to parental rights and the court may make such order relating to parental rights as it thinks fit.

(2) In any proceedings relating to parental rights the court shall regard the welfare of the child involved as the paramount consideration and shall not make any order relating to parental rights unless it is satisfied that to do so will be in the interests of the child.

(3) Any person appointed by a court to be a tutor to a child shall, unless the court otherwise orders, become curator to the child when the child attains the age of minority.

DEFINITIONS
"child": s.8.

"court": s.8.
"parental rights": s.8.
"tutor": s.8.

GENERAL NOTE

This section replaces and/or extends many of the provisions of the Guardianship of Infants Acts 1886–1925, s.2 of the Illegitimate Children (Scotland) Act 1930, s.5 of the Sheriff Courts (Scotland) Act 1907, s.10(3) of the Guardianship Act 1973 and the common law powers of the courts. There was some overlap between the various provisions. Some were restricted to legitimate or illegitimate children, while others could only be used if certain conditions obtained. The general formulation adopted by the section permits the provision to be drafted so as not to distinguish between children born within and outwith marriage.

The powers are conferred on the Court of Session and the sheriff courts. Jurisdiction in relation to tutory, curatory and custody is regulated in the Family Law Bill, currently before Parliament. An application relating to parental rights may be made on its own or in connection with other proceedings such as divorce, separation, parentage or aliment.

Subs. (1)

Mothers of children have parental rights by virtue of their status as mothers (s.2(1)(*a*)) as do married fathers (s.2(1)(*b*)). An unmarried father, however, can have parental rights conferred upon him only by a court (except where he is appointed as testamentary tutor or curator by the mother). This approach enables the claims of a particular father to be assessed so that unmeritorious fathers will not obtain parental rights. There is a danger that an unmeritorious father will apply merely to harass the mother. This is not a new problem although the range of rights that can be applied for is now greater.

The courts' powers in relation to parental rights applications are without prejudice to statutory provisions relating to taking into care and assumption of parental rights by local authorities or s.11 of the Sexual Offences (Scotland) Act 1976 (court can deprive parent who has committed specified crimes of authority over child).

"*any person claiming interest*": This includes not only a married or unmarried parent but also a grandparent, foster parent or anyone who has been looking after the child. As far as custody is concerned the courts have never closed the class of persons entitled to apply (*Syme* v. *Cunningham*, 1973 S.L.T(Notes) 40). The general provision supersedes s.47(1) of the Children Act 1975 (conferring statutory title to sue for custody on relatives, step or foster parents) which is now repealed.

"*parental rights*": This includes tutory, curatory, custody, access and any other legal right conferred on parents (see definition in s.8). An unmarried father with custody may now apply for tutory, curatory and other parental rights. In that way he can enjoy the full range of rights possessed by a married father. He can also apply for just some of the rights (direction of education for example) if that is all he wants.

"*such order . . . as it thinks fit*": The rights granted may be exercised solely or jointly with another person. A grant of full parental rights to an unmarried father to be exercised jointly with the mother would place an unmarried couple in exactly the same legal relationship to their children as a married couple. The court may deprive any person of parental rights conferred by law, appointment or a previous court order as well as recalling or varying its own orders under s.9(2). The court's discretionary power is unfettered and includes power to make ancillary orders necessary to make the principal order effective.

Subs. (2)

The criteria in the Guardianship of Infants Act 1925, s.1 (welfare of the child to be "the first and paramount consideration") and the Illegitimate Children (Scotland) Act 1930, s.2(1) (court to have regard "to the welfare of the child and to the conduct of the parents and to the wishes as well of the mother as of the father") applied in deciding applications are replaced by a single simpler criterion that the welfare of the child is the "paramount consideration". The change is intended to be verbal rather than substantive.

The court is expressly directed not to make an order unless it is satisfied that to do so will be in the child's interests, thus preventing undefended applications being granted without enquiry (as happened in *Beverley* v. *Beverley*, 1977 S.L.T.(Sh.Ct.) 3). "Satisfied" does not imply that a proof is required; the court may proceed on the basis of affidavits (where competent) or a report.

Subs. (3)

This subsection is modelled on s.11 of the Judicial Factors (Scotland) Act 1889 whereby a factor *loco tutoris* automatically becomes a *curator bonis* when the child becomes a minor.

It applies to any tutor other than a tutor *ad litem*. An unmarried father who had been appointed tutor would not have to reapply to the court for appointment as curator when the child attains minority. Married parents and unmarried mothers automatically become curators by virtue of s.2(1).

Power of parent to appoint tutor or curator

4.—(1) The parent of a child may appoint any person to be tutor or curator of the child after his death, but any such appointment shall be of no effect unless—

    (*a*) the appointment is in writing and signed by the parent; and

    (*b*) the parent at the time of his death was tutor or curator of the child or would have been such tutor if he had survived until after the birth of the child.

(2) Any person appointed under subsection (1) above to be tutor to a child shall, unless the appointment otherwise specifically provides, become curator to the child when the child attains the age of minority.

(3) Nothing in this section shall affect any power to appoint, or any appointment of, a tutor for the purposes of the administration of any property given or bequeathed to a child.

DEFINITIONS
    "child": s.8.
    "curator": s.8.
    "parent": s.8.
    "tutor": s.8.

GENERAL NOTE
Subs. (1)
This subsection largely reproduces the previous law so far as married parents are concerned. Either parent could by will or other deed appoint a person to act as tutor (Guardianship of Infants Act 1925, s.5) or curator (Tutors and Curators Act 1696 as applied to mothers by the Guardianship Act 1973, s.10(1)) to his or her child after death. One minor change is made. A parent who has been deprived of tutory or curatory by an order under s.3 or otherwise is not entitled to make an appointment. The relevant time for ascertaining whether the parent is a tutor or curator is the date of death not the date of the appointment.

Unmarried parents were not entitled to appoint testamentary tutors or curators (*Brand* v. *Shaws* (1888) 16 R. 315). The mother is now so entitled as long as she has not been deprived of her tutory or curatory, but the father is so entitled only if he has been appointed sole or joint tutor or curator by the court.

Subs. (2)
This subsection removes the need for an appointed tutor to apply to the court for appointment as curator when the child reaches minority if the will or deed does not provide for this. It remains competent for a parent to appoint a person other than the tutor to act as curator.

Subs. (3)
A person giving or bequeathing property to a child may appoint special tutors to administer the property (Fraser, *Parent and Child* (3rd ed.), p. 225). In default of such appointment the court may appoint tutors (strictly speaking factors *loco tutoris*) if the child's parents are considered unsuitable or there is a conflict of interest between parent and child (*Cochrane* (1891) 18 R. 456.)

Presumptions

5.—(1) A man shall be presumed to be the father of a child—

    (*a*) if he was married to the mother of the child at any time in the period beginning with the conception and ending with the birth of the child;

(b) where paragraph (a) above does not apply, if both he and the mother of the child have acknowledged that he is the father and he has been registered as such in any register kept under section 13 (register of births and still-births) or section 44 (register of corrections, etc.) of the Registration of Births, Deaths and Marriages (Scotland) Act 1965 or in any corresponding register kept under statutory authority in any part of the United Kingdom other than Scotland.

(2) Subsection (1)(a) above shall apply in the case of a void, voidable or irregular marriage as it applies in the case of a valid and regular marriage.

(3) Without prejudice to the effect under any rule of law which a decree of declarator in an action to which section 7 of this Act applies may have in relation to the parties, a decree of declarator in such an action shall give rise to a presumption to the same effect as the decree; and any such presumption shall displace any contrary presumption howsoever arising.

(4) Any presumption under this section may be rebutted by proof on a balance of probabilities.

GENERAL NOTE

This section restates previous presumptions and provides for new presumptions relating to a man's fatherhood of a child.

Subs. (1)

Para. (a) restates the common law presumption *pater est quem nuptiae demonstrant* and the related presumption that a man who has been familiar before marriage with a woman pregnant at the date of her marriage to him is the father of her child (*Gardner* v. *Gardner* (1877) 4 R. (H.L.) 56). Since the period ends with the birth of the child there is no presumption that a man who married a woman with a living child is the child's father. The law on this point is unchanged (*James* v. *McLennan*, 1971 S.L.T. 162 (H.L.)).

Para. (b) introduces a new presumption. Previously an entry in the register of births was only a piece of evidence tending to establish paternity (Walker and Walker, *Law of Evidence*, pp. 33 and 61). In order to be registered in the register of births a man not married to the mother must acknowledge paternity and be admitted to be the father by the mother (Registration of Births, Deaths and Marriages (Scotland) Act 1965, s.18 as amended by Sched. 1, para. 8). Similar requirements exist for other U.K. birth registers. The new presumption reflects these procedures and the general practice of treating the man who appears on the register as the father. The presumption does not apply to non U.K. registers; the evidential weight given to entries in such registers would depend on the procedures required by the registration authorities concerned.

The new presumption does not apply if one of the marriage based presumptions in para. (a) does. Thus if the mother is married but a man other than her husband is registered as the father, there is no presumption that he is the father. But the child's birth certificate will not alert outsiders to the presumption's absence in this case.

Subs. (2)

This subsection clarifies the law. It was doubtful whether the presumptions of fatherhood based on marriage applied to void, voidable and irregular marriages.

Subs. (3)

This subsection creates a new presumption without prejudice to the common law rule of *res judicata* whereby a declarator is binding on the parties to it. The wider effects of a declarator of a child's parentage or status were unclear (*Administrator of Austrian Property* v. *Von Lorang*, 1926 S.C. 598, *per* Lord Sands at pp. 622–3, declarator of status universally binding; but *Silver* v. *Walker*, 1938 S.C. 595, declarator of parentage binding on parties only). Now in relation to persons not parties to the declaratory action there is a presumption that the position is as stated in the declarator. This presumption prevails over the marriage and registration based presumptions in subs. (1). It arises in connection with declarators only since there the court must be satisfied by sufficient evidence (s.7(4)). Incidental findings of paternity, legitimacy, etc., no longer give rise to any presumption since s.11 of the Law

Reform (Miscellaneous Provisions) (Scotland) Act 1968 (paternity of man found to be father in action of affiliation and aliment presumed in other proceedings) is repealed. A pursuer in an action of affiliation and aliment who wants a decree with wider effect should seek a declarator of paternity rather than a finding.

Subs. (4)

This subsection changes the standard of proof required to rebut the marriage based presumptions from beyond reasonable doubt (*Brown* v. *Brown,* 1972 S.C. 123) to the normal civil standard of a balance of probabilities. If blood samples are available paternity can now be proved beyond reasonable doubt (see note on s.6).

Determination of parentage by blood sample

6.—(1) This section applies where, for the purpose of obtaining evidence relating to the determination of parentage in civil proceedings, a blood sample is sought by a party to the proceedings or by a curator ad litem.

(2) Where a blood sample is sought from a pupil child, consent to the taking of the sample may be given by his tutor or any person having custody or care and control of him.

(3) Where a blood sample is sought from any person who is incapable of giving consent, the court may consent to the taking of the sample where—

(a) there is no person who is entitled to give such consent, or

(b) there is such a person, but it is not reasonably practicable to obtain his consent in the circumstances, or he is unwilling to accept the responsibility of giving or withholding consent.

(4) The court shall not consent under subsection (3) above to the taking of a blood sample from any person unless the court is satisfied that the taking of the sample would not be detrimental to the person's health.

DEFINITIONS

"court": s.8.

"parentage": s.8.

"tutor": s.8.

GENERAL NOTE

The increasing accuracy of blood tests has led them to be used more frequently to resolve issues of disputed paternity and the courts attach greater weight to the results. Nevertheless, the usual tests can with certainty only exclude a particular man from being the father, although they may be able to suggest with a varying degree of probability that the particular man was the father. A new technique called DNA fingerprinting however can establish a particular man's paternity with virtually complete certainty using blood samples from the man, the mother and the child.

This section removes some obstacles to the use of such tests where an individual whose blood is to be tested is incapable of giving consent to the taking of a sample. The consent is of course only legal consent as the individual may not be willing to co-operate.

Subs. (2) deals with pupil children because minors are capable of giving their own consent. As well as the child's tutors—who will usually be the parents, including a husband presumed to be the father (*Docherty* v. *McGlynn,* 1983 S.L.T. 645)—any person having custody or care and control of the child may consent. Any dispute between parents or others about giving or withholding consent would have to be resolved by the court.

Subs. (3) deals mainly with incapacitated persons since it is most unlikely that a pupil has nobody with care and control of him or her. A *curator bonis* has no control over the ward's person and so cannot competently consent. A tutor-dative or a guardian appointed under the Mental Health (Scotland) Act 1984, s.40 can consent or refuse consent. It seems that the court has no power to override a positive refusal of consent.

Actions for declarator

7.—(1) An action for declarator of parentage, non-parentage, legitimacy, legitimation or illegitimacy may be brought in the Court of Session or the sheriff court.

(2) Such an action may be brought in the Court of Session if and only if the child was born in Scotland or the alleged or presumed parent or the child—

(*a*) is domiciled in Scotland on the date when the action is brought;
(*b*) was habitually resident in Scotland for not less than one year immediately preceding that date; or
(*c*) died before that date and either—
(i) was at the date of death domiciled in Scotland; or
(ii) had been habitually resident in Scotland for not less than one year immediately preceding the date of death.

(3) Such an action may be brought in the sheriff court if and only if—

(*a*) the child was born in the sheriffdom, or
(*b*) an action could have been brought in the Court of Session under subsection (2) above and the alleged or presumed parent or the child was habitually resident in the sheriffdom on the date when the action is brought or on the date of his death.

(4) In an action to which this section applies, the court shall not grant decree of declarator unless it is satisfied that the grounds of action have been established by sufficient evidence.

(5) Nothing in any rule of law or enactment shall prevent the court making in any proceedings an incidental finding as to parentage, non-parentage, legitimacy, legitimation or illegitimacy for the purposes of those proceedings.

(6) In this section "the alleged or presumed parent" includes a person who claims or is alleged to be or not to be the parent.

DEFINITIONS
"action for declarator": s.8.
"non-parentage": s.8.
"parent": s.8.
"parentage": s.8.
"the alleged or presumed parent": s.7(6).

GENERAL NOTE
This section clarifies the law, and makes new provision, in relation to actions of declarator of parentage, non-parentage, legitimacy, legitimation and illegitimacy. Declarators of legitimacy, etc., remain necessary for areas of the law where such status remains relevant (see note on s.1). Declarators of bastardy have been renamed declarators of illegitimacy.

Subs. (1)
Jurisdiction to hear any of the declarators is expressly extended to the sheriff courts thus ending any doubt whether a declarator of parentage or non-parentage was competent there.

Subss. (2) and (3)
These subsections set out the grounds of jurisdiction for the above declarators. They are virtually identical to the grounds for declarators of marriage or nullity of marriage (Domicile and Matrimonial Proceedings Act 1973, s.7(3)) but there is an additional ground—birth of the child in Scotland.

Subs. (4)
A declarator of parentage, etc., raises a presumption to the same effect as the declarator as far as persons who were not parties to the action are concerned (see s.5(3)). In order to justify this extended effect the court has to be satisfied by sufficient evidence even if the action is undefended. In connection with divorce actions sufficient evidence has been interpreted as requiring some evidence other than that of the parties (*Macfarlane* v. *Macfarlane*, 1956 S.C. 472; *Keenan* v. *Keenan*, 1974 S.L.T.(Notes) 10).

Subs. (5)
This subsection removes doubts about the competency of incidental findings of paternity. Persons who are content with such a finding pronounced in the course of obtaining another

remedy (aliment from the child's father for example) are not forced to incur the extra expense of declaratory proceedings. On the other hand a finding has no extended effect (see s.5(3)).

Interpretation

8. In this Act, unless the context otherwise requires, the following expressions shall have the following meanings respectively assigned to them—

"action for declarator" includes an application for declarator contained in other proceedings;

"child", except where used to express a relationship, means—

    (*a*) in relation to custody or access, a child under the age of 16 years;

    (*b*) in relation to tutory, a pupil;

    (*c*) in relation to curatory, a minor;

    (*d*) in relation to parental rights other than custody, access, tutory or curatory, a child under the age of 18 years;

"the court" means the Court of Session or the sheriff;

"curator" does not include curator ad litem;

"deed" means any disposition, contract, instrument or writing whether inter vivos or mortis causa;

"non-parentage" means that a person is not or was not the parent, or is not or was not the child, of another person;

"parent" includes natural parent;

"parentage" means that a person is or was the parent, or is or was the child, of another person;

"parental rights" means tutory, curatory, custody or access, as the case may require, and any right or authority relating to the welfare or upbringing of a child conferred on a parent by any rule of law;

"tutor" does not include tutor ad litem.

GENERAL NOTE

"*action for declarator*": This definition makes it clear that an application for a declarator mentioned in s.7 will be entertained only if the jurisdictional criteria in s.7(2) or (3) are met even though the application may be combined with other proceedings having different grounds of jurisdiction.

"*child*": Applications to the court under the Act for custody and access are competent in relation to children under 16. Applications under the common law remain competent in relation to children below the age of 18.

"*parent*": For the avoidance of doubt the term parent expressly includes a parent who is not or was not married to the other parent.

"*parental rights*": The definition is limited to common law rights in the case of parental rights other than tutory, curatory, custody and access. The rights of a parent under a statute (the Social Work (Scotland) Act 1968, for example) depend on the terms of the enactment in question.

Savings and supplementary provisions

9.—(1) Nothing in this Act shall—

    (*a*) affect any rule of law whereby a child born out of wedlock takes the domicile of his mother as a domicile of origin or dependence;

    (*b*) except to the extent that Schedules 1 and 2 to this Act otherwise provide, affect the law relating to adoption of children;

    (*c*) apply to any title, coat of arms, honour or dignity transmissible on the death of the holder thereof or affect the succession thereto or the devolution thereof;

(*d*) affect the right of legitim out of, or the right of succession to, the estate of any person who died before the commencement of this Act.

(2) The court may at any time vary or recall any order made under section 3 of this Act or consent given by it under section 6 of this Act.

DEFINITION
"court": s.8.

GENERAL NOTE
Subs. (1)
    As read together with s.1(3) and (4) this subsection contains the main exceptions to the general rule of equality of children set out in s.1(1).

Para. (a)
    The existing rules of domicile of origin and dependency are preserved. Where the parents are married the child's domicile of origin is the domicile of the father at the date of birth (*Udny* v. *Udny* (1869) 7 M. (H.L.) 89); a posthumous child is thought to take the domicile of the mother. The child's domicile thereafter changes with that of the father until minority is attained (*Shanks* v. *Shanks*, 1965 S.L.T. 330), but follows that of the mother if the father is dead (*Crumpton's J.F.* v. *Finch-Noyes*, 1918 S.C. 378), or the parents are separated and the child lives with the mother (Domicile and Matrimonial Proceedings Act 1973, s.4(2)).
    Where the child's parents are not married to each other the child's domicile of origin is that of the mother at the date of birth and follows her domicile thereafter until the child becomes a minor (*Udny* v. *Udny* (1869) 7 M. (H.L.) 89).

Para. (b)
    See note on s.1(2) and (4).

Para. (c)
    A person born outwith marriage is normally precluded from inheriting or transmitting a title, coat of arms or other dignity because the terms used in the grant to govern devolution such as "issue", "heirs" or "descendants" are deemed to mean legitimate or legitimated persons only. This rule continues to apply in relation to existing grants and also in relation to future grants except in the unlikely situation where the grant expressly permits devolution to persons born outwith marriage.

Para. (d)
    This paragraph preserves existing rights in relation to the estates of persons dying before commencement. Under the previous law a person born outwith marriage could not succeed to any relative who died intestate other than his or her children or their issue, his or her spouse, or his or her parents. A child could claim legitim out of the estate of his or her unmarried parents, but had no right to legitim by representation from the estates of grandparents or remoter ancestors.

Subs. (2)
    This subsection expressly empowers the court to vary or recall a previous order relating to parental rights (s.3(1)) or to withdraw consent it has already given on behalf of an incapacitated person to the taking of a blood sample (s.6(3)).

Transitional provisions, amendments and repeals

    10.—(1) The enactments specified in Schedule 1 to this Act shall have effect subject to the amendments set out in that Schedule.
    (2) The enactments specified in Schedule 2 to this Act are hereby repealed to the extent set out in the third column of that Schedule.

Citation, commencement and extent

    11.—(1) This Act may be cited as the Law Reform (Parent and Child) (Scotland) Act 1986.

(2) This Act shall come into operation on such day as the Secretary of State may appoint by order made by statutory instrument.

(3) An order under subsection (2) above may contain such transitional provisions and savings as appear to the Secretary of State necessary or expedient in connection with the coming into operation of this Act.

(4) This Act shall extend to Scotland only.

SCHEDULES

Section 10(1)   SCHEDULE 1

MINOR AND CONSEQUENTIAL AMENDMENTS

The Judicial Factors Act 1849 (c. 51)

1. In section 25 (application to certain tutors and curators) at the end there shall be inserted the following new subsection—
    "(2) Any person being an administrator-in-law, tutor-nominate, guardian appointed or acting under the Guardianship of Infants Acts 1886 and 1925 or tutor appointed under the Law Reform (Parent and Child) (Scotland) Act 1986 who shall, by virtue of his office, administer the estate of any pupil, shall be deemed to be a tutor within the meaning of this Act and shall be subject to the provisions thereof, but any such person shall not be bound to find caution in terms of sections 26 and 27 of this Act unless the court, on the application of any party having an interest, shall so direct."

The Conjugal Rights (Scotland) Amendment Act 1861 (c. 86)

2. For section 9 there shall be substituted the following section—

"Orders with respect to children
    9.—(1) In any action for divorce, judicial separation or declarator of nullity of marriage the court may make, with respect to any child of the marriage to which the action relates, such order (including an interim order) as it thinks fit relating to parental rights, and may vary or recall such order.
    (2) In this section—
        (*a*) "child" and "parental rights" have the same meaning as in section 8 of the Law Reform (Parent and Child) (Scotland) Act 1986;
        (*b*) "child of the marriage" includes any child who—
            (i) is the child of both parties to the marriage, or
            (ii) is the child of one party to the marriage and has been accepted as a child of the family by the other party; and
        (*c*) "court" in relation to divorce and separation includes the sheriff court."

The Sheriff Courts (Scotland) Act 1907 (c. 51)

3. In section 5 (extension of jurisdiction), after paragraph (2B) there shall be inserted—
    "(2C) Applications for orders relating to parental rights under section 3 of the Law Reform (Parent and Child) (Scotland) Act 1986".

The Trusts (Scotland) Act 1921 (c. 58)

4. In section 2 (definitions), in the definition of "trustee", after the word "tutor" there shall be inserted the words "(including a father or mother acting as tutor of a pupil)".

The National Assistance Act 1948 (c. 29)

5. In section 42 (liability to maintain wife or husband and children), for subsection (3) there shall be substituted the following subsection—
    "(3) Subsection (2) of this section shall not apply to Scotland and, in the application thereto of subsection (1) of this section, any reference to 'children' includes a reference to children whether or not their parents have ever been married to one another.".

The Matrimonial Proceedings (Children) Act 1958 (c. 40)

6. In section 9(1) (jurisdiction of court as respects children where action dismissed), for the words from "with respect" to "that child" there shall be substituted the words "relating to parental rights as could be made".

The Succession (Scotland) Act 1964 (c. 41)

7.—(1) In section 33(1) (construction of existing deeds), for the words "deed taking effect after the commencement of this Act", where those words second occur, there shall be substituted the words "such deed".

(2) In section 36 (interpretation), at the end there shall be added the following subsection—

"(5) Section 1(1) (legal equality of children) of the Law Reform (Parent and Child) (Scotland) Act 1986 shall apply to this Act; and any reference (however expressed) in this Act to a relative shall be construed accordingly".

The Registration of Births, Deaths and Marriages (Scotland) Act 1965 (c. 49)

8.—(1) In section 14 (duty to give information of particulars of birth), at the end there shall be added the following subsection—

"(5) In this section, any reference to the father or parent of the child shall not include a reference to a father who is not married to the mother and has not been married to her since the child's conception."

(2) In section 18 (births of illegitimate children), for subsection (1), there shall be substituted the following subsections—

"Births of children born out of wedlock

18.—(1) No person who is not married to the mother of a child and has not been married to her since the child's conception shall be required, as father of the child, to give information concerning the birth of the child and, save as provided in section 20 of this Act, the registrar shall not enter in the register the name and surname of any such person as father of the child except—

(a) at the joint request of the mother and the person acknowledging himself to be the father of the child (in which case that person shall sign the register together with the mother); or

(b) at the request of the mother—
    (i) on the production of—
        (aa) a declaration in the prescribed form made by the mother stating that that person is the father of the child; and
        (bb) a statutory declaration made by that person acknowledging himself to be the father of the child; or
    (ii) on production of a decree by a competent court finding or declaring that person to be the father of the child; or

(c) at the request of that person on production of—
    (i) a declaration in the prescribed form by that person acknowledging himself to be the father of the child; and
    (ii) a statutory declaration made by the mother stating that that person is the father of the child.

(1A) Where a person acknowledging himself to be the father of a child makes a request to the registrar in accordance with paragraph (c) of subsection (1) of this section, he shall be treated as a qualified informant concerning the birth of the child for the purposes of this Act; and the giving of information concerning the birth of the child by that person and the signing of the register by him in the presence of the registrar shall act as a discharge of any duty of any other qualified informant under section 14 of this Act."

(3) In section 18, in subsection (2)—

(a) for the words "an illegitimate" there shall be substituted the word "a",

(b) in paragraph (b) for heads (i) and (ii) there shall be substituted the words "a declaration and a statutory declaration such as are mentioned in paragraph (b) or (c) of subsection (1) of this section", and

(c) in paragraph (c) for the word "dead" there shall be substituted the words "dead or cannot be found or is incapable of making a request under subsection (1)(b) of this section, or a declaration under subsection (1)(*b*)(i)(*aa*) of this section, or a statutory declaration under subsection (1)(*c*)(ii) of this section", and the words "within the like period" shall be omitted.

(4) After section 18 there shall be inserted the following section—

"Decrees of parentage and non-parentage

18A.—(1) Where a decree of parentage or non-parentage has been granted by any court the clerk of court shall—

(*a*) where no appeal has been made against such decree, on the expiration of the time within which such an appeal may be made, or

(*b*) where an appeal has been made against such a decree, on the conclusion of any appellate proceedings,

notify the import of such decree in the prescribed form to the Registrar General.

(2) Where it appears to the Registrar General that the import of a decree notified to him under subsection (1) above does not correspond with the entry in the register of births in respect of any person to whom the decree relates he shall cause an appropriate entry to be made in the Register of Corrections Etc.".

(5) In section 20 (re-registration in certain cases)—

(*a*) in subsection (1)(*a*), for the words "or paternity" there shall be substituted the words, "parentage or non-parentage"; and

(*b*) in subsection (1)(*c*), for the words from "having been" to the end of paragraph (*c*) there shall be substituted the words "has been so made as to imply that his parents were not then married to one another and his parents have subsequently married one another".

(6) In section 20, at the end there shall be added the following subsection—

"(3) Subject to the proviso in subsection (1) of this section, an application for re-registration of a person's birth under this section may be made—

(*a*) if the person is under 16 years of age—

(i) by the person's mother, or

(ii) by the person's father if he is the person's guardian or is entitled to custody of the person or applies for such re-registration with the mother's consent; or

(*b*) if the person is of or over 16 years of age but under 18 years of age, by the person himself with the consent of a parent or guardian; or

(*c*) if the person is of or over 18 years of age, by the person himself; or

(*d*) in any case, by any person who may be prescribed by regulations made under this Act."

(7) In section 43(3) (recording of baptismal name or change of name or surname), for the words from "in the case" to "the mother is" there shall be substituted the words "if both parents are".

(8) In section 43, at the end there shall be added the following subsection—

"(10) In this section, "father" and "parent", in relation to a child, do not include a father who is not married to the mother and has not been married to her since the child's conception and who is not the child's tutor or curator and is not entitled to custody of the child."

(9) In section 56 (interpretation), in subsection (1), there shall be inserted (in their appropriate alphabetical place) the following definitions—

" "guardian" includes tutor or curator;

"parentage" has the meaning assigned to it in section 8 of the Law Reform (Parent and Child) (Scotland) Act 1986, and "non-parentage" shall be construed accordingly;

"tutor or curator" does not include tutor ad litem, curator ad litem or curator bonis".

(10) In section 56, at the end there shall be added the following subsection—

"(3) Section 1(1) (legal equality of children) of the Law Reform (Parent and Child) (Scotland) Act 1986 shall apply to this Act; and any reference (however expressed) in this Act to a relative shall, unless the contrary intention appears, be construed accordingly."

The Social Work (Scotland) Act 1968 (c. 49)

9.—(1) In section 16(11) (assumption of parental rights by local authority), for paragraph (*c*) there shall be substituted—

"(*c*) a tutor or curator to the child is appointed under the Law Reform (Parent and Child) (Scotland) Act 1986; or".

(2) In section 18(4) (duration and recission of resolutions under section 16), for the words from "section" to "1925" there shall be substituted the words "the Law Reform (Parent and Child) (Scotland) Act 1986" and for the word "guardian" there shall be substituted the words "tutor or curator".

(3) In section 81(2) (decrees for aliment)—

    (*a*) for the words from the beginning to "in force" there shall be substituted the words "Where a decree for aliment of a maintainable child is in force",

    (*b*) for the word "father" there shall be substituted the words "person liable under the decree", and

    (*c*) the words "for aliment" where those words second occur shall be omitted.

(4) In section 81(4)(*b*), for the words "father of a child" there shall be substituted the words "person liable to pay aliment for a child under a decree", and for the words "the father" where those words second occur there shall be substituted the words "that person".

(5) In section 88(3) (duty of parents to notify change of address), for the word "father" there shall be substituted the word "person".

(6) In section 94(1) (interpretation), in the definition of "guardian", for the words "the guardian" there shall be substituted the words "the tutor, curator or guardian", and for the word "charge" there shall be substituted the words "custody or charge".

The Law Reform (Miscellaneous Provisions) (Scotland) Act 1968 (c. 70)

10. In section 7 (protection of trustees and executors), at the end of paragraph (*b*) there shall be inserted the following paragraph—

    "and

    (*c*) that no paternal relative of an illegitimate person exists who is or may be entitled to an interest in that property or payment.".

The Sheriff Courts (Scotland) Act 1971 (c. 58)

11. In section 37(2A) (remits), after the word "custody" there shall be inserted the words "tutory, curatory".

The Guardianship Act 1973 (c. 29)

12. In section 13(1) (interpretation of Part II), after the definition of "child" there shall be inserted the following definition—

    " "guardian" means a tutor or curator or other guardian, but does not include a tutor or curator ad litem or a curator bonis;".

The Domicile and Matrimonial Proceedings Act 1973 (c. 45)

13. In Schedule 2 (ancillary and collateral orders (Scotland)), in paragraph 3 for the words from "or for" to the end there shall be substituted the words "and paragraph (2C) of the said section 5."

The Children Act 1975 (c. 27)

14.—(1) In section 47(2) (granting of custody)—

    (*a*) for the words from the beginning to "1930" there shall be substituted the words "Notwithstanding the generality of section 3(1) of the Law Reform (Parent and Child) (Scotland) Act 1986"; and

    (*b*) after the words "a parent" in each place where they occur there shall be inserted the words ", tutor, curator".

(2) In section 49(1) (notice to local authority of certain custody applications), for the words "a relative, step-parent or foster parent" there shall be substituted the words "not a parent".

(3) In section 55(1) (interpretation and extent of sections 47 to 55), at the end there shall be added the words "and 'relative' means a grand-parent, brother, sister, uncle or aunt, whether of the full blood or half blood or by affinity".

(4) In section 55(2), at the end there shall be added the words "and shall be construed in accordance with section 1(1) of the Law Reform (Parent and Child) (Scotland) Act 1986".

The Damages (Scotland) Act 1976 (c. 13)

15. In Schedule 1 (definition of relative), in paragraph 2, for sub-paragraph (*b*) there shall be substituted—

"(*b*) section 1(1) of the Law Reform (Parent and Child) (Scotland) Act 1986 shall apply; and any reference (however expressed) in this Act to a relative shall be construed accordingly."

The Supplementary Benefits Act 1976 (c. 71)

16.—(1) In section 17 (liability to maintain), after subsection (2) there shall be inserted the following subsection—

"(2A) Subsection (2) above shall not apply to Scotland, and in the application of subsection (1) to Scotland any reference to children shall be construed as a reference to children whether or not their parents have ever been married to one another."

(2) In section 18 (recovery of expenditure on supplementary benefits from persons liable for maintenance), at the end there shall be inserted the following subsection—

"(9) On an application under subsection (1) above a court in Scotland may make a finding as to the parentage of a child for the purpose of establishing whether a person is, for the purposes of this Act, liable to maintain him.".

The Marriage (Scotland) Act 1977 (c. 15)

17. At the end of section 2 (marriage of related persons) there shall be inserted the following subsection—

"(4) References in this section and in Schedule 1 to this Act to relationships and degrees of relationship shall be construed in accordance with section 1(1) of the Law Reform (Parent and Child) (Scotland) Act 1986.".

The Adoption (Scotland) Act 1978 (c. 28)

18.—(1) In section 18(7) (freeing child for adoption) for the words "an illegitimate child whose father is not its guardian" there shall be substituted "a child whose father is not married to the mother and who does not have any parental right in relation to the child" and for paragraphs (*a*) and (*b*) there shall be substituted the following paragraphs—

"(*a*) he has no intention of applying for any parental right under section 3 of the Law Reform (Parent and Child) (Scotland) Act 1986, or

(*b*) if he did apply for any parental right under that section the application would be likely to be refused."

(2) In section 39(2) (status conferred by adoption), for the words "an illegitimate" there shall be substituted "a".

(3) In section 46(1) (revocation of adoptions on legitimation), for the words "an illegitimate" there shall be substituted "a".

(4) In section 65(1) (interpretation), in the definition of "guardian", in paragraph (*b*), for the words from "an illegitimate" to the end there shall be substituted the words "a child whose father is not married to the mother, includes the father where he has, in relation to the child, tutory, curatory, custody, access or any other parental right by virtue of an order by a court of competent jurisdiction."

The Administration of Justice Act 1982 (c. 53)

19. In section 13(1) (interpretation of Part III), for the words from "an illegitimate" to the end there shall be substituted the words "section 1(1) of the Law Reform (Parent and Child) (Scotland) Act 1986 shall apply; and any reference (however expressed) in this Part of this Act to a relative shall be construed accordingly".

The Child Abduction Act 1984 (c. 37)

20. In section 6 (offence in Scotland of parent, etc. taking or sending child out of United Kingdom)—

(*a*) in subsection (2)(*c*), for the words "an illegitimate child" there shall be substituted the words "a child whose parents are not and have never been married to one another"; and (*b*) in subsection (7), after the word "means" there shall be inserted the words "a tutor or curator to the child appointed under the Law Reform (Parent and Child) (Scotland) Act 1986 or".

The Family Law (Scotland) Act 1985 (c. 37)

21. In section 27(1) (interpretation), in the definition of "child" for the words "an illegitimate child" there shall be substituted the words "a child whether or not his parents have ever been married to one another".

The Judicial Factors Act 1849

GENERAL NOTE

This amendment re-enacts s.12 of the Guardianship of Infants Act 1886 (repealed by Sched. 2) and includes a reference to tutors appointed under the present Act.

The Conjugal Rights (Scotland) Amendment Act 1861

GENERAL NOTE

Extended powers to make orders relating to children of the marriage are conferred. Previously only orders relating to custody, access and education were competent; now orders relating to any parental right (tutory, curatory, custody, access and other parental rights) can be made. Express power to vary or recall is given so that the practice of reserving leave to apply later should cease.

The National Assistance Act 1948

GENERAL NOTE

The liability of parents to maintain their children is now expressed in a way which does not differentiate between those born within and outwith marriage. S. 44 of the Act which provided for separate proceedings in respect of illegitimate children is repealed by Sched. 2.

The Succession (Scotland) Act 1964

GENERAL NOTE

Para. 7(2) removes any distinction in the rights of succession of and to persons between those born outwith and those born within marriage. Ss. 4 and 10A which made special provision for illegitimate children are repealed, as are other references to such children, by Sched. 2.

The Registration of Births, Deaths and Marriages (Scotland) Act 1965

GENERAL NOTE

The amendment to s.14 makes it clear that an unmarried father has no duty to give information about the birth of his child.

The amendments to s.18(1) implement the changes to the birth registration procedures for children born outwith marriage. See note to s.1(2) and (4). S. 18(2) as amended allows particulars of the father's paternity to be recorded in the Register of Corrections Etc. on production of the appropriate documents from the parents at any time after the birth. Formerly a decree of paternity was required after 12 months had elapsed.

The new s.20(3) added by para. 8(6) entitles an unmarried father to apply for reregistration of the child's birth, so as to incorporate particulars of his paternity omitted from the original registration, if he is a tutor or curator or the mother consents.

The Social Work (Scotland) Act 1968

GENERAL NOTE

The amendments to ss.16(1) and 18(4) are consequent upon the repeal of the Guardianship of Infants Acts 1886–1925.

S. 81 dealing with recovery by a local authority of aliment for children from liable relatives is now expressed without reference to illegitimate children.

S. 94(1) as amended means that an unmarried father who has sole or joint custody of his child is now a guardian for the purposes of the 1968 Act.

The Guardianship Act 1973

GENERAL NOTE

An unmarried father who has been appointed as a tutor or curator is now a guardian for the purposes of Part II of the 1973 Act. Sched. 2 repeals the whole of s.10. Most of its provisions have been superseded by the more general provisions of ss.2 to 4 of the present Act. S.10(2) has been repealed as unnecessary. Under the common law parental rights cannot be transferred by mere agreement, while agreements relating to the exercise of such rights are not prohibited.

The Children Act 1975

GENERAL NOTE

These amendments remove references to illegitimate children. S. 47 is repealed by Sched. 2 as it has been superseded by the more general provisions relating to title to sue for custody and the test used by the courts in deciding custody applications set out in s.3 of the present Act.

The Supplementary Benefits Act 1976

GENERAL NOTE

The effect of these amendments (together with the repeal of s.19 by Sched. 2) is that the provisions for the recovery from liable relatives of benefit provided for children are expressed in a way applicable to all children whether born within or outwith marriage.

The Adoption (Scotland) Act 1978

GENERAL NOTE

The distinction between married and unmarried fathers in relation to adoption is retained (see note to s.1(2) and (4)). By and large the amendments merely replace references to an illegitimate child by references to a child whose father is not married to the mother.

Section 10(2)   SCHEDULE 2

REPEALS

Chapter	Short title	Extent of repeal
1830 c. 69.	The Court of Session Act 1830.	In section 33, the words "and all actions of declarator of legitimacy and of bastardy,".
1836 c. 22.	The Bastards (Scotland) Act 1836.	The whole Act.
1886 c. 27.	The Guardianship of Infants Act 1886.	The whole Act.
1907 c. 51.	The Sheriff Courts (Scotland) Act 1907.	In section 5, in paragraph (1), the words from "and" to "individuals", paragraph (1A) and, in paragraph (2), the words from "and actions" to the end.
1925 c. 45.	The Guardianship of Infants Act 1925.	The whole Act.
1928 c. 26.	The Administration of Justice Act 1928.	Section 16.
1930 c. 33.	The Illegitimate Children (Scotland) Act 1930.	The whole Act.
1932 c. 47.	The Children and Young Persons (Scotland) Act 1932.	The whole Act.
1939 c. 4.	The Custody of Children (Scotland) Act 1939.	The whole Act.
1948 c. 29.	The National Assistance Act 1948.	Section 44.

Chapter	Short title	Extent of repeal
1958 c. 40.	The Matrimonial Proceed- ings (Children) Act 1958.	Section 7. In section 8(1), the words "maintenance and education". In section 10(1), the words "maintenance and education". In section 11(1), the words "maintenance and education". In section 13(1) and (1A), the words "maintenance and education." Section 14.
1964 c. 41.	The Succession (Scotland) Act 1964.	Section 4. In section 6, the words from "For the purposes" to the end. In section 9(1)(*a*) and (*b*), the words from "or by any" to "intestate". Section 10A. In section 11, in subsection (1), the words from "by virtue" to "rule of law" and the words from "In this" to the end, in subsection (2), the words from "For the purposes" to the end and, in subsection (4), the words "section 10A of this Act or of". In section 13, the words from "In this section" to the end. In section 33(1), the words from "(other than" to "said section 10A". In section 36(1), in the definition of "issue", the word "lawful".
1965 c. 49.	The Registration of Births, Deaths and Marriages (Scotland) Act 1965.	In section 18(2)(*c*), the words "within the like period". In section 43(3), the words from "in this definition" to the end.
1968 c. 49.	The Social Work (Scot-land) Act 1968.	In section 81, subsection (1); in subsection (2) the words "for aliment" where second occurring; and, in subsection (3), the words from the beginning to "section or".
1968 c. 70.	The Law Reform (Miscel-laneous Provisions) (Scotland) Act 1968.	Sections 1 to 6. In section 7, the words from the beginning to "this Act". In section 11, in subsection (1), paragraph (*b*) and the preceding "and", the words "or, as the case may be, is (or was) the father of that child" and the words "or paternity"; in subsection (2) the words from "or to" to "section", the words from "or, as" to "child" and the words "or affiliation"; in subsection (3) the words "or affiliation"; and in subsection (6) paragraph (*b*). Schedule 1.
1973 c. 29.	The Guardianship Act 1973.	Section 10. Section 11(6). In section 12(1)(*b*), the words "under the Guardianship of Infants Act 1886". Section 15(1)(*b*) Schedule 4. In Schedule 5, paragraphs 1 to 3.
1973 c. 45.	The Domicile and Matri-monial Proceedings Act 1973.	In Schedule 2, in paragraph 4, the words from "as extended" to the end, and paragraph 8.

Chapter	Short title	Extent of repeal
1975 c. 72.	The Children Act 1975.	In section 47, subsection (1); in subsection (2) the words from "having" to "decided)"; subsection (3); and in subsection (5) paragraphs (*b*) and (*c*). In section 48(1), the words from "and for this" to the end. In section 53, in subsection (1), the words from "the applicant" to "child and".
1976 c. 71.	The Supplementary Benefits Act 1976.	In section 17(2)(*a*), the words from "or, in Scotland," to "established". Section 19.
1977 c. 15.	The Marriage (Scotland) Act 1977.	Section 2(2)(*b*) and the word "and" preceding it.
1978 c. 28.	The Adoption (Scotland) Act 1978.	In section 65(1), in paragraph (*a*) of the definition of "guardian", the words from "in accordance" to "1971".
1983 c. 12.	The Divorce Jurisdiction, Court Fees and Legal Aid (Scotland) Act 1983.	In Schedule 1, paragraphs 3 and 4.

LOCAL GOVERNMENT ACT 1986*

(1986 c. 10)

An Act to require rating authorities to set a rate on or before 1st April; to prohibit political publicity and otherwise restrain local authority publicity; to require the mortgagor's consent and make other provision in connection with the disposal of local authority mortgages; to amend the law as to the effect of retirement and re-election of, and the allowances payable to, members of certain authorities; and for connected purposes.   [26th March 1986]

GENERAL NOTE

The main purpose of this Act is to restrict local authority publicity, particularly that of a political character. It also deals with a number of other unrelated matters.

Pt. I places a duty on local authorities to make a rate for a financial year on or before April 1 in that year and resulted from the failure of a number of authorities to do so in 1985.

Pt. II prohibits local authorities from publishing material which is likely to affect public support for a political party and places other restrictions on the powers of local authorities

* Annotations by H. W. Clarke, LL.M., D.P.A., Lecturer in Law, Chelmsford College of Further Education.

to incur expenditure on publicity. It is based on the recommendations of the Interim Report of the Committee of Inquiry into the Conduct of Local Authority Business set up under the chairmanship of Mr. David Widdicombe, Q.C., early in 1985.

One of the items to which the Committee was invited by the Secretary of State to pay particular attention was:

> "clarifying the limits and conditions governing discretionary spending, including the use of ss.137 and 142 of the Local Government Act 1972 (and sections 83 and 88 of the Local Government (Scotland) Act 1973) for political purposes in local government, or in relation to bodies set up, and largely financed by, local authorities."

The Secretary of State asked the Committee to submit an early interim report on this question in view of the growing public concern about the use made by some local authorities of their discretionary powers to engage in overt political campaigning at public expense.

The interim report, dated July 31, 1985 and published by H.M.S.O., summarised the Committee's proposals (at para. 244) as follows:

(a) there should be an express statutory prohibition of local authority publicity of a party political nature;

(b) local authorities' general powers to issue publicity should be contained in a single section—s.142 (s.88 in Scotland); accordingly;

(c) it should be made clear that s.137 (s.83 in Scotland) may not be used for publicity by local authorities;

(d) the exclusion of publicity from s.137 (s.83 in Scotland) should be so framed as not to prevent bodies funded under that section from issuing publicity to promote their own aims and objectives provided they are not acting as proxies for local authorities in unauthorised publicity;

(e) the scope of local authorities' general powers to issue publicity should be as currently set out in s.142 (s.88 in Scotland);

(f) local authorities' powers under s.111 (s.69 in Scotland) to issue publicity incidental to the discharge of their functions should remain unchanged;

(g) local authorities should be required by statute to keep a separate account of their advertising and information expenditure.

The committee indicated that they proposed to consider in their Main Report whether further means of challenge should be available to the citizen where a local authority is thought to have exceeded its publicity powers.

Pt. III deals with the disposal of local authority Housing Act mortgages and in particular requires the mortgagor's written consent to any transfer of any such mortgage.

Pt. IV remedies two inadvertent defects in the Local Government Act 1985. The first provides that a member appointed to the Inner London Education Authority or a joint authority established under the 1985 Act shall not cease to be a member of that authority on his retirement and re-election as a member of a constituent council. The second makes it clear that members of the Inner London Education Authority and council members of joint authorities established under the Act are eligible for attendance allowances.

During the passage of the Bill in the House of Lords a number of controversial amendments were made to Pt. II in connection with political publicity. These removed (a) the proposed test of whether publicity material could "reasonably be regarded as likely to affect" support for a political party; and (b) the obligation on local authorities to have regard to codes of recommended practice issued by the Secretary of State.

When the Bill was returned to the House of Commons the Minister for Environment, Countryside and Local Government indicated that the Government would not invite the House to disagree with the Lords' amendments as it was essential that the Bill should receive the Royal Assent before April 1, 1986 to ensure the enactment of the rate provisions for the next financial year.

However, legislation would be introduced next session to restore the effect of some of the amendments. In the meantime it would be better to "accept half a loaf than to have none at all in order to get something on the statute book" (Hansard H.C. Vol. 94, cols. 881–2). The Lords' amendments were accordingly accepted.

COMMENCEMENT

The Act received the Royal Assent on March 26, 1986. Pts. I, III (except s.8) and IV came into effect on that day. S. 8 and Pt. II (except s.5) came into force on April 1, 1986. S. 5 is to come into force on a day appointed by the Secretary of State.

EXTENT

Pt. II and s.12 extend to England and Wales and Scotland; the other provisions of the Act extend to England and Wales only. The Act does not apply to Northern Ireland.

PARLIAMENTARY DEBATES

Hansard: H.C. Vol. 86, col. 119; Vol. 87, col. 40; Vol. 90, col. 316; Vol. 94, col. 881; H.L. Vol. 470, cols. 385, 1013; Vol. 471, cols. 511, 823; Vol. 472, cols. 697, 869.
The Bill was considered by Standing Committee A on November 28 to December 19, 1985.

PART I

RATING

Duty to make rate on or before 1st April

1.—(1) A rating authority shall make a rate for a financial year on or before 1st April in that year.
    (2) In this section—
        (*a*) "rating authority" means an authority having power to make a rate under section 1 of the General Rate Act 1967;
        (*b*) "rate" means a general rate except that—
            (i) in the case of the City of London, it includes the poor rate, and
            (ii) in the case of the Inner Temple and the Middle Temple, it means any rate in the nature of a general rate levied in the Inner Temple or Middle Temple, as the case may be; and
        (*c*) "financial year" means a period of twelve months beginning with 1st April.
    (3) This section shall not be construed as invalidating a rate made by a rating authority for a financial year after 1st April in that year.

GENERAL NOTE

    Precepting authorities are required by s.1 of the Local Government Finance Act 1982 to issue a precept by March 10 in any year but, prior to this provision, there was no statutory time limit on the setting of a rate by rating authorities. In 1985, thirteen councils failed to set a rate by the commencement of the financial year in an attempt to put pressure on the Government to make more funds available to them. This section accordingly places a duty on rating authorities generally to set a rate for a financial year on or before April 1 in that year.
    There is no express penalty for non-compliance but an interested party may apply to the court for an order of mandamus and auditor may treat failure to comply as wilful misconduct and initiate action against the councillors concerned for the recovery of any loss sustained by the council as a result: see s.20 of the Local Government Act 1982.
    Even before this provision was enacted, it was held by the Court of Appeal in *Smith* v. *Skinner*; *Gladden and Others* v. *McMahon, The Times,* March 6, 1986, that Lambeth and Liverpool councillors were guilty of wilful misconduct when knowingly or with reckless indifference they caused their respective councils to act unlawfully by deferring, without valid reason, the making of a rate in 1985. They were accordingly jointly and severally liable for the loss or deficiency caused as a result. Where the loss certified by the auditor as due from a member of a local authority exceeds £2,000, that member, subject to an appeal to the High Court, is disqualified for five years from being a member of a local authority: s.20(4) of the Local Government Finance Act 1982.
    Subs. (3) saves the validity of any rate for a financial year made after the commencement of that year.

PART II

LOCAL AUTHORITY PUBLICITY

Prohibition of political publicity

2.—(1) A local authority shall not publish any material which, in whole or in part, appears to be designed to affect public support for a political party.

(2) In determining whether material falls within the prohibition—
  (a) regard shall be had to whether the material refers to a political party or to persons identified with a political party, and
  (b) where material is published as part of a campaign, regard shall be had to the effect which the campaign appears to be designed to achieve.

(3) A local authority shall not give financial or other assistance to a person for the publication of material which the authority are prohibited by this section from publishing themselves.

DEFINITIONS
  "local authority": s.6(2).
  "publicity": s.6(3).
  "publication": s.6(3).
  "publish": s.6(3).

GENERAL NOTE
  The Widdicombe Committee of Inquiry into the Conduct of Local Authority Business was asked to consider as a matter of urgency the question of political publicity by local authorities: see General Note, *ante*. It confirmed that some councils were producing material of a partisan nature for political ends beyond the proper scope of local authority advertising and this problem needed to be dealt with.
  This section implements that Committee's proposal that there should be an express statutory prohibition of local authority publicity of a party political nature.

Subs. (2)
  Lays down the criteria for determining whether material falls within the prohibition. Para. (b) seeks to ensure that material which might appear proper in isolation is considered in the context of any campaign of which it may form part.

Subs. (3)
  Debars local authorities from indirectly publishing prohibited material by giving financial or other help to persons for the purpose.

Other restrictions of existing powers

3.—(1) In section 142 of the Local Government Act 1972 and section 88 of the Local Government (Scotland) Act 1973 (general powers to provide information)—
  (a) in subsection (1) (power to make information available) after "other authorities" insert "mentioned in subsection (1B) below" and for "as to local government matters affecting the area" substitute "relating to the functions of the authority";
  (b) after that subsection insert—
      "(1A) A local authority may arrange for the publication within their area of information as to the services available in the area provided by them or by other authorities mentioned in subsection (1B) below.";
  (c) in subsection (2)(a) (power to publish certain information) for "on matters relating to local government" substitute "relating to the functions of the authority".
  (2) After the subsection (1A) inserted by subsection (1) above, in section 142 of the 1972 Act insert—
      "(1B) The other authorities referred to above are any other local authority, the Inner London Education Authority, a joint authority established by Part IV of the Local Government Act 1985 and any authority, board or committee which discharges functions which would otherwise fall to be discharged by two or more local or other such authorities.";

and in section 88 of the 1973 Act insert—

"(1B) The other authorities referred to above are any other local authority and any authority, board or committee which discharges functions which would otherwise fall to be discharged by two or more local authorities.".

(3) In section 137 of the Local Government Act 1972 (power to incur expenditure for purposes not otherwise authorised), after subsection (2B) insert—

"(2C) A local authority may incur expenditure under subsection (1) above on publicity only—

(*a*) for the purpose of promoting the economic development of the authority's area where the publicity is incidental to other activities undertaken or to be undertaken by the authority for that purpose, or

(*b*) by way of assistance to a public body or voluntary organisation where the publicity is incidental to the main purpose for which the assistance is given;

but the following provisions of this section apply to expenditure incurred by a local authority under section 142 below on information as to the services provided by them under this section, or otherwise relating to their functions under this section, as they apply to expenditure incurred under this section.

(2D) In subsection (2C) above—

"publicity" means any communication, in whatever form, addressed to the public at large or to a section of the public; and

"voluntary organisation" means a body which is not a public body but whose activities are carried on otherwise than for profit.";

and in section 83 of the Local Government (Scotland) Act 1973 (which makes corresponding provision for Scotland), after subsection (2B) insert—

"(2C) A local authority may incur expenditure under subsection (1) above on publicity only by way of assistance to a public body or voluntary organisation where the publicity is incidental to the main purpose for which the assistance is given; but the following provisions of this section apply to expenditure incurred by a local authority under section 88 below on information as to the services provided by them under this section, or otherwise relating to their functions under this section, as they apply to expenditure incurred under this section.

(2D) In subsection (2C) above—

"publicity" means any communication, in whatever form, addressed to the public at large or to a section of the public; and

"voluntary organisation" means a body which is not a public body but whose activities are carried on otherwise than for profit.".

General Note

This section amends ss.142 and 137 of the Local Government Act 1972 (and the corresponding sections of the Local Government (Scotland) Act 1973) so as to restrict the powers of local authorities to publish material under those provisions.

S. 142 of the 1972 Act deals with the provision of information, etc., relating to matters affecting local government. In *Meek* v. *Lothian Regional Council* (1983) S.L.T. 494, it was held that the provision did not restrict the council to publishing purely factual information but would also allow explanation and justification. Neither did it prohibit selection of information which would tend to show the majority political party in a favourable light.

However, in *R. v. Inner London Education Authority, ex p. Westminster City Council, The Times,* December 31, 1984, it was held that a decision of the ILEA under the section to retain an advertising agency to conduct a campaign with the object of informing the public of the effect of rate-capping and persuading them to the view held by the authority, was invalid because, in reaching its decision, the authority was pursuing an unauthorised purpose, namely that of persuasion, and this had materially influenced the making of the decision. Glidewell J., indicated some of the purposes coming within the phrase "information on matters relating to local government", including an explanation of legislation such as the Rates Act 1984 and a description of the extent to which the authority's activities and facilities would have to be curtailed if the maximum expenditure laid down by the Secretary of State was to be achieved. See also *R. v. Greater London Council, ex p. Westminster City Council, The Times,* January 22, 1985 (decided under s.111) (subsdiary powers of local authorities) where an interim injuction was granted to restrain the GLC from engaging advertising agencies for the purpose of its campaign against its abolition.

The Widdicombe Committee suggested that, in view of the above cases, s.142 (s.88 in Scotland) should be left unchanged, but the amendments enacted in subss. (1) and (2) restrict the publication by local authorities under the section to: (a) information concerning *services* available within their area provided by themselves or the other authorities specified or by government departments, charities or other voluntary organisations; and (b) to other information relating to the *functions* of the authority.

S. 137 of the Local Government Act 1972 authorises local authorities to incur in any financial year expenditure up to the product of a 2p rate which in their opinion is in the interests of the area or any part of it or some or all of its inhabitants, provided that the object of the expenditure is not the subject of other statutory provision. This is known as "the free twopence."

The Widdicombe Committee found that following the judgment of Glidewell J. in the ILEA case above, some authorities had relied on this power to authorise some of their advertising expenditure. Although the power had not been widely used for this purpose, the Committee recommended that it should be made clear that the section might not be used for local authority publicity.

The amendments enacted in subs. (3) accordingly limit the extent to which expenditure under s.137 (s.83 in Scotland) may be incurred on publicity and also provide that expenditure under s.142 (s.88 in Scotland) on information as to services provided by local authorities shall be subject to the provisions of subss. (2D) to (9) of s.137. This means *inter alia* that s.142 expenditure will count towards the 2p limit under s.137.

Codes of recommended practice as regards publicity

4.—(1) The Secretary of State may issue one or more codes of recommended practice as regards the content, style, distribution and cost of local authority publicity, and such other related matters as he thinks appropriate, for the guidance of local authorities in determining whether to incur expenditure on publicity.

(2) Codes may deal with different kinds of publicity or different kinds of local authority or the same kind of local authority in different circumstances or different areas.

(3) The Secretary of State may revise or withdraw a code issued under this section.

(4) The Secretary of State shall before issuing, revising or withdrawing a code consult such associations of local authorities as appear to him to be concerned and any local authority with whom consultation appears to him to be desirable.

(5) A code shall not be issued unless a draft of it has been laid before and approved by a resolution of each House of Parliament.

(6) Where the Secretary of State proposes to revise a code he shall lay a draft of the proposed alterations before each House of Parliament and—

> (*a*) he shall not make the revision until after the expiration of the period of 40 days beginning with the day on which the draft is laid (or, if copies are laid before each House of Parliament on different days, with the later of those days), and

(*b*) if within that period either House resolves that the alterations be withdrawn, he shall not proceed with the proposed alterations (but without prejudice to the laying of a further draft).

In computing the period of 40 days no account shall be taken of any time during which Parliament is dissolved or prorogued or during which both Houses are adjourned for more than four days.

DEFINITIONS
"local authority": s.6(2).
"publicity": s.6(3).

GENERAL NOTE
This section authorises the Secretary of State to issue codes of recommended practice as to the content, style, distribution and cost of publicity for the guidance of local authorities. The bill originally contained a sub-clause which placed a duty on local authorities to have regard to the provision of codes in force in determining whether to incur expenditure on publicity but this was removed by the House of Lords and not reinstated before the Royal Assent was given. The codes will therefore be purely advisory. An Outline of a Code of Practice was produced by the Secretary of State during the passage of the bill but it met with considerable criticism from MPs and the local authority associations and was subsequently withdrawn.

Subs. (4)
"*consultation*": The courts have been reluctant to define what constitutes consultation: see *Fletcher* v. *Minister of Town and Country Planning* [1947] 2 All E.R. 496 where Morris J. said (at p.500) "If a complaint is made of failure to consult, it will be for the court to examine the facts and circumstances of the particular case and decide whether consultation was in fact held." See also *Rollo* v. *Minister of Town and Country Planning* [1948] 1 All E.R. 13 (information to be supplied); and *R.* v. *Secretary of State for Social Services, ex p. Association of Metropolitan Authorities, The Times,* May 29 1985 (adequate time must be allowed to provide an informed response).

Subss. (5) and (6)
The discretion of the Secretary of State to issue or revise a code of recommended practice is subject to control by each House of Parliament.

Separate account of expenditure on publicity

5.—(1) A local authority shall keep a separate account of their expenditure on publicity.

(2) Any person interested may at any reasonable time and without payment inspect the account and make copies of it or any part of it.

(3) A person having custody of the account who intentionally obstructs a person in the exercise of the rights conferred by subsection (2) commits an offence and is liable on summary conviction to a fine not exceeding level 3 on the standard scale.

(4) The regulation making power conferred by section 23(1)(*e*) of the Local Government Finance Act 1982 or section 105(1)(*d*) of the Local Government (Scotland) Act 1973 (power to make provision as to exercise of right of inspection and as to informing persons of those rights) applies to the right of inspection conferred by subsection (2).

(5) The Secretary of State may by order provide that subsection (1) does not apply to publicity or expenditure of a prescribed description.

(6) Before making an order the Secretary of State shall consult such associations of local authorities as appear to him to be concerned and any local authority with whom consultation appears to him to be desirable.

(7) An order shall be made by statutory instrument which shall be subject to annulment in pursuance of a resolution of either House of Parliament.

DEFINITIONS
   "local authority": s.6(2).
   "publicity": s.6(3).

GENERAL NOTE
   Subject to any order made by the Secretary of State under subs. (5), local authorities are required to keep a separate account of expenditure on publicity. This applies to publicity expressly or impliedly authorised by any statutory provision: see s.6(4). Any interested person may inspect and make copies of the account.

Subs. (3)
   For the standard scale of fines on summary conviction, see Criminal Justice Act 1982, s.37(2) and the Criminal Penalties, etc. (Increase) Order 1984 (S.I. 1984 No. 447).

Subs. (4)
   See the Accounts and Audit Regulations 1983 (S.I. 1983 No. 1761) which apply to all bodies whose accounts are required to be audited in accordance with Pt. III of the Local Government Finance Act 1982.

Subs. (6)
   See note to s.4(4) above.

Subs. (7)
   The Procedure for making the type of statutory instrument specified is laid down in s.5 of the Statutory Instruments Act 1946.

Interpretation and application of Part II

   6.—(1) References in this Part to local authorities and to publicity, and related expressions, shall be construed in accordance with the following provisions.
   (2) "Local authority" means—
        (*a*) in England and Wales—
                a county, district or London borough council,
                the Common Council of the City of London,
                the Inner London Education Authority,
                a joint authority established by Part IV of the Local Government Act 1985,
                the Council of the Isles of Scilly, or
                a parish or community council;
        (*b*) in Scotland, a regional, islands or district council;
and includes any authority, board or committee which discharges functions which would otherwise fall to be discharged by two or more such authorities.
   (3) This Part applies to the Common Council of the City of London as local authority, police authority or port health authority.
   (4) "Publicity", "publish" and "publication" refer to any communication, in whatever form, addressed to the public at large or to a section of the public.
   (5) This Part applies to any such publicity expressly or impliedly authorised by any statutory provision, including—
        section 111 of the Local Government Act 1972 or section 69 of the Local Government (Scotland) Act 1973 (general subsidiary powers of local authorities),
        section 141 of the Local Government Act 1972 or section 87 of the Local Government (Scotland) Act 1973 (research and collection of information), and
        section 145(1)(*a*) of the Local Government Act 1972 or section 16(1)(*a*) of the Local Government and Planning (Scotland) Act 1982 (provision of entertainments, etc.).

(6) Nothing in this Part shall be construed as applying to anything done by a local authority in the discharge of their duties under Part VA of the Local Government Act 1972 or Part IIIA of the Local Government (Scotland) Act 1973 (duty to afford public access to meetings and certain documents).

GENERAL NOTE

"*Local authority*" is widely defined to include the Inner London Education Authority and joint authorities established following the abolition of the Greater London Council and the metropolitan county councils by the Local Government Act 1985. The additional reference to the Common Council of the City of London in subs. (3) is to deal with the unique character of the City Corporation.

Subss. (5) and (6)

The provisions on local authority publicity apply to any publicity authorised, whether expressly or by implication, by any statutory provision including those specified but not to anything required to be done under those parts of the Local Government Act 1972 or the Local Government (Scotland) Act 1973 added by the Local Government (Access to Information) Act 1985.

PART III

TRANSFER OF LOCAL AUTHORITY MORTGAGES

Transfer requires mortgagor's consent

7.—(1) A local authority shall not dispose of their interest as mortgagee of land without the prior written consent of the mortgagor (or, if there is more than one mortgagor, of all of them) specifying the name of the person to whom the interest is to be transferred.

(2) Consent given for the purposes of this section—

(*a*) may be withdrawn by notice in writing to the authority at any time before the disposal is made, and

(*b*) ceases to have effect if the disposal is not made within six months after it is given;

and if consent is withdrawn or ceases to have effect the authority shall return to the mortgagor any document in their possession by which he gave his consent.

(3) A disposal made without the consent required by this section is void, subject to subsection (4).

(4) If consent has been given and the local authority certify in the instrument effecting the disposal that it has not been withdrawn or ceased to have effect, the disposal is valid notwithstanding that consent has in fact been withdrawn or ceased to have effect.

(5) In such a case any person interested in the equity of redemption may, within six months of the disposal, by notice in writing served on the local authority, require the authority, the transferee and any person claiming under the transferee to undo the disposal, on such terms as may be agreed between them or determined by the court, and execute any documents and take any other steps necessary to vest back in the local authority the interest disposed of by them to the transferee.

(6) The Secretary of State may by regulations—

(*a*) require a local authority to give to a mortgagor whose consent is sought such information as may be prescribed,

(*b*) prescribe the form of the document by which a mortgagor's consent is given,

(*c*) require a local authority making a disposal to secure that notice of the fact that the disposal has been made is given to the mortgagor, and

10–9

(*d*) prescribe the form of that notice and the period within which it must be given.

(7) Regulations under this section shall be made by statutory instrument which shall be subject to annulment in pursuance of a resolution of either House of Parliament.

(8) This section applies—

> (*a*) to disposals on or after 24th July 1985 of a local authority's interest as mortgagee under a Housing Act mortgage, and
>
> (*b*) to disposals on or after 1st April 1986 of a local authority's interest as mortgagee under any description of mortgage,

except, in either case, where the disposal is carried out in pursuance of a contract entered into before that date.

(9) For this purpose a "Housing Act mortgage" means a mortgage entered into (whether by the local authority in question or a predecessor in title) under—

> the Small Dwellings Acquisition Acts 1899 to 1923,
>
> section 104 or 119 of the Housing Act 1957,
>
> section 43 of the Housing (Financial Provisions) Act 1958,
>
> section 100 of the Housing Act 1974, or
>
> section 1(1)(*c*) of the Housing Act 1980.

DEFINITIONS
  "Housing Act mortgage": s.7(9).
  "local authority": s.9(1).

GENERAL NOTE
  This section prevents local authorities from disposing of their interests as mortgagees without the written consent of the mortgagor. It arose from the action of a local authority which, without consulting the borrowers, sold £30 million of its mortgages to a consortium led by a French bank as a quick way of obtaining cash to meet its financial commitments.

  The consent lapses if the disposal is not made within six months. Any disposal made without consent is void except where the local authority wrongly certifies in the disposal instrument that the consent has not lapsed or been withdrawn. In that case arrangements may be made within six months for the interest to be transferred back to the local authority.

Subs. (6)
  The Secretary of State may make regulations as to the information to be supplied to the mortgagor, period of notice and prescribed forms.

Subs. (7)
  The procedure for making the type of statutory instrument specified is laid down in s.5 of the Statutory Instruments Act 1946.

Subs. (8)
  In the case of Housing Act mortgages as defined in subs. (9), the provisions are retrospective to July 24, 1985, the date on which the Secretary of State announced the proposed legislation. In other cases the provisions operate from April 1, 1986.

Certain transfers treated as not giving rise to capital receipts

8.—(1) A disposal by a local authority of their interest as mortgagee of land shall not, in the following circumstances, be treated as giving rise to a capital receipt for the purposes of Part VIII of the Local Government, Planning and Land Act 1980 (controls on capital expenditure).

(2) The circumstances are that, under the terms of the disposal or of any arrangement entered into in connection with the disposal—

> (*a*) any benefits or burdens of the mortgagee are retained by, or may be transferred to, the local authority, or
>
> (*b*) the transferee can call on the local authority to re-acquire any interest transferred or to redeem the mortgage, or

(*c*) the consideration for the transfer is other than a cash sum determined at the date of the transfer, or

(*d*) the transfer is carried out in consideration of some other transaction or the local authority may be required to enter into an agreement with a third party.

(3) The Secretary of State may by regulations amend subsection (2) or provide for other circumstances in which the disposal by a local authority of their interest as mortgagee of land is not to be treated as giving rise to a capital receipt for the purposes of Part VIII of the Local Government, Planning and Land Act 1980.

(4) Regulations under this section shall be made by statutory instrument which shall be subject to annulment in pursuance of a resolution of either House of Parliament.

DEFINITION
"local authority": s.9(1).

GENERAL NOTE
This section sets out the circumstances in which the sale of a mortgage by a local authority will not give rise to a capital receipt for the purpose of the control of expenditure under Pt. VIII of the Local Government, Planning and Land Act 1980.

The circumstances specified in subs. (2) are where the benefits and burdens are not unconditionally transferred to the buyer or where the consideration for the transaction is not a cash sum. Subs. (2) may be amended or the circumstances specified may be varied by regulations made by the Secretary of State.

Subs. (4)
The procedure for this type of statutory instrument is laid down in s.5 of the Statutory Instruments Act 1946.

Interpretation and application of Part III

9.—(1) In this Part—

(*a*) "local authority" means—

a county, district or London borough council,

the Common Council of the City of London,

the Inner London Education Authority,

a joint authority established by Part IV of the Local Government Act 1985,

the Council of the Isles of Scilly, or

any other authority prescribed for the purposes of this Part by regulations made by the Secretary of State,

and includes any authority, board or committee which discharges functions which would otherwise fall to be discharged by two or more such authorities,

(*b*) references to a local authority's interest as mortgagee of land include any interest of the authority in the land or in the debt secured, and

(*c*) references to the disposal of such an interest are to any transfer of the interest otherwise than by operation of law;

and for the purposes of this Part the disposal of an interest in registered land shall be taken to occur when the transfer is made and not when it is registered.

(2) Regulations under this section shall be made by statutory instrument which shall be subject to annulment in pursuance of a resolution of either House of Parliament.

(3) At the end of Schedule 13 to the Local Government Act 1985 (provisions with respect to residuary bodies) add—

"25. A residuary body shall be treated as a local authority for the purposes of Part III of the Local Government Act 1986 (transfer of local authority mortgages).".

GENERAL NOTE
Subs. (2)
The procedure for this type of statutory instrument is laid down in s.5 of the Statutory Instruments Act 1946.

Subs. (3)
The provisions of this Part of the Act apply to the residuary bodies established under Pt. IV of the Local Government Act 1985 to take over those rights and liabilities of the Greater London Council and the metropolitan county councils which were not transferred to other bodies on abolition. The residuary bodies are required by s.67 of the 1985 Act to complete their work as soon as practicable and, in any event, within five years and to submit to the Secretary of State within four years proposals for the transfer of any remaining property to a local authority or to a new authority.

PART IV

MISCELLANEOUS AND GENERAL

Miscellaneous

Retirement and re-election not to affect membership of joint authority

10.—(1) In section 32 of the Local Government Act 1985, after subsection (1) (appointment to joint authority to terminate if person appointed ceases to be a member of constituent council) insert—

"(1A) For the purposes of this section a person shall not be treated as ceasing to be a member of a constituent council where he retires by virtue of—

> (*a*) section 7(3) of the Local Government Act 1972 (retirement of metropolitan district councillors), or
>
> (*b*) paragraph 6(3) of Schedule 2 to that Act (retirement of London borough councillors),

and is re-elected to membership of the council not later than the day of his retirement.".

(2) In section 31 of that Act (replacement of members of joint authority), at the end add—

"(3) Where a constituent council exercises its powers under this section to replace a person who has continued to be a member of a joint authority by virtue of section 32(1A) below and notice is given not later than seven days after the council's annual meeting next following his retirement and re-election, his appointment shall terminate and the new appointment shall take effect upon the notice being given.";

and in subsection (2)(*b*) after "subject to" insert "subsection (3) below and to".

(3) In Schedule 12 to the Local Government Act 1972 for paragraph 6A (annual meeting of the new authorities) substitute—

"6A.—(1) Paragraph 1 above applies to a joint authority as it applies to a principal council, except that the annual meeting of the authority shall be held on such day between 1st March and 30th June (both inclusive) as the authority may fix.

(2) Paragraph 1 above applies to the Inner London Education Authority as it applies to the council of a London borough.".

This section remedies a technical defect in the Local Government Act 1985 in relation to the Local Government Act 1972 under which, in an election year, there might otherwise have been a period of about a month during which certain of the joint authorities established under the 1985 Act could have been without elected members.

Allowances payable to members of new authorities

11.—(1) Section 177 of the Local Government Act 1972 (supplementary provisions as to allowances payable to members of local authorities and other bodies) is amended as follows.

(2) In subsection (2) (meaning of "approved duty": things done as member of certain prescribed bodies), for "paragraphs (*b*) to (*f*) of subsection (1) above" (which does not reflect the amendment made to subsection (1) by paragraph 19 of Schedule 14 to the Local Government Act 1985) substitute "paragraphs (*ab*) to (*f*) of subsection (1) above".

(3) After that subsection insert—

"(2A) References in sections 173 and 173A above to a local authority and a councillor include references—

(*a*) to the Inner London Education Authority and a member of the Authority, and

(*b*) to a joint authority and a member of the authority appointed by one of the authority's constituent councils;

and in relation to such a member of a joint authority the references in section 173A(3) to his election shall be construed as references to his appointment.".

(4) In subsection (3) (co-opted members of committees to be treated as members of authority) after "For the purposes of sections 173 to 176 above", insert "(but not for the purposes of subsection (2A) above)".

(5) The reference in section 177(2A) of the Local Government Act 1972 (as inserted by subsection (3) above) to members of the Inner London Education Authority shall be construed, in relation to the period before elected members of the Authority first take office, as a reference to persons who are members of the Authority by virtue of section 18(5) of the Local Government Act 1985 and who are, or immediately before its abolition were, councillors of the Greater London Council.

(6) Section 84(2) and (3) of the Local Government Act 1985 (application of local authority provisions to new authorities) apply in relation to this section and the amendments made by this section as if they had been contained in Schedule 14 to that Act as originally enacted.

(7) A person who was a member of the Inner London Education Authority or a joint authority at any time before the commencement of this section may within one month of commencement give such notices under section 173A of the Local Government Act 1972 (right to opt for financial loss allowance) as he could have given if the amendments made by this section had come into force on the date on which they are, by virtue of subsection (6), deemed to have come into force and, in the case of a member of the Inner London Education Authority, as if he had been elected to membership of that authority on the date on which he became a member.

This section also remedies an inadvertent defect in the Local Government Act 1985 in relation to the Local Government Act 1972 to make it clear that members of the Inner London Education Authority and elected members of joint authorities established under Pt. IV of the 1985 Act are eligible to claim attendance or financial loss allowances.

General

Short title, commencement and extent

12.—(1) This Act may be cited as the Local Government Act 1986.

(2) The provisions of this Act come into force as follows—

Part I comes into force on the day this Act is passed;

Part II, except section 5, comes into force on 1st April 1986;

section 5 comes into force on such day as the Secretary of State may appoint by order made by statutory instrument;

Part III, except section 8, comes into force on the day this Act is passed;

section 8 comes into force on 1st April 1986;

Part IV comes into force on the day this Act is passed.

(3) Part II and this section extend to England and Wales and Scotland; the other provisions of this Act extend to England and Wales only.

GAMING (AMENDMENT) ACT 1986*

(1986 c. 11)

An Act to amend section 16 of the Gaming Act 1968 to make provision for the redemption of cheques; and to amend section 22 of that Act as to the records to be kept with respect to cheques.

[2nd May 1986]

GENERAL NOTE

In its regulation of commercial gaming, the Gaming Act 1968 prohibits licence holders from granting credit to players. In pursuit of this policy s.16 imposes strict conditions on the acceptance of players' cheques in exchange for gaming tokens. One of these conditions is that the licence holder "shall not more than two banking days later cause the cheque to be delivered to a bank for payment or collection" (s.16(3)).

This requirement means that players cannot redeem their cheques with their winnings (whether as cash or tokens) or with consolidating cheques, or a combination of these; while a casino runs the risk that having paid cash or a cheque to winning players, their cheques may subsequently be dishonoured. The Royal Commission on Gambling (1978: Cmnd. 7200, para. 18.67) found this aspect of the Gaming Act to be universally disliked, and this Act gives effect to its linked recommendations, that s.16 should be amended to enable players to redeem their cheques, provided that the redemption occurs during or immediately after the playing session in which they were tendered.

The Act was sponsored by Lord Harris of Greenwich and was supported by the Gaming Board for Great Britain, the British Casino Association and the government.

Ss. 1 and 2 textually amend s.16 of the 1968 Act; s.3 contains the short title and commencement.

COMMENCEMENT

The Act shall come into force on such a day as the Secretary of State may, by statutory instrument, appoint.

EXTENT

The Act does not extend to Northern Ireland.

ABBREVIATION

The 1968 Act: The Gaming Act 1968.

PARLIAMENTARY DEBATES

Hansard H.L. Vol. 470, cols. 390 and 1332; Vol. 471, col. 1172; H.C. Vol. 95, col. 1200.

Amendment of section 16 of Gaming Act 1968

1.—(1) Section 16 of the Act of 1968 (provision of credit for gaming) shall be amended as follows.

(2) In subsection (1), for the words "the next following subsection" there shall be inserted the words "subsections (2) and (2A) of this section".

(3) After subsection (2) there shall be inserted—

"(2A) Neither the holder of a licence under this Act nor any person acting on his behalf or under any arrangement with him shall permit to be redeemed any cheque (not being a cheque which has been dishonoured) accepted in exchange for cash or tokens for enabling any person to take part in gaming to which this Part of this Act applies unless the following conditions are fulfilled, that is to say—

(*a*) the cheque is redeemed by the person from whom it was accepted giving in exchange for it cash, or tokens, or a substitute cheque, or any combination of these, to an amount equal to the amount of the redeemed cheque or (where two or

* Annotations by David R. Miers, LL.M., D.Jur., Senior Lecturer in Law, University College, Cardiff.

more cheques are redeemed) the aggregate amount of the redeemed cheques;

(b) it is redeemed during the playing session in which it was accepted, or within thirty minutes after the end of the session;

(c) where a substitute cheque is given in whole or in part exchange for the redeemed cheque the substitute cheque is not a post-dated cheque; and

(d) where tokens are given in whole or in part exchange for the redeemed cheque, the value of each token is equal to the amount originally given in exchange for it or, if the token was won in the gaming, the value it represented when won;

but, where those conditions are fulfilled, the return of a redeemed cheque in exchange for cash, or tokens, or a substitute cheque, or any combination of these, shall not be taken to contravene subsection (1) of this section.".

(4) In subsection (3), after the words "of this Act applies" there shall be inserted the words "or a substitute cheque".

(5) After subsection (3) there shall be inserted—

"(3A) Subsection (3) of this section shall not apply to a redeemed cheque.".

(6) In subsection (4), after the words "of this Act applies" there shall be inserted the words "or any substitute cheque.".

(7) At the end of subsection (5) there shall be inserted—

" "playing session" means a continuous period during one day, or two consecutive days, throughout which gaming is permitted by or under this Act to take place on premises in respect of which a licence under this Act is for the time being in force;

"redeemed cheque" means a cheque accepted in fulfilment of the conditions specified in subsection (2) of this section and returned to the person from whom it was accepted in fulfilment of the conditions specified in subsection (2A) of this section;

"substitute cheque" means a cheque accepted in accordance with subsection (2A) of this section by either the holder of a licence under this Act or a person acting on behalf of or under any arrangement with the holder of such a licence.".

DEFINITION
"the Act of 1968": s.3(1).

GENERAL NOTE
S. 1 inserts s.16(2A) into the 1968 Act, defining those circumstances in which it shall be lawful for a player in a casino to redeem his cheque(s) during, or within 30 minutes of the close of, the playing session in which the cheques were exchanged for gaming tokens. The cheque(s) may be redeemed for cash, tokens, a substitute cheque, or any combination of these, provided that they jointly or severally equal the value of the redeemed cheque(s), and that any substitute cheque is not post-dated.

Subs. 1(3)
"gaming to which this part of the Act applies": that is, Part II of the 1968 Act.

Subs. 1(4)
The licence holder must deliver the substitute cheque to a bank for payment or collection within two banking days (s.16(3) of the 1968 Act).

Subs. 1(5)
The licence holder does not have to deliver the redeemed cheque(s) to a bank for payment or collection within two banking days (s.16(3) of the 1968 Act).

Subs. 1(6)

The legislation making gaming debts unenforceable at law does not apply to "substitute cheques" complying with s.16(2A).

Subs. 1(7)

"redeemed cheque": this must itself have complied with s.16(2) of the 1968 Act, *viz.*, be neither post-dated nor exchanged for any amount of cash or tokens less than the amount for which it was drawn.

Amendment of section 22 of Gaming Act 1968

2. Section 22 of the Act of 1968 (further powers to regulate licensed club premises) shall be amended by the insertion, in subsection (1)(*b*), after the words "on those premises", of the words "and with respect to redeemed cheques and substitute cheques within the meaning of section 16 of this Act".

GENERAL NOTE

In debate it was suggested that casinos keep a record of all transactions involving redeemed and substitute cheques for inspection by the Gaming Board. This section gives the Secretary of State power to make such regulations.

Interpretation, short title, commencement and extent

3.—(1) In this Act, "the Act of 1968" means the Gaming Act 1968.

(2) This Act may be cited as the Gaming (Amendment) Act 1986.

(3) This Act shall come into force on such day as the Secretary of State may by order made by statutory instrument appoint.

(4) This Act does not extend to Northern Ireland.

DEFINITION

"Secretary of State": one of Her Majesty's Principal Secretaries of State; Interpretation Act 1978, Sched. I.

STATUTE LAW (REPEALS) ACT 1986

(1986 c. 12)

ARRANGEMENT OF SECTIONS

An Act to promote the reform of the statute law by the repeal, in accordance with recommendations of the Law Commission and the Scottish Law Commission, of certain enactments which (except in so far as their effect is preserved) are no longer of practical utility, and to make other provision in connection with the repeal of those enactments.

[2nd May 1986]

PARLIAMENTARY DEBATES
   Hansard: Vol. 468, col. 978; Vol. 469, col. 111; Vol. 471, col. 728, 1172; H.C. Vol. 96, col. 136.

Repeals and associated amendments

1.—(1) The enactments in Schedule 1 to this Act are hereby repealed to the extent specified in the third column of that Schedule.

(2) Schedule 2 to this Act shall have effect.

Extent

2.—(1) This Act extends to Northern Ireland.

(2) Any amendment or repeal by this Act of an enactment which extends to the Channel Islands or the Isle of Man shall also extend there.

(3) The repeal of—

    (*a*) the Dentists Act 1878, and

    (*b*) the Medical Act 1886,

shall extend to any colony to which that Act extends.

(4) Subject to subsection (3) above, this Act does not repeal any enactment so far as the enactment forms part of the law of a country outside the British Islands; but Her Majesty may by Order in Council provide that the repeal by this Act of any enactment specified in the Order shall on a date so specified extend to any colony.

Short title

3. This Act may be cited as the Statute Law (Repeals) Act 1986.

SCHEDULES

Section 1(1)

SCHEDULE 1

REPEALS

PART I

ADMINISTRATION OF JUSTICE

Chapter	Short Title	Extent of Repeal
Group 1—General Repeals		
11 Geo. 4 & 1 Will 4. c.70.	Law Terms Act 1830.	The whole Act.
6 & 7 Will. 4. c.114.	Trials for Felony Act 1836.	The whole Act.
6 & 7 Vict. c.85.	Evidence Act 1843.	The whole Act.
8 & 9 Vict. c.16.	Companies Clauses Consolidation Act 1845.	Section 143.
8 & 9 Vict. c.17.	Companies Clauses Consolidation (Scotland) Act 1845.	Section 145.
8 & 9 Vict. c.19.	Lands Clauses Consolidation (Scotland) Act 1845.	Section 132.
8 & 9 Vict. c.72.	Rothwell Gaol Act 1845.	The whole Act.
14 & 15 Vict. c.100.	Criminal Procedure Act 1851.	The whole Act.
17 & 18 Vict. c.112.	Literary and Scientific Institutions Act 1854.	Section 22. In section 23, the words from "and writ of revivor" onwards.
44 & 45 Vict. c.24.	Summary Jurisdiction (Process) Act 1881.	Section 6 as it applies to the Isle of Man.
51 & 52 Vict. c.64.	Law of Libel Amendment Act 1888.	Section 9 as it applies to England and Wales.
23 & 24 Geo.5. c.36.	Administration of Justice (Miscellaneous Provisions) Act 1933.	In Schedule 2, paragraph 4.
24 & 25 Geo. 5. c.45.	Solicitors Act 1934.	The whole Act.
1965 c.32.	Administration of Estates (Small Payments) Act 1965.	In section 6(1)(*b*), the words "section 38(2) of the Finance Act 1918".
1970 c.17.	Proceedings against Estates Act 1970.	The whole Act.
1971 c.23.	Courts Act 1971.	In Schedule 8, paragraph 6.
1971 c.62.	Tribunals and Inquiries Act 1971.	In Schedule 1, paragraph 2.
1983 c.19.	Matrimonial Homes Act 1983.	In Schedule 2, the entry relating to the Matrimonial Homes Act 1967.
1984 c.28.	County Courts Act 1984.	In sections 14(1)(*b*), 92(1)(*b*) and 118(1)(i), the words "any" and "to which the judge has power to commit". Section 79(2). Section 141.

Chapter	Short Title	Extent of Repeal
Group 2—Judicial Committee		
58 & 59 Vict. c.44.	Judicial Committee Amendment Act 1895.	In section 1(1), the words from "of the Dominion" to "province of Canada".
8 Edw. 7. c.51.	Appellate Jurisdiction Act 1908.	In section 3, the words "or chief justice or judge of the Supreme Court of Newfoundland". In the Schedule, the entries relating to British India and the Dominion of Canada.
1970 c.37.	Republic of Gambia Act 1970.	Section 2(5).
1976 c.19.	Seychelles Act 1976.	Section 6.
1976 c.54.	Trinidad and Tobago Republic Act 1976.	Section 2(3).
1978 c.15.	Solomon Islands Act 1978.	Section 8.
1979 c.27.	Kiribati Act 1979.	Section 6(3).
1980 c.16.	New Hebrides Act 1980.	Section 3.
Group 3—Metropolitan Police Acts		
10 Geo. 4. c.44.	Metropolitan Police Act 1829.	Sections 14, 15 and 16.
2 & 3 Vict. c.47.	Metropolitan Police Act 1839.	Sections 32 & 74.
2 & 3 Vict. c.71.	Metropolitan Police Courts Act 1839.	Sections 39, 40 and 51.
24 & 25 Vict. c.124.	Metropolitan Police (Receiver) Act 1861.	In section 5, the words from "and may purchase" onwards. Section 8.
50 & 51 Vict. c.45.	Metropolitan Police Act 1887.	Section 4.
Group 4—Scottish Courts		
1555 c.6(Sc.).	Citation Act 1555.	The whole Act.
1661 c.47(Sc.).	Messengers of Arms Act 1661.	The whole Act.
10 Geo. 1. c.19.	Court of Session Act 1723.	The whole Act.
20 Geo. 2. c.43.	Heritable Jurisdictions (Scotland) Act 1746.	In section 34, the words from "except all cases" to "twelve pounds sterling".
24 Geo. 2. c.23.	Calendar (New Style) Act 1750.	In section 4, the words from the beginning to "Fens, and"; and from "the said Courts" to "April meeting, and".
54 Geo. 3. c.67.	Justiciary Courts (Scotland) Act 1814.	The whole Act.
6 Geo. 4, c.23.	Sheriff Courts (Scotland) Act 1825.	The whole Act.
1 & 2 Vict. c.119.	Sheriff Courts (Scotland) Act 1838.	The whole Act.
30 & 31 Vict. c.17.	Lyon King of Arms Act 1867.	In section 11, the words from "and after the death" onwards.
39 & 40 Vict. c.70.	Sheriff Courts (Scotland) Act 1876.	Part VII.
55 & 56 Vict. c.17.	Sheriff Courts (Scotland) Extracts Act 1892.	In section 2, the words from "to proceedings in" to "thirteen, or".
56 & 57 Vict. c.44.	Sheriff Courts Consignations (Scotland) Act 1893.	In section 2, the words "or the small debt court or debts recovery court". Section 6. In section 7, the words from the beginning to "and similarly".

Chapter	Short Title	Extent of Repeal
56 & 57 Vict. c.44—*cont.*	Sheriff Courts Consignations (Scotland) Act 1893—*cont.*	In section 8, the words from "shall report" to "and he". In section 9, the words from "to direct" to "Remembrancer" and the words "to them".
10 & 11 Geo. 6. c.14.	Exchange Control Act 1947.	In Part II of Schedule 5, paragraph 4.
1965 c.45.	Backing of Warrants (Republic of Ireland) Act 1965.	In section 8(2), the words from "and accordingly" onwards.
1972 c.38.	Matrimonial Proceedings (Polygamous Marriages) Act 1972.	Section 2(2)(*c*).
1980 c.55.	Law Reform (Miscellaneous Provisions) (Scotland) Act 1980.	Section 2(2)(*b*).
1980 c.62.	Criminal Justice (Scotland) Act 1980.	In Schedule 8, the entry relating to section 26(5) of the Criminal Justice Act 1961.
1983 c.12.	Divorce Jurisdiction, Court Fees and Legal Aid (Scotland) Act 1983.	In Schedule 1, paragraph 13.

Group 5—Tender of Amends and Payment into Court

Chapter	Short Title	Extent of Repeal
21 Jas. 1. c.16.	Limitation Act 1623.	The whole Act.
10 Chas. 1. Sess. 2 c.6 (Ir.).	Limitation Act (Ireland) 1634.	The whole Act.
11 Geo. 2, c.19.	Distress for Rent Act 1737.	Section 20.
11 Geo. 4 & 1 Will. 4. c.68.	Carriers Act 1830.	Section 10.
8 & 9 Vict. c.19.	Lands Clauses Consolidation (Scotland) Act 1845.	Section 129.
8 & 9 Vict. c.20.	Railways Clauses Consolidation Act 1845.	Section 139.
8 & 9 Vict. c.33.	Railways Clauses Consolidation (Scotland) Act 1845.	Section 131.
48 & 49 Vict. c.49.	Submarine Telegraph Act 1885.	Section 6(4).
53 & 54 Vict. c.37.	Foreign Jurisdiction Act 1890.	Section 13(2)

PART II

AGRICULTURE

Chapter	Short Title	Extent of Repeal
52 & 53 Vict. c.30.	Board of Agriculture Act 1889.	Section 2(1)(*c*) and the preceding "and". Section 9. Section 11(2) and (3). Section 13. In Part II of Schedule 1, the entries relating to the Public Schools Act 1868, the Universities of Oxford and Cambridge Act 1877 and statutes made thereunder, the Conveyancing and Law of Property Act 1881 and the Glebe Lands Act 1888.
3 Edw. 7. c.31.	Board of Agriculture and Fisheries Act 1903.	In section 1(2), the words from the beginning to "enactments, and". In section 1(4), the words "nine (transfer of officers) and". The Schedule.
1 & 2 Geo. 5. c.49.	Small Landholders (Scotland) Act 1911.	In Schedule 1, the entry relating to the Light Railways Act 1896.
1 Edw. 8 & 1 Geo. 6. c.70.	Agriculture Act 1937.	The whole Act.
2 & 3 Geo. 6. c.48.	Agricultural Development Act 1939.	The whole Act.
3 & 4 Geo. 6. c.14.	Agriculture (Miscellaneous War Provisions) Act 1940.	Section 27
4 & 5 Geo. 6. c.50.	Agriculture (Miscellaneous Provisions) Act 1941.	Section 1. Sections 12 to 14.
6 & 7 Geo. 6 c.16.	Agriculture (Miscellaneous Provisions) Act 1943.	The whole Act except sections 18 and 24 and Schedule 3.
9 & 10 Geo. 6. c.73.	Hill Farming Act 1946.	Section 12(13). Sections 13 to 17. Section 32(3). Section 37(1) (*c*), (*d*) and (*e*). Section 39(*d*).
10 & 11 Geo. 6. c.48.	Agriculture Act 1947.	Section 78(8), as it applies to Scotland. Section 97.
12, 13 & 14 Geo. 6. c.37.	Agriculture (Miscellaneous Provisions) Act 1949.	Section 12.
14 Geo. 6. c.17.	Agriculture (Miscellaneous Provisions) Act 1950.	The whole Act.
14 & 15 Geo. 6. c.18.	Livestock Rearing Act 1951.	Section 8(*b*).
15 & 16 Geo. 6. & 1 Eliz. 2. c.15.	Agriculture (Fertilisers) Act 1952.	The whole Act.
15 & 16 Geo. 6 & 1 Eliz. 2. c.35.	Agriculture (Ploughing Grants) Act 1952.	The whole Act.
15 & 16 Geo. 6 & 1 Eliz. 2. c.62.	Agriculture (Calf Subsidies) Act 1952.	The whole Act.
2 & 3 Eliz. 2. c.39.	Agriculture (Miscellaneous Provisions) Act 1954.	Section 2.
4 & 5 Eliz. 2. c.20.	Agriculture (Improvement of Roads) Act 1955.	The whole Act.
7 & 8 Eliz. 2. c.12.	Agriculture (Small Farmers) Act 1959.	The whole Act.

Chapter	Short Title	Extent of Repeal
1963 c.11.	Agriculture (Miscellaneous Provisions) Act 1963.	Sections 4, 5, 9, 10 and 12.
1967 c.22.	Agriculture Act 1967.	Sections 10 to 12. Section 26(11)(*b*). Sections 43 and 44. Section 61(8). In section 69(1), in paragraph (*a*), the words "or any payment under section 12 thereof, or", and paragraphs (*c*), (*d*) and (*e*).
1968 c.34.	Agriculture (Miscellaneous Provisions) Act 1968.	Sections 38 to 40.
1970 c.40.	Agriculture Act 1970.	Section 29(6) and (7). In section 34(2), in paragraph (*a*), the words "section 16 of the Agriculture Act 1937 or" and paragraph (*b*). Sections 35 and 36. In Schedule 5, Part I.
1974 c.39.	Consumer Credit Act 1974.	In Schedule 4, paragraph 10.
1976 c.55.	Agriculture (Miscellaneous Provisions) Act 1976.	In Schedule 3, the entries relating to the Agriculture Act 1937 and section 40(3)(*c*) of the Agriculture Act 1968.
1980 c.66.	Highways Act 1980.	Section 39. In Schedule 24, paragraph 6.

PART III

FINANCE

Chapter	Short Title	Extent of Repeal
5 Geo. 1. c.20.	Revenue of Scotland Act 1718.	The whole Act.
41 Geo. 3. c.32.	Irish Charges Act 1801.	The whole Act.
33 & 34 Vict. c.71.	National Debt Act 1870.	Sections 2 and 4. Part IV. Part V. Section 73. Schedule 2.
36 & 37 Vict. c.57.	Consolidated Fund (Permanent Charges Redemption) Act 1873.	In section 8, the words from "and any general rule" onwards.
47 & 48 Vict. c.23.	National Debt (Conversion of Stock) Act 1884.	In section 1(2), the words from "shall not be redeemable" to "such day". In section 1(5), the words from "and the Treasury" onwards. Sections 6 and 7. In section 9, the definition of "Three per cent. stock".
51 & 52 Vict. c.2.	National Debt (Conversion) Act 1888.	In section 2(2), the words from "shall not be redeemable" to "that day". In section 2(5), the words from "and the Treasury" onwards. Sections 19, 25, 27, 28 and 32.
51 & 52 Vict. c.15.	National Debt (Supplemental) Act 1888.	The whole Act.

Chapter	Short Title	Extent of Repeal
52 & 53 Vict. c.6.	National Debt Act 1889.	In section 4(1), the words "or by payment at a country branch".
53 & 54 Vict. c.8.	Customs and Inland Revenue Act 1890.	The whole Act.
55 & 56 Vict. c.39.	National Debt (Stockholders Relief) Act 1892.	Section 7.
2 Edw. 7. c.7.	Finance Act 1902.	Section 11.
6 Edw. 7. c.50.	National Galleries of Scotland Act 1906.	Section 8.
5 & 6 Geo. 5. c.89.	Finance (No. 2) Act 1915.	In section 48, the definition of "Government stock".
6 & 7 Geo. 5. c.24.	Finance Act 1916.	In section 66, the definition of "Government stock".
7 & 8 Geo. 5. c.31.	Finance Act 1917.	Section 35.
8 & 9 Geo. 5. c.15.	Finance Act 1918.	The whole Act.
8 & 9 Geo. 5. c.24.	Flax Companies (Financial Assistance) Act 1918.	The whole Act.
9 & 10 Geo. 5. c.37.	War Loan Act 1919.	The whole Act.
9 & 10 Geo. 5. c.53.	War Pensions (Administrative Provisions) Act 1919.	In section 8(1), the words from the beginning to "such service; or" and from "provided that" to "Ministry Appeal Tribunal". Section 8(3). In paragraph 8 of the Schedule, the words from "the transfer" to "nineteen".
11 & 12 Geo. 5. c.49.	War Pensions Act 1921.	In section 2(1) in paragraph (*d*), the words "or the special grants committee" and "or that committee, as the case may be"; paragraph (*e*); and in paragraph (*g*), the words "or the special grants committee". In section 3, the words "under the War Pensions Acts, 1915 to 1920, or". Section 4. In section 6(1), the words from "or after" to "later".
15 & 16 Geo. 5. c.29.	Gold Standard Act 1925.	The whole Act.
18 & 19 Geo. 5. c.17.	Finance Act 1928.	Section 26. Section 35(1).
21 & 22 Geo. 5. c.46.	Gold Standard (Amendment) Act 1931.	The whole Act.
24 & 25 Geo. 5. c.32.	Finance Act 1934.	Section 24.
1 Edw. 8 & 1 Geo. 6. c.54.	Finance Act 1937.	Section 29.
2 & 3 Geo. 6. c.41.	Finance Act 1939.	Section 38(6).
3 & 4 Geo. 6. c.23.	National Loans (No. 2) Act 1940.	The whole Act.
5 & 6 Geo. 6. c.10.	Securities (Validation) Act 1942.	The whole Act.

Chapter	Short Title	Extent of Repeal
5 & 6 Geo. 6. c.21.	Finance Act 1942.	In Part I of Schedule 11— (*a*) the entries relating to— Guaranteed 2¾% Stock, Guaranteed 3% Stock, 5% Conversion Loan 1944–64, 2½% Funding Loan 1956–61, 2¾% Funding Loan 1952–57, 3% Funding Loan 1959–69, 4% Funding Loan 1960–90, 2½% Conversion Loan 1944–49, 3% Conversion Loan 1948–53, 4% Victory Bonds, 2½% National Defence Bonds 1944–48, 3% National Defence Loan 1954–58, (*b*) the words "(other than National Defence Bonds and National Defence Loan of the descriptions aforesaid)". In Part II of Schedule 11, the entries relating to the National Debt Act 1870.
10 & 11 Geo. 6. c.35.	Finance Act 1947.	Section 58.
1947 c.15 (N.I.)	Finance Act (Northern Ireland) 1947.	Section 10.
12, 13 & 14 Geo. 6. c.2.	Debts Clearing Offices Act 1948.	The whole Act.
12, 13 & 14 Geo. 6. c.47.	Finance Act 1949.	Section 40(10) as it applies to Scotland. Section 48(3).
14 Geo. 6. c.21.	Miscellaneous Financial Provisions Act 1950.	The whole Act.
4 & 5 Eliz. 2. c.6.	Miscellaneous Financial Provisions Act 1955.	Section 5(10)(*b*).
8 & 9 Eliz. 2. c.1.	Mr. Speaker Morrison's Retirement Act 1959.	The whole Act.
8 & 9 Eliz. 2. c.58.	Charities Act 1960.	In Schedule 6, the entry relating to the National Debt (Conversion) Act 1888.
1963 c.25.	Finance Act 1963.	Section 71(6). Section 73(7)(*a*). Schedule 12. In Schedule 14, Part VIII.
1964 c.7.	Shipbuilding Credit Act 1964.	The whole Act.
1964 c.92.	Finance (No. 2) Act 1964.	The whole Act.
1965 c.25.	Finance Act 1965.	Schedules 1 to 4.
1967 c.47.	Decimal Currency Act 1967.	The whole Act.
1968 c.11.	Revenue Act 1968.	The whole Act.
1968 c.13.	National Loans Act 1968.	In Schedule 1, the entry relating to the Shipbuilding Credit Act 1964. In Schedule 5, the entries relating to the War Loan Act 1919 and the Finance Act 1934.
1968 c.32.	Industrial Expansion Act 1968.	Section 9.
1971 c.17.	Industry Act 1971.	The whole Act.
1971 c.56.	Pensions (Increase) Act 1971.	In Schedule 2, in paragraph 2, the words "Mr. Speaker Morrison's Retirement Act 1959 or".

Chapter	Short Title	Extent of Repeal
1972 c.41.	Finance Act 1972.	Sections 53, 54 and 122. Schedule 27. In Schedule 28, Parts I, II, VIII and IX.
1974 c.30.	Finance Act 1974.	Section 53. Schedule 13. In Schedule 14, Part V.
1979 c.2.	Customs and Excise Management Act 1979.	In section 171(2A), as inserted by the Finance Act 1984, the words from "and for the purposes" onwards. Section 177(2). In Part I of the Table in Schedule 4 the entries relating to the Finance (No. 2) Act 1964.
1979 c.8.	Excise Duties (Surcharges or Rebates) Act 1979.	In Schedule 1, paragraph 1.
1984 c. 51.	Capital Transfer Tax Act 1984.	Section 225(7).

Pension Funds

Chapter	Short Title	Extent of Repeal
2 Edw. 7. c.clxxxiv.	Aberdeen Accountants Order Confirmation Act 1902.	The whole Act.
8 Edw. 7. c.ii.	Clyde Navigation (Superannuation) Order Confirmation Act 1908.	The whole Act.
13 & 14 Geo. 5 c.lxv.	Church of Scotland Ministers' and Scottish University Professors' Widows' Fund Order Confirmation Act 1923.	The whole Act.
15 Geo. 5. c.ii.	Edinburgh Chartered Accountants Annuity &c. Fund Order Confirmation Act 1924.	The whole Act.
16 & 17 Geo. 5. c.lxviii.	Church of Scotland Ministers' and Scottish University Professors' Widows' Fund (Amendment) Order Confirmation Act 1926.	The whole Act.
17 & 18 Geo. 5. c.cxiv.	Edinburgh Chartered Accountants Annuity &c. Fund Order Confirmation Act 1927.	The whole Act.
20 & 21 Geo. 5. c.cxxxiv.	Churches & Universities (Scotland) Widows' and Orphans' Fund Order Confirmation Act 1930.	The whole Act.
1 Edw. 8 c.ii.	Edinburgh Chartered Accountants Annuity &c. Fund (Consolidation and Amendment) Order Confirmation Act 1936.	The whole Act.
6 & 7 Geo. 6. c.i.	Edinburgh Merchant Company Endowments (Amendment) Order Confirmation Act 1942.	The whole Act.
12 & 13 Geo. 6. c.vi.	Clyde Navigation (Superannuation) Order Confirmation Act 1949.	The whole Act.

Chapter	Short Title	Extent of Repeal
12 & 13 Geo. 6. cxiii.	Royal Bank of Scotland Officers' Widows' Fund Order Confirmation Act 1949.	The whole Act.
3 & 4 Eliz. 2. c.iv.	Clyde Navigation (Superannuation) Order Confirmation Act 1955.	The whole Act.

PART IV

IMPORTS AND EXPORTS

Chapter	Short Title	Extent of Repeal
39 & 40 Vict. c.36.	Customs Consolidation Act 1876.	Section 43.
42 & 43 Vict. c.21.	Customs and Inland Revenue Act 1879.	Section 8.
49 & 50 Vict. c.41.	Customs Amendment Act 1886.	The whole Act.
63 & 64 Vict. c.44.	Exportation of Arms Act 1900.	The whole Act.
4 & 5 Geo. 5. c.64.	Customs (Exportation Prohibition) Act 1914.	The whole Act.
5 & 6 Geo. 5. c.2.	Customs (Exportation Restriction) Act 1914.	The whole Act.
6 & 7 Geo. 5. c.52.	Trading with the Enemy and Export of Prohibited Goods Act 1916.	The whole Act.
11 & 12 Geo. 5. c.32.	Finance Act 1921.	Section 17.
22 & 23 Geo. 5. c.53.	Ottawa Agreements Act 1932.	The whole Act.

PART V

INDUSTRIAL RELATIONS

Chapter	Short Title	Extent of Repeal
5 & 6 Geo. 6. c.9.	Restoration of Pre-War Trade Practices Act 1942.	The whole Act.
14 & 15 Geo. 6. c.9.	Restoration of Pre-War Trade Practices Act 1950.	The whole Act.
1974 c.52.	Trade Union and Labour Relations Act 1974.	Section 1, except in subsection (2) the words "Schedule 1 to this Act shall have effect". Sections 20 to 24. In Schedule 4, paragraph 4.

PART VI

INTELLECTUAL PROPERTY

Chapter	Short Title	Extent of Repeal
15 Geo. 3. c.52.	Porcelain Patent Act 1775.	The whole Act.
7 Edw. 7. c.29.	Patents and Designs Act 1907.	Section 82.
1 & 2 Geo. 5. c.46.	Copyright Act 1911.	Section 34. Section 37(2).
22 & 23 Geo. 5. c.32.	Patents and Designs Act 1932.	The whole Act.
2 & 3 Geo. 6. c.32.	Patents and Designs (Limits of Time) Act 1939.	The whole Act.
9 & 10 Geo. 6. c.44.	Patents and Designs Act 1946.	The whole Act.
12, 13 & 14 Geo. 6. c.62.	Patents and Designs Act 1949.	In Schedule 1, the entry relating to section 82 of the Patents and Designs Act 1907.
12, 13 & 14 Geo. 6. c.88.	Registered Designs Act 1949.	In section 13(2), the words from "any British protectorate" to "United Nations". In section 13(3), the words "in accordance with a mandate from the League of Nations or".
4 & 5 Eliz. 2. c.74.	Copyright Act 1956.	In Schedule 7, paragraph 40.
1977 c.37.	Patents Act 1977.	In section 90(2), the words "or any British protectorate or protected state".

PART VII

LOCAL GOVERNMENT

Chapter	Short Title	Extent of Repeal
Group 1—General Repeals		
34 & 35 Vict. c.70.	Local Government Board Act 1871.	The whole Act.
8 Edw. 7. c.62.	Local Government (Scotland) Act 1908.	The whole Act.
3 & 4 Geo. 5. c.clvi.	Dunfermline District Water Order Confirmation Act 1913.	The whole Act.
3 & 4 Geo. 5. c.clx.	Lanarkshire (Middle Ward District) Water Order Confirmation Act 1913.	The whole Act.
6 & 7 Geo. 5. c.i.	Aberdeen Corporation Water Order Confirmation Act 1916.	The whole Act.
8 & 9 Geo. 5. c.i.	Dunfermline District Water Order Confirmation Act 1918.	The whole Act.
12 Geo. 5. c.i.	Lanarkshire County Council Order Confirmation Act 1922.	The whole Act.
15 & 16 Geo. 5. c.lxix.	Lanarkshire County Council Order Confirmation Act 1925.	The whole Act.

Chapter	Short Title	Extent of Repeal
20 Geo. 5. c.xviii.	Dundee Corporation Order Confirmation Act 1929.	The whole Act.
24 & 25 Geo. 5. c.xlii.	Dundee Corporation Order Confirmation Act 1934.	The whole Act.
9 & 10 Geo. 6. c.xxxviii.	Manchester Corporation Act 1946.	Section 35.
12 & 13 Geo. 6. c.xliii.	Bolton Corporation Act 1949.	Section 43.
12, 13 & 14 Geo. 6. c.84.	War Damaged Sites Act 1949.	The whole Act.
6 & 7 Eliz. 2. c.64.	Local Government and Miscellaneous Financial Provisions (Scotland) Act 1958.	In Schedule 4, paragraph 13(3).
1969 c.48.	Post Office Act 1969.	In Schedule 4, paragraph 49
1972 c.70.	Local Government Act 1972.	Section 101(9)(*g*).
1981 c.ix.	Greater Manchester Act 1981.	Sections 145 and 160.

Group 2—Exemptions from Corporate or Parochial Offices

Chapter	Short Title	Extent of Repeal
45 & 46 Vict. c.50.	Municipal Corporations Act 1882.	Section 257(4).
53 & 54 Vict. c.21.	Inland Revenue Regulation Act 1890.	Section 8.
1 & 2 Eliz. 2. c.37.	Registration Service Act 1953.	Section 17.

Group 3—Festival of Britain 1951

Chapter	Short Title	Extent of Repeal
12, 13 & 14 Geo. 6. c.26.	Public Works (Festival of Britain) Act 1949	The whole Act.
12, 13 & 14 Geo. 6. c.102.	Festival of Britain (Supplementary Provisions) Act 1949.	The whole Act.
15 & 16 Geo. 6. & 1 Eliz. 2. c.13.	Festival Pleasure Gardens Act 1952.	The whole Act.
1981 c.67.	Acquisition of Land Act 1981.	In Schedule 4— (*a*) in the Table in paragraph 1, the entry relating to the Public Works (Festival of Britain) Act 1949; (*b*) paragraph 5.

Group 4—Rating

Chapter	Short Title	Extent of Repeal
17 & 18 Vict. c.91.	Lands Valuation (Scotland) Act 1854.	In section 20, the words from "and the remuneration" onwards. Sections 28 and 29.
30 & 31 Vict. c.80.	Valuation of Lands (Scotland) Amendment Act 1867.	In section 6, the words from the beginning to "therein, and", Section 8.
19 & 20 Geo. 5. c.25.	Local Government (Scotland) Act 1929.	Sections 20, 47, 48 and 77(1).
24 & 25 Geo. 5. c.22.	Assessor of Public Undertakings (Scotland) Act 1934.	Sections 2 and 3.
1 & 2 Geo. 6. c.52.	Coal Act 1938.	In section 45(16), the words "or Supplementary Valuation Roll".
12, 13 & 14 Geo. 6. c.75.	Agricultural Holdings (Scotland) Act 1949.	In section 7(2)(*b*), the words from "the relief" to "that Act nor".

Chapter	Short Title	Extent of Repeal
10 & 11 Eliz. 2, c.9.	Local Government (Financial Provisions etc.) (Scotland) Act 1962.	Section 5.
1966 c.9.	Rating Act 1966.	The whole Act.
1972 c.11.	Superannuation Act 1972.	In Schedule 6, paragraphs 13 and 14.
1972 c.60.	Gas Act 1972.	Section 34(3).
1973 c.65.	Local Government (Scotland) Act 1973.	Section 117.
1975 c.30.	Local Government (Scotland) Act 1975.	Section 2(4). Section 5(1)(*c*). In section 5(4), the words "or (*c*)(i)", "or (*c*)(ii)" and "or (*c*)(iii)".
1976 c.45.	Rating (Charity Shops) Act 1976.	Section 1(3).
1984 c.31.	Rating and Valuation (Amendment) (Scotland) Act 1984.	In section 13(1), the words from the beginning to "1867 and". Section 13(2) and (4). Section 21(2). Schedule 3.

PART VIII

MEDICINE AND HEALTH SERVICES

Chapter	Short Title	Extent of Repeal
32 Hen. 8. c.42. (1540).	Concerning Barbers and Chirurgians.	The whole Act.
18 Geo. 2. c.15.	An Act for making the Surgeons of London and the Barbers of London two separate and distinct corporations.	The whole Act except sections 12 and 15 to 18.
21 & 22 Vict. c.90.	Medical Act 1858.	Sections 48 to 51.
23 & 24 Vict. c.66.	Medical Act 1860.	In section 2, the words from "and any such new charter", where first occurring, onwards.
38 & 39 Vict. c.43.	Medical Act (Royal College of Surgeons of England) 1875.	The whole Act.
41 & 42 Vict. c.33.	Dentists Act 1878.	The whole Act.
49 & 50 Vict. c.48.	Medical Act 1886.	The whole Act.
26 Geo. 5 and 1 Edw. 8. c.40.	Midwives Act 1936.	The whole Act.
2 & 3 Geo. 6. c.13.	Cancer Act 1939.	Section 4(4)(*a*)(ii). In section 5(1), the definition of "The National Radium Trust". In section 7(*b*), the words "except in section 3 of this Act".
1968 c.46.	Health Services and Public Health Act 1968.	In section 60(2), the words from "but the reception" onwards. In Schedule 3, the entries relating to the Disabled Persons (Employment) Act 1958 and the Mental Health Act 1959.

Chapter	Short Title	Extent of Repeal
1977 c.49.	National Health Service Act 1977.	In Schedule 15, paragraph 1.
1978 c.29.	National Health Service (Scotland) Act 1978.	In Schedule 16, paragraph 19.
1980 c.15.	National Health Service (Invalid Direction) Act 1980.	The whole Act.

PART IX

OVERSEAS JURISDICTION

Chapter	Short Title	Extent of Repeal
41 Geo. 3. c.103.	Malta Act 1801.	The whole Act.
23 & 24 Vict. c.5.	Indian Securities Act 1860.	The whole Act.
36 & 37 Vict. c.59.	Slave Trade (East African Courts) Act 1873.	The whole Act.
36 & 37 Vict. c.88.	Slave Trade Act 1873.	In section 2, in the definition of "British slave court", the words from "and every East African Court" onwards.
38 & 39 Vict. c.51.	Pacific Islanders Protection Act 1875.	The whole Act.
42 & 43 Vict. c.38.	Slave Trade (East African Courts) Act 1879.	The whole Act.
50 & 51 Vict. c.54.	British Settlements Act 1887.	Section 7.
53 & 54 Vict. c.27.	Colonial Courts of Admiralty Act 1890.	In section 9(2)(*a*), the words "in India or" and "other" and from "or the Pacific" to "1875". In section 13(1), the words from "and in and from East African Courts" onwards. Section 13(3). Sections 16, 17 and 18. Schedules 1 and 2.
53 & 54 Vict. c.37.	Foreign Jurisdiction Act 1890.	Section 18.
6 & 7 Geo. 5. c.9.	Pacific Islands Regulations (Validation) Act 1916.	The whole Act.
10 & 11 Geo. 5. c.27.	Nauru Island Agreement Act 1920.	The whole Act.
4 & 5 Eliz. 2. c.23.	Leeward Islands Act 1956.	The whole Act.
4 & 5 Eliz. 2. c.63.	British Caribbean Federation Act 1956.	The whole Act.
1967 c.4.	West Indies Act 1967.	The whole Act except sections 6, 8, 17(1) and (4), 19 and 21.

PART X

PARLIAMENTARY AND CONSTITUTIONAL PROVISIONS

Chapter	Short Title	Extent of Repeal
34 & 35 Vict. c.3.	Parliamentary Costs Act 1871.	In section 4, the words "provisional certificates".
42 & 43 Vict. c.17.	House of Commons Costs Taxation Act 1879.	In section 1, the words "or provisional certificate".
		In section 2, the words "or by the Local Government Board", "or provisional certificate" and "or to the Local Government Board, as the case may be".
11 & 12 Geo. 6. c.36.	House of Commons Members' Fund Act 1948.	Section 6.
11 & 12 Geo. 6. c.65.	Representation of the People Act 1948.	The whole Act except sections 1(1) and 81.
12, 13 & 14 Geo. 6. c.66.	House of Commons (Redistribution of Seats) Act 1949.	Section 5.
		In section 6, the words from "for any reference" (where first occurring) to "burgh, and" and from "whether" to "other Act".
		Sections 8 and 9(2).
12, 13 & 14 Geo. 6. c.103.	Parliament Act 1949.	In section 1, the proviso.
1975 c.33.	Referendum Act 1975.	The whole Act.

PART XI

SHIPPING, HARBOURS AND FISHERIES

Chapter	Short Title	Extent of Repeal
14 & 15 Vict. c.26.	Herring Fishery Act 1851.	The whole Act.
16 & 17 Vict. c.107.	Customs Consolidation Act 1853.	The whole Act.
16 & 17 Vict. c.129.	Pilotage Law Amendment Act 1853.	The whole Act.
27 & 28 Vict. c.58.	Hartlepool Pilotage Order Confirmation Act 1864.	The whole Act.
28 & 29 Vict. c.100.	Harbours Transfer Act 1865.	The whole Act.
57 & 58 Vict. c.60.	Merchant Shipping Act 1894.	Section 683(4).
9 Edw. 7. c.8.	Trawling in Prohibited Areas Prevention Act 1909.	The whole Act.
1 & 2 Geo. 5. c.42.	Merchant Shipping Act 1911.	The whole Act.
2 & 3 Geo. 5. c.31.	Pilotage Act 1913.	The whole Act as it applies to the Isle of Man.
26 Geo. 5 & 1 Edw. 8. c.36.	Pilotage Authorities (Limitation of Liability) Act 1936.	The whole Act as it applies to the Isle of Man.
3 & 4 Geo. 6. c.xlii.	Clyde Lighthouses Consolidation Order Confirmation Act 1940.	The whole Act.
3 & 4 Eliz. 2. c.7.	Fisheries Act 1955.	Section 3 as it applies to England and Wales.

Chapter	Short Title	Extent of Repeal
6 Eliz. 2. c.v.	Clyde Lighthouses Order Confirmation Act 1957.	The whole Act.
8 & 9 Eliz. 2. c.42.	Merchant Shipping (Minicoy Lighthouse) Act 1960.	The whole Act.
1973 c.27.	Bahamas Independence Act 1973.	Section 5.
1974 c.43.	Merchant Shipping Act 1974.	Section 24(4).
1981 c.29.	Fisheries Act 1981.	In Schedule 4, paragraphs 9 and 29.

Harbour Order Confirmation Acts

Chapter	Short Title	Extent of Repeal
9 & 10 Geo. 5. c.ii.	Leith Harbour and Docks Order Confirmation Act 1919.	The whole Act.
9 & 10 Geo. 5. c.xcviii.	Clyde Navigation Order Confirmation Act 1919.	The whole Act.
9 & 10 Geo. 5. c.civ.	Granton Harbour Order Confirmation Act 1919.	The whole Act.
11 & 12 Geo. 5. c.v.	Forth Conservancy Order Confirmation Act 1921.	The whole Act.
15 & 16 Geo. 5. c.cxxv.	Leith Harbour and Docks Order Confirmation Act 1925.	The whole Act.
23 & 24 Geo. 5. c.li.	Leith Harbour and Docks Order Confirmation Act 1933.	The whole Act.
25 & 26 Geo. 5. c.liv.	Leith Harbour and Docks Consolidation Order Confirmation Act 1935.	The whole Act.
4 & 5 Geo. 6. c.vii.	Greenock Port and Harbours Order Confirmation Act 1941.	The whole Act.
9 & 10 Geo. 6. c.lix.	Aberdeen Harbour Order Confirmation Act 1946.	The whole Act.
12 & 13 Geo. 6. c.liv.	Aberdeen Harbour Order Confirmation Act 1949.	The whole Act.
14 Geo. 6. c.xxv.	Leith Harbour and Docks Order Confirmation Act 1950.	The whole Act.
14 Geo. 6. c.xxviii.	Granton Harbour Order Confirmation Act 1950.	The whole Act.
14 Geo. 6. c.xxix.	Greenock Port and Harbours Order Confirmation Act 1950.	The whole Act.
15 & 16 Geo. 6 & 1 Eliz. 2. c.xviii.	Leith Harbour and Docks Order Confirmation Act 1952.	The whole Act.
1 & 2 Eliz. 2. c.xix.	Clyde Navigation Order Confirmation Act 1953.	The whole Act.
5 Eliz. 2. c.i.	Clyde Navigation Order Confirmation Act 1956.	The whole Act.
7 & 8 Eliz. 2. c.xxxv.	Leith Harbour and Docks Order Confirmation Act 1959.	The whole Act.
8 Eliz. 2. c.ii.	Clyde Navigation Order Confirmation Act 1959.	The whole Act.
10 & 11 Eliz. 2. c.xxxiv.	Leith Harbour and Docks Order Confirmation Act 1962.	The whole Act.

PART XII

SUBORDINATE LEGISLATION PROCEDURE

Chapter	Short Title	Extent of Repeal
7 & 8 Vict. c.69.	Judicial Committee Act 1844.	In section 1, the words "Provided also, that every such general order in council as aforesaid shall be published in the London Gazette within one calendar month next after the making thereof;".
18 & 19 Vict. c.68.	Burial Grounds (Scotland) Act 1855.	In section 5, the words from "and such Order in Council" to "this Act".
20 & 21 Vict. c.81.	Burial Act 1857.	In sections 10 and 23, the words "and every such Order in Council shall be published in the London Gazette;".
27 & 28 Vict. c.24.	Naval Agency and Distribution Act 1864.	In section 26, the words from "shall be published" to "Gazette, and" and from "within" (where first occurring) onwards.
27 & 28 Vict. c.25.	Naval Prize Act 1864.	In section 54, the words from "shall be published" to "Gazette, and" and from "within" (where first occurring) onwards.
28 & 29 Vict. c.89.	Greenwich Hospital Act 1865.	In section 60, the words from "shall be published" to "Gazette, and" and from "within" (where first occurring) onwards.
28 & 29 Vict. c.111.	Navy and Marines (Property of Deceased) Act 1865.	In section 18, the words from "shall be published" to "Gazette, and" and from "within" (where first occurring) onwards.
28 & 29 Vict. c.125.	Dockyard Ports Regulation Act 1865.	In section 7, the words from "and such rules" onwards. Sections 8, 9 and 10. In section 26, the words from "within" (where first occurring) onwards.
31 & 32 Vict. c.101.	Titles to Land Consolidation (Scotland) Act 1868.	In the proviso to section 162, the words from "within" to "same may" and from "and until" onwards.
33 & 34 Vict. c.78.	Tramways Act 1870.	In section 64, the words from "Any rules" (where first occurring) to "judicially noticed" and from "within three weeks" (where first occurring) onwards.
36 & 37 Vict. c.88	Slave Trade Act 1873.	In section 29, the words from "within six weeks" (where first occurring) to "Gazette".
38 & 39 Vict. c.17.	Explosives Act 1875.	In section 83, as it applies to Great Britain, the words from "Every Order" (where first occurring) to "whatever"; from "shall take effect" to "Gazette, and"; and from "within" (where first occurring) to "session of Parliament".
38 & 39 Vict. c.18.	Seal Fishery Act 1875.	In section 1, the words from "within six weeks" (where first occurring) onwards.
38 & 39 Vict. c.89.	Public Works Loans Act 1875.	In section 41, the words "as if it was enacted in this Act" and from "as soon as" to "powers of this Act".
39 & 40 Vict. c.18	Treasury Solicitor Act 1876.	In section 5, the words from "within" (where first occurring) onwards.
40 & 41 Vict. c.2.	Treasury Bills Act 1877.	In section 9, the words from "within one month" (where first occurring) to "enacted in this Act".

Chapter	Short Title	Extent of Repeal
40 & 41 Vict. c.41.	Crown Office Act 1877.	In section 3, provisos (1) and (2); and the words from "within one month" (where first occurring) onwards. In section 5, the words from "within one month" (where first occurring) onwards.
42 & 43 Vict. c.58.	Public Offices Fees Act 1879.	In section 2, the words from "Every such order" onwards. In section 3, the words from "and shall be binding" to "this Act".
47 & 48 Vict. c.31.	Colonial Prisoners Removal Act 1884.	Section 4(4) from "duly observed" onwards, except the words "laid before Parliament". In section 13(1), the words from "and every Order" onwards. In section 13(2), the words from "as soon as" (where first occurring) onwards.
47 & 48 Vict. c.55.	Pensions and Yeomanry Pay Act 1884.	In section 2(2), the words "as if enacted in this Act".
49 & 50 Vict. c.53.	Sea Fishing Boats (Scotland) Act 1886.	In section 14, the words from "and every such Order" onwards.
50 & 51 Vict. c.53	Escheat (Procedure) Act 1887.	In section 2(7), the words from "within" (where first occurring) onwards.
51 & 52 Vict. c.25.	Railway and Canal Traffic Act 1888.	In section 40(4), the words from "Any regulations" to "this Act".
52 & 53 Vict. c.53	Paymaster General Act 1889.	In section 1(2), the words from "within" (where first occurring) onwards.
53 & 54 Vict. c.27.	Colonial Courts of Admiralty Act 1890.	In section 7(1), in the proviso, the words "shall have full effect as if enacted in this Act, and". In section 14, the words from "and every such Order" onwards.
53 & 54 Vict. c.37.	Foreign Jurisdiction Act 1890.	In section 11, the words from "forthwith" (where first occurring) onwards.
55 & 56 Vict. c.6.	Colonial Probates Act 1892.	In section 4(1), the words from "as soon as" onwards.
55 & 56 Vict. c.23.	Foreign Marriage Act 1892.	In section 21(2), the words from "published" to "Stationery Office and" and from "and deemed" onwards.
57 & 58 Vict. c.2.	Behring Sea Award Act 1894.	In section 3(1), the words "this Act and" and from "and published" onwards.
57 & 58 Vict. c.28.	Notice of Accidents Act 1894.	In section 2(5), the words "in the London Gazette and" and "other". In sections 7 and 8, the words from "Every order" onwards.
57 & 58 Vict. c.60.	Merchant Shipping Act 1894.	In section 369(2), the words "published in the London Gazette" and "by an order published in like manner". Section 417(3). Section 479(2). In section 489, the words from "and those rules" onwards. In section 738(2), the words from "shall be published" to "Gazette, and" and from "within" (where first occurring) onwards. Section 738(3). Section 740.
58 & 59 Vict. c.21.	Seal Fisheries (North Pacific) Act 1985.	In section 6(1), the words "and published in the London Gazette".

Chapter	Short Title	Extent of Repeal
59 & 60 Vict. c.35.	Judicial Trustees Act 1896.	In section 4(2), the words from "have the same force" to "provided that".
59 & 60 Vict. c.48.	Light Railways Act 1896.	In section 10, the words from "shall have effect" to "Parliament, and".
2 Edw. 7. c.41.	Metropolis Water Act 1902.	In section 18(2)(*b*), the words from "and shall have effect" to "this Act".
3 Edw. 7. c.30.	Railways (Electrical Power) Act 1903.	Section 1(2).
8 Edw. 7. c.36.	Small Holdings and Allotments Act 1908.	In section 39(3), the words "and have effect as if enacted in this Act".
1 & 2 Geo. 5. c.28.	Official Secrets Act 1911.	In section 11, the words from "and the Order" to "in this Act".
3 & 4 Geo. 5. c.17.	Fabrics (Misdescription) Act 1913.	In section 2, the words from "as soon as" onwards.
4 & 5 Geo. 5. c.48.	Feudal Casualties (Scotland) Act 1914.	In section 23, the words from "and such Act of Sederunt" onwards.
5 & 6 Geo. 5. c.48.	Fishery Harbours Act 1915.	In section 2(3)(i), the words "and have effect as an Act of Parliament". In section 2(3)(ii) the words "as if enacted in this Act".
9 & 10 Geo. 5. c.51.	Checkweighing in Various Industries Act 1919.	In section 5(1), the words "and eighty-six". In Schedule 3, section 86 of the Factory and Workshop Act 1901.
10 & 11 Geo. 5. c.55.	Emergency Powers Act 1920.	In section 2(4), the words "shall have effect as if enacted in this Act, but".
11 & 12 Geo. 5. c.49.	War Pensions Act 1921.	In section 1(7), the words from "shall" to "Act, and". In section 9, the words "as if enacted in this Act".
13 & 14 Geo. 5. c.8.	Industrial Assurance Act 1923.	In section 43, the words from "If the Session" to the end of the section.
15 & 16 Geo. 5. c.21.	Land Registration Act 1925.	In section 126(5), the words from "All such regulations" to "this Act". In section 137(2), the words from "and any order" to "enacted in this Act".
16 & 17 Geo. 5. c.59.	Coroners (Amendment) Act 1926.	Section 12(6).
1 & 2 Geo. 6. c.22.	Trade Marks Act 1938.	Section 40(2). In section 40(4), the words from "if Parliament" onwards.
2 & 3 Geo. 6. c.69.	Import, Export and Customs Powers (Defence) Act 1939.	In section 2(3), the words from "as soon" onwards.
9 & 10 Geo. 6. c.17.	Police (Overseas Service) Act 1945.	In section 1(5), the words from "In reckoning" onwards. Section 1(6).
9 & 10 Geo. 6. c.36.	Statutory Instruments Act 1946.	Section 9(2).
9 & 10 Geo. 6. c.58.	Borrowing (Control and Guarantees) Act 1946.	Section 3(2) and (3)
9 & 10 Geo. 6. c.59.	Coal Industry Nationalisation Act 1946.	In section 62(2), the words from "In reckoning" onwards. Section 62(3).
10 & 11 Geo. 6. c.14.	Exchange Control Act 1947.	Section 36(3) and (4).
10 & 11 Geo. 6. c.54.	Electricity Act 1947.	Section 64(4) and (5).

PART XIII

MISCELLANEOUS

Chapter	Short Title	Extent of Repeal
17 Geo. 3. c.11.	Worsted Act 1776.	The whole Act.
33 & 34 Vict. c.69.	Statute Law Revision Act 1870.	The whole Act.
54 & 55 Vict. c.40.	Brine Pumping (Compensation for Subsidence) Act 1891.	In section 28, the words from "in accordance" to "1879".
59 & 60 Vict. c.48.	Light Railways Act 1896.	Section 5.
11 & 12 Geo. 5. c.55.	Railways Act 1921.	Section 70.
15 & 16 Geo. 5. c.24.	Universities and College Estates Act 1925.	In section 33(2), the words "the Augmentation of Benefices Act 1831 or", "by section 16 of the said Act of 1831 or" and the proviso.
23 & 24 Geo. 5. c.12.	Children and Young Persons Act 1933.	In section 107(1), the definition of "Metropolitan police court area".
26 Geo. 5 & 1 Edw. 8. c.44.	Air Navigation Act 1936.	The whole Act.
1 Edw. 8 & 1 Geo. 6. c.40.	Public Health (Drainage of Trade Premises) Act 1937.	In section 14(1), the definition of "joint sewerage authority".
1 Edw. 8 & 1 Geo. 6. c.48.	Methylated Spirits (Sale by Retail) (Scotland) Act 1937.	In section 2(1), the words from "(subject" to "licence)". Section 3.
1 & 2 Geo. 6. c.69.	Young Persons (Employment) Act 1938.	In section 7(1)(i), the words from "or of a licence" to "1952". In section 7(3)(a), the words from "(except" to "section)".
2 & 3 Geo. 6. c.31.	Civil Defence Act 1939.	In section 83(3), the words from "or in the case of grants" to "Minister of Health".
9 & 10 Geo. 6. c.17.	Police (Overseas Service) Act 1945.	Section 2(3). In section 3(1), in the definition of "Home police force", the words from "and in relation" to "constable".
8 & 9 Geo. 6. c.42.	Water Act 1945.	Section 41(9). In section 59(1), the definitions of "clerk" and "county district".
8 & 9 Geo. 6. c.43.	Requisitioned Land and War Works Act 1945.	Section 53(3).
9 & 10 Geo. 6. c.59.	Coal Industry Nationalisation Act 1946.	Section 50. In section 64(2), the words from "and for any reference" onwards.
10 & 11 Geo. 6 c.41.	Fire Services Act 1947.	In section 36(10), in the proviso, the words from "of any Defence Regulation" to "that Act".
11 & 12 Geo. 6. c.52.	Veterinary Surgeons Act 1948.	The whole Act.
12, 13 & 14 Geo. 6. c.5.	Civil Defence Act 1948.	Section 3(4). In section 6(1), the words from the beginning to "Air Raid Precautions Act 1937". Section 6(3).
3 & 4 Eliz. 2. c.27.	Public Libraries (Scotland) Act 1955.	Section 1.
6 & 7 Eliz. 2. c.67.	Water Act 1958.	The whole Act.

Chapter	Short Title	Extent of Repeal
9 & 10 Eliz. 2. c.34.	Factories Act 1961.	In Schedule 6, paragraph 3.
10 & 11 Eliz. 2. c.58.	Pipe-lines Act 1962.	In section 67(5), the proviso.
1963 c.37.	Children and Young Persons Act 1963.	In Schedule 3, paragraph 24.
1963 c.38.	Water Resources Act 1963.	Section 93(3) as it applies to Scotland. Section 134(6)(*a*) and (*b*). In section 137(2)(*a*), the reference to section 93(3).
1965 c.33.	Control of Office and Industrial Development Act 1965.	The whole Act.
1967 c.86.	Countryside (Scotland) Act 1967.	In section 60(7), paragraphs (*e*) and (*f*).
1968 c.65.	Gaming Act 1968.	Section 6(2)(*b*) and (*c*). Section 6(3)(*b*) and the preceding "or". In section 6(6)— (*a*) paragraph (*b*) and the preceding "or"; (*b*) the words "or to the Secretary of State, as the case may be". Section 7(3) and (4). In section 8(7), the words "or subsection (3)". In Schedule 9— (*a*) in paragraph 5(1)(*a*), the words "or (as the case may be) by the Secretary of State"; (*b*) in paragraphs 20(1)(*a*) and 20(2), the words "(not being the Secretary of State)".
1970 c.32.	Riding Establishments Act 1970.	In section 4, the proviso.
1971 c.40.	Fire Precautions Act 1971.	Section 27(2).
1971 c.65.	Licensing (Abolition of State Management) Act 1971.	The whole Act.
1971 c.77.	Immigration Act 1971.	Section 35(3), (4) and (5).
1972 c.52.	Town and Country Planning (Scotland) Act 1972.	In section 275(1), the proviso to the definition of "authority possessing compulsory purchase powers".
1974 c.37.	Health and Safety at Work etc. Act 1974.	Section 60(3).
1976 c.44.	Drought Act 1976.	Section 5(7). Schedule 3.
1982 c.13.	Fire Service College Board (Abolition) Act 1982.	The whole Act.
1982 c.25.	Iron and Steel Act 1982.	In Schedule 6, paragraph 3.
1982 c.51.	Mental Health (Amendment) Act 1982.	In section 70(2), the words from the beginning to "Northern Ireland and".
1983 c.2.	Representation of the People Act 1983.	In Schedule 8, paragraph 27.
1983 c.20.	Mental Health Act 1983.	In Schedule 4, paragraph 61(*a*).

Church Assembly Measure

6 & 7 Geo. 6. No. 3.	Diocesan Education Committees Measures 1943.	The whole Measure.

      SCHEDULE 2

CONSEQUENTIAL PROVISIONS

Sheriff Courts Consignations (Scotland) Act 1893

1. In section 7 of the Sheriff Courts Consignations (Scotland) Act 1893, for the words from "in each succeeding year" to "shall be made" there shall be substituted "in each year the sheriff clerk shall lodge with the Secretary of State a detailed return of unclaimed consignations".

Trade Marks Act 1938

2. After section 40 of the Trade Marks Act 1938 there shall be inserted the following section (which replaces section 82 of the Patents and Designs Act 1907)—

"Hours of business and excluded days

40A.—(1) Rules under section 40 of this Act may specify the hour at which the Patent Office shall be deemed to be closed on any day for purposes of the transaction by the public of business under this Act or of any class of such business, and may specify days as excluded days for any such purposes.

(2) Any business done under this Act on any day after the hour specified as aforesaid in relation to business of that class, or on a day which is an excluded day in relation to business of that class, shall be deemed to have been done on the next following day not being an excluded day; and where the time for doing anything under this Act expires on an excluded day, that time shall be extended to the next following day not being an excluded day."

Patents, Designs, Copyright and Trade Marks (Emergency) Act 1939

3. Section 6(1) of the Patents, Designs, Copyright and Trade Marks (Emergency) Act 1939 shall continue to have effect with the amendment made by section 6(2) of the Patents and Designs Act 1946, that is, with the substitution of "that the act was not done within the time so limited by reason that a person was on active service or by reason of" for "that the doing of the act within the time so limited was prevented by a person's being on active service or by".

Representation of the People Act 1948

4.—(1) In section 1 of the Representation of the People Act 1948 the following subsection shall be substituted for subsection (1)—

"(1) There shall for the purpose of parliamentary elections be the county and borough constituencies (or in Scotland the county and burgh constituencies), each returning a single member, which are described in Orders in Council made under the House of Commons (Redistribution of Seats) Acts 1949 to 1979."

(2) Neither sub-paragraph (1) above nor the repeal by this Act of Schedule 1 to the Representation of the People Act 1948 shall affect the constitution of the Northern Ireland Assembly in being at the commencement of this Act or any election to the Assembly before the next general election to the Assembly.

HIGHWAYS (AMENDMENT) ACT 1986

(1986 *c.* 13)

An Act to amend the Highways Act 1980 so as to impose penalties in cases where a user of a highway is injured, interrupted or endangered in consequence of the lighting of a fire on the highway or elsewhere.

[2nd May 1986]

PARLIAMENTARY DEBATES
Hansard H.C. Vol. 92, cols. 646, 1234; H.L. Vol. 472, cols. 11, 951; Vol. 473, col. 82; Vol. 474, col. 45.

Amendment of Highways Act 1980

1.—(1) The Highways Act 1980 shall be amended as follows.

(2) For section 161(2) (penalty for lighting a fire or discharging a firearm or firework within 50 feet of the centre of a highway) there shall be substituted the following subsection—

"(2) If a person without lawful authority or excuse—
> (*a*) lights any fire on or over a highway which consists of or comprises a carriageway; or
> (*b*) discharges any firearm or firework within 50 feet of the centre of such a highway,

and in consequence a user of the highway is injured, interrupted or endangered, that person is guilty of an offence and liable to a fine not exceeding level 3 on the standard scale.".

(3) After section 161 there shall be inserted the following section—

"Danger or annoyance caused by fires lit otherwise than on highways
161A.—(1) If a person—
> (*a*) lights a fire on any land not forming part of a highway which consists of or comprises a carriageway; or
> (*b*) directs or permits a fire to be lit on any such land,

and in consequence a user of any highway which consists of or comprises a carriageway is injured, interrupted or endangered by, or by smoke from, that fire or any other fire caused by that fire, that person is guilty of an offence and liable to a fine not exceeding level 5 on the standard scale.

(2) In any proceedings for an offence under this section it shall be a defence for the accused to prove—
> (*a*) that at the time the fire was lit he was satisfied on reasonable grounds that it was unlikely that users of any highway consisting of or comprising a carriageway would be injured, interrupted or endangered by, or by smoke from, that fire or any other fire caused by that fire; and
> (*b*) either—
>>   (i) that both before and after the fire was lit he did all he reasonably could to prevent users of any such highway from being so injured, interrupted or endangered, or
>>   (ii) that he had a reasonable excuse for not doing so.".

Short title, commencement etc.

2.—(1) This Act may be cited as the Highways (Amendment) Act 1986.

(2) This Act shall come into force at the end of the period of two months beginning with the date on which it is passed.

(3) Nothing in this Act shall apply in relation to any act done before this Act comes into force.

(4) This Act extends to England and Wales only.

ANIMALS (SCIENTIFIC PROCEDURES) ACT 1986

(1986 c.14)

ARRANGEMENT OF SECTIONS

Preliminary

An Act to make new provision for the protection of animals used for experimental or other scientific purposes.

[20th May 1986]

PARLIAMENTARY DEBATES

Hansard: H.L. Vol. 468, cols. 388, 991, 1002; Vol. 469, cols. 369, 411, 735, 755 and 1190; Vol. 470, col. 895; Vol. 474, cols. 587 and 606; H.C. Vol. 92, col. 81; Vol. 96, col. 77.
The Bill was considered by Standing Committee A on February 27 to March 25, 1986.

Protected animals

1.—(1) Subject to the provisions of this section, "a protected animal" for the purposes of this Act means any living vertebrate other than man.

(2) Any such vertebrate in its foetal, larval or embryonic form is a protected animal only from the stage of its development when—

(a) in the case of a mammal, bird or reptile, half the gestation or incubation period for the relevant species has elapsed; and

(b) in any other case, it becomes capable of independent feeding.

(3) The Secretary of State may by order—

(a) extend the definition of protected animal so as to include invertebrates of any description;

(b) alter the stage of development specified in subsection (2) above;

(c) make provision in lieu of subsection (2) above as respects any animal which becomes a protected animal by virtue of an order under paragraph (a) above.

(4) For the purposes of this section an animal shall be regarded as continuing to live until the permanent cessation of circulation or the destruction of its brain.

(5) In this section "vertebrate" means any animal of the Sub-phylum Vertebrata of the Phylum Chordata and "invertebrate" means any animal not of that Sub-phylum.

Regulated procedures

2.—(1) Subject to the provisions of this section, "a regulated procedure" for the purposes of this Act means any experimental or other scientific procedure applied to a protected animal which may have the effect of causing that animal pain, suffering, distress or lasting harm.

(2) An experimental or other scientific procedure applied to an animal is also a regulated procedure if—

(a) it is part of a series or combination of such procedures (whether the same or different) applied to the same animal; and

(b) the series or combination may have the effect mentioned in subsection (1) above; and

(c) the animal is a protected animal throughout the series or combination or in the course of it attains the stage of its development when it becomes such an animal.

(3) Anything done for the purpose of, or liable to result in, the birth or hatching of a protected animal is also a regulated procedure if it may as respects that animal have the effect mentioned in subsection (1) above.

(4) In determining whether any procedure may have the effect mentioned in subsection (1) above the use of an anaesthetic or analgesic, decerebration and any other procedure for rendering an animal insentient shall be disregarded; and the administration of an anaesthetic or analgesic to a protected animal, or decerebration or any other such procedure applied to such an animal, for the purposes of any experimental or other scientific procedure shall itself be a regulated procedure.

(5) The ringing, tagging or marking of an animal, or the application of any other humane procedure for the sole purpose of enabling an animal to be identified, is not a regulated procedure if it causes only momentary pain or distress and no lasting harm.

(6) The administration of any substance or article to an animal by way of a medicinal test on animals as defined in subsection (6) of section 32 of the Medicine Act 1968 is not a regulated procedure if the substance or article is administered in accordance with the provisions of subsection (4) of that section or of an order under section 35(8)(*b*) of that Act.

(7) Killing a protected animal is a regulated procedure only if it is killed for experimental or other scientific use, the place where it is killed is a designated establishment and the method employed is not one appropriate to the animal under Schedule 1 to this Act.

(8) In this section references to a scientific procedure do not include references to any recognised veterinary, agricultural or animal husbandry practice.

(9) Schedule 1 to this Act may be amended by orders made by the Secretary of State.

Personal and project licences

Prohibition of unlicensed procedures

3. No person shall apply a regulated procedure to an animal unless—
   (*a*) he holds a personal licence qualifying him to apply a regulated procedure of that description to an animal of that description;
   (*b*) the procedure is applied as part of a programme of work specified in a project licence authorising the application, as part of that programme, of a regulated procedure of that description to an animal of that description; and
   (*c*) the place where the procedure is carried out is a place specified in the personal licence and the project licence.

Personal licences

4.—(1) A personal licence is a licence granted by the Secretary of State qualifying the holder to apply specified regulated procedures to animals of specified descriptions at a specified place or specified places.

(2) An application for a personal licence shall be made to the Secretary of State in such form and shall be supported by such information as he may reasonably require.

(3) Except where the Secretary of State dispenses with the requirements of this subsection any such application shall be endorsed by a person who—
   (*a*) is himself the holder of a personal licence or a licence treated as such a licence by virtue of Schedule 4 to this Act; and
   (*b*) has knowledge of the biological or other relevant qualifications and of the training, experience and character of the applicant;
and the person endorsing an application shall, if practicable, be a person occupying a position of authority at a place where the applicant is to be authorised by the licence to carry out the procedures specified in it.

(4) No personal licence shall be granted to a person under the age of eighteen.

(5) A personal licence shall continue in force until revoked but the Secretary of State shall review each personal licence granted by him at intervals not exceeding five years and may for that purpose require the holder to furnish him with such information as he may reasonably require.

Project licences

5.—(1) A project licence is a licence granted by the Secretary of State specifying a programme of work and authorising the application, as part of that programme, of specified regulated procedures to animals of specified descriptions at a specified place or specified places.

(2) A project licence shall not be granted except to a person who undertakes overall responsibility for the programme to be specified in the licence.

(3) A project licence shall not be granted for any programme unless the Secretary of State is satisfied that it is undertaken for one or more of the following purposes—

(a) the prevention (whether by the testing of any product or otherwise) or the diagnosis or treatment of disease, ill-health or abnormality, or their effects, in man, animals or plants;

(b) the assessment, detection, regulation or modification of physiological conditions in man, animals or plants;

(c) the protection of the natural environment in the interests of the health or welfare of man or animals;

(d) the advancement of knowledge in biological or behavioural sciences;

(e) education or training otherwise than in primary or secondary schools;

(f) forensic enquiries;

(g) the breeding of animals for experimental or other scientific use.

(4) In determining whether and on what terms to grant a project licence the Secretary of State shall weigh the likely adverse effects on the animals concerned against the benefit likely to accrue as a result of the programme to be specified in the licence.

(5) The Secretary of State shall not grant a project licence unless he is satisfied that the applicant has given adequate consideration to the feasibility of achieving the purpose of the programme to be specified in the licence by means not involving the use of protected animals.

(6) The Secretary of State shall not grant a project licence authorising the use of cats, dogs, primates or equidae unless he is satisfied that animals of no other species are suitable for the purposes of the programme to be specified in the licence or that it is not practicable to obtain animals of any other species that are suitable for those purposes.

(7) Unless revoked and subject to subsection (8) below, a project licence shall continue in force for such period as is specified in the licence and may be renewed for further periods but (without prejudice to the grant of a new licence in respect of the programme in question) no such licence shall be in force for more than five years in all.

(8) A project licence shall terminate on the death of the holder but if—

(a) the holder of a certificate under section 6 below in respect of a place specified in the licence; or

(b) where by virtue of subsection (2) of that section the licence does not specify a place in respect of which there is such a certificate, the holder of a personal licence engaged on the programme in question,

notifies the Secretary of State of the holder's death within seven days of its coming to his knowledge the licence shall, unless the Secretary of State otherwise directs, continue in force until the end of the period of twenty-eight days beginning with the date of the notification.

Scientific procedure establishments

6.—(1) Subject to subsection (2) below, no place shall be specified in a project licence unless it is a place designated by a certificate issued by the Secretary of State under this section as a scientific procedure estabishment.

(2) Subsection (1) above shall not apply in any case in which it appears

to the Secretary of State that the programme or procedures authorised by the licence require him to specify a different place.

(3) An application for a certificate in respect of a scientific procedure establishment shall be made to the Secretary of State in such form and shall be supported by such information as he may reasonably require.

(4) A certificate shall not be issued under this section—

    (a) except to a person occupying a position of authority at the establishment in question; and

    (b) unless the application nominates for inclusion in the certificate pursuant to subsection (5) below a person or persons appearing to the Secretary of State to be suitable for that purpose.

(5) A certificate under this section shall specify—

    (a) a person to be responsible for the day-to-day care of the protected animals kept for experimental or other scientific purposes at the establishment; and

    (b) a veterinary surgeon or other suitably qualified person to provide advice on their health and welfare;

and the same person may, if the Secretary of State thinks fit, be specified under both paragraphs of this subsection.

(6) If it appears to any person specified in a certificate pursuant to subsection (5) above that the health or welfare of any such animal as is mentioned in that subsection gives rise to concern he shall—

    (a) notify the person holding a personal licence who is in charge of the animal; or

    (b) if there is no such person or it is not practicable to notify him, take steps to ensure that the animal is cared for and, if it is necessary for it to be killed, that it is killed by a method which is appropriate under Schedule 1 to this Act or approved by the Secretary of State.

(7) In any case to which subsection (6) above applies the person specified in the certificate pursuant to paragraph (a) of subsection (5) above may also notify the person (if different) specified pursuant to paragraph (b) of that subsection; and the person specified pursuant to either paragraph of that subsection may also notify one of the inspectors appointed under this Act.

(8) A certificate under this section shall continue in force until revoked.

Breeding and supplying establishments

7.—(1) A person shall not at any place breed for use in regulated procedures (whether there or elsewhere) protected animals of a description specified in Schedule 2 to this Act unless that place is designated by a certificate issued by the Secretary of State under this section as a breeding establishment.

(2) A person shall not at any place keep any such protected animals which have not been bred there but are to be supplied for use elsewhere in regulated procedures unless that place is designated by a certificate issued by the Secretary of State under this section as a supplying establishment.

(3) An application for a certificate in respect of a breeding or supplying establishment shall be made to the Secretary of State in such form and shall be supported by such information as he may reasonably require.

(4) A certificate shall not be issued under this section unless the application nominates for inclusion in the certificate pursuant to subsection (5) below a person or persons appearing to the Secretary of State to be suitable for that purpose.

(5) A certificate under this section shall specify—

    (a) a person to be responsible for the day-to-day care of the animals bred or kept for breeding at the establishment or, as the case may be, kept there for the purpose of being supplied for use in regulated procedures; and

(b) a veterinary surgeon or other suitably qualified person to provide advice on their health and welfare;

and the same person may, if the Secretary of State thinks fit, be specified under both paragraphs of this subsection.

(6) If it appears to any person specified in a certificate pursuant to subsection (5) above that the health or welfare of any such animal as is mentioned in that subsection gives rise to concern he shall take steps to ensure that it is cared for and, if it is necessary for it to be killed, that it is killed by a method appropriate under Schedule 1 to this Act or approved by the Secretary of State.

(7) In any case to which subsection (6) above applies the person specified in the certificate pursuant to paragraph (a) of subsection (5) above may also notify the person (if different) specified pursuant to paragraph (b) of that subsection; and the person specified pursuant to either paragraph of that subsection may also notify one of the inspectors appointed under this Act.

(8) A certificate under this section shall continue in force until revoked.

(9) Schedule 2 to this Act may be amended by orders made by the Secretary of State.

8. The holder of a certificate issued under section 6 or 7 above shall pay such periodical fees to the Secretary of State as may be prescribed by or determined in accordance with an order made by him.

Licences and designation certificates: general provisions

Consultation

9.—(1) Before granting a licence or issuing a certificate under this Act the Secretary of State shall consult one of the inspectors appointed under this Act and may also consult an independent assessor or the Animal Procedures Committee established by this Act.

(2) Where the Secretary of State proposes to consult an independent assessor he shall notify the applicant of that fact, and in selecting the assessor he shall have regard to any representations made by the applicant.

Conditions

10.—(1) Subject to the provisions of this section, a licence or certificate under this Act may contain such conditions as the Secretary of State thinks fit.

(2) The conditions of a personal licence shall include—

(a) a condition to the effect that the holder shall take precautions to prevent or reduce to the minimum consistent with the purposes of the authorised procedures any pain, distress or discomfort to the animals to which those procedures may be applied; and

(b) an inviolable termination condition, that is to say, a condition specifying circumstances in which a protected animal which is being or has been subjected to a regulated procedure must in every case be immediately killed by a method appropriate to the animal under Schedule 1 to this Act or by such other method as may be authorised by the licence.

(3) The conditions of a project licence shall, unless the Secretary of State considers that an exception is justified, include a condition to the effect—

(a) that no cat or dog shall be used under the licence unless it has been bred at and obtained from a designated breeding establishment; and

(b) that no other protected animal of a description specified in Schedule 2 to this Act shall be used under the licence unless it has been bred at a designated breeding establishment or obtained from a designated supplying establishment;

but no exception shall be made from the condition required by paragraph (a) above unless the Secretary of State is satisfied that no animal suitable for the purpose of the programme specified in the licence can be obtained in accordance with that condition.

(4) If the conditions of a personal licence permit the holder to use assistants to perform, under his direction, tasks not requiring technical knowledge nothing done by an assistant in accordance with such a condition shall constitute a contravention of section 3 above.

(5) The conditions of a certificate issued under section 6 above shall include a condition prohibiting the killing otherwise than by a method which is appropriate under Schedule 1 to this Act or approved by the Secretary of State of any protected animal kept at the establishment for experimental or other scientific purposes but not subjected to a regulated procedure or required to be killed by virtue of section 15 below; and the conditions of a certificate issued under section 7 above shall include a condition prohibiting the killing otherwise than by such a method of an animal of a description specified in Schedule 2 to this Act which is bred or kept for breeding or, as the case may be, kept at the establishment for the purposes of being supplied for use in regulated procedures but not used, or supplied for use, for that purpose.

(6) The conditions of a certificate issued under section 6 or 7 above shall include conditions requiring the holder of the certificate—

(a) to secure that a person competent to kill animals in the manner specified by conditions imposed in accordance with subsection (5) above will be available to do so; and

(b) to keep records as respects the source and disposal of and otherwise relating to the animals kept at the establishment for experimental or other scientific purposes or, as the case may be, bred or kept for breeding there or kept there for the purposes of being supplied for use in regulated procedures.

(7) Breach of a condition in a licence or certificate shall not invalidate the licence or certificate but shall be a ground for its variation or revocation.

Variation and revocation

11. A licence or certificate under this Act may be varied or revoked by the Secretary of State—

(a) on the ground mentioned in section 10(7) above;

(b) in any other case in which it appears to the Secretary of State appropriate to do so; or

(c) at the request of the holder.

Right to make representations

12.—(1) Where the Secretary of State proposes—

(a) to refuse a licence or certificate under this Act; or

(b) to vary or revoke such a licence or certificate otherwise than at the request of the holder,

he shall serve on the applicant or the holder a notice of his intention to do so.

(2) The notice shall state the reasons for which the Secretary of State

proposes to act and give particulars of the rights conferred by subsection (3) below.

(3) A person on whom a notice is served under subsection (1) above may make written representations and, if desired, oral representations to a person appointed for that purpose by the Secretary of State if before such date as is specified in the notice (not being less than twenty-eight days after the date of service) he notifies the Secretary of State of his wish to do so.

(4) The holder of a licence or certificate who is dissatisfied with any condition contained in it may, if he notifies the Secretary of State of his wish to do so, make written representations and, if desired, oral representations to a person appointed for that purpose by the Secretary of State; but the making of such representations shall not affect the operation of any condition unless and until it is varied under section 11 above.

(5) The person appointed to receive any representations under this section shall be a person who holds or has held judicial office in the United Kingdom or a barrister, solicitor or advocate of at least seven years' standing and the Secretary of State may, if he thinks fit, appoint a person with scientific or other appropriate qualifications to assist the person receiving the representations in his consideration of them.

(6) The person appointed to receive any such representations shall after considering them make a report to the Secretary of State; and the Secretary of State shall furnish a copy of the report to the person who made the representations and take it into account in deciding whether to refuse the application or to vary or revoke the licence or certificate, as the case may be.

(7) The Secretary of State may by order make rules with respect to the procedure to be followed in the making and consideration of representations under this section, including provision requiring any such representations to be made within a specified time.

(8) A notice under subsection (1) above may be served either personally or by post.

Suspension in cases of urgency

13.—(1) If it appears to the Secretary of State to be urgently necessary for the welfare of any protected animals that a licence or certificate under this Act should cease to have effect forthwith he shall by notice served on the holder suspend its operation for a period not exceeding three months.

(2) If during that period a notice of proposed variation or revocation of the licence or certificate is served under section 12 above but at the end of that period—

(a) the time for notifying the Secretary of State under subsection (3) of that section has not expired; or

(b) representations are to be or are being made in accordance with that subsection; or

(c) such representations have been made but the Secretary of State has not received or has not completed his consideration of the report of the person to whom the representations were made,

he may by notice served on the holder further suspend the licence or certificate until he is able to decide whether to vary or revoke it but no further suspension shall be for longer than three months at a time.

(3) A notice under this section may be served personally or by post.

Additional controls

Re-use of protected animals

14.—(1) Where a protected animal—

(*a*) has been subjected to a series of regulated procedures for a particular purpose; and

(*b*) has been given a general anaesthetic for any of those procedures and allowed to recover consciousness,

it shall not be used for any further regulated procedures.

(2) Subsection (1) above shall not preclude the use of an animal with the consent of the Secretary of State if—

(*a*) the procedure, or each procedure, for which the anaesthetic was given consisted only of surgical preparation essential for a subsequent procedure; or

(*b*) the anaesthetic was administered soley to immobilise the animal; or

(*c*) the animal is under general anaestheia throughout the further procedures and not allowed to recover consciousness.

(3) Where a protected animal—

(*a*) has been subjected to a series of regulated procedures for a particular purpose; but

(*b*) has not been given a general anaesthetic for any of those procedures.

it shall not be used for any further regulated procedures except with the consent of the Secretary of State.

(4) Any consent for the purposes of this section may relate to a specified animal or to animals used in specified procedures or specified circumstances.

Killing animals at conclusion of regulated procedures

15.—(1) Where a protected animal—

(*a*) has been subjected to a series of regulated procedures for a particular purpose; and

(*b*) at the conclusion of the series is suffering or likely to suffer adverse effects,

the person who applied those procedures, or the last of them, shall cause the animal to be immediately killed by a method appropriate to the animal under Schedule 1 to this Act or by such other method as may be authorised by the personal licence of the person by whom the animal is killed.

(2) Subsection (1) above is without prejudice to any condition of a project licence requiring an animal to be killed at the conclusion of a regulated procedure in circumstances other than those mentioned in that subsection.

Prohibition of public displays

16.—(1) No person shall carry out any regulated procedure as an exhibition to the general public or carry out any such procedure which is shown live on television for general reception.

(2) No person shall publish a notice or advertisement announcing the carrying out of any regulated procedure in a manner that would contravene subsection (1) above.

Neuro-muscular blocking agents

17. No person shall in the course of a regulated procedure—

(*a*) use any neuromuscular blocking agent unless expressly authorised to do so by the personal and project licences under which the procedure is carried out; or

(*b*) use any such agent instead of an anaesthetic.

The inspectorate and the committee

Inspectors

18.—(1) The Secretary of State shall, with the consent of the Treasury as to number and remuneration, appoint as inspectors for the purposes of this Act persons having such medical or veterinary qualifications as he thinks requisite.

(2) It shall be the duty of an inspector—

(*a*) to advise the Secretary of State on applications for personal and project licences, on requests for their variation or revocation and on their periodical review;

(*b*) to advise him on applications for certificates under this Act and on requests for their variation or revocation;

(*c*) to visit places where regulated procedures are carried out for the purpose of determining whether those procedures are authorised by the requisite licences and whether the conditions of those licences are being complied with;

(*d*) to visit designated establishments for the purpose of determining whether the conditions of the certificates in respect of those establishments are being complied with;

(*e*) to report to the Secretary of State any case in which any provision of this Act or any condition of a licence or certificate under this Act has not been or is not being complied with and to advise him on the action to be taken in any such case.

(3) If an inspector considers that a protected animal is undergoing excessive suffering he may require it to be immediately killed by a method appropriate to the animal under Schedule 1 to this Act or by such other method as may be authorised by any personal licence held by the person to whom the requirement is addressed.

The Animal Procedures Committee

19.—(1) There shall be a committee to be known as the Animal Procedures Committee.

(2) The Committee shall consist of a chairman and at least twelve other members appointed by the Secretary of State.

(3) Of the members other than the chairman—

(*a*) at least two-thirds shall be persons having such a qualification as is mentioned in subsection (4) below; and

(*b*) at least one shall be a barrister, solicitor or advocate,

but so that at least half of those members are persons who neither hold nor within the previous six years have held any licence under this Act or under the Cruelty to Animals Act 1876; and in making appointments to the Committee the Secretary of State shall have regard to the desirability of ensuring that the interests of animal welfare are adequately represented.

(4) The qualifications referred to in subsection (3)(*a*) above are full registration as a medical practitioner, registration as a veterinary surgeon or qualifications or experience in a biological subject approved by the Secretary of State as relevant to the work of the Committee.

(5) Members of the Committee shall be appointed for such periods as the Secretary of State may determine but no such period shall exceed four years and no person shall be re-appointed more than once.

(6) Any member may resign by notice in writing to the Secretary of State; and the chairman may by such a notice resign his office as such.

(7) The Secretary of State may terminate the appointment of a member if he is satisfied that—

(*a*) for a period of six months beginning not more than nine months previously he has, without the consent of the other members, failed to attend the meetings of the Committee;

(*b*) he is an undischarged bankrupt or has made an arrangement with his creditors;

(*c*) he is by reason of physical or mental illness, or for any other reason, incapable of carrying out his duties; or

(*d*) he has been convicted of such a criminal offence, or his conduct has been such, that it is not in the Secretary of State's opinion fitting that he should remain a member.

(8) The Secretary of State may make payments to the chairman by way of remuneration and make payments to him and the other members in respect of expenses incurred by them in the performance of their duties.

(9) The Secretary of State may also defray any other expenses of the Committee.

Functions of the Committee

20.—(1) It shall be the duty of the Animal Procedures Committee to advise the Secretary of State on such matters concerned with this Act and his functions under it as the Committee may determine or as may be referred to the Committee by the Secretary of State.

(2) In its consideration of any matter the Committee shall have regard both to the legitimate requirements of science and industry and to the protection of animals against avoidable suffering and unnecessary use in scientific procedures.

(3) The Committee may perform any of its functions by means of sub-committees and may co-opt as members of any sub-committee any persons considered by the Committee to be able to assist that sub-committee in its work.

(4) The Committee may promote research relevant to its functions and may obtain advice or assistance from other persons with knowledge or experience appearing to the Committee to be relevant to those functions.

(5) The Committee shall in each year make a report on its activities to the Secretary of State who shall lay copies of the report before Parliament.

Miscellaneous and Supplementary

Guidance, codes of practice and statistics

21.—(1) The Secretary of State shall publish information to serve as guidance with respect to the manner in which he proposes to exercise his power to grant licences and certificates under this Act and with respect to the conditions which he proposes to include in such licences and certificates.

(2) The Secretary of State shall issue codes of practice as to the care of protected animals and their use for regulated procedures and may approve such codes issued by other persons.

(3) The Secretary of State shall consult the Animal Procedures Committee before publishing or altering any information under subsection (1) above or issuing, approving, altering or approving any alteration in any code issued or approved under subsection (2) above.

(4) A failure on the part of any person to comply with any provision of a code issued or approved under subsection (2) above shall not of itself render that person liable to criminal or civil proceedings but—

(*a*) any such code shall be admissible in evidence in any such proceedings; and

(*b*) if any of its provisions appears to the court conducting the proceedings to be relevant to any question arising in the proceedings it shall be taken into account in determining that question.

(5) The Secretary of State shall lay before Parliament—

(a) copies of any information published or code issued by him under subsection (1) or (2) above and of any alteration made by him in any such information or code; and

(b) copies of any code approved by him under subsection (2) above and of any alteration approved by him in any such code;

and if either House of Parliament passes a resolution requiring the information, code or alteration mentioned in paragraph (a) above, or the approval mentioned in paragraph (b) above, to be withdrawn the Secretary of State shall withdraw it accordingly; and where he withdraws information published or a code issued by him or his approval of a code he shall publish information or issue or approve a code, as the case may be, in substitution for the information or code previously published, issued or approved.

(6) No resolution shall be passed by either House under subsection (5) above in respect of any information, code or alteration after the end of the period of forty days beginning with the day on which a copy of the information, code or alteration was laid before that House; but for the purposes of this subsection no account shall be taken of any time during which Parliament is dissolved or prorogued or during which both Houses are adjourned for more than four days.

(7) The Secretary of State shall in each year publish and lay before Parliament such information as he considers appropriate with respect to the use of protected animals in the previous year for experimental purposes.

Penalties for contraventions

22.—(1) Any person who contravenes section 3 above shall be guilty of an offence and liable—

(a) on conviction on indictment, to imprisonment for a term not exceeding two years or to a fine or to both:

(b) on summary conviction, to imprisonment for a term not exceeding six months or to a fine not exceeding the statutory maximum or to both.

(2) Any person who, being the holder of a project licence—

(a) procures or knowingly permits a person under his control to carry out a regulated procedure otherwise than as part of the programme specified in the licence; or

(b) procures or knowingly permits a person under his control to carry out a regulated procedure otherwise than in accordance with that person's personal licence,

shall be guilty of an offence and liable to the penalties specified in subsection (1) above.

(3) Any person who—

(a) contravenes section 7(1) or (2), 14, 15, 16 or 17 above; or

(b) fails to comply with a requirement imposed on him under section 18(3) above,

shall be guilty of an offence and liable on summary conviction to imprisonment for a term not exceeding three months or to a fine not exceeding the fourth level on the standard scale or to both.

(4) A person shall not be guilty of an offence under section 3 or 17(a) above by reason only that he acted without the authority of a project licence if he shows that he reasonably believed, after making due enquiry, that he had such authority.

(5) A person guilty of an offence under section 1 of the Protection of Animals Act 1911 or section 1 of the Protection of Animals (Scotland) Act 1912 in respect of an animal at a designated establishment shall be liable to the penalties specified in subsection (1) above.

False statements

23.—(1) A person is guilty of an offence if for the purpose of obtaining or assisting another person to obtain a licence or certificate under this Act he furnishes information which he knows to be false or misleading in a material particular or recklessly furnishes information which is false or misleading in a material particular.

(2) A person guilty of an offence under this section shall be liable on summary conviction to imprisonment for a term not exceeding three months or to a fine not exceeding the fourth level on the standard scale or to both.

Protection of confidential information

24.—(1) A person is guilty of an offence if otherwise than for the purpose of discharging his functions under this Act he discloses any information which has been obtained by him in the exercise of those functions and which he knows or has reasonable grounds for believing to have been given in confidence.

(2) A person guilty of an offence under this section shall be liable—

(*a*) on conviction on indictment, to imprisonment for a term not exceeding two years or to a fine or to both;

(*b*) on summary conviction, to imprisonment for a term not exceeding six months or to a fine not exceeding the statutory maximum or to both.

Powers of entry

25.—(1) If a justice of the peace or in Scotland a sheriff is satisfied by information on oath that there are reasonable grounds for believing that an offence under this Act has been or is being committed at any place, he may issue a warrant authorising a constable to enter that place if need be by such force as is reasonably necessary, to search it and to require any person found there to give his name and address.

(2) A warrant under this section may authorise a constable to be accompanied by an inspector appointed under this Act and shall require him to be accompanied by such an inspector if the place in question is a designated establishment.

(3) Any person who—

(*a*) intentionally obstructs a constable or inspector in the exercise of his powers under this section; or

(*b*) refuses on demand to give his name and address or gives a false name or address

shall be guilty of an offence and liable on summary conviction to imprisonment for a term not exceeding three months or to a fine not exceeding the fourth level on the standard scale or to both.

Prosecutions

26.—(1) No proceedings for—

(*a*) an offence under this Act; or

(*b*) an offence under section 1 of the Protection of Animals Act 1911 which is alleged to have been committed in respect of an animal at a designated establishment,

shall be brought in England and Wales except by or with the consent of the Director of Public Prosecutions.

(2) Summary proceedings for an offence under this Act may (without prejudice to any jurisdiction exercisable apart from this subsection) be taken against any person at any place at which he is for the time being.

(3) Notwithstanding anything in section 127(1) of the Magistrates' Courts Act 1980, an information relating to an offence under this Act which is triable by a magistrates' court in England and Wales may be so tried if it is laid at any time within three years after the commission of the offence and within six months after the date on which evidence sufficient in the opinion of the Director of Public Prosecutions to justify the proceedings comes to his knowledge.

(4) Notwithstanding anything in section 331 of the Criminal Procedure (Scotland) Act 1975, summary proceedings for an offence under this Act may be commenced in Scotland at any time within three years after the commission of the offence and within six months after the date on which evidence sufficient in the opinion of the Lord Advocate to justify the proceedings comes to his knowledge; and subsection (3) of that section shall apply for the purposes of this subsection as it applies for the purposes of that section.

(5) For the purposes of subsections (3) and (4) above a certificate of the Director of Public Prosecutions or, as the case may be, the Lord Advocate as to the date on which such evidence as is there mentioned came to his knowledge shall be conclusive evidence of that fact.

Repeal, consequential amendments and transitional provisions

27.—(1) The Cruelty to Animals Act 1876 is hereby repealed.

(2) The enactments mentioned in Schedule 3 to this Act shall have effect with the amendments there specified, being amendments consequential on the provisions of this Act.

(3) The Breeding of Dogs Act 1973 shall not apply to the breeding of dogs for use in regulated procedures if they are bred at a designated establishment.

(4) Schedule 4 to this Act shall have effect with respect to the transitional matters there mentioned.

(5) The Secretary of State may by order make such further transitional provisions as he considers necessary or expedient.

Orders

28.—(1) Any power of the Secretary of State to make an order under this Act shall be exercisable by statutory instrument.

(2) A statutory instrument containing an order under any of the foregoing provisions of this Act shall be subject to annulment in pursuance of a resolution of either House of Parliament.

Application to Northern Ireland

29.—(1) This Act applies to Northern Ireland with the following modifications.

(2) For any reference to the Secretary of State in any provision of this Act except sections 19 and 20(1) there shall be substituted a reference to the Department of Health and Social Services for Northern Ireland; and for the reference in section 18(1) above to the Treasury there shall be substituted a reference to the Department of Finance and Personnel for Northern Ireland.

(3) The functions of the Secretary of State under sections 19 and 20(1) shall be exercisable by him jointly with the Department of Health and Social Services for Northern Ireland; and any notice under section 19(6) or advice under section 20(1) may be given to either of them.

(4) In section 20(5) above for the reference to Parliament there shall be substituted a reference to the Northern Ireland Assembly; and in section 21 above—

(*a*) for the references to Parliament or either House of Parliament there shall be substituted references to the Assembly;

(*b*) in subsection (5) after the word "if" there shall be inserted the words "within the statutory period (within the meaning of the Interpretation Act (Northern Ireland) 1954)"; and

(*c*) subsection (6) shall be omitted.

(5) In sections 22(5) and 26(1)(*b*) above for the references to section 1 of the Protection of Animals Act 1911 there shall be substituted references to sections 13 and 14 of the Welfare of Animals Act (Northern Ireland) 1972.

(6) In section 25(1) above for the reference to information on oath there shall be substituted a reference to a complaint on oath.

(7) In section 26 above—

(*a*) in subsections (1) and (3) for the words "England and Wales" there shall be subtituted the words "Northern Ireland";

(*b*) in subsections (1), (3) and (5) for the references to the Director of Public Prosecutions there shall be substituted references to the Director of Public Prosecutions for Northern Ireland; and

(*c*) in subsection (3) for the reference to section 127(1) of the Magistrates' Courts Act 1980 there shall be substituted a reference to Article 19(1) of the Magistrates' Courts (Northern Ireland) Order 1981.

(8) In section 27(3) above for the reference to the Breeding of Dogs Act 1973 there shall be substituted a reference to Articles 12, 13 and 43 of the Dogs (Northern Ireland) Order 1983.

(9) Section 28 above shall not apply and any order made by the Department of Health and Social Services for Northern Ireland under this Act shall be a statutory rule for the purposes of the Statutory Rules (Northern Ireland) Order 1979 and shall be subject to negative resolution within the meaning of section 41(6) of the Interpretation Act (Northern Ireland) 1954.

Short title, interpretation and commencement

30.—(1) This Act may be cited as the Animals (Scientific Procedures) Act 1986.

(2) In this Act—

"designated", in relation to an establishment, means designated by a certificate under section 6 or 7 above;

"personal licence" means a licence granted under section 4 above;

"place" includes any place within the seaward limits of the territorial waters of the United Kingdom, including any vessel other than a ship which is not a British ship;

"project licence" means a licence granted under section 5 above;

"protected animal" has the meaning given in section 1 above but subject to any order under subsection (3) of that section;

"regulated procedure" has the meaning given in section 2 above.

(3) This Act shall come into force on such a date as the Secretary of State may by order appoint; and different dates may be appointed for different provisions or different purposes.

SCHEDULES

**Sections 2, 6, 7, 10,
15(1) and 18(3).**   SCHEDULE 1

STANDARD METHODS OF HUMANE KILLING

Method	*Animals for which appropriate*
A. *Animals other than foetal, larval and embryonic forms*	
1. Overdose of anaesthetic suitable for the species—	
(i) by injection	(i) All animals
(ii) by inhalation	(ii) All animals up to 1kg bodyweight except reptiles, diving birds and diving mammals.
(iii) by immersion.	(iii) Fishes Amphybia up to 250g bodyweight.
(Followed by destruction of the brain in cold-blooded vertebrates and by exsanguination or by dislocation of the neck in warm blooded vertebrates except where *rigor mortis* has been confirmed).	
2. Dislocation of the neck.	Rodents up to 500g bodyweight other than guinea-pigs.
(Followed by destruction of the brain in fishes).	Guinea-pigs and lagomorphs up to 1kg bodyweight. Birds up to 3kg bodyweight. Fishes up to 250g bodyweight.
3. Concussion by striking the back of the head.	Rodents up to 1kg bodyweight. Birds up to 250g bodyweight. Fishes.
(Followed by exsanguination or dislocation of the neck in rodents and birds and destruction of the brain in fishes).	
4. Decapitation followed by destruction of the brain.	Cold-blooded vertebrates.
5. Exposure to carbon dioxide in a rising concentration using a suitable technique followed by exsanguination or by dislocation of the neck except where *rigor mortis* has been confirmed.	Rodents over 10 days of age up to 1½kg bodyweight. Birds over 1 week of age up to 3kg bodyweight.
B. *Foetal, larval and embryonic forms*	
1. Overdose of anaesthetic suitable for the species—	
(i) by injection	(i) All animals.
(ii) by immersion.	(ii) Fishes Amphibia.
2. Decapitation.	Mammals.

14–16

SCHEDULE 2

ANIMALS TO BE OBTAINED ONLY FROM DESIGNATED BREEDING OR SUPPLYING ESTABLISHMENTS

Mouse
Rat
Guinea-pig
Hamster
Rabbit
Dog
Cat
Primate

SCHEDULE 3

CONSEQUENTIAL AMENDMENTS

1. In section 1(3) of the Protection of Animals Act 1911 for the words "the Cruelty to Animals Act 1876" there shall be substituted the words "the Animals (Scientific Procedures) Act 1986".

2. In section 1(3) of the Protection of Animals (Scotland) Act 1912 for the words "the Cruelty to Animals Act 1876" there shall be substituted the words "the Animals (Scientific Procedures) Act 1986".

3. In paragraph 1 of Schedule 1 to the Protection of Animals (Anaesthetics) Act 1954 for the words "Any experiment duly authorised under the Cruelty to Animals Act 1876" there shall be substituted the words "Any procedure duly authorised under the Animals (Scientific Procedures) Act 1986".

4. In section 12 of the Pests Act 1954 for the words "any experiment duly authorised under the Cruelty to Animals Act 1876" there shall be substituted the words "any procedure duly authorised under the Animals (Scientific Procedures) Act 1986".

5. In section 19(4)(*a*) of the Veterinary Surgeons Act 1966 for the words "any experiment duly authorised under the Cruelty to Animals Act 1876" there shall be substituted the words "any procedure duly authorised under the Animals (Scientific Procedures) Act 1986".

6. In section 1(2A)(*b*) of the Slaughter of Poultry Act 1967 for the words "an experiment in respect of which restrictions are imposed by the Cruelty to Animals Act 1876, being an experiment performed subject to any restrictions so imposed" there shall be substituted the words "a procedure duly authorised under the Animals (Scientific Procedures) Act 1986".

7. In section 1(2) of the Agriculture (Miscellaneous Provisions) Act 1968 for the words "the Cruelty to Animals Act 1876" there shall be substituted the words "the Animals (Scientific Procedures) Act 1986".

8. In sections 1(2) and 15(*a*) of, and paragraph 1 of Schedule 1 to, the Welfare of Animals Act (Northern Ireland) 1972 for the words "the Cruelty to Animals Act 1876" there shall be substituted the words "the Animals (Scientific Procedures) Act 1986".

9. In section 8(3) of the Badgers Act 1973 for the words from "something done" onwards there shall be substituted the words "doing anything which is authorised under the Animals (Scientific Procedures) Act 1986".

10. In section 5(4) of the Dangerous Wild Animals Act 1976 for the words "registered pursuant to the Cruelty to Animals Act 1876 for the purpose of performing experiments" there shall be substituted the words "which is a designated establishment within the meaning of the Animals (Scientific Procedures) Act 1986".

SCHEDULE 4

TRANSITIONAL PROVISONS

Existing licences

1. Any licence which immediately before the coming into force of section 3 of this Act is in force under the Cruelty to Animals Act 1876 (in this Schedule referred to as "the previous Act") shall until such date as it would have expired under that Act be treated for the purposes of this Act as if it were a personal licence.

Current experiments

2.—(1) Subject to sub-paragraph (2) below, any experiment or series of experiments which is lawfully in progress under the previous Act immediately before the coming into force of section 3 of this Act shall be treated for the purposes of this Act as authorised by a project licence.

(2) The Secretary of State may direct that sub-paragraph (1) above shall cease to have effect on such a date as he may specify; and different dates may be specified in relation to different cases.

Existing certificates

3. A person shall not by virtue of paragraphs 1 or 2 above be entitled to do anything which would have been unlawful under the previous Act without such a certificate as is mentioned in paragraph (2) or (3) of the proviso to section 3 of that Act or in section 5 of that Act unless immediately before the coming into force of section 3 of this Act he holds the appropriate certificate under that Act.

Registered premises

4. Until such date as the Secretary of State may direct there shall be treated as a designated scientific procedure establishment for the purposes of this Act any place registered under the previous Act or approved by the Secretary of State.

Inspectors

5. Any person who at the coming into force of section 18 of this Act holds office as an inspector under the previous Act shall be treated for the purposes of this Act as an inspector appointed under that section.

INDUSTRIAL TRAINING ACT 1986

(1986 c. 15)

An Act to make provision with respect to the functions of industrial training boards.

[20th May 1986]

Parliamentary Debates
Hansard: H.C. Vol. 91, col. 611; Vol. 92, col. 1234; H.L. Vol. 472, cols. 11, 1350; Vol. 474, cols. 587, 1039.

Training overseas or for overseas employment

1.—(1) For subsection (1) of section 10 of the Industrial Training Act 1982 (training for employment overseas) there shall be substituted the following subsections—

"(1) An industrial training board may, with the consent of the Commission given with the approval of the Secretary of State, exercise such functions in connection with training for employment in a similar industry outside Great Britain as are exercisable by it under the relevant provisions in connection with the training of persons employed or intending to be employed in the industry in Great Britain.

(1A) In subsection (1) above 'the relevant provisions' means—
(a) in relation to the training of persons in Great Britain, section 5(1), (3)(d) and (4) above; and
(b) in relation to the training of persons outside Great Britain, paragraphs (a), (c), (d), (e), (f) and (g) of section 5(1) and paragraph (d) of section 5(3) above."

(2) In section 5 of that Act (general functions of boards), after subsection (6), there shall be inserted the following subsection—

"(7) The functions conferred by this section which are exercisable outside Great Britain are those which are exercisable under provisions of it which are applied by section 10(1A) below in connection with the training of persons outside Great Britain under that section."

Short title and commencement

2.—(1) This Act may be cited as the Industrial Training Act 1986.
(2) This Act shall come into force at the end of the period of two months beginning on the day on which it is passed.

MARRIAGE (PROHIBITED DEGREES OF RELATIONSHIP) ACT 1986

(1986 c.16)

An Act to make further provision with regard to the marriage of persons
related by affinity.

[20th May 1986]

PARLIAMENT
  Hansard: H.L. Vol. 468, col. 555; Vol. 469, col. 39; Vol. 470, col. 932; Vol. 471, col. 883;
Vol. 472, col. 1253; H.C. Vol. 97, col. 1029.

Marriage between certain persons related by affinity not to be void

1.—(1) A marriage solemnized after the commencement of this Act
between a man and a woman who is the daughter or granddaughter of a
former spouse of his (whether the former spouse is living or not) or who
is the former spouse of his father or grandfather (whether his father or
grandfather is living or not) shall not be void by reason only of that
relationship if both the parties have attained the age of twenty-one at the
time of the marriage and the younger party has not at any time before
attaining the age of eighteen been a child of the family in relation to the
other party.

(2) A marriage solemnized after the commencement of this Act
between a man and a woman who is the grandmother of a former spouse
of his (whether the former spouse is living or not) or is a former spouse
of his grandson (whether his grandson is living or not) shall not be void
by reason only of that relationship.

(3) A marriage solemnized after the commencement of this Act
between a man and a woman who is the mother of a former spouse of his
shall not be void by reason only of that relationship if the marriage is
solemnized after the death of both that spouse and the father of that
spouse and after both the parties to the marriage have attained the age of
twenty-one.

(4) A marriage solemnized after the commencement of this Act
between a man and a woman who is a former spouse of his son shall not
be void by reason only of that relationship if the marriage is solemnized
after the death of both his son and the mother of his son and after both
the parties to the marriage have attained the age of twenty-one.

(5) In this section "child of the family" in relation to any person, means
a child who has lived in the same household as that person and been
treated by that person as a child of his family.

(6) The Marriage Act 1949 shall have effect subject to the amendments
specified in the Schedule to this Act, being amendments consequential on
the preceding provisions of this section.

(7) Where, apart from this Act, any matter affecting the validity of a
marriage would fall to be determined (in accordance with the rules of
private international law) by reference to the law of a country outside
England and Wales nothing in this Act shall preclude the determination
of that matter in accordance with that law.

(8) Nothing in this section shall affect any marriage solemnized before
the commencement of this Act.

Marriage between certain persons related by affinity—Scotland

2. Schedule 2 (which amends the Marriage (Scotland) Act 1977 so as to
permit—

(*a*) the marriage of a man and a woman who is the grandmother of a former spouse of his or is a former spouse of his grandson;

(*b*) the marriage of a woman and a man who is the grandfather of a former spouse of hers or is a former spouse of her grand-daughter; and

(*c*) under certain conditions, the marriage of persons related in certain other degrees of affinity)

shall have effect.

Marriage according to rites of Church of England or the Church in Wales

3. In the Marriage Act 1949 after section 5 there shall be inserted the following section—

"Marriages between certain persons related by affinity

5A. No clergyman shall be obliged—

(*a*) to solemnize a marriage which, apart from the Marriage (Prohibited Degrees of Relationship) Act 1986, would have been void by reason of the relationship of the persons to be married; or

(*b*) to permit such a marriage to be solemnized in the church or chapel of which he is the minister."

Amendment of s.3 of Perjury Act 1911

4. In section 3(1) of the Perjury Act 1911 (false statements relating to marriage) after paragraph (*c*) there shall be inserted the words "or

(*d*) with respect to a declaration made under section 16(1A) or 27B(2) of the Marriage Act 1949—

(i) enters a caveat under subsection (2) of the said section 16, or

(ii) makes a statement mentioned in subsection (4) of the said section 27B,

which he knows to be false in a material particular,".

Amendment of Schedule 1 to Supreme Court Act 1981

5. In Schedule 1 to the Supreme Court Act 1981 in paragraph 3(*c*) (assignment of business to the Family Division) after the words "marriage of a minor" there shall be inserted the words "or for a declaration under section 27B(5) of the Marriage Act 1949."

Short title, citation, commencement and extent

6.—(1) This Act may be cited as the Marriage (Prohibited Degrees of Relationship) Act 1986.

(2) This Act so far as it extends to England and Wales may be cited with the Marriage Acts 1949 to 1983 and the Marriage (Wales) Act 1986 as the Marriage Acts 1949 to 1986.

(3) This Act so far as it relates to the Marriage (Scotland) Act 1977 may be cited with that Act as the Marriage (Scotland) Acts 1977 and 1986.

(4) In section 11(*a*) of the Matrimonial Causes Act 1973 for the words "Marriage Acts 1949 to 1983" there shall be substituted the words "Marriage Acts 1949 to 1986."

(5) This Act shall come into force on such day as the Secretary of State may by order made by statutory instrument appoint and different days may be so appointed for different provisions.

(6) Section 2 and Schedule 2 shall extend to Scotland only, but save as aforesaid this Act shall not extend to Scotland or to Northern Ireland.

SCHEDULES

SCHEDULE 1

AMENDMENTS OF MARRIAGE ACT 1949

1. The Marriage Act 1949 shall have effect subject to the following amendments.

2. In section 1 (prohibited degrees) after subsection (1) there shall be inserted the following subsections—

"(2) Subject to subsection (3) of this section, a marriage solemnized between a man and any of the persons mentioned in the first column of Part II of the First Schedule to this Act, or between a woman and any of the persons mentioned in the second column of the said Part II, shall be void.

(3) Any such marriage as is mentioned in subsection (2) of this section shall not be void by reason only of affinity if both the parties to the marriage have attained the age of twenty-one at the time of the marriage and the younger party has not at any time before attaining the age of eighteen been a child of the family in relation to the other party.

(4) Subject to subsection (5) of this section, a marriage solemnized between a man and any of the persons mentioned in the first column of Part III of the First Schedule to this Act or between a woman and any of the persons mentioned in the second column of the said Part III shall be void.

(5) Any such marriage as is mentioned in subsection (4) of this section shall not be void by reason only of affinity if both the parties to the marriage have attained the age of twenty-one at the time of the marriage and the marriage is solemnized—

(*a*) in the case of a marriage between a man and the mother of a former wife of his, after the death of both the former wife and the father of the former wife;

(*b*) in the case of a marriage between a man and the former wife of his son, after the death of both his son and the mother of his son;

(*c*) in the case of a marriage between a woman and the father of a former husband of hers, after the death of both the former husband and the mother of the former husband;

(*d*) in the case of a marriage between a woman and a former husband of her daughter, after the death of both her daughter and the father of her daughter."

3. In section 5 (marriages according to rites of Church of England) there shall be added at the end the words "except that paragraph (*a*) of this section shall not apply in relation to the solemnization of any marriage mentioned in subsection (2) of section 1 of this Act."

4. In section 16 (common licences)—

(*a*) after subsection (1) there shall be inserted the following subsections—

"(1A) A common licence shall not be granted for the solemnization of a marriage mentioned in subsection (2) of section 1 of this Act unless—

(*a*) the person having authority to grant the licence is satisfied by the production of evidence that both the persons to be married have attained the age of twenty-one; and

(*b*) he has received a declaration in writing made by each of those persons specifying their affinal relationship and declaring that the younger of those persons has not at any time before attaining the age of eighteen been a child of the family in relation to the other.

(1B) In the case of a marriage mentioned in subsection (4) of section 1 of this Act which by virtue of subsection (5) of that section is valid only if at the time of the marriage both the parties to the marriage have attained the age of twenty-one and the death has taken place of two other persons related to those parties in the manner mentioned in the said subsection (5), a common licence shall not be granted for the solemnization of the marriage unless the person having authority to grant the licence is satisfied by the production of evidence—

(*a*) that both the parties to the marriage have attained the age of twenty-one; and

(*b*) that both those other persons are dead.";

(*b*) in subsection (2) at the beginning there shall be inserted the words "Subject to subsection (2A) of this section"; and

(*c*) after subsection (2) there shall be inserted the following subsections—

"(2A) Where in the case of a marriage mentioned in subsection (2) of section 1 of this Act a caveat is entered under subsection (2) of this section on the ground that the persons to be married have not both attained the age of twenty-one or that one of those persons has at any time before attaining the age of eighteen been a child of the family in relation to the other, then, notwithstanding that the caveat is withdrawn by the person who entered it, no licence shall be issued unless the judge has certified that he has examined into that ground of objection and is satisfied that that ground ought not to obstruct the grant of the licence.

(2B) In the case of a marriage mentioned in subsection (2) of section 1 of this Act, one of the persons to be married may apply to the ecclesiastical judge out of whose office the licence is to issue for a declaration that, both those persons having attained the age of twenty-one and the younger of those persons not having at any time before attaining the age of eighteen been a child of the family in relation to the other, there is no impediment of affinity to the solemnization of the marriage; and where any such declaration is obtained the common licence may be granted notwithstanding that no declaration has been made under the said subsection (1A)."

5. After section 27A there shall be inserted the following sections—

"Provisions relating to section 1(3) marriages

27B.—(1) This section applies in relation to any marriage mentioned in subsection (2) of section 1 of this Act which is intended to be solemnized on the authority of a certificate of a superintendent registrar.

(2) The superintendent registrar shall not enter notice of the marriage in the marriage notice book unless—

(a) he is satisfied by the production of evidence that both the persons to be married have attained the age of twenty-one; and

(b) he has received a declaration made in the prescribed form by each of those persons, each declaration having been signed and attested in the prescribed manner, specifying their affinal relationship and declaring that the younger of those persons has not at any time before attaining the age of eighteen been a child of the family in relation to the other.

(3) The fact that a superintendent registrar has received a declaration under subsection (2) of this section shall be entered in the marriage notice book together with the particulars given in the notice of marriage and any such declaration shall be filed and kept with the records of the office of the superintendent registrar or, where notice of marriage is required to be given to two superintendent registrars, of each of them.

(4) Where the superintendent registrar receives from some person other than the persons to be married a written statement signed by that person which alleges that the declaration made under subsection (2) of this section is false in a material particular, the superintendent registrar shall not issue a certificate or licence unless a declaration is obtained from the High Court under subsection (5) of this section.

(5) Either of the persons to be married may, whether or not any statement has been received by the superintendent registrar under subsection (4) of this section, apply to the High Court for a declaration that, both those persons having attained the age of twenty-one and the younger of those persons not having at any time before attaining the age of eighteen been a child of the family in relation to the other, there is no impediment of affinity to the solemnization of the marriage; and where such a declaration is obtained the superintendent registrar may enter notice of the marriage in the marriage notice book and may issue a certificate, or certificate and licence, whether or not any declaration has been made under subsection (2) of this section.

(6) Section 29 of this Act shall not apply in relation to a marriage to which this section applies, except so far as a caveat against the issue of a certificate or licence for the marriage is entered under that section on a ground other than the relationship of the persons to be married.

Provisions relating to section 1(5) marriages

27C. In the case of a marriage mentioned in subsection (4) of section 1 of this Act which by virtue of subsection (5) of that section is valid only if at the time of the marriage both the parties to the marriage have attained the age of twenty-one and the death has taken place of two other persons related to those parties in the manner mentioned in the said subsection (5), the superintendent registrar shall not enter notice of the marriage in the marriage notice book unless satisfied by the production of evidence—

(a) that both the parties to the marriage have attained the age of twenty-one, and

(b) that both those other persons are dead.".

6. In section 39 (notice of marriage given on board Her Majesty's ships)—
    (*a*) in subsection (2) for the words "excluding section 27A" there shall be substituted the words "excluding sections 27A and 27B";
    (*b*) in subsection (3) for the words "excluding section 27A" there shall be substituted the words "excluding sections 27A and 27B".
7. In section 78 (interpretation) after the definition of "brother" there shall be inserted—
    "'child of the family', in relation to any person, means a child who has lived in the same household as that person and been treated by that person as a child of his family".
8. In the First Schedule—
    (*a*) in Part I—
        (i) in the first column the words from "Wife's mother" to "Daughter's son's wife"; and
        (ii) in the second column the words from "Husband's father" to "Daughter's daughter's husband" shall cease to have effect; and
    (*b*) at the end of Part I there shall be added—

"Part II

Degrees of affinity referred to in section 1(2) and (3) of this Act

Daughter of former wife	Son of former husband
Former wife of father	Former husband of mother
Former wife of father's father	Former husband of father's mother
Former wife of mother's father	Former husband of mother's mother
Daughter of son of former wife	Son of son of former husband
Daughter of daughter of former wife	Son of daughter of former husband

Part III

Degrees of affinity referred to in section 1(4) and (5) of this Act

Mother of former wife	Father of former husband
Former wife of son	Former husband of daughter"

Amendments of Marriage (Scotland) Act 1977

1. The Marriage (Scotland) Act 1977 shall be amended as follows.
2. In section 2 (prohibited degrees for marriage of related persons)—
    (*a*) at the beginning of subsection (1) there shall be inserted the words "Subject to subsections (1A) and (1B) below,";
    (*b*) after subsection (1) there shall be inserted the following subsections—
    "(1A) Subsection (1) above does not apply to a marriage between a man and any woman related to him in a degree specified in column 1 of paragraph 2 of Schedule 1 to this Act, or between a woman and any man related to her in a degree specified in column 2 of that paragraph, if—
    (*a*) both parties have attained the age of 21 at the time of the marriage; and
    (*b*) the younger party has not at any time before attaining the age of 18 lived in the same household as the other party and been treated by the other party as a child of his family.
    (1B) Subsection (1) above does not apply to a marriage between a man and any woman related to him in a degree specified in column 1 of paragraph 2A of Schedule 1 to this Act or between a woman and any man related to her in a degree specified in column 2 of that paragraph, if both parties to the marriage have attained the age of 21 and the marriage is solemnized—
    (*a*) in the case of a man marrying the mother of a former wife of his, after the death of both the former wife and the former wife's father;
    (*b*) in the case of a man marrying a former wife of his son, after the death of both his son and his son's mother;

  (c) in the case of a woman marrying the father of a former husband of hers, after the death of both the former husband and the former husband's mother;

  (d) in the case of a woman marrying a former husband of her daughter, after the death of both her daughter and her daughter's father."; and

 (c) after subsection (4) there shall be inserted the following new subsection—

  "(5) Where the parties to an intended marriage are related in a degree specified in paragraph 2 of Schedule 1 to this Act, either party may (whether or not an objection to the marriage has been submitted in accordance with section 5(1) of this Act) apply to the Court of Session for a declarator that the conditions specified in paragraphs (a) and (b) of subsection (1A) above are fulfilled in relation to the intended marriage.".

 3. In section 3(1) (notice of intention to marry), after paragraph (c) there shall be inserted the following paragraph—

  "(d) where he is related to the other party in a degree specified in paragraph 2 of Schedule 1 to this Act, a declaration in the prescribed form stating—

   (i) the degree of relationship; and

   (ii) that the younger party has not at any time before attaining the age of 18 lived in the same household as the other party and been treated by the other party as a child of his family.".

 4. In section 5 (objections to marriage)—

  (a) at the beginning of subsection (3) there shall be inserted the words "Subject to subsection (3A) below,";

  (b) after subsection (3) there shall be inserted the following subsection—

   "(3A) Where—

   (a) an objection of which the Registrar General has received notification under subsection (2)(b)(i) above is on the ground that—

    (i) the parties are related in a degree specified in paragraph 2 of Schedule 1 to this Act; and

    (ii) the conditions specified in paragraphs (a) and (b) of section 2(1A) of this Act are not satisfied; and

   (b) an extract decree of declarator that those conditions are satisfied, granted on an application under section 2(5) of this Act, is produced to the Registrar General,

   the Registrar General shall inform the district registrar that there is no legal impediment to the marriage on that ground."; and

  (c) in subsection (4), for the words "subsection (3) above" there shall be substituted the words "this section".

 5. In section 6(1) (the Marriage Schedule), after "5(3)(b)" there shall be inserted "or (3A)".

 6. In section 7(1) (marriage outside Scotland where a party resides in Scotland), for the words "(a) and (b)" there shall be substituted the words "(a), (b) and (d)".

 7. For paragraph 2 of Schedule 1 (relationships by affinity) there shall be substituted the following paragraphs—

  "2—*Relationships by affinity referred to in section 2(1A)*

Daughter of former wife;	Son of former husband;
Former wife of father;	Former husband of mother;
Former wife of father's father;	Former husband of father's mother;
Former wife of mother's father;	Former husband of mother's mother;
Daughter of son of former wife;	Son of son of former husband;
Daughter of daughter of former wife;	Son of daughter of former husband.

  2A.—*Relationships by affinity referred to in section 2(1B)*

Mother of former wife;	Father of former husband;
Former wife of son;	Former husband of daughter."

DRAINAGE RATES (DISABLED PERSONS) ACT 1986

(1986 c. 17)

An Act to make provision for reducing drainage rates in respect of premises used by disabled persons and invalids.   [26th June 1986]

PARLIAMENTARY DEBATES
Hansard: H.C. Vol. 88, col. 311; Vol. 91, col. 1257; Vol. 95; col. 549; H.L. Vol. 473, col. 669; Vol. 474, col. 875; Vol. 475, cols. 137, 1091.

Relief from drainage rates

1.—(1) Where a rating authority grant a rebate under section 1 or 2 of the Rating (Disabled Persons) Act 1978 in respect of the rates chargeable on a hereditament situated in an internal drainage district the authority shall, as soon as practicable, give the internal drainage board for that district written notice of the grant of the rebate stating—

(*a*) its amount and the hereditament and period in respect of which it was granted; and

(*b*) the amount of the rates that would have been chargeable in respect of that hereditament and period apart from the rebate.

(2) On receiving a notice under subsection (1) above the internal drainage board shall grant corresponding relief in respect of any drainage rates made by it so far as chargeable in respect of the hereditament and the period specified in the notice.

(3) In subsection (2) above "corresponding relief", in relation to a rebate, means relief of an amount which bears to the amount of the drainage rates chargeable as mentioned in that subsection the same proportion as the rebate bears to the amount of the rates that would have been chargeable in respect of the hereditament and the period in question apart from the rebate.

(4) The foregoing provisions apply also where part of a hereditament is in an internal drainage district; and where different parts are in different districts a notice shall be given under subsection (1) above to the internal drainage board for each of those districts.

(5) Relief under this section shall be granted by reducing the drainage rates chargeable as mentioned in subsection (2) above or by repaying or allowing the amount overpaid.

Short title, commencement and extent

2.—(1) This Act may be cited as the Drainage Rates (Disabled Persons) Act 1986.

(2) This Act shall come into force on 1st April 1987.

(3) This Act does not extend to Scotland or Northern Ireland.

CORNEAL TISSUE ACT 1986

(1986 c. 18)

An Act to permit the removal of eyes or parts of eyes for therapeutic purposes and purposes of medical education and research by persons who are not medically qualified, subject to appropriate safeguards.

[26th June 1986]

PARLIAMENTARY DEBATES
 Hansard: H.C. Vol. 88, col. 312; Vol. 89, col. 1412; Vol. 95, col. 1153; H.L. Vol. 473, col. 1123; Vol. 475, col. 70; Vol. 475, col. 711; Vol. 476, col. 592.
 The Bill was considered by Standing Committee C on December 12, 1985.

Amendment of Human Tissue Act 1961

1.—(1) Section 1 of the Human Tissue Act 1961 (removal of parts of bodies for medical purposes) shall be amended as follows.

(2) In subsection (3), after "(4)" there shall be inserted ", (4A)".

(3) For subsection (4) (removals to be effected only by registered medical practitioners) there shall be substituted the following subsections—

"(4) No such removal, except of eyes or parts of eyes, shall be effected except by a registered medical practitioner, who must have satisfied himself by personal examination of the body that life is extinct.

(4A) No such removal of an eye or part of an eye shall be effected except by—

    (*a*) a registered medical practitioner, who must have satisfied himself by personal examination of the body that life is extinct; or

    (*b*) a person in the employment of a health authority acting on the instructions of a registered medical practitioner who must, before giving those instructions, be satisfied that the person in question is sufficiently qualified and trained to perform the removal competently and must also either—

        (i) have satisfied himself by personal examination of the body that life is extinct, or

        (ii) he satisfied that life is extinct on the basis of a statement to that effect by a registered medical practitioner who has satisfied himself by personal examination of the body that life is extinct.".

(4) After subsection (9) there shall be added the following subsection—

"(10) In this section 'health authority'—

    (*a*) in relation to England and Wales, has the meaning given by section 128(1) of the National Health Service Act 1977;

    (*b*) in relation to Scotland, means a Health Board constituted under section 2 of the National Health Service (Scotland) Act 1978.".

Short title, commencement and extent

2.—(1) This Act may be cited as the Corneal Tissue Act 1986.

(2) This Act shall come into force at the end of the period of two months beginning with the day on which it is passed.

(3) This Act does not extend to Northern Ireland.

BRITISH SHIPBUILDERS (BORROWING POWERS) ACT 1986

(1986 c. 19)

An Act to raise the limits imposed by section 11 of the Aircraft and
Shipbuilding Industries Act 1977 in relation to the finances of British
Shipbuilders and its wholly owned subsidiaries.

[26th June 1986]

PARLIAMENTARY DEBATES
Hansard: H.C. Vol. 95, col. 1035; Vol. 96, col. 685; Vol. 97, col. 202; H.L. Vol. 474, col.
875; Vol. 475, col. 75; Vol. 476, col. 592.

Limit on borrowing etc. of British Shipbuilders

1.—(1) In subsection (7) of section 11 of the Aircraft and Shipbuilding
Industries Act 1977 (which imposes an overall limit, increased from £1,000
million to £1,100 million by the British Shipbuilders Borrowing Powers
(Increase of Limit) Order 1984 and further increased to £1,200 million by
the British Shipbuilders Borrowing Powers (Increase of Limit) Order
1985, on certain sums borrowed by British Shipbuilders and its wholly
owned subsidiaries and on its public dividend capital), for "£1,000 million"
(the limit initially specified in that subsection as amended by the British
Shipbuilders (Borrowing Powers) Act 1983) and "£1,200 million" (the
maximum to which that limit could be increased by order under that
subsection as so amended) there shall be substituted respectively "£1,300
million" and "£1,400 million".

(2) The British Shipbuilders Borrowing Powers (Increase of Limit)
Order 1984 and the British Shipbuilders Borrowing Powers (Increase of
Limit) Order 1985 are hereby revoked.

Short title and extent

2.—(1) This Act may be cited as the British Shipbuilders (Borrowing
Powers) Act 1986.

(2) This Act extends to Northern Ireland.

HORTICULTURAL PRODUCE ACT 1986

(1986 c. 20)

An Act to confer on authorised officers (within the meaning of Part III of the Agriculture and Horticulture Act 1964) powers in relation to the movement of horticultural produce; and for purposes connected therewith.

[26th June 1986]

PARLIAMENTARY DEBATES
  Hansard: H.C. Vol. 88, col. 312; Vol. 90, col. 1249; Vol. 95, col. 1196; H.L. Vol. 473, col. 1014; Vol. 475, col. 212; Vol. 476, cols. 392 and 592.
  The Bill was considered by Standing Committee C on April 16, 1986.

Power to control the movement of produce

1.—(1) Where an authorised officer inspects any produce which he is entitled to inspect under section 13 of the Act of 1964, he may prohibit its movement if he is satisfied that a grading offence is being committed in respect of it.

(2) An officer who exercises the power conferred by subsection (1) above shall, without delay, give to the person who appears to him to be in charge of the produce concerned notice in writing—

(a) specifying the produce in relation to which the power has been exercised; and

(b) stating that the produce may not be moved without the written consent of an authorised officer.

(3) If the person to whom the officer gives the notice does not appear to him to be the owner of the produce or an agent or employee of the owner, the officer shall use his best endeavours to bring the contents of the notice to the attention of such a person as soon as practicable.

(4) An authorised officer may affix to any produce in relation to which the power conferred by subsection (1) above has been exercised, or to any container in which the produce is packed, labels warning of the exercise of the power.

Consents to the movement of controlled produce

2.—(1) An authorised officer may, at any time give written consent to the movement of controlled produce.

(2) An authorised officer shall, upon request, give written consent to the movement of controlled produce if—

(a) he is satisfied that no grading offence would be committed in respect of the produce if it were sold in circumstances in which grading rules apply; or

(b) he, or another authorised officer, has been given a written undertaking that the produce will be disposed of in a specified manner, he is satisfied that if the produce is disposed of in that manner no grading offence will be committed in respect of it and he has no reason to doubt that the terms of the undertaking will be met.

(3) An authorised officer shall, upon request, give written consent to the movement of controlled produce if—

(a) he, or another authorised officer, has been given a written undertaking to the effect that—

(i) the produce will be moved to a place approved by an authorised officer;

(ii) there will be taken there the steps required to ensure that the produce may be sold in circumstances in which grading rules apply without a grading offence being committed in respect of it; and

(iii) the produce will not be moved from that place without the written consent of an authorised officer; and

(b) he has no reason to doubt that the terms of the undertaking will be met.

(4) A consent given by an authorised officer under this section shall—

(a) specify the produce to which it relates; and

(b) where the consent is given under subsection (3) above, state that the produce continues to be controlled.

Power to change the circumstances in which consent must be given

3.—(1) The Ministers may by order made by statutory instrument make such amendments of this Act as they think fit for the purpose of changing the circumstances in which an authorised officer is required to give written consent to the movement of produce.

(2) Before making such an order, the Ministers shall consult such organisations as appear to them to represent interests likely to be affected by the order.

(3) An order under this section shall be subject to annulment in pursuance of a resolution of either House of Parliament.

(4) In this section "the Ministers" means the Minister of Agriculture, Fisheries and Food and the Secretary of State, acting jointly.

Offences

4.—(1) Any person who, knowing produce to be controlled, knowingly—

(a) moves it, or

(b) causes it to be moved,

without the written consent of an authorised officer shall be guilty of an offence.

(2) Any person who, knowing produce to be controlled, knowingly—

(a) removes from it, or

(b) causes to be removed from it,

a label which has been affixed under section 1(4) of this Act shall be guilty of an offence.

(3) Any person who fails to comply with an undertaking given by him for the purposes of section 2 of this Act shall be guilty of an offence.

(4) It shall be a defence—

(a) for a person charged with any offence under this section, to prove that, when the power conferred by section 1(1) of this Act was exercised, no grading offence was being committed in respect of the produce concerned;

(b) for a person charged with an offence under subsection (1) or (2) above, to prove that there was a reasonable excuse for the act or omission in respect of which he is charged; and

(c) for a person charged with an offence under subsection (3) above, to prove that he took all reasonable precautions and exercised all due diligence to avoid the commission of such an offence.

(5) A person guilty of an offence under this section shall be liable, on summary conviction, to a fine not exceeding level 5 on the standard scale.

Extension of the Act of 1964

5. The following provisions of the Act of 1964 shall have effect as if the provisions of this Act were contained in Part III of that Act—

    (*a*) section 15 (which penalises the obstruction of an authorised officer acting under that Part);

    (*b*) section 19 (which applies in relation to the commission by corporations of offences under that Part); and

    (*c*) section 20(3) (which provides that proceedings in England and Wales for an offence under that Part may only be instituted with the consent of the Attorney General or, in England, the Minister of Agriculture, Fisheries and Food and, in Wales, the Secretary of State).

Interpretation

6. In this Act—

    "the Act of 1964" means the Agriculture and Horticulture Act 1964;

    "authorised officer" means a person who is an authorised officer for the purposes of Part III of the Act of 1964 (grading of fresh horticultural produce);

    "controlled", in relation to produce, means that the power conferred by section 1(1) of this Act has been exercised in relation to it and that no consent to its movement has been given under section 2(1) or (2) of this Act;

    "grading offence" means an offence under section 14(1) or (2) of the Act of 1964;

    "grading rules" means the rules enforced under Part III of the Act of 1964.

Short title, repeals, commencement and extent

7.—(1) This Act may be cited as the Horticultural Produce Act 1986.

(2) In sections 19 and 20(3) of the Act of 1964, the word "foregoing" shall be repealed.

(3) This Act shall come into force at the end of the period of two months beginning with the day on which it is passed.

(4) This Act does not extend to Northern Ireland.

ARMED FORCES ACT 1986*

(1986 c. 21)

An Act to continue the Army Act 1955, the Air Force Act 1955 and the Naval Discipline Act 1957 and to amend those Acts and the Armed

---

* Annotations by Peter Rowe, LL.M., Barrister, Senior Lecturer in Law, University of Liverpool.

Forces Act 1976 and the Armed Forces Act 1981.   [26th June 1986]

GENERAL NOTE

Until 1955 Parliament passed an annual Act to continue in forc̄ the law governing the Army and the R.A.F. This rather cumbersome procedure was due, in part, to the Bill of Rights 1688 which prohibited the "raising and keeping of a standing army in the Kingdom in time of peace without the consent of Parliament". In 1955 renewal of the Army Act and the Air Force Act was put on a quinquennial basis but became subject to the annual consent of Parliament by means of a continuation order after the affirmative resolutions of both Houses of Parliament. Naval discipline was never subject to the Bill of Rights procedure but in 1971 it too was brought within this framework, which has been likened to a 'naval refit' or to a 'quinquennial visitation' when "members of the presbytery visit the kirk and review the spiritual welfare of the congregation and the fabric of its building" (Mr. J. Wallace, M.P.). The principal Acts are the Army Act 1955, the Air Force Act 1955 and the Naval Discipline Act 1957.

It is one of the guiding principles of each successive Armed Forces Act that wherever possible military and civilian law should not differ. Debate on the Bill tends, therefore, to centre on those areas of proposed differences between the two legal systems. In this way the burden is placed upon the military authorities to justify the special position of the serviceman, especially where his "civil rights" are concerned. Debate in Parliament and in the Select Committee ranged over many issues including homosexuality in the armed forces, the continuation of the death penalty for certain offences, immunity of the Crown under s.10 of the Crown Proceedings Act 1947 and emergency powers in war-time. None of these matters has, however, found its way into the Act.

This Act amends the Service Discipline Acts of 1955 and 1957. Each successive Armed Forces Act makes the principal changes to the 1955 and 1957 Acts but amendments may also be introduced by other legislation. The Police and Criminal Evidence Act 1984, by s.113, for instance, applies parts of that Act to the Service Discipline Acts. On occasions Parliament is able to make changes to the criminal law or to the law of evidence that applies in courts-martial in advance of alteration to the civilian law. An example of this was s.9 of the Armed Forces Act 1981 which made a computer print-out admissible as evidence of the facts contained in it. This is now admissible in civilian and military courts by s.69 of the Police and Criminal Evidence Act 1984. The same procedure is at work in ss.2 and 3 of this Act, which deal with the problem of interference with a computer program. Courts, whose jurisdiction is based under the Service Discipline Acts, have powers to deal with servicemen and women but also civilians. The Army Act 1955, for instance, applies military law to civilians outside the United Kingdom when the force is not on active service (s.209 and Sched. 5).

These civilians will generally be those employed by the armed forces abroad and the families of servicemen. They can be dealt with by court-martial or by a Standing Civilian Court (introduced by the Armed Forces Act 1976) for offences against the criminal law of England and Wales and for certain purely military offences. This Act makes further progress in bringing the military legal system in line with the procedure when a civilian is tried for the same offence within the United Kingdom. There are, however, important differences relating to the sentencing of civilians; the Select Committee went so far as to recommend that a Standing Civilian Court should have the power to award suspended, or partly suspended, sentences and suggested that this might be included in the forthcoming Criminal Justice Bill.

COMMENCEMENT

See s.17

SCOTLAND AND NORTHERN IRELAND

The Service Discipline Acts apply to Scotland and Northern Ireland (see 1955 Acts, sections 214, 215).

TABLE OF ABBREVIATIONS

Civil offence	: an offence against the criminal law of England and Wales, see s.70 of the 1955 Acts, s.42 of the 1957 Act.
The 1955 Acts	: The Army Act 1955, the Air Force Act 1955.
The 1957 Act	: The Naval Discipline Act 1957.
Service Discipline Acts	: the three above Acts.
Select Committee	: Select Committee on the Armed Forces Bill, 1985–86, H.C. 170.

PARLIAMENTARY DEBATES
Hansard: H.C. Vol. 87, col. 433; Vol. 95, col. 403; H.L. Vol. 473, col. 418; Vol. 474, col. 66; Vol. 475, cols. 7 and 23; Vol. 476, cols. 192, 1036.
The Bill was considered by the Commons Select Committee on January 22 to March 24, 1986.

PART I

CONTINUANCE OF SERVICES ACTS

Continuance of Services Acts

1.—(1) The 1955 Acts and the 1957 Act shall, instead of expiring on 31st August 1986, continue in force until 31st August 1987, and shall then expire unless continued in force in accordance with the following provisions of this section.

(2) Subject to subsection (3) below, Her Majesty may from time to time by Order in Council provide for the 1955 Acts and the 1957 Act to continue in force for a period not exceeding twelve months beyond the day on which they would otherwise expire.

(3) No Order in Council shall be made under subsection (2) above so as to continue the 1955 Acts and the 1957 Act beyond the end of the year 1991.

(4) No recommendation shall be made to Her Majesty in Council to make an Order under subsection (2) above unless a draft thereof has been laid before Parliament and approved by resolution of each House of Parliament.

GENERAL NOTE
Section 1 of the Armed Forces Act 1981 provided for the continuance in force of the Army Act 1955, the Air Force Act 1955 and the Naval Discipline Act 1957 until August 31, 1986. The effect of s.1 is that these Acts will continue in force for one year and then can be extended on a yearly basis by Order in Council for a further four years until 1991, giving a life to the Act of a total of five years. The Order in Council must be laid annually and approved by resolution of both Houses. The next Armed Forces Act will then come before Parliament in 1990–91 and the process of quinquennial review will begin again.

PART II

AMENDMENTS OF SERVICES ACTS ETC.

Offences

Interference etc. with equipment, messages or signals

2.—(1) After section 44A of the Army Act 1955 (damage to and loss of Her Majesty's aircraft or aircraft material) there shall be inserted the following section—

"Interference etc. with equipment, messages or signals

44B.—(1) Any person subject to military law who by any conduct of his—

    (*a*) intentionally impairs the efficiency or effectiveness of any equipment which is public or service property; or

    (*b*) intentionally interferes with or modifies any message or other signal which is being transmitted, by means of a telecommunication system, directly or indirectly to or from any such equipment,

shall, on conviction by court-martial, be liable to imprisonment or any less punishment provided by this Act.

(2) Any person subject to military law who is guilty of any conduct which is likely to have the effect—

    (*a*) of impairing the efficiency or effectiveness of any such equipment; or

    (*b*) of interfering with or modifying any such message or signal,

shall (whether or not that conduct has that effect) be liable, on conviction by court-martial, to imprisonment for a term not exceeding two years or any less punishment provided by this Act.

(3) It shall be a defence for a person charged with an offence under subsection (2) of this section in respect of any conduct likely to have a particular effect that, in the circumstances, his conduct was in all respects consistent with the exercise of reasonable care to avoid producing that effect.

(4) For the purposes of this section the efficiency or effectiveness of any equipment is impaired if, whether or not it is damaged, the equipment is made temporarily or permanently less efficient or effective either for all purposes or for a particular purpose for which it has been designed, adapted, adjusted or programmed.

(5) In this section—

'conduct' includes any act or omission;

'equipment' includes any apparatus, any computer and any vessel, aircraft or vehicle; and

'telecommunication system' has the same meaning as in the Telecommunications Act 1984."

(2) The provisions set out in subsection (1) above shall also be inserted after section 44A of the Air Force Act 1955 and, as section 29B, after section 29A of the 1957 Act, but as if—

    (*a*) in those provisions, as inserted in the Air Force Act 1955, for the words "military law", in each place where they occur, there were substituted the words "air-force law"; and

    (*b*) in those provisions, as inserted in the 1957 Act—

        (i) for the words "military law", in each place where they occur, there were substituted the words "this Act";

        (ii) the words "on conviction by court-martial", in each place where they occur, were omitted; and

        (iii) for the words "punishment provided", in each place where they occur, there were substituted the words "punishment authorised".

GENERAL NOTE

This section creates a new offence to be added to the Service Discipline Acts of intentionally impairing the efficiency or effectiveness of any equipment which is public or service property, or interfering with, or modifying, any message or signal. It also creates an offence of doing anything which is likely to have the same effect. Other offences in the Service Discipline Acts deal with causing *damage* to public or service property (see ss.44 and 44A of the Army Act 1955). In addition, a suitable charge under the Criminal Damage Act 1971 might be framed where damage has been caused. However, a serviceman may interfere with a computer program by, for example, erasing part without necessarily damaging it. Section 2 avoids problems that might arise if the offence required damage to be caused. An example was given in the Select Committee of a soldier who erased an entry in a computer that showed his British Forces Germany driving licence had been withdrawn. Other cases might be more serious and in the nature of sabotage if a computer controlling a weapon system was intentionally interfered with. For the view that this section creates offences of too wide a nature see the Select Committee at pp.247–248.

Subs. (1)

This subsection inserts a new section 44B into the Army Act 1955.

New s.44B

Subs. (1): Any person subject to military law. A person will be subject to military law if he comes within ss.208, 209 and the Fifth Sched. to the Army Act 1955 or ss.205–208 of the Air Force Act 1955 or ss.111–115 of the Naval Discipline Act 1957. The *mens rea* required for the offence is intention to produce the consequences outlined and not recklessness or negligence. For the meaning of intention see *R.* v. *Hancock* [1986] 1 All E.R. 641. It should be noted that there is no defence provided of 'without lawful excuse' to justify an intentional interference.

Conduct is defined in subs. (5).

Equipment is defined in subs. (5).

Impairs is defined in subs. (4).

Telecommunication system is defined in subs. (5).

The punishment provided for the offence is an indefinite one. This is because in the 1955 Acts there are only two levels of sentence. One is unlimited and the other is imprisonment for a maximum of two years. What are considered to be serious offences attract the former while less serious offences the latter. *Any less punishment provided by this Act* refers to sentences not involving imprisonment that are set out in the Service Discipline Acts, see for example s.71 Army Act 1955 and Sched. 1, para. 4 of this Act.

Subs. (2): An accused need only engage in conduct that is likely to (whether it does or does not) have the prohibited effect. There is no requirement of *mens rea* in this subsection. The punishment of a maximum of two years' imprisonment can be contrasted with that provided for in subs. (1).

Conduct is defined in subs. (5) so as to include any act or omission.

Subs. (3) This subsection contributes the *mens rea* to subs. (2) above. It is necessary for the prosecution to prove that the accused engaged in conduct that had the prohibited effect and for the accused to prove that he took all reasonable care to avoid producing that effect. He will be required to prove this on a balance of probabilities (*R.* v. *Carr-Briant* [1943] K.B. 607) whereas the prosecution's task is to prove its case beyond reasonable doubt. The combined effect of subss. (2) and (3) is to create a strict liability offence subject to the accused being unable to prove 'no negligence'. It is to be contrasted with self-defence where the accused bears an evidential burden only and the prosecution must prove the accused was not acting in self-defence.

Subs. (2)

This subsection inserts the corresponding provisions into the Air Force Act 1955 and the Naval Discipline Act 1957.

Offences in relation to official documents

3.—(1) In section 62 of each of the 1955 Acts and in section 35 of the 1957 Act (making of false documents), for paragraphs (*a*) to (*c*) there shall be substituted the following paragraphs—

"(*a*) makes an official document or official record which is to his knowledge false in a material particular, or

(*b*) makes in any official document or official record an entry which is to his knowledge false in a material particular, or

(*c*) tampers with the whole or any part of any official document or official record (whether by altering it, destroying it, suppressing it, removing it or otherwise), or

(*d*) with intent to deceive, fails to make an entry in any official document or official record,".

(2) Each of the sections amended by subsection (1) above shall be renumbered subsection (1) of that section and after each of those provisions, as so re-numbered, there shall be inserted the following subsections—

"(2) For the purposes of this section—

(*a*) a document or record is official if it is or is likely to be made use of, in connection with the performance of his functions as such, by a person who holds office under, or is in the service of, the Crown; and

(*b*) a person who has signed or otherwise adopted as his own a document or record made by another shall be treated, as well as that other, as the maker of the document or record.

(3) In this section—

'document' includes, in addition to a document in writing—

    (*a*) any map, plan, graph or drawing;

    (*b*) any photograph;

    (*c*) any disc, tape, sound-track or other device in which sounds or other data (not being visual images) are embodied so as to be capable (with or without the aid of some other equipment) of being reproduced therefrom; and

    (*d*) any film, negative, tape or other device in which one or more visual images are embodied so as to be capable as aforesaid of being reproduced therefrom;

'film' includes a microfilm; and

'record' includes any account, any information recorded otherwise than in a document by mechanical, electronic or other means and any program in a computer."

GENERAL NOTE

This section amends s.62 of the 1955 Acts and s.35 of the 1957 Act (which deal with the making of false documents) by making it clear that the term 'document' has a wide meaning and that 'record' includes a computer program. A narrow interpretation of s.62 would lead to the conclusion in that section that the term 'or other official document' was intended to deal only with documents relating to pay.

Subs. (1)

This subsection sets out the *actus reus* in relation to official documents and records.
Document is defined in subs. (3).
Record is defined in subs. (3).

Subs. (2)

This subsection introduces a new subs. (2) to s.62 of the 1955 Acts and in the corresponding section in the 1957 Act. It defines when a document or record is official and who is its maker. It is interesting to note that a person may be the maker of the document if he has 'signed or otherwise treated it as his own'; see *Groves* v. *Redbart* [1975] Crim.L.R. 158 and *R.* v. *Mathews* (1958) 42 Cr.App.R. 93 (C.M.A.C.).

Elimination of distinctions between certain offences

4.—(1) In sections 28(*a*), 29(*b*), 33(1)(*a*), 55(1) and (2) and 65(*a*) and (*b*) of each of the 1955 Acts and in sections 6(*b*), 11(*a*), 24(*a*), 33B(1) and (2) and 36A(*a*) and (*b*) of the 1957 Act (offences consisting in striking a person or in otherwise ill-treating him or using violence to him or force against him), the words "strikes or otherwise", wherever occurring, shall be omitted.

(2) In section 69 of each of the 1955 Acts and in section 39 of the 1957 Act (conduct or neglect to the prejudice of good order and military discipline), for the words "of any conduct or neglect" there shall be substituted the words ", whether by any act or omission or otherwise, of conduct".

GENERAL NOTE

A number of textual changes are made by this section to the Service Discipline Acts.

Subs. (1)

This subsection alters a number of sections of the Service Discipline Acts that use the words 'strikes or otherwise' (uses force, s.29 of the 1955 Acts, or ill-treats, ss.28 and 65 of the 1955 Acts, or uses violence, ss.33 and 55 of the 1955 Acts) and removes these words. To 'strike' had been interpreted as meaning a blow with the hand or with something which is held in the hand, but the words 'strikes or otherwise' added nothing of substance. The section can clearly stand without these words, so that, for instance, ill-treatment could encompass striking.

Subs. (2)

Section 69 of the 1955 Acts is a very wide offence-creating section which could, in theory, cover any conduct that prejudices good order and military discipline and that was not a substantive offence. This section removes the word 'neglect' and defines conduct so as to include an omission. For an example of s.69 see *R.* v. *Davies*; *R.* v. *Hamilton* [1980] Crim.L.R. 582 (conviction upheld by C.M.A.C. where accused had taken paintings and etchings from a German civilian without the intention permanently to deprive the owner).

Sentence, reconsideration and limitation

Maximum periods of imprisonment or detention for default in payment of fines

5. For subsection (2) of section 71B of each of the 1955 Acts and for subsection (2) of section 43B of the 1957 Act (maximum periods of imprisonment or detention for default in payment of fines) there shall be substituted the following subsection—

"(2) Subject to subsections (4) and (5) below, the Table in section 31(3A) of the Powers of Criminal Courts Act 1973 (maximum periods of imprisonment for default in payment of fines etc.), as from time to time amended under section 143 of the Magistrates' Courts Act 1980, shall have effect for the purpose of determining the maximum periods of further imprisonment or detention that may be specified under subsection (1) above for fines of the amounts set out in that Table."

GENERAL NOTE

This section brings the Service Discipline Acts into line with civilian law in connection with the periods of imprisonment applicable in default of payment of a fine. The civilian law is to be found in s.31(3A) of the Powers of Criminal Courts Act 1973.

Repeal of power of reconsideration

6. Neither section 114 of the Army Act 1955 nor section 114 of the Air Force Act 1955 (reconsideration of sentences of imprisonment or detention) shall apply in the case of a sentence awarded after the coming into force of this section.

GENERAL NOTE

Section 114 of the 1955 Acts permitted an officer not below the rank of brigadier to reconsider sentences of imprisonment and detention and to remit the sentence in whole or in part. There was no power under this section to reconsider the verdict itself or to impose any alternative punishment. This can now be done by the process of review contained in s.113 (as well as that of confirmation under s.107). S.114 was considered otiose and is repealed by this section.

Removal of three year limit for commencement of certain proceedings

7.—(1) For subsection (1) of section 132 of each of the 1955 Acts (which, subject to any limit imposed in relation to a corresponding civil offence and to a power of the Attorney General to consent to proceedings in certain cases, imposes a three year limit on the commencement of proceedings for certain offences under the relevant service law) there shall be substituted the following subsection—

"(1) Where by virtue of any enactment proceedings on indictment for any civil offence must be brought within a limited period, no proceedings shall be taken against any person for an offence against section 70 of this Act corresponding to that civil offence unless the trial or proceedings on a summary dealing with the charge is or are begun before the end of that period."

(2) For subsection (1) of section 52 of the 1957 Act (which, with subsection (3) of that section, makes provision equivalent to that made by section 132(1) of each of the 1955 Acts) there shall be substituted the following subsection—

"(1) Where by virtue of any enactment proceedings on indictment for any civil offence must be brought with a limited period, a person shall not be tried for that offence under section 42 of this Act unless the trial is begun within that period."

(3) In subsection (3) of the said section 52—

    (*a*) for the words "Subsections (1) and (2)" there shall be substituted the words "Subsection (2)"; and

    (*b*) for the words from "and in the case of a civil offence" onwards there shall be substituted the words "or, without prejudice to subsection (1) above, to a civil offence punishable under section 42 of this Act where the civil offence is alleged to have been committed outside the United Kingdom and the Attorney General consents to the trial."

(4) Section 7(3) of the Armed Forces Act 1976 (which imposes a three year limit on the commencement of proceedings before a Standing Civilian Court) shall cease to have effect.

(5) In section 7(4) of the said Act of 1976 (application to trial by Standing Civilian Court of time limit for corresponding civil offence), after the word "proceedings" there shall be inserted the words "on indictment".

(6) Nothing in this section shall affect the operation of section 132(1) of either of the 1955 Acts, section 52 of the 1957 Act or section 7(3) or (4) of the said Act of 1976 in relation to an offence if the offence was committed before the date on which this section comes into force and—

    (*a*) the period of three years beginning with the commission of the offence expired before that date; or

    (*b*) the offence is an offence under section 70 of either of the 1955 Acts or punishable under section 42 of the 1957 Act and the period between the commission of the offence and that date was longer than the period within which proceedings for the corresponding civil offence must be taken.

GENERAL NOTE

    This section brings service law into line with the civil law by removing the time limit by which a trial by court-martial must begin.

Subs. (1)

    Section 132 of the 1955 Acts required a person to be tried by court-martial within three years of the commission of the offence of which he was charged. This related to all offences save mutiny, failure to suppress a mutiny and desertion. The time limit caused difficulty, particularly in relation to fraud where the offence may not have been discovered for some time. There is no corresponding provision, that a trial must begin within three years of the offence, in civil law, although some statutes do require any information to be laid before a magistrate within specified time limits. Where such a statute does lay down a time limit for trial on indictment the three-year period remains so that the trial or, if the offence is to be dealt with by way of summary disposal, the proceedings must begin within that time. To this extent military law is more favourable to an accused serviceman than the civilian system to an accused civilian. The real practical effect of the section will relate to offences against English law committed by a serviceman abroad and in which there is jurisdiction within the military legal system but none by the courts in England and Wales.

Subs. (2)

    This subsection makes a similar amendment to the Naval Discipline Act 1957.

Subss. (4 & 5)

These subsections make similar provisions in trials and proceedings before the Standing Civilian Court (established by s.6 of the Armed Forces Act 1976).

Subs. (6)

This subsection ensures that an accused serviceman is not prejudiced by the change produced by this section.

Civilians

Application of limitation period to civilians ceasing to be subject to service law

8.—(1) Subsection (3A) of section 209 of each of the 1955 Acts (application of Act to civilians) shall be renumbered subsection (3B) and before that subsection, as so renumbered, there shall be inserted the following subsection—

"(3A) For the purposes of paragraph (*g*) of subsection (3) of this section a person shall be deemed not to have ceased to be in such circumstances as are mentioned in that paragraph if he has so ceased by reason only of one or both of the following, namely—

(*a*) the fact that he has ceased to be within the limits of a command within whose limits he continues to have his ordinary residence or to serve or to be employed;

(*b*) the fact that there has been an interruption of his residence with a family of persons whose place of residence continues to be his home."

(2) In Schedule 4 to the 1957 Act (application of Act to certain civilians), after paragraph 4 there shall be inserted the following paragraph—

"4A. For the purposes of section 52(2) of this Act a person shall be deemed not to have ceased to be a person to whom this Act applies by virtue of section 118(2) of this Act if he has so ceased by reason only of one or both of the following, namely—

(*a*) the fact that he has ceased to be within the limits of a command within whose limits he continues to have his ordinary residence or to serve or to be employed;

(*b*) the fact that there has been an interruption of his residence with a family of persons whose place of residence continues to be his home."

(3) Nothing in this section shall affect the operation of any of the relevant provisions in relation to proceedings for an offence by a person who ceased, after the commission of the offence and more than the specified period before the coming into force of this section, to be in such circumstances that Part II of either of the 1955 Acts or any provision specified in section 118 of the 1957 Act applied to him.

(4) In subsection (3) above—

"the relevant provisions" means section 132(3) of each of the 1955 Acts and section 52(2) of the 1957 Act; and

"the specified period", in relation to any proceedings, means the period specified in relation to those proceedings in the relevant provisions.

GENERAL NOTE

A civilian is subject to military law outside the United Kingdom if he comes within the class of person described in Sched. 5 to the 1955 Acts. S.209 limits his liability to military law to a situation where he is within the limits of the command of any officer commanding a body of the regular forces outside the United Kingdom and also as to certain offences. By s.132(3) of the 1955 Acts and s.52(2) of the 1957 Act a person who has ceased to be subject to military law must be tried by court-martial within six months of so ceasing or within three months if he is to be proceeded with summarily. Any temporary departure by a civilian (for example, on holiday) from the limits of command of an officer commanding a body of the regular forces outside the United Kingdom will therefore mean that he has ceased to be subject to military law and the time limit will therefore begin to run. This was so even if it was his intention to return after his holiday.

Subs. (1)
Adds a new subs. (3A) to s.209 of the 1955 Acts to provide that a civilian does not cease to be subject to military law if, despite his leaving the limits of a command, he continues to have his ordinary residence or to serve or to be employed there or if he is to continue to reside with a person subject to military law.

Subs. (2)
Makes the same amendment to the 1957 Act.

Subs. (3)
Ensures that a civilian is not to be prejudiced retroactively by this change in the law.

Power of Standing Civilian Court to defer sentence

9.—(1) In Schedule 5A to the Army Act 1955 (powers of court on trial of civilian), after paragraph 2 there shall be inserted the following paragraph—

"Deferment of award of sentence

2A.—(1) Subject to the provisions of this paragraph, where a civilian is found guilty of an offence by a Standing Civilian Court, the Standing Civilian Court may defer the award of sentence against him for the purpose of enabling the Standing Civilian Court, or any other court to which it falls to deal with him, to have regard, in dealing with him, to his conduct after conviction (including, where appropriate, the making by him of reparation for his offence) or to any change in his circumstances.

(2) Any deferment under this paragraph shall be until such date as may be specified by the Standing Civilian Court, being a date not more than six months after the date on which the Standing Civilian Court announces the deferment; and where the award of sentence against an offender has been deferred on one occasion, it shall not be further deferred.

(3) The power conferred by this paragraph shall be exercisable only if the offender consents and the Standing Civilian Court is satisfied, having regard to the nature of the offence and the character and circumstances of the offender, that it would be in the interests of justice to exercise the power.

(4) A Standing Civilian Court which has deferred the award of sentence against an offender may deal with him at a time when the period of deferment has not expired if—

(a) he is during that period found guilty of an offence by a court-martial under any of the Services Acts or by a Standing Civilian Court; or

(b) such conditions as may be specified for the purposes of this paragraph in an order under paragraph 12 of Schedule 3 to the Armed Forces Act 1976 (proceedings in Standing Civilian Courts) are satisfied in relation to him.

(5) Without prejudice to sub-paragraph (4) above, where a Standing Civilian Court has deferred the award of sentence against an offender in respect of one or more offences and the offender is, during the period of the deferment, found guilty of an offence ('the

subsequent offence') by a court-martial under any of the Services Acts or by a Standing Civilian Court, then, subject to subsection (6) below, the court which (whether during that period or not) deals with the offender for the subsequent offence may also, if this has not already been done, deal with him for the offence or offences in respect of which the award of sentence was deferred.

(6) Subject to sub-paragraph (7) below, the power of a court under this paragraph to deal with an offender for an offence in respect of which the award of sentence has been deferred shall be a power to deal with him in any way in which the Standing Civilian Court which deferred the award of sentence could have dealt with him for that offence.

(7) In a case falling within sub-paragraph (5) above a court-martial which awards a sentence of imprisonment or a sentence under a custodial order for the subsequent offence may (subject to the application to the aggregate of the sentences of any limit imposed by, or by any provision corresponding to, section 85 of this Act or paragraph 10(1A) below) order that the sentence shall begin to run from the expiry of any sentence which, being a sentence of imprisonment or a sentence under a custodial order, is awarded for the offence or offences in respect of which the award of sentence was deferred.

(8) Where a Standing Civilian Court has deferred the award of sentence against an offender, the Court or the directing officer may order the offender's arrest either—

(a) in order to secure the offender's appearance on the day specified by the Standing Civilian Court as the day on which it proposes to deal with him (including a day before the end of the period of deferment); or

(b) where the offender has failed to appear on a day so specified.

(9) Where the arrest of an offender has been ordered under sub-paragraph (8) above, then, whether or not the offender continues to be subject to service law—

(a) he may be arrested—

(i) by a provost officer; or

(ii) by any warrant officer or non-commissioned officer legally exercising authority under or on behalf of a provost officer; or

(iii) by order of any officer of the regular forces or of the regular air force (within the meaning of the Air Force Act 1955); and

(b) a warrant for the offender's arrest may be issued to any officer or officers of police by the directing officer or by any superior officer or authority.

(10) A warrant under sub-paragraph (9)(b) above shall specify the name of the person for whose arrest it is issued and shall refer to the order of the Standing Civilian Court or directing officer that that person be arrested.

(11) A person arrested under this paragraph shall be delivered into military or air force custody and may be kept in such custody until his appearance before the Standing Civilian Court which deferred the award of sentence against him.

(12) Where under this section an officer of police delivers a person into military or air force custody, there shall be handed over with him a certificate which shall—

(a) be in such form as may be specified by order under paragraph 12 of Schedule 3 to the Armed Forces Act 1976;

(b) be signed by that officer of police; and

(*c*) state the fact, date, time and place of arrest;
and such a certificate shall for the purposes of this Act be evidence of the matters stated therein.

(13) In this paragraph 'the directing officer', in relation to an offender, means the higher authority by whom the offender was sent for trial for the offence in respect of which the award of sentence was deferred, or any officer for the time being discharging the functions of that authority."

(2) The provisions set out in subsection (1) above shall also be inserted after paragraph 2 of Schedule 5A to the Air Force Act 1955 but as if in sub-paragraph (9)(*a*) for the words from "regular forces" to "1955)" there were substituted the words "regular air force or of the regular forces (within the meaning of the Army Act 1955)".

(3) In paragraph 12 of Schedule 3 to the Armed Forces Act 1976 (power to make orders with respect to procedures before Standing Civilian Courts), after sub-paragraph (3) there shall be inserted the following sub-paragraph—

"(3A) An order under this paragraph may, for the purposes of paragraph 2A of Schedule 5A to the Army Act 1955 and paragraph 2A of Schedule 5A to the Air Force Act 1955, specify the conditions to be satisfied, in relation to an offender, before a Standing Civilian Court that has deferred the award of sentence against the offender may award sentence during the period of deferment."

DEFINITION
Directing officer: see s.2(A)(13).

GENERAL NOTE
This section is concerned with increasing the range of sentence possessed by a Standing Civilian Court. The Standing Civilian Court was created by s.6 of the Armed Forces Act 1976 to try civilians abroad who are subject to military law (see General Note to s.8). It is presided over by a senior member of the staff of the Judge Advocate General and is similar to a magistrate's court in England and Wales. It can impose a term of imprisonment of up to 6 months (or 12 months for more than one conviction) and a fine not exceeding £400 (s.8(1) Armed Forces Act 1976). The full range of sentences that can be imposed on a civilian by this court can be found in Sched. 5A of the 1955 Acts and, in particular, it should be noted that there is no power to suspend (or part suspend) a sentence. The Select Committee considered (at p.viii) that the court should have this power and invited the Government to include such a proposal in the forthcoming Criminal Justice Bill.

Subs. (1)
Creates a power to defer a sentence for up to 6 months. A similar sentencing option exists in the civil legal system by virtue of s.1(1) of the Powers of Criminal Courts Act 1973, see generally, *R.* v. *George* [1984] 3 All E.R. 13. The power can only be exercised once and it requires the consent of the convicted person. If he is subsequently convicted by a court-martial or by the Standing Civilian Court during the period of deferment he may, in addition, be dealt with for the offence on which sentence was deferred. There are also powers of arrest in order to secure the offender's presence in court.

Subs. (2)
A similar alteration is made to the Air Force Act 1955.

Subs. (3)
Deals with the case where an offender has had his sentence deferred during that period and has failed to comply with the specified conditions. These conditions are to be made under the power granted by Sched. 3, para. 12 of the Armed Forces Act 1976.

Extension of power to make community supervision orders in relation to civilians

10.—(1) In Schedule 5A to each of the 1955 Acts and Schedule 4A to the 1957 Act, in paragraph 4(1) (power to make community supervision order in relation to a civilian under 21 years of age), the words "under 21 years of age" shall be omitted.

(2) In the first column of the Table in paragraph 15(3) of each of the Schedules amended by subsection (1) above (scale of punishments and orders for offenders of 21 and over), after paragraph 3 there shall be inserted the following paragraph—

"3A. Community supervision order."

GENERAL NOTE

Paragraph 4(1) of Sched. 5A of the 1955 Acts inserted by Sched. 4 of the Armed Forces Act 1976, enables a Standing Civilian Court to pass sentence of a community supervision order, under which a civilian is to be supervised in the military community. The 1976 Act required the offender to be under the age of 21 years. The community supervision order has 'no exact equivalence in civilian life, but [is] in essence a mixture in varying proportions of probation orders, community service orders and supervision orders' (*Manual of Military Law Part I, Civilian Supplement*, p.68). An offender may be required to perform up to 90 hours of unpaid work. There is no power to place an offender on probation or to impose a community service order.

Subs. (1)

This deletes the requirement that the offender be under the age of 21. A community supervision order can now be passed on an offender of any age.

Subs. (2)

Paragraph 15(3) of Sched. 5A to the 1955 Act sets out in tabular form the punishments that may be imposed on a civilian. This subsection inserts the community supervision order under the heading in the table of 'Offender 21 or over'.

Extension of power to make custodial orders in relation to civilians

11.—(1) In Schedule 5A to each of the 1955 Acts and Schedule 4A to the 1957 Act, in paragraph 10(1) (custodial orders in respect of offender under 21 but not less than 17 years of age)—

(a) for the words "17 years of age" there shall be substituted the words "the minimum age"; and

(b) at the end there shall be inserted the words—
"and in this sub-paragraph 'the minimum age', in relation to a male offender, means 15 years of age and, in relation to a female offender, means 17 years of age."

(2) In paragraph 10(1A) of each of the Schedules amended by subsection (1) above (restriction on making of custodial orders), at the end there shall be inserted the words "and the court shall not make a custodial order committing an offender under 17 years of age to be detained for a period which exceeds twelve months or for a period such that the continuous period for which he is committed to be detained under that order and any one or more other custodial orders exceeds twelve months."

(3) In paragraph 10(6)(b) of each of the said Schedules (appropriate institution in Scotland), for sub-paragraph (i) there shall be substituted the following sub-paragraphs—

"(i) if the offender is a male person who is under the age of 16 years, such place as the Secretary of State may direct;

(ia) subject to sub-paragraph (ib) below, if the offender is a male person who has attained 16 years of age and the period specified in the order is not less than twenty-eight days nor more than four months, a detention centre;

(ib) where detention in a detention centre would be required by sub-paragraph (ia) above but the offender has already served such a sentence, a young offenders institution; and".

(4) In paragraph 10(6)(c) of each of the said Schedules (appropriate institution in Northern Ireland), for the words "a young offenders centre" there shall be substituted the following sub-paragraphs—

"(i) if the offender is a male person who is under the age of 17 years, a remand home; and
(ii) in any other case, a young offenders centre;".
(5) In the third column of the Table in paragraph 15(3) of each of the said Schedules (scale of punishments and orders for offenders under 17), after paragraph 1 there shall be inserted the following paragraph—
"1A. Custodial order."
(6) This section shall not have effect in relation to offences committed before the coming into force of this section.

GENERAL NOTE
This section permits a court-martial or a Standing Civilian Court to impose a custodial order in relation to a male aged between 15 and 21 years. The Armed Forces Act 1976 had stipulated the minimum age to be 17 years and, upon conviction, a young offender between 15 and 17 had therefore to be returned to the United Kingdom and placed in care until his or her majority. This new sentence is similar to youth custody introduced by s.6 of the Criminal Justice Act 1982 except that it does not apply to females aged between 15 and 17 years.

Subs. (1)
This reduces the minimum age from 17 to 15 years for the imposition of a custodial order by a court-martial or a Standing Civilian Court.

Subs. (2)
Contains a restriction in respect of an offender under 17 years of age. He may not be sentenced to a custodial order for a period greater than 12 months for an offence or offences taken together.

Subs. (3)
Deals with the precise type of sentence, depending on the age of the offender and the length of his sentence.

Subs. (4)
Makes a similar amendment to deal with the particular type of sentence that can be served where an offender is removed to Northern Ireland.

Subs. (5)
The Table in para. 15(3) of Sched. 5A of the 1955 Acts of the sentence by age that may be imposed on a civilian is correspondingly amended to reflect the age change introduced by this section.

Subs. (6)
This ensures that the section does not have a retroactive effect.

Power of court-martial to suspend sentence on appeal from Standing Civilian Court

12.—(1) In paragraph 18 of Schedule 3 to the Armed Forces Act 1976 (appeals from Standing Civilian Courts), after sub-paragraph (11) there shall be inserted the following sub-paragraph—
"(12) Where a court-martial passes a sentence on an appeal under this paragraph in a case in which the sentence of the Standing Civilian Court was suspended under paragraph 20(4) below, the court-martial may, if it thinks fit, direct that the suspension shall apply to the sentence of the court-martial in the same way as it would have applied to the sentence of the Standing Civilian Court."
(2) Accordingly, in sub-paragraph (8) of that paragraph, after the word "above" there shall be inserted the words "and sub-paragraph (12) below".

GENERAL NOTE

An appeal from a Standing Civilian Court lies to a court-martial by Sched. 3 (para. 18) of the Armed Forces Act 1976. Para. 20 of that Schedule provides that a finding or sentence of a Standing Civilian Court may be reviewed and the Armed Forces Act 1981 in Sched. 1 (para. 4) provided that the reviewing authority may at any time suspend a sentence of a Standing Civilian Court. Where a convicted civilian appealed to a court-martial, under para. 18 of Sched. 3 of the Armed Forces Act 1976, and the court-martial upheld the conviction the sentence was to be treated as if it had been passed by a court-martial. But prior to this section a court-martial had no power to suspend a sentence. The court-martial can now order that a sentence suspended by the reviewing authority may continue to be suspended.

Subss. 1 & 2

These provide that the suspended sentence shall apply to the court-martial decision as it did to the sentence of the Standing Civilian Court. It does this by making the necessary amendments to Sched. 3 of the Armed Forces Act 1976.

Change of place of safety and return to United Kingdom of children in need of care or control

13.—(1) Section 14 of the Armed Forces Act 1981 (temporary removal to and detention in a place of safety abroad of children of service families in need of care or control) shall be amended as follows.

(2) For subsection (3) (power to order removal of child to place of safety outside United Kingdom) there shall be substituted the following subsection—

"(3) If an officer having jurisdiction in relation to a child to whom this section applies thinks fit, he may, on being satisfied on one or more of the grounds specified in subsection (4) below that the child is in need of care or control, order the child to be removed to and detained in a place of safety."

(3) After subsection (4) there shall be inserted the following subsection—

"(4A) A place of safety in which a child is required to be detained under this section may be situated either in the country or territory where the child resides or elsewhere (including in the United Kingdom); and an officer having jurisdiction in relation to a child detained in a place of safety outside the United Kingdom may make an order (including an order involving the return of the child to the United Kingdom) modifying the order by which the child is detained so as to require the child to be removed to and detained in another place of safety."

(4) In subsection (5) (officers having power to make orders)—

(*a*) for the words from the beginning to "say" there shall be substituted the words "The officers having jurisdiction in relation to a child to whom this section applies or a child detained in a place of safety are"; and

(*b*) in paragraph (*b*), after the word "resides" there shall be inserted the words "or, as the case may be, was residing when he was removed to a place of safety".

(5) For subsections (7) to (9) (matters to be specified in order and effect and duration of orders) there shall be substituted the following subsections—

"(7) An order made by virtue of subsection (3) or (4A) above shall specify the place of safety to which the child is to be removed and shall be sufficient authority for—

(*a*) the removal of the child to the place specified in the order;

(*b*) the detention of the child for the purpose of that removal in any other place or on board any ship or aircraft; and

(*c*) the detention of the child in the place so specified in accordance with the order.

(8) An order made by virtue of subsection (3) above in relation to a child shall specify the period for which it is to have effect, being—

(a) in a case where the order is made by the commanding officer of the person to whose family the child belongs or with whose family the child resides, a period not exceeding the period of eight days, beginning with the date of the order; and

(b) in a case where the order is made by an officer superior in command to the commanding officer of either of those persons, a period not exceeding the period of twenty-eight days beginning with that date;

and, subject to the following provisions of this section, neither that order nor any order under subsection (4A) above modifying that order shall authorise the detention of the child after the end of the specified period.

(9) Where it at any time appears to an officer having jurisdiction in relation to a child detained by virtue of an order under this section—

(a) that the period for which the order is to have effect is less than the maximum period applicable under subsection (8) above in relation to an order made by that officer; and

(b) that it is appropriate, for any reason, for the effect of the order to be extended or further extended,

that officer may order the effect of the order to continue until a time no later after the making of the original order than the end of the said maximum period.

(9A) Where a child is removed under this section to a place of safety in the United Kingdom—

(a) the order in pursuance of which he is so removed shall not authorise his detention in that place after the end of the period of twenty-four hours beginning with his arrival in that place; but

(b) the powers conferred by the Children and Young Persons Act 1933, the Children and Young Persons Act 1969, the Social Work (Scotland) Act 1968 and the Children and Young Persons Act (Northern Ireland) 1968 shall be exercisable in relation to the child as if everything which was relevant to the question under this section whether the child was in need of care or control were relevant, notwithstanding that the child is or has been detained in a place of safety, to the question whether the conditions for the exercise of any of those powers are satisfied."

(6) In subsection (10) (right of parent to make representations before order made), for the words "for the time being" there shall be substituted the words "or, as the case may be, was residing when he was removed to a place of safety under this section".

GENERAL NOTE

Section 14 of the Armed Forces Act 1981 established the right of the service authorities to order that a child, whose family is serving outside the United Kingdom, be removed to a place of safety on similar grounds to those contained in s.1 of the Children and Young Persons Act 1969. An order can therefore be made, *inter alia*, if the health of the child is being neglected or he is being ill-treated or he is beyond the control of his parent or guardian. The order is made administratively by either the commanding officer of the person to whose family the child belongs or resides or by an officer superior in command to that commanding officer, (s.14(5)). Unlike civilian law the parent or guardian of the child has a right to make representations to the officer by whom the case is being considered unless that officer considers that it is undesirable to do so (s.14(10)). The place of safety may be a service hospital and it is usually preceded by a case conference. There was no power given by the Armed Forces Act 1981 to transfer the child to the United Kingdom although this could be achieved administratively by sending the whole family back to the United Kingdom. This procedure was considered by the Select Committee in 1981 (H.C. 253) to be unsatisfactory since a child could quite lawfully be intercepted by a parent or guardian before he or she reached the United Kingdom. The opportunity has been taken to correct this difficulty. Under s.14 of the 1981 Act a place of safety order could be made by a commanding officer for a period of eight days but if it required to be extended an officer superior in command had to make a fresh order. Further, the place of safety order could not be varied to enable the child to be removed to a different place than that originally specified. The Select Committee was told that in 1984 one place of safety order was made and in the following year the figure was four, one of which was extended to 28 days.

Subs. (2)

The effect of this subsection is that the place of safety is no longer restricted to a place outside the United Kingdom. It should be read in the light of subss. (3) and (5) below.

Subs. (3)

This subsection directly permits a place of safety order to be made in respect of a place in the United Kingdom and it allows an order to be varied so that a child who is originally placed in a service hospital overseas may be subsequently transferred to the United Kingdom.

Subs. (5)

This replaces subss. (7) to (9) of s.14 of the 1981 Act. The new subs. (7) creates the necessary powers to enable the child to be transferred to the United Kingdom and, in effect, prevents interference with his passage. New subs. (8) enables an officer superior in command to the family's commanding officer to make one order to extend for a maximum of 28 days. New subs. (9) allows an order to be "topped up" if it was made for a period short of the maximum. New subs. (9A) provides that where the designated place of safety is in the United Kingdom it will expire at the end of 24 hours after the arrival of the child. This will enable a local authority to take up the case and the child will then be dealt with as if he were the child of a civilian in the United Kingdom. A court that is seised with the matter under the legislation that is referred to in the subsection, can take into account the grounds for the making of the place of safety order.

Reserve liability of women

Reserve liability of women

14. Paragraph (*a*) of section 213 of the Army Act 1955 (so much of Part I of that Act as relates to service in and transfer to the reserve not to apply in relation to women members of the regular forces) shall cease to have effect.

GENERAL NOTE

Part I (ss.9 to 13) of the Army Act 1955 relates to enlistment and terms of service and by s.213(*a*) this Part did not apply to women members of the Army in relation to transfer to, or service in, the reserve. No such restriction applies in the R.A.F. or in the Royal Navy. In order to impose a reserve liability on completion of their regular service the repeal of s.213(*a*) was required. Women members will be liable, as male soldiers, to be transferred to the reserve and be liable to be called to the colours on mobilisation.

PART III

SUPPLEMENTAL

Interpretation

15. In this Act—
   "the 1955 Acts" means the Army Act 1955 and the Air Force Act 1955; and
   "the 1957 Act" means the Naval Discipline Act 1957.

Correction of minor deficiencies, repeals and transitional provision

16.—(1) Schedule 1 to this Act shall have effect for correcting certain minor deficiencies in the 1955 Acts and in the 1957 Act.

(2) The enactments mentioned in Schedule 2 to this Act are hereby repealed to the extent specified in the third column of that Schedule.

(3) The repeals made by this Act in Schedule 3 to each of the 1955 Acts and the repeals of section 29 of the Armed Forces Act 1966 and of paragraph 1(12) and (13) of Schedule 1 to the Armed Forces Act 1971 shall not have effect in relation to proceedings for an offence committed before the coming into force of section 4 above.

Short title and commencement

17.—(1) This Act may be cited as the Armed Forces Act 1986.

(2) Subject to subsection (3) below, Part II of this Act, section 16 above and the provisions of Schedules 1 and 2 to this Act shall come into force on such day as the Secretary of State may, by order made by statutory instrument, appoint; and different days may be so appointed for different provisions and for different purposes.

(3) The repeal by this Act of section 1 of the Armed Forces Act 1981 shall come into force on 1st September 1986.

SCHEDULES

Section 16(1)   SCHEDULE 1

CORRECTION OF MINOR DEFICIENCIES IN SERVICES ACTS

References to summary sentence for offence in relation to court-martial

1.—(1) Each of the 1955 Acts shall have effect, and shall be deemed always to have had effect, with the following amendments (being amendments relating to the effect of a summary sentence for an offence in relation to a court-martial), namely—
  (*a*) in subsections (3) and (4) of section 71 (certain sentences to be accompanied by dismissal or reduction to the ranks), before the word "sentenced", in the first place where it occurs in each of those subsections, there shall be inserted the words "who, otherwise than under section 57(2) of this Act, is";
  (*b*) in the proviso to section 107(2) (which qualifies the provision requiring confirmation of a finding or sentence of a court-martial), after the word "not" there shall be inserted the words "require a sentence under section 57(2) of this Act to be confirmed or";
  (*c*) in section 108 (petitions against finding or sentence), after the word "completed" there shall be inserted the words "or, in the case of a sentence under section 57(2) of this Act, after the award of the sentence"; and
  (*d*) in section 113(1) (review of findings and sentences which have been confirmed)—
        (i) after the word "confirmed" there shall be inserted the words "or a sentence under subsection (2) of section 57 of this Act"; and
        (ii) for the words from "after confirmation" to "against the" there shall be substituted the words "a petition is duly presented under section 108 of this Act against a".

(2) Subsections (3) and (4) of section 43 of the 1957 Act (certain sentences to be accompanied by dismissal or disrating) shall have effect, and shall be deemed always to have had effect, as if before the word "sentenced", in the first place where it occurs in each of those subsections, there were inserted the words "who, otherwise than under section 38(3) of this Act, is".

(3) In section 70 of the 1957 Act (review of finding and sentence)—
  (*a*) in subsection (1), after the words "such a finding" there shall be inserted the words "or under section 38(3) of this Act"; and
  (*b*) in subsection (2), for the words "or found thereunder" there shall be substituted the words "sentenced under section 38(3) of this Act or found under section 63(1) of this Act".

Correction of wrong cross-reference in provision relating to custodial orders

2. Subsection (3A) of section 38 of the 1957 Act (which, for the purpose of modifying a reference to a power to impose a sentence of imprisonment, refers to subsection (2) of that section) shall have effect, and shall be deemed always to have had effect, as if for the words "subsection (2)" there were substituted the words "subsection (3)".

Punishment for civil offences

3. In section 42(1)(*c*) of the 1957 Act (maximum punishment for civil offence to be same as could be imposed on the offender by a civil court), the words "on the offender" shall be omitted.

Position of custodial orders in scale of punishments

4. In section 71 of each of the 1955 Acts and in section 43 of the 1957 Act (scale of punishments and supplementary provisions), for the proviso in subsection (1) there shall be substituted the following proviso—

"Provided that a punishment such as is mentioned in paragraph (*e*) of this subsection shall not be treated as a less punishment than a punishment such as is mentioned in paragraph (*b*) or (*bb*) if the term of detention is longer than the term of imprisonment or, as the case may be, than the term of detention by virtue of the custodial order."

Consecutive periods of detention under custodial order etc.

5.—(1) The 1955 Acts and the 1957 Act shall have effect in relation to the making of a custodial order at any time after the coming into force of this paragraph with the following amendments (being amendments which enable a period of detention under a custodial order to run consecutively with another such period and, except where the order is made under either of the 1955 Acts by a Standing Civilian Court, to exceed two years.

(2) For subsection (5) of section 71AA of each of the 1955 Acts there shall be substituted the following subsection—

"(5) The following provisions of this Act shall apply in the case of a sentence under a custodial order as they apply in the case of a sentence of imprisonment, that is to say—
(*a*) sections 71(3) and (4), 118(1), 118A(1) and (3), 119A(3) and 145; and
(*b*) for the period before a person sentenced under a custodial order is received into the institution where he is to be detained (or for the currency of the sentence if its term ends before he is so received), sections 119(2), (4) and (5), 122, 123, 129, 142 and 190B;
and, accordingly, references in those provisions to a sentence of imprisonment shall include for the purposes of this subsection references to a sentence under a custodial order."

(3) For sub-paragraph (5A) of paragraph 10 of Schedule 5A to each of the 1955 Acts there shall be substituted the following sub-paragraph—

"(5A) The following provisions shall apply in the case of a sentence under a custodial order as they apply in the case of a sentence of imprisonment by the same court, that is to say—
(*a*) where the court is a court-martial, sections 118(1) and 118A(1) and (3) of this Act; and
(*b*) where the court is a Standing Civilian Court, section 8(2) of the Armed Forces Act 1976;
and, accordingly, references in those provisions to a sentence of imprisonment shall include for the purposes of this sub-paragraph references to a sentence under a custodial order."

(4) In sub-paragraph (5B) of each of the paragraphs amended by sub-paragraph (3) above, for the word "detention" there shall be substituted the word "imprisonment".

(5) For subsection (5) of section 43AA of the 1957 Act there shall be substituted the following subsection—

"(5) The following provisions of this Act shall apply in the case of a sentence under a custodial order as they apply in the case of a sentence of imprisonment, that is to say—
(*a*) sections 43(3) and (4), 85(1), 86(1) and (3), 89(3) and 92(1); and
(*b*) for the period before a person sentenced under a custodial order is received into the institution where he is to be detained (or for the currency of the sentence if

its term ends before he is so received), sections 81, 82, 87, 88, 104, 119 and 130A;

and, accordingly, references in those provisions to a sentence of imprisonment shall include for the purposes of this subsection references to a sentence under a custodial order."

(6) For sub-paragraph (5A) of paragraph 10 of Schedule 4A to the 1957 Act there shall be substituted the following sub-paragraph—

"(5A) The following provisions of this Act shall apply in the case of a sentence under a custodial order as they apply in the case of a sentence of imprisonment, that is to say—

(*a*) sections 85(1), 86(1) and (3) and 92(1); and

(*b*) for the period before a person sentenced under a custodial order is received into the institution where he is to be detained (or for the currency of the sentence if its term ends before he is so received), sections 81, 82, 87, 88, 104, 119 and 130A;

and, accordingly, references in those provisions to a sentence of imprisonment shall include for the purposes of this sub-paragraph references to a sentence under a custodial order."

Correction of modification of section 132(3) of each of the 1955 Acts

6.—(1) In paragraph 7 of Schedule 6 to the Army Act 1955 (which provides for the limitation of time for trial of attached members of Her Majesty's naval or air forces), for the words from "substitution" onwards there shall be substituted the words "substitution for references to military law of references to service law."

(2) In paragraph 7 of Schedule 6 to the Air Force Act 1955 (which provides for the limitation of time for trial of attached members of Her Majesty's naval or military forces), for the words from "substitution" onwards there shall be substituted the words "substitution for references to air-force law of references to service law."

Financial penalties enforcement orders

7.—(1) Section 133A of each of the 1955 Acts and section 128F of the 1957 Act (financial penalty enforcement orders) shall be amended as follows.

(2) For paragraph (*b*) of subsection (1) there shall be substituted the following paragraph—

"(*b*) the penalty was—

(i) a fine awarded in respect of a qualifying offence (or in respect of such an offence together with other offences) on the conviction of a qualifying offence either of that person or of the person as whose parent or guardian that person is to pay the penalty; or

(ii) stoppages or a compensation order awarded in respect of a qualifying offence, (whether on the conviction of any person of the offence or on a request by any person for the offence to be taken into consideration); and"

(3) In subsection (4)(*d*) (contents of certificate), for the words "charge or charges" there shall be substituted the words "offence or offences".

(4) After subsection (10) there shall be inserted the following subsection—

"(11) Where a fine has been awarded together with stoppages or a compensation order, this section shall have effect in relation to the fine and to the stoppages or compensation order as if they were separate penalties."

Application of 1957 Act to passengers on board H.M. vessels

8. In section 117 of the 1957 Act (application of Act to passengers on board H.M. ships), after the word "ships" there shall be inserted the word ", vessels".

Deductions from naval pay

9.—(1) Section 128A of the 1957 Act shall have effect, and shall be deemed always to have had effect, as if—

(*a*) in subsection (1) (which limits the deductions that may be made from pay), for the words from "by Her Majesty by an Order in Council made under this section" onwards there were substituted the words "by or under an Order in Council made under the Naval and Marine Pay and Pensions Act 1865";

(*b*) in subsection (2) (Orders in Council not to authorise penal deductions), for the words

"An Order in Council under this section" there were substituted "Such an Order in Council"; and

(*c*) in subsection (3) (power to make supplemental provision with respect to deductions), for the words "Her Majesty may by Order in Council under this section and" there were substituted the words "and without prejudice to the power conferred on Her Majesty in Council by section 3 of the said Act of 1865".

(2) Accordingly, section 128D of the 1957 Act (remission of deductions) shall have effect, and shall be deemed always to have had effect, as if for the words "under an Order in Council made under section 128A above" there were substituted the words "by or under an Order in Council made under section 3 of the Naval and Marine Pay and Pensions Act 1865".

(3) For the purposes of deductions made before the coming into force of this paragraph from the pay of persons subject to the 1957 Act the reference in subsection (3) of the said section 128A to a deduction authorised by Act shall be deemed at all relevant times to have included a reference to the deduction of a sum due to the Crown.

Construction of references to the holding of a commission

10.—(1) Section 225 of the Army Act 1955 and section 223 of the Air Force Act 1955 (general interpretation) shall each have effect, and be deemed always to have had effect, as if before subsection (2) there were inserted the following subsection—

"(1C) References in this Act, in relation to any of Her Majesty's forces, to an officer holding a commission include references to a person to whom a commission is required to be issued; and for the purposes of this Act, where a commission issued to any person takes effect from a date earlier than the date of its issue, that earlier date shall be conclusively presumed to be the date on which the requirement to issue the commission arose."

(2) Section 135 of the 1957 Act (general interpretation) shall have effect, and be deemed always to have had effect, as if after subsection (2) there were inserted the following subsection—

"(2A) References in this Act, in relation to any of the armed forces of the Crown, to an officer holding a commission include references to a person to whom a commission is required to be issued; and for the purposes of this Act, where a commission issued to any person takes effect from a date earlier than the date of its issue, that earlier date shall be conclusively presumed to be the date on which the requirement to issue the commission arose."

Awards against parents and guardians

11. Sub-paragraph (1) of paragraph 13 of Schedule 5A to each of the 1955 Acts (fines and compensation orders against parents and guardians) shall have effect, and shall be deemed to have had effect since the coming into force of paragraph 9 of Schedule 8 to the Criminal Justice Act 1982, as if for paragraphs (*a*) and (*b*) (which were contained in the amendment of the said paragraph 13 made by the said paragraph 9) there were substituted the following paragraphs—

"(*a*) a civilian under 17 years of age is found guilty of an offence; and
(*b*) the court is of the opinion that the case would best be met (whether or not in conjunction with any other punishment) by the exercise of any power of the court to impose a fine in respect of the offence or to make a compensation order in respect of the offence or of any other offence taken into consideration in determining sentence,".

Application to 1957 Act of Amendments of 1955 Acts made by Criminal Justice Act 1982

12.—(1) Schedule 4A to the 1957 Act (powers of court on trial of civilian) shall have effect with the following amendments (being amendments which correspond to those made in Schedule 5A to each of the 1955 Acts by paragraphs 9, 10 and 11 of Schedule 8 to the Criminal Justice Act 1982 and by paragraph 11 above).

(2) In paragraph 13, for sub-paragraphs (1) and (2) there shall be substituted the following sub-paragraphs—

"(1) Where—
(*a*) a civilian under 17 years of age is found guilty of any offence; and
(*b*) the court is of the opinion that the case would best be met (whether or not in conjunction with any other punishment) by the exercise of any power of the court to impose a fine in respect of the offence or to make a compensation order in respect of the offence or any other offence taken into consideration in determining sentence,

it shall be the duty of the court to order that the fine or compensation awarded be paid by any parent or guardian of his who is a service parent or guardian, instead of by the person himself, unless the court is satisfied—
　　　　(i) that the parent or guardian cannot be found; or
　　　　(ii) that it would be unreasonable to make an order for payment, having regard to the circumstances of the case.
　(2) An order under this paragraph may be made against the parent or guardian if—
　　　(a) he has been required to attend in the manner prescribed by General Orders under section 58 of this Act, and
　　　(b) he has failed to do so,
but, save as aforesaid, no such order shall be made without giving the parent or guardian an opportunity of being heard."
　(3) In paragraph 14(1), for "£50" there shall be substituted "£500".
　(4) In paragraph 15(3)—
　　　(a) in the second column of the Table, in paragraph 2, for the word "Imprisonment" there shall be substituted the words "Custody for life"; and
　　　(b) in paragraph (i) of the Note following the Table for the word "imprisonment" there shall be substituted the words "custody for life".
　(5) Sub-paragraph (3) above has effect only in relation to offences committed after the coming into force of this paragraph.

GENERAL NOTE
Para. 1
This provides for the case of a person who is sentenced summarily for an offence in relation to court-martial by the court itself. It ensures that a person so dealt with is not deprived of the procedures of confirmation, petition and review (ss.107, 108 and 113 respectively of the 1955 Acts).

Para. 4
Offences under the Service Discipline Acts generally impose a maximum, or any less punishment provided by the Act. S.71 of the 1955 Acts and s.43 of the 1957 Act set out a ranking of punishments, ranging from death as the greatest and minor punishments as the least punishment. Imprisonment is considered a greater punishment than detention. The effect of this paragraph is to treat detention as a greater punishment if its length exceeds that of imprisonment or custodial order.

Para. 5
Custodial orders are made under Sched. 5A to the 1955 Acts and Sched. 4A to the 1957 Act, as amended by s.11 of this Act. This paragraph enables a court-martial to pass consecutive custodial sentences on a civilian. The sentences may exceed two years unless made by a Standing Civilian Court.

Para. 7
S.133A of the 1955 Acts permits fines, stoppages of pay and compensation orders following conviction of a qualifying offence (s.133A(3)) to be registered in a civil court of the United Kingdom where the offender has left the armed forces or is a civilian. This paragraph permits the same procedure to be followed in relation to a qualifying offence even if imposed along with a non-qualifying offence and also in relation to such an offence taken into consideration.

Para. 9
This paragraph makes minor alterations to s.128A of the Naval Discipline Act 1957 relating to deductions from pay.

Para. 10
This paragraph directs that a commissioned officer is one to whom a commission is required to be issued even though he has not received the commissioning document. The relevance of this paragraph can be noted by considering s.88 of the 1955 Acts.

Para. 11

Schedule 5A to the 1955 Acts enables a court to order a parent or guardian of a civilian under the age of 17 years to pay a fine or to make compensation instead of imposing the sentence on the young person. This paragraph enables the court to do this in respect of offences taken into consideration as well as to offences of which he has been convicted.

Para. 12

This paragraph makes amendments to the Naval Discipline Act 1957 which bring that Act into line with the 1955 Acts.

Section 16(2)   SCHEDULE 2

REPEALS

Chapter	Short title	Extent of repeal
3 & 4 Eliz. 2 c.18.	The Army Act 1955.	In section 28(*a*), the words "strikes or otherwise". In section 29(*b*), the words "strikes or otherwise". In section 33(1)(*a*), the words "strikes or otherwise". In section 55(1) and (2), the words "strikes or otherwise". In section 65(*a*) and (*b*), the words "strikes or otherwise". In section 71B(1), the words "such as is specified in subsection (2) below". Section 114. In section 120, in subsection (3), the words "or reconsideration" and "or reconsidering" and, in subsection (4), the words "or reconsideration". In section 133A(10), paragraph (*d*) of the definition of "financial penalty" and the word "or" immediately preceding it. Section 205(3). Section 213(*a*). In Schedule 3, paragraphs 1A, 2, 4A, 11, 13 and 14 and in paragraphs 3 and 12, the words "otherwise than by striking him" and "other than striking", respectively. In Schedule 5A, in paragraph 4(1), the words "under 21 years of age".
3 & 4 Eliz. 2 c.19.	The Air Force Act 1955.	In section 28(*a*), the words "strikes or otherwise". In section 29(*b*), the words "strikes or otherwise". In section 33(1)(*a*), the words "strikes or otherwise". In section 55(1) and (2), the words "strikes or otherwise". In section 65(*a*) and (*b*), the words "strikes or otherwise".

Chapter	Short title	Extent of repeal
3 & 4 Eliz. 2 c.19—*cont.*	The Air Force Act 1955—*cont.*	In section 71B(1), the words "such as is specified in subsection (2) below". Section 114. In section 120, in subsection (3), the words "or reconsideration" and "or reconsidering" and, in subsection (4), the words "or reconsideration". In section 133A(10), paragraph (*d*) of the definition of "financial penalty" and the word "or" immediately preceding it. Section 205(4). In Schedule 3, paragraphs 1A, 2, 4A, 11, 13 and 14 and in paragraphs 3 and 12, the words "otherwise than by striking him" and "other than striking", respectively. In Schedule 5A, in paragraph 4(1), the words "under 21 years of age".
5 & 6 Eliz. 2 c.53.	The Naval Discipline Act 1957.	In section 6(*b*), the words "strikes or otherwise". In section 11(*a*), the words "strikes or otherwise". In section 24(*a*), the words "strikes or otherwise". In section 33B(1) and (2), the words "strikes or otherwise". In section 36A(*a*) and (*b*), the words "strikes or otherwise". In section 42(1)(*c*), the words "on the offender". In section 43B(1), the words "such as is specified in subsection (2) below". In section 128F(10), paragraph (*d*) of the definition of "financial penalty" and the word "or" immediately preceding it. In Schedule 4A, in paragraph 4(1), the words "under 21 years of age".
1966 c.45.	The Armed Forces Act 1966.	Section 29.
1971 c.33.	The Armed Forces Act 1971.	Section 26(1). In section 33, the words "by substituting the word 'conduct' for the words 'act, disorder'". Section 54(1). In Schedule 1, paragraph 1(12) and (13).
1976 c.52.	The Armed Forces Act 1976.	Section 7(3).
1980 c.9.	The Reserve Forces Act 1980.	In section 6(3)(*b*), the words "(including one entitled to the issue of such a commission)". In section 117(2), the words "(including a person entitled to the issue of one)".
1981 c.55.	The Armed Forces Act 1981.	Section 1. Section 6(3)(*a*) and (*b*).
1982 c.48.	The Criminal Justice Act 1982.	Section 69(2).

CIVIL PROTECTION IN PEACETIME ACT 1986

(1986 c. 22)

An Act to enable local authorities to use their civil defence resources in connection with emergencies and disasters unconnected with any form of hostile attack by a foreign power. [26th June 1986]

PARLIAMENTARY DEBATES
Hansard: H.C. Vol. 92, cols. 587 and 1165; Vol. 97, col. 404; H.L. Vol. 474, col. 1024; Vol. 475, col. 1057; Vol. 476, col. 730; Vol. 477, col. 10.
The Bill was considered by Standing Committee A on April 30, 1986.

Preliminary

1.—(1) This Act applies to any local authority within the meaning of the Civil Defence Act 1948 on whom any functions are for the time being conferred under section 2 (civil defence functions) of that Act; and in the following provisions of this Act "local authority" means a local authority to whom this Act applies.

(2) In this Act—

"civil defence" has the same meaning as in the Civil Defence Act 1948;

"civil defence functions", in relation to a local authority, means all such functions as are for the time being conferred on the authority under section 2 of the Civil Defence Act 1948;

"civil defence resources", in relation to a local authority, means all the resources maintained, provided, used or held by the authority for civil defence purposes, including personnel (whether employees or volunteers), premises, equipment, services and facilities.

Use of civil defence resources in emergencies or disasters

2.—(1) Where an emergency or disaster involving destruction of or danger to life or property occurs or is imminent or there is reasonable ground for apprehending such an emergency or disaster, and a local authority are of opinion that it is likely to affect the whole or part of their area or all or some of its inhabitants, the authority may use any of their civil defence resources in taking action (either alone or jointly with any other person or body and either in their area or elsewhere in or outside the United Kingdom) which is calculated to avert, alleviate or eradicate in their area or among its inhabitants the effects or potential effects of the event, notwithstanding that the event is unconnected with any form of hostile attack by a foreign power.

(2) A local authority whose civil defence functions include the function of making, keeping under review and revising plans for any matter may perform that function so as to allow for the possible occurrence of such an emergency or disaster and facilitate the use of all or any of their civil defence resources in connection with any such emergency or disaster that may occur or become imminent or which there may be reasonable ground for apprehending.

(3) References in the Civil Defence Act 1948 to functions conferred on a local authority under section 2 of that Act do not include any power conferred on them by subsection (1) or (2) above; but the fact that expenses incurred by a local authority in or in connection with the discharge of functions conferred on them under section 2 of that Act are incurred (whether in the repair or replacement of damaged or expended

equipment or otherwise) in circumstances resulting from the exercise of any such power shall not prevent those expenses from qualifying for grant under regulations made under section 3 of that Act.

(4) There shall be paid out of money provided by Parliament any increase attributable to this section in the sums payable out of money so provided under any other Act.

Short title, commencement and extent

3.—(1) This Act may be cited as the Civil Protection in Peacetime Act 1986.

(2) This Act shall come into force at the end of the period of two months beginning with the day on which it is passed.

(3) This Act does not extend to Northern Ireland.

SAFETY AT SEA ACT 1986

(1986 c. 23)

ARRANGEMENT OF SECTIONS

PART I

SAFETY OF FISHING VESSELS

The vessel's equipment

PART II

MISCELLANEOUS AND GENERAL

Miscellaneous

General

An Act to promote the safety of fishing and other vessels at sea and the persons in them; and for related purposes.   [26th June 1986]

PARLIAMENTARY DEBATES
Hansard: H.C. Vol. 88, col. 309, H.C. Vol. 91, cols. 541, 575, H.C. Vol. 97, col. 360; H.L. Vol. 474, col. 1024; H.L. Vol. 475, col. 1075; H.L. Vol. 477, col. 157.
This Bill was considered by Standing Committee C on April 23, 1986.

PART I

SAFETY OF FISHING VESSELS

The vessel's equipment

Emergency position indicating radio beacon

1.—(1) A fishing vessel shall carry a radio beacon which in the event of an emergency will indicate its position by transmitting on a prescribed frequency.

(2) This section applies to all United Kingdom fishing vessels of 12 metres or more in length and to such other United Kingdom fishing vessels as may be prescribed.

Automatic release life rafts

2.—(1) The life rafts carried by a fishing vessel shall be secured in such a way that they are automatically released and float free if the vessel sinks.

(2) This section applies to all United Kingdom fishing vessels of 12 metres or more in length and to such other United Kingdom fishing vessels as may be prescribed.

Lifejackets

3.—(1) A United Kingdom fishing vessel of less than 12 metres in length shall carry a lifejacket of an appropriate size for each person on board and extra lifejackets as follows—

(*a*) if lifejackets of different sizes are required to be carried, at least one extra lifejacket of each size;

(*b*) otherwise, one extra lifejacket if there are 10 or fewer persons and two extra lifejackets if there are 11 or more.

(2) The lifejackets shall comply with the requirements for the time being of Part I or, as the case may be, Part II of Schedule 11 to the Fishing Vessels (Safety Provisions) Rules 1975 (general requirements for lifejackets).

Power to prescribe further requirements

4.—(1) The Secretary of State may by regulations—

(*a*) prescribe anything required to be prescribed for the purposes of sections 1 and 2; and

(*b*) amplify or extend the requirements of sections 1 to 3, in particular, by laying down further technical requirements in relation to the equipment required by those sections.

(2) References in this Act or elsewhere to the requirements of sections 1 to 3 are to those requirements as amplified or extended under this section.

Enforcement

5.—(1) In section 2(1) of the Fishing Vessels (Safety Provisions) Act 1970 (fishing vessel survey rules) for "and the rules for radio navigational aids" substitute ", the rules for radio navigational aids and sections 1 and 2 of the Safety at Sea Act 1986 (safety requirements for fishing vessels)".

(2) In section 3(1) of the Fishing Vessels (Safety Provisions) Act 1970 (fishing vessel certificates) omit "or" at the end of paragraph (*b*) and after paragraph (*c*) insert—", or

(*d*) sections 1 and 2 of the Safety at Sea Act 1986 (safety requirements for fishing vessels)".

(3) The references to "the Merchant Shipping Acts" in section 3(1) of the Fishing Vessels (Safety Provisions) Act 1970 and in section 76(1) of the Merchant Shipping Act 1970 (powers of inspection) include this Act.

(4) In Schedule 1 to the Merchant Shipping Act 1984 (relevant statutory provisions for purposes of improvement and prohibition notices), at the appropriate place add—

"1986 c.23 The Safety at Sea Act   Sections 1 to 3."
                 1986.

Offences

6.—(1) No fishing vessel to which any of the requirements of sections 1 to 3 applies shall go to sea unless the requirement is complied with.

(2) If a fishing vessel goes to sea in contravention of this section the owner and skipper of the vessel are each liable on summary conviction to a fine not exceeding level 5 on the standard scale.

(3) In proceedings for an offence under this section it is a defence for the accused to show that he used all due diligence and took all reasonable precautions to avoid the commission of an offence under this section.

The skipper and crew

Training in safety matters

7.—(1) The Secretary of State may make regulations for securing that the skipper of and every seaman employed or engaged in a United Kingdom fishing vessel is trained in safety matters.

(2) The regulations may provide that if a person goes to sea on a fishing vessel in contravention of a requirement of the regulations—

(a) he commits an offence and is liable on summary conviction to a fine not exceeding level 2, or if he is the skipper or an owner of the vessel level 5, on the standard scale; and

(b) the skipper and each owner of the vessel is (except in respect of a contravention by himself) liable on summary conviction to a fine not exceeding level 5 on the standard scale.

Supplementary provisions

Exemptions

8.—(1) The Secretary of State may exempt a fishing vessel or description of fishing vessel from any requirement of this Part.

(2) He may do so generally or for a specified time or with respect to a specified voyage or to voyages in a specified area, and may do so subject to any specified conditions.

Regulations

9.—(1) Regulations under this Part may make different provision for different cases, or descriptions of case, including different provision for different descriptions of vessel or according to the circumstances of operation of a vessel.

(2) Regulations under this Part shall be made by statutory instrument which shall be subject to annulment in pursuance of a resolution of either House of Parliament.

(3) Before making regulations under this Part the Secretary of State shall carry out such consultation with organisations or persons likely to be affected by the regulations as appears to him to be appropriate.

(4) If it appears to the Secretary of State that regulations under a power conferred by any other enactment supersede any of the provisions of this Part, or of regulations made under them, he may in exercise of that power repeal or revoke the superseded provisions and make such consequential repeals or amendments of any other provision of this Part or any enactment amended by this Part as appear to him appropriate.

Part II

Miscellaneous and General

Miscellaneous

Drunkenness, &c., of skipper of fishing vessel

10. In section 28 of the Merchant Shipping Act 1970 (drunkenness, &c., on board fishing vessel)—
  (*a*) for "a seaman employed" substitute "the skipper of or a seaman employed or engaged", and
  (*b*) for "carry out the duties of his employment" substitute "fulfil his responsibility for the vessel or, as the case may be, carry out the duties of his employment or engagement".

Extension of power to make safety regulations

11.—(1) In section 21 of the Merchant Shipping Act 1979 (power to make safety regulations), in subsection (1) after paragraph (*b*) add—
  "(*c*) for securing the safety of other ships and persons on them while they are within a port in the United Kingdom.".
(2) In subsection (3) of that section (matters for which regulations may provide) for the opening words substitute—
  "Regulations in pursuance of paragraph (*a*) or (*b*) of subsection (1) of this section may make provision with respect to any of the following matters, and regulations in pursuance of paragraph (*c*) of that subsection may make provision with respect to any of the following matters so far as relates to safety, namely—".
(3) In section 49 of the Merchant Shipping Act 1979 (general provisions as to orders and regulations) after subsection (4) insert—
  "(4A) Regulations of the following descriptions under section 21(1) of this Act shall be subject to annulment in pursuance of a resolution of either House of Parliament—
  (*a*) regulations under paragraph (*a*) of that subsection,
  (*b*) regulations under paragraph (*b*) of that subsection which—
      (i) relate to an international agreement laid before Parliament before 4th April 1979, or
      (ii) relate to safety matters and give effect to amendments in force to an international agreement already implemented under that paragraph, and
  (*c*) regulations under paragraph (*c*) of that subsection which contain a statement that they are made only for the purpose of applying to certain other ships the provisions of an international agreement implemented under paragraph (*b*) of that subsection;
  and regulations of any other description under section 21(1) of this Act shall not be made unless a draft of the regulations has been approved by resolution of each House of Parliament.".

(4) In consequence of the above amendments the following amendments and repeals in the Merchant Shipping Act 1979 have effect—

(a) in section 21(1), after "regulations" insert "(hereafter in this section and in the following section referred to as 'safety regulations')",

(b) in section 21(3), at the end add "; but the mention of specific matters in this subsection shall not be construed as restricting the generality of the power conferred by paragraph (a), (b) or (c) of subsection (1) of this section.",

(c) in section 49(3) omit the words from "and no regulations" to "section 21(1)(b) of this Act" and "or regulations", and

(d) in section 49(4) omit the words "21(1)" and the words "(except regulations" to "preceding subsection)".

General

Expenses

12.—(1) There shall be paid out of money provided by Parliament—

(a) any administrative expenses incurred by a Minister of the Crown or a government department under this Act; and

(b) any increase attributable to this Act in the sums payable out of money so provided under any other Act.

Interpretation

13.—(1) In this Act—

"fishing vessel" means a vessel which is for the time being used for or in connection with sea fishing but does not include a vessel used for fishing other than for profit;

"length" means the register length shown on the vessel's certificate of registry;

"prescribed" means prescribed by regulations under section 4;

"United Kingdom fishing vessel" means a fishing vessel registered in the United Kingdom.

(2) This Act shall be construed as one with the Merchant Shipping Acts 1894 to 1984.

Power to extend provisions to other territories and vessels

14.—(1) Her Majesty may by Order in Council direct that the provisions of Part I of this Act and of regulations made under those provisions extend to any of the Channel Islands, with such exceptions, adaptations or modifications as may be specified in the Order.

(2) Sections 92 to 94 of the Merchant Shipping Act 1970 (unregistered ships and ships registered outside the United Kingdom) apply to section 10 of this Act as they apply to the provisions of that Act.

(3) Section 47 of the Merchant Shipping Act 1979 (power to extend Act to certain countries) applies to section 11 of this Act as it applies to the provisions of that Act.

(4) The references above to specified provisions of this Act include references to other provisions of this Act so far as they have effect for the interpretation of, or otherwise for the purposes of, the specified provisions.

Short title, citation, commencement and extent

15.—(1) This Act may be cited as the Safety at Sea Act 1986.

(2) This Act and the Merchant Shipping Acts 1894 to 1984 may be cited together as the Merchant Shipping Acts 1894 to 1986.

(3) This Act comes into force on such day as may be appointed by the Secretary of State by order made by statutory instrument.

(4) Different days may be appointed for different provisions and for different descriptions of vessel.

(5) This Act extends to England and Wales, Scotland and Northern Ireland.

HEALTH SERVICE JOINT CONSULTATIVE COMMITTEES (ACCESS TO INFORMATION) ACT 1986

(1986 c. 24)

An Act to provide for access by the public to meetings of, and to certain documents and information relating to, joint consultative committees and sub-committees constituted under section 22 of the National Health Service Act 1977.

[26th June 1986]

PARLIAMENTARY DEBATES
Hansard: H.C. Vol. 90, col. 1247; Vol. 96, col. 1263; H.L. Vol. 474, col. 772; Vol. 475, col. 1143; Vol. 476, col. 730; Vol. 477, col. 157.
The Bill was considered by Standing Committee C on April 9, 1986.

Interpretation

1.—(1) In this Act—
"joint committee" means—
    (*a*) a joint consultative committee appointed pursuant to an order under section 22 of the National Health Service Act 1977 or deemed by virtue of such an order to be so appointed, or
    (*b*) a sub-committee of such a committee, or
    (*c*) a joint sub-committee of two or more such committees; and
"local authority" means a county council, a district council, a London borough council, the Common Council of the City of London or the Inner London Education Authority.

(2) Any reference in this Act to a constituent authority shall be construed, in relation to a joint committee, as a reference to a District Health Authority, Family Practitioner Committee or local authority which—

(*a*) if the committee in question is a joint consultative committee, is represented on that committee, or

(*b*) if the committee in question is a sub-committee or joint sub-committee, is represented on the joint consultative committee, or (as the case may be) one of the joint consultative committees, that appointed that committee.

Access to meetings and documents of joint committees

2.—(1) Sections 100A to 100D of the Local Government Act 1972 (access to meetings and documents of certain authorities) shall apply to a joint committee as they apply to a principal council (within the meaning of Part VA of that Act), but subject to the following modifications, namely—

(*a*) any reference to the offices of a principal council shall be construed as a reference to the offices of each of the constituent authorities;

(*b*) any reference to the proper officer in relation to a principal council shall be construed as a reference to the person appointed for the purpose by the joint committee; and

(*c*) in section 100A(6)(*c*) the reference to premises not belonging to a principal council shall be construed as a reference to premises not belonging to any of the constituent authorities nor vested in the Secretary of State.

(2) In section 100H of that Act (supplemental provisions and offences)—

    (*a*) any reference to any provision of Part VA of that Act or to any right conferred by Part VA includes a reference to any such provision as it applies to a joint committee by virtue of this section or to any right conferred by Part VA as it so applies (as the case may be);

    (*b*) in subsection (3), as it so applies, the reference to a principal council shall be construed as a reference to a constituent authority; and

    (*c*) subsection (5) shall apply to any meeting of a joint committee.

(3) The power conferred on the Secretary of State by section 100I(2) of that Act to vary Schedule 12A to that Act (exempt information) shall include power to vary that Schedule as it applies in relation to a joint committee by virtue of this section.

(4) In that Schedule, as it so applies—

    (*a*) Part I shall have effect with the insertion after paragraph 6 of the following paragraphs—

        "6A. Information relating to the physical or mental health of any particular person.

        6B. Information relating to—

        (*a*) any particular person who is or was formerly included in a list of persons undertaking to provide services under Part II of the National Health Service Act 1977, or is an applicant for inclusion in such a list, or

        (*b*) any particular employee of such a person.";

    (*b*) paragraph 1 of Part II shall have effect with the insertion after "paragraphs 1 to 5" of "or 6B"; and

    (*c*) any reference to "the authority" shall be construed as a reference to a constituent authority (and paragraph 1(2) of Part III shall accordingly not apply).

Access to information relating to members of joint committees etc.

3.—(1) A joint committee shall maintain a register containing the name and address of every member of the committee, and stating in the case of each member—

    (*a*) the name and address of the constituent authority which he represents and whether he is or is not a member of that authority, or

    (*b*) if he has been appointed by any voluntary organisations (within the meaning of the National Health Service Act 1977), that he has been so appointed.

(2) A written summary of the rights—

    (*a*) to attend meetings of a joint committee, and

    (*b*) to inspect and copy, and to be furnished with, documents relating to a joint committee,

which are for the time being conferred by virtue of section 2 of this Act shall be kept at the offices of each of the constituent authorities.

(3) Any such register or summary as is mentioned in subsection (1) or (2) above shall be open to inspection by the public, at all reasonable hours and without payment, at the offices of each of the constituent authorities; and any of those authorities shall, at the request of any person, supply him with a copy of any such register or summary on payment of such reasonable fee as the authority may determine.

Short title, commencement and extent

4.—(1) This Act shall be cited as the Health Service Joint Consultative Committees (Access to Information) Act 1986.

(2) This Act shall come into force at the end of the period of two months beginning with the day on which this Act is passed.

(3) Nothing in this Act applies in relation to any meeting of a joint committee held before the coming into force of this Act.

(4) This Act extends to England and Wales only.

COMMONWEALTH DEVELOPMENT CORPORATION ACT 1986

(1986 c. 25)

An Act to extend the powers of the Commonwealth Development Corporation; to enable the Secretary of State to make grants to the Corporation; and to enable him to impose restrictions on, and to give guarantees in respect of, borrowing by the Corporation's subsidiaries.

[26th June 1986]

PARLIAMENTARY DEBATES
   Hansard: H.L. Vol. 468, cols. 387, 981; H.L. Vol. 469, cols. 904, 1165; H.L. Vol. 470, col. 346; H.C. Vol. 92, col. 1164; H.C. Vol. 100, col. 279.
   The Bill was considered by Standing Committee F on June 5, 1986.

Amendments of Commonwealth Development Corporation Act 1978

1.—(1) The Commonwealth Development Corporation Act 1978 shall be amended as follows.

(2) In section 2 (powers of Corporation)—

(a) in subsection (2)(b) for the words "in those countries" there shall be substituted the words "in those or other overseas countries";

(b) in subsection (2)(e) for the words "any such functions as are mentioned in paragraph (d) above" there shall be substituted the words "any functions which the Corporation is empowered to perform by virtue of any of paragraphs (a) to (d) above or to assist the Corporation to perform any of those functions";

(c) at the end of subsection (3) there shall be inserted the words "; and the power conferred by paragraph (d) of that subsection to give assistance may be exercised indirectly by giving assistance to a body which will in turn assist other bodies or persons to perform any of the functions mentioned in that paragraph."

(3) In section 9 (borrowing by Corporation)—

(a) after subsection (2) there shall be inserted—

"(2A) It shall be the duty of the Corporation to secure that none of its wholly-owned subsidiaries borrows otherwise than from the Corporation or from another of its wholly-owned subsidiaries except with the approval of the Secretary of State given with the consent of the Treasury as to the matters mentioned in subsection (2) above.";

(b) in subsection (3) for the words "subsection (2) above" there shall be substituted the words "subsection (2) or (2A) above".

(4) After section 10 (advances by Secretary of State) there shall be inserted—

Grants to Corporation by Secretary of State

10A.—(1) The Secretary of State may, after consultation with the Corporation and with the consent of the Treasury, make to the Corporation grants of amounts to be applied by the Corporation in accordance with such directions, if any, as may be given to it by the Secretary of State.

(2) Any sums required by the Secretary of State for the purpose of grants made to the Corporation under this section shall be paid out of money provided by Parliament."

(5) In section 11 (guarantees)—

(a) after subsection (1) there shall be inserted—

"(1A) The Secretary of State may, with the approval of the Treasury, guarantee in such manner and on such conditions as he thinks fit the repayment of the principal of, and the payment of interest and other charges on, any borrowings of a subsidiary of the Corporation made otherwise than from the Corporation.";

(b) after subsection (3) there shall be inserted—

"(3A) Immediately after any guarantee is given under subsection (1A) above or any sum is issued for fulfilling such a guarantee, the Secretary of State shall lay a statement of the guarantee or, as the case may be, a statement relating to that sum before each House of Parliament."; and

(c) at the end of subsection (4) there shall be inserted the words "and any sums required by the Secretary of State for fulfilling any guarantee given under subsection (1A) above shall be paid out of money provided by Parliament.".

(6) In section 12(2)(a) (repayment by Corporation of sums issued in fulfilment of guarantees) for the words "section 11(1) above" there shall be substituted the words "section 11(1) or (1A) above".

(7) In section 17(1) (definitions) the word "and" at the end of the definition of "new Commonwealth country" shall be omitted and after the definition of "overseas country" there shall be inserted the words "and

"subsidiary" and "wholly-owned subsidiary" shall be construed in accordance with section 736 of the Companies Act 1985.";

and paragraph (b) of section 9A(6) (which is replaced by the foregoing provision) is hereby repealed together with the word "and" immediately preceding it.

Short title, citation and extent

2.—(1) This Act may be cited as the Commonwealth Development Corporation Act 1986.

(2) The Commonwealth Development Corporation Act 1978, the Commonwealth Development Corporation Act 1982 and this Act may be cited together as the Commonwealth Development Corporation Acts 1978 to 1986.

(3) This Act extends to Northern Ireland.

LAND REGISTRATION ACT 1986*

(1986 c. 26)

An Act to make amendments of the Land Registration Act 1925 relating to the conversion of title and to leases, to abolish the Minor Interests Index, and for connected purposes.   [26th June 1986]

GENERAL NOTE

The Act, which received the Royal Assent on June 26, 1986 gives effect to the recommendations of the Law Commission in their report in 1983, *Property Law: Land Registration* (Law Com: No. 125). The Report dealt with a number of specific topics arising out of four working papers published between 1970 and 1976, reviewing various aspects of the land registration system, and the comments received on these. The Law Commission made specific recommendations for amendments to the law relating to land registration in order to simplify and improve this in three distinct areas; the conversion of title, the registration and protection of leases and the abolition of the Minor Interests Index. The Act follows closely the terms of the draft clauses annexed to the Law Commission Report and deals with the topics concerned as follows:

S.1: Simplification of the system for conversion of inferior titles.

Ss.2 to 4: Extension to the categories of leases subject to compulsory registration; registration of inalienable leases made possible and extension of the categories of overriding interest to include gratuitous leases and leases granted at a premium.

S.5: Abolition of the Minor Interests Index.

COMMENCEMENT

The Act will come into force on a day to be appointed.

EXTENT

The Act applies to England and Wales only.

ABBREVIATIONS

The LPA 1925: The Law of Property Act 1925.
The LRA 1925: The Land Registration Act 1925.

PARLIAMENTARY DEBATES

Hansard: H.L. Vol. 471, col. 1171, Vol. 472, col. 744; Vol. 473, cols. 82 and 1078; H.C. Vol. 98, col. 627; Vol. 100, col. 297.

The Bill was considered by Standing Committee B on June 10, 1986.

Conversion of title

1.—(1) In the Land Registration Act 1925 ("the 1925 Act") the following shall be substituted for section 77 (conversion of title)—
"Conversion of title
    77.—(1) Where land is registered with a good leasehold title, or satisfies the conditions for such registration under this section, the registrar may, and on application by the proprietor shall, if he is satisfied as to the title to the freehold and the title to any intermediate leasehold, enter the title as absolute.

* Annotations by Richard Fearnley, B.A., Solicitor, Assistant Land Registrar at H.M. Land Registry.

(2) Where land is registered with a possessory title, the registrar may, and on application by the proprietor shall—

(a) if he is satisfied as to the title, or

(b) if the land has been so registered for at least twelve years and he is satisfied that the proprietor is in possession,

enter the title in the case of freehold land as absolute and in the case of leasehold land as good leasehold.

(3) Where land is registered with a qualified title, the registrar may, and on application by the proprietor shall, if he is satisfied as to the title, enter it in the case of freehold land as absolute and in the case of leasehold land as good leasehold.

(4) If any claim adverse to the title of the proprietor has been made, an entry shall not be made in the register under this section unless and until the claim has been disposed of.

(5) No fee shall be charged for the making of an entry in the register under this section at the instance of the registrar or on an application by the proprietor made in connection with a transfer for valuable consideration of the land to which the application relates.

(6) Any person, other than the proprietor, who suffers loss by reason of any entry on the register made by virtue of this section shall be entitled to be indemnified under this Act as if a mistake had been made in the register."

(2) In the case of land registered with a possessory title before the commencement of this Act—

(a) subsection (2)(b) of section 77 of the 1925 Act as substituted by this section applies only where the land has been so registered for a period of at least 12 years after that commencement, but

(b) nothing in this section affects the operation of subsection (3)(b) of section 77 of the 1925 Act as originally enacted (which provides for conversion of a possessory title after 15 years' registration in the case of freehold land and 10 years' registration in the case of leasehold land) in relation to a period of registration beginning before that commencement.

GENERAL NOTE

This section implements the recommendations of the Law Commission intended to simplify and improve the provisions of the LRA 1925 concerning the conversion of inferior titles. The LRA 1925 established four classes of title which may be granted by the registrar on first registration of title to land; absolute, good leasehold, possessory and qualified (of which absolute, possessory and qualified titles may each be freehold or leasehold). Only absolute titles carry with them the full indemnity provisions of the LRA 1925 and they are therefore the best titles available. The other classes of title may be regarded as inferior since they are associated with different kinds of defect, identified by the registrar at the time of first registration, which are reflected in the lesser degree to which such titles are "guaranteed" under the land registration system. In the case of good leasehold title, usually granted where the title of the original lessor is not deduced or is found to be inadequate, in some way, s.10 of the LRA 1925 provides that the registration does not affect or prejudice the enforcement of any estate right or interest affecting or in derogation of the title of the lessor to grant the lease. In the case of possessory title, where there is found on first registration to be the possibility of a third party claim which may upset the title of the first proprietor, s.6 (freeholds) or s.11 (leaseholds) of the LRA 1925 provides that registration does not affect or prejudice the enforcement of any estate right or interest adverse to or in derogation of the title of the first proprietor and subsisting or capable of arising at the time of first registration. Qualified title is rare but may be granted where an applicant's title is found to be subject to some specific defect or limitation. In such cases, under s.7 (freeholds) or s.12 (leaseholds) of the LRA 1925, a special entry may be made in the register excepting from the effects of registration any estate right or interest arising before a specified date or arising under a specified instrument or otherwise particularly described in the register.

Registration with an inferior class of title is not immutable and it is generally desirable, where possible, to arrange for registration with a particular class of inferior title to be upgraded by the process of conversion, for which provision is made in s.77 of the LRA 1925. However this section, in its original terms, was criticised by the Law Commission as unsatisfactory, lacking in clarity, illogical and difficult to read and to grasp as a coherent whole. The Commission particularly criticised subs. (4) which may be taken to imply (contrary to principle) that a good leasehold title may be converted to absolute title without production of the reversionary title. They also criticised subs. (3)(*b*) (under which possessory freehold titles and possessory leasehold titles may "mature" after 15 years registration and 10 years registration respectively into absolute freehold title or good leasehold title as appropriate) because of the apparently arbitrary difference in the periods required to elapse for conversion of freehold and leasehold titles and the fact that neither period accorded with the standard limitation period of 12 years (see s.15 of the Limitation Act 1980).

Accordingly, the Law Commission recommended the substitution of a new s.77 to remove the difficulties identified in the original section and to provide a more coherent and understandable system for the conversion of title. S.1 of the new Act does this by enacting, in substantially the same terms, the equivalent draft clause annexed to the Law Commission Report.

Subs. (1)

This subsection substitutes a new s.77 in the LRA 1925. The new section does not carry forward the special provisions of the original section relating to the conversion of titles registered before January 1, 1926. Other changes are dealt with below.

Subs. (1) of the new section 77: Good leasehold titles (and qualified and possessory leasehold titles capable of being converted under the section to good leasehold title) can only be converted to absolute leasehold if the registrar is satisfied as to the title to the freehold and any intermediate leasehold (and is therefore satisfied as to the matters which are excepted from the effects of registration with good leasehold title). Such title will therefore need to be deduced in all cases before conversion can take place. Provided the registrar is satisfied as to the superior title, conversion must be effected on specific application being made by the proprietor of the title but may be effected by the registrar himself without such application.

Satisfies the conditions for such registration under this section: Possessory and qualified leasehold titles may be converted to good leasehold titles under subss. (2) and (3) of the new section.

Subs. (2) of the new s.77: A single standard period of 12 years (to accord with the standard limitation period provided by s.15 of the Limitation Act 1980 for the barring of actions for recovery of land in general cases) is specified for the registration of possessory titles after which the title can be converted to absolute title (in the case of freehold) and good leasehold title (in the case of leasehold) on the registrar being satisfied only that the proprietor is in possession (para. (*b*)). Otherwise, provided the registrar is satisfied as to the title, conversion may take place at any time and not only on the occasion of a transfer for valuable consideration, as required by the original s.77 (para. (*a*)).

Subs. (3) of the new s.77: As with possessory titles, provided the registrar is satisfied as to the title, the conversion of qualified freehold and leasehold titles to absolute title and good leasehold title respectively may take place at any time and not only on the occasion of a transfer for value.

Subs. (4) of the new s.77: This subsection re-enacts subs. (5) of the original s.77 and prevents conversion of title where an adverse claim is pending.

Subs. (5) of the new s.77: This subsection provides for no fee to be charged where conversion takes place at the instance of the registrar or is connected with a transfer for valuable consideration of the land. This accords with the policy of the original section.

Subs. (6) of the new s.77: This subsection re-enacts subs. (6) of the original s.77 and provides for indemnity to be paid out of public funds to anyone who suffers loss (*e.g.* by the shutting out of a valid claim) as a result of conversion of title in the same manner as if a mistake has been made in the register (see s.83 of the LRA 1925 for the relevant provisions governing the payment of indemnity).

Subs. (2)

This subsection of s.1 contains transitional provisions affecting subs. (2) of the new s.77 in relation to possessory titles already registered at the commencement of the Act.

Para. (a): The new 12 year period for the conversion of possessory titles to absolute freehold or good leasehold titles (subs. (2)(*b*) of the new s.77) will only apply so as to enable possessory titles to be converted where such period has elapsed since the commencement of the Act.

Para. (b): Where, because registration was effected prior to the commencement of the Act, the 15 year registration period (in relation to possessory freehold titles) or the 10 year registration period (in relation to possessory leasehold titles) specified in the original s.77(3)(*b*) has started to run, the proprietor will still be able to take advantage of that period if it will result in conversion being available before 12 years after the commencement of the Act.

The effect of the provisions relating to the conversion of possessory titles are shown by the following examples which assume the Act comes into force on January 2, 1987:

(i) a possessory freehold title registered on July 1, 1980 will be eligible for conversion from July 1, 1995 onward (15 years having elapsed under the original s.77(3)(*b*)) but such a title registered on any date between January 2, 1984 and December 31, 1986 will be eligible for conversion from January 2, 1999 onwards (12 years having elapsed since the commencement of the Act in accordance with the new s.77(2)(*b*) as applied by s.1(2) of the new Act);

(ii) a possessory leasehold title registered on July 1, 1985 will be eligible for conversion from July 1, 1995 onwards (10 years having elapsed under the original s.77(3)(*b*)) but such a title registered on July 1, 1987 will not be eligible for conversion until July 1, 1999 (rather than July 1, 1997) since 12 years will be required to elapse from the date of registration, under the new s.77(2)(*b*).

Compulsory registration of certain leases

2.—(1) In section 123(1) of the 1925 Act (which requires an application for registration to be made upon the grant or assignment of certain leases)—

(*a*) for "a term of years absolute not being less than forty years from the date of the delivery of the grant" there shall be substituted "a term of years absolute of more than twenty-one years from the date of delivery of the grant", and

(*b*) for "having not less than forty years to run from the date of delivery of the assignment" there shall be substituted "having more than twenty-one years to run from the date of delivery of the assignment".

(2) The following shall be inserted after section 8(1) of the 1925 Act (which provides that application for registration may be made by an estate owner holding under a lease with more than 21 years unexpired)—

"(1A) An application for registration in respect of leasehold land held under a lease in relation to the grant or assignment of which section 123(1) of this Act applies (whether by virtue of this Act or any later enactment) may be made within the period allowed by section 123(1), or any authorised extension of that period, notwithstanding that the lease was granted for a term of not more than twenty-one years or that the unexpired term of the lease is not more than twenty-one years."

(3) In consequence of subsection (1) above, in section 154(1) of the Housing Act 1985 (section 123 of the 1925 Act to apply in relation to certain leases whether or not for 40 years or more) for "not less than 40 years" there shall be substituted "more than 21 years".

(4) The following shall be added at the end of section 154 of the Housing Act 1985—

"(7) Section 70(1)(*k*) of the Land Registration Act 1925 (overriding interests) shall not apply to a lease granted in pursuance of this Part."

(5) The amendments made by subsections (1) and (2) above apply only in relation to the grant or assignment of a lease after the commencement of this Act.

GENERAL NOTE
This section implements the recommendation of the Law Commission that, in areas of compulsory registration, all leases granted for more than 21 years out of unregistered titles

should be compulsorily registrable on grant, and existing leases with more than 21 years unexpired at the date of assignment should be compulsorily registrable on assignment. The recommended periods of "more than 21 years" replace the equivalent periods of "not less than 40 years" originally specified in s.123(1) of the LRA 1925 (which sets out the categories of transaction following which registration of title is compulsory). This eliminates in areas of compulsory registration the anomaly that, in relation to leases which are granted for a term of more than 21 years but less than 40 years or which are assigned having more than 21 years but less than 40 years unexpired at the date of assignment, registration is compulsory, under ss.19(2) and 22(2) of the LRA 1925, if the superior title is registered but only optional, under s.8(1) of the LRA 1925, if the superior title is not registered. The section is in substantially the same terms as the equivalent draft clause annexed to the Law Commission Report except for one amendment and a new subs. (3) which were made necessary by modifications to the provisions for compulsory registration of titles contained in the Housing and Building Control Act 1984 now consolidated in the Housing Act 1985.

Subs. (1)

   This subsection effects the substitution of references to periods of "more than twenty-one years" for the references to periods of "not less than forty years" in s.123 of the LRA 1925. Following commencement of the Act, in areas of compulsory registration, registration of all leases granted for terms of more than 21 years, whether or not the lessors' title is registered, and of all assignments of leases having more than 21 years to run at the date of assignment, will be mandatory.

Subs. (2)

   This subsection contains a consequential amendment of s.8 of the LRA 1925. S.8 enables estate owners holding under leases to apply for registration of those leases but only where they have more than 21 years to run at the time the application is made. However in compulsory areas, under the revised s.123 the category of leases subject to compulsory registration will include leases granted for a term of only slightly over 21 years or assigned having only slightly over 21 years to run. Because there may be a period of up to two months (or more where the registrar authorises extension of this) before application for registration is made there may be cases where there are no longer more than 21 years unexpired under the lease at the date of application for registration so that s.8, unless amended, will not apply to enable such applications to be made. The subsection resolves the potential conflict by inserting a new subsection (1A) after subs. (1) of s.8 to enable applications for registration to be made in those circumstances.

   Or any later enactment: The amendment is also required for an entirely separate reason. The words in brackets in the new subs. (1A) were added to the equivalent provision in the draft clause annexed to the Law Commission Report and the particular "later enactment" which is intended is the Housing and Building Control Act 1984, now consolidated in the Housing Act 1985. S.154(1) of the 1985 Act applies the compulsory registration provision of s.123 of the LRA 1925 to all conveyances of freehold or grants of leases under the "right to buy" provisions of Pt. V of the 1985 Act (whether or not in areas of compulsory registration) and, as a result of the 1984 Act, leases granted under these provisions can, in some circumstances, be for 21 years or less. The potential conflict with s.8 of the LRA 1925 is again removed by the new subs. (1A).

Subs. (3)

   This is purely a consequential amendment to s.154(1) of the Housing Act 1985 following upon the changes effected by subs. (1).

Subs. (4)

   This subsection adds a new subsection to s.154 of the Housing Act 1985 to remove from the category of leases which are overriding interests under s.70(1)(*k*) of the LRA 1925 (leases granted for a term not exceeding 21 years—see s.4(1) of the new Act below) those leases which are for not more than 21 years but which are nevertheless subject to compulsory registration, as explained above. Overriding interests are those matters not entered on the register of a title, for the most part set out in s.70(1) of the LRA 1925, to which the land in the title will nevertheless be subject despite the lack of such entry on the register. Where leases are subject to compulsory registration the proper method of ensuring their protection is to apply for registration and it is undesirable that they should also benefit from the protection afforded to overriding interests where registration has been neglected.

Subs. 5

The extension of compulsory registration to leases granted or assigned and having more than 21 years but not more than 40 years to run relates only to leases granted or assigned after the commencement of the Act.

Inalienable leases: registration to be allowed

3.—(1) The following shall be substituted for section 8(2) of the 1925 Act (which prohibits registration of leasehold land if the lease contains an absolute prohibition on alienation and requires that a restriction on alienation be protected by entry on the register or otherwise)—

"(2) Leasehold land held under a lease containing a prohibition or restriction on dealings therewith inter vivos shall not be registered under this Act unless and until provision is made in the prescribed manner for preventing any dealing therewith in contravention of the prohibition or restriction by an entry on the register to that effect, or otherwise."

(2) The amendment made by subsection (1) above applies in relation to a lease granted before the commencement of this Act subject to an absolute prohibition on any dealings therewith inter vivos—

(*a*) so as to enable an application for registration to be made, and

(*b*) as regards dealings therewith after that commencement,

but not so as to alter the effect of any grant, assignment or other dealing before that commencement.

GENERAL NOTE

The Law Commission considered the position of leases which contain an absolute prohibition on alienation and concluded that s.8(2) of the LRA 1925 (which precludes registration of such leases) should be amended so as to permit their registration on the same basis as other leases not containing such a prohibition. The registration of leases containing such a prohibition was no doubt considered unnecessary originally because one of the main functions of land registration is to facilitate transfers and other dispositions of land, which function would not be thought relevant in the case of inalienable leases. However, as the Law Commission pointed out, such leases can be transferred if the lessor waives the prohibition on alienation, and there appeared to be no good reason to exclude such leases from registration. S.3 of the new Act is in substantially the same terms as the recommended draft clause annexed to the Law Commission Report.

Subs. (1)

This subsection replaces s.8(2) of the LRA 1925 with a new subsection in which the words preventing registration of an inalienable lease are deleted and whereby the prohibition on alienation contained in such a lease is to be protected in the same way as restrictions on alienation are at present; *i.e.* by entry on the register.

Subs. (2)

Under this subsection the new s.8(2) of the LRA 1925 will apply to all inalienable leases whether created before or after commencement of the Act. However, in relation to existing inalienable leases, the provision will not alter the effect of any grant assignment or dealing prior to commencement so that it is only on a subsequent dealing inducing compulsory registration that application for registration will need to be made. In the meantime voluntary registration (in compulsory areas) will be permissible under subs. (2)(*a*).

Gratuitous leases and leases granted at a premium

4.—(1) In section 70(1) of the 1925 Act (the list of overriding interests) the following shall be substituted for paragraph (*k*) (leases for 21 years or less granted at a rent without taking a fine)—

"(*k*) Leases granted for a term not exceeding twenty-one years;".

(2) In sections 18(3) and 21(3) of the 1925 Act (powers of disposition of registered freeholds and leaseholds: lease to take effect notwithstanding caution, restriction, etc.) the words "at a rent without taking a fine" shall be omitted.

(3) In sections 19(2) and 22(2) of the 1925 Act (dispositions to be completed by registration) in paragraph (*a*) the words "if it is granted at a rent without taking a fine" shall be omitted.

(4) Where a lease granted before the commencement of this Act was not an overriding interest because it was not granted at a rent or without taking a fine, the amendment made by subsection (1) above applies in relation to it only if the land was subject to it immediately before that commencement.

(5) The amendments made by subsections (2) and (3) above apply only in relation to dispositions after the commencement of this Act.

GENERAL NOTE

This section implements the recommendations of the Law Commission as to the enlarging of the category of leases which are treated as overriding interests in relation to a superior registered title. Overriding interests are those interests to which registered land and dispositions thereof are subject, notwithstanding they are not protected by entry on the register (ss.5(*b*), 9(*c*), 20(1)(*b*) and 23(1)(*c*) of the LRA 1925). Any interests which are not overriding interests can only be protected against dealings with the lessor's title by being noted on the register of title. The principal categories of overriding interest are set out in s.70(1) of the LRA 1925 and these include, at para. (*k*), "Leases for any term or interest not exceeding twenty-one years granted at a rent without taking a fine". Since such leases will be protected by virtue of their status as overriding interests and since leases which are registrable will be protected by notice on the lessor's title entered as part of the process of registration of the lease or the lessor's title, whichever is later, there remain two categories of lease which are not automatically protected because they are neither overriding interests nor themselves capable of being substantively registered. These are leases for a term not exceeding 21 years which are either not granted at a rent or are granted at a premium. In order to protect such leases against dealings with the lessor's registered title, specific application must be made for their protection by entry of notice on the lessor's title under the procedure governed by section 48 of the LRA 1925. The Law Commission saw no good reason why such leases should be excluded from protection as overriding interests, in the same manner as all other leases for terms not exceeding 21 years and they therefore recommended that s.70(1)(*k*) of the LRA 1925 should be amended to include them. S.4 of the new Act does this in substantially the same terms as the relevant draft clause annexed to the Law Commission Report.

Subs. (1)

This subsection replaces para. (*k*) of s.70(1) of the LRA 1925 with a new paragraph which removes the previous qualification that leases for terms not exceeding 21 years should be granted at a rent without taking a fine and all leases for such terms affecting registered land will therefore be overriding interests.

Subss. (2) and (3)

These subsections make consequential amendments to the provisions concerning the powers of proprietors of registered land to effect dispositions, and the registration of such dispositions, to reflect the new category of leases which qualify as overriding interests.

Subs. (4)

The changes made by subs. (1) are to apply to existing leases so that leases granted gratuitously or at a premium out of registered land will become overriding interests if not already noted on the lessor's title. Thus, where there has been a failure to protect such leases prior to commencement of the Act by entry of notice on the lessor's title, those leases will acquire protection as overriding interests following commencement. The subsection is intended to prevent subs. (1) operating to the detriment of persons who have dealt with the original lessor prior to commencement, so as to acquire interests which would have been free from leases which were unprotected by notice, and who might otherwise be prejudiced by such leases becoming protected as overriding interests following commencement. It does so by providing that, in relation to a lease granted gratuitously or at a premium prior to commencement, subs. (1) only applies "If the land was subject to it immediately before that commencement". The example is given in the Law Commission Report of a lessor, L1, who has granted a lease for 21 years at a premium in 1975 to T, who has never protected the lease by notice on the register. It is stated that if L1 assigns to L2 after commencement then L2 will be bound by the lease as an overriding interest because the reversion was subject to the lease immediately before commencement but if L1 has assigned the reversion to L2 prior to commencement and L2 assigns to L3 after commencement, L3 will take free of the lease because the reversion was not subject to the lease immediately before commencement. However it is not quite clear that the subsection achieves its aim since this may depend upon the meaning of the word *land* in the subsection. If it is taken to mean only the lessor's legal estate in the land then a transferee of the lessor's title will have acquired a legal estate free from any lease which is not an overriding interest or noted on the register by virtue of section 20(1) or 23(1) of the LRA 1925. But if *land* means the property registered under a particular title it is arguable that the land itself remains subject to such a lease even in circumstances where the lessor's estate is free of it as a matter of title. In either case subs. (4) does not appear to prevent subs. (1) operating where a lessor has not disposed of his interest, but has, for instance, created a legal charge over the land prior to commencement of the Act but after granting a lease for not more than 21 years gratuitously or at a premium not noted on the register. After commencement such lease would become an overriding interest affecting both the lessor's and the mortgagee's interests. However the mortgagee's interests would not usually be prejudiced by this because, in most cases, the lessee under such a lease will be in occupation or in receipt of rent and profits so that his rights under the lease (as distinct from the lease itself) will have been an overriding interest binding on the mortgagee prior to commencement of the Act by virtue of s.70(1)(g) of the LRA 1925 ("The rights of every person in actual occupation of the land or in receipt of the rents and profits thereof; save where enquiry is made of such persons and the rights are not disclosed").

Abolition of Minor Interests Index

5.—(1) In section 102 of the 1925 Act, subsection (2) (under which priorities between certain dealings with equitable interests are regulated by the order of lodging of priority cautions and inhibitions) is repealed, and accordingly—

(a) the index maintained for the purposes of that subsection and known as the Minor Interests Index shall cease to be kept, and

(b) any question of priority which would have fallen to be determined in accordance with that subsection shall be determined in accordance with the rule of law referred to in section 137(1) of the Law of Property Act 1925 (which applies to dealings with equitable interests in land the rule commonly known as the rule in *Dearle* v. *Hall*).

(2) The following provisions have effect for the purposes of the application of the rule in *Dearle* v. *Hall,* and of sections 137 and 138 of the Law of Property Act 1925, to dealings in respect of which a priority caution or inhibition was entered in the Minor Interests Index—

(a) the notice of the making of the entry which was given under the Land Registration Rules 1925 before the commencement of this Act to the proprietor or, in the case of settled land, to the trustees of the settlement, shall be treated for those purposes as a notice of the dealing to which the entry relates given (at the time it was issued by the registrar) by the person on whose behalf the entry was made to the trustees or other persons appropriate to receive it for the purposes of establishing priority under the rule in *Dearle* v. *Hall*;

(b) where a trust corporation has been nominated to receive notices of dealings in accordance with section 138, subsection (4) of that section (under which the notice does not affect priority until received by the corporation) does not apply but the trustees shall, if the notice has not already been transmitted to the corporation, deliver it or send it by post to the corporation as soon as practicable after the commencement of this Act.

(3) A person who suffers loss as a result of the operation of this section is entitled to be indemnified in the same way as a person suffering loss by reason of an error or omission in the register, except that in relation to a

claim under this subsection the reference in section 83(6)(*a*) of the 1925 Act (restriction on amount of indemnity in certain cases) to the value of the relevant estate, interest or charge at the time when the error or omission was made shall be construed as a reference to its value immediately before the commencement of this Act.

(4) For the purposes of subsection (3) above, a loss resulting from trustees failing to comply with their duty under subsection (2)(*b*) above shall be treated as a loss resulting from the operation of this section; but this is without prejudice to the liability of the trustees for breach of that duty or to the registrar's right of recourse against them under section 83(10) of the 1925 Act (under which the registrar may enforce a right which a person indemnified would have been entitled to enforce in relation to a matter in respect of which an indemnity has been paid).

(5) In consequence of the repeal of section 102(2) of the 1925 Act, the following provisions of that Act are also repealed—

(*a*) in section 54(1), the words from "but this provision" to the end,
(*b*) section 102(3), and
(*c*) in section 144(1)(xxiii), the words "and of priority cautions and inhibitions".

GENERAL NOTE

The Minor Interests Index, which this section abolishes, was created, under s.102(2) of the LRA 1925, in order to regulate the priority of dealings effected between assignees and encumbrancers of certain limited categories of equitable interest in registered land (such interests are also minor interests as defined by s.3(xv) of the LRA 1925 hence the name of the Index). The categories of equitable interest mentioned are life interests, remainders, reversions and executory interests and priority of dealings with them is governed by the order of priority cautions or inhibitions (being the terms used for the entries made in the Index) lodged against the proprietor of the registered estate affected. The Index itself is provided for by Rule 11 of the Land Registration Rules 1925 which specifically provides that entries are not to affect the powers of disposition of the proprietor of the land, that the entries are not to form part of the register of title and that purchasers are not to be concerned with the Index. Rule 229 of the 1925 Rules regulates the making and vacation of entries in the Index and provision is made for notice of entries made to be given by the registrar to the proprietor of the land and, in the case of settled land, to the trustees of the settlement. The function of the Index is extraneous to that of the land registration system as a whole and, in practice, very little use has been made of it (at the time of the Law Commission Report fewer than 100 entries had been made in it in the previous 20 years and there had been fewer than 50 searches). The Index is not applicable to dealings affecting equitable interests in unregistered land or personalty and does not even apply to dealings with all equitable interests in registered land—only those already mentioned. Confusion and duplication of effort could therefore result where a dealing with an equitable interest in one of the categories mentioned affects a fund comprising both registered land and other property, such as unregistered land or personalty, since the service of notices required to establish priority outside the ambit of the Minor Interests Index would still be necessary in relation to the property other than registered land. Accordingly the Law Commission recommended that the Index be abolished and that the priority of dealings with the specified equitable interests in registered land should instead be governed by the rule which applies to unregistered land, whereby priority is determined by the order in which notice of dealings is given to the trustees of the property (commonly known as the "rule in *Dearle* v. *Hall*") as referred to in subs. (1) of s.137 of the LPA 1925 (Dealings with life interests, reversions and other equitable interests). The Commission also recommended that, in order to assimilate the system of priorities governed by the Minor Interests Index in the system governed by s.137 of the LPA 1925, the notice of an application for an entry in the Index already served by the registrar on the proprietor of the land or trustees of the settlement, as required by Rule 229 of the Land Registration Rules 1925, should be treated as the equivalent of an assignee's or mortgagee's notice under section 137 and as establishing priority accordingly. S.5 of the new Act gives effect to the recommendations by enacting, in substantially the same terms, the relevant draft clause annexed to the Law Commission Report.

Subs. (1)

This repeals s.102(2) of the LRA 1925 and provides that the Minor Interests Index shall cease to be kept. It also applies to dealings with equitable interests in registered land the rule in *Dearle* v. *Hall* and, in the process, will render effective notices, given in relation to registered land to the trustees only which, prior to the commencement of the Act, would be ineffective under the system governed by the Minor Interests Index.

Subs. (2)

Para. (a) provides that the notice of the making of entry of a priority caution or inhibition in the Minor Interests Index which the registrar will have served on the proprietor of the land, or in the case of settlements, the trustees, is to act as the equivalent of the giving of notice by the person on whose behalf the entry was made to the person appropriate to receive it for the purpose of establishing priority under the rule in *Dearle* v. *Hall* (see General Note above).

Para. (b): S.138 of the LPA 1925 enables a settlement or other instrument creating a trust to designate a trust corporation for the purpose of receiving notices of dealings affecting real or personal property, including equitable interests, and in such cases subs. (4) of that section provides that priority is dependent upon the receipt of notices by the trust corporation and not the trustees. Para. (*b*) provides that, in those cases, the notice issued by the registrar will determine priority rather than s.138(4) of the LPA 1925 but if the registrar's notice has not already been transmitted to the relevant trust corporation the trustees will be required to do this as soon as possible after the commencement of the Act. Prudent trustees will no doubt already have forwarded notices to any relevant trust corporation but it is understood that HM Land Registry will be able to assist where necessary by providing copies of notices relating to entries of priority cautions and inhibitions served in the past.

Subs. (3)

Indemnity will be available under s.83 of the LRA 1925 in respect of loss occasioned as a result of the operation of the section in the same way as loss resulting from an error or omission in the register except that the amount of indemnity payable will be restricted to the value of the relevant estate interest or charge immediately before the commencement of the Act. Indemnity might need to be paid, for example, where the priority determined by the date of the registrar's notice differs from that determined by the abolished Index.

Subs. (4)

Indemnity will also be payable if loss is caused by failure of trustees to transmit notices to the relevant trust corporation (if any) as provided in subs. (2)(*b*). The registrar will, however, be entitled to enforce against such trustees any claim which the indemnified person would have had against them.

Subs. (5)

This subsection effects various consequential repeals.

Citation etc.

6.—(1) This Act may be cited as the Land Registration Act 1986.

(2) The Land Registration Acts 1925 to 1971 and this Act may be cited together as the Land Registration Acts 1925 to 1986.

(3) This Act shall be construed as one with the 1925 Act.

(4) This Act shall come into force on such day as the Lord Chancellor may appoint by order made by statutory instrument.

(5) This Act extends to England and Wales only.

GENERAL NOTE

The section contains provisions for citation of the Act and for joint citation with the Land Registration Acts 1925 to 1971. The provision that the Act shall be construed as one with the LRA 1925 means that expressions used in the Act have the same meaning as the same expressions where used in the LRA 1925. The Act will commence on a date to be appointed by the Lord Chancellor.

ROAD TRAFFIC REGULATION (PARKING) ACT 1986

(1986 c. 27)

An Act to amend the Road Traffic Regulation Act 1984 in relation to parking.   [8th July, 1986]

PARLIAMENTARY DEBATES
Hansard: H.C. Vol. 93, col. 1385; Vol. 95, col. 1203; H.L. Vol. 473, col. 1014; Vol. 476, col. 654; Vol. 477, cols. 11 and 589.

Parking schemes

1. In subsection (2) of section 45 of the Road Traffic Regulation Act 1984 (designation of paying parking places on highways)—
 (*a*) after the words "parking place", in the second place where they occur, there shall be inserted the words "or both by such persons or vehicles or classes of persons or vehicles and also, with or without charge and subject to such conditions as to duration of parking or times at which parking is authorised, by such other persons or vehicles, or persons or vehicles of such other class, as may be specified";
 (*b*) in paragraph (*a*), the words ", instead of making a charge as mentioned in subsection (1) above," shall be omitted.

Parking devices

2.—(1) The following section shall be substituted for section 51 of the Road Traffic Regulation Act 1984—

"Parking devices for designated parking places

51.—(1) Any power of a local authority to make charges under section 45 of this Act for vehicles left in a designated parking place shall include power to require those charges, or any part of them, to be paid by means of the hire or purchase in advance, or the use, of parking devices in accordance with any relevant provision of an order under section 46 of this Act.

(2) Any power of a local authority to make orders under section 46(2) of this Act shall include power by any such order to make provision—
 (*a*) for regulating the issue, use and surrender of parking devices;
 (*b*) for requiring vehicles to display parking devices when left in any parking place in respect of which the parking devices may be used;
 (*c*) without prejudice to the generality of paragraph (*b*) above, for regulating the manner in which parking devices are to be displayed or operated;
 (*d*) for prescribing the use, and the manner of use, of apparatus, of such type as may be approved by the Secretary of State either generally or specially, designed to be used in connection with parking devices;
 (*e*) for treating—
   (i) The indications given by a parking device; or
   (ii) the display or the failure to display a parking device on or in any vehicle left in any parking place,
  as evidence of such facts as may be provided by the order;
 (*f*) for the refund, in such circumstances and in such manner as may be prescribed in the order, of the whole or part of the

amount of any charge paid in advance in respect of a parking device;

(g) for the payment of a deposit in respect of the issue of a parking device and for the repayment of the whole or part of any such deposit.

(3) For the purposes of subsection (2) above—

(a) the references to parking meters in section 46(2)(b) and (c) of this Act shall include references to the apparatus referred to in subsection (2)(d) above; and

(b) the reference in section 46(2)(c) of this Act to the insertion in a parking meter of coins additional to those inserted by way of payment of any charge shall include (so far as is appropriate) a reference to insertions or re-insertions in any such apparatus of parking devices additional to the original insertion of those devices.

(4) In this Act "parking device" means a card, disc, token, meter, permit, stamp or other similar device, whether used in a vehicle or not, of such type or design as may be approved by the Secretary of State, which, being used either by itself, or in conjunction with any such apparatus as is referred to in subsection (2)(d) above, indicates, or causes to be indicated, the payment of a charge, and—

(a) the period in respect of which it has been paid and the time of the beginning or end of the period; or

(b) whether the period for which it has been paid or any further period has elapsed.

(5) Subject to subsection (6) below, the approval of the Secretary of State of—

(a) the type or design of a parking device; or

(b) the type of apparatus designed to be used in connection with parking devices,

may be given, in respect of any device or apparatus, either without limit of time or for such period, being not less than 2 years, as the Secretary of State considers appropriate.

(6) Before the expiry of any such period, or of any such period as extended under this subsection, the Secretary of State—

(a) may direct that the period shall be extended for such further period as he may specify; or

(b) may approve the device without limit of time.".

(2) The following subsection shall be substituted for section 115(1) of that Act (mishandling of parking documents and related offences)—

"(1) A person shall be guilty of an offence who, with intent to deceive—

(a) uses, or lends to, or allows to be used by, any other person,—

(i) any parking device or apparatus designed to be used in connection with parking devices;

(ii) any ticket issued by a parking meter, parking device or apparatus designed to be used in connection with parking devices;

(iii) any authorisation by way of such a certificate, other means of identification or device as is referred to in any of sections 4(2), 4(3), 7(2) and 7(3) of this Act; or

(iv) any such permit or token as is referred to in section 46(2)(i) of this Act;

(b) makes or has in his possession anything so closely resembling any such thing as is mentioned in paragraph (a) above as to be calculated to deceive; or (*c*) in Scotland, forges or alters any such thing as is mentioned in that paragraph.".

Short title, repeal, commencement and extent

3.—(1) This Act may be cited as the Road Traffic Regulation (Parking) Act 1986.

(2) Paragraph 4(20) of Schedule 5 to the Local Government Act 1985 shall cease to have effect.

(3) This Act shall come into force at the end of two months beginning with the date on which it is passed.

(4) This Act does not extend to Northern Ireland.

CHILDREN AND YOUNG PERSONS (AMENDMENT) ACT 1986*

(1986 c. 28)

An Act to amend the law in relation to children and young persons in care and to proceedings connected therewith. [8th July 1986]

INTRODUCTION AND GENERAL NOTE

The Bill that was initially introduced in the House of Commons by Mr. Dennis Walters made some radical changes in the balance of power between the courts and local authorities. By the time the Bill reached the end of its Parliamentary passage it was in almost every respect different from the one that was introduced because it had, in effect, been taken over by the Government which used it to make "limited changes where they can sensibly be made ahead of a major Bill", *per* the Parliamentary Under-Secretary of State, H.C. Vol. 96, No. 106, col. 1234.

COMMENCEMENT

The Act received the Royal Assent on July 8, 1986. It will come into force on such days as the Secretary of State (s.1) or the Lord Chancellor (ss.2 and 3) may appoint (s.5).

EXTENT

The Act does not extend to Scotland and Northern Ireland (s.8).

ABBREVIATION

The 1969 Act. The Children and Young Persons Act 1969.

PARLIAMENTARY DEBATES

Hansard: H.C. Vol. 90, col. 1196; Vol. 93, col. 912; Vol. 96, col. 1201; H.L. Vol. 474, col. 772; Vol. 475, col. 1065; Vol. 476, col. 949; Vol. 477, cols. 157 and 589.

The Bill was considered by Standing Committee C on March 19, 1986.

Regulations as to accommodation of children in care

1.—(1) After section 22 of the Child Care Act 1980 there shall be inserted—

"Regulations as to accommodation with parents etc.

22A.—(1) The Secretary of State may by regulations make provision as to the accommodation under the charge and control of a parent, guardian, relative or friend of children who are in the care of a local authority.

(2) Without prejudice to the generality of subsection (1) above, regulations under this section may—

(*a*) make provision as to the making by a local authority of a decision to accommodate children under the charge and control of a parent, guardian, relative or friend and, in particular, as to the persons who must be consulted before such a decision is made and the persons to whom notification of any such decision must be given; and

(*b*) impose requirements on a local authority as to the supervision or medical examination of children in such accommodation or their removal from such accommodation in such circumstances as may be specified in the regulations.".

(2) In section 85 of that Act (regulations and orders) in subsection (4) after the word "21A" there shall be inserted the words "22, 22A".

(3) In section 43(5) of the Matrimonial Causes Act 1973 (which

---

* Annotations by Richard M. Jones, M.A., Solicitor, C.Q.S.W., Assistant Director of Social Services, Mid Glamorgan County Council.

provides that the exercise by the local authority of their powers under sections 18, 21 and 22 of the Child Care Act 1980 shall be subject to any directions given by the court) for the words "and 22" there shall be substituted the words ", 22 and 22A".

GENERAL NOTE

The Bill originally provided that a local authority should apply to a court for permission to place "home on trial" a child who is subject to a care order or parental rights resolution. The Government objected to such an involvement by the courts because of their fear that the necessity to make an application could cause delay, their concern that such a procedure might either discourage local authorities from attempting rehabilitation or alternatively, encourage authorities to seek prematurely to discharge a care order without a prior period "home on trial", and their concern that the ability of the courts to attach conditions to a child's return home would restrict the authority's ability to respond flexibly to the child's needs. Apart from these practical objections the Government also had reservations about the principle of court involvement in the decision to return a child in care "home on trial".

The approach favoured by the Government is to "start from the premise that the right way to promote the welfare of abused children is, in broad terms, through improving the performance of the local authorities which are statutorily charged with that task. There can be no satisfactory external substitute for the involvement of experienced staff acting within a well-considered framework of policies directed towards and centred on the welfare of the child", *per* the Under-Secretary of State for Health and Social Security, H.C. Vol. 96, No. 106, cols. 1233, 4.

This section gives the Secretary of State power to make regulations in respect of the discharge of the responsibilities for *all* children in their care where a return "home on trial" is contemplated. This fills a gap in the Secretary of State's powers, as he is already able to make, and has made, regulations to govern the way in which local authorities discharge their responsibilities for children in their care whom they place with foster parents or in children's homes. The regulations will cover not only the placement of children at home with their parents, but also placements with the relatives, guardians and friends not covered by the Boarding Out of Children Regulations 1955.

S.22A(1)

Parent, guardian, relative. Are defined in s.87(1) of the Child Care Act 1980.

Children who are in the care of a local authority. Include children who are in care under the Child Care Act 1980 and the 1969 Act; see s.17 of the 1980 Act.

Para. (a). "This subsection would be wide enough . . . to provide for some involvement of local authority members in the decision-making process, should it be thought desirable", *per* the Under-Secretary of State, H.C. Vol. 96, col. 1235.

Appeals

2.—(1) In subsection (12) of section 2 of the Children and Young Persons Act 1969 (right of relevant infant to appeal against order made in care proceedings) after the words "the relevant infant" there shall be inserted the words "or, in a case where a parent or guardian of his was a party to the care proceedings by virtue of an order under section 32A of this Act, the parent or guardian" and for the word "him" there shall be substituted the words "the relevant infant".

(2) In section 16(8) of that Act (appeals by the supervised person against certain supervision orders and dismissal of application to discharge such orders) after the words "the supervised person" there shall be inserted the words "or, in a case where a parent or guardian of his was a party to the proceedings on an application under the preceding section by virtue of an order under section 32A of this Act, the parent or guardian".

(3) After subsection (4) of section 21 of that Act (variation and discharge of care orders) there shall be inserted—

"(4A) In a case where a parent or guardian is a party to the proceedings on an application under subsection (2) of this section by virtue of an order under section 32A of this Act, the parent or guardian may appeal to the Crown Court against the making of a supervision order or the refusal of the court to discharge the care order.".

(4) In section 22(4) of that Act (power of High Court, on application of person to whom interim order relates, to discharge order) after the word "relates" there shall be inserted the words ", or, in a case where the order was made in proceedings to which a parent or guardian was a party by virtue of an order under section 32A of this Act, of the parent or guardian,".

GENERAL NOTE

This section overcomes the effect of the decision of the Divisional Court in *A-R* v. *Avon County Council* [1985] 2 All E.R. 981, by allowing a parent or guardian who was a party to care and related proceedings by virtue of the insertion of s.32A(4A) of the 1969 Act by s.3 of this Act, to have a right of appeal to the Crown Court. It also allows a parent or guardian who was a party to proceedings in which an interim order was made to apply to the High Court to have the interim order discharged.

Subs. (1)
Parent; guardian. See the note on s.3(1), below.

Parties to care proceedings

3.—(1) In section 32A of the Children and Young Persons Act 1969 (conflict of interest between parent and child or young person), after subsection (4) there shall be inserted—

"(4A) Where an order is made under this section in respect of a parent or guardian in relation to any proceedings he shall by virtue of the order be made a party to the proceedings."

(2) After section 32B of that Act there shall be inserted—

"Applications by grandparents to be parties to proceedings

32C.—(1) Where in any such proceedings as are mentioned in section 32A(1) of this Act any grandparent of the child or young person in respect of whom the proceedings are brought makes an application to the court under this section, the court may, in such circumstances as may be specified in rules of court, give leave for the grandparent to be made a party to the proceedings.

(2) Rules of court shall make provision as to the circumstances in which the court may give leave under subsection (1) above.

(3) In this section "the court" includes a single justice.".

(3) For the first sentence of subsection (6A) of section 28 of the Legal Aid Act 1974 (power to order legal aid be given to parent or guardian in respect of whom an order has been made under section 32A of the said Act of 1969) there shall be substituted—

"Where a court—

(a) makes an order under section 32A of the Children and Young Persons Act 1969 by virtue of which a parent or guardian is made a party to any proceedings; or

(b) gives leave for a grandparent to be made a party to any proceedings under section 32C of that Act,

it may order that the parent or guardian or, as the case may be, grandparent shall be given legal aid for the purpose of those proceedings.".

GENERAL NOTE

This section deals with party status in care proceedings. Subs. (1) has the effect of making parents and guardians automatically parties if a separate representation order is made under s.32A of the 1969 Act, subs. (2) adds a new section to the 1969 Act providing for grandparents in circumstances specified in rules of court to be made parties, and subs. (3) provides for legal aid to be granted for parents, guardians and grandparents when they have been granted party status.

Subs. (1)
   Parent. Including both parents of a legitimate child, and the mother but not the putative father of an illegitimate child.
   Order made under this section. Ordering that the parents of a child who is the subject of care proceedings shall not represent the child or otherwise act for him in the proceedings.
   Guardian. Probably has the meaning given to it by s.107(1) of the Children and Young Persons Act 1933, *viz.*: "any person who, in the opinion of the court . . . has for the time being the charge of or control over the child."

Subs. (2)
   Grandparent. This would not include grandparents whose relationship derive through the putative father of an illegitimate child.
   Rules of court. "I should like to take the opportunity to say a little more about the rules of court, as I indicated at Second Reading. The detail will need to be worked out but I can say that our intention would be for a grandparent who wished to be joined as a party to make an application to the court in writing stating why it would be in the child's best interests for him or her to be made a party. The criteria would be, first, that the grandparent had had the actual custody of the child or young person for such and such a time; secondly, that the court considered that the grandparent had exercised some or all of the parental rights on behalf of a parent or parental duties as relate to the person of the child or young person and had maintained a continuing interest in that child or young person; and, thirdly, that joining the grandparent as a party was in the child's best interests", *per* Baroness Trumpington, H.L. Vol. 476, No. 111, cols. 954, 5.

Rules of court

   4.—(1) An authority having power to make rules of court may make such provision for giving effect to this Act as appears to that authority to be necessary or expedient.
   (2) Without prejudice to the generality of subsection (1) above rules of court may make provision with respect to the procedure in any proceedings to which a parent or guardian becomes a party by virtue of an order under section 32A of the Children and Young Persons Act 1969 or a grandparent becomes a party under section 32C of that Act.

Commencement

   5.—(1) Section 1 above shall come into force on such date as the Secretary of State may by order made by statutory instrument appoint.
   (2) Sections 2 and 3 above shall come into force on such date as the Lord Chancellor may by order made by statutory instrument appoint and different dates may be appointed for different provisions.

GENERAL NOTE
   The Government intend to bring this Act into effect, "as soon as possible", *per* the Parliamentary Under-Secretary of State, H.C. Vol. 96, No. 106, col. 1256.

Transitional provisions

   6. No provision of this Act shall have effect in relation to any proceedings which were commenced before the commencement of that provision.

Application to Isles of Scilly

7. This Act shall, in its application to the Isles of Scilly, have effect subject to such exceptions, adaptions and modifications as the Secretary of State may by order prescribe.

Short title and extent

8.—(1) This Act may be cited as the Children and Young Persons (Amendment) Act 1986.

(2) This Act does not extend to Scotland and Northern Ireland.

CONSUMER SAFETY (AMENDMENT) ACT 1986

(1986 c.29)

ARRANGEMENT OF SECTIONS

An Act to make further provision with respect to the safety of consumers and others.

[8th July 1986]

PARLIAMENTARY DEBATES
    Hansard: H.C. Vol. 91, col. 611; Vol. 92, col. 1165; Vol. 97, col. 415; H.L. Vol. 474, col. 1024; Vol. 476, col. 61; Vol. 477, cols. 225, 589.
    The Bill was considered by Standing Committee C on April 30 to May 7, 1986.

Power of Commissioners to disclose information

1.—(1) The Commissioners of Customs and Excise may, if they think it appropriate to do so for the purpose of facilitating the exercise by any person to whom subsection (2) below applies of any functions conferred on that person by or under the safety legislation, authorise the disclosure to that person, in such manner and through such persons acting on behalf of that person as they may direct, of any information obtained for the purposes of the exercise by the Commissioners of their functions in relation to imported goods.

(2) This subsection applies to an enforcement authority and to any officer of an enforcement authority.

(3) Information may be disclosed to a person under subsection (1) above whether or not the disclosure of the information has been requested by or on behalf of that person.

Power of Commissioners to detain goods

2.—(1) A customs officer may, for the purpose of facilitating the exercise by any enforcement authority or officer of such an authority of any functions conferred on the authority or officer by or under the safety legislation, seize any imported goods and detain them for not more than forty-eight hours.

29–1

(2) Anything seized and detained under this section shall be dealt with during the period of its detention in such manner as the Commissioners of Customs and Excise may direct.

(3) In this section "customs officer" means any officer within the meaning of the Customs and Excise Management Act 1979.

Suspension notices

3.—(1) Where an enforcement authority has reasonable cause to suspect that any relevant provisions have been contravened in relation to any goods, the authority may serve a notice ("a suspension notice") prohibiting the person on whom it is served, for such period ending not more than six months after the date of the notice as is specified therein, from doing any of the following things without the consent of the authority, that is to say, supplying the goods, offering to supply them, agreeing to supply them or exposing them for supply.

(2) A suspension notice served by an enforcement authority in respect of any goods shall—

(a) describe the goods in a manner sufficient to identify them;

(b) set out the grounds on which the authority suspects that relevant provisions have been contravened in relation to the goods; and

(c) state that, and the manner in which, the person on whom the notice is served may appeal against the notice under section 4 or 5 below.

(3) Where a suspension notice has been served on any person in respect of any goods, no further such notice shall be served on that person in respect of the same goods unless—

(a) proceedings against that person for an offence in respect of a contravention in relation to the goods of any relevant provisions (not being an offence under this section); or

(b) proceedings for the forfeiture of the goods under section 6 or 7 below,

are pending at the end of the period specified in the first-mentioned notice.

(4) A consent given by an enforcement authority for the purposes of subsection (1) above may impose such conditions on the doing of anything for which the consent is required as the authority thinks appropriate.

(5) Any person who contravenes a suspension notice shall be guilty of an offence and liable on summary conviction to imprisonment for a term not exceeding three months or to a fine not exceeding level 5 on the standard scale or to both.

(6) Paragraphs 14(2) and 15 of Schedule 2 to the 1978 Act (liability of enforcement authority to pay compensation) shall apply where an enforcement authority exercises its power to serve a suspension notice in respect of any goods as they apply where an officer of such an authority exercises his power to seize and detain any goods.

(7) References in this section, in relation to any goods, to supplying include references to supplying the goods—

(a) to a person who carries on a business of buying such goods as those in question and repairing or reconditioning them; or

(b) by a sale of articles as scrap (that is to say for the value of the materials included in the articles and not of the articles themselves).

Appeals against suspension notices and seizures

4.—(1) Any person having an interest in any goods—

(a) in respect of which a suspension notice under section 3 above is for the time being in force; or (*b*) which are for the time being detained under any provision of Schedule 2 to the 1978 Act,

may apply under this section for an order setting aside the suspension notice or, as the case may be, requiring the goods to be released to him or to any other person.

(2) An application under this section may be made—

    (*a*) to any court in which proceedings have been commenced—

        (i) for an offence in respect of a contravention in relation to the goods of any relevant provisions; or

        (ii) for the forfeiture of the goods under section 6 below;

    (*b*) where no such proceedings have been commenced—

        (i) in England and Wales, by way of complaint to a magistrates' court;

        (ii) in Northern Ireland, by way of complaint to a court of summary jurisdiction.

(3) On an application under this section the court shall make an order setting aside a suspension notice in respect of any goods or requiring any goods to be released to the applicant or to any other person only if the court is satisfied—

    (*a*) that there has been no contravention in relation to the goods of any relevant provisions; or

    (*b*) in the case of goods that have been seized and detained, that more than six months have expired since the seizure without proceedings being commenced—

        (i) for an offence in respect of a contravention in relation to the goods of any relevant provisions; or

        (ii) for the forfeiture of the goods under section 6 below.

Setting aside suspension notices etc. in Scotland

5.—(1) Any person having an interest in any goods—

    (*a*) in respect of which a suspension notice under section 3 above is for the time being in force; or

    (*b*) which are for the time being detained under any provision of Schedule 2 to the 1978 Act,

may apply to the sheriff under this section for an order setting aside the suspension notice or, as the case may be, requiring the goods to be released to him or to any other person.

(2) The sheriff may make an order under this section only if he is satisfied—

    (*a*) in any case, that at the date of making the order, no proceedings have been commenced—

        (i) for an offence of contravening a relevant provision in relation to the goods; or

        (ii) under section 7(1)(*a*) below,

    or if they have been commenced, that they have been concluded; and

    (*b*) where subsection (1)(*b*) above applies, that more than six months have elapsed since the goods were seized, without any such proceedings having been commenced.

Forfeiture: England and Wales and Northern Ireland

6.—(1) An enforcement authority may apply under this section for an order for the forfeiture of any goods on the grounds that there has been a contravention in relation to the goods of any relevant provisions.

(2) An application under this section may be made—

(*a*) where proceedings have been commenced in any court for an offence in respect of a contravention in relation to some or all of the goods of any relevant provisions, to that court;

(*b*) where an application with respect to some or all of the goods has been made to a court under section 4 above, to that court; and

(*c*) where no application for the forfeiture of the goods has been made to a court under paragraph (*a*) or (*b*) above—
  (i) in England and Wales, by way of complaint to a magistrates' court;
  (ii) in Northern Ireland, by way of complaint to a court of summary jurisdiction.

(3) On an application under this section the court shall make an order for the forfeiture of any goods only if it is satisfied that there has been a contravention in relation to the goods of any relevant provisions.

(4) For the avoidance of doubt it is hereby declared that a court may infer for the purposes of this section that there has been a contravention in relation to any goods of any relevant provisions if it is satisfied that those provisions have been contravened in relation to any goods which are representative of those goods (whether by reason of being of the same design or part of the same consignment or batch or otherwise).

(5) Subject to subsection (6) and section 9(3) below, where a court makes an order under this section, the goods to which it relates shall be destroyed in accordance with such directions as the court may give.

(6) On making an order under this section a court may, if it thinks it appropriate to do so, direct that the goods to which the order relates shall (instead of being destroyed) be released to such person as the court may specify on condition that that person—

(*a*) does not supply those goods to any person otherwise than as mentioned in section 3(7)(*a*) or (*b*) above; and

(*b*) complies with any order to pay costs or expenses (including any order under section 13 below) which has been made against that person in the proceedings for the order.

Forfeiture: Scotland

7.—(1) A sheriff may make an order for forfeiture of any goods in relation to which there has been a contravention of any relevant provisions—

(*a*) on an application by the procurator-fiscal made in the manner specified in section 310 of the Criminal Procedure (Scotland) Act 1975; or

(*b*) where a person is convicted of any offence of contravening any relevant provisions, in addition to any other penalty which the sheriff may impose.

(2) The procurator-fiscal making an application under subsection (1)(*a*) above shall serve on any person appearing to him to be the owner of, or otherwise to have an interest in, the goods to which the application relates a copy of the application, together with a notice giving him the opportunity to appear at the hearing of the application to show cause why the goods should not be forfeited.

(3) Service under subsection (2) above shall be carried out, and such service may be proved, in the manner specified for citation of an accused in summary proceedings under the Criminal Procedure (Scotland) Act 1975.

(4) Any person upon whom notice is served under subsection (2) above and any other person claiming to be the owner of, or otherwise to have

an interest in, goods to which an application under this section relates shall be entitled to appear at the hearing of the application to show cause why the goods should not be forfeited.

(5) The sheriff shall not make an order following an application under subsection (1)(*a*) above—

(*a*) if any person on whom notice is served under subsection (2) above does not appear, unless service of the notice on that person is proved; or

(*b*) if no notice under subsection (2) above has been served, unless the court is satisfied that in the circumstances it was reasonable not to serve notice on any person.

(6) The sheriff shall make an order under this section only if he is satisfied that there has been a contravention in relation to those goods of any relevant provisions.

(7) For the avoidance of doubt it is declared that the sheriff may infer, for the purposes of this section, that there has been a contravention in relation to goods of any relevant provisions, if he is satisfied that those provisions have been contravened in relation to any goods which are representative of those goods (whether by reason of being of the same design or part of the same consignment or batch or otherwise).

Effect of order under section 7

8.—(1) An order following an application under section 7(1)(*a*) above shall not take effect—

(*a*) until the end of the period of twenty-one days beginning with the day after the day on which the order is made; or

(*b*) if an appeal is made under section 10 below within that period, until the appeal is determined or abandoned.

(2) An order under section 7(1)(*b*) above shall not take effect—

(*a*) until the expiry of the period within which an appeal against the order could be brought under the Criminal Procedure (Scotland) Act 1975; or

(*b*) if an appeal is made within that period, until the appeal is determined or abandoned.

(3) Subject to subsection (4) below, goods forfeited under section 7 above shall be destroyed in accordance with such directions as the sheriff may give.

(4) If he thinks fit, the sheriff may direct that the goods be released to such person as he may specify, on condition that that person does not supply those goods to any other person otherwise than as mentioned in section 3(7)(*a*) or (*b*) above.

Appeal, to Crown court or county court

9.—(1) In England and Wales, any person aggrieved by an order of a magistrates' court under section 4 or 6 above or by a decision of a magistrates' court not to make such an order may appeal against that order or decision to the Crown Court.

(2) In Northern Ireland, any person aggrieved by an order of a court of summary jurisdiction under section 4 or 6 above or by a decision of a court of summary jurisdiction not to make such an order may appeal against that order or decision to the county court.

(3) An order made by a court under section 4 or 6 above may contain such provision as appears to the court to be appropriate for delaying the coming into force of the order pending the making and determination of any appeal.

(4) In subsection (3) above "appeal" includes any proceedings on or in consequence of—

(*a*) an application under section 111 of the Magistrates' Courts Act 1980 (statement of case by magistrates' court); or

(*b*) an application under Article 146 of the Magistrates' Courts (Northern Ireland) Order 1981 (statement of case by magistrates' court).

Appeals relating to section 7

10. Where an order is made following an application under section 7(1)(*a*) above, any person who appeared, or was entitled to appear, to show cause why goods should not be forfeited may, within twenty-one days of the making of the order appeal to the High Court by Bill of Suspension on the ground of an alleged miscarriage of justice; and section 452(4)(*a*) to (*e*) of the Criminal Procedure (Scotland) Act 1975 shall apply to an appeal under this subsection as it applies to a stated case under Part II of that Act.

Restrictions on disclosure of information

11.—(1) Subject to the following provisions of this section, a person shall be guilty of an offence if he discloses any information—

(*a*) which was disclosed to or through him under section 1 above; or

(*b*) which was obtained in exercise of the power conferred by section 4 of the 1978 Act; or

(*c*) which consists in a secret manufacturing process or a trade secret and was obtained in consequence of the inclusion of the information—

(i) in written or oral representations made in pursuance of Part II or Part III of Schedule 1 to that Act (prohibition orders etc.); or

(ii) in a statement of a witness in connection with any such oral representations; or

(*d*) which was obtained by any person in or in connection with the exercise of any power conferred by Schedule 2 to that Act.

(2) Subsection (1) above shall not apply to any disclosure of information if the information is publicised information or the disclosure is made—

(*a*) for the purpose of facilitating the performance by an enforcement authority of any functions of the authority under the safety legislation (including the functions of the Secretary of State with respect to the making, variation and revocation of regulations and his functions under section 3 of and Part II of Schedule 1 to the 1978 Act);

(*b*) for the purpose of facilitating the performance by the Director General of Fair Trading of his functions under Part III of the Fair Trading Act 1973 or for the purposes of proceedings under that Part;

(*c*) for the purposes of compliance with a Community obligation;

(*d*) in connection with the investigation of any criminal offence or for the purposes of any criminal proceedings; or

(*e*) for the purposes of any civil proceedings in respect of a contravention of any provision made by or under the safety legislation or in respect of an infringement of a trade mark or certification trade mark.

(3) Subsection (2)(*e*) above shall not authorise the disclosure of any secret manufacturing process or trade secret.

(4) Any person guilty of an offence under this section shall be liable—

(*a*) on summary conviction, to a fine not exceeding the statutory maximum;

(*b*) on conviction on indictment, to imprisonment for a term not exceeding two years or to a fine or to both.

(5) In this section—

"publicised information" means any information which has been disclosed in any such proceedings as are mentioned in subsection (2) above or is or has been required to be contained in a warning published in pursuance of a notice to warn served under section 3(1)(*c*) of the 1978 Act; and

"trade mark" and "certification trade mark" have the same meanings as in the Trade Marks Act 1938.

Defence of due diligence etc.

12.—(1) This section applies to—

(*a*) an offence under section 3 above;

(*b*) an offence in pursuance of subsections (1) to (3) of section 2 of the 1978 Act (contravention of safety regulations);

(*c*) an offence under subsection (3) of section 3 of that Act (contravention of prohibition order, prohibition notice or notice to warn); and

(*d*) an offence under section 3 of the Consumer Protection Act 1961 or section 3 of the Consumer Protection Act (Northern Ireland) 1965 (contraventions of safety requirements).

(2) Subject to the following provisions of this section, in proceedings against any person for an offence to which this section applies it shall be a defence for that person to show that he took all reasonable steps and exercised all due diligence to avoid committing the offence.

(3) Where in any proceedings against any person for such an offence the defence provided by subsection (2) above involves an allegation that the commission of the offence was due—

(*a*) to the act or default of another; or

(*b*) to reliance on information supplied by another,

that person shall not, without the leave of the court, be entitled to rely on the defence unless he has, more than seven clear days before the hearing of the proceedings, served a notice on the person bringing the proceedings.

(4) A notice under subsection (3) above shall give such information identifying or assisting in the identification of the person who committed the act or default or supplied the information as is in the possession of the person serving the notice at the time he serves it.

(5) For the removal of doubt it is hereby declared that a person shall not be entitled to rely on the defence provided by subsection (2) above by reason of his reliance on information supplied by another, unless he shows that it was reasonable in all the circumstances for him to have relied on the information, having regard in particular—

(*a*) to the steps which he took, and those which might reasonably have been taken, for the purpose of verifying the information; and

(*b*) to whether he had any reason to disbelieve the information.

(6) Where the commission by any person of an offence to which this section applies is due to the act or default of some other person the other person shall be guilty of the offence and may be proceeded against and convicted of the offence by virtue of this subsection whether or not proceedings are taken against the first-mentioned person.

Recovery of expenses of enforcement

13.—(1) This section applies where a court in England and Wales or Northern Ireland—

(*a*) convicts a person of an offence in respect of a contravention in relation to any goods of any relevant provisions; or

(*b*) makes an order under section 6 above for the forfeiture of any goods.

(2) The court may (in addition to any other order it may make as to costs) order the person convicted or, as the case may be, any person having an interest in the goods to reimburse any enforcement authority for any expenditure which has been or may be incurred by that authority—

(*a*) in connection with any seizure or detention of the goods by or on behalf of the authority; or

(*b*) in connection with any compliance by the authority with directions given by the court for the purposes of any order for the forfeiture of the goods.

Enforcement of the 1978 Act

14. For Schedule 2 to the 1978 Act (enforcement) there shall be substituted the Schedule set out in Schedule 1 to this Act.

Interpretation

15.—(1) In this Act—

"the 1978 Act" means the Consumer Safety Act 1978;

"safety legislation" means the Consumer Protection Act 1961, the Consumer Protection Act (Northern Ireland) 1965, the Consumer Safety Act 1978 and this Act.

(2) Sections 7(1) to (5) and 9 of the 1978 Act (supplemental provisions as to notices and offences and interpretation) shall have effect in relation to this Act as they have effect in relation to that Act, and expressions defined in paragraph 1 of Schedule 2 to that Act (enforcement) have the same meanings in this Act as in that Schedule.

Consequential amendments and repeals

16.—(1) In section 5(1) of the 1978 Act (duty to enforce), for the words from "the provisions of safety regulations" onwards there shall be substituted the words "the relevant provisions, within the meaning of Schedule 2 to this Act."

(2) Any reference to the 1978 Act in any provision of the Gas Act 1986 relating to the disclosure of information shall include a reference to this Act.

(3) The enactments mentioned in Schedule 2 to this Act are hereby repealed to the extent specified in the third column of that Schedule.

Short title, commencement and extent

17.—(1) This Act may be cited as the Consumer Safety (Amendment) Act 1986.

(2) This Act shall come into force at the end of the period of one month beginning with the day on which it is passed.

(3) Sections 4, 6, 9 and 13 above shall not extend to Scotland and sections 5, 7, 8 and 10 above shall extend only to Scotland.

(4) Subject to subsection (3) above, this Act extends to Northern Ireland.

SCHEDULES

Section 14　　　　　　　　　　SCHEDULE 1

SCHEDULE TO BE SUBSTITUTED FOR SCHEDULE 2 TO 1978 ACT

SCHEDULE 2

ENFORCEMENT

Preliminary

1.—(1) In this Schedule—

"enforcement authority" means the Secretary of State, any person on whom a duty is imposed by or under section 5 of this Act and any other person by whom that duty may be discharged in pursuance of arrangements made by virtue of any enactment;

"officer", in relation to an enforcement authority, means a person authorised in writing by the authority to assist the authority in performing such a duty as aforesaid or, where the authority is the Secretary of State, to assist him in enforcing relevant provisions;

"premises" includes any place, any stall, and any ship, aircraft and other vehicle of any kind;

"relevant provisions" means provisions of—

    (*a*) regulations made under the Consumer Protection Act 1961 or the Consumer Protection Act (Northern Ireland) 1965;

    (*b*) safety regulations;

    (*c*) a prohibition order;

    (*d*) a prohibition notice; or

    (*e*) a suspension notice under section 3 of the Consumer Safety (Amendment) Act 1986.

(2) Except in so far as the context otherwise requires, references in this Schedule, in relation to any goods, to a contravention of any relevant provisions shall include references to anything which, if the goods were supplied to any person—

(*a*) would constitute such a contravention; or

(*b*) by virtue of any such provision, would constitute an offence under section 3 of the Consumer Protection Act 1961 or section 3 of the Consumer Protection Act (Northern Ireland) 1965.

(3) References in this Schedule to any goods in relation to which any relevant provisions have been or may have been contravened shall include references to any goods which it is not reasonably practicable to separate from any such goods.

Purchases

2. An enforcement authority shall have the power to purchase goods and to authorise any of its officers to purchase goods on behalf of the authority for the purpose of ascertaining whether any relevant provisions have been contravened in relation to any goods.

Powers to enter premises and to inspect and seize goods

3. An officer of an enforcement authority may, at all reasonable hours and on production if required of his credentials, exercise the following powers, that is to say—

(*a*) he may for the purpose of ascertaining whether any relevant provisions have been contravened in relation to any goods inspect any of those goods and enter any premises other than premises used only as a dwelling;

(*b*) he may for the purpose of ascertaining whether any relevant provisions have been contravened in relation to any goods examine any procedure (including any arrangements for carrying out a test) connected with the production of the goods;

(*c*) if he has reasonable cause to suspect that any relevant provisions have been contravened in relation to any goods or that any goods are goods that have not been supplied in the United Kingdom since they were manufactured or imported, he may, for the purpose of ascertaining whether any such provisions have been contravened in relation to the goods, require any person carrying on a business or employed in connection with a business to produce any books or documents relating to the business and may take copies of, or of any entry in, any such book or document;

(*d*) if he has reasonable cause to believe that any relevant provisions have been contravened in relation to any goods or that any goods are goods that have not been supplied in the United Kingdom since they were manufactured or imported, he may seize and detain the goods for the purpose of ascertaining by testing or otherwise whether any such provisions have been contravened in relation to those goods;

(*e*) he may seize and detain any goods (including documents) which he has reason to believe may be required as evidence in proceedings for an offence in respect of a contravention of any relevant provisions or which may be liable to be forfeited under section 6 or 7 of the Consumer Safety (Amendment) Act 1986;

(*f*) he may, for the purpose of exercising his powers under sub-paragraph (*d*) or (*e*) above to seize goods, but only if and to the extent that it is reasonably necessary in order to secure that relevant provisions are complied with, require any person having authority to do so to break open any container and, if that person does not comply with the requirement, he may do so himself.

4.—(1) An officer seizing any goods or documents in the exercise of his powers under the preceding paragraph shall inform the person from whom they are seized that the officer has seized them.

(2) In sub-paragraph (1) above the reference to the person from whom goods are seized includes, in the case of imported goods seized on any premises under the control of the Commissioners of Customs and Excise, the importer of those goods (within the meaning of the Customs and Excise Management Act 1979).

5. If a justice of the peace on sworn information in writing or, in Scotland, on evidence on oath—

(*a*) is satisfied that there is reasonable ground to believe either—

(i) that any goods (including books and documents) which an officer of an enforcement authority has power under paragraph 3 of this Schedule to inspect are on any premises and that their inspection is likely to disclose evidence that relevant provisions have been contravened in relation to any goods, or

(ii) that relevant provisions have been or are being or are about to be contravened on any premises in relation to any goods; and

(*b*) is also satisfied either—

(i) that admission to the premises has been or is likely to be refused and that notice of intention to apply for a warrant under this paragraph has been given to the occupier, or

(ii) that an application for admission, or the giving of such a notice would defeat the object of the entry or that the premises are unoccupied or that the occupier is temporarily absent and it might defeat the object of the entry to await his return, the justice may by warrant under his hand, which shall continue in force for a period of one month, authorise an officer of an enforcement authority to enter the premises, if need be by force.

In the application of this paragraph to Scotland "justice of the peace" shall be construed as including a sheriff.

6. An officer entering any premises by virtue of this Schedule may take with him such other persons and such equipment as may appear to him necessary; and on leaving any premises which he has entered by virtue of a warrant under the preceding paragraph he shall, if the premises are unoccupied or the occupier is temporarily absent, leave the premises as effectively secured against trespassers as he found them.

7. If any person who is not an officer of an enforcement authority purports to act as such under this Schedule he shall be guilty of an offence and liable on summary conviction to a fine not exceeding level 5 on the standard scale.

8. Nothing in this Schedule shall be taken to compel the production by a barrister, advocate or solicitor of a document containing a privileged communication or, in Scotland, a confidential communication made by or to him in that capacity or to authorise the taking of possession of any such document which is in his possession.

Obstruction

9. Any person who—

(*a*) wilfully obstructs an officer of an enforcement authority acting in pursuance of this Schedule; or

(*b*) wilfully fails to comply with any requirement made to him by such an officer under this Schedule; or

(*c*) without reasonable cause fails to give such an officer so acting any other

assistance or information which he may reasonably require of him for the purpose of the performance of his functions under this Schedule,
shall be guilty of an offence and liable on summary conviction to a fine not exceeding level 3 on the standard scale.

10. If any person, in giving such information as is mentioned in the preceding paragraph, makes any statement which he knows is false in a material particular or recklessly makes a statement which is false in a material particular, he shall be guilty of an offence and liable on conviction on indictment to a fine and on summary conviction to a fine of an amount not exceeding level 5 on the standard scale.

11. Nothing in this Schedule shall be construed as requiring a person to answer any question or give any information if to do so might incriminate the person or the person's spouse.

Tests

12. Where any goods seized or purchased by an officer in pursuance of this Schedule are submitted to a test, then—

(a) if the goods were seized, the officer shall inform the person mentioned in paragraph 4 of this Schedule of the result of the test;

(b) if the goods were purchased and the test leads to—

(i) the institution of proceedings for an offence in respect of a contravention of any relevant provisions;

(ii) the service in respect of any goods of a suspension notice under section 3 of the Consumer Safety (Amendment) Act 1986; or

(iii) the making of an application for the forfeiture of any goods under section 6 or 7 of that Act,

the officer shall inform the person from whom the goods were purchased of the result of the test;

and the officer shall, where as a result of the test such proceedings are instituted, such a notice served or such an application made, allow the person against whom the proceedings are instituted or any person having an interest in the goods to have the goods tested if it is reasonably practicable to do so.

13. The Secretary of State may by regulations provide that any test of goods seized or purchased by or on behalf of an enforcement authority in pursuance of this Schedule shall, in such cases as are specified in the regulations—

(a) be carried out at the expense of the authority in a manner so specified and by a person specified in or determined under the regulations; or

(b) be carried out either as mentioned in sub-paragraph (a) above, or by the authority in a manner specified in the regulations.

Compensation

14.—(1) This paragraph shall apply where an officer of an enforcement authority exercises any power under this Schedule to seize and detain goods.

(2) The enforcement authority shall be liable to pay compensation to any person having an interest in the goods in respect of any loss or damage caused by reason of the exercise of the power if—

(a) there has been no contravention in relation to the goods of any relevant provisions; and

(b) the exercise of the power is not attributable to any neglect or default by that person.

15. Any disputed question as to the right to or the amount of any compensation payable under the preceding paragraph shall be determined by arbitration and, in Scotland, by a single arbiter appointed, failing agreement between the parties, by the sheriff.

Section 16   SCHEDULE 2

REPEALS

Chapter	Short title	Extent of repeal
1978 c.38.	The Consumer Safety Act 1978.	In section 2, subsections (5) and (6). In section 3, in subsection (3), the words from "but" onwards and subsections (4) and (5). In section 4, subsections (3) and (4). In section 5, in subsection (3), the words from "for the purpose" to the end of paragraph (*b*) and, in subsection (4), the words from "or, while" to "that Act". In section 9, in subsection (4), the definition of "publicised information". In section 10, subsections (4) and (5). In section 11, in paragraph (*h*), the words "(3) to" and the words from "and in section 10(4)" onwards. In Schedule 1, paragraphs 24 and 25 and in paragraph 27 the words "to 25", subparagraph (*e*) and the word "and" immediately preceding it.

FORESTRY ACT 1986

(1986 c. 30)

An Act to empower the Forestry Commissioners to require the restocking of land with trees after unauthorised felling. [8th July 1986]

PARLIAMENTARY DEBATES
Hansard: H.C. Vol. 96, col. 1270; Vol. 97, col. 1029; H.L. Vol. 475, cols. 69 and 787; Vol. 476, col. 795; Vol. 477, col. 760.
The Bill was considered by Standing Committee C on May 14, 1986.

Restocking

1. In the Forestry Act 1967—
(*a*) after section 17 (tree felling without a licence) there shall be inserted the following sections—

"Power of Commissioners to require restocking after unauthorised felling
17A.—(1) Where a person is convicted of an offence under section 17 of this Act and he is a person having, as regards the land on which the felling which gave rise to the conviction took place, such estate or interest as is mentioned in section 10(1) of this Act, the Commissioners may serve on him a notice (in this Act referred to as a "restocking notice") requiring him—
  (*a*) to restock or stock with trees the land or such other land as may be agreed between the Commissioners and him; and
  (*b*) to maintain those trees in accordance with the rules and practice of good forestry for a period, not exceeding ten years, specified in the notice.
(2) A restocking notice shall be served within three months after the date of the conviction or of the dismissal or withdrawal of any appeal against the conviction.
(3) Subject to the provisions of this Act, in considering whether to issue a restocking notice the Commissioners shall—
  (*a*) have regard to the interests of good forestry and agriculture and of the amenities of the district;
  (*b*) have regard to their duty of promoting the establishment and maintenance in Great Britain of adequate reserves of growing trees; and
  (*c*) take into account any advice tendered by the regional advisory committee for the conservancy comprising the land to which the restocking notice would relate.
(4) This section shall not apply in relation to trees to which a tree preservation order relates or in relation to trees the felling of which took place before the date of coming into force of the Forestry Act 1986.

Appeal against restocking notice
17B.—(1) A person on whom a restocking notice has been served who objects to the notice or to any condition contained therein may by notice served within the prescribed

time and in the prescribed manner request the Minister to refer the matter to a committee appointed in accordance with section 27 of this Act; and—

    (*a*) the Minister shall, unless he is of the opinion that the grounds of the request are frivolous, refer the matter accordingly; and

    (*b*) the committee, after compliance with subsection (3) of that section, shall thereupon make a report to the Minister.

(2) The Minister may, after considering the committee's report, direct the Commissioners to withdraw the notice or to notify the objector that it shall have effect subject to such modification as the Minister shall direct.

Enforcement of restocking notice

17C. The provisions of sections 24 (notice to require compliance with conditions or directions), 25 (appeal against notice under section 24) and 26(1), (3) and (4) (expenses) of this Act shall apply in relation to a restocking notice as they apply in relation to a felling licence; and for the purposes of such application—

    (*a*) references in those sections to a felling licence shall be construed as references to a restocking notice; and

    (*b*) the reference in the said subsection (3) to the applicant for the licence shall be construed as a reference to the person on whom the restocking notice has been served.";

  (*b*) in section 27 (committees of reference) after the words "sections 16," there shall be inserted the words "17B,"; and

  (*c*) in section 35 (interpretation) after the definition of "prescribed" there shall be inserted the following definition—

""restocking notice" shall be construed in accordance with section 17A(1) of this Act;".

Citation, commencement and extent

2.—(1) This Act may be cited as the Forestry Act 1986 and shall come into force at the end of the period of two months beginning with the day on which it is passed.

(2) This Act shall not apply to Northern Ireland.

AIRPORTS ACT 1986

(1986 c.31)

PART VI

MISCELLANEOUS AND SUPPLEMENTARY

An Act to provide for the dissolution of the British Airports Authority and the vesting of its property, rights and liabilities in a company nominated by the Secretary of State; to provide for the reorganisation of other airport undertakings in the public sector; to provide for the regulation of the use of airports and for the imposition of economic controls at certain airports; to make other amendments of the law relating to airports; to make provision with respect to the control of capital expenditure by local authority airport undertakings; and for connected purposes.

[8th July 1986]

PARLIAMENTARY DEBATES
   Hansard: H.C. Vol. 89, col. 1241; H.C. Vol. 90, col. 691; H.C. Vol. 95, cols. 168, 271; H.C. Vol. 100, col. 1097; H.L. Vol. 473, cols. 378, 957, 974; H.L. Vol. 474, col. 1279; H.L. Vol. 475, col. 408; H.L. Vol. 476, col. 128; H.L. Vol. 477, col. 74.
   The Bill was considered in committee by the House of Commons in Standing Committee J between February 2 and March 18, 1986.

PART I

TRANSFER OF UNDERTAKING OF BRITISH AIRPORTS AUTHORITY
Preliminary

Power to direct reorganisation of BAA's undertaking prior to appointed day

1.—(1) If the Secretary of State so directs at any time before the day appointed under section 2(1), the BAA shall, before the end of such period as the Secretary of State may specify in his direction, submit to the Secretary of State for his approval written proposals for the carrying on of any of the activities of the BAA by such companies as may be nominated by it in the proposals.

(2) Any company so nominated shall be a company limited by shares and registered under the Companies Act 1985; and any proposals submitted to the Secretary of State under this section shall include a copy of the memorandum and articles of association of each of the companies so nominated.

(3) The Secretary of State may approve any such proposals either without modifications or with such modifications as, after consulting the BAA, he thinks fit; and where the Secretary of State approves them with modifications the BAA shall, before such date as the Secretary of State may, in giving his approval, specify—

(a) secure that such alterations are made to the memorandum and articles of association of any nominated company, or

(b) form such company or companies to carry on any of the activities of the BAA,

as may be necessary to give effect to those modifications.

(4) Any company so formed shall be a company limited by shares and registered under the Companies Act 1985.

(5) Together with the proposals submitted to the Secretary of State under this section the BAA shall submit to the Secretary of State for his approval a scheme providing, in the case of each of the nominated companies, for the transfer to that company of any property, rights or liabilities of the BAA relevant to the carrying on of any activities which the BAA has power to carry on and which are within the scope of the objects of that company.

(6) A scheme under this section shall not come into force until it has been approved by the Secretary of State or until such date as the Secretary of State may, in giving his approval, specify, and the Secretary of State may approve any such scheme either without modifications or with such modifications as, after consulting the BAA, he thinks fit.

(7) Any such modifications may, in particular, provide for property, rights or liabilities of the BAA to be transferred to any company required to be formed in pursuance of subsection (3)(b).

(8) On the coming into force of a scheme under this section the property, rights and liabilities affected by the scheme shall, subject to section 75(3), be transferred and vest in accordance with the scheme.

(9) If such a scheme has not come into force before the day appointed under section 2(1), any direction, proposals, scheme or approval previously given or made under this section shall cease to have effect.

Dissolution of BAA and vesting of its property etc. in a successor company

Dissolution of BAA and vesting of its property etc. in a successor company

2.—(1) On such day as the Secretary of State may by order appoint—

(*a*) the BAA shall cease to exist; and

(*b*) (subject to section 3) all the property, rights and liabilities to which the BAA was entitled or subject immediately before that day shall become by virtue of this section property, rights and liabilities of a company nominated for the purposes of this section by the Secretary of State;

and references in this Act to the appointed day or to the successor company are references to the day so appointed or to the company so nominated respectively.

(2) The Secretary of State may, after consulting the BAA, by order nominate for the purposes of this section any company formed and registered under the Companies Act 1985; but on the appointed day the company in question must be a company limited by shares which is wholly owned by the Crown.

(3) References in this Act to property, rights and liabilities of the BAA are references to all such property, rights and liabilities, whether or not capable of being transferred or assigned by the BAA.

(4) In the House of Commons Disqualification Act 1975, in Part III of Schedule 1 (other disqualifying offices) there shall be inserted at the appropriate place—

"Director of the successor company (within the meaning of the Airports Act 1986) being a director nominated or appointed by a Minister of the Crown or by a person acting on behalf of the Crown";

and the like insertion shall be made in Part III of Schedule 1 to the Northern Ireland Assembly Disqualification Act 1975.

(5) An order under this section appointing a day under subsection (1) or nominating any company for the purposes of this section may be varied or revoked by a subsequent order at any time before any property, rights or liabilities vest in any company by virtue of this section.

Cancellation of liabilities of BAA to the Secretary of State

3.—(1) Subject to subsections (2) and (3), any liability of the BAA to the Secretary of State—

(*a*) in respect of the BAA's commencing capital debt, or

(*b*) in respect of loans made, or having effect as if made, under section 6 of the 1975 Act (Government loans to BAA),

shall be extinguished immediately before the appointed day; and the assets of the National Loans Fund shall be reduced accordingly.

(2) Subsection (1)(*a*) shall not operate to extinguish any liability of the BAA under section 4 of the 1975 Act (commencing capital debt of the BAA)—

(*a*) to repay any part of the principal of its commencing capital debt which falls due for repayment before the appointed day, or

(*b*) to pay interest on its commencing capital debt in respect of a period falling before that day.

(3) Subsection (1)(*b*) shall not operate to extinguish any liability of the BAA under section 6 of the 1975 Act—

(*a*) to repay any part of the principal of any such loan as is referred to in subsection (1)(*b*) which falls due for repayment before the appointed day, or

(*b*) to pay interest on any such loan in respect of a period falling before that day.

(4) References in this section to the BAA's commencing capital debt are references to the debt referred to in section 4(1) of the 1975 Act.

Initial Government holding in the successor company

4.—(1) As a consequence of the vesting in the successor company by virtue of section 2 of property, rights and liabilities of the BAA, the successor company shall issue such securities of the company as the Secretary of State may from time to time direct—

    (*a*) to the Treasury or the Secretary of State; or

    (*b*) to any person entitled to require the issue of the securities following their initial allotment to the Treasury or the Secretary of State.

(2) The Secretary of State shall not give a direction under subsection (1) at a time when the successor company has ceased to be wholly owned by the Crown.

(3) Securities required to be issued in pursuance of this section shall be issued or allotted at such time or times and on such terms (as to allotment) as the Secretary of State may direct.

(4) Shares issued in pursuance of this section—

    (*a*) shall be of such nominal value as the Secretary of State may direct; and

    (*b*) shall be issued as fully paid and treated for the purposes of the Companies Act 1985 as if they had been paid up by virtue of the payment to the successor company of their nominal value in cash.

(5) The Secretary of State may not exercise any power conferred on him by this section, or dispose of any securities issued or of any rights to securities initially allotted to him in pursuance of this section, without the consent of the Treasury.

(6) Any dividends or other sums received by the Treasury or the Secretary of State in right of, or on the disposal of, any securities or rights acquired by virtue of this section shall be paid into the Consolidated Fund.

Government investment in securities of the successor company

5.—(1) Subject to section 7(5), the Treasury or, with the consent of the Treasury, the Secretary of State may at any time, acquire—

    (*a*) securities of the successor company; or

    (*b*) rights to subscribe for any such securities.

(2) The Secretary of State may not dispose of any securities or rights acquired by him under this section without the consent of the Treasury.

(3) Any expenses incurred by the Treasury or the Secretary of State in consequence of the provisions of this section shall be paid out of money provided by Parliament.

(4) Any dividends or other sums received by the Treasury or the Secretary of State in right of, or on the disposal of, any securities or rights acquired under this section shall be paid into the Consolidated Fund.

Exercise of functions through nominees

6.—(1) The Treasury or, with the consent of the Treasury, the Secretary of State may, for the purposes of section 4 or 5, appoint any person to act as the nominee, or one of the nominees, of the Treasury or the Secretary of State; and—

    (*a*) securities of the successor company may be issued under section 4 to any nominee of the Treasury or the Secretary of State appointed for the purposes of that section or to any person entitled to require the issue of the securities following their initial allotment to any such nominee, and (*b*) any such nominee appointed for the purposes of section 5 may acquire securities or rights under that section,

in accordance with directions given from time to time by the Treasury or, with the consent of the Treasury, by the Secretary of State.

(2) Any person holding any securities or rights as a nominee of the Treasury or the Secretary of State by virtue of subsection (1) shall hold the deal with them (or any of them) on such terms and in such manner as the Treasury or, with the consent of the Treasury, the Secretary of State may direct.

Target investment limit for Government shareholding

7.—(1) As soon after the date when the successor company ceases to be wholly owned by the Crown as he considers expedient, and in any case not later than six months after that date, the Secretary of State shall by order fix a target investment limit in relation to the shares for the time being held in the successor company by virtue of any provision of this Part by the Treasury and their nominees and by the Secretary of State and his nominees ("the Government shareholding").

(2) The target investment limit shall be expressed as a proportion of the voting rights which are exercisable in all circumstances at general meetings of the successor company ("the ordinary voting rights").

(3) The first target investment limit fixed under this section shall be equal to the proportion of the ordinary voting rights which is carried by the Government shareholding at the time when the order fixing the limit is made.

(4) The Secretary of State may from time to time by order fix a new target investment limit in place of the one previously in force under this section; but—

(*a*) any new limit must be lower than the one it replaces; and

(*b*) an order under this section may only be revoked by an order fixing a new limit.

(5) It shall be the duty of the Treasury and of the Secretary of State so to exercise—

(*a*) their powers under section 5 and any power to dispose of any shares held by virtue of any provision of this Part, and

(*b*) their power to give directions to their respective nominees,

as to secure that the Government shareholding does not carry a proportion of the ordinary voting rights exceeding any target investment limit for the time being in force under this section.

(6) Notwithstanding subsection (5), the Treasury or the Secretary of State may take up, or direct any of their respective nominees to take up, any rights for the time being available to them or him, or to that nominee, as an existing holder of shares or other securities of the successor company; but if, as a result, the proportion of the ordinary voting rights carried by the Government shareholding at any time exceeds the target investment limit, it shall be the duty of the Treasury or (as the case may be) the Secretary of State to comply with subsection (5) as soon after that time as is reasonably practicable.

(7) For the purposes of this section the temporary suspension of any of the ordinary voting rights shall be disregarded.

Financial structure of the successor company

8.—(1) If the Secretary of State so directs at any time before the successor company ceases to be wholly owned by the Crown, such sum (not exceeding the accumulated realised profits of the BAA) as may be specified in the direction shall be carried by the successor company to a reserve ("the statutory reserve").

(2) The statutory reserve may only be applied by the successor company in paying up unissued shares of the company to be allotted to members of the company as fully paid bonus shares.

(3) Notwithstanding subsection (2), the statutory reserve shall not count as an undistributable reserve of the successor company for the purposes of section 264(3)(*d*) of the Companies Act 1985; but, for the purpose of determining under that section whether the successor company may make a distribution at any time, any amount for the time being standing to the credit of the statutory reserve shall be treated for the purposes of section 264(3)(*c*) as if it were unrealised profit of the company.

(4) For the purposes of any statutory accounts of the successor company, the value of any asset and the amount of any liability of the BAA vesting in the successor company on the appointed day shall be taken to be the value or (as the case may be) the amount assigned to that asset or liability for the purposes of the corresponding statement of accounts prepared by the successor company under this Act for the period from the end of that dealt with in the last annual statement of accounts published by the BAA down to the appointed day.

(5) For the purposes of any statutory accounts of the successor company the amount to be included in respect of any item shall be determined as if anything done by the BAA (whether by way of acquiring, revaluing or disposing of any asset or incurring, revaluing or discharging any liability, or by carrying any amount to any provision or reserve, or otherwise) had been done by the successor company.

Accordingly (but without prejudice to the generality of the preceding provision) the amount to be included from time to time in any reserves of the successor company as representing its accumulated realised profits shall be determined as if any profits realised and retained by the BAA had been realised and retained by the successor company.

(6) References in this section to the statutory accounts of the successor company are references to any accounts prepared by the successor company for the purposes of any provision of the Companies Act 1985 (including group accounts).

Temporary restrictions on successor company's borrowings etc.

9.—(1) If articles of association of the successor company confer on the Secretary of State powers exercisable with the consent of the Treasury for, or in connection with, restricting the sums of money which may during any period be borrowed or raised by the successor company and its subsidiaries, taken as a whole, those powers shall be exercisable in the national interest notwithstanding any rule of law and the provisions of any enactment.

(2) For the purposes of this section any alteration of the articles of association of the successor company which—

(*a*) has the effect of conferring or extending any such power as is mentioned in subsection (1), and

(*b*) is made at a time when that company has ceased to be wholly owned by the Crown,

shall be disregarded.

Supplementary

Statements in connection with flotation

10.—(1) This section shall apply where—

(*a*) an offer for sale to the public of any securities of the successor company is made by or on behalf of the Crown;

(*b*) any invitation or advertisement is issued (whether or not in documentary form) by or on behalf of the Crown in connection with the offer; and

(*c*) that invitation or advertisement does not contain all the listing particulars.

(2) None of the persons mentioned in subsection (3) shall incur any civil liability by reason of the invitation or advertisement, or any omission from it, if—

(*a*) the contents of the invitation or advertisement were submitted to the Council of The Stock Exchange;

(*b*) the Council did not object to the contents of the invitation or advertisement; and

(*c*) the invitation or advertisement and the listing particulars, taken together, would not be likely to mislead persons of the kind likely to consider the offer.

(3) The persons referred to in subsection (2) are—

(*a*) the Crown;

(*b*) any person acting on behalf of the Crown in connection with the offer;

(*c*) the maker of any statement contained in the invitation or advertisement;

(*d*) any person responsible for the preparation of, or of any part of, the listing particulars.

(4) The reference in subsection (2) to a person mentioned in subsection (3) incurring civil liability shall include a reference to any other person being entitled as against the person so mentioned to be granted any civil remedy or to rescind or repudiate any agreement.

(5) In this section "the listing particulars", in relation to the offer, means such particulars as, by virtue of any provision of any enactment other than this section or of any subordinate legislation, have been approved by the Council of The Stock Exchange for the purposes of the admission of the securities to which the offer relates to the Official List of The Stock Exchange.

Application of Trustee Investments Act 1961 in relation to investment in the successor company

11.—(1) For the purpose of applying paragraph 3(*b*) of Part IV of Schedule 1 to the Trustee Investments Act 1961 (which provides that shares and debentures of a company shall not count as wider-range and narrower-range investments respectively within the meaning of that Act unless the company has paid dividends in each of the five years immediately preceding that in which the investment is made) in relation to investment in shares or debentures of the successor company during the calendar year in which the appointed day falls ("the first investment year") or during any year following that year, the successor company shall be deemed to have paid a dividend as there mentioned—

(*a*) in any year preceding the first investment year which is included in the relevant five years; and

(*b*) in the first investment year, if that year is included in the relevant five years and the successor company does not in fact pay such a dividend in that year.

(2) In subsection (1) "the relevant five years" means the five years immediately preceding the year in which the investment in question is made or proposed to be made.

PART II

TRANSFER OF AIRPORT UNDERTAKINGS OF LOCAL AUTHORITIES

Preliminary

Interpretation of Part II

   12.—(1) In this Part—
"local authority"—
     (*a*) in relation to England and Wales, means a local authority
       within the meaning of the Local Government Act 1972 or the
       Common Council of the City of London; and
     (*b*) in relation to Scotland, has the same meaning as in the Local
       Government (Scotland) Act 1973; and
"principal council"—
     (*a*) in relation to England and Wales, means the council of a
       non-metropolitan county, of a district, or of a London borough;
       and
     (*b*) in relation to Scotland, means a regional or islands council.
   (2) References in this Part to—
     (*a*) a public airport company;
     (*b*) the controlling authority of a public airport company;
     (*c*) a composite authority;
     (*d*) constituent councils of a composite authority; or
     (*e*) an associated company,
shall be read in accordance with the relevant provisions of section 16.
   (3) For the purposes of this Part an airport shall be treated as controlled
by a principal council or (as the case may be) by two or more principal
councils jointly if it is for the time being owned—
     (*a*) by that council or jointly by those councils; or
     (*b*) by a subsidiary of that council or those councils; or
     (*c*) by that council or those councils jointly with any such subsidiary.
   (4) Any reference in this Part, in relation to two or more principal
councils, to a subsidiary of those councils shall be read as a reference to
a body corporate which would, if those councils were a single body
corporate, be a subsidiary of that body corporate.

Transfer of airport undertakings of local authorities

**Transfer of airport undertakings of local authorities to companies owned
    by such authorities**

   13.—(1) The Secretary of State may give to any principal council who
control (whether alone or jointly with one or more other principal
councils) an airport to which this section applies in accordance with
section 14, a direction requiring the council to form a company for the
purpose of carrying on—
     (*a*) the business of operating the airport as a commercial undertaking;
       and
     (*b*) any activities which appear to the council to be incidental to or
       connected with carrying on that business.
   (2) The company shall be a company limited by shares and registered
under the Companies Act 1985, and shall be formed by the council before
such date as the Secretary of State may specify in his direction under
subsection (1).
   (3) In the case of an airport which is jointly controlled by two or more
principal councils the Secretary of State may give a direction under
subsection (1) to such one of those councils as he thinks fit; but in any

such case the council to whom the direction is given must consult the other principal council or councils before forming a company in accordance with the direction.

(4) The Secretary of State may revoke a direction given by him under subsection (1) at any time before a company has been formed in accordance with the direction.

(5) References in subsection (1) to carrying on the business of operating an airport as a commercial undertaking include references to carrying on any activities which, at the time when the direction in question is given, are carried on at the airport or on airport land—

> (a) by the principal council, or (as the case may be) any of the principal councils, who control the airport,
>
> (b) by any subsidiary by whom the airport is owned as mentioned in section 12(3),
>
> (c) by any person managing the airport under the terms of any lease or other arrangement made by or on behalf of the principal council or councils who control it or by any such subsidiary, or
>
> (d) by any person who has been granted a right to carry on activities there by any council, subsidiary or person falling within any of the preceding paragraphs,

with the exception of any activities which the Secretary of State has, before the date referred to in subsection (2), agreed with the principal council or councils who control the airport should not be carried on by the company to be formed in pursuance of the direction.

(6) In subsection (5) "airport land", in relation to an airport, means land which is attached to the airport and was on 1st April 1986 administered with the airport as a single unit.

(7) This section and section 15 (together with section 12(3) and (4)) shall apply to a metropolitan county passenger transport authority as they apply to a principal council.

Airports to which s.13 applies

14.—(1) Section 13 applies to an airport if the annual turnover of the business carried on at the airport by the airport operator exceeded £1 million in the case of at least two of the last three financial years ending before the relevant date.

(2) In subsection (1)—

> "annual turnover", in relation to the business carried on at an airport by the airport operator, means the aggregate, as stated or otherwise shown in the accounts of the business, of all sums received in the course of the business during a financial year, including grants from any public or local authority but excluding—
>
> > (a) capital receipts; and
> >
> > (b) loans made by any person;
>
> "financial year" means a period of twelve months ending with 31st March; and
>
> "the relevant date", in relation to an airport, means the date of any direction given by the Secretary of State in respect of the airport under section 13(1).

(3) The Secretary of State may by order substitute for the sum for the time being specified in subsection (1) such greater sum as may be specified in the order.

(4) An order under subsection (3) shall not affect the validity of any direction in force under section 13(1) immediately before the coming into operation of the order.

Transfer schemes

15.—(1) Where a principal council have formed a company in pursuance of section 13, the council shall, before such date as the Secretary of State may specify in a direction given to the council, submit to the Secretary of State a scheme providing for the transfer to the company of any property, rights or liabilities of the council, or of any subsidiary of theirs, which it appears to the council to be appropriate to transfer to that company.

(2) In preparing a scheme in pursuance of subsection (1) a council shall take into account any advice given by the Secretary of State as to the provisions he regards as appropriate for inclusion in the scheme (and in particular any advice as to the description of property, rights and liabilities which it is in his view appropriate to transfer to the company).

(3) A scheme under subsection (1) shall not come into force until it has been approved by the Secretary of State or until such date as the Secretary of State may, in giving his approval, specify; and the Secretary of State may approve a scheme either without modifications or with such modifications as he thinks fit after consulting the council who submitted the scheme.

(4) If it appears to the Secretary of State that a scheme submitted under subsection (1) does not accord with any advice given by him as mentioned in subsection (2), he may do one or other of the following things, as he thinks fit, namely—

(*a*) approve the scheme under subsection (3) with modifications, or

(*b*) after consulting the council who submitted the scheme, substitute for it a scheme of his own, to come into force on such date as may be specified in the scheme.

(5) In the case of a scheme relating to an airport which is jointly controlled by two or more principal councils ("the relevant authorities") the authority required to submit the scheme under subsection (1) must consult the other relevant authority or authorities before submitting the scheme under that subsection; and the Secretary of State shall not approve the scheme (whether with or without modifications), or substitute a scheme of his own, unless—

(*a*) he has given that other authority or (as the case may be) those other authorities an opportunity of making, within such time as he may allow for the purpose, written representations with respect to the scheme; and

(*b*) he has considered any such representations made to him within that time.

(6) In relation to a scheme relating to any such airport, subsection (1) shall be read as if—

(*a*) the reference to any property, rights or liabilities of the council submitting the scheme were a reference to any property, rights or liabilities vested in, or in any person on behalf of, the relevant authorities; and

(*b*) the reference to any subsidiary of the council submitting the scheme were a reference to any subsidiary of the relevant authorities.

(7) On the coming into force of a scheme under this section the property, rights and liabilities affected by the scheme shall, subject to section 75(3), be transferred and vest in accordance with the scheme.

(8) The Secretary of State may, if he thinks fit, give a council a direction specifying a date under subsection (1) above at the same time as he gives the council a direction under section 13(1); and the Secretary of State may revoke any direction given by him under subsection (1) above at any time before any property, rights or liabilities vest in any company by virtue of this section.

(9) Section 13(7) applies for the purposes of this section.

Public airport companies

Public airport companies and their controlling authorities

16.—(1) References in this Part to a public airport company are references to a company (whether formed under section 13 or not) which carries on the business of operating an airport as a commercial undertaking and is for the time being either—

(*a*) a subsidiary of a single principal council, or

(*b*) a subsidiary of two or more such councils.

(2) In this Part of this Act—

(*a*) references to the controlling authority of a public airport company are references to the principal council or principal councils of whom it is for the time being a subsidiary as mentioned in subsection (1); and

(*b*) references to a composite authority are references to a controlling authority consisting of two or more principal councils, the councils concerned being referred to as the constituent councils of that authority.

(3) For the purposes of this Part a public airport company is an associated company of a principal council if that council are its controlling authority or one of the constituent councils of a composite authority who are its controlling authority.

Control over constitution and activities of public airport companies

17.—(1) Subject to subsection (2), it shall be the duty of the controlling authority of a public airport company to exercise their control over the company so as to ensure that at least three of the directors of the company, or at least one-quarter of their number (whichever is less), are full-time employees of the company who are suitably qualified to act as directors of the company by virtue of their experience in airport management.

(2) Where at any time it appears to the Secretary of State—

(*a*) that a public airport company has made arrangements for the management of the airport operated by it to be carried on otherwise than through its officers or employees, and

(*b*) that any such arrangements are adequate to secure that those participating in the management of the airport under the arrangements are suitably qualified to do so by virtue of their experience in airport management,

the Secretary of State may direct that subsection (1) shall not apply in relation to that company.

(3) Any direction given by the Secretary of State under subsection (2) may provide—

(*a*) that it is to have effect only for such period, or in such circumstances, as may be specified in it, or

(*b*) that its continuation in force is to be subject to compliance with such conditions specified in it as the Secretary of State thinks fit.

(4) It shall be the duty of the controlling authority of a public airport company to exercise their control over the company so as to ensure that the company does not—

(*a*) engage in activities in which the controlling authority have no power to engage, or

(*b*) permit any subsidiary of the company to engage in any such activities.

(5) Where the controlling authority of a public airport company are a composite authority, the duties imposed by subsections (1) and (4) are joint duties of both or all of the constituent councils of that authority; and

subsection (4) shall apply in any such case as if it referred to activities in which none of the constituent councils have power to engage.

Disabilities of directors of public airport companies

18.—(1) A director of a public airport company who is paid for acting as such, or who is an employee of the company or of a subsidiary of the company, shall be disqualified for being elected, or being, a member—
  (a) where the company's controlling authority is a single principal council, of that council; or
  (b) where the company's controlling authority are a composite authority, of any of the councils who are the constituent councils of that authority.

(2) Where a director of a public airport company is a member of any such council as is mentioned in subsection (1)(a) or (b) he shall not at any meeting of the council—
  (a) take part in the consideration or discussion of any contract or proposed contract between the company or a subsidiary of the company and the council; or
  (b) vote on any question with respect to any contract or proposed contract between the company or a subsidiary of the company and—
      (i) the council, or
      (ii) (if they are a constituent council), any of the constituent councils,
  or with respect to any other matter relating to the activities of the company or such a subsidiary.

(3) Any person who contravenes paragraph (a) or (b) of subsection (2) shall be guilty of an offence and liable on summary conviction to a fine not exceeding the fourth level on the standard scale, unless he proves that he did not know that the matter in relation to which the contravention occurred was such a contract or proposed contract as is mentioned in that paragraph or (as the case may be) was a matter otherwise relating to the activities of the company or subsidiary concerned.

(4) A prosecution for an offence under this section shall not, in England and Wales, be instituted except by or on behalf of the Director of Public Prosecutions.

(5) A principal council who are the controlling authority of a public airport company or one of the constituent councils of such an authority may by standing orders provide for the exclusion of a member of the council who is a director of the company from a meeting of the council while there is under consideration by the council—
  (a) any contract or proposed contract between the company or a subsidiary of the company and the council, or
  (b) any other matter relating to the activities of the company or such a subsidiary.

(6) Subsections (2) and (5) above shall apply in relation to members of—
  (a) a committee of any principal council who are the controlling authority of a public airport company or one of the constituent councils of such an authority, or
  (b) a joint committee of two or more local authorities one or more of whom are such a council,
(including, in either case, a sub-committee) as they apply in relation to members of any such council, but with the substitution of references to meetings of any such committee for references to meetings of the council.

(7) This section shall apply in relation to a director of a subsidiary of a public airport company as it applies in relation to a director of such a company.

Prohibition on employment by public airport company of officers etc. of controlling authority

19.—(1) No person who is a full-time officer or employee of a principal council shall hold any office or employment under an associated company except as a director who is not also an employee of the company.

(2) Any person who contravenes subsection (1) shall be guilty of an offence and liable on summary conviction to a fine not exceeding the fourth level on the standard scale.

Powers of investment and disposal in relation to public airport companies

20.—(1) Without prejudice to the powers of a principal council—

(a) to subscribe for shares on the formation of a company formed by them in pursuance of section 13, or

(b) to acquire any shares in or other securities of a company formed in pursuance of that section by way of consideration for any transfer of property, rights and liabilities to that company under section 15(7),

a principal council shall have power at any time to subscribe for, take up or acquire (as the case may be) any securities of any associated company.

(2) A principal council shall have power to provide for the disposal, in such manner as they think fit, of any such securities.

(3) A local authority shall have power, with the consent of the Secretary of State, to acquire securities of any company which carries on the business of operating an airport as a commercial undertaking and is not an associated company (whether or not it is a public airport company or was formed in pursuance of section 13).

(4) Subsections (1) and (3) are without prejudice to the operation of section 30(1)(a) of the 1982 Act (need for consent of Secretary of State to the maintenance of airports by local authorities).

(5) A principal council who are the controlling authority of a public airport company, or (as the case may be) both or all of the constituent councils of a composite authority who are such a controlling authority, may, in exercising their power under subsection (2) in relation to the disposal of any securities of the company, provide for an employees' share scheme to be established in respect of the company; and any such scheme may provide for the transfer of shares without consideration.

(6) In subsection (5) "employees' share scheme" means a scheme for encouraging or facilitating the holding of shares or debentures in a public airport company by or for the benefit of—

(a) the bona fide employees or former employees of the company or of a subsidiary of the company; or

(b) the wives, husbands, widows, widowers or children or step-children under the age of 18 of such employees or former employees.

Capital controls relating to investment in public airport companies by local authorities in England and Wales

21.—(1) Where a local authority dispose of any securities of a public airport company (whether it continues to be such a company after the disposal or not)—

(a) any amount received by the authority in respect of the disposal shall be treated for the purposes of section 72 of the 1980 Act (expenditure which authorities may make) as a receipt of the authority which, by virtue of section 75(1) of that Act, is a capital receipt of the authority for the purposes of Part VIII of that Act (capital expenditure of local authorities etc.), but

(b) only the relevant sum shall be taken into account under section 72(3)(d) of that Act.

(2) In subsection (1) "the relevant sum", in relation to an amount falling within paragraph (a) of that subsection, means—

(a) three-tenths of that amount, or

(b) if regulations are made for the purposes of section 72(3)(d) of the 1980 Act which prescribe a proportion other than three-tenths in relation to disposals falling within subsection (1), the proportion of that amount so prescribed.

(3) Where a local authority incur any expenditure in respect of the acquisition of any securities—

(a) of a public airport company, or

(b) of any company which, as a result of the acquisition by the authority of those securities, becomes a public airport company,

the amount of that expenditure shall, in so far as it is not prescribed expenditure of the authority for the purposes of Part VIII of the 1980 Act by virtue of Schedule 12 to that Act, be treated as prescribed expenditure of the authority for those purposes.

(4) In this section and section 22 "the 1980 Act" means the Local Government, Planning and Land Act 1980; and this section and section 22 apply to England and Wales only.

Other local authority capital controls in England and Wales

22.—(1) For the purposes of Part VIII of the 1980 Act—

(a) the amount of any advance of a capital nature made—

(i) to a public airport company by any person other than a subsidiary of the company or an authority to whom Part VIII of that Act applies, or

(ii) to a subsidiary of a public airport company by a person other than that company, any other subsidiary of that company or such an authority, and

(b) subject to subsection (2), any amount raised by the issue of any securities—

(i) by a public airport company to any person other than such an authority, or

(ii) by a subsidiary of a public airport company to any person other than that company,

shall be treated as prescribed expenditure of the controlling authority of that company.

(2) Subsection (1)(b) shall not apply to any amount raised by the issue of any securities—

(a) by a public airport company where, as a result of the issue of those securities, it ceases to be such a company; or

(b) by a subsidiary of a public airport company where, as a result of the issue of those securities, it ceases to be such a subsidiary.

(3) Any amount repaid by a public airport company or a subsidiary of such a company in respect of any such advance as is mentioned in subsection (1)(a) shall be treated for the purposes of section 72 of the 1980 Act as a receipt of the controlling authority of that company which, by virtue of section 75(1) of that Act, is a capital receipt of the authority for the purposes of Part VIII of that Act.

(4) Where the controlling authority of a public airport company are a composite authority, subsections (1) and (3) shall have effect as if the references to the controlling authority were references to such one of the

constituent councils of that authority as may be determined by agreement between those councils.

(5) It shall be the duty of the controlling authority of a public airport company to exercise their control over the company so as to ensure that the company appoints as auditors of the company only persons who, in addition to being qualified for appointment as such auditors in accordance with section 389 of the Companies Act 1985, are approved for appointment as such auditors by the Audit Commission for Local Authorities in England and Wales.

(6) Where the controlling authority of a public airport company are a composite authority, the duty imposed by subsection (5) is a joint duty of both or all of the constituent councils of that authority.

(7) Section 21(4) applies for the purposes of this section.

Local authority capital controls in Scotland

23.—(1) Any liability to meet capital expenses incurred by a public airport company, or by a subsidiary of such a company, shall, in the case of a company whose controlling authority are an authority to whom section 94 of the Local Government (Scotland) Act 1973 (consent of Secretary of State required for the incurring of liability to meet capital expenses) applies, be treated for the purposes of that section as a liability to meet capital expenses incurred by the company's controlling authority.

(2) It shall be the duty of the controlling authority of a public airport company to exercise their control over the company so as to ensure that the company appoints as auditors of the company only persons who, in addition to being qualified for appointment as such auditors in accordance with section 389 of the Companies Act 1985, are approved for appointment as such auditors by the Commission for Local Authority Accounts in Scotland.

(3) This section applies to Scotland only.

Provision of services for public airport companies

24.—(1) A principal council shall have power to enter into an agreement with any associated company, or with any subsidiary of an associated company, for the provision by the council for that company or (as the case may be) for that subsidiary of any administrative, professional or technical services.

(2) Any agreement under this section shall include provision for payment of proper commercial charges in respect of services to be provided under the agreement.

(3) Where a principal council have entered into an agreement under this section, the accounts of that council shall include a separate account in respect of that agreement and—

(*a*) in England and Wales, section 24 of the Local Government Finance Act 1982 (rights of inspection) shall apply in relation to any such separate account as it applies in relation to any statement of accounts prepared by the council pursuant to regulations under section 23 of that Act; and

(*b*) in Scotland, sections 101 and 105 of the Local Government (Scotland) Act 1973 (rights of inspection and regulations as to accounts) shall have effect as if any reference to an abstract of the accounts of an authority included a reference to any such separate account.

Financial backing for establishment and operations of public airport companies

25.—(1) A principal council shall have power to make loans to any associated company, or to guarantee loans made to any associated company by any other person, for the provision of working capital.

(2) The reference in subsection (1) to guaranteeing loans is a reference to guaranteeing the repayment of the principal of, the payment of interest on, and the discharge of any other financial obligation in connection with, the loans.

(3) A principal council shall have power to make loans—

(*a*) to any associated company, or

(*b*) to any subsidiary of an associated company,

for the purpose of meeting any expenses incurred or to be incurred by that company or subsidiary in connection with the provision or improvement of assets in connection with its business.

(4) Any loan under subsection (1) or (3) must be made on terms, both as to rates of interest and otherwise, no more favourable than the terms on which the council making the loan would themselves be able to borrow at the time when the loan is made.

(5) A principal council shall have power to give any guarantees and do any other things which appear to the council to be necessary or expedient for the purpose of or in connection with—

(*a*) any disposal authorised under section 20(2); or

(*b*) any disposal by any associated company of the whole or any part of that company's undertaking, or of any property, rights or liabilities of that company.

(6) A principal council shall have power to provide financial assistance by way of grants, loans or guarantees for any associated company which has incurred losses affecting the viability of its business.

(7) A principal council shall have power, where on the winding up of any associated company the assets of the company are not sufficient to meet the company's liabilities, to make to the creditors of the company such payments as may be necessary to meet the balance of those liabilities (and may accordingly give to persons dealing or proposing to deal with any such company such guarantees with respect to the exercise of their power under this subsection in relation to the company as they think fit).

Supplementary

Avoidance of restrictions on transfer of securities of public airport companies

26.—(1) Any provision to which this section applies shall be void in so far as it operates—

(*a*) to preclude the holder of any securities of a public airport company from disposing of those securities, or

(*b*) to require the holder of any such securities to dispose, or offer to dispose, of those securities to particular persons or to particular classes of persons, or

(*c*) to preclude the holder of any such securities from disposing of those securities except—

(i) at a particular time or at particular times, or

(ii) on the fulfilment of particular conditions or in other particular circumstances.

(2) This section applies to any provision relating to any securities of a public airport company and contained in—

(*a*) the memorandum or articles of association of the company or any other instrument purporting to regulate to any extent the respective rights and liabilities of the members of the company,

(b) any resolution of the company, or

(c) any instrument issued by the company and embodying terms and conditions on which any such securities are to be held by persons for the time being holding them.

Consents under s.30 of the 1982 Act

27. Where any airport controlled by a principal council, or jointly by two or more principal councils, comes into the ownership of a public airport company as a result of a transfer under section 15(7), any consent given to that council or (as the case may be) to any of those councils under section 30(1)(a) of the 1982 Act, or any consent having effect as if so given, shall (together with any conditions to which it is subject) continue in force so as to enable the council in question, through the company, to maintain that airport; but that council may not by virtue of the consent establish or maintain (whether directly or indirectly) any other airport.

Compensation for loss or diminution of pension rights

28.—(1) The Secretary of State may provide by regulations for the payment, by such persons as may be prescribed by or determined under the regulations, in such cases and to such extent as may be so prescribed or determined, of pensions, allowances or gratuities by way of compensation to or in respect of persons who have suffered loss or diminution of pension rights by reason of—

(a) any transfer of property, rights and liabilities under section 15(7), or

(b) the disposal under section 20(2) of any interests held by a principal council in a public airport company.

(2) Regulations under this section may—

(a) include provision as to the manner in which and the persons to whom any claim for compensation is to be made, and for the determination of all questions arising under the regulations;

(b) make or authorise the Secretary of State to make exceptions and conditions in relation to any classes of persons or any circumstances to which the regulations apply; and

(c) be framed so as to have effect from a date earlier than the making of the regulations;

but regulations having effect from a date earlier than their making shall not place any individual who is qualified to participate in the benefits for which the regulations provide in a worse position than he would have been in if the regulations had been framed so as to have effect only from the date of their making.

(3) Regulations under this section may include either or both of the following provisions, namely—

(a) provision authorising the payment, without probate (or, in Scotland, confirmation) and without other proof of title, of any sum due under the regulations in respect of a person who has died to his personal representatives or such other persons as may be prescribed by the regulations; and

(b) provision rendering void any assignment of (or, in Scotland, assignation of) or charge on, or any agreement to assign or charge, any benefit under the regulations, and provision that on the bankruptcy of a person entitled to such a benefit (or, in Scotland, sequestration of the estate of, or granting of a trust deed for creditors by, such a person) no part of it shall pass to any trustee or other person acting on behalf of the creditors, except in accordance with an order made by a court in pursuance of any enactment specified in the regulations.

(4) Subject to subsection (5), where regulations under this section have made provision for the payment of pensions, allowances or gratuities as mentioned in subsection (1), compensation in respect of any such loss or diminution of pension rights as is mentioned in that subsection shall be paid only in accordance with those regulations in any case to which those regulations apply; and accordingly such compensation shall not be paid under any other statutory provision, by virtue of any provision in a contract or otherwise.

(5) Subsection (4) shall not prevent the payment of any sum to which a person is entitled by virtue of contractual rights acquired by him before such date as the Secretary of State may by order specify.

(6) Any regulations or order made under this section by the Secretary of State may make different provision for different cases to which those regulations or that order apply or applies, as the case may be, and may in particular make different provision as respects different areas.

(7) In this section—

"pension", in relation to a person, means a pension, whether contributory or not, of any kind whatsoever payable to or in respect of him, and includes—

(*a*) a gratuity so payable;

(*b*) a return of contributions to a pension fund, with or without interest on or any other addition to those contributions; and

(*c*) any sums payable on or in respect of the death of that person;

"pension rights" includes, in relation to any person, all forms of right to or eligibility for the present or future payment of a pension, and any expectation of the accruer of a pension under any customary practice, and includes a right of allocation in respect of the present or future payment of a pension.

PART III

REGULATION OF USE OF AIRPORTS, ETC.

Interpretation of Part III, etc.

29.—(1) In this Part—

"air transport licensing functions" means the functions conferred on the CAA in relation to the grant of such licences as are referred to in section 64(1)(*a*) of the 1982 Act and in relation to the revocation, suspension or variation of such licences (whether on the application of any person or otherwise);

"movement", in relation to an airport, means a take-off or landing by an aircraft at the airport.

(2) For the purposes of this Part any class or description may be framed by reference to any matters or circumstances whatever.

Directions to airport operators in the interests of national security etc.

30.—(1) The Secretary of State may give to any airport operator or to airport operators generally such directions of a general character as appear to the Secretary of State to be necessary or expedient in the interests of national security or of relations with a country or territory outside the United Kingdom.

(2) The Secretary of State may give to any airport operator a direction requiring him (according to the circumstances of the case) to do, or not to do, a particular thing specified in the direction, if the Secretary of State considers it necessary or expedient to give such a direction in the interests of national security.

(3) The Secretary of State may give to the appropriate person in relation to any airport a direction requiring that person (according to the circumstances of the case)—

(*a*) to do, or not to do, in connection with any operational activities relating to the airport a particular thing specified in the direction, or

(*b*) to secure that a particular thing specified in the direction is done or not done in connection with any such activities,

if the Secretary of State considers it necessary or expedient to give such a direction in order to discharge or facilitate the discharge of any international obligation of the United Kingdom.

(4) In subsection (3)—

"the appropriate person", in relation to an airport, means—

(*a*) the airport operator, or

(*b*) an associated company of the airport operator; and

"operational activities", in relation to an airport, means any activities—

(*a*) which are carried on wholly or mainly for the benefit of users of the airport, or

(*b*) the revenues from which are wholly or mainly attributable to payments by such users;

but the Secretary of State may by order make such modifications of the definition of "operational activities" as he thinks necessary or expedient having regard to any international obligation of the United Kingdom.

(5) In so far as any direction applying to an airport operator by virtue of subsection (1), (2) or (3) conflicts with the requirements of any other enactment or instrument having effect in relation to him as an airport operator, those requirements shall be disregarded; and it is hereby declared that nothing in Part IV of this Act is to be construed as prejudicing the generality of subsection (3).

(6) The Secretary of State shall lay before each House of Parliament a copy of every direction given under this section unless he is of the opinion that disclosure of the direction is against the interests of national security or of relations with a country or territory outside the United Kingdom, or against the commercial interests of any person.

(7) A person shall not disclose, or be required by virtue of any enactment or otherwise to disclose, any direction given or other thing done by virtue of this section if the Secretary of State has notified him that the Secretary of State is of the opinion that disclosure of that direction or thing is against the interests of national security or of relations with a country or territory outside the United Kingdom, or against the commercial interests of some other person.

(8) Any person who in contravention of subsection (7) discloses any direction given, or other thing done, by virtue of this section shall be guilty of an offence and liable—

(*a*) on summary conviction, to a fine not exceeding the statutory maximum;

(*b*) on conviction on indictment, to imprisonment for a term not exceeding two years or to a fine, or to both.

(9) Before giving any direction or directions under this section to a particular person the Secretary of State shall consult that person; and before giving any directions under subsection (1) to airport operators

generally the Secretary of State shall consult such of the following, namely—

(a) airport operators who appear to him to be likely to be affected by the directions, and

(b) organisations representing airport operators,

as he considers appropriate.

Traffic distribution rules

31.—(1) Where—

(a) it appears to the Secretary of State that two or more airports are airports serving the same area in the United Kingdom, and

(b) he considers it appropriate to do so,

he may in accordance with this section make rules (to be known as traffic distribution rules) providing for air traffic, or any class or description of air traffic, to be distributed between those airports in such manner as he thinks fit.

(2) It shall be the duty of the CAA so to perform its air transport licensing functions as to secure that any traffic distribution rules in force under this section are complied with.

(3) Traffic distribution rules may do any of the following things (and no more), namely—

(a) specify classes or descriptions of air traffic that are permitted under the rules to use any of the airports concerned;

(b) impose prohibitions or restrictions in relation to the use of any of those airports by air traffic of any class or description specified in the rules;

(c) provide for the rules to come into operation (in whole or in part) at such time or in such circumstances as may be specified in the rules.

(4) Before making any traffic distribution rules the Secretary of State shall consult the CAA who shall in turn, before giving advice to the Secretary of State, consult such of the following namely—

(a) airport operators who appear to it to be likely to be affected by the rules,

(b) operators of aircraft who appear to it to be likely to be so affected, and

(c) organisations representing airport operators or operators of aircraft,

as it considers appropriate.

(5) Where—

(a) the subject-matter of any particular rules made by the Secretary of State under this section is a matter in relation to which the CAA has given advice to the Secretary of State (whether before or after the passing of this Act), and

(b) those rules are so made not later than five years after the giving of that advice,

the requirements of subsection (4) shall be taken to have been satisfied with respect to those rules.

(6) In subsection (1) the reference to airports serving the same area in the United Kingdom is a reference to airports in the case of which a substantial number of the passengers departing from, or arriving at, the airports by air (other than those interrupting their flights there or transferring from one flight to another) have as their original points of departure, or (as the case may be) as their ultimate destinations, places situated within the same area in the United Kingdom.

Power to limit aircraft movements at certain airports

32.—(1) The Secretary of State may, if he considers it appropriate to do so in the case of a particular airport to which this section applies, make an order in accordance with this section which does either or both of the following things, namely—

(*a*) imposes an overall limit on the number of occasions on which, during any period specified in the order, aircraft may take off or land at the airport,

(*b*) imposes such other limit or limits applying to the taking off or landing of aircraft at the airport during any such period in circumstances or cases specified in the order as the Secretary of State thinks fit.

(2) This section applies to an airport if it appears to the Secretary of State that the existing runway capacity of the airport is not fully utilised for a substantial proportion of the time during which its runway or runways is or are available for the take-off or landing of aircraft.

(3) It shall be the duty of the airport operator to secure that any limit imposed under this section is complied with; and in performing its air transport licensing functions the CAA shall have regard to the existence of any such limit.

(4) An order under this section may—

(*a*) provide for aircraft taking off or landing at the airport in circumstances or cases specified in the order to be disregarded for the purposes of any specified limit falling within subsection (1)(*a*) or (*b*) or for the purposes of every such limit imposed by the order;

(*b*) provide for the number of occasions on which aircraft of any description specified in the order take off or land at the airport in any period so specified to be determined, for any such purposes as are mentioned in paragraph (*a*), in any manner so specified (whether or not involving the counting of two or more such occasions as a single occasion).

(5) The Secretary of State shall not make an order under this section imposing any limit in relation to a particular period by virtue of which the level of the movements to be permitted at the airport during that period is lower than—

(*a*) the highest level of any corresponding movements at the airport occurring during any equivalent period within the three years preceding the making of the order, or

(*b*) where any limit is for the time being in force under this section in relation to any corresponding movements at the airport during an equivalent period, the level of such movements permitted during that period by virtue of that limit.

(6) Before making an order under this section the Secretary of State shall consult the CAA, the airport operator affected by the order and such of the following, namely—

(*a*) operators of aircraft who appear to the Secretary of State to be likely to be affected by the order,

(*b*) organisations representing operators of aircraft, and

(*c*) any local authority or authorities who appear to the Secretary of State to be affected by operations at the airport,

as the Secretary of State considers appropriate.

(7) In subsection (6) "local authority"—

(*a*) in relation to England, Wales and Scotland, has the meaning given by section 12(1);

(*b*) in relation to Northern Ireland, means a district council established under the Local Government Act (Northern Ireland) 1972.

Schemes for allocating capacity at airports

33.—(1) Where—

(a) an order is for the time being in force in relation to an airport under section 32, or

(b) it appears to the Secretary of State that the demand for the use of an airport exceeds, or is likely in the near future to exceed, the operational capacity of the airport, and as a result he considers it appropriate that a scheme under this section should apply in relation to the airport,

the Secretary of State may give the CAA a direction requiring it to prepare and submit for his approval a scheme under this section in relation to the airport.

(2) Any direction of the Secretary of State under subsection (1) shall specify the matters which are to be dealt with in the scheme; and the Secretary of State shall consult the CAA before giving it any such direction.

(3) A scheme under this section in relation to an airport may do either or both of the following things, namely—

(a) provide for an aircraft to be precluded from performing a movement at the airport unless (in addition to satisfying any requirements or conditions having effect otherwise than under the scheme) the operator of the aircraft has acquired a right under the scheme to cause it to perform that movement;

(b) provide for special charges to be payable to the airport operator by operators of aircraft in respect of the performance by the aircraft of movements at the airport.

(4) A scheme under this section may—

(a) where it provides for the acquisition of rights in pursuance of subsection (3)(a), provide—

(i) for the allocation of such rights on such basis or by such method as may be specified in the scheme,

(ii) for such rights to be framed by reference to particular times or periods of time,

(iii) for such rights to be transferable,

(iv) for such rights to be subject to such conditions as may be specified in the scheme;

(b) where it provides for the payment of special charges in pursuance of subsection (3)(b), provide for different charges to apply in the case of operators of different classes or descriptions, or in different circumstances;

(c) in either case, provide for provisions of the scheme not to apply to operators, or to movements, of any specified class or description.

(5) A scheme under this section shall not come into force until it has been approved by the Secretary of State or until such date as the Secretary of State may, in giving his approval, specify; and the Secretary of State may approve a scheme either without modifications or with such modifications as, after consulting the CAA, he thinks fit.

(6) Before submitting a scheme under this section for the approval of the Secretary of State, the CAA shall consult the airport operator and such of the following, namely—

(a) operators of aircraft who appear to it to be likely to be affected by the scheme, and

(b) organisations representing airport operators or operators of aircraft,

as it considers appropriate.

(7) Where a scheme under this section is in force in relation to an airport it shall be the duty of the airport operator to give effect to the scheme.

(8) A scheme under this section in relation to an airport—

(a) may be varied or revoked by any subsequent such scheme; and

(b) may, with the approval of the Secretary of State, be revoked by the CAA otherwise than in connection with its replacement by any such scheme;

and where any such scheme was prepared in pursuance of a direction given by virtue of subsection (1)(a), the scheme shall in any event cease to have effect if the airport ceases to be subject to such an order as is mentioned in that provision (but without prejudice to the power of the Secretary of State to give a further direction in relation to the airport by virtue of subsection (1)(b)).

(9) The revocation or termination of a scheme as mentioned in subsection (8) shall be without prejudice to the recovery of sums already owing to the airport operator.

Matters to be taken into account by CAA

34.—(1) This section applies to the following functions of the CAA, namely—

(a) the function of giving advice to the Secretary of State on being consulted by him under any of sections 31 to 33, and

(b) the function of preparing a scheme under section 33 where directed to do so under that section.

(2) Section 4 of the 1982 Act (general objectives of the CAA) shall not apply to any function to which this section applies; and instead, in performing any such function, the CAA shall take into account—

(a) such of the international obligations of the United Kingdom as the Secretary of State may notify to it for the purposes of this section; and

(b) any advice received from the Secretary of State with respect to the relations of the United Kingdom with a country or territory outside the United Kingdom;

and, subject to that, shall have regard to the matters referred to in subsection (3).

(3) Those matters are—

(a) the need to secure the sound development of civil aviation throughout the United Kingdom;

(b) the reasonable interests of users of air transport services; and

(c) such policy considerations as the Secretary of State may notify to the CAA for the purposes of this section.

Regulation of availability of airports by reference to airport licences

35. An Order in Council under section 60 of the 1982 Act (Air Navigation Orders) may provide for regulating the availability of an airport for the take-off or landing of aircraft, or of aircraft of any specified class or description, by reference to the nature of the licence for the time being in force in respect of the airport by virtue of subsection (3)(c) of that section.

PART IV

ECONOMIC REGULATION OF AIRPORTS

Preliminary

Interpretation of Part IV, etc.

36.—(1) In this Part—
"the 1973 Act" means the Fair Trading Act 1973;
"the 1980 Act" means the Competition Act 1980;
"airport charges", in relation to an airport, means—
(*a*) charges levied on operators of aircraft in connection with the landing, parking or taking off of aircraft at the airport (including charges that are to any extent determined by reference to the number of passengers on board the aircraft, but excluding charges payable by virtue of regulations under section 73 of the 1982 Act (air navigation services etc.)); and
(*b*) charges levied on aircraft passengers in connection with their arrival at, or departure from, the airport by air;
"the Commission" means the Monopolies and Mergers Commission;
"operational activities" has the same meaning as it has for the time being in section 30(3);
"prescribed" has the meaning given by subsection (3);
"relevant activities", in relation to an airport, means the provision at the airport of any services or facilities for the purposes of—
(*a*) the landing, parking or taking off of aircraft;
(*b*) the servicing of aircraft (including the supply of fuel); or
(*c*) the handling of passengers or their baggage or of cargo at all stages while on airport premises (including the transfer of passengers, their baggage or cargo to and from aircraft).

(2) It is hereby declared that the reference in the definition of "relevant activities" in subsection (1) to the provision of facilities for the purposes of the handling of passengers does not include the provision of facilities for car parking, for the refreshment of passengers at the airport or for the supply of consumer goods or services there.

(3) Without prejudice to the generality of section 7(2) of the 1982 Act (special provisions as respects certain functions of the CAA), regulations made by the Secretary of State in pursuance of that provision may prescribe for the purposes of that provision any functions conferred on the CAA by this Part; and in this Part "prescribed" means prescribed by regulations so made.

Permissions

Airports subject to economic regulation: requirement for permission to levy airport charges

37.—(1) Where an airport is subject to economic regulation under this Part no airport charges shall be levied at the airport unless—
(*a*) they are levied by the airport operator, and
(*b*) a permission to levy airport charges is for the time being in force in respect of the airport.

(2) Where the annual turnover of the business carried on at an airport by the airport operator exceeded the relevant sum in the case of at least two of the last three financial years ending before the date when this section comes into force, then (subject to section 53(3)) the airport shall

be subject to economic regulation under this Part as from the end of the period of six months beginning with that date.

(3) Where—

    (*a*) an airport is not one to which subsection (2) applies, but

    (*b*) the annual turnover of the business carried on at the airport by the airport operator exceeded the relevant sum in the case of at least two of the last three financial years ending before a date later than the date when this section comes into force,

the airport shall be subject to economic regulation under this Part as from the end of the period of nine months beginning with that later date.

(4) Nothing in this section applies—

    (*a*) to any airport managed by the Secretary of State;

    (*b*) to any airport owned or managed by the CAA or by any subsidiary of the CAA; or

    (*c*) to any airport for the time being exempted from economic regulation under this Part by virtue of subsection (5).

(5) Where at any time the Secretary of State is satisfied as respects any airport which is subject to economic regulation under this Part that the annual turnover of the business carried on at the airport by the airport operator did not exceed the relevant sum in the case of each of the two last financial years ending before that time, he may, after consulting the CAA, determine that the airport shall cease to be subject to economic regulation under this Part as from the date of his determination.

(6) Any such determination may be made by the Secretary of State either of his own motion or on the application of the airport operator.

(7) A determination under subsection (5) shall not—

    (*a*) preclude subsection (3) from applying to the airport in question on a subsequent occasion; or

    (*b*) affect any rights or liabilities accruing by virtue of this Part before the determination is made.

(8) Where any person levies any airport charges in contravention of subsection (1)—

    (*a*) he shall not be guilty of an offence by reason only of his contravening that subsection; but

    (*b*) any airport charges so levied shall not be recoverable by him, and, in so far as they have been paid to him, shall be recoverable from him.

(9) In this section "the relevant sum" means £1 million or such other sum as is for the time being specified in subsection (1) of section 14, and "annual turnover" and "financial year" have the meaning given by subsection (2) of that section.

(10) Where at the coming into operation of an order under section 14(3) any airport is, or is due to become, subject to economic regulation under this Part in accordance with subsection (2) or (3) above, that subsection shall continue to apply to the airport notwithstanding any increase in the relevant sum effected by the order.

Grant or refusal of permissions

38.—(1) Where an airport is by virtue of section 37(2) or (3) due to become subject to economic regulation under this Part at the end of the period of either six or nine months referred to in that provision, the airport operator may, at any time after the beginning of that period, make an application to the CAA for the grant in respect of the airport of a permission to levy airport charges.

(2) Any such application—

    (*a*) must be in writing and contain such particulars with respect to such matters as the CAA may specify in a notice published in the prescribed manner; and

   (*b*) must be accompanied by such fee as may be specified in a scheme or regulations made under section 11 of the 1982 Act.

(3) Where an application is made in relation to an airport by the airport operator in accordance with this section, then, as from the date of the application or the date when the airport becomes subject to economic regulation under this Part (whichever is the later), there shall, by virtue of this subsection, be deemed for all purposes to be a permission in force under this Part in respect of the airport until such time as—

   (*a*) the CAA grants a permission in pursuance of the application; or

   (*b*) the airport operator is notified by the CAA that it has refused the application.

(4) Where—

   (*a*) any such application has been so made by an airport operator, and

   (*b*) he has complied with any requirement to produce any documents, or to furnish any accounts, estimates, returns or other information, to the CAA which the CAA may have imposed on him under this Act for the purpose of enabling it to determine whether, and (if so) what, conditions should be imposed under this Part in relation to the airport in question,

the CAA shall grant the application within such period as may be prescribed.

(5) Where—

   (*a*) any such application has been so made by an airport operator, but

   (*b*) he has failed to comply with any such requirement as is mentioned in subsection (4)(*b*) within such time as may have been allowed for the purpose,

the CAA may, if it thinks fit, allow him further time (not exceeding such period as may be prescribed) to comply with the requirement; and if he has still not complied with it when that further time expires the CAA shall refuse the application.

(6) The grant or refusal of an application made by an airport operator under this section shall be notified to him in such manner as may be prescribed.

(7) Any permission granted under this section in respect of an airport shall come into force on whichever is the later of the following dates, namely—

   (*a*) the date when it is granted, and

   (*b*) the date when the airport becomes subject to economic regulation under this Part,

and shall remain in force unless and until it is revoked in pursuance of section 49(9) or the airport ceases to be subject to economic regulation under this Part by virtue of a determination of the Secretary of State under section 37(5) (and shall so remain in force notwithstanding any change of airport operator).

Conditions

Imposition of conditions by CAA

39.—(1) So long as a permission is for the time being in force under this Part in respect of an airport, the airport operator shall comply with such conditions as are for the time being in force in relation to the airport by virtue of the following sections of this Part.

(2) The CAA shall perform its functions under those sections in the manner which it considers is best calculated—

(*a*) to further the reasonable interests of users of airports within the United Kingdom;

(*b*) to promote the efficient, economic and profitable operation of such airports;

(*c*) to encourage investment in new facilities at airports in time to satisfy anticipated demands by the users of such airports; and

(*d*) to impose the minimum restrictions that are consistent with the performance by the CAA of its functions under those sections;

and section 4 of the 1982 Act (general objectives of the CAA) shall accordingly not apply in relation to the performance by the CAA of those functions.

(3) In performing those functions the CAA shall take into account such of the international obligations of the United Kingdom as may be notified to it by the Secretary of State for the purposes of this section.

(4) The duty of an airport operator under subsection (1) to comply with any such conditions as are there mentioned shall be enforceable in accordance with sections 48 to 50 (and not otherwise).

(5) Nothing in this Part shall be read as requiring or authorising the CAA to impose or modify any conditions in relation to an airport otherwise than on granting a permission under this Part in respect of it or while any such permission is in force.

(6) Without prejudice to the generality of section 11 of the 1982 Act, a scheme or regulations under that section may make provision for charges to be paid in respect of the performance by the CAA of any of its functions under the following sections of this Part.

Mandatory conditions in case of designated airports

40.—(1) Where an airport is designated for the purposes of this section by an order made by the Secretary of State, then (subject to subsection (9))—

(*a*) if the airport is so designated at the time when a permission under this Part is granted in respect of it under section 38(4), the CAA shall, at the time of granting the permission, impose in relation to the airport such conditions as to accounts and airport charges as are mentioned in subsections (2) and (3); and

(*b*) if the airport is so designated at any later time, the CAA shall impose any such conditions in relation to the airport within the period of nine months beginning with the date of the designation.

(2) The conditions as to accounts referred to in subsection (1) are—

(*a*) such conditions as the CAA considers appropriate to secure that the accounts of the airport operator disclose—

(i) any subsidy furnished (whether by the making of loans on non-commercial terms or otherwise) by any person or authority to the airport operator in connection with his business so far as consisting of the carrying on of operational activities relating to the airport, and the identity of any such person or authority,

(ii) any subsidy so furnished to that business by the airport operator out of funds attributable to any other activities carried on by him,

(iii) the aggregate income and expenditure of the airport operator attributable to the levying by him of airport charges at the airport,

(iv) the aggregate income and expenditure of the airport operator attributable to operational activities relating to the airport (whether carried on by the airport operator or any other person) being income and expenditure which are taken into account by him in fixing airport charges, and

(v) where the airport operator has for the time being the management of two or more airports, the aggregate income and expenditure of the airport operator attributable to the business carried on by him at each of those airports; and

(b) where the accounts of the airport operator are not required to be delivered to the registrar of companies in accordance with the Companies Act 1985, such conditions as the CAA considers appropriate with respect to the publication of those accounts;

and the reference in paragraph (a) to the accounts of the airport operator shall be read as referring to accounts delivered to the registrar of companies in accordance with that Act or published in pursuance of paragraph (b).

(3) The conditions as to airport charges referred to in subsection (1) are such conditions as the CAA considers appropriate for regulating the maximum amounts that may be levied by the airport operator by way of airport charges at the airport during the period of five years beginning with such date as may be specified by the CAA when imposing the conditions, being a date falling not later than the end of the period of twelve months beginning with the date when the conditions are imposed.

(4) Subject to subsection (9), the CAA shall—

(a) at the end of the period of five years specified in subsection (3), and

(b) at the end of each succeeding period of five years,

make such modifications in the conditions imposed in pursuance of subsection (3) (as they are for the time being in force) as it thinks appropriate for regulating during the succeeding period of five years the maximum amounts that may be levied by the airport operator by way of airport charges at the airport; and any reference in this Part to the making of modifications in any such conditions includes a reference to the making of a modification whose effect is merely to extend the application of a particular condition or conditions for a further period of five years.

(5) Without prejudice to the generality of subsections (3) and (4), conditions imposed or modified in pursuance of those provisions—

(a) may provide—
(i) for an overall limit on the amount that may be levied by the airport operator by way of all airport charges at the airport, or
(ii) for limits to apply to particular categories of charges, or
(iii) for a combination of any such limits;

(b) may operate to restrict increases in any such charges, or to require reductions in them, whether by reference to any formula or otherwise;

(c) may provide for different limits to apply in relation to different periods of time falling within the period of five years for which the conditions are in force.

(6) Except with the agreement of the airport operator concerned, conditions imposed in pursuance of subsection (3) shall not be modified by the CAA otherwise than in pursuance of subsection (4).

(7) The CAA may, if it thinks fit and after consultation with the airport operator concerned, determine, at any time during any period of five years for which conditions under subsection (3) are in force in accordance with the preceding provisions of this section, that that period shall be extended by such period (not exceeding twelve months) as may be specified in its determination; and in any such case any reference in this Part to that period shall be read as a reference to that period as extended by virtue of this subsection.

(8) Where the CAA makes any such determination in the case of conditions providing for different limits to apply in relation to different periods of time, any limit applying in relation to the last of those periods

shall apply also in relation to the additional period for which the conditions are to remain in force in accordance with the determination, unless the CAA and the airport operator concerned agree that some other limit shall apply instead.

(9) Before imposing any conditions in pursuance of subsection (3), or making any modifications in pursuance of subsection (4), in relation to any airport, the CAA shall, unless the Secretary of State otherwise directs, make a reference to the Commission in respect of the airport under section 43(1).

(10) The Secretary of State may by order under this section either designate particular airports for the purposes of this section or designate any class of airports for those purposes; and any such class may be framed by reference to annual turnover, as defined in the order, or by reference to any other matter whatever.

Discretionary conditions

41.—(1) The CAA may, if it thinks fit in the case of any airport which is not a designated airport, impose in relation to the airport such conditions as are mentioned in section 40(2), either at the time of granting a permission under this Part in respect of the airport or at any other time while it is in force.

(2) Where, at the time of granting a permission under this Part in respect of an airport (whether a designated airport or not) or at any other time while such a permission is in force, it appears to the CAA that the airport operator is pursuing one of the courses of conduct specified in subsection (3), then (subject to subsection (6) and section 42) the CAA may, if it thinks fit, impose in relation to the airport such conditions as it considers appropriate for the purpose of remedying or preventing what it considers are the adverse effects of that course of conduct.

(3) The courses of conduct referred to in subsection (2) are—

(*a*) the adoption by the airport operator, in relation to any relevant activities carried on by him at the airport, of any trade practice, or any pricing policy, which unreasonably discriminates against any class of users of the airport or any particular user or which unfairly exploits his bargaining position relative to users of the airport generally;

(*b*) the adoption by the airport operator, in relation to the granting of rights by virtue of which relevant activities may be carried on at the airport by any other person or persons, of any practice which—

(i) unreasonably discriminates against persons granted any class of such rights, or any particular grantee of such a right, or unfairly exploits his bargaining position relative to the grantees of such rights generally, or

(ii) unreasonably discriminates against any class of persons applying for such rights or any particular applicant, or unreasonably limits the number of such rights that are granted in the case of any particular services or facilities,

or which has resulted in the adoption by any other person of a practice that does any of those things;

(*c*) the fixing by the airport operator of any charges levied by him at the airport in relation to any relevant activities carried on by him there at levels which—

(i) are insufficient, even after taking into account such other revenues (if any) as are relevant to the fixing of such charges, to cover the costs of providing the services or facilities to which the charges relate or are, in the opinion of the CAA, artificially low, and

(ii) materially harm (or are intended materially to harm) the business carried on by an airport operator at any other airport in the United Kingdom.

(4) In subsection (3)(*c*)(i) the reference to levels at which charges are fixed being artificially low is a reference to such levels being significantly lower than they would otherwise have been—

(*a*) by reason of any subsidy—

(i) furnished by any person or authority to the airport operator in connection with his business so far as consisting of the carrying on of operational activities relating to the airport, or

(ii) furnished to that business by the airport operator out of funds attributable to any other activities carried out by him, whether by the making of loans on non-commercial terms or otherwise; or

(*b*) where the airport operator is a company, by reason of any conduct on the part of the company which, in the opinion of the CAA, has resulted, or will result, in—

(i) a failure by the company to achieve a reasonable return on the capital employed by it in carrying on operational activities relating to the airport, or

(ii) a failure by the company to distribute to members of the company a reasonable proportion of the profits available for distribution, or

(iii) a failure by the company to reach a level of borrowing which is appropriate having regard to its equity share capital (within the meaning of the Companies Act 1985).

(5) In determining for the purposes of subsection (4) what is reasonable or (as the case may be) appropriate in the case of a company, the CAA—

(*a*) shall disregard the fact that the relevant conduct on the part of the company was in conformity with any policy for the time being of a person having control over the company, but

(*b*) shall have regard to any circumstances which, in the opinion of the CAA, would affect any company carrying on the business of operating the airport as a commercial undertaking.

(6) Before imposing any conditions under subsection (2) in relation to an airport, the CAA shall notify the airport operator concerned of the course of conduct within subsection (3)(*a*), (*b*) or (*c*) which it appears to the CAA that he is pursuing and of the conditions which the CAA proposes to impose; and if, within such period as may be prescribed, the airport operator notifies the CAA that he objects to its proposals, the CAA—

(*a*) shall not proceed with the implementation of those proposals; but

(*b*) may instead make a reference to the Commission in respect of the airport under section 43(3).

(7) In this section "designated airport" means an airport for the time being designated for the purposes of section 40.

Discretionary conditions: supplementary provisions

42.—(1) Nothing in section 41(2) shall be read as authorising the CAA to impose under that provision—

(*a*) any condition providing for any such overall limit as is mentioned in paragraph (*a*)(i) of section 40(5); or

(*b*) any condition for regulating the maximum amount that may be levied by an airport operator by means of any particular category of charges levied by him at an airport if the same category of charges is for the time being subject to any limit or limits imposed in pursuance of paragraph (*a*)(ii) or (iii) of section 40(5).

(2) The CAA shall, in determining—

(*a*) whether an airport operator is pursuing a course of conduct within section 41(3)(*a*), or

(*b*) (where it determines that an airport operator is pursuing such a course of conduct) whether, and (if so) what, conditions should be imposed by it under section 41(2) in relation to the airport in question,

take into account any advice given to it by the Secretary of State for the purposes of this subsection as to practices currently adopted at airports in countries or territories outside the United Kingdom.

(3) Where the CAA receives from any operator of aircraft whose principal place of business is in any such country or territory any representations to the effect that the powers of the CAA under section 41(2) appear to be exercisable in relation to an airport on the grounds that the airport operator is pursuing a course of conduct within section 41(3)(*a*), the CAA shall notify those representations to the Secretary of State for the purpose of enabling him to determine whether to give any advice to the CAA for the purposes of subsection (2) above.

References to Commission

References to Commission in relation to imposition or modification of conditions

43.—(1) Where the CAA is, by virtue of section 40(9), required to make a reference to the Commission under this subsection in respect of any airport, that reference shall be so framed as to require the Commission to investigate and report on—

(*a*) the question as to what are the maximum amounts that should be capable of being levied by the airport operator by way of airport charges at the airport during such period of five years as the CAA may specify in the reference; and

(*b*) the questions specified in subsection (2).

(2) Those questions are—

(*a*) whether the airport operator has, at any time during the relevant period, pursued—

(i) in relation to any airport charges levied by him at the airport, or

(ii) in relation to any operational activities carried on by him and relating to the airport, or

(iii) in relation to the granting of a right by virtue of which any operational activities relating to the airport may be carried on by any other person or persons,

a course of conduct which has operated or might be expected to operate against the public interest; and

(*b*) if so, whether the effects adverse to the public interest which that course of conduct has had, or might be expected to have, could be remedied or prevented by the imposition of any conditions in relation to the airport or by the modification of any conditions already in force in relation to it.

(3) Where the CAA is, by virtue of section 41(6), authorised to make a reference to the Commission under this subsection in respect of any airport, that reference shall be so framed as to require the Commission to investigate and report on the questions—

(*a*) whether the airport operator has, at any time during the relevant period, pursued the course of conduct referred to in the CAA's notification under section 41(6); and

(b) if so, whether any such course of conduct has operated or might be expected to operate against the public interest; and

(c) if so, whether the effects adverse to the public interest which that course of conduct has had, or might be expected to have, could be remedied or prevented by the imposition of any conditions in relation to the airport or by the modification of any conditions already in force in relation to it.

(4) The CAA may, at any time, by notice given to the Commission vary any reference under subsection (3) by adding to the matters specified in the reference or by excluding from the reference some or all of the matters so specified; and on receiving such a notice the Commission shall give effect to the variation.

(5) In determining for the purposes of this section whether any particular matter has operated, or might be expected to operate, against the public interest, the Commission—

(a) shall have regard to the objectives specified in paragraphs (a) to (d) of section 39(2); and

(b) in the case of a matter relating to the granting of a right by virtue of which any operational activities relating to an airport may be carried on by any person or persons, shall in addition have regard to the following objective, namely the furtherance of the reasonable interests of persons granted such rights.

(6) In this section "the relevant period"—

(a) in relation to any reference in respect of an airport under subsection (1), means—

(i) in the case of the first reference in respect of that airport under that subsection, the period of twelve months ending with the date of the reference; and

(ii) in the case of any subsequent such reference, the period ending with the date of that reference and beginning with the date of the reference immediately preceding it; and

(b) in relation to any reference in respect of an airport under subsection (3), means the period of twelve months ending with the date of the reference.

Supplementary provisions relating to references

44.—(1) For the purpose of assisting the Commission in carrying out an investigation on a reference under section 43, the CAA may—

(a) in the case of a reference under subsection (1) of that section, specify in the reference—

(i) any view that the CAA has formed as to what the maximum amounts referred to in paragraph (a) of that subsection should be,

(ii) any course of conduct which, in its opinion, has been pursued by the airport operator in relation to any of the matters specified in subsection (2)(a) of that section and has operated, or might be expected to operate, against the public interest,

(iii) any effects adverse to the public interest which, in its opinion, any such course of conduct has had or might be expected to have, and

(iv) any conditions or modifications of conditions by which, in its opinion, its view as to those maximum amounts could be implemented or (as the case may be) those adverse effects could be remedied or prevented;

(b) in the case of a reference under subsection (3) of that section, or a variation of such a reference, specify in the reference or variation—

(i) any effects adverse to the public interest which, in the opinion of the CAA, any course of conduct specified in the reference or variation has had or might be expected to have, and

(ii) any conditions or modifications of conditions by which, in its opinion, those adverse effects could be remedied or prevented.

(2) It shall be the duty of the CAA, for the purpose of assisting the Commission in carrying out an investigation on any reference under section 43, to give to the Commission—

(a) any information in the possession of the CAA which—

(i) it is within the power of the CAA to give, and

(ii) relates to matters falling within the scope of the investigation, and

(iii) either is requested by the Commission for that purpose or is information that it would in the CAA's opinion be appropriate to give to the Commission for that purpose without any such request, and

(b) any other assistance which the Commission may require, and which it is within the power of the CAA to give, in relation to any such matters;

and the Commission shall, for the purpose of carrying out the investigation, take account of any information given to them in pursuance of paragraph (a).

(3) The following provisions of the 1973 Act, namely sections 70 (time limit for report on merger reference), 81 (procedure in carrying out investigations) and 85 (attendance of witnesses and production of documents) and Part II of Schedule 3 (performance of functions of the Commission), together with section 24 of the 1980 Act (modification of provisions about performance of Commission's functions), shall apply in relation to references under section 43 of this Act as if—

(a) the functions of the Commission in relation to such references were functions under the 1973 Act;

(b) the expression "merger reference" included a reference under this section;

(c) in section 70 of the 1973 Act, references to the Secretary of State were references to the CAA and the reference to three months were a reference to six months;

(d) in paragraph 11 of Schedule 3 to the 1973 Act, the reference to section 71 of that Act were a reference to section 43(4) of this Act; and

(e) paragraph 16(2) of that Schedule were omitted.

(4) The CAA shall—

(a) publish particulars of any reference under section 43, and of any variation of such a reference, in such manner as it considers appropriate for the purpose of bringing the reference or variation to the attention of persons likely to be affected by it; and

(b) send a copy of the reference or variation to the Secretary of State and to the airport operator concerned.

Reports on references

45.—(1) In making a report on any reference under section 43, the Commission—

(a) shall include in the report definite conclusions on the questions comprised in the reference together with such an account of their reasons for those conclusions as, in their opinion, is expedient for facilitating proper understanding of those questions and of their conclusions;

(b) where they conclude that any course of conduct specified in the reference has operated, or might be expected to operate, against the public interest, shall specify in the report the effects adverse to the public interest which that course of conduct has had or might be expected to have; and

(c) where they conclude that any adverse effects so specified could be remedied or prevented by the imposition of any conditions in relation to the airport in question, or by the modification of any conditions already in force in relation to it, shall specify in the report the conditions that should be imposed or (as the case may be) the modifications that should be made.

(2) The Commission's conclusions on a reference under section 43(1) so far as relating to the maximum amounts referred to in paragraph (a) of that provision shall take the form of recommendations as to what those maximum amounts should be during the five years in question; and any such recommendations may do any of the things referred to in paragraphs (a) to (c) of section 40(5).

(3) Where, on any reference under section 43, the Commission conclude that an airport operator is a party to an agreement to which the Restrictive Trade Practices Act 1976 applies, the Commission, in making their report on that reference, shall exclude from their consideration the question whether the provisions of that agreement, in so far as they are provisions by virtue of which it is an agreement to which that Act applies, have operated, or might be expected to operate, against the public interest; and paragraph (b) of subsection (1) above shall have effect subject to the provisions of this subsection.

(4) Section 82 of the 1973 Act (general provisions as to reports) shall apply in relation to reports of the Commission on references under section 43 above as it applies to reports of the Commission under that Act.

(5) A report of the Commission on any reference under section 43 shall be sent to the CAA.

(6) On receiving such a report, the CAA—

(a) shall send a copy of the report to the Secretary of State and to the airport operator concerned; and

(b) subject to any direction given by the Secretary of State under subsection (7), shall publish the report in such manner as the CAA considers appropriate for bringing the report to the attention of persons likely to be affected by it.

(7) If it appears to the Secretary of State that the publication of any matter in such a report would be against the public interest or the commercial interests of any person, he may, before the end of the period of 21 days beginning with the day on which he receives the copy of the report, direct the CAA to exclude that matter from the report as published under subsection (6).

Imposition or modification of conditions following Commission's report

46.—(1) Where the CAA—

(a) is required to impose any such conditions as are mentioned in section 40(3), or to make any such modifications as are mentioned in section 40(4), in respect of any such maximum amounts as are there mentioned, and

(b) has received a report made by the Commission under section 45 and containing their recommendations as to what those maximum amounts should be, the CAA shall impose any such conditions in accordance with section 40(3) or make any such modifications in accordance with section 40(4) (as the case may be).

(2) Where the CAA has received a report of the Commission on a reference under section 43 and the report—

    (a) includes conclusions to the effect that any course of conduct within the scope of the reference has operated or might be expected to operate against the public interest,

    (b) specifies effects adverse to the public interest which that course of conduct has had or might be expected to have,

    (c) includes conclusions to the effect that those effects could be remedied or prevented by the imposition of any conditions in relation to the airport in question or by the modification of any conditions already in force in relation to it, and

    (d) specifies conditions or modifications by which those effects could be remedied or prevented,

the CAA shall, subject to subsection (3), impose such conditions, or make such modifications of any conditions already in force, in relation to the airport in question as the CAA considers appropriate for the purpose of remedying or preventing the adverse effects specified in the report.

(3) In the case of a report of the Commission on a reference under section 43(1), the Secretary of State may, if he thinks fit, direct that, notwithstanding that the report satisfies the requirements of paragraphs (a) to (d) of subsection (2) above, the CAA shall not impose any conditions or make any modifications as mentioned in that subsection.

(4) Before imposing any conditions or making any modifications as mentioned in subsection (1) the CAA shall have regard to the recommendations referred to in paragraph (b) of that subsection; and before imposing any conditions or making any modifications as mentioned in subsection (2) the CAA shall have regard to the conditions or modifications referred to in paragraph (d) of that subsection.

(5) Where the CAA has imposed any conditions or made any modifications as mentioned in subsection (1) or (2), it shall publish the following matters, namely—

    (a) particulars of the conditions or modifications in question, and

    (b) in so far as those conditions or modifications do not accord with the recommendations referred to in subsection (1)(b), or (as the case may be) with the conditions or modifications referred to in subsection (2)(d), a statement of the CAA's reasons for not implementing the Commission's report,

in such manner as it considers appropriate for the purpose of bringing those matters to the attention of persons likely to be affected by them.

Charges to be paid by airport operators in respect of Commission's expenses

47.—(1) The Secretary of State may, in accordance with the following provisions of this section, provide by regulations for annual charges to be payable by airport operators in respect of the expenses incurred by the Commission in carrying out investigations, and reporting, on references to which this subsection applies.

(2) Subsection (1) applies to any reference made to the Commission under section 43 other than a reference under subsection (1) of that section which relates to the first period of five years for which any such conditions as are mentioned in section 40(3) are to be in force in relation to a particular airport.

(3) Any such regulations as are mentioned in subsection (1) shall—

    (a) require the Commission—

(i) to prepare, in such form and including such information as may be prescribed by the regulations, an annual statement containing an assessment of the expenses incurred by it as mentioned in subsection (1) in the preceding period of twelve months, and

(ii) to send a copy of any such statement to the CAA;

(b) prescribe the circumstances in which airport operators, being persons having the management of airports in respect of which permissions under this Part are in force, are to be liable to charges under this section in respect of the expenses of the Commission specified in any such statement;

(c) provide that, where a particular airport operator is liable to such a charge, the amount of the charge payable by him shall (subject to paragraph (d)) be a proportion of the expenses referred to in paragraph (b) to be determined by reference to such matters or circumstances as may be specified in the regulations; and

(d) prescribe the maximum amount of any charge under this section.

(4) Without prejudice to the generality of subsection (3)(b), any such regulations may provide for an airport operator falling within that provision to be liable to a charge under this section notwithstanding that none of the expenses there referred to relate to a reference made in respect of an airport managed by him.

(5) Where by virtue of any such regulations a charge under this section is payable by any airport operator, the CAA shall notify him that he is required to pay that charge to the CAA; and where an airport operator has been so notified the amount of any such charge shall be recoverable from him as a debt due to the CAA.

(6) Any sums received by the CAA by virtue of this section shall be paid to the Secretary of State, who shall then pay them into the Consolidated Fund.

Enforcement of conditions

Breach of conditions other than accounts conditions: complaints and compliance orders

48.—(1) Where—

(a) a complaint is made to the CAA in relation to any airport that the airport operator is failing to comply, or has failed to comply and is likely again to fail to comply, with any condition in contravention of section 39(1); and

(b) that complaint is made—

(i) by any person on whom any airport charges have been levied by the airport operator at the airport (whether actually paid by that person or not), or

(ii) by any other airport operator who claims that the business carried on by him at another airport in the United Kingdom has been or is being materially harmed by the alleged failure to comply with the condition in question,

the CAA shall investigate that complaint (unless the CAA considers that it is frivolous); but nothing in this section applies to a condition to which any provision of section 50 applies.

(2) Where any such complaint is made to the CAA by a person not falling within subsection (1)(b)(i) or (ii), the CAA may investigate the complaint if it thinks fit.

(3) If, having investigated any such complaint, the CAA is satisfied that an airport operator is failing to comply, or has failed to comply and is

likely again to fail to comply, with any condition in contravention of section 39(1), the CAA shall either—

   (a) by order make such provision as it considers appropriate for the purpose of securing compliance with that condition and for remedying any loss or damage sustained, or injustice suffered, by any person in consequence of the failure to comply with that condition; or

   (b) subject to section 40(6) and subsection (4) below, modify the condition in such manner as it considers appropriate in all the circumstances.

(4) The CAA shall not under subsection (3)(b) modify a condition in such a manner as would permit of the occurrence, or (as the case may be) recurrence, of any effects adverse to the public interest which have been specified by the Commission in a report made by them on any reference under section 43 in respect of the airport in question.

(5) If, having investigated any such complaint, the CAA is satisfied that an airport operator has failed to comply with any condition in contravention of section 39(1) (but not that he is for the time being failing to comply with it or is likely again to fail to comply with it) the CAA may by order make such provision as it considers appropriate for remedying any loss or damage sustained, or injustice suffered, by any person in consequence of the failure to comply with that condition.

(6) An order under subsection (3)(a) or (5)—

   (a) shall require the airport operator concerned (according to the circumstances of the case) to do, or not to do, such things as are specified in the order or are of a description so specified; and

   (b) shall, as respects any such requirement, take effect (according to the terms of the order) either as soon as a copy of it is served on the airport operator or at such later time as may be specified in it by the CAA; and

   (c) may be revoked by the CAA at any time.

(7) A copy of any such order shall be served by the CAA on the airport operator in the prescribed manner; and references in this and the following section to the service of a copy of such an order on an airport operator shall be construed accordingly.

Validity and effect of compliance orders

49.—(1) If an airport operator is aggrieved by any compliance order applying to him by virtue of section 48 and desires to question the validity of the order on the ground—

   (a) that the order is not within the powers of that section; or

   (b) where any regulations under section 7(2) of the 1982 Act provide for regulating the procedure to be followed by the CAA in the performance of its functions under section 48, that any requirement of those regulations has not been complied with in relation to the order,

he may, within 42 days from the date of service on him of a copy of the order, make an application to the court under this section.

(2) On any such application the court may, if satisfied—

   (a) that the compliance order is not within the powers of section 48, or

   (b) that the interests of the applicant have been substantially prejudiced by a failure to comply with any such requirement as is mentioned in subsection (1)(b) above,

quash the order or any provision of the order.

(3) Except as provided by this section, the validity of a compliance order shall not be questioned in any legal proceedings whatever.

(4) No criminal proceedings shall, by virtue of the making of a compliance order, lie against any person on the ground that he has committed, or aided, abetted, counselled or procured the commission of, or conspired or attempted to commit, or incited others to commit, any contravention of the order.

(5) The obligation to comply with a compliance order is a duty owed to any person who may be affected by a contravention of it.

(6) Where a duty is owed by virtue of subsection (5) to any person—

(*a*) any breach of the duty which causes that person to sustain loss or damage, and

(*b*) any act which, by inducing a breach of that duty or interfering with its performance, causes that person to sustain loss or damage and which is done wholly or partly for the purpose of achieving that result,

shall be actionable at the suit or instance of that person.

(7) In any proceedings brought against any person in pursuance of subsection (6)(*a*), it shall be a defence for him to prove that he took all reasonable steps and exercised all due diligence to avoid contravening the order.

(8) Without prejudice to any right which any person may have by virtue of subsection (6)(*a*) to bring civil proceedings in respect of any contravention or apprehended contravention of a compliance order, the CAA may enforce compliance with any such order by civil proceedings for an injunction or interdict or for any other appropriate relief.

(9) Where it appears to the CAA that an airport operator has contravened a compliance order and is unlikely to comply with it in the immediate future the CAA may, instead of proceeding under subsection (8), revoke the permission for the time being in force under this Part in respect of the airport to which the contravention relates.

(10) Where any such permission is revoked by reason of an airport operator's contravention of a compliance order, then (notwithstanding section 38(4)) a permission shall not again be granted under this Part in respect of the airport in question so long as he remains the airport operator unless it appears to the CAA that, if the CAA were to impose in relation to the airport any condition corresponding to the one whose breach gave rise to the making of the compliance order, he would comply with that condition.

(11) In this section—

"act", in relation to any person, includes any failure to do an act which he is under a duty to do and "done" shall be construed accordingly;

"compliance order" means an order under section 48(3)(*a*) or (5);

"contravention", in relation to a compliance order, includes any failure to comply with it;

"the court"—

(*a*) in relation to England and Wales, means the High Court; and

(*b*) in relation to Scotland, means the Court of Session.

Breach of accounts conditions: criminal penalties etc.

50.—(1) Any airport operator who fails to comply with any condition imposed in accordance with section 40(2)(*a*) (in pursuance of either section 40(1) or section 41(1)) shall be guilty of an offence and liable—

(*a*) on summary conviction, to a fine not exceeding the statutory maximum;

(*b*) on conviction on indictment, to a fine.

(2) Any airport operator who, in the case of any condition imposed in accordance with section 40(2)(*b*) (in pursuance of either section 40(1) or section 41(1)), fails to comply with that condition before the end of the period allowed for compliance with it by virtue of that or any other such condition shall be guilty of an offence and liable—

(*a*) on summary conviction, to a fine not exceeding the fifth level on the standard scale; and

(*b*) on a second or subsequent summary conviction, to a fine of one-tenth of the amount corresponding to that level for each day on which the contravention is continued.

(3) Where an airport operator has failed to comply with any such condition as is mentioned in subsection (1) above, then (whether or not proceedings are brought under that subsection in respect of that contravention) the CAA may impose, in relation to the airport to which the contravention relates, such conditions as the CAA considers appropriate with respect to the publication of any matter to whose non-disclosure the contravention relates; and if the airport operator fails to comply with any condition so imposed before the end of the period allowed for compliance with it by virtue of that or any other such condition he shall be guilty of an offence and liable as mentioned in paragraphs (*a*) and (*b*) of subsection (2).

(4) In any proceedings for an offence under this section it shall be a defence for the person charged to prove—

(*a*) in the case of an offence under subsection (1), that he took all reasonable steps for securing compliance with the condition in question;

(*b*) in the case of an offence under subsection (2) or (3), that he took all reasonable steps for securing compliance with the condition in question before the end of the period mentioned in that subsection.

(5) Any reference in this section to an airport operator failing to comply with a condition is a reference to his failing to do so in contravention of section 39(1).

Supplementary

Supplementary provisions relating to conditions

51.—(1) Any condition imposed by the CAA under this Part otherwise than in pursuance of section 40(3) shall (subject to the provisions of this section and to the continuation in force of a permission under this Part in respect of the airport in question) either remain in force for a particular period or remain in force without limit of time, as the CAA may determine; and when imposing any such condition the CAA shall accordingly either—

(*a*) specify the period in question, or

(*b*) specify that it is a condition whose duration is unlimited, as the case may require.

(2) Where the CAA has in the case of any condition specified a period under subsection (1)(*a*), the CAA may, if it thinks fit, determine that that period shall be extended by such period as may be specified in its determination.

(3) Where any such conditions as are mentioned in section 40(2) are in force in relation to an airport, the CAA may at any time modify or revoke those conditions; but the CAA shall not revoke any such conditions otherwise than in connection with replacing them with further conditions unless the conditions revoked were imposed in pursuance of section 41(1).

(4) Where any such conditions as are mentioned in section 41(2) are in force in relation to an airport (being conditions imposed otherwise than following a reference to the Commission under section 43(3)) the CAA may at any time modify or revoke those conditions unless—

(a) subsection (5)(a) operates to preclude the modification of the conditions under this subsection, or

(b) that provision has previously so operated and the conditions were modified following a reference to the Commission made in pursuance of subsection (5)(b).

(5) Before making any modifications under subsection (4) whose object is the more effective securing of the purpose for which the conditions concerned were imposed the CAA shall notify the airport operator concerned of the course of conduct within section 41(3)(a), (b) or (c) which it appears to the CAA that he is still pursuing and of the modifications which it proposes to make; and, if within such period as may be prescribed, the airport operator notifies the CAA that he objects to its proposals, the CAA—

(a) shall not proceed with the implementation of those proposals, but

(b) may instead make a reference to the Commission in respect of the airport under section 43(3);

and, in relation to any such reference, section 43(3) shall have effect as if references to section 41(6) were references to this subsection.

(6) Where any conditions have been imposed or modified by the CAA in relation to an airport for the purpose of remedying or preventing any such adverse effects as are mentioned in section 46(2), the CAA may—

(a) make such modifications or further modifications of those conditions as it considers appropriate, or

(b) revoke the conditions,

as long as the modifications or revocation in question would not permit of the occurrence or (as the case may be) recurrence of any of those adverse effects.

(7) Where under this Part the CAA imposes any condition in relation to an airport or modifies, extends the period of operation of, or revokes, any such condition the CAA shall notify the airport operator of the imposition, modification or revocation of the condition, or (as the case may be) of the extension of the period of its operation, in such manner as may be prescribed.

(8) Where a permission is in force under this Part in respect of an airport, the airport operator shall, if so required by any person and on payment of such reasonable fee as the airport operator may determine, provide that person with a copy of that permission and of any conditions for the time being in force under this Part in relation to the airport.

Special provisions relating to groups of airports

52.—(1) Where it appears to the CAA that two or more airports are airports serving the same area in the United Kingdom and either—

(a) that they are managed by the same airport operator, or

(b) that they are owned by the same person, or by members of the same group of companies, and they operate as a group of airports whose activities are co-ordinated by the airport operators concerned,

any conditions imposed or modified by the CAA in pursuance of section 40(3) or (4) in relation to any one of those airports may be framed so as to prescribe a limit or limits operating by reference to the aggregate of amounts levied by way of airport charges at that airport and amounts so levied at the other airport or airports.

(2) In subsection (1) the reference to airports serving the same area in the United Kingdom shall be construed in accordance with section 31(6); and, for the purposes of that subsection, a body corporate and each of its subsidiaries shall be treated as members of a group of companies.

Functions in relation to permissions and conditions initially exercisable by Secretary of State

53.—(1) If the Secretary of State, at any time during the period of six months beginning with the date of the coming into force of section 37 notifies the CAA that he proposes to perform, in relation to any airport which is—

(a) due to become subject to economic regulation under this Part at the end of that period by virtue of section 37(2), and

(b) specified in the notification,

the functions of the CAA specified in subsection (2), those functions shall (subject to subsection (4)) be performed in relation to the airport by the Secretary of State and not by the CAA, and references to the CAA in the provisions mentioned in subsection (2) and in sections 51 and 73 shall, so far as may be necessary for the purpose or in consequence of the transfer of those functions, be read as references to the Secretary of State.

(2) The functions of the CAA referred to in subsection (1) are—

(a) its functions under section 38 with respect to the grant or refusal of a permission under this Part, and

(b) if the airport in question is for the time being designated for the purposes of section 40, its functions under that section and section 52 with respect to the imposition of conditions in accordance with section 40(1)(a), and

(c) if the airport in question is not so designated, its functions under section 41(1) with respect to the imposition of such conditions as are there mentioned at the time of granting a permission under this Part.

(3) If the Secretary of State so determines at the time of granting a permission under this Part in respect of an airport in pursuance of this section, that airport shall, instead of becoming subject to economic regulation under this Part at the end of the period of six months referred to in subsection (1), become so subject on such earlier date as may be specified by the Secretary of State in his determination.

(4) Where functions of the CAA under section 40 or 41(1) fall to be performed by the Secretary of State by virtue of this section, the Secretary of State—

(a) shall perform those functions in the manner which he considers is best calculated to achieve the objectives specified in paragraphs (a) to (d) of section 39(2); and

(b) shall perform those functions with respect to the imposition of conditions in pursuance of section 40(3) without there having been made any prior reference to the Commission in connection with the imposition of any such conditions.

(5) Where, before a notification is given by the Secretary of State under subsection (1) in the case of an airport, the airport operator has already made an application in accordance with section 38 to the CAA, then, as from the date when the notification is given—

(a) the application shall be treated as if it had been so made to the Secretary of State, and

(b) anything previously done by or in relation to the CAA in connection with the application shall be treated as if done by or in relation to the Secretary of State, and any fee paid by him in pursuance of section 38(2)(*b*) shall be refunded to him by the CAA.

Orders under the 1973 Act or 1980 Act modifying or revoking conditions

54.—(1) Where, in the circumstances mentioned in subsection (3), the Secretary of State by order exercises any of the powers specified in Parts I and II of Schedule 8 to the 1973 Act or section 10(2)(*a*) of the 1980 Act, the order may also provide for the revocation or modification of any relevant conditions to such extent as may be requisite to give effect to or to take account of any provision made by the order.

(2) In subsection (1) "relevant conditions" means any conditions for the time being in force under this Part other than any conditions imposed or modified in pursuance of section 40(3) or (4).

(3) Subsection (1) shall have effect where—

(*a*) the circumstances are as mentioned in section 56(1) of the 1973 Act (order on report on monopoly reference) and the monopoly situation exists in relation to the carrying on of any operational activities relating to one or more airports;

(*b*) the circumstances are as mentioned in section 73(1) of that Act (order on report on merger reference) and at least one of the two or more enterprises which ceased to be distinct enterprises was an airport operator; or

(*c*) the circumstances are as mentioned in section 10(1) of the 1980 Act (order on report on competition reference) and the anti-competitive practice relates to the carrying on of any operational activities relating to one or more airports.

(4) Expressions used in this section which are also used in the 1973 Act or the 1980 Act have the same meanings as in that Act.

Application of Part IV to associated companies of airport operators

55. Schedule 1 shall have effect with respect to the application of the preceding provisions of this Part to associated companies of airport operators.

Co-ordination of exercise of functions by CAA and Director General of Fair Trading

56. The Secretary of State may by regulations make such provision as he thinks expedient—

(*a*) for the purpose of regulating—

(i) the performance by the CAA of functions under this Part, and

(ii) the performance by the Director General of Fair Trading of functions under the 1973 Act or the 1980 Act,

in cases where, apart from the regulations, such functions would be authorised or required to be performed by the CAA and the Director respectively in relation to the same matter; and

(*b*) for the purpose of prescribing the procedure to be followed in such cases by the CAA and the Director.

PART V

STATUS OF CERTAIN AIRPORT OPERATORS AS STATUTORY UNDERTAKERS, ETC.

Scope of Part V

57.—(1) Subject to subsection (3), this Part applies to—

(*a*) any airport in respect of which a permission to levy airport charges is in force under Part IV, or in respect of which there subsists a pending application for such a permission made in accordance with section 38, other than an airport excluded by virtue of subsection (2); and

(b) any airport which is owned or managed by any subsidiary of the CAA.

(2) The airports excluded by virtue of this subsection are—

(a) any airport owned by the BAA, and

(b) any airport owned by a principal council (within the meaning of Part II of this Act) or by a metropolitan county passenger transport authority or jointly owned by two or more principal councils or by such an authority and one or more such councils.

(3) During the period beginning with the coming into force of this section and ending with the coming into force of section 37 this Part applies to—

(a) any airport which is managed by a company to which any property, rights or liabilities have been transferred in pursuance of a scheme made under section 1 or 15; and

(b) any such airport as is mentioned in subsection (1)(b) above.

(4) In this Part "relevant airport operator" means the airport operator in the case of an airport to which this Part applies.

Application of enactments relating to statutory undertakings

58. Schedule 2 shall have effect with respect to the application of the enactments mentioned in that Schedule (which relate to statutory undertakers etc.) to airports to which this Part applies and to relevant airport operators.

Acquisition of land and rights over land

59.—(1) The Secretary of State may authorise any relevant airport operator to acquire land in Great Britain compulsorily for any purpose connected with the performance of the operator's functions as such; and the following enactments, namely—

(a) if the land is in England and Wales, the Acquisition of Land Act 1981, except Part VI, and

(b) if the land is in Scotland, the Acquisition of Land (Authorisation Procedure) (Scotland) Act 1947, except section 3,

shall apply in relation to the compulsory purchase of land by a relevant airport operator under this section; and, in the case of the latter Act, shall so apply as if the operator were a local authority and as if this subsection were contained in an Act in force immediately before the commencement of that Act.

(2) For the purpose of the acquisition by a relevant airport operator of land in Great Britain by agreement the following provisions shall apply, namely—

(a) if the land is in England and Wales, the provisions of Part I of the Compulsory Purchase Act 1965 (so far as applicable) except sections 4 to 8, 27 and 31, and

(b) if the land is in Scotland, the provisions of the Lands Clauses Acts (so far as applicable) except sections 120 to 125, 127, 142 and 143 of the Lands Clauses Consolidation (Scotland) Act 1845.

(3) The provisions of the 1982 Act which are specified in subsection (4) below shall apply in relation to any relevant airport operator as they apply in Great Britain to the CAA and, in the case of Schedule 10 to the 1982 Act, as if the references to an order made or proposed to be made under Part II of that Act or to the making of such an order included an order for the compulsory purchase of land by a relevant airport operator which

the Secretary of State has confirmed or proposes to confirm or (as the case may be) the confirmation of such an order.

(4) The provisions of the 1982 Act mentioned in subsection (3) are—

section 44 (power to obtain rights over land);

section 45 (power to restrict use of land for purpose of securing safety at airports);

section 46 (power to exercise control over land in interests of civil aviation);

section 48 (power to stop up and divert highways), except subsection (9);

section 50 (power of entry for purposes of survey);

section 52 (displacements from land); and

Schedules 7 to 10 (supplemental provisions and provisions relating to statutory undertakers).

(5) The power of a relevant airport operator to acquire land compulsorily under this section may be exercised for the purpose of providing or improving any highway which is to be provided or improved in pursuance of an order under section 48 of the 1982 Act, as applied by this section, or for any other purpose for which land is required in connection with such an order.

(6) The following enactments (which refer to consecrated land and burial grounds), namely—

(*a*) section 128 of the Town and Country Planning Act 1971; and

(*b*) section 118 of the Town and Country Planning (Scotland) Act 1972,

shall have effect in relation to any land acquired by a relevant airport operator as they have effect in relation to land acquired by statutory undertakers under Part VI of that Act of 1971 or (as the case may be) under Part VI of that Act of 1972.

Disposal of compulsorily acquired land

60.—(1) This section applies to the disposal of any land—

(*a*) which was acquired compulsorily by a relevant airport operator or any predecessor in title of his under section 59(1) or any other enactment; and

(*b*) which, at the time of the disposal, forms part of an airport or is attached to an airport and administered with it as a single unit or has, at any time since the date of its acquisition, formed part of an airport or been so attached and administered.

(2) A relevant airport operator shall not dispose of any land to which this section applies, or any interest or right in or over such land, within the period of 25 years beginning with the date of its acquisition as mentioned in subsection (1), unless—

(*a*) the disposal is for the purposes of the provision of any of the services and facilities associated with the operation of an airport; or

(*b*) the disposal is of a leasehold interest in the land for a term of less than 7 years; or

(*c*) the Secretary of State consents to the disposal.

(3) Any consent of the Secretary of State under this section may be given subject to such conditions as he thinks fit.

Compensation in respect of planning decisions relating to safety of airports etc.

61.—(1) In the case of an airport to which this Part applies, a local planning authority ("a planning authority") shall be entitled to recover from the airport operator a sum equal to any compensation which the planning authority has become liable to pay, if—

(*a*) it has become so liable under section 164, 165, 169, 187(2), or 237(1) of the Town and Country Planning Act 1971 ("the 1971 Act") or under section 153, 154, 158, 176(2) or 226(1) of the Town and Country Planning (Scotland) Act 1972 ("the 1972 Act") (which relate to compensation for certain planning restrictions, for purchase notices which do not take effect and in respect of undertakers' operational land); and

(*b*) the liability is attributable to a planning decision which would not have been taken, or (in the case of compensation under section 164 of the 1971 Act or section 153 of the 1972 Act) to an order under section 45 of the 1971 Act or section 42 of the 1972 Act which would not have been made, but for the need—

(i) to secure the safe and efficient operation of the airport, or

(ii) to prevent persons or buildings from being struck by aircraft using the airport, or

(iii) to secure the safe and efficient operation of apparatus owned by the airport operator and provided for the purpose of assisting air traffic control or as an aid to air navigation.

(2) Where a sum equal to any compensation is payable or paid to a planning authority by an airport operator in pursuance of subsection (1), the planning authority shall pay the airport operator any amount received by the planning authority in respect of the compensation under section 168 of the 1971 Act or section 157 of the 1972 Act (which relate to the recovery of compensation on subsequent development).

(3) Where a purchase notice is served under section 180 of the 1971 Act or section 169 of the 1972 Act in respect of a planning decision which would not have been taken but for such a need as is mentioned in subsection (1) in the case of any airport to which this Part applies, any local authority who are deemed under section 181(2) or 186(1) of the 1971 Act or section 170(2) or 175(1) of the 1972 Act to have served a notice to treat in respect of the interest to which the purchase notice relates may, by notice in writing given to the airport operator not later than one month from the time when the amount of compensation payable by the local authority for the interest is agreed or determined, require the airport operator to purchase the interest from the local authority for a sum equal to the amount of compensation so agreed or determined.

(4) Where a notice in writing is given to an airport operator under subsection (3) he shall, subject to any agreement between him and the local authority, be deemed to have contracted with the local authority to purchase the interest at that price.

(5) Any dispute as to whether a planning decision would not have been taken, or an order under section 45 of the 1971 Act or section 42 of the 1972 Act would not have been made, but for such a need as is mentioned in subsection (1) shall be referred to and determined by the Secretary of State.

(6) In the preceding provisions of this section "planning decision" means a decision made on an application under Part III of the 1971 Act or Part III of the 1972 Act; and references in those provisions to a local planning authority shall be construed—

(*a*) in relation to England and Wales, as including references to any authority to whom functions of a local planning authority are delegated; and

(*b*) in relation to Scotland, as references to a planning authority.

Provisions as to telecommunication apparatus

62.—(1) Paragraph 23 of the telecommunications code (undertakers' works) shall apply for the purposes—

(a) of any work in pursuance of an order or direction under section 44 or 46 of the 1982 Act, as applied by section 59 above, and

(b) of anything done with respect to a highway in pursuance of an order under section 48 of the 1982 Act (as so applied) to which subsection (2) below applies,

to the person doing that work or, as the case may be, the highway authority; and, in the case of any such order as is mentioned in paragraph (b), any person entitled to land over which the highway passes shall be entitled to require the alteration of the telecommunications apparatus in question.

(2) This subsection applies to an order under section 48 of the 1982 Act where the order provides—

(a) for the stopping up or diversion of the highway, or

(b) unless the highway is a trunk road, for the improvement of the highway,

and immediately before the order comes into operation any telecommunication apparatus is kept installed for the purposes of a telecommunications code system under, in, on, over, along or across the highway.

(3) Subject to the preceding provisions of this section, the operator of a telecommunications code system shall, in a case falling within subsection (2)(a), have the same rights in respect of any apparatus kept installed for the purposes of that system as if the order had not come into operation.

(4) Paragraph 23 of the telecommunications code shall not apply by virtue of subsection (2)(b) in relation to the alteration of any telecommunication apparatus where the alteration is for the purpose of authority's works as defined in Part II of the Public Utilities Street Works Act 1950.

(5) Sub-paragraph (8) of paragraph 23 (offence) shall be deemed to be omitted for the purposes of the application by this section of that paragraph to the Secretary of State.

(6) Paragraph 1(2) of the telecommunications code (alteration of apparatus to include moving, removal or replacement of apparatus) shall apply for the purposes of the preceding provisions of this section as it applies for the purposes of the code.

(7) Paragraph 21 of the telecommunications code (restriction on removal of apparatus) shall apply in relation to any entitlement conferred by this section to require the alteration, moving or replacement of any telecommunication apparatus as it applies in relation to an entitlement to require the removal of any such apparatus.

(8) In this section "the telecommunications code" and other expressions defined by paragraph 1(1) of Schedule 4 to the Telecommunications Act 1984 shall be construed in accordance with that provision.

(9) In the application of this section to Scotland, the reference to the highway authority shall be read as a reference to the roads authority as defined by section 151(1) of the Roads (Scotland) Act 1984, and any reference to a highway shall be read as a reference to a road as defined in that provision.

PART VI

MISCELLANEOUS AND SUPPLEMENTARY

Byelaws

Airport byelaws

63.—(1) Where an airport is either—

(a) designated for the purposes of this section by an order made by the Secretary of State, or

(*b*) managed by the Secretary of State,
the airport operator (whether the Secretary of State or some other person) may make byelaws for regulating the use and operation of the airport and the conduct of all persons while within the airport.

(2) Any such byelaws may, in particular, include byelaws—

(*a*) for securing the safety of aircraft, vehicles and persons using the airport and preventing danger to the public arising from the use and operation of the airport;

(*b*) for controlling the operation of aircraft within, or directly above, the airport for the purpose of limiting or mitigating the effect of noise, vibration and atmospheric pollution caused by aircraft using the airport;

(*c*) for preventing obstruction within the airport;

(*d*) for regulating vehicular traffic anywhere within the airport, except on roads within the airport to which the road traffic enactments apply, and in particular (with that exception) for imposing speed limits on vehicles within the airport and for restricting or regulating the parking of vehicles or their use for any purpose or in any manner specified in the byelaws;

(*e*) for prohibiting waiting by hackney carriages except at standings appointed by such person as may be specified in the byelaws;

(*f*) for prohibiting or restricting access to any part of the airport;

(*g*) for preserving order within the airport and preventing damage to property within it;

(*h*) for regulating or restricting advertising within the airport;

(*i*) for requiring any person, if so requested by a constable or airport official, to leave the airport or any particular part of it, or to state his name and address and the purpose of his being within the airport;

(*j*) for securing the safe custody and redelivery of any property which, while not in proper custody, is found within the airport or in an aircraft within the airport, and in particular—

(i) for requiring charges to be paid in respect of any such property before it is redelivered; and

(ii) for authorising the disposal of any such property if it is not redelivered before the end of such period as may be specified in the byelaws;

(*k*) for restricting the area which is to be taken as constituting the airport for the purposes of the byelaws.

(3) In paragraph (*d*) of subsection (2) "the road traffic enactments" means the enactments (whether passed before or after this Act) relating to road traffic, including the lighting and parking of vehicles, and any order or other instrument having effect by virtue of any such enactment.

(4) In paragraph (*i*) of subsection (2) "airport official" means a person authorised by the airport operator; and any such official shall not exercise any power under a byelaw made by virtue of that paragraph without producing written evidence of his authority if required to do so.

(5) Byelaws made under this section by a person other than the Secretary of State shall not have effect until they are confirmed by the Secretary of State, and the provisions of Schedule 3 shall apply to any such byelaws.

(6) Before any byelaws are made by the Secretary of State under this section, he shall take such steps as appear to him to be appropriate for giving public notice of the proposed byelaws and for affording an opportunity for representations to be made with respect to them; and the Secretary of State, shall have regard to any such representations and may then make the byelaws in the form proposed or in that form with such modifications as he thinks fit.

(7) Any byelaws made by the Secretary of State under this section shall be made by statutory instrument.

(8) Section 236(9) of the Local Government Act 1972 and section 202(13) of the Local Government (Scotland) Act 1973 (notice of byelaws made by one local authority to be given to another) and section 237 of the Act of 1972 and section 203 of the Act of 1973 (penalties) shall not apply to any byelaws made by a local authority under this section.

Byelaws: penalties and power to revoke in certain cases

64.—(1) Any person contravening any byelaws made under section 63 shall be liable on summary conviction to a fine not exceeding such amount as, subject to subsection (2) of this section, may be specified by the byelaws in relation to the contravention.

(2) The maximum fines that byelaws may specify by virtue of subsection (1) are fines of an amount at the fourth level on the standard scale or of a lower amount.

(3) Where any person other than the Secretary of State has made any byelaw in relation to any airport by virtue of section 63(2)(*b*), the Secretary of State may, after consulting that person, by order—

(*a*) revoke or vary that byelaw if the Secretary of State considers it appropriate to do so by reason of his having designated the airport for the purposes of section 78 of the 1982 Act (regulation of noise and vibration from aircraft); or

(*b*) revoke or vary that byelaw to the extent that it appears to the Secretary of State to be inconsistent with the safety of persons or vehicles using the airport, of aircraft or of the general public or to be inconsistent with any international obligation of the United Kingdom.

Other provisions relating to airports

Control of road traffic at designated airports

65.—(1) Subject to the provisions of this section, the road traffic enactments shall apply in relation to roads which are within a designated airport but to which the public does not have access as they apply in relation to roads to which the public has access.

(2) The Secretary of State may by order direct that in their application to roads within such an airport the road traffic enactments shall have effect subject to such modifications as appear to him necessary or expedient for the purpose of, or in consequence of, conferring—

(*a*) on the airport operator functions exercisable under those enactments by a highway authority or local authority; or

(*b*) on the chief officer of any airport constabulary functions so exercisable by a chief officer of police.

(3) An order under subsection (2) may exempt from the application of the road traffic enactments particular roads or lengths of road to which the public does not have access and may require the airport operator to indicate the roads or lengths of roads so exempted in such manner as may be specified in the order.

(4) Before making an order under this section in relation to any airport (other than one managed by the Secretary of State) the Secretary of State shall consult the airport operator.

(5) Any road or place within an airport in the metropolitan police district shall be deemed to be a street or place within the meaning of section 35 of the London Hackney Carriage Act 1831.

(6) In this section—

"airport constabulary" means, in relation to an airport owned or managed by the Secretary of State, the special constables appointed under section 57 of the 1982 Act and, in relation to any airport owned or managed by a local authority, any body of constables which the authority have power to maintain at that airport;

"designated airport" means an airport which is designated for the purposes of this section by an order made by the Secretary of State; and

"the road traffic enactments" has the meaning given by section 63(3).

(7) In the application of subsection (2) to Scotland, for "highway authority or local authority" there shall be substituted "roads authority as defined in section 151(1) of the Roads (Scotland) Act 1984".

Functions of operators of designated airports as respects abandoned vehicles

66.—(1) The Secretary of State may by order direct that, in their application to land within any designated airport, the provisions of—

(a) sections 3, 4 and 5 of the Refuse Disposal (Amenity) Act 1978 (powers and duties of local authorities to remove and dispose of vehicles abandoned on land in their area) and section 8 of that Act (powers of entry etc.) so far as relating to section 3 of that Act, and

(b) any regulations for the time being in force under any of those sections,

shall have effect subject to such modifications as appear to him necessary or expedient for the purpose of, or in consequence of, conferring on the airport operator the functions exercisable under those provisions by local authorities or local authorities of any description.

(2) In relation to the provisions of—

(a) sections 99 to 102 of the Road Traffic Regulation Act 1984 (removal of vehicles from roads if illegally, obstructively or dangerously parked or broken down, and from roads or open land if abandoned), and

(b) any regulations for the time being in force under any of those sections,

the powers of the Secretary of State under section 65(2) shall be exercisable not only as respects the application of those provisions to roads within an airport but also as respects their application to other land within the airport.

(3) Where the provisions of—

(a) section 3 of the Refuse Disposal (Amenity) Act 1978,

(b) section 99, 100 or 102 of the Road Traffic Regulation Act 1984, or

(c) any regulations for the time being in force under any of those sections,

apply to any land within any airport in accordance with an order made under or by virtue of this section, those provisions shall have effect in relation to vehicles in a building on that land which is used for providing facilities for the parking of vehicles as they have effect in relation to vehicles on land in the open air.

(4) Before making an order under subsection (1) in relation to an airport (other than one managed by the Secretary of State) the Secretary of State shall consult the airport operator.

(5) In this section—

"designated airport" means an airport which is designated for the purposes of this section by an order made by the Secretary of State; and "the road traffic enactments" has the meaning given by section 63(3).

Provision of special accommodation at airports

67.—(1) The Secretary of State may, in the case of any airport—

(a) give the airport operator a direction requiring him to make available for the exclusive use of designated persons using the airport such special accommodation and any associated facilities as may be specified in the direction;

(b) give the airport operator a direction requiring him to take such steps as may be specified in the direction for the purposes of, or in connection with, the use of such accommodation and facilities by such persons;

(c) where it appears to the Secretary of State that the airport lacks special accommodation and associated facilities suitable for being made available as mentioned in paragraph (a), give the airport operator a direction requiring him to take such steps as may be specified in the direction for the purpose of, or in connection with, securing the provision at the airport of such accommodation and facilities.

(2) In subsection (1) "designated persons", in relation to an airport, means such persons, or classes of persons, as may from time to time be notified to the airport operator by the Secretary of State for the purposes of this section.

(3) Without prejudice to the generality of subsection (1)(c), a direction given by virtue of that provision may require an airport operator to carry out works of construction or alteration, and may specify the manner in which the accommodation in question is to be equipped in any respect.

(4) The Secretary of State may, with the consent of the Treasury, make grants to airport operators for the purpose of defraying or contributing towards expenses incurred by them in complying with directions given to them under this section.

(5) Before giving a direction under this section the Secretary of State shall consult the airport operator concerned.

Monitoring of aircraft movements

68.—(1) Where an airport is designated for the purposes of section 78 of the 1982 Act (regulation of noise and vibration from aircraft), the Secretary of State may, after consultation with the airport operator, by order require him—

(a) to provide, maintain and operate such equipment as is specified in the order (in accordance with any instructions so specified) for the purpose of monitoring the movements, within an area so specified, of aircraft on flights to and from the airport, and

(b) to make to the Secretary of State such reports as are so specified with respect to the movements monitored by the equipment in pursuance of paragraph (a), and to permit any person authorised by the Secretary of State for the purpose to inspect the equipment on demand at any time;

and it shall be the duty of the airport operator to comply with the requirements of the order.

(2) Any reference in subsection (1) to the movements of aircraft shall be read as a reference to the routes taken by them measured by reference to both direction and height.

(3) Subsections (9) and (10) of the said section 78 (enforcement) shall apply for the purposes of this section as if, in subsection (9) of that

section, any reference to subsection (8) of that section were a reference to subsection (1) of this section.

Duty of CAA with respect to implementation of recommendations concerning airport capacity

69.—(1) If, after considering any recommendations made to him by the CAA in pursuance of section 16(2) of the 1982 Act (recommendations concerning airport capacity), the Secretary of State so directs, the CAA shall take such steps as it considers appropriate for the purpose of encouraging or facilitating the provision (whether by an airport operator or any other person) of any facilities or services that are necessary for the implementation of those recommendations.

(2) The steps taken by the CAA in pursuance of subsection (1)—

(*a*) may, without prejudice to the generality of that subsection, include the furnishing of information, the provision of assistance to persons requesting it and the provision of advice (whether or not requested); but

(*b*) shall not include the carrying out of any works of construction or alteration or the defraying of, or the making of any contribution towards, expenses incurred by any other person in carrying out any such works.

(3) Before embarking on the performance of its duty under subsection (1) with respect to any recommendations the CAA shall consult the airport operator in the case of any relevant airport as to the manner in which that duty is to be performed by the CAA.

(4) Without prejudice to the generality of section 11 of the 1982 Act, a scheme or regulations under that section may make provision for charges to be paid in respect of the performance by the CAA of its duty under subsection (1) above with respect to any recommendations, and for such charges to be paid by—

(*a*) the airport operator in the case of any relevant airport, and

(*b*) any person for whom assistance or advice has, at his request, been provided by the CAA in pursuance of that duty;

but if such provision is not made by any such scheme or regulations the CAA shall be entitled to recover an amount or amounts in respect of any expenses reasonably incurred by it in performing that duty from such one or more persons falling within paragraphs (*a*) and (*b*) above as the CAA considers appropriate.

(5) An airport is a relevant airport for the purposes of subsection (3) or (4) if—

(*a*) the recommendations referred to in that subsection relate to the airport, or

(*b*) the airport is subject to economic regulation under Part IV, and it and any new airport to which those recommendations relate would be airports serving the same area in the United Kingdom;

and the reference in paragraph (*b*) above to airports serving the same area in the United Kingdom shall be construed in accordance with section 31(6).

(6) Section 4 of the 1982 Act applies in relation to the performance by the CAA of its functions under this section.

Extension of Shops (Airports) Act 1962

70. Section 1 of the Shops (Airports) Act 1962 (exemption of traders at certain airports from restrictions under Part I of the Shops Act 1950 on hours of closing) shall have effect in relation to the provisions of Part IV of the Shops Act 1950 (Sunday trading) as well as in relation to the provisions of Part I of that Act; and accordingly, in subsection (1) of that section, after "hours of closing)" there shall be inserted "and of Part IV of that Act (which relates to Sunday trading)".

Capital controls in relation to local authority airport undertakings other than public airport companies

71.—(1) Where an authority to whom Part VIII of the Local Government, Planning and Land Act 1980 applies own any airport (which is accordingly not an airport operated by a public airport company within the meaning of Part II of this Act) then, for the purposes of that Part of that Act—

(a) the amount of any grant or advance of a capital nature made by any person for the purposes of the authority's airport undertaking shall be treated as prescribed expenditure of the authority, but

(b) no expenditure by the authority for the purposes of that undertaking other than any amount expended on the making of any such grant or advance shall be treated as prescribed expenditure of the authority;

and any amount repaid in respect of any such grant or advance as is mentioned in paragraph (a) shall be treated for the purposes of section 72 of that Act as a receipt of the authority which, by virtue of section 75(1) of that Act, is a capital receipt of the authority for the purposes of Part VIII of that Act.

(2) The profits to which any such authority are entitled from their airport undertaking shall not be taken into account for the purposes of subsection (3)(e) of section 72 of that Act; and accordingly—

(a) in subsection (3)(e) "trading undertaking" shall not include an airport undertaking; and

(b) subsection (4)(iii) of that section shall cease to have effect.

(3) Any amount received by any such authority in respect of the disposal of any assets held by the authority for the purposes of their airport undertaking shall not be taken into account for the purposes of section 75(1)(b) of that Act.

(4) This section shall apply in relation to an airport owned jointly by two or more authorities to whom Part VIII of that Act applies as it applies in relation to an airport owned by one such authority alone (references to the airport undertaking of a particular authority being read as references to the airport undertaking of the authorities in question), but the provisions of subsection (1) requiring any amount to be treated as prescribed expenditure of any authority, or (as the case may be) as such a receipt of an authority as is there mentioned, shall have effect only in relation to such one of the authorities in question as may be determined by agreement between those authorities.

(5) This section applies to England and Wales only.

Constitution of CAA

Increase in maximum number of members of CAA

72. In section 2(2) of the 1982 Act (which provides that the CAA shall consist of not less than six nor more than twelve members), for "twelve" there shall be substituted "sixteen".

Supplementary

Furnishing of information etc. to CAA

73.—(1) The CAA may by notice in writing served on any person require him at such time or times as may be specified in the notice—

(a) to produce to the CAA such documents or descriptions of documents specified in the notice, and

(b) to furnish to the CAA, in such form as may be specified in the notice, such accounts, estimates, returns or other information,

as the CAA may reasonably require for the purpose of performing its functions under this Act or for the purpose of giving any advice, assistance or information to the Secretary of State in connection with the performance by him of any functions under this Act.

(2) A person shall not by virtue of subsection (1) be compelled—

(a) to produce any documents which he could not be compelled to produce in civil proceedings before the High Court or (in Scotland) the Court of Session, or

(b) in complying with any requirement for the furnishing of information, to give any information which he could not be compelled to give in evidence in such proceedings.

(3) Any person who fails without reasonable excuse to comply with the requirements of a notice served on him under subsection (1) shall be guilty of an offence and liable on summary conviction to a fine not exceeding the fifth level on the standard scale.

(4) Any person who, in purported compliance with the requirements of any such notice, knowingly or recklessly furnishes information which is false in a material particular shall be guilty of an offence and liable—

(a) on summary conviction, to a fine not exceeding the statutory maximum;

(b) on conviction on indictment, to a fine.

Restriction on disclosure of information

74.—(1) Subject to the following provisions of this section, no information with respect to any particular business which has been obtained under or by virtue of the provisions of this Act shall, so long as the business continues to be carried on, be disclosed without the consent of the person for the time being carrying it on.

(2) Subsection (1) does not apply to any disclosure of information which is made—

(a) for the purpose of facilitating the performance of any functions under this Act or any of the enactments specified in subsection (3) of any Minister, any Northern Ireland department, the head of any such department, the CAA, the Commission, the Director General of Fair Trading or a local weights and measures authority in Great Britain;

(b) in connection with the investigation of any criminal offence or for the purposes of any criminal proceedings;

(c) for the purposes of any civil proceedings brought under or by virtue of this Act or any of the enactments specified in subsection (3);

(d) in pursuance of any Community obligation.

(3) The enactments referred to in subsection (2) are—

(a) the Trade Descriptions Act 1968;

(b) the Fair Trading Act 1973;

(c) the Consumer Credit Act 1974;

(d) the Restrictive Trade Practices Act 1976;

(e) the Resale Prices Act 1976;

(f) the Estate Agents Act 1979;

(g) the Competition Act 1980; and

(h) the 1982 Act and any Order in Council made under section 60 of that Act (Air Navigation Orders).

(4) Nothing in subsection (1) shall be construed—

(*a*) as limiting the matters which may be included in, or made public as part of, a report of the Commission under section 45; or

(*b*) as applying to any information which has been made public as part of such a report.

(5) Any person who discloses any information in contravention of this section shall be guilty of an offence and liable—

(*a*) on summary conviction, to a fine not exceeding the statutory maximum;

(*b*) on conviction on indictment, to imprisonment for a term not exceeding two years or to a fine, or to both.

(6) In this section "the Commission" means the Monopolies and Mergers Commission.

Supplementary provisions relating to transfer schemes

75.—(1) A scheme under section 1 or 15 may define the property, rights and liabilities to be transferred by the scheme—

(*a*) by specifying the property, rights and liabilities in question, or

(*b*) by referring to all the property, rights and liabilities comprised in the whole or any specified part of the transferor's undertaking,

(or partly in one way and partly in the other) and may contain such supplementary, incidental and consequential provisions as may appear to the authority making the scheme to be necessary or expedient (including, in particular, provision with respect to the consideration to be furnished by the transferee for any transfer under the scheme, whether in the case of a scheme under section 15 it is to be furnished to the transferor or to any other person).

(2) A scheme under section 1 or 15 may—

(*a*) provide that any functions of the transferor under any statutory provision not contained in this Act shall, to the extent to which that provision relates—

(i) to property transferred by the scheme, or

(ii) to any undertaking of the transferor, or part of such an undertaking, so transferred,

be transferred to the transferee under the scheme; and

(*b*) define any such functions—

(i) by specifying the statutory provision in question,

(ii) by referring to all the statutory provisions (not contained in this Act) which relate to the property, or to the undertaking or part of the undertaking, to be transferred by the scheme, or

(iii) by referring to all the statutory provisions within sub-paragraph (ii), but specifying certain excepted provisions.

(3) Subject to the following provisions of this section, Schedule 4 to the Transport Act 1968 (supplementary provisions as to certain transfers of property, rights and liabilities) shall apply to any transfer under section 1(8) or 15(7); and each of those provisions shall have effect subject to the provisions of that Schedule.

(4) In Schedule 4 to that Act as it applies by virtue of subsection (3)—

(*a*) any reference to a transfer by, or a vesting by virtue of, that Act shall be read as a reference to a transfer by, or a vesting by virtue of, the scheme in question;

(*b*) the reference in paragraph 8 to any of the transferred rights and liabilities shall be read as including a reference to any property or functions transferred by the scheme;

(*c*) the reference in paragraph 10, in relation to pending legal proceedings or applications, to any transferred property, right or liability shall be read as including a reference to any functions transferred by the scheme; and

(d) the reference in paragraph 13(5) to the relevant provisions of that Act shall be read as including a reference to the relevant provisions of this Act.

(5) The Secretary of State may by order make modifications in Schedule 4 for the purposes of its application to transfers under section 1(8) or 15(7) of this Act.

(6) For the purposes of this Act, and of Schedule 4 as it applies by virtue of subsection (3), the granting of a lease of any property by a scheme under section 1 or 15 to the transferee under the scheme shall be regarded as a transfer of that property to him by the scheme.

(7) In this section "statutory provision" means any provision (whether of a general or special nature) contained in, or having effect under, any Act (whether public general or local).

Stamp duty

76.—(1) Stamp duty shall not be chargeable under section 47 of the Finance Act 1973 in respect of—

(a) the formation of a company in pursuance of section 1(3) or 13, or
(b) any increase in the capital of a company—
  (i) nominated under section 1(1), or
  (ii) formed in pursuance of section 1(3) or 13,

if the transaction concerned is certified by the Treasury as satisfying the requirements of subsection (2) below.

(2) A transaction satisfies the requirements of this subsection if—

(a) it is effected solely in connection with a transfer to be effected in pursuance of a scheme made under section 1 or 15; and
(b) it takes place on or before the transfer date; and
(c) in a case falling within subsection (1)(a) above, the total issued capital of the company does not on the transfer date exceed the total value of the assets less liabilities transferred; and
(d) in a case falling within subsection (1)(b) above, the aggregate amount of the increase of issued capital of the company does not on that date exceed that total value;

and in this subsection "issued capital" means issued share capital or loan capital.

(3) Stamp duty shall not be chargeable—

(a) on any scheme made under section 1 or 15; or
(b) on any instrument which is certified to the Commissioners of Inland Revenue by the transferring authority, or (as the case may be) by both or all of the transferring authorities, as having been made or executed in pursuance of Schedule 4 to the Transport Act 1968 as it applies in relation to any such scheme by virtue of section 75(3).

(4) An instrument such as is mentioned in subsection (3)(b) shall not be treated as duly stamped unless it is stamped with the duty to which it would be liable but for subsection (3), or it has, in accordance with section 12 of the Stamp Act 1891, been stamped with a particular stamp denoting that it is not chargeable with any duty or that it is duly stamped.

(5) Stamp duty shall not be chargeable under section 47 of the Finance Act 1973 in respect of any increase in the capital of the successor company which is effected by the issue of shares allotted at a time when the successor company is wholly owned by the Crown and which is certified by the Treasury as having been—

(a) effected for the purpose of complying with the requirements of section 4 above; or
(b) where any convertible securities have been issued in pursuance of

that section, effected in consequence of the exercise of the conversion rights attached to those securities; or

(c) effected by the issue of shares subscribed for by the Treasury or the Secretary of State under section 5(1)(a) above.

Corporation Tax

77.—(1) Subject to subsection (2), the successor company shall be treated for all purposes of corporation tax as if it were the same person as the BAA.

(2) The successor company shall not by virtue of subsection (1) be regarded as a body falling within section 272(5) of the 1970 Act (bodies established for carrying on industries or undertakings under national ownership or control).

(3) Where any debentures are issued in pursuance of section 4, any annual payment secured by those debentures shall be treated for all purposes of corporation tax as if it were a charge on income of the successor company.

(4) For the avoidance of doubt it is hereby declared that—

(a) any issue of shares in pursuance of section 4 is to be regarded as a subscription for shares for the purposes of section 48(10) of the Finance Act 1981 (write-off of government investment: restriction of tax losses); and

(b) where any debentures are issued in pursuance of section 4, the principal sums payable under the debentures are to be regarded as money lent for those purposes.

(5) Where in the case of a claim for group relief—

(a) the claimant company is the BAA or the successor company and the surrendering company is a company to whom property, rights or liabilities have been transferred by a scheme made under section 1, and

(b) the claim relates to the accounting period of the surrendering company first ending after that transfer, and

(c) the corresponding accounting period of the claimant company ends with the same date as that accounting period,

then, for the purposes of section 261(2) of the 1970 Act (corresponding accounting periods) as it applies in relation to the claim, those accounting periods shall be taken to coincide and, for the purposes of section 262(1) of the 1970 Act (companies joining or leaving group) as it so applies, the claimant company and the surrendering company shall be taken to have been members of the same group throughout each of those periods (notwithstanding anything in section 262(2) and (3) of that Act).

(6) In this section ' the 1970 Act" means the Income and Corporation Taxes Act 1970, and in subsection (5) above expressions used in sections 258 to 264 of that Act (group relief) have the same meanings as in those sections.

Offences by bodies corporate

78.—(1) Where a body corporate is guilty of an offence under this Act and that offence is proved to have been committed with the consent or connivance of, or to be attributable to any neglect on the part of, any director, manager, secretary or other similar officer of the body corporate or any person who was purporting to act in any such capacity he, as well as the body corporate, shall be guilty of an offence and shall be liable to be proceeded against and punished accordingly.

(2) Where the affairs of a body corporate are managed by its members, subsection (1) shall apply in relation to the acts and defaults of a member

in connection with his functions of management as if he were a director of the body corporate.

Orders and regulations

79.—(1) Any power conferred on the Secretary of State by this Act to make an order or regulations shall be exercisable by statutory instrument.

(2) Any statutory instrument containing—

(*a*) an order made by the Secretary of State under this Act, other than an order appointing a day or an order under section 2(2) or 32, or

(*b*) any regulations under this Act,

shall be subject to annulment in pursuance of a resolution of either House of Parliament.

(3) No order shall be made under section 32 unless a draft of the order has been laid before and approved by a resolution of each House of Parliament.

(4) A draft of an order under that section which would, apart from the provisions of this subsection, be treated for the purposes of the Standing Orders of either House of Parliament as a hybrid instrument shall proceed in that House as if it were not such an instrument.

(5) Any regulations under section 28 or order under section 64(3) or 85(5) may make such transitional, incidental or supplementary provision as appears to the Secretary of State to be necessary or expedient.

Directions etc.

80.—(1) It shall be the duty of any person to whom the Secretary of State gives directions under this Act to give effect to those directions.

(2) Subject to any express provision contained in this Act, any direction given by the Secretary of State under a provision of this Act may be varied or revoked by a subsequent direction given under that provision.

(3) Any determination made by the Secretary of State under this Act shall be notified by him to such persons appearing to him to be likely to be affected by it as he considers appropriate.

(4) Any direction or notification given under this Act shall be in writing.

Financial provisions

81. There shall be paid out of money provided by Parliament—

(*a*) any administrative expenses incurred by the Secretary of State in consequence of the provisions of this Act;

(*b*) any sums required by him for making grants under section 67; and

(*c*) any increase attributable to this Act in the sums payable out of money so provided under any other Act.

General interpretation

82.—(1) In this Act—

"the 1975 Act" means the Airports Authority Act 1975;

"the 1982 Act" means the Civil Aviation Act 1982;

"airport" means the aggregate of the land, buildings and works comprised in an aerodrome within the meaning of the 1982 Act;

"airport operator" means the person for the time being having the management of an airport, or, in relation to a particular airport, the management of that airport;

"air transport services" means services for the carriage by air of passengers or cargo;

"the appointed day" means the day appointed under section 2(1);

"the BAA" means the British Airports Authority;

"the CAA" means the Civil Aviation Authority;

"cargo" includes mail;

"debenture" includes debenture stock;

"functions" includes powers and duties;

"modifications" includes additions, omissions and amendments;

"operator", in relation to an aircraft, means the person for the time being having the management of the aircraft;

"the registrar of companies" has the same meaning as in the Companies Act 1985;

"securities", in relation to a company, includes shares, debentures, bonds and other securities of the company, whether or not constituting a charge on the assets of the company;

"shares" includes stock;

"subordinate legislation" has the same meaning as in the Interpretation Act 1978;

"subsidiary" has the same meaning as in the Companies Act 1985;

"the successor company" means the company nominated for the purposes of section 2;

"user", in relation to an airport, means—

    (*a*) a person for whom any services or facilities falling within the definition of "relevant activities" in section 36(1) are provided at the airport, or

    (*b*) a person using any of the air transport services operating from the airport.

(2) A company shall be regarded for the purposes of this Act as wholly owned by the Crown at any time when each of the issued shares in the company is held by, or by a nominee of, the Treasury or the Secretary of State.

(3) Any reference in section 14 or 37 to the business carried on at any airport by the airport operator shall, in a case where the person for the time being having the management of the airport has not had its management for the whole or any part of any period relevant for the purposes of that section, be construed as including a reference to the business carried on there by any other person who had the management of the airport for the whole or any part of that period.

(4) For the purposes of this Act a body corporate shall be treated as an associated company of an airport operator if either that body or the airport operator is a body corporate of which the other is a subsidiary or if both of them are subsidiaries of one and the same body corporate.

Amendments, transitional provisions and repeals

83.—(1) The enactments mentioned in Schedule 4 shall have effect subject to the amendments there specified (being amendments consequential on the preceding provisions of this Act).

(2) The Secretary of State may by order make such consequential modifications of any provision contained in any Act (whether public general or local) passed, or subordinate legislation made, before the appointed day as appear to him to be necessary or expedient in respect of any reference in that Act or subordinate legislation to the BAA.

(3) The Secretary of State may, after consulting any local authority which appears to him to be concerned, by order repeal or amend any enactment in a local Act which appears to him to be unnecessary having regard to the provisions of this Act or to be inconsistent with any provision of this Act.

(4) The transitional provisions and savings contained in Schedule 5 shall have effect; but nothing in that Schedule shall be taken as prejudicing the

operation of sections 16 and 17 of the Interpretation Act 1978 (which relate to repeals).

(5) The enactments mentioned in Schedule 6 are hereby repealed to the extent specified in the third column of that Schedule.

Application of provisions of Act to certain overseas territories

84.—(1) Her Majesty may by Order in Council direct that any of the following, namely—

(*a*) sections 30 and 35, and

(*b*) any provision of section 78, 80 or 82,

shall extend, with such modifications (if any) as may be specified in the Order, to any of the Channel Islands or to any colony.

(2) An Order in Council under this section may make such transitional, incidental or supplementary provision as appears to Her Majesty to be necessary or expedient.

Short title, commencement and extent

85.—(1) This Act may be cited as the Airports Act 1986.

(2) The following provisions of this Act shall come into force on the day on which this Act is passed—

section 1;
section 3;
section 75;
section 76(1) to (4);
section 77(5) and (6);
sections 79 to 82;
this section.

(3) The following provisions of this Act shall come into force on the appointed day—

section 2;
sections 4 to 11;
section 76(5);
section 77(1) to (4);
paragraph 9 of Schedule 4 and section 83(1) so far as relating thereto;
section 83(2) and (4) and Schedule 5;
Part I of Schedule 6 and section 83(5) so far as relating thereto.

(4) The following provisions of this Act shall come into force at the end of the period of two months beginning with the day on which this Act is passed—

Part II;
Part III;
sections 68 and 70 to 72;
section 78;
section 84.

(5) The following provisions of this Act shall come into force on such date as the Secretary of State may by order appoint—

Part IV (including Schedule 1);
Part V (including Schedule 2);
sections 63 to 66 and Schedule 3;
section 67;
section 69;
sections 73 and 74;
paragraphs 1 to 8 and 10 of Schedule 4 and section 83(1) so far as relating thereto;
section 83(3);
Part II of Schedule 6 and section 83(5) so far as relating thereto.

(6) An order under subsection (5) may appoint different days for different provisions or for different purposes.

(7) With the exception of the provisions mentioned in subsection (8), this Act does not extend to Northern Ireland.

(8) Those provisions are—

section 2(4);

Part III;

section 68;

sections 72 to 74;

sections 78 to 82;

section 83(1) and (5) and Schedules 4 and 6 so far as they amend or
    repeal any enactment extending to Northern Ireland; and

this section.

SCHEDULES

Section 55 ## SCHEDULE 1

APPLICATION OF PART IV TO ASSOCIATED COMPANIES OF AIRPORT OPERATORS

Preliminary

1. This Schedule has effect for the purpose of authorising or requiring the imposition by the CAA under this Part (as it applies in accordance with this Schedule) of the following conditions in relation to an airport, namely—

(a) conditions under section 40(1) or 41(1) with respect to the accounts of an associated company of the airport operator, and

(b) conditions under section 41(2) or 46(2) in respect of a course of conduct pursued by such a company,

and for related purposes; and in this Schedule any such conditions are referred to as "subsidiary conditions".

Section 39

2. Section 39(1) and (4) shall apply to any subsidiary conditions for the time being in force in relation to an airport as if—

(a) references to the airport operator were references to the associated company of the airport operator with respect to whose accounts the conditions were imposed or (as the case may be) that pursued the course of conduct in respect of which the conditions were imposed, and

(b) references to any such conditions as are mentioned in section 39(1) were references to any such conditions as are mentioned above.

Section 40

3.—(1) Where an associated company of the airport operator in the case of any airport either carries on operational activities relating to the airport or is entitled to grant rights by virtue of which any such activities may be carried on by other persons, section 40(2) shall have effect in relation to the airport with the modifications specified in sub-paragraphs (2) to (4) below.

(2) After paragraph (a) there shall be inserted the following paragraph—

"(aa) such conditions as the CAA considers appropriate to secure that the accounts of any associated company of the airport operator, being a company which either carries on operational activities relating to the airport or is entitled to grant rights by virtue of which any such activities may be carried on by other persons, disclose—

(i) any subsidy furnished (whether by the making of loans on non-commercial terms or otherwise) by any person or authority to the company in connection with its business so far as consisting of the carrying on of operational activities relating to the airport, and the identity of any such person or authority,

(ii) any subsidy so furnished to that business by the company out of funds attributable to any other activities carried on by it, and

(iii) the aggregate income and expenditure of the company attributable to any such operational activities (whether carried on by the company or by some other person); and".

(3) After "the airport operator" where it occurs in paragraph (b) there shall be inserted "or the associated company".

(4) After "the airport operator" where it last occurs there shall be inserted "or in paragraph (aa) to the accounts of any associated company of the airport operator".

(5) Where—

(a) sub-paragraph (1) above does not apply to an airport at the time when conditions are imposed in relation to the airport under section 40(1)(a) or (b), but

(b) at any later time it appears to the CAA that that subparagraph then applies to the airport,

the CAA shall thereupon impose in relation to the airport such conditions as are mentioned in paragraphs (aa) and (b) of section 40(2) as modified by this paragraph.

Section 41

4. In section 41—

(a) in subsection (1), the reference to section 40(2) shall be construed as including, in relation to an airport to which sub-paragraph (1) of paragraph 3 above applies, a reference to section 40(2) as modified by that paragraph,

(b) in subsections (2), (3)(a) and (b) and (6), references to the airport operator shall be construed as including references to an associated company of the airport operator, and

(c) in relation to such a company—

(i) the reference in subsection (2) to subsection (3) shall be construed as a reference to subsection (3)(a) and (b) (as modified by paragraph (b) above), and

(ii) the reference in subsection (6) to subsection (3)(a), (b) or (c) shall be construed as a reference to subsection (3)(a) or (b) (as so modified).

Section 42

5. In section 42(2) and (3)—

(a) references to an airport operator shall be construed as including references to an associated company of an airport operator, and

(b) in relation to such a company, references to any provision of section 41 shall be construed as references to that provision as modified by paragraph 4 above.

Section 43

6.—(1) Where an associated company of the airport operator in the case of any airport either carries on operational activities relating to the airport or is entitled to grant rights by virtue of which any such activities may be carried on by other persons, section 43(2) shall have effect in relation to any reference under section 43(1) with respect to the airport with the insertion after paragraph (a) of the following paragraph—

"(aa) whether any associated company of the airport operator has, at any time during the relevant period, pursued—

(i) in relation to any operational activities carried on by the company and relating to the airport, or

(ii) in relation to the granting of a right by virtue of which any operation activities relating to the airport may be carried on by any other person or persons,

a course of conduct which has operated or might be expected to operate against the public interest; and".

(2) In section 43(3), as it applies in relation to an associated company of an airport operator in accordance with this Schedule, the reference to the airport operator shall be construed as a reference to the associated company in question.

Section 44

7.—(1) In relation to any reference to which paragraph 6(1) above applies, section 44(1)(a) shall have effect with the insertion at the end of sub-paragraph (ii) of "and any course of conduct which, in its opinion, has been pursued by an associated company of the airport operator in relation to any of the matters specified in subsection (2)(*aa*) of that section and has operated, or might be expected to operate, against the public interest,".

(2) In section 44(4) the reference to the airport operator concerned shall—

  (*a*) in the case of a reference or variation under section 43 relating only to a course of conduct pursued by an associated company of an airport operator, be construed as a reference to that company, and

  (*b*) in the case of a reference or variation under that section relating to courses of conduct pursued by an airport operator and such a company respectively, be construed as a reference to both the airport operator and the company.

Section 45

8.—(1) In section 45(3) the reference to an airport operator shall, in the case of a reference under section 43 relating wholly or in part to a course of conduct pursued by an associated company of an airport operator, be construed as, or as including, a reference to any such company (as the case may require).

(2) In section 45(6) the reference to the airport operator concerned shall be construed as mentioned in paragraph 7(2) above according to the nature of the reference under section 43.

Section 48

9.—(1) In section 48(1)(*a*) the reference to the airport operator in relation to an airport shall be construed as including a reference to an associated company of the airport operator.

(2) Section 48(3), (5), (6) and (7) shall have effect in relation to any complaint against an associated company of an airport operator made by virtue of sub-paragraph (1) above as if any reference to an airport operator or to the airport operator concerned were a reference to any such company or to the company against which the complaint is made (as the case may require).

Section 49

10.—(1) In section 49(1) and (9) any reference to an airport operator shall be construed as including a reference to an associated company of an airport operator.

(2) Where the permission for the time being in force in respect of an airport is revoked under section 49(9) (as it applies in accordance with sub-paragraph (1) above) by reason of an associated company's contravention of a compliance order, then (notwithstanding section 38(4)) a permission shall not again be granted under this Part in respect of that airport unless it appears to the CAA that, if the CAA were to impose in relation to the airport any condition corresponding to the one whose breach gave rise to the making of the compliance order, that condition would be complied with by the person (whether the airport operator or an associated company of the airport operator) to whose activities any such condition would relate.

(3) In this paragraph "compliance order" and "contravention" shall be construed in accordance with section 49(11).

Section 50

11.—(1) In section 50 any reference to an airport operator shall be construed as including a reference to an associated company of an airport operator.

(2) In that section, as it applies to any such company in accordance with sub-paragraph (1)—

  (*a*) in subsection (1), the reference to section 40(2)(*a*) shall be construed as a reference to paragraph (*aa*) of section 40(2) (as modified by paragraph 3(2) and (4) above).

  (*b*) in subsection (2), the reference to section 40(2)(*b*) shall be construed as a reference to that provision as modified by paragraph 3(3), and

  (*c*) the references to section 39(1) and section 41(1) shall be construed as references to those provisions as modified by paragraph 2 and paragraph 4(*a*) above.

Section 51

12.—(1) Section 51(3) shall apply in relation to any subsidiary conditions as if the reference to section 40(2) were a reference to that provision as modified by paragraph 3 above.

(2) Section 51(5) shall apply in relation to any subsidiary conditions as if—

(*a*) references to the airport operator concerned were references to the associated company of the airport operator that pursued the course of conduct in respect of which the conditions were imposed; and

(*b*) the reference to section 41(3)(*a*), (*b*) or (*c*) were a reference to section 41(3)(*a*) or (*b*) (as modified by paragraph 4(*b*) above).

(3) Section 51(7) shall apply in relation to any subsidiary conditions as if the reference to the airport operator were a reference to the associated company with respect to whose accounts the conditions were imposed or (as the case may be) that pursued the course of conduct in respect of which the conditions were imposed.

Section 54

13. In section 54(3)(*b*), the reference to an airport operator shall be construed as including a reference to an associated company of an airport operator engaged in carrying on any operational activities relating to one or more airports.

Section 58   SCHEDULE 2

APPLICATION OF ENACTMENTS RELATING TO STATUTORY UNDERTAKERS ETC.

General application of enactments

1.—(1) Any airport to which this Part applies shall be deemed to be a statutory undertaking, and a relevant airport operator a statutory undertaker, for the purposes of the following enactments, namely—

the Acquisition of Land (Authorisation Procedure) (Scotland) Act 1947;

the New Towns (Scotland) Act 1968;

the Town and Country Planning Act 1971;

the Town and Country Planning (Scotland) Act 1972;

Part I of the Local Government (Miscellaneous Provisions) Act 1976;

the Development of Rural Wales Act 1976;

the New Towns Act 1981;

the Acquisition of Land Act 1981; and

sections 283, 296 and 611 of the Housing Act 1985;

and for the purposes of any other enactment in which "statutory undertakers" or "statutory undertaking" has the meaning assigned to it by section 275(1) of the Town and Country Planning (Scotland) Act 1972.

(2) In the following enactments, namely—

the Town and Country Planning Act 1971,

the Town and Country Planning (Scotland) Act 1972, and

the New Towns Act 1981,

"the appropriate Minister" shall, in relation to a relevant airport operator, mean the Secretary of State for Transport.

Application of particular enactments

2. In the Public Health Act 1936—

(*a*) section 330 (power of certain undertakers in England and Wales to alter sewers), and

(*b*) section 333 (protection of certain such undertakers from works executed under that Act),

shall apply in relation to a relevant airport operator and the airport in question as they apply in relation to a railway company and its railway.

3.—(1) The following provisions (which relate to the protection of certain statutory undertakers), namely—

section 93 of Schedule 3 to the Water Act 1945, and

section 45 of Schedule 4 to the Water (Scotland) Act 1980,

shall apply with the necessary modifications in relation to any works which statutory water undertakers propose to execute along, upon or under any airport to which this Part applies, whether or not section 93 or section 45 has been applied to the undertakers by an order under that Act of 1945 or (as the case may be) under that Act of 1980.

(2) In sub-paragraph (1) "statutory water undertakers" means—

(*a*) in relation to England and Wales, statutory water undertakers within the meaning of the Water Act 1973 and includes a person authorised to construct works by an order under section 23 of the Water Act 1945; and

(b) in relation to Scotland, a water authority within the meaning of the Water (Scotland) Act 1980.

4. A relevant airport operator shall be deemed to be a public undertaker for the purposes of section 56 of the Housing (Scotland) Act 1966 (demolition of obstructive buildings).

5. For the purposes of section 112 of the Land Drainage Act 1976 (protection of nationalised undertakings, etc.) an airport to which this Part applies shall be deemed to be an undertaking to which that section applies and the airport operator shall accordingly be deemed to be a person carrying on such an undertaking.

6. In the Building Act 1984—

(a) section 4(1)(b) (exemption of buildings of statutory undertakers from building regulations), and

(b) section 59(4) (exemption of such buildings from provisions relating to drainage),

shall apply in relation to a relevant airport operator as they apply in relation to statutory undertakers, but as if in those provisions any reference to a house included a hotel, and any reference to offices or showrooms did not include offices or showrooms on any airport to which this Part applies.

Section 63(5)　　　　　　　SCHEDULE 3

AIRPORT BYELAWS MADE BY PERSONS OTHER THAN THE SECRETARY OF STATE

1. References in this Schedule to the airport operator in relation to any byelaws are references to the person making those byelaws as mentioned in section 63(5).

2. Where the airport operator is a body corporate, the byelaws shall be made under its common seal.

3. At least one month before application for confirmation of the byelaws is made to the Secretary of State, notice of the intention to apply for confirmation shall be given by the airport operator in one or more local newspapers circulating in the locality in which the airport to which the byelaws relate is situated or (if the byelaws relate to more than one airport) circulating respectively in the several localities in which those airports are situated; and the notice shall specify a period of not less than one month during which representations on the byelaws may be made to the Secretary of State.

4. For at least one month before application for confirmation is made, a copy of the byelaws shall be deposited at the offices of the airport operator at each airport to which the byelaws relate and shall, at all reasonable hours, be open to public inspection free of charge.

5. The airport operator shall, on application made by any person before the byelaws are confirmed, furnish him with a copy of the byelaws or of any part of them on payment of such reasonable fee as the airport operator may determine.

6. The Secretary of State may confirm with or without modifications, or refuse to confirm, any byelaw submitted to him for confirmation, and may fix the date on which a byelaw confirmed by him is to come into operation; and if no date is so fixed, the byelaw shall come into operation at the end of the period of one month beginning with the day on which it is confirmed.

7. A copy of the byelaws, when confirmed, shall be printed and deposited at the offices of the airport operator at each airport to which they relate and shall, at all reasonable hours, be open to public inspection free of charge; and a copy of the byelaws shall on application be furnished to any person on payment of such reasonable fee as the airport operator may determine.

8. The production of a printed copy of a byelaw purporting to be made by an airport operator upon which is endorsed a certificate purporting to be signed by a person authorised for the purpose by the airport operator and stating—

(a) that the byelaw was made by the airport operator,

(b) that the copy is a true copy of the byelaw,

(c) that on a specified date the byelaw was confirmed by the Secretary of State, and

(d) the date, if any, fixed by the Secretary of State for the coming into operation of the byelaw,

shall be evidence, and in Scotland sufficient evidence, of the facts stated in the certificate, without proof of the handwriting or authorisation of the person by whom it purports to be signed.

SCHEDULE 4

CONSEQUENTIAL AMENDMENTS

TOWN AND COUNTRY PLANNING ACT 1971 (c. 78)

1. In section 223(2)(*b*) (cases in which land is to be treated as not being operational land), after "the Gas Act 1986" insert ", the Airports Act 1986".

TOWN AND COUNTRY PLANNING (SCOTLAND) ACT 1972 (c. 52)

2. In section 212(2)(*b*) (cases in which land is to be treated as not being operational land), after "the Gas Act 1986" insert ", the Airports Act 1986".

FAIR TRADING ACT 1973 (c. 41)

3. In section 133(2) (exceptions to general restriction on disclosure of information), after "the Director General of Gas Supply," insert "the Civil Aviation Authority," and after "or the Gas Act 1986," insert "or the Airports Act 1986,".

CONSUMER CREDIT ACT 1974 (c. 39)

4. In section 174(3)(*a*) (exceptions to general restriction on disclosure of information), after "or the Gas Act 1986" insert "or the Airports Act 1986" and after "the Director General of Gas Supply" insert "the Civil Aviation Authority".

RESTRICTIVE TRADE PRACTICES ACT 1976 (c. 34)

5. In section 41(1)(*a*) (disclosure of information), after "the Director General of Gas Supply," insert "the Civil Aviation Authority," and after "the Gas Act 1986" insert "or the Airports Act 1986".

ESTATE AGENTS ACT 1979 (c. 38)

6. In section 10(3)(*a*) (exceptions to general restriction on disclosure of information), after "or the Gas Act 1986" insert "or the Airports Act 1986" and after "the Director General of Gas Supply," insert "the Civil Aviation Authority,".

COMPETITION ACT 1980 (c. 21)

7. In section 19 (restriction on disclosure of information)—
(*a*) in subsection (2), after "the Director General of Gas Supply," insert "the Civil Aviation Authority,"; and
(*b*) in subsection (3), after paragraph (*h*), insert—
    "(*i*) the Airports Act 1986."

CIVIL AVIATION ACT 1982 (c. 16)

8.—(1) In section 23(6) (disclosure of information), for "28 and 29" substitute "and 28".
(2) In section 108(1) (extension of 1982 Act outside United Kingdom), for "27, 32 to 35, 37," substitute "34, 35,".

AVIATION SECURITY ACT 1982 (c. 36)

9. In section 29 (control of road traffic at designated airports)—
(*a*) in subsection (1), for the words from "section 13(1) to (3)" to "1982" substitute "section 65 of the Airports Act 1986" and for "those sections" substitute "that section"; and
(*b*) in subsection (3), for the words from "section 13(1) to (3)" to "thereof" substitute "section 65 of the Airports Act 1986 includes a reference to subsection (2) of that section as extended by section 66(2) of that Act".

LOCAL GOVERNMENT ACT 1985 (C. 51)

10. In section 40(3) (airports), for "to 33, 35, 37(3), (4) and (5), 60(3)(*o*)" substitute
", 31, 35".

Section 83(4)   SCHEDULE 5

TRANSITIONAL PROVISIONS

Supplementary provisions as to vesting of property etc. of BAA

1. Any agreement made, transaction effected or other thing done by, to or in relation to the BAA which is in force or effective immediately before the appointed day shall have effect as from that day as if made, effected or done by, to or in relation to the successor company, in all respects as if the successor company were the same person, in law, as the BAA; and accordingly references to the BAA—
   (*a*) in any agreement (whether or not in writing) and in any deed, bond or instrument,
   (*b*) in any process or other document issued, prepared or employed for the purpose of any proceeding before any court or other tribunal or authority, and
   (*c*) in any other document whatever (other than an enactment) relating to or affecting any property, right or liability of the BAA which vests by virtue of section 2 in the successor company,
shall be taken as from the appointed day as referring to the successor company.
2. Where immediately before the appointed day there is in force an agreement which—
   (*a*) confers or imposes on the BAA any rights or liabilities which vest in the successor company by virtue of section 2, and
   (*b*) refers (in whatever terms and whether expressly or by implication) to a member or officer of the BAA,
the agreement shall have effect, in relation to anything falling to be done on or after that day, as if for that reference there were substituted a reference to such person as that company may appoint or, in default of appointment, to the officer of that company who corresponds as nearly as may be to the member or officer of the BAA in question.
3. It is hereby declared for the avoidance of doubt that—
   (*a*) the effect of section 2 in relation to any contract of employment with the BAA in force immediately before the appointed day is merely to modify the contract (as from that day) by substituting the successor company as the employer (and not to terminate the contract or vary it in any other way); and
   (*b*) that section is effective to vest the rights and liabilities of the BAA under any agreement or arrangement for the payment of pensions, allowances or gratuities in the successor company along with all other rights and liabilities of the BAA;
and accordingly for the purposes of any such agreement or arrangement (as it has effect by virtue of paragraph 1 in relation to employment with the successor company) any period of employment with the BAA shall count as employment with the successor company.

Financial provisions

4. The terms which, by virtue of section 4(2) of the 1975 Act, are applicable immediately before the appointed day to any such liability of the BAA as is mentioned in section 3(2) of this Act shall continue to apply to that liability after it becomes a liability of the successor company by virtue of section 2 of this Act, and section 4(3) of that Act shall continue to apply to sums received by the Secretary of State from the successor company by virtue of this paragraph.
5. The terms which, by virtue of section 6(2) of the 1975 Act, are applicable immediately before the appointed day to any such liability of the BAA as is mentioned in section 3(3) of this Act shall continue to apply to that liability after it becomes a liability of the successor company by virtue of section 2 of this Act, and section 6(4) of that Act shall continue to apply to sums received by the Secretary of State from the successor company by virtue of this paragraph.
6. Subsections (2) to (5) of section 7 of the 1975 Act (Treasury guarantees) shall continue to apply in relation to any guarantee given by the Treasury under that section with respect to a liability of the BAA which becomes a liability of the successor company by virtue of section 2 of this Act, but as if the reference to the BAA in subsection (4) of that section were a reference to the successor company.

7.—(1) The successor company shall prepare a statement of the BAA's accounts for the period from the end of that dealt with in the last annual statement of accounts published by the BAA down to the appointed day (referred to in this paragraph and paragraph 8 as "the final period").

(2) The statement shall be in such form and contain such particulars, compiled in such a manner, as the Secretary of State may, with the approval of the Treasury, direct.

(3) The successor company shall arrange for the accounts of the BAA for the final period to be audited by auditors appointed by the Secretary of State; and a person shall not be qualified to be so appointed unless that person is a member of, or is a Scottish firm in which all the partners are members of, one or more bodies of accountants established in the United Kingdom and for the time being recognised by the Secretary of State for the purposes of section 389(1)(*a*) of the Companies Act 1985.

8.—(1) The successor company shall make to the Secretary of State a report on the performance by the BAA of its functions during the final period.

(2) The report shall—

(*a*) set out any direction given to the BAA under section 2(7) of the 1975 Act during the final period, unless the Secretary of State has notified the successor company that in his opinion it is against the national interest to do so; and

(*b*) include such information relating to the activities of the BAA and its financial position during that period as the Secretary of State may direct.

(3) There shall be attached to the report a copy of the statement of accounts prepared in respect of the final period under paragraph 7 and a copy of any report made on the statement by the auditors.

(4) The Secretary of State shall lay a copy of the report, and of the statements attached to it, before each House of Parliament.

9.—(1) Where it is proposed to declare a distribution during the accounting reference period of the successor company which includes the appointed day, or before any accounts are laid or delivered to the registrar of companies in respect of that period, sections 270 to 276 of the Companies Act 1985 (relevant accounts) shall have effect as if—

(*a*) such accounts as are mentioned in sub-paragraph (2) were accounts relevant under section 270, and

(*b*) references in section 273 to initial accounts included references to any such accounts.

(2) The accounts referred to in sub-paragraph (1)(*a*) and (*b*) are such accounts as, on the assumptions stated in sub-paragraph (3), would have been prepared under section 227 of the Companies Act 1985 in respect of the relevant year.

(3) Those assumptions are—

(*a*) that the relevant year had been a financial year of the successor company;

(*b*) that the vesting effected by section 2 of this Act had been a vesting of all the property, rights and liabilities to which the BAA was entitled or subject immediately before the beginning of the relevant year and had been effected immediately after the beginning of that year;

(*c*) that the value of any asset and the amount of any liability of the BAA vested in the successor company by virtue of that section had been the value or (as the case may be) the amount assigned to that asset or liability for the purposes of the statement of accounts prepared by the BAA in respect of its accounting year immediately preceding the relevant year;

(*d*) that any securities of the successor company issued or allotted before the declaration of the distribution had been issued or allotted before the end of the relevant year; and

(*e*) such other assumptions (if any) as may appear to the directors of the successor company to be necessary or expedient for the purposes of this paragraph.

(4) For the purposes of such accounts as are mentioned in sub-paragraph (2) the amount to be included in respect of any item shall be determined as if anything done by the BAA (whether by way of acquiring, revaluing or disposing of any asset or incurring, revaluing or discharging any liability, or by carrying any amount to any provision or reserve, or otherwise) had been done by the successor company.

Accordingly (but without prejudice to the generality of the preceding provision) the amount to be included in any reserves of the successor company as representing its accumulated realised profits shall be determined as if any profits realised and retained by the BAA had been realised and retained by the successor company.

(5) Any such accounts shall not be regarded as statutory accounts for the purposes of section 8 of this Act.

(6) In this paragraph "the relevant year" means the accounting year of the BAA ending with the 31st March immediately preceding the appointed day.

Compulsory purchase orders

10. A compulsory purchase order made under section 17 of the 1975 Act which is in force immediately before the appointed day shall have effect as if made under section 59 of this Act; and the provisions of section 59 shall apply accordingly.

Byelaws and regulations relating to airports

11.—(1) Any byelaws made or having effect as if made under section 9 of the 1975 Act and in force in relation to any airport immediately before the appointed day shall, as from that day, have effect as if they were byelaws made under section 63 of this Act and the airport were an airport designated for the purposes of that section.

(2) The provisions of any regulations made or having effect as if made under subsection (2)(*j*) of section 63 of this Act and the airport the 1975 Act, and in force in relation to any airport immediately before the appointed day shall, as from that day, have effect (with any necessary modifications) as if they were contained in byelaws made under subsection (2)(*j*) of section 63 of this Act and the airport were an airport designated for the purposes of that section; and any such provisions may accordingly be varied or revoked by byelaws so made.

Control of road traffic

12. Where immediately before the appointed day section 13 of the 1975 Act (control of road traffic) applies to any airport, then, as from that day and until such time as the airport is designated by an order under section 65 of this Act—

    (*a*) the airport shall be deemed to be an airport designated for the purposes of that section, and

    (*b*) any order which, immediately before that day, is in force in relation to the airport under section 13(2) of the 1975 Act shall have effect as if made under section 65(2) of this Act.

Abandoned vehicles

13. Where immediately before the appointed day any order is in force in relation to an airport under section 14 of the 1975 Act (functions of BAA as respects abandoned vehicles) then, as from that day and until such time as the airport is designated by an order under section 66 of this Act—

    (*a*) the airport shall be deemed to be an airport designated for the purposes of that section, and

    (*b*) the order shall have effect as if made under section 66(1).

Cargo areas

14. Notwithstanding the repeal by this Act of section 12 of the 1975 Act (prevention of theft from cargo areas at BAA's airports) any area which, immediately before the appointed day, is to be treated as a cargo area for the purposes of section 27 of the Aviation Security Act 1982 (prevention of thefts at designated airports) in accordance with subsection (7) of that section shall continue to be so treated as if this Act had not been passed.

Extension of Shops (Airports) Act 1962

15. Any order designating an airport for the purposes of the Shops (Airports) Act 1962 and in force at the commencement of section 70 of this Act shall, as from that commencement, be treated as designating that airport for the purposes of that Act as amended by this Act.

SCHEDULE 6

REPEALS

PART I

REPEALS COMING INTO FORCE ON THE APPOINTED DAY

Chapter	Short title	Extent of repeal
1966 c.34.	Industrial Development Act 1966.	In Schedule 2, the entry relating to the British Airports Authority.
1971 c.78.	Town and Country Planning Act 1971.	In section 224(1)(*c*), the words "the British Airports Authority or".
1972 c.52.	Town and Country Planning (Scotland) Act 1972.	In section 213(1)(*c*), the words "the British Airports Authority or".
1975 c.24.	House of Commons Disqualification Act 1975.	In Part II of Schedule 1, the entry relating to the British Airports Authority.
1975 c.78.	Airports Authority Act 1975.	The whole Act.
1976 c.57.	Local Government (Miscellaneous Provisions) Act 1976.	In section 15(3), the words "the British Airports Authority,".
1976 c.70.	Land Drainage Act 1976.	In section 112(2), the words "the British Airports Authority,".
1976 c.75.	Development of Rural Wales Act 1976.	In section 34(1), in the definition of "statutory undertakers", the words "the British Airports Authority,".
1978 c.3.	Refuse Disposal (Amenity) Act 1978.	Section 12(1). Schedule 1.
1978 c.8.	Civil Aviation Act 1978.	Section 8. In Schedule 1, paragraph 7.
1979 c.46.	Ancient Monuments and Archaeological Areas Act 1979.	In section 61(2)(*b*), the words "the British Airports Authority,".
1980 c.60.	Civil Aviation Act 1980.	Sections 24 and 25.
1980 c.65.	Local Government, Planning and Land Act 1980.	In section 108(1)(*b*), the words "the British Airports Authority,". In section 120(3), in the definition of "statutory undertakers", the words "the British Airports Authority,". In section 170(1)(*b*), the words "the British Airports Authority,". In Schedule 16, paragraph 10.
1981 c.64.	New Towns Act 1981.	In section 78(1)(*c*), the words "the British Airports Authority or". In section 79(1)(*b*), the words "or the British Airports Authority". In Schedule 12, paragraph 19.
1981 c.67.	Acquisition of Land Act 1981.	In section 8, in subsection (1)(*b*), the words "the British Airports Authority or", and subsection (2). In section 32(8), the words from "section 17(1)" to the end. In Schedule 4, paragraph 25.
1982 c.1.	Civil Aviation (Amendment) Act 1982.	Section 1.
1982 c.16.	Civil Aviation Act 1982.	Section 34(2). In section 35(1), the words "is managed by a person other than the BAA and". In section 88(10), the words ", the BAA". In section 105(1), the definition of the BAA. In Schedule 15, paragraph 17.

Chapter	Short title	Extent of repeal
1982 c.36.	Aviation Security Act 1982.	Section 27(7). Section 29(2)(*b*). Section 30(3)(*b*). In section 38(1), in the definition of "manager", the words "the British Airports Authority,".
1982 c.48.	Criminal Justice Act 1982.	Section 44. In section 81(3), the words "section 44".
1983 c.44.	National Audit Act 1983.	In Part I of Schedule 4, the entry relating to the British Airports Authority.
1984 c.12.	Telecommunications Act 1984.	In Schedule 4, paragraph 64.
1984 c.22.	Public Health (Control of Disease) Act 1984.	In section 14(1), the words "or the British Airports Authority".
1984 c.27.	Road Traffic Regulation Act 1984.	In section 43(1), the words "and no such regulations" onwards. In Schedule 13, paragraph 33.
1984 c.55.	Building Act 1984.	In section 4(1)(*b*) the words ", the British Airports Authority", in sub-paragraph (i) the words "or in the case of the British Airports Authority a house or a hotel,", and in sub-paragraph (ii) the words "the British Airports Authority or" and "in question". In section 59(4), the words ", the British Airports Authority", in paragraph (*a*) the words "or in the case of the British Airports Authority a house or a hotel,", and in paragraph (*b*) the words "the British Airports Authority or" and "in question".
1985 c.71.	Housing (Consequential Provisions) Act 1985.	In Schedule 2, paragraph 29.

PART II

REPEALS COMING INTO FORCE ON A DATE APPOINTED UNDER SECTION 85(5)

Chapter	Short title	Extent of repeal
1973 c.41.	Fair Trading Act 1973.	In Part II of Schedule 7, paragraph 13.
1980 c.65.	Local Government, Planning and Land Act 1980.	Section 72(4)(iii).
1982 c.16.	Civil Aviation Act 1982.	Section 27. Section 29. Sections 32 and 33. Section 37. In section 38(2), the words "Without prejudice to section 60(3)(*o*),". Section 40. Section 58. Section 60(3)(*o*). Section 61(6). Section 99(5)(*a*). Schedule 5. In Part II of Schedule 13, the entries relating to sections 32(5), 33(1), 37, 40(2) and 61(6) of the 1982 Act. In Schedule 14, paragraph 5(1).
1982 c.48.	Criminal Justice Act 1982.	Section 45. In section 81(5), the words "section 45".

DRUG TRAFFICKING OFFENCES ACT 1986*

(1986 c.32)

ARRANGEMENT OF SECTIONS

* Annotations by D. A. Thomas, LL.D.

An Act to make provision for the recovery of the proceeds of drug trafficking and other provision in connection with drug trafficking, to make provision about the supply of articles which may be used or adapted for use in the administration of controlled drugs or used to prepare a controlled drug for administration and to increase the number of assistant commissioners of police for the metropolis.

[8th July 1986]

INTRODUCTION AND GENERAL NOTE

This statute makes entirely new provision for the Crown Court to make confiscation orders against persons convicted of drug trafficking offences, and for their enforcement.

Ss.1 to 5 deal with the procedure to be followed in the Crown Court when a person is convicted of a drug trafficking offence. The procedure specified in those sections is mandatory and must be completed before the offender is sentenced for the offence. S.6 provides for the enforcement of confiscation orders through the machinery provided for the enforcement of fines, but with an extended table of terms in default. An alternative procedure for the enforcement of confiscation orders through the appointment of a receiver by the High Court is provided by s.11. Ss.7 to 10 provide machinery to prevent a person suspected of drug trafficking from disposing of property before it can be dealt with under a confiscation order: the High Court is empowered to make restraint orders and charging orders in cases where proceedings are in process or have not yet been instituted. S.19 provides for the payment of compensation to persons whose property is affected by such orders, and who suffer substantial losses as a result, if the criminal proceedings do not lead to an effective conviction for a drug trafficking offence. The Act provides for the enforcement of confiscation orders in Scotland, and for the enforcement in England and Wales of equivalent orders made in other jurisdictions, including Northern Ireland. Ss.27 to 31 make provision for the investigation of drug trafficking, providing for orders for production for material relevant to such investigations and for search warrants to be issued in certain cases: there is also a procedure for orders to be made for the production and disclosure of confidential material held by government departments, and for the inspection of the Land Register. The Act creates a number of new offences—making a disclosure likely to prejudice a drug trafficking investigation, assisting a drug trafficker to retain the proceeds of drug trafficking, and supplying or offering to supply items to be used in the unlawful administration of drugs, or in the preparation of drugs for administration.

PARLIAMENTARY DEBATES

Hansard: H.C. Vol. 90, col. 241; Vol. 92, col. 196; H.L. Vol. 471, col. 727; Vol. 472, cols. 90 and 1158; Vol. 474, col. 1094; Vol. 476, col. 447.

The Bill was considered by Standing Committee H on January 28 and 30, 1986.

Confiscation of proceeds of drug trafficking

Confiscation orders

1.—(1) Subject to subsection (7) below, where a person appears before the Crown Court to be sentenced in respect of one or more drug trafficking offences (and has not previously been sentenced or otherwise dealt with in respect of his conviction for the offence or, as the case may be, any of the offences concerned), the court shall act as follows.

(2) The court shall first determine whether he has benefited from drug trafficking.

(3) For the purposes of this Act, a person who has at any time (whether before or after the commencement of this section) received any payment or other reward in connection with drug trafficking carried on by him or another has benefited from drug trafficking.

(4) If the court determines that he has so benefited, the court shall, before sentencing or otherwise dealing with him in respect of the offence or, as the case may be, any of the offences concerned, determine in accordance with section 4 of this Act the amount to be recovered in his case by virtue of this section.

(5) The court shall then, in respect of the offence or offences concerned—
(*a*) order him to pay that amount,
(*b*) take account of the order before—
   (i) imposing any fine on him, or
   (ii) making any order involving any payment by him, or
   (iii) making any order under section 27 of the Misuse of Drugs Act 1971 (forfeiture orders), section 39 of the Powers of Criminal Courts Act 1973 (criminal bankruptcy orders) or section 43 of that Act (deprivation orders), and
(*c*) subject to paragraph (*b*) above, leave the order out of account in determining the appropriate sentence or other manner of dealing with the defendant.

(6) No enactment restricting the power of a court dealing with an offender in a particular way from dealing with him also in any other way shall by reason only of the making of an order under this section restrict the Crown Court from dealing with an offender in any way the court considers appropriate in respect of a drug trafficking offence.

(7) Subsection (1) above does not apply in relation to any offence for which a person appears before the Crown Court to be sentenced if—
(*a*) he has been committed to the Crown Court for sentence in respect of that offence under section 37(1) of the Magistrates' Courts Act 1980 (committal to Crown Court with a view to sentence of youth custody), or
(*b*) the powers of the court (apart from this section) to deal with him in respect of that offence are limited to dealing with him in any way in which a magistrates' court might have dealt with him in respect of the offence.

(8) In this Act—
(*a*) an order under this section is referred to as a "confiscation order", and
(*b*) a person against whom proceedings have been instituted for a drug trafficking offence is referred to (whether or not he has been convicted) as "the defendant".

DEFINITIONS
"drug trafficking, drug trafficking offences": s.38.

GENERAL NOTE
This section imposes on the Crown Court the obligation to take certain steps before sentencing a defendant who appears before the court to be sentenced for one or more drug trafficking offences. "Drug trafficking offences" is defined in s.38: it includes offences of producing, supplying and possessing with intent to supply controlled drugs of all classes, offences relating to the importation of drugs whose importation is prohibited by Misuse of Drugs Act 1971, s.3, and attempting, conspiring, inciting or aiding any of those offences. The obligation to take the steps indicated by the section applies to a person convicted on indictment, or committed for sentence under Magistrates' Courts Act 1980, s.38, but not to persons committed for sentence under Magistrates' Courts Act 1980, s.37 (committal of juvenile with view to youth custody sentence) and Criminal Justice Act 1967, s.56 (committal in respect of lesser offences.) (See s.1(7)(*a*) and (*b*)). The obligation to take the steps required by the section does not apply to a defendant who appeals to the Crown Court against conviction or sentence (see s.1(7)(*b*)), nor does it apply in the case of a person who appears before the Crown Court in breach of a probation order, community service order, or to be dealt with in respect of a suspended sentence or for the revocation of a parole licence: in all of these cases the defendant has "previously been sentenced or otherwise dealt with in respect of his conviction" for the offence (see s.1(1)).
Where the obligation to proceed under the Act arises, the court must first determine whether the defendant has "benefited from drug trafficking". A person who has received any payment or reward in connection with drug trafficking carried on by him or another has "benefited from drug trafficking" for this purpose (see s.1(3)). No detailed procedure is

provided by the Act for making this determination. The Crown Court may make the assumptions mentioned in s.2, although it is not bound to do so. The assumptions are that any property which appears to have been held by the defendant at any time since his conviction, or to have been transferred by him at any time within the six years immediately preceding the institution of the proceedings against him, was received by him as a payment or reward in connection with drug trafficking, and that any expenditure since the beginning of that period was met out of payments received by him in connection with drug trafficking (see s.2(3)). The prosecution may tender a statement of any matters relevant to the determination whether the defendant has benefited from drug trafficking, but is not obliged to do so (see s.3(1)). If such a statement is tendered, and the defendant admits the allegations in the statement, the admission may be treated as conclusive. If the defendant does not admit the allegation, the court may "require" him to "indicate any matters he proposes to rely on". The defendant's failure to comply with such a requirement allows him to be treated as accepting any allegation, except an allegation that he has benefited from drug trafficking or that any payment or other reward has been received by him in connection with drug trafficking (see s.3(3)(*b*)). If the statement tendered by the prosecution merely alleges that the defendant has been in possession of certain property since his conviction, his failure to comply with a requirement to "indicate any matters he proposes to rely on" may be treated as an admission of the allegation that he held the property in question, and the court may then make the assumption under s.2(3)(*a*) that the property is the proceeds of drug trafficking.

It appears to be implicit in the section that the prosecution may allege, in a statement tendered under s.3(1)(*a*) or otherwise, that the defendant has committed or been concerned in offences which are not included in the indictment or formally taken into consideration (see s.(3(6), which provides that no acceptance of an allegation in this connection is admissible in evidence in any proceedings for an offence). In normal circumstances, a court would not be entitled to impose a sentence on the assumption that the defendant is guilty of offences which have not been charged or taken into consideration. In a case where the court determines that the defendant has benefited from drug trafficking on the basis of such allegations, it seems that such allegations must be left out of account in determining the sentence (other than a confiscation order made under this Act) for the offences of which he is convicted. The Act makes no specific provision for the case where the prosecution alleges that the defendant has been involved in drug trafficking on other occasions than those which form the basis of the charges in the indictment, and the defendant denies that this is so. If the prosecution satisfies the court that at the time of this conviction the defendant held any property, the court may (but is not bound to) assume that it was the proceeds of drug trafficking, "except to the extent" that such an assumption is "shown to be incorrect in the defendant's case". Where the defendant is prepared to call evidence to show that the property concerned was not the proceeds of drug trafficking, it is not clear how the court is to proceed. Presumably there must be a hearing, at which the prosecution will prove that the defendant has held particular property since his conviction, and it may be that it will be up to the defendant to call evidence to show why the statutory assumptions in s.2(2) should not be made. Presumably the prosecution may also call evidence to show that there has been a benefit from drug trafficking, either to rebut the evidence that the defendant's property has been legitimately acquired, or more directly bearing on the question of previous drug trafficking. The same will apply where the prosecution prove particular expenditures made by the defendant. The Act makes no specific provision for the incidence of the burden and standard of proof on such a question. S.2(2) (which allows the court to make certain assumptions) appears to be permissive rather than mandatory: it does not require the court to make the assumptions in question unless it is satisfied to the contrary.

If the court determines that the defendant has "benefited from drug trafficking", it must determine the amount to be recovered from him. This determination must be made before the defendant is sentenced for the offences involving drug trafficking, and presumably in many cases will require an adjournment. (It appears that if the defendant is before the court for other offences which are not drug trafficking offences, the court may sentence him for those offences without waiting until the processes required by the Act have been completed (see s.1(4)). To determine the amount to be recovered from the defendant, the court must first determine the value of the defendant's proceeds of drug trafficking in accordance with s.2, and then determine the amount that may be realised from the defendant, if that amount is less than the value of his proceeds of drug trafficking. In determining the amount that may be realised, the court must comply with the detailed provisions of s.5, which relates to the valuation of various kinds of property and the extent to which gifts made by the defendant are caught by the Act. Having made these determinations, the court must make a "confiscation order" requiring him to pay the appropriate amount. Only when that order has been made may the court proceed to sentence the defendant. A confiscation order must be taken into account before the court imposes a fine, any other order involving payment, or any order depriving the defendant of property, but the court must leave the confiscation order out of account in determining the appropriate sentence (presumably of imprisonment, youth custody, etc.) or other means of dealing with the defendant. The making of a confiscation order does not preclude the making of a probation order or discharge (see s.1(6)). It appears that a confiscation order, unlike a fine or a compensation order, is not a sentence which can be imposed in isolation, and some other sentence must be imposed in conjunction with such an order. A confiscation order is clearly a sentence for the purpose of Criminal Appeal Act 1968, s.11, and may be the subject of an appeal against sentence.

Assessing the proceeds of drug trafficking

2.—(1) For the purposes of this Act—

(*a*) any payments or other rewards received by a person at any time (whether before or after the commencement of section 1 of this Act) in connection with drug trafficking carried on by him or another are his proceeds of drug trafficking, and

(*b*) the value of his proceeds of drug trafficking is the aggregate of the values of the payments or other rewards.

(2) The Court may, for the purpose of determining whether the defendant has benefited from drug trafficking and, if he has, of assessing the value of his proceeds of drug trafficking, make the following assumptions, except to the extent that any of the assumptions are shown to be incorrect in the defendant's case.

(3) Those assumptions are—

(*a*) that any property appearing to the court—

(i) to have been held by him at any time since his conviction, or

(ii) to have been transferred to him at any time since the beginning of the period of six years ending when the proceedings were instituted against him,

was received by him, at the earliest time at which he appears to the court to have held it, as a payment or reward in connection with drug trafficking carried on by him,

(*b*) that any expenditure of his since the beginning of that period was met out of payments received by him in connection with drug trafficking carried on by him, and

(*c*) that, for the purpose of valuing any property received or assumed to have been received by him at any time as such a reward, he received the property free of any other interests in it.

(4) Subsection (2) above does not apply if the only drug trafficking offence in respect of which the defendant appears before the court to be sentenced is an offence under section 24 of this Act.

(5) For the purpose of assessing the value of the defendant's proceeds of drug trafficking in a case where a confiscation order has previously been made against him, the court shall leave out of account any of his proceeds of drug trafficking that are shown to the court to have been taken into account in determining the amount to be recovered under that order.

DEFINITIONS

"drug trafficking, drug trafficking offence, interest, property": s.38.

GENERAL NOTE

This section provides for a court to make certain assumptions in the course of determining whether a defendant has benefited from drug trafficking, and if he has, the "value of his proceeds of drug trafficking" (the aggregate of all the payments or other rewards he has received in connection with drug trafficking at any time). It does not apply to the third stage of the process, the determination of the "amount that might be realised" in accordance with s.4(3). The court is not obliged to make any of the assumptions, and the court may not make any of the assumptions which is shown to be incorrect in the defendant's case. No particular procedure is provided by the Act for the purpose of calling evidence on which the making of an assumption can be founded, or showing that the assumption is incorrect in the defendant's case, except the provisions of s.3 relating to statements tendered by the prosecution (see the General Note to s.1). Only the first two assumptions are relevant to the first determination, whether the defendant has benefited from drug trafficking: all three apply to the determination of the value of his proceeds of drug trafficking.

The three assumptions are set out in s.2(3). They may be summarised as that any property which the defendant has held since his conviction or has received during the six years prior to the institution of the proceedings against him (including property which is abroad, see s.38(3)) are the proceedings of drug trafficking, that any expenditures he has made during this period are made out of payments received by him in connection with drug trafficking, and that any property which he has received as a reward for drug trafficking (including presumably any property which the court has assumed him to have received as a reward for drug trafficking) has been received free of any other interest in it.

The assumptions may not be made in the case of a defendant convicted only of offences under s.24 of the Act, which deals with assisting another to retain the benefits of drug trafficking.

Statements relating to drug trafficking

3.—(1) Where—
>   (a) there is tendered to the Crown Court by the prosecutor a statement as to any matters relevant to the determination whether the defendant has benefited from drug trafficking or to the assessment of the value of his proceeds of drug trafficking, and
>   (b) the defendant accepts to any extent any allegation in the statement,

the court may, for the purposes of that determination and assessment, treat his acceptance as conclusive of the matters to which it relates.

(2) Where—
>   (a) a statement is tendered under subsection (1)(a) above, and
>   (b) the court is satisfied that a copy of that statement has been served on the defendant,

the court may require the defendant to indicate to what extent he accepts each allegation in the statement and, so far as he does not accept any such allegation, to indicate any matters he proposes to rely on.

(3) If the defendant fails in any respect to comply with a requirement under subsection (2) above he may be treated for the purposes of this section as accepting every allegation in the statement apart from—
>   (a) any allegation in respect of which he has complied with the requirement, and
>   (b) any allegation that he has benefited from drug trafficking or that any payment or other reward was received by him in connection with drug trafficking carried on by him or another.

(4) Where—
>   (a) there is tendered to the Crown Court by the defendant a statement as to any matters relevant to determining the amount that might be realised at the time the confiscation order is made, and
>   (b) the prosecutor accepts to any extent any allegation in the statement,

the court may, for the purposes of that determination, treat the acceptance by the prosecutor as conclusive of the matters to which it relates.

(5) An allegation may be accepted or a matter indicated for the purposes of this section either—
>   (a) orally before the court, or

(*b*) in writing in accordance with Crown Court Rules.

(6) No acceptance by the defendant under this section that any payment or other reward was received by him in connection with drug trafficking carried on by him or another shall be admissible in evidence in any proceedings for an offence.

DEFINITIONS
"benefited from drug trafficking": s.1(3).
"value of his proceeds of drug trafficking": s.2(2).

GENERAL NOTE
This section provides for statements to be tendered by the prosecution in relation to matters relevant to the determination whether the defendant has benefited from drug trafficking, and the assessment of the value of his proceeds of drug trafficking. It does not apply to statements tendered by the prosecution relevant to the final determination which the court must make before fixing the amount of a confiscation order, the assessment of the "amount that might be realised" (see s.4(3)).

The prosecution are not obliged to tender any statement, but where a statement is tendered by the prosecution, the defendant may accept any allegation in the statement, in which case his acceptance is conclusive of that allegation. If the defendant does not accept any allegation in such a statement, he may be required by the court to "indicate any matters he proposes to rely on". The defendant may be treated as accepting any allegation in respect of which he does not comply with such a requirement. This provision does not however, apply to an allegation that the defendant has benefited from drug trafficking, (that is, an allegation that he has received any payment or other reward in connection with drug trafficking), or that any payment or reward was received by him in connection with drug trafficking (s.3(3)(*b*)). It seems that it can apply only to allegations that the defendant possesses specified items of property or has made specified expenditures. If these facts are established in this manner, the court may make one of the assumptions mentioned in s.2 on the basis of such fact, but only for the purposes of determining whether he has benefited from drug trafficking or assessing the value of his proceeds of drug trafficking. Neither the provisions of s.2 relating to the three assumptions, nor those of s.3 relating to the consequences of the defendant's failure to comply with a requirement under s.3(2) to indicate any matters he proposes to rely on, has any application to the third stage of the process which leads to the making of a confiscation order, the determination of the "amount that might be realised" for the purposes of s.4(3). The statute appears to assume that when the court has determined that the defendant has benefited from drug trafficking, and assessed the value of his proceeds of drug trafficking, on the basis of material put forward by the prosecution and with the assistance of the procedures provided by ss.2 and 3, in so far as they apply, the defendant will take the initiative and submit a statement of his means and assets in accordance with s.3(4). If the prosecution accept any allegation contained in such a statement, they are bound by it, but there is no provision equivalent to s.3(3) allowing the court to treat the prosecution as accepting the contents of such a statement.

Amount to be recovered under confiscation order

4.—(1) Subject to subsection (3) below, the amount to be recovered in the defendant's case under the confiscation order shall be the amount the Crown Court assesses to be the value of the defendant's proceeds of drug trafficking.

(2) If the court is satisfied as to any matter relevant for determining the amount that might be realised at the time the confiscation order is made (whether by an acceptance under section 3 of this Act or otherwise), the court may issue a certificate giving the court's opinion as to the matters concerned and shall do so if satisfied as mentioned in subsection (3) below.

(3) If the court is satisfied that the amount that might be realised at the time the confiscation order is made is less than the amount the court assesses to be the value of his proceeds of drug trafficking, the amount to be recovered in the defendant's case under the confiscation order shall be the amount appearing to the court to be the amount that might be so realised.

DEFINITIONS
"value of the defendant's proceeds of drug trafficking": s.2(1)(*b*).

GENERAL NOTE
This section provides for the determination of the amount of a confiscation order under s.1. The amount of the order is to be the value of the defendant's proceeds of drug trafficking, as determined by the court in accordance with ss.2 and 3. If, as may often be the case, the whole of that amount cannot be realised, the court must proceed to the third stage, and determine "the amount that might be realised". If the court does this, it must issue a certificate in accordance with s.4(2), "giving the court's opinion as to the matters concerned". Presumably such a certificate should set out the finding that the defendant has benefited from drug trafficking, the value of his proceeds of drug trafficking as assessed by the court, and the amount that might be realised, and possibly and subsidiary findings relevant to the determination of the amount in accordance with s.5. Although the statute does not make any explicit provision on the matter, it appears to be assumed that the onus of satisfying the court that "the amount that might be realised" is less than the "value of his proceeds of drug trafficking" rests on the defendant, who will submit a statement of his assets under s.3(4) for this purpose.

Definition of principal terms used

5.—(1) In this Act, "realisable property" means, subject to subsection (2) below—
　(*a*) any property held by the defendant, and
　(*b*) any property held by a person to whom the defendant has directly or indirectly made a gift caught by this Act.
　(2) Property is not realisable property if—
　　(*a*) an order under section 43 of the Powers of Criminal Courts Act 1973 (deprivation orders),
　　(*b*) an order under section 27 of the Misuse of Drugs Act 1971 (forfeiture orders), or
　(*c*) an order under section 223 or 436 of the Criminal Procedure (Scotland) Act 1975 (forfeiture of property),
is in force in respect of the property.
　(3) For the purposes of sections 3 and 4 of this Act the amount that might be realised at the time a confiscation order is made against the defendant is—
　　(*a*) the total of the values at that time of all the realisable property held by the defendant, less
　　(*b*) where there are obligations having priority at that time, the total amounts payable in pursuance of such obligations,
together with the total of the values at that time of all gifts caught by this Act.
　(4) Subject to the following provisions of this section, for the purposes of this Act the value of property (other than cash) in relation to any person holding the property—
　　(*a*) where any other person holds an interest in the property, is—
　　　(i) the market value of the first mentioned person's beneficial interest in the property, less
　　　(ii) the amount required to discharge any incumbrance (other than a charging order) on that interest, and
　　(*b*) in any other case, is its market value.
　(5) Subject to subsection (10) below, references in this Act to the value at any time (referred to in subsection (6) below as "the material time") of a gift caught by this Act or of any payment or reward are references to—
　　(*a*) the value of the gift, payment or reward to the recipient when he received it adjusted to take account of subsequent changes in the value of money, or
　　(*b*) where subsection (6) below applies, the value there mentioned,
whichever is the greater.

(6) Subject to subsection (10) below, if at the material time the recipient holds—

(*a*) the property which he received (not being cash), or

(*b*) property which, in whole or in part, directly or indirectly represents in his hands the property which he received,

the value referred to in subsection (5)(*b*) above is the value to him at the material time of the property mentioned in paragraph (*a*) above or, as the case may be, of the property mentioned in paragraph (*b*) above so far as it so represents the property which he received, but disregarding in either case any charging order.

(7) For the purposes of subsection (3) above, an obligation has priority at any time if it is an obligation of the defendant to—

(*a*) pay an amount due in respect of a fine, or other order of a court, imposed or made on conviction of an offence, where the fine was imposed or order made before the confiscation order, or

(*b*) pay any sum which would be included among the preferential debts (within the meaning given by section 386 of the Insolvency Act 1986) in the defendant's bankruptcy commencing on the date of the confiscation order or winding up under an order of the court made on that date.

(8) In the case of a confiscation order made before the coming into force of the Insolvency Act 1986, subsection (7) above shall have effect as if for paragraph (*b*) there were substituted—

"(*b*) pay any sum which, if the defendant had been adjudged bankrupt or was being wound up, would be among the preferential debts.";

and in that paragraph "the preferential debts"—

(*a*) in relation to bankruptcy, means the debts to be paid in priority under section 33 of the Bankruptcy Act 1914 (assuming the date of the confiscation order to be the date of the receiving order) and

(*b*) in relation to winding up, means the preferential debts listed in Schedule 19 to the Companies Act 1985 (assuming the date of the confiscation order to be the relevant date for the purpose of that Schedule).

(9) A gift (including a gift made before the commencement of section 1 of this Act) is caught by this Act if—

(*a*) it was made by the defendant at any time since the beginning of the period of six years ending when the proceedings were instituted against him, or

(*b*) it was made by the defendant at any time and was a gift of property—

(i) received by the defendant in connection with drug trafficking carried on by him or another, or

(ii) which in whole or in part directly or indirectly represented in the defendant's hands property received by him in that connection.

(10) For the purposes of this Act—

(*a*) the circumstances in which the defendant is to be treated as making a gift include those where he transfers property to another person directly or indirectly for a consideration the value of which is significantly less than the value of the consideration provided by the defendant, and

(*b*) in those circumstances, the preceding provisions of this section shall apply as if the defendant had made a gift of such share in the property as bears to the whole property the same proportion as the difference between the values referred to in paragraph (*a*) above bears to the value of the consideration provided by the defendant.

DEFINITION
"charging order": s.9.

GENERAL NOTE
This section provides detailed rules for the third stage of the process which leads towards a confiscation order under s.1. Having determined that the defendant has benefited from drug trafficking, and assessed the value of his proceeds of drug trafficking, the court must determine "the amount that might be realised". The amount of the confiscation order will be the value of the defendant's proceeds of drug trafficking, or the amount that might be realised, whichever is the less.

"The amount that might be realised" is the total value of all realisable property held by the defendant at the time of the confiscation order, less the total value of any obligations having priority at that time, together with the total value of all gifts which are "caught by this Act." (Property is not realisable if it is subject to an order under Powers of Criminal Courts Act 1973, s.43 or Misuse of Drugs Act 1971, s.27, or the equivalent provisions of the Criminal Procedure (Scotland) Act 1975). The only obligations which have priority for this purpose are those specified in s.5(7)—broadly speaking, existing fines and compensation orders, or debts which would be treated as preferential debts for the purposes of bankruptcy proceedings.

"Gifts caught by this Act," which are included in the "amount that might be realised", are those which were either made within the period of six years before the institution of the proceedings against the defendant, or were gifts either of property received in connection with drug trafficking, or were of property which in whole or part directly or indirectly represented property received by the defendant in connection with drug trafficking. A transaction whereby property is transferred by the defendant at significantly less that its true value is treated as a gift for this purpose: the value of such a gift is to be determined in accordance with s.5(10).

Enforcement etc. of confiscation orders

Application of procedure for enforcing fines

6.—(1) Where the Crown Court orders the defendant to pay any amount under section 1 of this Act, sections 31(1) to (3C) and 32(1) and (2) of the Powers of Criminal Courts Act 1973 (powers of Crown Court in relation to fines and enforcement of Crown Court fines) shall have effect as if—

(a) that amount were a fine imposed on him by the Crown Court, and

(b) in the Table in section 31(3A) (imprisonment in default), for the entry relating to an amount exceeding £10,000 there were substituted—

"An amount exceeding £10,000
but not exceeding £20,000 ....12 months
An amount exceeding £20,000
but not exceeding £50,000 ....18 months
An amount exceeding £50,000
but not exceeding £100,000 ....2 years
An amount exceeding £100,000
but not exceeding £250,000 ....3 years
An amount exceeding £250,000
but not exceeding £1 million ....5 years
An amount exceeding £1 million ....10 years".

(2) Where—

(a) a warrant of commitment is issued for a default in payment of an amount ordered to be paid under section 1 of this Act in respect of an offence or offences, and

(b) at the time the warrant is issued, the defendant is liable to serve a term of custody in respect of the offence or offences,

the term of imprisonment or of detention under section 9 of the Criminal Justice Act 1982 (detention of persons aged 17 to 20 for default) to be served in default of payment of the amount shall not begin to run until after the term mentioned in paragraph (b) above.

(3) The reference in subsection (2) above to the term of custody which the defendant is liable to serve in respect of the offence or offences is a reference to the term of imprisonment, youth custody or detention under section 4 or 9 of the said Act of 1982 which he is liable to serve in respect of the offence or offences; and for the purposes of this subsection—

(*a*) consecutive terms and terms which are wholly or partly concurrent shall be treated as a single term, and

(*b*) there shall be disregarded—

(i) any sentence suspended under section 22(1) of the said Act of 1973 which has not taken effect at the time the warrant is issued,

(ii) in the case of a sentence of imprisonment passed with an order under section 47(1) of the Criminal Law Act 1977, any part of the sentence which the defendant has not at that time been required to serve in prison, and

(iii) any term of imprisonment or detention fixed under section 31(2) of the said Act of 1973 for which a warrant of commitment has not been issued at that time.

(4) In the application of Part III of the Magistrates' Courts Act 1980 to amounts payable under confiscation orders—

(*a*) such an amount is not a sum adjudged to be paid by a conviction for the purposes of section 81 (enforcement of fines imposed on young offenders) or a fine for the purposes of section 85 (remission of fines), and

(*b*) in section 87 (enforcement by High Court or county court), subsection (3) shall be omitted.

(5) The reference in section 143(2) of that Act (power to alter sums specified in certain provisions) to the Table in section 31(3A) of the Powers of Criminal Courts Act 1973 includes a reference to that Table as it has effect by virtue of subsection (1) above.

(6) This section applies in relation to confiscation orders made by the criminal division of the Court of Appeal, or by the House of Lords on appeal from that division, as it applies in relation to confiscation orders made by the Crown Court, and the reference in subsection (1)(*a*) above to the Crown Court shall be construed accordingly.

GENERAL NOTE

This section provides for the enforcement of confiscation orders. Confiscation orders will be treated substantially as if they were fines imposed by the Crown Court, and the relevant provisions of Powers of Criminal Courts Act 1973, ss.31 to 32 apply, with some amendment. The Crown Court has power on making a confiscation order to allow time to pay and direct payment by instalments: it must fix the term to be served in the event of default, in accordance with the table set out in Powers of Criminal Courts Act 1973, s.31(3A), as that table is extended to apply to larger amounts by s.6(1)(*b*). Powers of Criminal Courts Act 1973, s.31(3), which restricts the power of the court to order immediate committal in default of payment of a fine, applies to confiscation orders, but it may be that in practice the majority of confiscation orders will accompany custodial sentences. This situation will be covered by Powers of Criminal Courts Act 1973, s.31(3)(*c*), which allows an immediate committal where the defendant is sentenced to custody on the same occasion. Any term of custody ordered to be served in default of a confiscation order must run consecutively to any custodial sentence which the defendant is serving for the offences in respect of which the confiscation order is made, and any terms which he is serving concurrently or consecutively with them, whether he is committed at the time he is sentenced or later (s.6(2)), but if the defendant is serving a term of custody for unrelated offences when he is committed in default of payment of a confiscation order, it appears that the court will have power to order that the default term be served concurrently with the sentence.

Alternative procedures for the enforcement of confiscation orders are provided by ss.11–13.

Cases in which restraint orders and charging orders may be made

7.—(1) The powers conferred on the High Court by sections 8(1) and 9(1) of this Act are exercisable where—

    (*a*) proceedings have been instituted in England and Wales against the defendant for a drug trafficking offence,

    (*b*) the proceedings have not been concluded, and

    (*c*) the court is satisfied that there is reasonable cause to believe that the defendant has benefited from drug trafficking.

(2) Those powers are also exercisable where the court is satisfied—

    (*a*) that an information is to be laid under section 1 of the Magistrates' Courts Act 1980 that a person has or is suspected of having committed a drug trafficking offence, and

    (*b*) that there is reasonable cause to believe that he has benefited from drug trafficking.

(3) For the purposes of sections 8, 9 and 22 of this Act, at any time when those powers are exercisable before proceedings have been instituted—

    (*a*) references in this Act to the defendant shall be construed as references to the person referred to in subsection (2)(*a*) above,

    (*b*) references in this Act to the prosecutor shall be construed as references to the person who the High Court is satisfied is to have the conduct of the proposed proceedings, and

    (*c*) references in this Act to realisable property shall be construed as if, immediately before that time, proceedings had been instituted against the person referred to in subsection (2)(*a*) above for a drug trafficking offence.

(4) Where the court has made an order under section 8(1) or 9(1) of this Act by virtue of subsection (2) above, the court shall discharge the order if the proposed proceedings are not instituted within such time as the court considers reasonable.

GENERAL NOTE

Ss.7 to 10 provide for charging and restraint orders to be made by the High Court on the application of the prosecution, in respect of property which is held by a person against whom a confiscation order may be made or has been made. S.7 sets out the conditions which are common to both types of order. The powers may be exercised where a prosecution is in process, but has not yet been concluded, and there is reasonable cause to believe that the defendant has benefited from drug trafficking, or where a prosecution is about to be commenced by the laying of an information under the Magistrates' Courts Act 1980, s.1 and there is reasonable cause to believe that the intended defendant has benefited from drug trafficking. The conditions for the exercise of either power before the institution of a prosecution do not require that the laying of the information is imminent—it is sufficient that a definite decision has been taken to lay an information—but any order made in anticipation of a prosecution must be discharged if the proposed proceedings are not instituted within such time as the court considers reasonable. This provision appears to allow the court, on making either kind of order in anticipation of a prosecution, to set a time limit within which the information must be laid, but it appears that a further application must be made to the court for the discharge of the order if such a time limit is exceeded.

Restraint orders

8.—(1) The High Court may by order (in this Act referred to as a "restraint order") prohibit any person from dealing with any realisable property, subject to such conditions and exceptions as may be specified in the order.

(2) A restraint order may apply—

    (*a*) to all realisable property held by a specified person, whether the property is described in the order or not, and

    (*b*) to realisable property held by a specified person, being property transferred to him after the making of the order.

(3) This section shall not have effect in relation to any property for the time being subject to a charge under section 9 of this Act.

(4) A restraint order—

    (*a*) may be made only on an application by the prosecutor,

    (*b*) may be made on an ex parte application to a judge in chambers, and

    (*c*) shall provide for notice to be given to persons affected by the order.

(5) A restraint order—

    (*a*) may be discharged or varied in relation to any property, and

    (*b*) shall be discharged when proceedings for the offences are concluded.

(6) Where the High Court has made a restraint order, the court may at any time appoint a receiver—

    (*a*) to take possession of any realisable property, and

    (*b*) in accordance with the court's directions, to manage or otherwise deal with any property in respect of which he is appointed,

subject to such exceptions and conditions as may be specified by the court; and may require any person having possession of property in respect of which a receiver is appointed under this section to give possession of it to the receiver.

(7) For the purposes of this section, dealing with property held by any person includes (without prejudice to the generality of the expression)—

    (*a*) where a debt is owed to that person, making a payment to any person in reduction of the amount of the debt, and

    (*b*) removing the property from Great Britain.

(8) Where the High Court has made a restraint order, a constable may for the purpose of preventing any realisable property being removed from Great Britain, seize the property.

(9) Property seized under subsection (8) above shall be dealt with in accordance with the court's directions.

DEFINITIONS

    "confiscation order: s.1(8).
    "defendant": s.7(3)(*a*).
    "proceedings for the offence are concluded": s.38(12).
    "property held by any person": ss.38(7), 38(8), 38(9).
    "prosecutor": s.7(3)(*b*).
    "realisable property": s.5.

GENERAL NOTE

This section empowers the High Court to make a restraint order, authorising the seizure of realisable property where criminal proceedings are either in process or are about to be instituted in accordance with s.7. The order, which will be made in chambers on the *ex parte* application of the prosecutor, may apply to all the realisable property held by the person specified in the order (either the defendant or intended defendant, or a person to whom the defendant has made a gift caught by the Act in the manner specified in s.5(5)) at the time of the order, and any property which may be transferred to him after the making of the restraint order. It is not necessary to specify the property in the order, but the property may be specified. Where a restraint order is made, the court may appoint a receiver to manage the property and otherwise deal with it, subject to conditions specified by the court. Where property subject to a restraint order is about to be removed from Great Britain, it may be seized by a constable without further authority from the court. A restraint order may be discharged or varied by the court, and must be discharged when the proceedings for the offences are concluded. The discharge of an order on the conclusion of the proceedings appears to require an order of the High Court: there is no power in the Crown Court to discharge an order in the event of an acquittal.

The powers given to the court and to the receiver by this section must be exercised in accordance with the general principles set out in s.13.

Charging orders in respect of land, securities etc.

9.—(1) The High Court may make a charging order on realisable property for securing the payment to the Crown—

(*a*) where a confiscation order has not been made, of an amount equal to the value from time to time of the property charged, and

(*b*) in any other case, of an amount not exceeding the amount payable under the confiscation order.

(2) For the purposes of this Act, a charging order is an order made under this section imposing on any such realisable property as may be specified in the order a charge for securing the payment of money to the Crown.

(3) A charging order—

(*a*) may be made only on an application by the prosecutor, and

(*b*) may be made on an ex parte application to a judge in chambers.

(4) Subject to subsection (6) below, a charge may be imposed by a charging order only on—

(*a*) any interest in realisable property, being an interest held beneficially by the defendant or by a person to whom the defendant has directly or indirectly made a gift caught by this Act—

    (i) in any asset of a kind mentioned in subsection (5) below, or

    (ii) under any trust, or

(*b*) any interest in realisable property held by a person as trustee of a trust if the interest is in such an asset or is an interest under another trust and a charge may by virtue of paragraph (*a*) above be imposed by a charging order on the whole beneficial interest under the first-mentioned trust.

(5) The assets referred to in subsection (4) above are—

(*a*) land in England and Wales, or

(*b*) securities of any of the following kinds—

    (i) government stock,

    (ii) stock of any body (other than a building society) incorporated within England and Wales,

    (iii) stock of any body incorporated outside England and Wales or of any country or territory outside the United Kingdom, being stock registered in a register kept at any place within England and Wales,

    (iv) units of any unit trust in respect of which a register of the unit holders is kept at any place within England and Wales.

(6) In any case where a charge is imposed by a charging order on any interest in an asset of a kind mentioned in subsection (5)(*b*) above, the court may provide for the charge to extend to any interest or dividend payable in respect of the asset.

(7) The court may make an order discharging or varying the charging order and shall make an order discharging the charging order if the proceedings for the offence are concluded or the amount payment of which is secured by the charge is paid into court.

Definitions

"confiscation order": s.1(8).
"proceedings for the offence are concluded": s.38(12).
"property held by any person": ss.38(7), 38(8), 38(9).
"realisable property": s.5.

General Note

This section empowers the High Court to make a charging order, imposing a charge on any land or securities held by a defendant or potential defendant, for the purpose of securing the payment of money ordered to be paid by way of a confiscation order. A charging order may be made either before the making of a confiscation order, in the circumstances specified in s.7, or after a confiscation order has been made. It will be made on an *ex parte* application by the prosecution to a judge in chambers, and may apply to property specified in s.9(4). The order may be discharged by the court or varied, and must be discharged if the proceedings for the offence are concluded (either by the determination of the proceedings without a confiscation order or the satisfaction of a confiscation order), or the amount for which payment is secured by the charge is paid into court.

The powers given to the court and to the receiver by this section must be exercised in accordance with the general principles set out in s.13.

Charging orders: supplementary provisions

10.—(1) A charging order may be made either absolutely or subject to conditions as to notifying any person holding any interest in the property to which the order relates or as to the time when the charge is to become enforceable, or as to other matters.

(2) The Land Charges Act 1972 and the Land Registration Act 1925 shall apply in relation to charging orders as they apply in relation to orders or writs issued or made for the purpose of enforcing judgments.

(3) Where a charging order has been registered under section 6 of the Land Charges Act 1972, subsection (4) of that section (effect of non-registration of writs and orders registrable under that section) shall not apply to an order appointing a receiver made in pursuance of the charging order.

(4) Subject to any provision made under section 11 of this Act or by rules of court, a charge imposed by a charging order shall have the like effect and shall be enforceable in the same courts and in the same manner as an equitable charge created by the person holding the beneficial interest or, as the case may be, the trustees by writing under their hand.

(5) Where a charging order has been protected by an entry registered under the Land Charges Act 1972 or the Land Registration Act 1925, an order under section 9(7) of this Act discharging the charging order may direct that the entry be cancelled.

(6) The Secretary of State may by order made by statutory instrument amend section 9 of this Act by adding to or removing from the kinds of asset for the time being referred to there any asset of a kind which in his opinion ought to be so added or removed.

An order under this subsection shall be subject to annulment in pursuance of a resolution of either House of Parliament.

(7) In this section and section 9 of this Act, "building society", "dividend", "government stock", "stock" and "unit trust" have the same meanings as in the Charging Orders Act 1979.

DEFINITION
  "charging order": s.9.

GENERAL NOTE
  This section contains detailed provisions relating to the registration and form of charging orders made under s.9.

Realisation of property

11.—(1) Where—
  (*a*) in proceedings instituted for a drug trafficking offence, a confiscation order is made,
  (*b*) the order is not subject to appeal, and
  (*c*) the proceedings have not been concluded,
the High Court may, on an application by the prosecutor, exercise the powers conferred by subsections (2) to (6) below.

(2) The court may appoint a receiver in respect of realisable property.

(3) The court may empower a receiver appointed under subsection (2) above, under section 8 of this Act or in pursuance of a charging order—

(*a*) to enforce any charge imposed under section 9 of this Act on realisable property or on interest or dividends payable in respect of such property, and

(*b*) in relation to any realisable property other than property for the time being subject to a charge under section 9 of this Act, to take possession of the property subject to such conditions or exceptions as may be specified by the court.

(4) The court may order any person having possession of realisable property to give possession of it to any such receiver.

(5) The court may empower any such receiver to realise any realisable property in such manner as the court may direct.

(6) The court may order any person holding an interest in realisable property to make such payment to the receiver in respect of any beneficial interest held by the defendant or, as the case may be, the recipient of a gift caught by this Act as the court may direct and the court may, on the payment being made, by order transfer, grant or extinguish any interest in the property.

(7) Subsections (4) to (6) above do not apply to property for the time being subject to a charge under section 9 of this Act.

(8) The court shall not in respect of any property exercise the powers conferred by subsection (3)(*a*), (5) or (6) above unless a reasonable opportunity has been given for persons holding any interest in the property to make representations to the court.

DEFINITIONS
"confiscation order": s.1(8).
"proceedings concluded": s.38(12).
"realisable property": s.5(1).

GENERAL NOTE
This section provides for the appointment of a receiver by the High Court, on the application of the prosecutor, for the purpose of enforcing a confiscation order made under s.1. With the authority of the court, the receiver may enforce any charge imposed by a charging order under s.9, where such an order has been made, and take possession of any realisable property which has not been made the subject of a charging order. The receiver may be authorised to realise any realisable property which is not subject to a charging order under s.9, or receive any payments due to the defendant in respect of property which is not subject to a charging order under s.9. The powers given to the court and to the receiver by this section must be exercised in accordance with the general principles set out in s.13.

Application of proceeds of realisation and other sums

12.—(1) Subject to subsection (2) below, the following sums in the hands of a receiver appointed under section 8 or 11 of this Act or in pursuance of a charging order, that is—

(*a*) the proceeds of the enforcement of any charge imposed under section 9 of this Act,

(*b*) the proceeds of the realisation, other than by the enforcement of such a charge, of any property under section 8 or 11 of this Act, and

(*c*) any other sums, being property held by the defendant,

shall, after such payments (if any) as the High Court may direct have been made out of those sums, be applied on the defendant's behalf towards the satisfaction of the confiscation order.

(2) If, after the amount payable under the confiscation order has been fully paid, any such sums remain in the hands of such a receiver, the receiver shall distribute those sums—

(*a*) among such of those who held property which has been realised
under this Act, and

(*b*) in such proportions,

as the High Court may direct after giving a reasonable opportunity for
such persons to make representations to the court.

(3) The receipt of any sum by a justices' clerk on account of an amount
payable under a confiscation order shall reduce the amount so payable,
but the sum shall be applied as follows—

(*a*) if paid by a receiver under subsection (1) above, it shall first be
applied in payment of his remuneration and expenses,

(*b*) subject to paragraph (*a*) above, it shall be applied in reimbursement
of any sums paid by the prosecutor under section 18(2) of this Act,

and the balance shall be treated for the purposes of section 61 of the
Justices of the Peace Act 1979 (application of fines, etc.) as if it were a
fine imposed by a magistrates' court.

In this subsection, "justices' clerk" has the same meaning as in the
Justices of the Peace Act 1979.

DEFINITIONS
"charging order": s.9.
"confiscation order": s.1(8).

GENERAL NOTE
This section provides for the application of sums realised by a receiver appointed under
s.8 (restraint orders), s.11 (enforcement of confiscation orders), or by a receiver appointed
in pursuance of a charging order under s.9. Subject to any payments made by direction of
the High Court, sums in the hands of the receiver will be applied towards the satisfaction of
the confiscation order: any sums remaining in the hands of the receiver after the confiscation
order has been fully paid will then be distributed as the High Court may direct in accordance
with s.12(2). Any sums of money paid on account of a confiscation order, whether directly
by the defendant or on his behalf, or by a receiver appointed under the relevant provisions,
go to reduce the amount payable under the confiscation order, but the sums must be applied
in the manner specified in s.12(3). The justices' clerk to whom the sums are paid must first
pay out of the money received from a receiver the receiver's expenses and remuneration, or
reimburse the prosecutor if the prosecutor has met these expenses, and the balance is treated
as if it were a fine imposed by a magistrate's court.

Exercise of powers by High Court or receiver

13.—(1) The following provisions apply to the powers conferred on the
High Court by sections 8 to 12 of this Act, or on the Court of Session by
sections 20 to 22 of this Act, or on a receiver appointed under section 8
or 11 of this Act or in pursuance of a charging order.

(2) Subject to the following provisions of this section, the powers shall
be exercised with a view to making available for satisfying the confiscation
order or, as the case may be, any confiscation order that may be made in
the defendant's case the value for the time being of realisable property
held by any person by the realisation of such property.

(3) In the case of realisable property held by a person to whom the
defendant has directly or indirectly made a gift caught by this Act, the
powers shall be exercised with a view to realising no more than the value
for the time being of the gift.

(4) The powers shall be exercised with a view to allowing any person
other than the defendant or the recipient of any such gift to retain or
recover the value of any property held by him.

(5) An order may be made or other action taken in respect of a debt
owed by the Crown.

(6) In exercising those powers, no account shall be taken of any
obligations of the defendant or of the recipient of any such gift which
conflict with the obligation to satisfy the confiscation order.

DEFINITIONS
  "confiscation order": s.1(8).
  "realisable property": s.5(1).

GENERAL NOTE
  This section lays down general principles affecting the exercise by the court and by any receiver appointed by the court of the various powers given by the provisions mentioned in s.13(1). The powers must be exercised primarily with a view to the satisfaction of the confiscation order or potential confiscation order, and no account may be taken of any obligation which conflicts with the obligation to satisfy the confiscation order: however, where the powers are exercised against a person who is the recipient of a gift caught by the Act, the powers must be exercised with a view to recovering no more than the value of the gift, and where they are exercised against any person other than the defendant or the recipient of a gift caught by the Act, they must be exercised with a view to allowing him to retain or recover the value of any property held by him.

Variation of confiscation orders

14.—(1) If, on an application by the defendant in respect of a confiscation order, the High Court is satisfied that the realisable property is inadequate for the payment of any amount remaining to be recovered under the order the court shall issue a certificate to that effect, giving the court's reasons.

(2) For the purposes of subsection (1) above—

    (*a*) in the case of realisable property held by a person who has been adjudged bankrupt or whose estate has been sequestrated the court shall take into account the extent to which any property held by him may be distributed among creditors, and

    (*b*) the court may disregard any inadequacy in the realisable property which appears to the court to be attributable wholly or partly to anything done by the defendant for the purpose of preserving any property held by a person to whom the defendant had directly or indirectly made a gift caught by this Act from any risk of realisation under this Act.

(3) Where a certificate has been issued under subsection (1) above, the defendant may apply to the Crown Court for the amount to be recovered under the order to be reduced.

(4) The Crown Court shall, on an application under subsection (3) above—

    (*a*) substitute for the amount to be recovered under the order such lesser amount as the court thinks just in all the circumstances of the case, and

    (*b*) substitute for the term of imprisonment or of detention fixed under subsection (2) of section 31 of the Powers of Criminal Courts Act 1973 in respect of the amount to be recovered under the order a shorter term determined in accordance with that section (as it has effect by virtue of section 6 of this Act) in respect of the lesser amount.

DEFINITIONS
  "confiscation order": s.1(8).
  "gift caught by this Act": s.5(5).
  "realisable property": s.5(1).

GENERAL NOTE
  This section provides a procedure for the variation of a confiscation order. The defendant may apply to the High Court for a certificate that the realisable property is inadequate to meet any amount which remains to be recovered under the confiscation order. It is not clear whether this application is to be made *ex parte*, or whether the prosecutor must be notified of the application (compare the express provisions of s.8(4) and 9(3)). If the High Court, having considered the matters mentioned in s.14(2), in particular any attempts by the

defendant to protect property held by a person to whom he has made a gift caught by the Act, is satisfied that the realisable property is insufficient to discharge the outstanding balance of the confiscation order, it must issue a certificate to that effect, stating its reasons. The defendant may then take the certificate to the Crown Court, and apply for a reduction of the amount to be recovered under the confiscation order. The Crown Court must apparently substitute some lesser amount for the amount specified in the original confiscation order as the amount to be recovered, and make any consequential orders in relation to default terms, but the Crown Court does not appear to be bound to accept the High Court's certificate at face value: it may substitute such lesser amount "as the court thinks just in all the circumstances of the case".

Bankruptcy of defendant etc.

15.—(1) Where a person who holds realisable property is adjudged bankrupt—

(*a*) property for the time being subject to a restraint order made before the order adjudging him bankrupt, and

(*b*) any proceeds of property realised by virtue of section 8(6) or 11(5) or (6) of this Act for the time being in the hands of a receiver appointed under sections 8 or 11 of this Act,

is excluded from the bankrupt's estate for the purposes of Part IX of the Insolvency Act 1986.

(2) Where a person has been adjudged bankrupt, the powers conferred on the High Court by sections 8 to 12 of this Act or on a receiver so appointed or on the Court of Session by sections 20 to 22 of this Act shall not be exercised in relation to—

(*a*) property for the time being comprised in the bankrupt's estate for the purposes of that Part,

(*b*) property in respect of which his trustee in bankruptcy may (without leave of court) serve a notice under section 307 or 308 of that Act (after-acquired property and tools, clothes etc. exceeding value of reasonable replacement), and

(*c*) property which is to be applied for the benefit of creditors of the bankrupt by virtue of a condition imposed under section 280(2)(*c*) of that Act.

(3) Nothing in that Act shall be taken as restricting, or enabling the restriction of, the exercise of those powers.

(4) Subsection (2) above does not affect the enforcement of a charging order—

(*a*) made before the order adjudging the person bankrupt, or

(*b*) on property which was subject to a restraint order when the order adjudging him bankrupt was made.

(5) Where, in the case of a debtor, an interim receiver stands appointed under section 286 of that Act and any property of the debtor is subject to a restraint order—

(*a*) the powers conferred on the receiver by virtue of that Act do not apply to property for the time being subject to the restraint order,

(*b*) section 287(4) of that Act (receiver's immunity), as it applies to the receiver by virtue of section 286(3) of that Act, shall have effect in relation to such property as if references to such property were substituted for references to property which is not comprised in the bankrupt's estate, and

(*c*) any such property in the hands of the receiver shall, subject to a lien for any expenses (including his remuneration) properly incurred in respect of the property, be dealt with in such manner as the High Court may direct.

(6) Where a person is adjudged bankrupt and has directly or indirectly made a gift caught by this Act—

(*a*) no order shall be made under section 339 or 423 of that Act (avoidance of certain transactions) in respect of the making of the gift at any time when proceedings for a drug trafficking offence have been instituted against him and have not been concluded or when property of the person to whom the gift was made is subject to a restraint order or charging order, and

(*b*) any order made under either of those sections after the conclusion of the proceedings shall take into account any realisation under this Act of property held by the person to whom the gift was made.

(7) In any case in which a petition in bankruptcy is presented, or a receiving order or adjudication in bankruptcy is made, before the date on which the Insolvency Act 1986 comes into force, this section has effect with the following modifications—

(*a*) for references to the bankrupt's estate for the purposes of Part IX of that Act there are substituted references to the property of the bankrupt for the purposes of the Bankruptcy Act 1914.

(*b*) for references to the Act of 1986 and sections 280(2)(*c*), 286, 339 and 423 of that Act there are respectively substituted references to the Act of 1914 and to sections 26(2), 8, 27 and 42 of that Act,

(*c*) the references in subsection (5) to an interim receiver appointed as there mentioned include, where a receiving order has been made, a reference to the receiver constituted by virtue of section 7 of the Act of 1914, and

(*d*) subsections (2)(*b*) and (5)(*a*) and (*b*) are omitted.

DEFINITIONS
"realisable property": s.5(1).
"restraint order": s.8.

GENERAL NOTE
  This section deals with the case where a person holding realisable property is adjudged bankrupt. Its general effect is that any property which has already been made subject to a restraint order, or has been realised by a receiver appointed under this Act, is excluded from the bankruptcy: where the person is adjudged bankrupt before action is taken under this Act, the powers to make charging or restraint orders, or to enforce the order under s.11, are restricted in the manner specified in s.15(2), but not otherwise.

Sequestration in Scotland of defendant etc.

16.—(1) Where the estate of a person who holds realisable property is sequestrated—

(*a*) property for the time being subject to a restraint order made before the award of sequestration, and

(*b*) any proceeds of property realised by virtue of section 8(6) or 11(5) or (6) of this Act for the time being in the hands of a receiver appointed under section 8 or 11 of this Act,

is excluded from the debtor's estate for the purposes of the Bankruptcy (Scotland) Act 1985.

(2) Where an award of sequestration has been made, the powers conferred on the High Court by sections 8 to 12 of this Act or on a receiver so appointed or on the Court of Session by sections 20 to 22 of this Act shall not be exercised in relation to—

(*a*) property comprised in the whole estate of the debtor within the meaning of section 31(8) of that Act,

(*b*) any income of the debtor which has been ordered, under subsection (2) of section 32 of that Act, to be paid to the permanent trustee or any estate which, under subsection (6) of that section, vests in the permanent trustee.

(3) Nothing in that Act shall be taken as restricting, or enabling the restriction of, the exercise of those powers.

(4) Subsection (2) above does not affect the enforcement of a charging order–

(*a*) made before the award of sequestration, or

(*b*) on property which was subject to a restraint order when the award of sequestration was made.

(5) Where, during the period before sequestration is awarded, an interim trustee stands appointed under the proviso to section 13(1) of that Act and any property in the debtor's estate is subject to a restraint order—

(*a*) the powers conferred on the trustee by virtue of that Act do not apply to property for the time being subject to the restraint order,

(*b*) the trustee, if he seizes or disposes of any property for the time being subject to the restraint order and, when he does so, believes and has reasonable grounds for believing that he is entitled (whether in pursuance of an order of a court or otherwise) to do so—

(i) shall not (except insofar as the same has been caused by his negligence) be liable to any person in respect of any loss or damage resulting from his seizure or disposal of the property, and

(ii) shall have a lien on the property, or the proceeds of its sale, for such of the expenses of the sequestration as were incurred in connection with the seizure or disposal, and

(*c*) any such property in the hands of the trustee shall, subject to a lien for any expenses (including his remuneration) properly incurred in respect of the property, be dealt with in such manner as the High Court may direct.

(6) Where the estate of a person is sequestrated and he has directly or indirectly made a gift caught by this Act—

(*a*) no decree shall be granted under section 34 or 36 of that Act (gratuitous alienations and unfair preferences) in respect of the making of the gift at any time when proceedings for a drug trafficking offence have been instituted against him and have not been concluded or when property of the person to whom the gift was made is subject to a restraint order or charging order, and

(*b*) any decree made under either of those sections after the conclusion of the proceedings shall take into account any realisation under this Act of property held by the person to whom the gift was made.

(7) In any case in which, notwithstanding the coming into force of the Bankruptcy (Scotland) Act 1985 the Bankruptcy (Scotland) Act 1913 applies to a sequestration, subsection (2) above shall have effect as if for paragraphs (*a*) and (*b*) thereof there were substituted the following paragraphs—

"(*a*) property comprised in the whole property of the debtor which vests in the trustee under section 97 of the Bankruptcy (Scotland) Act 1913,

(*b*) any income of the bankrupt which has been ordered under subsection (2) of section 98 of that Act, to be paid to the trustee or any estate which, under subsection (1) of that section, vests in the trustee";

and subsection (3) above shall have effect as if for the reference therein to the Act of 1985 there were substituted a reference to the Act of 1913.

Winding up of company holding realisable property

17.—(1) Where realisable property is held by a company and an order for the winding up of the company had been made or a resolution has been passed by the company for the voluntary winding up, the functions of the liquidator (or any provisional liquidator) shall not be exercisable in relation to—

(*a*) property for the time being subject to a restraint order made before the relevant time, and

(*b*) any proceeds of property realised by virtue of section 8(6) or 11(5) or (6) of this Act for the time being in the hands of a receiver appointed under section 8 of 11 of this Act;

but there shall be payable out of such property any expenses (including the remuneration of the liquidator or provisional liquidator) properly incurred in the winding up in respect of the property.

(2) Where, in the case of a company, such an order has been made or such a resolution had been passed, the powers conferred on the High Court by sections 8 to 12 of this Act or on a receiver so appointed or on the Court of Session by sections 20 to 22 of this Act shall not be exercised in relation to any realisable property held by the company in relation to which the functions of the liquidator are exercisable—

(*a*) so as to inhibit him from exercising those functions for the purpose of distributing any property held by the company to the company's creditors, or

(*b*) so as to prevent the payment out of any property of expenses (including the remuneration of the liquidator or any provisional liquidator) properly incurred in the winding up in respect of the property.

(3) Nothing in the Insolvency Act 1986 shall be taken as restricting, or enabling the restriction of, the exercise of those powers.

(4) Subsection (2) above does not affect the enforcement of a charging order made before the relevant time or on property which was subject to a restraint order at the relevant time.

(5) In this section—

"company" means any company which may be wound up under the Insolvency Act 1986; and

"the relevant time" means—

(*a*) where no order for the winding up of the company has been made, the time of the passing of the resolution for voluntary winding up,

(*b*) where such an order has been made and, before the presentation of the petition for the winding up of the company by the court, such a resolution had been passed by the company, the time of the passing of the resolution, and

(*c*) in any other case where such an order has been made, the time of the making of the order.

(6) In any case in which a winding up of a company has commenced, or is treated as having commenced, before the date on which the Insolvency Act 1986 comes into force, this section has effect with the substitution for references to that Act of references to the Companies Act 1985

DEFINITIONS

"charging order": s.9.
"realisable property": s.5(1).
"restraint order": s.8.

GENERAL NOTE

This section makes provision for the case where realisable property is held by a company which is in the process of winding up. Its general effect is similar to that of s.15 in relation to personal bankruptcy. Property which has already been subjected to a restraint order, or which has been realised by a receiver acting under either a restraint order or an existing confiscation order, does not fall to be distributed by the liquidator: but where the company is already in liquidation, the court may not exercise the powers to make restraint orders, charging orders or to enforce the confiscation order in such a way as to inhibit the liquidator from distributing the company's property among its creditors. Similarly a charging order made before the relevant time (as defined by s.17(5)) will be enforceable, notwithstanding that the company is subsequently in liquidation.

Receivers: supplementary provisions

18.—(1) Where a receiver appointed under section 8 or 11 of this Act or in pursuance of a charging order takes any action—

(*a*) in relation to property which is not realisable property, being action which he would be entitled to take if it were such property,

(*b*) believing, and having reasonable grounds for believing, that he is entitled to take that action in relation to that property,

he shall not be liable to any person in respect of any loss of damage resulting from his action except in so far as the loss or damage is caused by his negligence.

(2) Any amount due in respect of the renumeration and expenses of a receiver so appointed shall, if no sum is available to be applied in payment of it under section 12(3)(*a*) of this Act, be paid by the prosecutor or, in a case where proceedings for a drug trafficking offence are not instituted, by the person on whose application the receiver was appointed.

DEFINITIONS
   "charging order": s.9.
   "realisable property": s.5(1).

GENERAL NOTE
   Subs. (1) of this section provides a defence to a receiver appointed in connection with a restraint order under s.8, a charging order under s.9, or in conection with the enforcement of a confiscation order under s.11, in respect of any acts done in relation to property which is not realisable property for the purposes of s.5, if he acts in the reasonable belief that he is entitled to take such action, and is not negligent.
   Subs. (2) deals with the payment of the receiver's remuneration and expenses in a case where the amount realised under the confiscation order is insufficient to cover them.

Compensation

19.—(1) If proceedings are instituted against a person for a drug trafficking offence or offences and either—

(*a*) the proceedings do not result in his conviction for any drug trafficking offence, or

(*b*) where he is convicted of one or more drug trafficking offences—

(i) the conviction or convictions concerned are quashed (and no conviction for any drug trafficking offence is substituted), or

(ii) he is pardoned by Her Majesty in respect of the conviction or convictions concerned,

the High Court may, on an application by a person who held property which was realisable property, order compensation to be paid to the applicant.

(2) The High Court shall not order compensation to be paid in any case unless the court is satisfied—

(*a*) that there has been some serious default on the part of a person concerned in the investigation or prosecution of the offence or offences concerned, being a person mentioned in subsection (4) below, and that, but for that default, the proceedings would not have been instituted or continued, and

(*b*) that the applicant has suffered substantial loss in consequence of anything done in relation to the property by or in pursuance of—

(i) an order of the High Court under sections 8 to 11 of this Act, or

      (ii) an order of the Court of Session under section 20, 21 or 22 of this Act.

(3) The amount of compensation to be paid under this section shall be such as the High Court thinks just in all the circumstances of the case.

(4) Compensation payable under this section shall be paid—

     (*a*) where the person in default was or was acting as a member of a police force, out of the police fund out of which the expenses of that police force are met,

     (*b*) where the person in default was a member of the Crown Prosecution Service or acting on behalf of the service, by the Director of Public Prosecutions, and

     (*c*) where the person in default was an officer within the meaning of the Customs and Excise Management Act 1979, by the Commissioners of Customs and Excise.

DEFINITION

"realisable property": s.5(1).

GENERAL NOTE

This section provides for the payment of compensation to a person who held realisable property which has been the subject of orders by the High Court or Court of Session, and who has suffered substantial loss as a result. Compensation may be ordered to be paid to such a person only if the proceedings for the drug trafficking offence in connection with which the order was made end in an acquittal, the quashing of a conviction or a pardon, and there has been serious default on the part of a member of the relevant investigation or prosecuting department, which has lead to the institution or continuance of the proceedings. Compensation may be paid either to a defendant or to the recipient of a gift caught by the Act.

Enforcement in Scotland

Recognition and enforcement in Scotland of orders and functions under sections 8, 11, 12 and 30

20.—(1) An order to which this section applies shall, subject to this section and section 21 of this Act, have effect in the law of Scotland but shall be enforced in Scotland only in accordance with this section and that section.

(2) A receiver's functions under or for the purposes of section 8, 11 or 12 of this Act shall, subject to this section and section 21 of this Act, have effect in the law of Scotland.

(3) If an order to which this section applies is registered under this section—

     (*a*) the Court of Session shall have, in relation to its enforcement, the same power,

     (*b*) proceedings for or with respect to its enforcement may be taken, and

     (*c*) proceedings for or with respect to any contravention of such an order (whether before or after such registration) may be taken,

as if the order had originally been made in that Court.

(4) Nothing in this section enables any provision of an order which empowers a receiver to do anything in Scotland under section 11(3)(*a*) of this Act to have effect in the law of Scotland.

(5) The orders to which this section applies are orders of the High Court—

     (*a*) made under sections 8, 11, 12 or 30 of this Act,

     (*b*) relating to the exercise by that Court of its powers under those sections, or

     (*c*) relating to receivers in the performance of their functions under sections 8, 11 or 12 of this Act, but not including an order in proceedings for enforcement of any such order.

(6) References in this section to an order under section 8 of this Act include references to a discharge under section 7(4) of this Act of such an order.

(7) In this section and in sections 21 and 23, "order" means any order, direction or judgment (by whatever name called).

(8) Nothing in any order of the High Court under section 11(6) of this Act prejudices any enactment or rule of law in respect of the recording of deeds relating to heritable property in Scotland or the registration of interests therein.

Provisions supplementary to section 20

21.—(1) The Court of Session shall, on application made to it in accordance with rules of court for registration of an order to which section 20 applies, direct that the order shall, in accordance with such rules, be registered in that Court.

(2) Subsections (1) and (3) of section 20 of this Act and subsection (1) above are subject to any provision made by rules of court—

(*a*) as to the manner in which and conditions subject to which orders to which that section applies are to be enforced in Scotland,

(*b*) for the sisting of proceedings for enforcement of such an order,

(*c*) for the modification or cancellation of the registration of such an order if the order is modified or revoked or ceases to have effect.

(3) This section and section 20 are without prejudice to any enactment or rule of law as to the effect of notice or the want of it in relation to orders of the High Court.

(4) The Court of Session shall have the like power to make an order under section 1 of the Administration of Justice (Scotland) Act 1972 (extended power to order inspection of documents etc.) in relation to proceedings brought or likely to be brought under this Act in the High Court as if those proceedings had been brought or were likely to be brought in the Court of Session.

(5) The Court of Session may, additionally, for the purpose of—

(*a*) assisting the achievement in Scotland of the purposes of orders to which section 20 of this Act applies, or

(*b*) assisting receivers performing functions there under or for the purposes of section 8, 11 or 12 of this Act,

make such orders and do otherwise as seems to it appropriate.

Inhibition and arrestment of property in Scotland

22.—(1) On the application of the prosecutor, the Court of Session may, in respect of any property in Scotland, being property to which a restraint order registered in that Court relates—

(*a*) where the property is heritable, grant warrant for inhibition in respect of the property against any person with an interest in it, or

(*b*) where the property is moveable and would, if the person entitled to it were a debtor, be arrestable property, grant warrant for arrestment of the property,

and on the grant of such a warrant the enactments and rules of law relating to inhibition and arrestment shall, subject to the provisions of this section, apply respectively as if the warrant had been granted on the dependence of an action for debt at the instance of the prosecutor against the person against whom the warrant for inhibition is granted or, as the case may be, whose property falls to be arrested.

(2) Section 155 of the Titles to Land Consolidation (Scotland) Act 1868 (effective date of inhibitions) shall apply in relation to an inhibition proceeding upon a warrant under this section.

(3) In the application of section 158 of the said Act of 1868 (recall of inhibitions) to an inhibition proceeding upon a warrant under this section, the references to a particular Lord Ordinary in the Court of Session shall be construed as references to any such Lord Ordinary.

(4) Any power of the Court of Session to recall, loose or restrict inhibitions or arrestments shall, in relation to an inhibition or arrestment proceeding upon a warrant under this section and without prejudice to any other consideration lawfully applying to the exercise of the power, be exercised with a view to achieving the purposes specified in section 13 of this Act.

(5) The Court of Session shall have power to restrict the effect of an inhibition proceeding upon a warrant under this section to particular property.

(6) The fact that such an inhibition or arrestment has been executed as respects any property shall not prejudice the exercise of a receiver's powers under or for the purposes of section 8, 11 or 12 of this Act in respect of that property.

(7) An inhibition or arrestment under this section shall cease to have effect upon the restraint order to which it relates ceasing to have effect and, where an inhibition ceases to have effect, it shall thereupon be the duty of the prosecutor to discharge it.

Proof in Scotland of High Court Orders

23. A document purporting to be a copy of an order under or for the purposes of this Act by the High Court and to be certified as such by a proper officer of that Court shall, in Scotland, be sufficient evidence of the order.

Offence of assisting drug traffickers

Assisting another to retain the benefit of drug trafficking

24.—(1) Subject to subsection (3) below, if a person enters into or is otherwise concerned in an arrangement whereby—

    (*a*) the retention or control by or on behalf of another (call him "A") of A's proceeds of drug trafficking is facilitated (whether by concealment, removal from the jurisdiction, transfer to nominees or otherwise), or

    (*b*) A's proceeds of drug trafficking—

        (i) are used to secure that funds are placed at A's disposal, or

        (ii) are used for A's benefit to acquire property by way of investment,

knowing or suspecting that A is a person who carries on or has carried on drug trafficking or has benefited from drug trafficking, he is guilty of an offence.

(2) In this section, references to any person's proceeds of drug trafficking include a reference to any property which in whole or in part directly or indirectly represented in his hands his proceeds of drug trafficking.

(3) Where a person discloses to a constable a suspicion or belief that any funds or investments are derived from or used in connection with drug trafficking or any matter on which such a suspicion or belief is based—

    (*a*) the disclosure shall not be treated as a breach of any restriction upon the disclosure of information imposed by contract, and

    (*b*) if he does any act in contravention of subsection (1) above and the disclosure relates to the arrangement concerned, he does not commit an offence under this section if the disclosure is made in accordance with this paragraph, that is—

(i) it is made before he does the act concerned, being an act done with the consent of the constable, or

(ii) it is made after he does the act, but is made on his initiative and as soon as it is reasonable for him to make it.

(4) In proceedings against a person for an offence under this section, it is a defence to prove—

(*a*) that he did not know or suspect that the arrangement related to any person's proceeds of drug trafficking, or

(*b*) that he did not know or suspect that by the arrangement the retention or control by or on behalf of A of any property was facilitated or, as the case may be, that by the arrangement any property was used as mentioned in subsection (1) above, or

(*c*) that—

(i) he intended to disclose to a constable such a suspicion, belief or matter as is mentioned in subsection (3) above in relation to the arrangement, but

(ii) there is reasonable excuse for his failure to make disclosure in accordance with subsection (3)(*b*) above.

(5) A person guilty of an offence under this section shall be liable—

(*a*) on conviction on indictment to imprisonment for a term not exceeding fourteen years or to a fine or to both, and

(*b*) on summary conviction, to imprisonment for a term not exceeding six months or to a fine not exceeding the statutory maximum or to both.

(6) In Part II of Schedule 1 to the Criminal Justice Act 1982 (persons convicted of offences under certain enactments not eligible for early release), after paragraph 25 there is inserted—

"DRUG TRAFFICKING OFFENCES ACT 1986 (c.32)

26. Section 24 (assisting another to retain the benefit of drug trafficking)."

DEFINITIONS

"drug trafficking": s.38.

"proceeds of drug trafficking": s.2(1)(*a*).

GENERAL NOTE

This section creates a new offence relating to assisting another (who is to be known as A) to retain or control his proceeds of drug trafficking. The offence is triable either way, with a maximum sentence on indictment of 14 years' imprisonment: it is a drug trafficking offence for the purposes of this Act, and an excluded offence for the purpose of Criminal Justice Act 1982, Sched. 1. It is always a serious arrestable offence for the purposes of Police and Criminal Evidence Act 1984 (see s.36, below).

The offence under the section can be committed in a variety of ways, as specified in s.24(1)(*a*) and (*b*). The prosecution must establish that the person accused of the offence knew or suspected that A was or had been a drug trafficker, but not apparently that the particular arrangement which is the subject of the charge related to the proceeds of drug trafficking. S.24(4) places on the accused the burden of proving that he did not know or suspect that the arrangement related to the proceeds of drug trafficking, among other matters. S24(3) creates a special defence to a charge under s.24(1), that the accused had made a disclosure of information as indicated by s.24(3)(*b*)(1) and (2): s.24(3)(*a*) provides that the disclosure of information of this kind will not constitute a breach of any contract requiring confidentiality.

Enforcement of external orders

Enforcement of Northern Ireland orders

25.—(1) Her Majesty may by Order in Council provide that, for the purposes of sections 7 to 19 of this Act, this Act shall have effect as if—

   (*a*) references to confiscation orders included a reference to orders made by courts in Northern Ireland which appear to Her Majesty to correspond to confiscation orders,

   (*b*) references to drug trafficking offences included a reference to any offence under the law of Northern Ireland (not being a drug trafficking offence) which appears to Her Majesty to correspond to such an offence,

   (*c*) references to proceedings in England and Wales or to the institution or conclusion in England and Wales of proceedings included a reference to proceedings in Northern Ireland or to the institution or conclusion in Northern Ireland of proceedings, as the case may be, and

   (*d*) references to the laying of an information or the issue of a summons or warrant under section 1 of the Magistrates' Courts Act 1980 included a reference to making a complaint or issuing a summons or warrant (as the case may be) under Article 20 of the Magistrates' Courts (Northern Ireland) Order 1981.

(2) An Order in Council under this section may provide for those sections to have effect in relation to anything done or to be done in Northern Ireland subject to such further modifications as may be specified in the order.

(3) An Order in Council varying or revoking a previous Order in Council under this section may contain such incidental, consequential and transitional provisions as Her Majesty considers expedient.

(4) An Order in Council under this section shall not be made unless a draft of the order has been laid before Parliament and approved by resolution of each House of Parliament.

DEFINITIONS
   "conclusion of proceedings": s.38.
   "confiscation order": s.1(8).
   "drug trafficking offences": s.38.
   "institution of proceedings": s.38.

GENERAL NOTE
   This section provides for the enforcement provisions (including those relating to restraint and charging orders made before the making of a confiscation order) of the Act to be made applicable to confiscation orders or their equivalent made by courts in Northern Ireland.
   No order has been made under this section at the time of going to press.

Enforcement of other external orders

26.—(1) Her Majesty may by Order in Council apply this section to any order made after the Order in Council comes into force by a court of a country or territory outside the United Kingdom, being an order—

   (*a*) of a description specified in the Order in Council, and

   (*b*) made for the purpose of recovering payments or other rewards received in connection with drug trafficking or their value.

(2) An order to which this section applies is referred to below in this section as an "external confiscation order"; and in this section "designated country" means a country or territory outside the United Kingdom designated by an Order in Council under this section.

(3) The High Court may, on an application by or on behalf of the government of a designated country, register an external confiscation order made there, subject to subsection (4) below.

(4) The High Court shall not register an external confiscation order unless—

   (*a*) the court is satisfied that at the time of registration the order is in force in the designated country and is not subject to appeal in the designated country,

   (*b*) the court is satisfied, where the person against whom the order is made did not appear in the proceedings, that he received notice of the proceedings in sufficient time to enable him to defend them, and

   (*c*) the court is of the opinion that enforcing the order in England and Wales would not be contrary to the interests of justice.

(5) The High Court shall cancel the registration of an external confiscation order if it appears to the court that the order has been satisfied (whether by payment of the amount due under the order, by the person against whom the order is made serving imprisonment in default or otherwise).

(6) In relation to an external confiscation order registered under this section, sections 8 to 18 of this Act shall have effect subject to such modifications as may be specified in an Order in Council under this section as they have effect in relation to a confiscation order.

(7) In subsection (4) above, "appeal" includes any proceedings by way of discharging or setting aside a judgment or an application for a new trial or a stay of execution.

(8) In any case where the High Court is satisfied, on an application by or on behalf of the government of a designated country, that proceedings which might result in an external confiscation order being made against a person have been instituted in the designated country and have not been concluded, sections 8 to 10 of this Act shall have effect in relation to those proceedings—

   (*a*) as they would have effect in relation to proceedings instituted in England and Wales against that person for a drug trafficking offence which have not been concluded, and

   (*b*) as if references to a confiscation order were references to an external confiscation order and references to an application by the prosecutor were references to an application by or on behalf of that government, and

   (*c*) subject to such other modifications as may be specified in an Order in Council under this section.

(9) An Order in Council under this section may include such provision—

   (*a*) as to evidence or proof of any matter for the purposes of this section, and

   (*b*) as to the circumstances in which proceedings are to be treated for those purposes as instituted or concluded in any designated country,

as Her Majesty considers expedient.

(10) An Order in Council varying or revoking a previous Order in Council under this section may contain such incidental, consequential and transitional provisions as Her Majesty considers expedient.

(11) An Order in Council under this section shall not be made unless a draft of the order has been laid before Parliament and approved by resolution of each House of Parliament.

DEFINITIONS

  "conclusion of proceedings": s.38(12).
  "confiscation order": s.1(8).
  "designated country": s.26(2).
  "drug trafficking offences": s.38(1).

external confiscation order": s.26(2).
"institution of proceedings": s.38(11).

General Note
This section provides for the enforcement provisions of the Act to be applied to orders of courts in foreign countries which are analogous to confiscation orders. Countries whose orders will be recognised will be designated by Order in Council (s.2(2)): orders made by the courts of those countries will then be capable of being registered as "external confiscation orders" on application to the High Court, subject to the conditions specified in s.26(4), and any special conditions included in the Order in Council relating to the particular country (s.26(9). While an external confiscation order remains registered, ss.8 to 18 apply to it as they do to a confiscation order under s.1(8), subject to any modifications made by the relevant order in Council. Where proceedings in designated foreign countries have been instituted but are not yet concluded, apppication may be made to the High Court for a restraint or charging order under ss.8 and 9, which will apply subject to such modifications as may be stipulated in the Order designating the country concerned. These provisions will not apply to cases in which proceedings in the designated country are about to be instituted, as they do to cases in England and Wales where an information is to be laid (see s.7(2)).
No Order has been made under this section.

Investigations into drug trafficking

Order to make material available

27.—(1) A constable or, in Scotland, the procurator fiscal may, for the purpose of an investigation into drug trafficking, apply to a Circuit Judge or, in Scotland, the sheriff for an order under subsection (2) below in relation to particular material or material or a particular description.

(2) If on such an application the judge or, as the case may be, the sheriff is satisfied that the conditions in subsection (4) below are fulfilled, he may make an order that the person who appears to him to be in possession of the material to which the application relates shall—

(*a*) produce it to a constable for him to take away, or
(*b*) give a constable access to it,

within such period as the order may specify.
This subsection is subject to section 30(11) of this Act.

(3) The period to be specified in an order under subsection (2) above shall be seven days unless it appears to the judge or, as the case may be, the sheriff that a longer or shorter period would be appropriate in the particular circumstances of the application.

(4) The conditions referred to in subsection (2) above are—

(*a*) that there are reasonable grounds for suspecting that a specified person has carried on or has benefited from drug trafficking,
(*b*) that there are reasonable grounds for suspecting that the material to which the application relates—
(i) is likely to be of substantial value (whether by itself or together with other material) to the investigation for the purpose of which the application is made, and
(ii) does not consist of or include items subject to legal privilege or excluded material, and
(*c*) that there are reasonable grounds for believing that it is in the public interest, having regard—
(i) to the benefit likely to accrue to the investigation if the material is obtained, and
(ii) to the circumstances under which the person in possession of the material holds it,
that the material should be produced or that access to it should be given.

(5) Where the judge or, as the case may be, the sheriff makes an order under subsection (2)(*b*) above in relation to material on any premises he may, on the application of a constable or, in Scotland, the procurator fiscal order any person who appears to him to be entitled to grant entry

to the premises to allow a constable to enter the premises to obtain access to the material.

(6) Provision may be made by Crown Court Rules or, as respects Scotland, rules of court as to—

(a) the discharge and variation of orders under this section, and

(b) proceedings relating to such orders.

(7) An order of a Circuit Judge under this section shall have effect as if it were an order of the Crown Court.

(8) Where the material to which an application under this section relates consists of information contained in a computer—

(a) an order under subsection (2)(a) above shall have effect as an order to produce the material in a form in which it can be taken away and in which it is visible and legible, and

(b) an order under subsection (2)(b) above shall have effect as an order to give access to the material in a form in which it is visible and legible.

(9) An order under subsection (2) above—

(a) shall not confer any right to production of, or access to, items subject to legal privilege or excluded material,

(b) shall have effect notwithstanding any obligation as to secrecy or other restriction upon the disclosure of information imposed by statute or otherwise, and

(c) may be made in relation to material in the possession of an authorised government department.

DEFINITIONS

"constable": s.38(1).

"drug trafficking": s.38(1).

"excluded material": s.29.

"premises": s.29.

"subject to legal privilege": s.29.

GENERAL NOTE

This section provides for an order to be made by a Circuit judge (or a sheriff in Scotland) for the production of material which may be relevant to an investigation into drug trafficking, on the application of a constable or officer of the Customs and Excise (see s.38(1).) In Scotland, an order may be made by a sheriff on the application of a procurator fiscal. There is no provision for an application to be made in England and Wales by the Crown prosecution service. The material must be specified, or must be material of a particular kind: the Circuit judge or sheriff must be satisfied of the matters set out in s.27(4). The order may be made against any person holding the material to which the order relates, not necessarily the person who is suspected of having carried on or benefited from drug trafficking, but the name of that person must be specified in the order. An application may be made at any time in relation to the criminal proceedings against the person suspected of drug trafficking—before or during the criminal proceedings, or after a conviction, for the purpose of establishing any of the matters necessary to the making or enforcement of a confiscation order.

An order may not be made in relation to material which is subject to legal privilege or is "excluded material" as defined in Police and Criminal Evidence Act 1984, ss.10 and 11. Apart from this, an order under the section will override any obligation as to secrecy or confidentiality imposed on the holder of the material whether statutory or not, and may apply to material in the possession of a government department.

Authority for search

28.—(1) A constable or, in Scotland, the procurator fiscal may, for the purpose of an investigation into drug trafficking, apply to a Circuit Judge or, in Scotland, the sheriff for a warrant under this section in relation to specified premises.

(2) On such application the judge or, as the case may be, the sheriff may issue a warrant authorising a constable to enter and search the premises if he is satisfied—

(*a*) that an order made under section 27 of this Act in relation to material on the premises has not been complied with, or

(*b*) that the conditions in subsection (3) below are fulfilled, or

(*c*) that the conditions in subsection (4) below are fulfilled.

(3) The conditions referred to in subsection (2)(*b*) above are—

    (*a*) that there are reasonable grounds for suspecting that a specified person has carried on or has benefited from drug trafficking, and

    (*b*) that the conditions in section 27(4)(*b*) and (*c*) of this Act are fulfilled in relation to any material on the premises, and

    (*c*) that it would not be appropriate to make an order under that section in relation to the material because—

        (i) it is not practicable to communicate with any person entitled to produce the material, or

        (ii) it is not practicable to communicate with any person entitled to grant access to the material or entitled to grant entry to the premises on which the material is situated, or

        (iii) the investigation for the purposes of which the application is made might be seriously prejudiced unless a constable could secure immediate access to the material.

(4) The conditions referred to in subsection (2)(*c*) above are—

    (*a*) that there are reasonable grounds for suspecting that a specified person has carried on or has benefited from drug trafficking, and

    (*b*) that there are reasonable grounds for suspecting that there is on the premises material relating to the specified person or to drug trafficking which is likely to be of substantial value (whether by itself or together with other material) to the investigation for the purpose of which the application is made, but that the material cannot at the time of the application be particularised, and

    (*c*) that—

        (i) it is not practicable to communicate with any person entitled to grant entry to the premises, or

        (ii) entry to the premises will not be granted unless a warrant is produced, or

        (iii) the investigation for the purpose of which the application is made might be seriously prejudiced unless a constable arriving at the premises could secure immediate entry to them.

(5) Where a constable has entered premises in the execution of a warrant issued under this section, he may seize and retain any material, other than items subject to legal privilege and excluded material, which is likely to be of substantial value (whether by itself or together with other material) to the investigation for the purpose of which the warrant was issued.

DEFINITIONS

  "constable": s.38(1).

  "drug trafficking": s.38(1).

  "premises": s.29.

GENERAL NOTE

  This section provides for the issue of a search warrant by a Circuit judge or sheriff in Scotland where an order for the production of material made under s.27 has not been complied with, or such an order is impractical or inappropriate for the reasons specified in either s.28(3) or s.28(4).

Sections 27 and 28: supplementary provisions

29.—(1) For the purposes of sections 21 and 22 of the Police and Criminal Evidence Act 1984 (access to, and copying and retention of, seized material)—

(a) an investigation into drug trafficking shall be treated as if it were an investigation of or in connection with an offence, and

(b) material produced in pursuance of an order under section 27(2)(a) of this Act shall be treated as if it were material seized by a constable.

(2) Subject to subsection (3) below, in sections 27 and 28 of this Act "items subject to legal privilege", "excluded material" and "premises" have the same meanings as in the said Act of 1984.

(3) As respects Scotland, in sections 27 and 28 of this Act the references to excluded material shall be omitted, and—

"items subject to legal privilege" means—

(a) communications between a professional legal adviser and his client,

(b) communications made in connection with or in contemplation of legal proceedings and for the purposes of these proceedings,

being communications which would in legal proceedings be protected from disclosure by virtue of any rule of law relating to the confidentiality of communications, and

"premises" includes any place and, in particular, includes—

(a) any vehicle, vessel, aircraft or hovercraft,

(b) any offshore installation within the meaning of section 1 of the Mineral Workings (Offshore Installations) Act 1971, and

(c) any tent or movable structure.

GENERAL NOTE

This section applies to material produced in compliance with an order under s.27, or seized under a warrant under s.28, the provisions of Police and Criminal Evidence Act 1984 which relate to the handling and retention of material seized under the powers granted by that Act, and adopts the definitions of certain expressions defined in the Police and Criminal Evidence Act 1984.

Disclosure of information held by government departments

30.—(1) Subject to subsection (4) below, the High Court may on an application by the prosecutor order any material mentioned in subsection (3) below which is in the possession of an authorised government department to be produced to the court within such period as the court may specify.

(2) The power to make an order under subsection (1) above is exercisable if—

(a) the powers conferred on the court by sections 8(1) and 9(1) of this Act are exercisable by virtue of subsection (1) of section 7 of this Act, or

(b) those powers are exercisable by virtue of subsection (2) of that section and the court has made a restraint or charging order which has not been discharged;

but where the power to make an order under subsection (1) above is exercisable by virtue only of paragraph (b) above, subsection (3) of section 7 of this Act shall apply for the purposes of this section as it applies for the purposes of sections 8 and 9 of this Act.

(3) The material referred to in subsection (1) above is any material which—

(*a*) has been submitted to an officer of an authorised government department by the defendant or by a person who has at any time held property which was realisable property,

(*b*) has been made by an officer of an authorised government department in relation to the defendant or such a person, or

(*c*) is correspondence which passed between an officer of an authorised government department and the defendant or such a person,

and an order under that subsection may require the production of all such material or of a particular description of such material, being material in the possession of the department concerned.

(4) An order under subsection (1) above shall not require the production of any material unless it appears to the High Court that the material is likely to contain information that would facilitate the exercise of the powers conferred on the court by sections 8 to 11 of this Act or on a receiver appointed under section 8 or 11 of this Act or in pursuance of a charging order.

(5) The court may by order authorise the disclosure to such a receiver of any material produced under subsection (1) above or any part of such material; but the court shall not make an order under this subsection unless a reasonable opportunity has been given for an officer of the department to make representations to the court.

(6) Material disclosed in pursuance of an order under subsection (5) above may, subject to any conditions contained in the order, be further disclosed for the purposes of the functions under this Act of the receiver or the Crown Court.

(7) The court may by order authorise the disclosure to a person mentioned in subsection (8) below of any material produced under subsection (1) above or any part of such material; but the court shall not make an order under this subsection unless—

(*a*) a reasonable opportunity has been given for an officer of the department to make representations to the court, and

(*b*) it appears to the court that the material is likely to be of substantial value in exercising functions relating to drug trafficking.

(8) The persons referred to in subsection (7) above are—

    (*a*) any member of a police force,

    (*b*) any member of the Crown Prosecution Service, and

    (*c*) any officer within the meaning of the Customs and Excise Management Act 1979.

(9) Material disclosed in pursuance of an order under subsection (7) above may, subject to any conditions contained in the order, be further disclosed for the purposes of functions relating to drug trafficking.

(10) Material may be produced or disclosed in pursuance of this section notwithstanding any obligation as to secrecy or other restriction upon the disclosure of information imposed by statute or otherwise.

(11) An order under subsection (1) above and, in the case of material in the possession of an authorised government department, an order under section 27(2) of this Act may require any officer of the department (whether named in the order or not) who may for the time being be in possession of the material concerned to comply with it, and such an order shall be served as if the proceedings were civil proceedings against the department.

(12) The person on whom such an order is served—

(*a*) shall take all reasonable steps to bring it to the attention of the officer concerned, and

(*b*) if the order is not brought to that officer's attention within the period referred to in subsection (1) above, shall report the reasons for the failure to the court;

and it shall also be the duty of any other officer of the department in receipt of the order to take such steps as are mentioned in paragraph (*a*) above.

DEFINITIONS
"authorised government department": s.38.
"charging order": s.9.
"defendant": s.7.
"drug trafficking": s.38.
"prosecutor": s.7.
"realisable property": s.5(1).
"restraint order": s.8.

GENERAL NOTE
This section provides a procedure which may lead to the disclosure of material held by a government department, in cases where it would be possible for the High Court to make a charging order or a restraint order in connection with proceedings which have been instituted, or in connection with a restraint order or charging order which has been made in connection with proceedings which have not yet been instituted. The effect of s.30(2) is simply to adapt the definitions of "prosecutor", "defendant" and "realisable property" to the latter case.

The procedure under the section falls into two stages—an application by the prosecutor to the High Court for production to the High Court of material thought likely to contain information that would facilitate the exercise of the powers of the High Court under ss.8 to 11 (restraint orders, charging orders and enforcement), or the exercise of his powers by a receiver appointed under ss.8 to 11 or under a charging order. An order for production to the High Court may be made without allowing a hearing to an officer of the department holding the material. When material has been produced to the High Court under a production order, the court may make a further order for the disclosure of the material either to a receiver or to a police officer, a member of the Crown Prosecution service or an officer of the Customs and Excise. No order for disclosure may be made unless the government department holding the material has been given an opportunity to make representations to the court, and if the disclosure is to be to any official other than a receiver, it must appear to the High Court that the material "is likely to be of substantial value in exercising functions relating to drug trafficking". Material disclosed to a police officer, Crown Prosecutor or Customs and Excise officer may be further disclosed for the purpose of functions relating to drug trafficking.

Offence of prejudicing investigation

31.—(1) Where, in relation to an investigation into drug trafficking, an order under section 27 of this Act has been made or has been applied for and has not been refused or a warrant under section 28 of this Act has been issued, a person who, knowing or suspecting that the investigation is taking place, makes any disclosure which is likely to prejudice the investigation is guilty of an offence.

(2) In proceedings against a person for an offence under this section, it is a defence to prove—
(*a*) that he did not know or suspect that the disclosure was likely to prejudice the investigation, or
(*b*) that he had lawful authority or reasonable excuse for making the disclosure.

(3) A person guilty of an offence under this section shall be liable—
(*a*) on conviction on indictment, to imprisonment for a term not exceeding five years or to a fine or to both, and
(*b*) on summary conviction, to imprisonment for a term not exceeding six months or to a fine not exceeding the statutory maximum or to both.

DEFINITION
"drug trafficking": s.38.

GENERAL NOTE

This section creates an offence of making a disclosure likely to prejudice an investigation into drug trafficking. The offence can be committed only where an application has been made for an order for production of material under s.27, or an order has been made under that section, or a warrant has been issued under s.28. It will be necessary to prove that the person accused of an offence under this section knew or suspected that an investigation into drug trafficking was taking place, but not that he knew that an application had been made under s.27 or warrant issued under s.28. It will be a defence for the defendant to prove the matters set out in s.31(2): the offence is triable either way and punishable with a maximum of five years' imprisonment on indictment. The offence is an arrestable offence for the purposes of Police and Criminal Evidence Act 1984, but it is not a drug trafficking offence for the purposes of this Act.

Authorisation of delay in notifying arrest

32.—(1) In section 56 of the Police and Criminal Evidence Act 1984 (right to have someone informed when arrested), at the beginning of subsection (5) there is inserted "Subject to subsection (5A) below" and after that subsection there is inserted—

"(5A) An officer may also authorise delay where the serious arrestable offence is a drug trafficking offence and the officer has reasonable grounds for believing—

(*a*) that the detained person has benefited from drug trafficking, and

(*b*) that the recovery of the value of that person's proceeds of drug trafficking will be hindered by telling the named person of the arrest."

(2) In section 58 of that Act (access to legal advice) at the beginning of subsection (8) there is inserted "Subject to subsection (8A) below" and after that subsection there is inserted—

"(8A) An officer may also authorise delay where the serious arrestable offence is a drug trafficking offence and the officer has reasonable grounds for believing—

(*a*) that the detained person has benefited from drug trafficking, and

(*b*) that the recovery of the value of that person's proceeds of drug trafficking will be hindered by the exercise of the right conferred by subsection (1) above."

(3) In section 65 of that Act (interpretation)—

(*a*) after the definition of "appropriate consent" there is inserted—

""drug trafficking" and "drug trafficking offence" have the same meaning as in the Drug Trafficking Offences Act 1986", and

(*b*) at the end of that section there is inserted "and references in this Part to any person's proceeds of drug trafficking are to be construed in accordance with the Drug Trafficking Offences Act 1986".

(4) Without prejudice to section 20(2) of the Interpretation Act 1978, the Police and Criminal Evidence Act 1984 (Application to Customs and Excise) Order 1985 applies to sections 56 and 58 of the Police and Criminal Evidence Act 1984 as those sections have effect by virtue of this section.

GENERAL NOTE

Police and Criminal Evidence Act 1984, s.56 provides that any person who has been arrested and who is being held in custody is entitled to have one person notified that he has been arrested and where he is being detained, subject to exceptions set out in s.56(5). This provision creates a new exception, as set out in the new subs. 5A to be inserted in s.56. A similar exception is added to s.58, which gives a person who is in custody after arrest the right to consult a solicitor at any time.

Miscellaneous and Supplemental

Power to inspect Land Register etc.

33.—(1) The Chief Land Registrar (in this section referred to as "the registrar") shall, on an application under subsection (2) or (4) below made in relation to a person specified in the application or to property so specified, provide the applicant with any information kept by the registrar under the Land Registration Act 1925 which relates to the person or property so specified.

(2) An application may be made by—

    (*a*) any police officer not below the rank of superintendent,

    (*b*) any Crown Prosecutor, or

    (*c*) any person commissioned by the Commissioners of Customs and Excise not below the rank of senior executive officer,

and on an application under this subsection an appropriate certificate shall be given to the registrar.

(3) In subsection (2) above, "appropriate certificate" means a certificate—

    (*a*) that there are reasonable grounds for suspecting that there is information kept by the registrar which is likely to be of substantial value (whether by itself or together with other information) to an investigation into drug trafficking, or

    (*b*) that—

        (i) a person specified in the certificate has committed or there are reasonable grounds for suspecting that a person so specified has committed a drug trafficking offence, and

        (ii) there are reasonable grounds for suspecting that there is information kept by the registrar which is likely to be of substantial value (whether by itself or together with other information) to an investigation into whether the person so specified has benefited from drug trafficking or in facilitating the recovery of the value of his proceeds of drug trafficking.

(4) An application may be made by a receiver appointed under section 8 or 11 of this Act and on an application under this subsection there shall be given to the registrar—

    (*a*) a document certified by the proper officer of the court to be a true copy of the order appointing the receiver, and

    (*b*) a certificate that there are reasonable grounds for suspecting that there is information kept by the registrar which is likely to facilitate the exercise of the powers conferred on the receiver in respect of the person or property specified in the application.

(5) The reference in subsection (1) above to the provision of information is a reference to its provision in documentary form.

D<small>EFINITIONS</small>

    "benefited from drug trafficking": s.1(3).

    "drug trafficking, drug trafficking offence": s.38.

G<small>ENERAL</small> N<small>OTE</small>

    This section provides for the disclosure of information kept on the Land Register, on application made by a police officer not below the rank of superintendent, a Crown Prosecutor, an officer of the Customs and Excise not below the rank of senior executive officer, or a receiver appointed under ss.8 to 11 of the Act (which relate to restraint orders, charging orders, and the enforcement of confiscation orders). The application may relate either to a specified person (who will normally be a defendant or a recipient of a gift caught by the Act) or to specified property, and must be accompanied by the appropriate certificate, in accordance with either s.33(3)(*b*) or (if the application is made by a receiver), s.33(4)(*b*). The Chief Registrar is bound to comply with the application.

Drug administration kits etc.

Prohibition of supply etc. of articles for administering or preparing controlled drugs

34.—(1) After section 9 of the Misuse of Drugs Act 1971 there is inserted the following section—

"Prohibition of supply etc. of articles for administering or preparing controlled drugs

9A.—(1) A person who supplies or offers to supply any article which may be used or adapted to be used (whether by itself or in combination with another article or other articles) in the administration by any person of a controlled drug to himself or another, believing that the article (or the article as adapted) is to be so used in circumstances where the administration is unlawful, is guilty of an offence.

(2) It is not an offence under subsection (1) above to supply or offer to supply a hypodermic syringe, or any part of one.

(3) A person who supplies or offers to supply any article which may be used to prepare a controlled drug for administration by any person to himself or another believing that the article is to be so used in circumstances where the administration is unlawful is guilty of an offence.

(4) For the purposes of this section, any administration of a controlled drug is unlawful except—

(*a*) the administration by any person of a controlled drug to another in circumstances where the administration of the drug is not unlawful under section 4(1) of this Act, or

(*a*) the administration by any person of a controlled drug to himself in circumstances where having the controlled drug in his possession is not unlawful under section 5(1) of this Act.

(5) In this section, references to administration by any person of a controlled drug to himself include a reference to his administering it to himself with the assistance of another".

(2) In Schedule 4 to that Act, after the entry relating to section 9 there is inserted—

"Section 9A.	Prohibition of supply etc. of articles for admininstering or preparing controlled drugs.	Summary	—	—	—	6 months or level 5 on the standard scale, or both."

GENERAL NOTE

This section creates two new summary offences under Misuse of Drugs Act 1971. The first consists of supplying or offering to supply articles (other than a hypodermic syringe) for the purpose of administering a controlled drug, where the administration of the drug will be unlawful, and the second of supplying or offering to supply articles to be used in the preparation of a controlled drug for unlawful administration. These offences are not drug trafficking offences for the purpose of this Act. Misuse of Drugs Act 1971 generally penalises the possession of a drug, rather than the administration: presumably, the administration of a drug will be unlawful for the purpose of this section when its possession is unlawful.

Miscellaneous and Supplemental

Power to appoint additional assistant commissioner

35. In section 2 of the Metropolitan Police Act 1856 (power to appoint two assistant commissioners of police for the metropolis, increased to five by the Metropolitan Police Act 1933) for the word "two" there is substituted "six"; and the Metropolitan Police Act 1933 is repealed.

GENERAL NOTE
This section has no obvious connection with anything else in the Act.

Drug trafficking offences to be serious arrestable offences

36. In section 116(2) of the Police and Criminal Evidence Act 1984 (arrestable offences that are always serious) after paragraph (*a*) there is inserted—
> "(*aa*) any of the offences mentioned in paragraphs (*a*) to (*d*) of the definition of "drug trafficking offence" in section 38(1) of the Drug Trafficking Offences Act 1986".

GENERAL NOTE
This section adds any offence which is a drug trafficking offence for the purpose of s.38, to the list of "serious arrestable offences" in Police and Criminal Evidence Act 1984, s.116. This is relevant in particular for the purposes of ss.4 (road checks), 8 (search warrants), and 42 and 43 (continued detention of arrested persons) of Police and Criminal Evidence Act 1984.

Expenses

37. There shall be paid out of money provided by Parliament any increase attributable to this Act in the sums payable out of money so provided under any other Act.

General interpretation

38.—(1) In this Act—
> "authorised government department" means a government department which is an authorised department for the purposes of the Crown Proceedings Act 1947;
>
> "constable" includes a person commissioned by the Commissioners of Customs and Excise;
>
> "corresponding law" has the same meaning as in the Misuse of Drugs Act 1971;
>
> "drug trafficking" means doing or being concerned in any of the following, whether in England and Wales or elsewhere—
>> (*a*) producing or supplying a controlled drug where the production or supply contravenes section 4(1) of the Misuse of Drugs Act 1971 or a corresponding law;
>>
>> (*b*) transporting or storing a controlled drug where possession of the drug contravenes section 5(1) of that Act or a corresponding law;
>>
>> (*c*) importing or exporting a controlled drug where the importation or exportation is prohibited by section 3(1) of that Act or a corresponding law;
>
> and includes a person doing the following, whether in England and Wales, or elsewhere, that is entering into or being otherwise concerned in an arrangement whereby—
>> (i) the retention or control by or on behalf of another person of the other person's proceeds of drug trafficking is facilitated, or
>>
>> (ii) the proceeds of drug trafficking by another person are used to secure that funds are placed at the other person's disposal or are used for the other person's benefit to acquire property by way of investment;

"drug trafficking offence" means any of the following—

(*a*) an offence under section 4(2) or (3) or 5(3) of the Misuse of Drugs Act 1971 (production, supply and possession for supply of controlled drugs);

(*b*) an offence under section 20 of that Act (assisting in or inducing commission outside United Kingdom of offence punishable under a corresponding law);

(*c*) an offence under—

  (i) section 50(2) or (3) of the Customs and Excise Management Act 1979 (improper importation),

  (ii) section 68(2) of that Act (exportation), or

  (iii) section 170 of that Act (fraudulent evasion),

in connection with a prohibition or restriction on importation or exportation having effect by virtue of section 3 of the Misuse of Drugs Act 1971;

(*d*) an offence under section 24 of this Act;

(*e*) an offence under section 1 of the Criminal Law Act 1977 of conspiracy to commit any of the offences in paragraphs (*a*) to (*d*) above;

(*f*) an offence under section 1 of the Criminal Attempts Act 1981 of attempting to commit any of those offences;

(*g*) an offence of inciting another to commit any of those offences, whether under section 19 of the Misuse of Drugs Act 1971 or at common law; and

(*h*) aiding, abetting, counselling or procuring the commission of any of those offences;

"interest", in relation to property, includes right;

"property" includes money and all other property, real or personal, heritable or moveable, including things in action and other intangible or incorporeal property.

(2) The expressions listed in the left hand column below are respectively defined or (as the case may be) fall to be construed in accordance with the provisions of this Act listed in the right hand column in relation to those expressions.

Expression	*Relevant provision*
Benefited from drug trafficking	Section 1(3)
Charging order	Section 9(2)
Confiscation order	Section 1(8)
Dealing with property	Section 8(7)
Defendant	Section 1(8)
Gift caught by this Act	Section 5(9)
Making a gift	Section 5(10)
Proceeds of drug trafficking	Section 2(1)(*a*)
Realisable property	Section 5(1)
Restraint order	Section 8(1)
Value of gift, payment or reward	Section 5
Value of proceeds of drug trafficking	Section 2(1)(*b*)
Value of property	Section 5(4).

(3) This Act applies to property whether it is situated in England and Wales or elsewhere.

(4) References in this Act to offences include a reference to offences committed before the commencement of section 1 of this Act; but nothing in this Act imposes any duty or confers any power on any court in or in connection with proceedings against a person for a drug trafficking offence instituted before the commencement of that section.

(5) References in this Act to anything received in connection with drug trafficking include a reference to anything received both in that connection and in some other connection.

(6) The following provisions shall have effect for the interpretation of this Act.

(7) Property is held by any person if he holds any interest in it.

(8) References to property held by a person include a reference to property vested in his trustee in bankruptcy, permanent or interim trustee within the meaning of the Bankruptcy (Scotland) Act 1985 or liquidator.

(9) References to an interest held by a person beneficially in property include a reference to an interest which would be held by him beneficially if the property were not so vested.

(10) Property is tranferred by one person to another if the first person transfers or grants to the other any interest in the property.

(11) Proceedings for an offence are instituted in England and Wales—

(*a*) when a justice of the peace issues a summons or warrant under section 1 of the Magistrates' Courts Act 1980 in respect of the offence,

(*b*) when a person is charged with the offence after being taken into custody without a warrant,

(*c*) when a bill of indictment is preferred under section 2 of the Administration of Justice (Miscellaneous Provisions) Act 1933 in a case falling within paragraph (*b*) of subsection (2) of that section;

and where the application of this subsection would result in there being more than one time for the institution of proceedings, they shall be taken to have been instituted at the earliest of those times.

(12) Proceedings in England and Wales for an offence are concluded on the occurrence of one of the following events—

(*a*) the discontinuance of the proceedings;

(*b*) the acquittal of the defendant;

(*c*) the quashing of his conviction for the offence;

(*d*) the grant of Her Majesty's pardon in respect of his conviction for the offence;

(*e*) the court sentencing or otherwise dealing with him in respect of his conviction for the offence without having made a confiscation order; and

(*f*) the satisfaction of a confiscation order made in the proceedings (whether by payment of the amount due under the order or by the defendant serving imprisonment in default).

(13) An order is subject to appeal so long as an appeal or further appeal is pending against the order or (if it was made on a conviction) against the conviction; and for this purpose an appeal or further appeal shall be treated as pending (where one is competent but has not been brought) until the expiration of the time for bringing that appeal.

Minor amendments

39.—(1) Section 28 of the Bankruptcy Act 1914 (effect of order of discharge) shall have effect as if amounts payable under confiscation orders were debts excepted under subsection (1)(*a*) of that section.

(2) In section 49(1)(*g*) of the Land Registration Act 1925 (protection of certain interests by notice) after "Charging Orders Act 1979" there is inserted "or the Drug Trafficking Offences Act 1986".

(3) In section 1(2)(*a*) of the Rehabilitation of Offenders Act 1974 (failure to pay fines etc. not to prevent person becoming rehabilitated) the reference to a fine or other sum adjudged to be paid by or imposed

on a conviction does not include a reference to an amount payable under a confiscation order.

(4) After subsection (4) of section 18 of the Civil Jurisdiction and Judgments Act 1982 there is inserted the following subsection—

"(4A) This section does not apply as respects the enforcement in Scotland of orders made by the High Court in England and Wales under or for the purposes of the Drug Trafficking Offences Act 1986."

(5) Section 281(4) of the Insolvency Act 1986 (discharge of bankrupt not to release him from liabilities in respect of fines, etc.) shall have effect as if the reference to a fine included a reference to a confiscation order.

(6) Section 55(2) of the Bankruptcy (Scotland) Act 1985 (discharge of debtor not to release him from liabilities in respect of fines etc.) shall have effect as if the reference to a fine included a reference to a confiscation order.

Short title, commencement and extent

40.—(1) This Act may be cited as the Drug Trafficking Offences Act 1986.

(2) This Act, except section 35 (which comes into force on the day on which this Act is passed), shall come into force on such day as the Secretary of State may by order made by statutory instument appoint and different days may be appointed for different provisions and for different purposes.

(3) Subject to subsections (4) and (5) below, this Act extends to England and Wales only.

(4) This Act has effect in Scotland as follows—

    (*a*) sections 7(4), 8 (but not subsection (8) or (9)), 11, 12 and 30 (but not subsection (10), (11) or (12)) extend also to Scotland, but only as provided by sections 20 and 21 of this Act;

    (*b*) section 7(3);

        section 8(8) and (9);

        section 13;

        sections 15 to 17;

        section 18(1);

        section 24(3)(*a*);

        sections 27 to 29;

        section 30(10), (11) and (12);

        section 34;

        section 38, so far as relating to other provisions of this Act extending to Scotland;

        section 39(3), (4) and (6); and

        this section, so far as relating to other provisions of this Act extending to Scotland,

    extend also to Scotland;

    (*c*) sections 20 to 23 extend to Scotland only.

(5) Section 34 extends also to Northern Ireland.

DISABLED PERSONS (SERVICES, CONSULTATION AND REPRESENTATION) ACT 1986 *

(1986 c. 33)

An Act to provide for the improvement of the effectiveness of, and the co-ordination of resources in, the provision of services for people with mental or physical handicap and for people with mental illness; to make further provision for the assessment of the needs of such people; to establish further consultative processes and representational rights for such people; and for connected purposes.

[8th July 1986]

GENERAL NOTE

The Disabled Persons (Services, Consultation and Representation) Bill was a Private Member's measure introduced by Mr. Tom Clarke, the Labour M.P. for Monklands West. The Government's proposals for amendments to the Bill were the subject of a public

---

* Annotations by Richard M. Jones M.A., Solicitor, C.Q.S.W., Assistant Director of Social Services, Mid Glamorgan County Council.

consultation exercise. The Government's approach to the Bill can be best summarised by the following extract from its consultation paper: "it could provide a basis for a useful if modest development of the present legislative basis on which services for disabled people are provided." Although the Act is not as radical as Mr. Clarke hoped for (H.C., Vol. 95, No. 91, col. 341), by improving the rights of disabled people by enabling them to have a greater say in the provision of services and by clarifying the obligations of local authorities to assess the needs of disabled persons it has made a significant addition to the body of law that has been established by two other Acts which started their Parliamentary lives as Private Members' measures, the Chronically Sick and Disabled Persons Act 1970 and the Disabled Persons Act 1981.

COMMENCEMENT AND EXTENT
See s.18.

PARLIAMENTARY DEBATES
Hansard: H.C. Vol. 89, col. 1348; Vol. 100, col. 1306; H.L. Vol. 473, col. 785; Vol. 474, col. 1221; Vol. 476, col. 956; Vol. 477, cols. 573 and 760.
The Bill was considered by Standing Committee C on January 29 to February 5, 1986.

PART I

REPRESENTATION AND ASSESSMENT

Appointment of authorised representatives of disabled persons

1.—(1) In this Act "authorised representative", in relation to a disabled person, means a person for the time being appointed by or on behalf of that disabled person (in accordance with regulations made under this section) to act as his authorised representative for the purposes of this Act.

(2) The Secretary of State may by regulations make provision with respect to the appointment of persons to act as the authorised representatives of disabled persons, including provision—
   (*a*) for the manner in which the appointment of a person as an authorised representative is to be made; and
   (*b*) for any such appointment to be notified to the relevant local authority (as defined in the regulations) if made otherwise than by that authority.

(3) Any such regulations—
   (*a*) may provide for the parent or guardian of a disabled person under the age of 16 to appoint himself or some other person as the authorised representative of the disabled person (but shall not permit a person under that age himself to appoint a person as his authorised representative);
   (*b*) may provide for the appointment of a person as the authorised representative of a disabled person who is a child in the care of a local authority to be made by that authority in such circumstances as may be specified in the regulations;
   (*c*) may, in accordance with subsection (4), provide for the appointment of a person as the authorised representative of a disabled person to be made by, or under arrangements made by, a local authority in a case where the disabled person appears to the authority to be unable to appoint a person as his authorised representative by reason of any mental or physical incapacity;
   (*d*) may contain such incidental or supplementary provisions as the Secretary of State thinks fit.

(4) Regulations under paragraph (*c*) of subsection (3) may make provision—

(*a*) for requiring a local authority, for the purpose of enabling them to determine whether a disabled person is unable to appoint a person as his authorised representative as mentioned in that paragraph, to obtain the opinion of a registered medical practitioner;

(*b*) for authorising a local authority, where they determine that a disabled person is so unable, either—

(i) themselves to appoint a person as the disabled person's authorised representative, or

(ii) to make with any voluntary organisation, person or persons approved by them for the purpose such arrangements as they think fit for such an appointment to be made by the organisation, person or persons concerned;

(*c*) for requiring or authorising a local authority, before determining the question specified in paragraph (*a*), or (as the case may be) before making any appointment of an authorised representative, or any arrangements, in pursuance of paragraph (*b*), to consult any of the following, namely—

(i) a person or persons appointed by them for the purpose, or

(ii) a person or persons falling within any class or description specified in the regulations;

(*d*) for requiring a local authority, in such circumstances as may be specified in the regulations, to review the case of a disabled person whose authorised representative has been appointed in pursuance of paragraph (*b*) (whether by the local authority or under any arrangements made by them) for the purpose of determining whether he is still unable to appoint a person as his authorised representative as mentioned in subsection (3)(*c*).

(5) Subsections (2) to (4) shall apply, with any necessary modifications, in relation to the termination of the appointment of a person as an authorised representative as they apply in relation to the making of such an appointment.

(6) It is hereby declared that any person exercising under Part II of the 1983 Act or Part V of the 1984 Act—

(*a*) the functions of the nearest relative of a disabled person, or

(*b*) the functions of the guardian of a disabled person received into guardianship under that Part of that Act,

may, if appointed as such in accordance with this section, also act as that person's authorised representative.

DEFINITIONS

"disabled person": s.16
"local authority": s.16
"parent": s.16
"guardian": s.16
"voluntary organisation": s.16
"1983 Act": s.16
"1984 Act": s.16

GENERAL NOTE

This section enables regulations to be made to provide for the appointment of authorised representatives by disabled persons or on their behalf. The rights of authorised representatives are set out in ss.2 and 3, below. A person who is the nearest relative or guardian of a mentally disordered person may be appointed as that person's authorised representative.

Subs. (1)

Authorised representative: Who will not be paid or receive expenses out of public funds.

Appointed by . . . that disabled person: A disabled person is not required to appoint an authorised representative.

Subs. (2)
   With respect to the appointment: Or termination of appointment (subs. (5)).

Subs. (3) enables regulations to be made to provide for the appointment of authorised representatives for disabled people who are children or who, because of physical or mental incapacity, are unable to appoint someone themselves. It does not cover the situation of a disabled child who has neither parent nor guardian and who is not in the care of a local authority.

Subs. (4) provides for regulations to set out the procedure that would be followed where a local authority has ascertained that a disabled person is unable to appoint an authorised representative.
   para. (a): Enabling them to determine: After having consulted with other people (para. (*c*)).
   para. (b): Authorising a local authority: "We are not proposing a compulsory duty on local authorities to set up arrangements for appointing representatives for people unable to act. We feel that that should be left to local decision in the light of local priorities", *per* the Minister of State, H.C. Vol. 100, No. 143, col. 1314. The local authority must consult with other persons before taking action under this provision (para. (*c*)).

Rights of authorised representatives of disabled persons

   2.—(1) A local authority shall permit the authorised representative of a disabled person, if so requested by the disabled person—
     (*a*) to act as the representative of the disabled person in connection with the provision by the authority of any services for him in the exercise of any of their functions under the welfare enactments, or
     (*b*) to accompany the disabled person (otherwise than as his representative) to any meeting or interview held by or on behalf of the authority in connection with the provision by them of any such services.
   (2) For the purpose of assisting the authorised representative of a disabled person to do any of the things mentioned in subsection (1)(*a*) and (*b*) a local authority shall, if so requested by the disabled person—
     (*a*) supply to the authorised representative any information, and
     (*b*) make available for his inspection any documents,
that the disabled person would be entitled to require the authority to supply to him or (as the case may be) to make available for his inspection.
   (3) In relation to a disabled person whose authorised representative has been appointed by virtue of subsection (3) of section 1, subsections (1) and (2) above shall each have effect as follows—
     (*a*) if the appointment was made by virtue of subsection (3)(*a*) of that section, the words "the parent or guardian of" shall be inserted after the words "if so requested by"; and
     (*b*) if the appointment was made by virtue of subsection (3)(*b*) or (*c*) of that section, the words "if so requested by the disabled person" shall be omitted.
   (4) A local authority shall not be required by virtue of subsection (1) or (2)—
     (*a*) to permit an authorised representative to be present at any meeting or interview or part of a meeting or interview, or
     (*b*) to supply any information to an authorised representative or to make any documents available for the inspection of an authorised representative,
if the authority are satisfied that to do so would be likely to be harmful to the interests of the disabled person by whom or on whose behalf the representative has been appointed; and in determining that matter the authority shall have regard to any wishes expressed by the disabled person.
   (5) Where a disabled person is residing—
     (*a*) in hospital accommodation provided by the Secretary of State under section 3(1)(*a*) of the 1977 Act or, in Scotland, in

hospital accommodation (other than accommodation at a State hospital) provided by the Secretary of State under section 36(1)(*a*) of the 1978 Act, or

(*b*) in accommodation provided by a local authority under Part III of the 1948 Act or Schedule 8 to the 1977 Act or, in Scotland, under Part IV of the 1968 Act or section 7 of the 1984 Act, or

(*c*) in accommodation provided by a voluntary organisation in accordance with arrangements made by a local authority under section 26 of the 1948 Act or, in Scotland, provided by a voluntary organisation or other persons in accordance with arrangements made by a local authority under section 59(2)(*c*) of the 1968 Act, or

(*d*) in a residential care home within the meaning of Part I of the Registered Homes Act 1984 or, in Scotland, in an establishment (other than accommodation falling within paragraph (*c*) above) registered under section 61 of the 1968 Act, or

(*e*) at any place specified by a person having the guardianship of the disabled person under Part II of the 1983 Act or Part V of the 1984 Act,

the disabled person's authorised representative may at any reasonable time visit him there and interview him in private.

(6) In paragraph (*c*) of subsection (5) "voluntary organisation" in relation to England and Wales includes a housing association within the meaning of the Housing Associations Act 1985.

(7) The Secretary of State may, after consulting such bodies representing health authorities or local authorities as appear to him to be appropriate and such other bodies as appear to him to be concerned, provide by order for any of the preceding provisions of this section to have effect (with such modifications as may be prescribed by the order) in relation to—

(*a*) the provision of services by health authorities in the exercise of such of their functions under the 1977 Act or the 1978 Act as may be prescribed by the order, or

(*b*) the provision of services by local authorities in the exercise of such of their functions as may be so prescribed.

(8) An order under subsection (7) may provide for any provision of regulations made under section 1 to have effect for the purposes of the order with such modifications as may be prescribed by the order, and in that event the reference in subsection (1) of that section to regulations made under that section shall be read as a reference to any such regulations as they have effect in accordance with the order.

(9) In subsection (7)—
"health authority"—

(*a*) in relation to England and Wales, has the meaning given by section 128(1) of the 1977 Act, and

(*b*) in relation to Scotland, means a Health Board; and
"local authority"—

(*a*) in relation to England and Wales, has the meaning given by section 270(1) of the Local Government Act 1972; and

(*b*) in relation to Scotland, means a regional, islands or district council.

Definitions
"authorised representative": s.16
"disabled person": s.16
"services": s.16
"welfare enactments": s.16
"parent": s.16

"guardian": s.16
"hospital": s.16
"1977 Act": s.16
"State hospital": s.16
"1978 Act": s.16
"1948 Act": s.16
"1968 Act": s.16
"1984 Act": s.16
"voluntary organisation": s.16
"1983 Act": s.16

GENERAL NOTE

This section establishes the right of an authorised representative to act on behalf of a disabled person in connection with services to be provided for the disabled person by social services departments. The authorised representative can either directly act for the disabled person or can accompany him to meetings and interviews. He also has the right to receive any information or documentation that the disabled person would be entitled to have. The local authority can prevent the authorised representative from attending interviews or meetings or from receiving documentation or information if the authority considers that such an involvement would be likely to be harmful to the interests of the disabled person. Where the disabled person is residing in accommodation specified in subs. (5), the authorised person may visit him there and interview him in private.

This section also provides for the rights of authorised representatives to be extended to take in services provided by health authorities and other services provided by local authorities.

Subs. (1)
Local authority: Is defined in subs. (9).
Shall permit: Subject to subs. (4).
Requested: If the authorised representative has been appointed on behalf of the disabled person under s.1(3), above, this provision should be read as amended by subs. (3).
Act as the representative: And therefore speak for the disabled person.
Accompany: To offer support and advice to the disabled person.

Subs. (4)
Harmful to the interests of the disabled person: This provision could be used to prevent the involvement of an authorised representative who was thought to be likely to exploit the disabled person.

Subs. (5)
para. (c): voluntary organisation: see subs. (6).

Subs. (7)
Health authority: Is defined in subs. (9).

Assessment by local authorities of needs of disabled persons

3.—(1) Where—
   (a) on any assessment carried out by them in pursuance of any provision of this Act, or
   (b) on any other occasion,
it falls to a local authority to decide whether the needs of a disabled person call for the provision by the authority (in accordance with any of the welfare enactments) of any statutory services for that person, the authority shall afford an opportunity to the disabled person or his authorised representative to make, within such reasonable period as the authority may allow for the purpose, representations to an officer of the authority as to any needs of the disabled person calling for the provision by the authority (in accordance with any of those enactments) of any statutory services for him.

(2) Where any such representations have been made to a local authority in accordance with subsection (1) or the period mentioned in that subsection has expired without any such representations being made, and the authority have reached a decision on the question referred to in that

subsection (having taken into account any representations made as mentioned above), the authority shall, if so requested by the disabled person or his authorised representative, supply the person making the request with a written statement—

(*a*) either specifying—
    (i) any needs of the disabled person which in the opinion of the authority call for the provision by them of any statutory services, and
    (ii) in the case of each such need, the statutory services that they propose to provide to meet that need.
    or stating that, in their opinion, the disabled person has no needs calling for the provision by them of any such services; and
(*b*) giving an explanation of their decision; and
(*c*) containing particulars of the right of the disabled person or his authorised representative to make representations with respect to the statement under subsection (4).

(3) Where the local authority do not propose to provide any statutory services to meet a particular need identified in any representations under subsection (1), any statement supplied under subsection (2) must state that fact together with the reasons why the authority do not propose to provide any such services.

(4) If the disabled person or his authorised representative is dissatisfied with any matter included in the statement supplied under subsection (2), that person may, within such reasonable period as the authority may allow for the purpose, make representations to an officer of the authority with respect to that matter.

(5) Where any such representations have been made to the authority in accordance with subsection (4), the authority shall—

(*a*) consider (or, as the case may be, reconsider) whether any, and (if so) what, statutory services should be provided by them for the disabled person to meet any need identified in the representations; and
(*b*) inform the disabled person or his authorised representative in writing of their decision on that question and their reasons for that decision.

(6) Where—

(*a*) the disabled person or his authorised representative is unable to communicate, or (as the case may be) be communicated with, orally or in writing (or in each of those ways) by reason of any mental or physical incapacity, or
(*b*) both of those persons are in that position (whether by reason of the same incapacity or not),

the local authority shall provide such services as, in their opinion, are necessary to ensure that any such incapacity does not—

(i) prevent the authority from discharging their functions under this section in relation to the disabled person, or
(ii) prevent the making of representations under this section by or on behalf of that person.

(7) In determining whether they are required to provide any services under subsection (6) to meet any need of the disabled person or his authorised representative, and (if so) what those services should be, the local authority shall have regard to any views expressed by either of those persons as to the necessity for any such services or (as appropriate) to any views so expressed as to the services which should be so provided.

(8) In this section "representations" means representations made orally or in writing (or both).

DEFINITIONS
"local authority": s.16
"disabled person": s.16
"welfare enactments": s.16
"statutory services": s.16
"authorised representative": s.16

GENERAL NOTE

This section requires local authorities, when assessing a disabled person's need for social services, to provide an opportunity for the disabled person, or his authorised representative, to make representations on their perception of the need for such services. After the assessment has been made the local authority can be requested by the disabled person or his representative to supply a statement giving an explanation of the basis upon which the assessment has been made which would include an explanation of why a particular need identified by the disabled person or his representative cannot be met.

On receipt of the statement the disabled person or his representative is given an opportunity to make further representations. The local authority must consider the further representations and inform the disabled person or his representative of the outcome and the reasons for the decision.

The local authority must provide appropriate interpretation services for disabled people, or their representatives, who are unable to communicate normally because of their disability and who are thereby prevented from exercising their rights under this section.

When assessing the needs of a disabled person the local authority must take into account the ability of that person's care; see s.8, below.

Subs. (1)
Representations: see subs. (8).

Subs. (2) "requires the statement to specify the needs of the disabled person as well as the services to meet them. This . . . will prove useful if there is a dispute as to how the needs should be met—for example the common choice between a stairlift or downstairs adaptations on which there is often disagreement between disabled people and the social services", *per* the Minister of State, H.C. Vol. 100, No. 143, col. 1318.

If so requested: the disabled person or his authorised representative does not have an automatic right to receive a written statement.

Needs . . . which . . . call for the provision of statutory services: For the position where the local authority does not propose to provide a service for a need identified by the disabled person; see subs. (3).

Subs. (4)
Representations: see subs. (8).

Subs. (6) provides for interpretation services to be provided for disabled people and their authorised representatives who are unable to communicate normally by reason of mental or physical incapacity and who would otherwise be prevented from exercising their rights under this section. In appropriate circumstances local authorities are required to provide interpretation services for people who cannot communicate in English; see s.71 of the Race Relations Act 1976.

Subs. (7): "In determining both the need for communication assistance and the nature of that assistance [under subs. (6)] the local authority must have regard to the views expressed by the disabled person or his representative, who are, of course, uniquely qualified to identify what is required", *per* the Minister of State, H.C. Vol. 11, No. 143, col. 1318.

Services under s.2 of the 1970 Act: duty to consider needs of disabled persons

4. When requested to do so by—
    (*a*) a disabled person.
    (*b*) his authorised representative, or
    (*c*) any person who provides care for him in the circumstances mentioned in section 8,
a local authority shall decide whether the needs of the disabled person call for the provision by the authority of any services in accordance with section 2(1) of the 1970 Act (provision of welfare services).

DEFINITIONS
"disabled person": s.16
"authorised representative": s.16
"local authority": s.16
"services": s.16

GENERAL NOTE
This section removes some uncertainty about the responsibilities of local authorities by placing a clear duty on local social services authorities to decide whether the needs of a disabled person require the provision of welfare services under s.2 of the Chronically Sick and Disabled Persons Act 1970. A local authority will be required to make this decision when requested to do so by a disabled person, his authorised representative or carer. The request for a decision will trigger the procedure set out in s.3 above.

Disabled persons leaving special education

5.—(1) Where—
    (a) a local education authority have made a statement under section 7 of the Education Act 1981 (statement of child's educational needs) in respect of a child under the age of 14, and
    (b) the statement is still maintained by the authority at whichever is the earlier of the following times, namely—
        (i) the time when they institute the first annual review of the statement following the child's fourteenth birthday, and
        (ii) any time falling after that birthday when they institute a re-assessment of his educational needs,
the authority shall at that time require the appropriate officer to give to the authority his opinion as to whether the child is or is not a disabled person.

(2) Where—
    (a) a local education authority make any such statement in respect of a child after he has attained the age of 14, or
    (b) a local education authority maintain any such statement in respect of a child in whose case the appropriate officer has, in pursuance of subsection (1), given his opinion that the child is not a disabled person, but the authority have become aware of a significant change in the mental or physical condition of the child giving them reason to believe that he may now be a disabled person.
the authority shall, at the time of making the statement or (as the case may be) of becoming aware of that change, require the appropriate officer to give to the authority his opinion as to whether the child is or is not a disabled person.

(3) Where an opinion has in pursuance of subsection (1) or (2) been given in the case of a child that he is a disabled person and it subsequently appears to the responsible authority—
    (a) that the child will cease to receive full-time education at school on a particular date and will not subsequently be receiving full-time education at a further education establishment, or
    (b) that the child will cease to receive full-time education at such an establishment on a particular date.
and (in either case) that he will be under the age of 19 on the relevant date, the authority shall give to the appropriate officer written notification for the purposes of subsection (5) of the date referred to in paragraph (a) or (b); and any such notification shall be given not later than the relevant date and not earlier than four months before that date.
In this subsection "the relevant date" means the date falling 8 months before the date referred to in paragraph (a) or (b) above.

(4) If at any time it appears to a local education authority—

(*a*) that a person has on a particular date ceased to receive full-time education as mentioned in paragraph (*a*) or (*b*) of subsection (3) or will cease to do so on a particular date falling less that 8 months after that time, and

(*b*) that no notification of that date has been given to the appropriate officer under that subsection with respect to that person, but

(*c*) that, had that or any other authority (as the responsible authority for the time being) been aware of his intentions 8 months or more before that date, they would have been required to give notification of that date under that subsection with respect to him,

that authority shall, as soon as is reasonably practicable, give to the appropriate officer written notification for the purposes of subsection (5) of that date.

(5) When the appropriate officer receives a notification given with respect to any person under subsection (3) or (4), he shall (subject to subsections (6) and (7)) make arrangements for the local authority of which he is an officer to carry out an assessment of the needs of that person with respect to the provision by that authority of any statutory services for that person in accordance with any of the welfare enactments, and any such assessment shall be carried out—

(*a*) in the case of a notification under subsection (3), not later than the end of the period of 5 months beginning with the date of receipt of the notification, or

(*b*) in the case of a notification under subsection (4), before the date specified in the notification, if reasonably practicable, and in any event not later than the end of the period referred to in paragraph (*a*) above.

(6) If—

(*a*) a notification has been given to the appropriate officer with respect to any person under subsection (3) or (4), but

(*b*) it subsequently appears to a local education authority that that person will be receiving full-time education (whether at school or at a further education establishment) at a time later than the date specified in the notification,

the authority shall give written notification of the relevant facts to that officer as soon as is reasonably practicable; and on receiving any such notification that officer shall cease to be required under subsection (5) to make arrangements for the assessment of the needs of the person in question (but without prejudice to the operation of that subsection in relation to any further notification given with respect to that person under subsection (3) or (4)).

(7) Nothing in subsection (5) shall require the appropriate officer to make arrangements for the assessment of the needs of a person—

(*a*) if, having attained the age of 16, he has requested that such arrangements should not be made under that subsection, or

(*b*) if, being under that age, his parent or guardian has made such a request.

(8) Regulations under paragraph 4 of Schedule 1 to the Education Act 1981 (assessments and statements of special educational needs) may, in relation to the transfer of statements made under section 7 of that Act, make such provision as appears to the Secretary of State to be necessary or expedient in connection with the preceding provisions of this section.

(9) In this section—

"the appropriate officer", in relation to the child or person referred to in the provision of this section in question, means such officer as may be appointed for the purposes of this section by the local authority for the area in which that child or person is for the time being ordinarily resident;

"child" means a person of compulsory school age or a person who has attained that age but not the age of 19 and is registered as a pupil at a school or a further education establishment; and

"the responsible authority"—

(*a*) in relation to a child at school, means the local education authority who are responsible for the child for the purposes of the Education Act 1981;

(*b*) in relation to a child at a further education establishment, means the local education authority who were responsible for the child immediately before he ceased to receive full-time education at school;

in each case whether any such opinion as is mentioned in subsection (3) was given to that authority or not;

and other expressions used in this section and in the Education Act 1944 (and not defined in this Act) have the same meaning in this section as in that Act.

(10) This section applies to England and Wales only.

DEFINITIONS
"disabled person": s.16
"local authority": s.16
"statutory services": s.16
"welfare enactments": s.16
"parent": s.16
"guardian": s.16
"local authority": s.16

GENERAL NOTE
This section, which only applies in England and Wales, is aimed at facilitating social services planning for children with special education needs who are assessed as being disabled. It requires local education authorities to seek an assessment as to whether a child is or is not a disabled person in his or her fifteenth year. If the child is assessed as being disabled the education authority must notify the appropriate officer of the date when the child will cease to receive full time education. The appropriate officer will then arrange for the social services department to carry out an assessment of the child's needs. If it subsequently appears to the education authority that the child will be receiving full time education at a time later than that specified in the notification to the appropriate officer he is relieved of his duty to arrange for an assessment to be made. The appropriate officer is also not required to arrange for an assessment if the child's parents or the child himself, if he is over sixteen, request that an assessment be not made.

Subs. (1) requires the education authority to seek an opinion as to whether a child is disabled or not during the child's fifteenth year either as part of the mandatory reassessment of the first annual review or the statement of the child's educational needs, whichever is the sooner.

Subs. (2) requires the education authority to seek similar advice in respect of a child over fourteen who has been made subject to a statement of his educational needs for the first time and to seek further advice in respect of a child whose physical or mental condition has changed and for whom revised advice may be appropriate.

Subs. (3) requires the education authority to notify the appropriate officer of the cessation of full time education by a disabled child eight months before the relevant date as long as the child is under nineteen on the day eight months prior to his leaving date.

Under the age of 19: "The Government have no wish to deprive disabled young people who stay on in full-time education after the age of nineteen of rights which they would have enjoyed had they decided to leave full time education at nineteen. We shall make that clear in guidance to local education authorities and social services departments", *per* the Minister of State, H.C. Vol. 100, No. 143, col. 1328. The reason for this restriction is that full time schooling under the Education Act 1944 and the making of statements for those at school under the Education Act 1981 is geared to the maximum age of nineteen years.

Subs. (4) provides that where a child decides to leave full time education at short notice, the education authority shall notify the appropriate officer as soon as possible. It covers the case where a child moves to the area of a new education authority and ensures that that authority gives notice to the new appropriate officer.

Subs. (5) places a duty on the appropriate officer to arrange for an assessment of the child to be carried out within five months of the date of the receipt of the notification by the education authority or, in cases of late notification under subs. (4), before the child leaves full time education if that is practicable, but in any event within five months.

Subs. (6) provides that where a child changes his mind and decides not to leave full time education as anticipated, the education authority must notify the appropriate officer as soon as possible. The appropriate officer will then not be required to complete the arrangements for the assessment until a further notification giving a revised leaving date is received.

Subs. (9)
Compulsory school age: Five to Sixteen (Education Act 1944, s.35).

Review of expected leaving dates from full-time education of disabled persons

6.—(1) A local education authority shall for the purposes of section 5 above keep under review the dates when the following children are expected to cease to receive full-time education at school or (as the case may be) at a further education establishment, namely—

(*a*) children for whom that authority are responsible for the purposes of the Education Act 1981 and in the case of each of whom an opinion has been given in pursuance of subsection (1) or (2) of section 5 above that he is a disabled person (whether it was given to that authority or not); and

(*b*) children at further education establishments for whom that authority were so responsible immediately before they ceased to receive full-time education at school and in the case of each of whom any such opinion had been given as mentioned in paragraph (*a*).

(2) Subsection (9) of section 5 shall have effect for the purposes of this section as it has effect for the purposes of that section.

DEFINITIONS
"child": s.16
"disabled person": s.16

GENERAL NOTE
This section requires education authorities to establish a procedure which keeps disabled children under review and thus permits them to have available the necessary information to enable them to comply with the notification requirements of s.5.

Persons discharged from hospital

7.—(1) When a person is to be discharged from a hospital after having received medical treatment for mental disorder as an in-patient for a continuous period of not less than 6 months ending with the date on which he is to be discharged, the managers of the hospital shall give written notification of that date—

(*a*) to the health authority in whose district or area it appears to the managers that that person is likely to reside after his discharge (unless the managers are that authority),

(*b*) to the local authority in whose area it appears to them that that person is likely then to reside, and

(*c*) in the case of a person under the relevant age on that date, to the appropriate officer or authority, as soon as is reasonably practicable after that date is known to the managers.

(2) Where—

    (a) a person liable to be detained under the 1983 Act or the 1984 Act is discharged from a hospital in pursuance of an order for his immediate discharge made by a Mental Health Review Tribunal or, in Scotland, by the Mental Welfare Commission for Scotland or by the sheriff, and

    (b) he is so discharged after having received medical treatment for mental disorder as an in-patient for a continuous period of not less than 6 months ending with the date of his discharge,

the managers of the hospital shall give written notification of that person's discharge in accordance with paragraphs (a), (b), and (c) of subsection (1) above as soon as is reasonably practicable.

(3) Where—

    (a) a health authority receive a notification given with respect to a person under subsection (1) or (2), or

    (b) the managers of a hospital from which a person is to be, or is, discharged as mentioned in subsection (1) or (2) are the health authority referred to in subsection (1)(a),

that authority shall (subject to subsection (7)) make arrangements for an assessment of the needs of that person with respect to the provision of any services under the 1977 Act or 1978 Act which the Secretary of State is under a duty to provide; and in making any such arrangements a health authority falling within paragraph (a) above shall consult the managers of the hospital in question.

(4) Where a local authority receive a notification given with respect to a person under subsection (1) or (2), the authority shall (subject to subsection (7)) make arrangements for an assessment of the needs of that person with respect to the provision of any services under any of the welfare enactments.

(5) A health authority and a local authority who are by virtue of subsections (3) and (4) each required to make arrangements for an assessment of the needs of a particular person shall co-operate with each other in the making of those arrangements.

(6) Any assessment for which arrangements are required to be made by virtue of subsection (3) or (4) shall be carried out—

    (a) where the notification in question was given under subsection (1), not later than the date mentioned in that subsection, or

    (b) where the notification in question was given under subsection (2), as soon as is reasonably practicable after receipt of the notification.

(7) A health authority or a local authority shall not be required to make arrangements for an assessment of the needs of a person by virtue of subsection (3) or (4) if that person has requested them not to make any such arrangements.

(8) Nothing in this section shall apply in relation to a person who is being discharged from a hospital for the purpose of being transferred to another hospital in which he will be an in-patient (whether or not he will be receiving medical treatment for mental disorder); but any reference in subsection (1) or (2) to a person's having received medical treatment for mental disorder as an in-patient for the period mentioned in that subsection is a reference to his having received such treatment for that period as an in-patient in one or more hospitals (any interruption of that period attributable to his being transferred between hospitals being disregarded).

(9) In this section—

    "the appropriate officer or authority" means—

        (a) where the local authority referred to in subsection 1(a) are a local education authority or, in Scotland, an education authority, such officer discharging functions of that authority in their capacity as a local education authority or (as the case may be) education authority as may be appointed by them for the purposes of this section;

(b) where, in England and Wales, that local authority are not a local education authority, the Inner London Education Authority;

"health authority"—

(a) in relation to England and Wales, means a District Health Authority, and

(b) in relation to Scotland, means a Health Board;

"the managers"—

(a) in relation to—

(i) a health service hospital within the meaning of the 1977 Act (other than a special hospital),

(ii) a health service hospital within the meaning of the 1978 Act (other than a State hospital), or

(iii) any accommodation provided by a local authority and used as a hospital by or on behalf of the Secretary of State under the 1977 Act,

means the District Health Authority or special health authority, or (as the case may be) the Health Board who are responsible for the administration of the hospital;

(b) in relation to a special hospital, means the Secretary of State;

(c) in relation to a State hospital, means a State Hospital Management Committee constituted by the Secretary of State to manage the hospital on his behalf or (where no such committee has been constituted) the Secretary of State; and

(d) in relation to any other hospital, means the persons for the time being having the management of the hospital;

"medical treatment"—

(a) in relation to England and Wales, has the meaning given by section 145(1) of the 1983 Act; and

(b) in relation to Scotland, has the meaning given by section 125(1) of the 1984 Act; and

"the relevant age"—

(a) in relation to England and Wales, means the age of 19; and

(b) in relation to Scotland, means the age of 18.

DEFINITIONS
"hospital": s.16.
"mental disorder": s.16.
"local authority": s.16.
"the 1983 Act": s.16.
"the 1984 Act": s.16.
"the 1977 Act": s.16.
"the 1978 Act": s.16.
"services": s.16.
"welfare enactments": s.16.
"Health Board": s.16.
"special hospital": s.16.
"State hospital": s.16.

GENERAL NOTE
This section applies to patients who have been receiving hospital treatment for mental disorder for six months or more. It requires the hospital managers to send written

notification of the date of the patient's discharge from hospital to the health authority and the local authority for the area in which the patient is to live. Notification also has to be sent to the local education authority if the patient is under 19. Following notification the local authority and the health authority are required to co-operate in assessing the patient's need for services for which they are responsible. The assessments must be made before the patient is discharged. However, if the patient's discharge follows the order of a Mental Health Review Tribunal or, in Scotland, by the Mental Welfare Commission or the sheriff, the assessment must take place as soon as practicable after discharge. Neither authority is required to make an assessment if the patient has requested them not to make an assessment.

Under s.117 of the Mental Health Act 1983 local authorities are required to co-operate in the provision of after-care services for certain categories of patients who cease to be detained and then leave hospital.

Subs. (1)
Medical treatment: see subs. (9).
Not less than 6 months: The patient need not have been treated in the same hospital during this period; see subs. (8).
The managers; health authority: see subs. (9).
The appropriate officer or authority; relevant age: see subs. (9).

Subs. (3)
Assessment of needs: Which will bring into play s.3, above.

Subs. (5)
Co-operate: "In many cases authorities may wish to undertake joint assessments; but it was not felt right to tie their hands in primary legislation and tie the practical arrangements to a precise formula which may not be credible or operable in all circumstances", *per* Mr. Tom Clarke, H.C. Vol. 100, No. 143, col 1331.

Subs. (6)
Date mentioned in that subsection: Which is the date of the patient's discharge. Where a discharge is properly planned there should be no fear of it being held up by this provision. Note that subs. (7) allows patients to waive their rights to an assessment.

Subs. (8) stops assessments being triggered by transfers between hospitals and also confirms that time spent in different hospitals will be added together for the purposes of the six months mentioned in subs. (1).

Duty of local authority to take into account abilities of carer

8.—(1) Where—
   (*a*) a disabled person is living at home and receiving a substantial amount of care on a regular basis from another person (who is not a person employed to provide such care by any body in the exercise of its functions under any enactment), and
   (*b*) it falls to a local authority to decide whether the disabled person's needs call for the provision by them of any services for him under any of the welfare enactments,
the local authority shall, in deciding that question, have regard to the ability of that other person to continue to provide such care on a regular basis.

(2) Where that other person is unable to communicate, or (as the case may be) be communicated with, orally or in writing (or in each of those ways) by reason of any mental or physical incapacity, the local authority shall provide such services as, in their opinion, are necessary to ensure that any such incapacity does not prevent the authority from being properly informed as to the ability of that person to continue to provide care as mentioned in subsection (1).

(3) Section 3(7) shall apply for the purposes of subsection (2) above as it applies for the purposes of section 3(6), but as if any reference to the disabled person or his authorised representative were a reference to the person mentioned in subsection (2).

DEFINITIONS
"disabled person": s.16
"local authority": s.16
"services": s.16
"welfare enactments": s.16
"authorised representative": s.16

GENERAL NOTE
This section requires social services departments, when assessing the needs of a disabled person who receives a substantial amount of regular care from any person other than an employee of the statutory services, to have regard to the carer's ability to continue to provide that care. It probably does little more than to reflect current local authority practice.

It also requires the local authority to provide an interpretation service if the carer is unable to communicate effectively by reason of mental or physical incapacity. In determining whether such a service is required the local authority is required to take into account any views expressed by the carer (subs. (3)). Also see the note on s.3(6), above.

PART II

INFORMATION AND CONSULTATION

Information

9. In subsection (2)(b) of section 1 of the 1970 Act—
    (a) for the words "any other of those services" there shall be substituted the words "any other service provided by the authority (whether under any such arrangements or not)"; and
    (b) at the end there shall be inserted the words "and of any service provided by any other authority or organisation which in the opinion of the authority is so relevant and of which particulars are in the authority's possession.".

DEFINITIONS
"the 1970 Act": s.16

GENERAL NOTE
This section amends the Chronically Sick and Disabled Persons Act 1970 by extending the scope of the information that a local authority is required to provide to any disabled person who receives any of its services.
Service . . . which . . . is . . . relevant: "The list of what may be included is endless, but would obviously include all the activities of voluntary organisations, transport schemes, leisure opportunities, and I hope also education and employment opportunities. Basic information on benefits should be included as well as all the personal services provided by the Council and the N.H.S.", *per* Baroness Masham, H.L. Vol. 474, No. 92, col.1227.

Co-option to committees etc. of persons representing interests of disabled persons

10. Where any enactment provides for the appointment or co-option to any council, committee or body of one or more persons with special knowledge of the needs of disabled persons, such appointment or co-option shall only be made after consultation with such organisation or organisations of disabled people as may be appropriate in each case.

DEFINITIONS
"disabled person": s.16

GENERAL NOTE
This section provides that where under statute persons with special knowledge of the needs of the disabled are appointed to public bodies or organisations, organisations of disabled persons should be consulted.

Reports to Parliament

11.—(1) The Secretary of State shall annually lay before Parliament a report containing the following information, namely—

(a) such information as the Secretary of State considers appropriate with respect to the development of health and social services in the community for persons suffering from mental illness or mental handicap who are not resident in hospitals;

(b) information with respect to—

   (i) the number of persons receiving treatment for mental illness as in-patients in health service hospitals, and

   (ii) the number of persons receiving treatment for mental handicap as in-patients in such hospitals,

in each case analysed by reference to age and length of stay; and

(c) such other information (if any) as the Secretary of State considers appropriate to be included in the report.

(2) In this section—

"health service hospital"—

    (a) in relation to England and Wales, has the same meaning as in the 1977 Act, except that it does not include a special hospital, and

    (b) in relation to Scotland, has the same meaning as in the 1978 Act, except that it does not include a State hospital; and

"mental handicap" has, in relation to England and Wales, the same meaning as in Group D in Schedule 1 to the Juries Act 1974.

DEFINITIONS
   "hospitals": s.16
   "the 1977 Act": s.16
   "special hospital": s.16
   "the 1978 Act": s.16
   "State hospital": s.16

GENERAL NOTE
This section requires the Secretary of State to make an annual report to Parliament giving information on the development of health and social services in the community for mentally ill and mentally handicapped people; a breakdown of numbers, by age and length of stay, of hospital patients receiving treatment for mental illness and mental handicap; and such other information, if any, as he considers appropriate. It enables "the commitment that I gave in committee to provide information on small units with four beds or under to be met", *per* the Minister of State, H.C. Vol. 95, No. 91, col. 504.

Subs. (2)
Mental handicap: Is defined in Group D in Schedule 1 to the Juries Act 1974 (as amended) as "a state of arrested or incomplete development of mind (not amounting to severe mental handicap) which includes significant impairment of intelligence and social functioning".

PART III

SCOTLAND

Amendment of the 1970 Act and the 1968 Act

12.—(1) In section 29 of the 1970 Act in subsection (2) (which extends the Act to Scotland) for paragraph (a) there shall be substituted the following paragraph—

"(a) any references to functions under section 29 of the National

Assistance Act 1948 shall be construed as references to duties to—

      (i) chronically sick or disabled persons; or

      (ii) persons suffering from mental disorder,

(being persons in need) to whom section 12 of the Social Work (Scotland) Act 1968 applies;".

(2) In section 2 of the 1968 Act (social work committees and functions referred to them) in paragraph (*a*) of subsection (2) after the word "Act" there shall be inserted the words "as read with sections 1 and 2(1) of the Chronically Sick and Disabled Persons Act 1970 and the Disabled Persons (Services, Consultation and Representation) Act 1986".

(3) The foregoing provisions of this section extend to Scotland only.

DEFINITIONS
"the 1970 Act": s.16

GENERAL NOTE
Subs. (1) clarifies the position of mentally disordered persons in Scotland in relation to local authority duties under ss.1 and 2 of the Chronically Sick and Disabled Persons Act 1970. Subs. (2) makes an addition to the list of provisions containing functions which stand referred to the social work committees of regional authorities in Scotland under the Social Work (Scotland) Act 1968.

Disabled persons leaving special education: Scotland

13.—(1) Before an education authority make a report under section 65B(1) of the 1980 Act on a child they shall require the appropriate authority to give an opinion as to whether or not the child is a disabled person.

(2) Where the appropriate authority have given an opinion that the child is a disabled person, the education authority shall make a note of this opinion in the Record kept under section 60(2) of the 1980 Act and in the report made under section 65B(1) of that Act.

(3) Where an education authority—

    (*a*) intend to record a child or young person under section 60(2) of the 1980 Act (recording of children with special educational needs) after the period mentioned in section 65B(2) of that Act; or

    (*b*) after making a report under the said section 65B(1) on a child or young person who was not at the time of the report a disabled person, become aware of a significant change in the mental or physical condition of the child or young person giving them reason to believe that he may now be a disabled person,

they shall before opening the Record or, as the case may be, on becoming aware of the change, require the appropriate authority to give an opinion as to whether or not the child or young person is a disabled person and if the appropriate authority give an opinion that he is, this opinion shall be recorded in the Record and (where applicable) the report.

(4) Where the appropriate authority have given an opinion that a child or young person is a disabled person it shall be the duty of that authority to make an assessment of the needs of that child or young person with respect to the provision by the authority of any statutory services for that person in accordance with the welfare enactments, and for that assessment to be carried out—

    (*a*) in the case of a child in relation to whom a report is made under section 65B(1) of the 1980 Act, within the period mentioned in section 65B(2) of that Act; and

    (*b*) in the case of a child or young person who is considered to be

disabled under subsection (3) above, as soon as is reasonably practicable (but, in any event, not later than 6 months from the time the appropriate authority was asked for an opinion as to whether or not the child or young person was a disabled person),
and to make a report thereon.

(5) Where the appropriate authority have given an opinion that a child or young person is a disabled person and it subsequently appears to the education authority—

(*a*) that the child or young person will cease to receive full-time education at school at a particular date and will not subsequently be receiving full-time education at a further education establishment; or

(*b*) that the child or young person will cease to receive full-time education at such an establishment on a particular date,

the education authority shall, not later than 6 months before that date, record the date in the report or (if no report has been made) give written notification of the date to the appropriate authority.

(6) If at any time it appears to the education authority—

(*a*) that a child or young person who has been recorded as being disabled has ceased to receive full-time education; and

(*b*) the authority did not at the appropriate time—

(i) record that date in the report made under section 65B of the 1980 Act; or (as the case may be)

(ii) give notification to the appropriate authority; and

(*c*) a copy of the report has not been sent to the bodies mentioned in section 65B(6) of the said Act,

they shall, as soon as is reasonably practicable, record the date in the report and send a copy of the report to the appropriate authority or (if no report has been made) give written notification of the date to the appropriate authority.

(7) The education authority and the appropriate authority shall keep under consideration the cases of all children and young persons on whom a report has been made under section 65B of the 1980 Act or, as the case may be, under subsection (4) and shall at such times as they consider appropriate review the information contained in the report.

(8) Nothing in subsection (4) shall require the appropriate authority to make an assessment of the needs of a child or young person—

(*a*) if, having attained the age of 16, he has requested that such an assessment should not be made under that subsection; or

(*b*) if, being under that age or unable to make such a request by reason of any mental or physical incapacity, his parent has made such a request.

(9) In this section "appropriate authority" means the local authority for the purposes of the 1968 Act falling to perform functions in relation to the child or young person; and expressions used in the 1980 Act have the same meaning in this section as in that Act.

(10) The foregoing provisions of this section extend to Scotland only.

DEFINITIONS
"disabled person": s.16
"statutory services": s.16
"welfare enactments": s.16

GENERAL NOTE
This is the Scottish equivalent of s.3, above. "In considering this clause we had to have regard to the very different statutory provisions covering children and young persons with special educational needs in Scotland. For example, we have had to have regard to the fact that in Scotland arrangements already exist for these children to have their future needs

assessed. This assessment, made under section 65B of the Education (Scotland) Act 1980, takes place during the period when a child is between 14 years and 15 years 3 months. In bringing forward this new clause we have taken care to ensure not only that there should be no duplication of effort, which could easily occur if the two assessments needed are not carefully co-ordinated, but also that we build upon existing arrangements in a way which both improves them and makes the extension of assessment more effective. I am confident that those objectives have been achieved in this clause and that no disabled recorded child will leave special education without the benefit of an up-to-date assessment by both education authority and social work departments of his future needs and welfare requirements", *per* Lord Skelmersdale, H.L. Vol. 476, No. 112, col. 996.

Subs. (1)
   Appropriate authority: see subs. (9).

Assessment and recording of children and young persons

14.—(1) The 1980 Act is amended in accordance with the provisions of this section.

(2) In section 4 (duty of education authorities to provide child guidance service)—

   (a) for the words "a child guidance service in child guidance clinics" there shall be substituted the words "a regional or island authority psychological service in clinics"; and

   (b) in sub-paragraph (c) the words "child guidance" shall be omitted.

(3) In section 61 (examination and assessment of children and young persons)—

   (a) in subsection (1)—

      (i) for the words from "process of assessment" to "in his educa-tion" there shall be substituted the words "process of obser-vation and assessment (including educational, psychological and medical assessments)";

      (ii) in paragraphs (a) and (b) for the words "a medical examination and a psychological examination" there shall be substituted the word "assessment";

   (b) in subsection (2)—

      (i) for the words "a medical examination" there shall be substi-tuted the word "assessment";

      (ii) for the words "that examination" there shall be substituted the words "any medical examination held in connection with the assessment";

   (c) in subsection (3)—

      (i) in paragraph (a) for the word "examinations" there shall be substituted the word "assessment";

      (ii) in paragraph (b) for the words "the examinations" there shall be substituted the words "any examinations held in connection with the assessment";

      (iii) in paragraph (c) for the words "the medical examination" there shall be substituted the words "any medical examination held in connection with the assessment";

   (d) in subsection (6) after the words "process of" there shall be inserted the words "observation and";

   (e) in subsection (7) in paragraph (a) after the words "process of" there shall be inserted the words "observation and".

(4) In section 62 (recording of children and young persons)—

   (a) in subsection (1) in paragraphs (a) and (b) after the words "process of" there shall be inserted the words "observation and";

   (b) in subsection (2) in paragraph (c) at the end there shall be added the words "unless the parent of the child or of the young person or, as the case may be, the young person has requested the education authority not to appoint such a person".

(5) In section 63 (appeals against decisions about recorded children or young persons)—

(*a*) in subsection (1) after paragraph (*a*) there shall be inserted—
> "(*aa*) a decision of an education authority not to record the child or, following a review under section 65A of this Act, not to continue to record him;";

(*b*) in subsection (2) before paragraph (*a*) there shall be inserted—
> "(*aa*) a decision of an education authority not to record the young person or, following a review under section 65A of this Act, not to continue to record him;".

(6) In section 64 (provisions supplementary to section 63) in subsection (1) in paragraph (*a*)—

(*a*) after the words "(1)(*a*)" there shall be inserted ", (*aa*)";

(*b*) for the words "(2)(*a*)" substitute "(2)(*aa*) or (*a*)".

(7) The foregoing provisions of this section extend to Scotland only.

Definition
"the 1980 Act": s.16

General Note
This section makes amendments to the Education (Scotland) Act 1980.

Subs. (2) amends s.4 of the Act so that the child guidance service should in future be called the regional or island authority psychological service.

Subs. (3) amends s.61 of the Act which sets out the elements of the examination and assessment of a child which must be undertaken before that child may be recorded as having special educational needs.

Subs. (4) amends s.2 of the Act to enable parents to opt out of the appointment of a named person. The named person is someone appointed by the education authority under s.62 of the Act to whom parents may go for advice and information about their children's special educational needs.

Subs. (5) amends s.63 of the Act to enable parents to appeal against the decision of the education authority not to record a child or young person as having special educational needs.

Co-operation in planning

15.—(1) In relation to disabled persons the duty under section 13 of the 1978 Act of Health Boards and local authorities to co-operate with one another shall include—

(*a*) joint planning of services of common concern to those authorities;

(*b*) consultation with voluntary organisations providing services similar in function to those mentioned in the preceding paragraph;

(*c*) the publication at such times and in such manner as they consider appropriate of joint plans for the development of such services.

(2) The foregoing provisions of this section extend to Scotland only.

Definitions
"disabled person": s.16
"Health Board": s.16
"local authority": s.16
"voluntary organisation": s.16
"services": s.16
"the 1978 Act": s.16

General Note
This section extends the duty of health boards and local authorities in Scotland to co-operate in the joint planning of services for disabled people, to consult with voluntary organisations and to publish joint plans.

PART IV

SUPPLEMENTAL

Interpretation

16. In this Act—

"the 1948 Act" means the National Assistance Act 1948;

"the 1968 Act" means the Social Work (Scotland) Act 1968;

"the 1970 Act" means the Chronically Sick and Disabled Persons Act 1970;

"the 1977 Act" means the National Health Service Act 1977;

"the 1978 Act" means the National Health Service (Scotland) Act 1978;

"the 1980 Act" means the Education (Scotland) Act 1980;

"the 1983 Act" means the Mental Health Act 1983;

"the 1984 Act" means the Mental Health (Scotland) Act 1984;

"authorised representative" has the meaning given by section 1(1) above;

"disabled person"—

    (*a*) in relation to England and Wales, means a person to whom section 29 of the 1948 Act applies; and

    (*b*) in relation to Scotland, means—

        (i) a chronically sick or disabled person, or

        (ii) a person suffering from mental disorder,

(being a person in need) to whom section 12 of the 1968 Act applies;

"guardian" (except in section 1(6))—

    (*a*) in relation to England and Wales, means a person appointed by deed or will or by order of a court of competent jurisdiction to be the guardian of a child; and

    (*b*) in relation to Scotland, means a person appointed by deed or will or by order of a court of competent jurisdiction to be the tutor, curator or guardian of a child;

"Health Board" means a Health Board within the meaning of the 1978 Act;

"hospital"—

    (*a*) in relation to England and Wales, means—

        (i) a health service hospital within the meaning of the 1977 Act, or

        (ii) any accommodation provided by any person pursuant to arrangements made under section 23(1) of that Act (voluntary organisations and other bodies) and used as a hospital; and

    (*b*) in relation to Scotland, means a health service hospital within the meaning of the 1978 Act;

"local authority" (except in section 2(7))—

    (*a*) in relation to England and Wales, means a council which is a local authority for the purposes of the Local Authority Social Services Act 1970 or, so long as an order under section 12 of that Act is in force, the Council of the Isles of Scilly; and

    (*b*) in relation to Scotland, means a regional or islands council on whom functions are imposed by section 1, as read with section 2, of the 1968 Act;

"mental disorder"—
>   (*a*) in relation to England and Wales, has the meaning given by section 1 of the 1983 Act; and
>   (*b*) in relation to Scotland, has the meaning given by section 1(2) of the 1984 Act;

"modifications" includes additions, omissions and amendments;

"parent"—
>   (*a*) in relation to England and Wales, means, in the case of a child who is illegitimate, his mother, to the exclusion of his father; and
>   (*b*) in relation to Scotland, means, in the case of a child whose father is not married to the mother, his mother, to the exclusion of his father;

"services" includes facilities;

"special hospital" means a special hospital within the meaning of the 1977 Act;

"State hospital" means a State hospital within the meaning of the 1984 Act;

"statutory services"—
>   (*a*) in relation to England and Wales, means services under any arrangements which a local authority are required to make by virtue of any of the welfare enactments, and
>   (*b*) in relation to Scotland, means services which a local authority find it necessary to provide themselves or by arrangement with another local authority, or with any voluntary or other body, in connection with the performance of the local authority's functions under the welfare enactments;

"voluntary organisation" means a body the activities of which are carried on otherwise than for profit, but does not include any public or local authority;

"the welfare enactments" means Part III of the 1948 Act, section 2 of the 1970 Act and—
>   (*a*) in relation to England and Wales, Schedule 8 to the 1977 Act, and
>   (*b*) in relation to Scotland, section 27 of the National Health Service (Scotland) Act 1947, the 1968 Act and sections 7 and 8 of the 1984 Act.

GENERAL NOTE

A person to whom section 29 of the 1948 Act applies: *I.e.* persons who are blind, deaf or dumb, or who suffer from mental disorder of any description and other persons who are substantially and permanently handicapped by their illness, injury, or congenital deformity.

Otherwise than for profit: It seems that if the making of a profit is not one of the main objects of an organisation, but is only a subsidiary object, *i.e.* it is only a means whereby the organisations main objects can be furthered or achieved, then the organisation can be said to be "carried on otherwise than for profit" (*National Deposit Friendly Society Trustees* v. *Skegness Urban District Council* [1959] A.C. 293, *per* Lord Denning at 319, 320).

Financial provisions

17. There shall be paid out of money provided by Parliament any increase attributable to this Act in the sums payable out of money so provided under any other Act.

Short title, commencement, regulations, orders and extent

18.—(1) This Act may be cited as the Disabled Persons (Services, Consultation and Representation) Act 1986.

(2) This Act shall come into force on such date as the Secretary of State may by order appoint and different dates may be appointed for different provisions or different purposes, and different provision may be made under this subsection for England and Wales and for Scotland.

(3) Any regulations or order made under this Act shall be made by statutory instrument and (except in the case of an order under subsection (2)) shall be subject to annulment in pursuance of a resolution of either House of Parliament.

(4) This Act does not extend to Northern Ireland.

PROTECTION OF CHILDREN (TOBACCO) ACT 1986

(1986 c. 34)

An Act to amend the Children and Young Persons Act 1933, and the
Children and Young Persons (Scotland) Act 1937, to make it an offence
to sell any tobacco product to persons under the age of sixteen; and for
connected purposes.   [8th July 1986]

PARLIAMENTARY DEBATES
Hansard: H.C. Vol. 88, col. 311; H.C. Vol. 90, col. 1235; H.C. Vol. 95, col. 1172; H.L.
Vol. 473, col. 1123; H.L. Vol. 475, col. 687; H.L. Vol. 476, col. 1151; H.L. Vol. 477, cols.
476, 758.
The Bill was also considered in committee by the House of Commons in Standing
Committee C on March 26, 1986.

Amendment of section 7 of the Children and Young Persons Act 1933

1.—(1) In section 7 of the Children and Young Persons Act 1933 (sale
of tobacco &c. to persons under sixteen)—
  (*a*) the proviso to subsection (1) (person not guilty of the offence of
       selling tobacco otherwise than in form of cigarettes if he did not
       know and had no reason to believe that it was intended for use of
       purchaser) is repealed;
  (*b*) in subsection (2) (powers of court in respect of tobacco vending
       machines used by young persons) for the word "may" in the first
       place where it occurs there shall be substituted the word "shall";
  (*c*) in subsection (5) (definition of "tobacco") after the words "includes
       cigarettes" there shall be inserted the words ", any product con-
       taining tobacco and intended for oral or nasal use".
(2) Paragraph (*a*) of subsection (1) above does not affect any offence
alleged to have been committed before the date on which this Act comes
into force and paragraph (*b*) of that subsection does not affect the powers
of the court on a complaint made before that date.

Amendment of section 18 of the Children and Young Persons (Scotland) Act 1937

2.—(1) In section 18 of the Children and Young Persons (Scotland)
Act 1937 (sale of tobacco &c. to persons under sixteen)—
  (*a*) the proviso to subsection (1) (person not guilty of the offence of
       selling tobacco otherwise than in form of cigarettes if he did not
       know and had no reason to believe that it was intended for use of
       purchaser) is repealed;
  (*b*) in subsection (2) (powers of court in respect of tobacco vending
       machines used by young persons) for the word "may" in the first
       place where it occurs there shall be substituted the word "shall";
  (*c*) in subsection (5) (definition of "tobacco") after the words "includes
       cigarettes" there shall be inserted the words ", any product con-
       taining tobacco and intended for oral or nasal use";
  (*d*) after subsection (5) there shall be inserted the following
       subsections—
       "(6) For the purposes of subsections (1) and (2) of this
       section, any substance sold in a container (whether sealed or
       not) shall, subject to subsections (7) to (9) of this section, be
       presumed to conform to the description of the substance on the
       container.

(7) Where a prosecutor (within the meaning of section 462 of the Criminal Procedure (Scotland) Act 1975) intends to rely on subsection (6) of this section, he shall give notice of his intention to the accused or his agent not less than 14 days before the commencement of the trial.

(8) The accused shall not be entitled to challenge the presumption in subsection (6) of this section, unless he or his agent gives notice to the said prosecutor of intention to do so not less than 7 days before the commencement of the trial.

(9) A notice under subsection (7) or (8) of this section shall be by recorded delivery letter, and the execution of the recorded delivery shall be sufficient evidence of the date of posting and of intimation of the notice, which shall be presumed to have been intimated to the addressee on the day after the day on which it was posted, except that, in the case of a notice posted on a Friday or a Saturday, it shall be presumed to have been so intimated on the Monday next following.".

(2) Paragraph (*a*) of subsection (1) above does not affect any offence alleged to have been committed before the date on which this Act comes into force and paragraph (*b*) of that subsection does not affect the powers of the court on an application made before that date.

Short title, extent and commencement

3.—(1) This Act may be cited as the Protection of Children (Tobacco) Act 1986.

(2) This Act does not extend to Northern Ireland.

(3) This Act shall come into force at the end of the period of three months beginning with the day on which it is passed.

PROTECTION OF MILITARY REMAINS ACT 1986

(1986 c.35)

ARRANGEMENT OF SECTIONS

An Act to secure the protection from unauthorised interference of the remains of military aircraft and vessels that have crashed, sunk or been stranded and of associated human remains; and for connected purposes.

[8th July 1986]

PARLIAMENTARY DEBATES
Hansard: H.C. Vol. 90, col. 1227; Vol. 91, col. 611; Vol. 100, col. 1283; H.L. Vol. 471, col. 73; Vol. 473, col. 811; Vol. 475, col. 768; Vol. 476, col. 1156; Vol. 477, col. 589.

Application of Act

1.—(1) This Act applies to any aircraft which has crashed (whether before or after the passing of this Act) while in military service.

(2) Subject to the following provisions of this section, the Secretary of State may by order made by statutory instrument—

(*a*) designate as a vessel to which this Act applies any vessel which appears to him to have sunk or been stranded (whether before or after the passing of this Act) while in military service;

(*b*) designate as a controlled site any area (whether in the United Kingdom, in United Kingdom waters or in international waters) which appears to him to contain a place comprising the remains of, or of a substantial part of, an aircraft to which this Act applies or a vessel which has so sunk or been stranded;

and the power of the Secretary of State to designate a vessel as a vessel to which this Act applies shall be exercisable irrespective of whether the situation of the remains of the vessel is known.

(3) The Secretary of State shall not designate a vessel as a vessel to which this Act applies unless it appears to him—

(*a*) that the vessel sank or was stranded on or after 4th August 1914; and

(*b*) in the case of a vessel which sank or was stranded while in service with, or while being used for the purposes of, any of the armed forces of a country or territory outside the United Kingdom, that remains of the vessel are in United Kingdom waters.

(4) The Secretary of State shall not designate any area as a controlled site in respect of any remains of an aircraft or vessel which has crashed, sunk or been stranded unless it appears to him—

(*a*) that less than two hundred years have elapsed since the crash, sinking or stranding;

(*b*) that the owners and occupiers of such land in the United Kingdom as is to be designated as, or as part of, that site do not object to the terms of the designating order which affect them; and

(c) where the aircraft or vessel crashed, sank or was stranded while in service with, or while being used for the purposes of, any of the armed forces of a country or territory outside the United Kingdom, that the remains are in the United Kingdom or in United Kingdom waters.

(5) An area designated as a controlled site shall not extend further around any place appearing to the Secretary of State to comprise remains of an aircraft or vessel which has crashed, sunk or been stranded while in military service than appears to him appropriate for the purpose of protecting or preserving those remains or on account of the difficulty of identifying that place; and no controlled site shall have a boundary in international waters any two points on which are more than two nautical miles apart.

(6) For the purposes of this Act a place (whether in the United Kingdom, in United Kingdom waters or in international waters) is a protected place if—

(a) it comprises the remains of, or of a substantial part of, an aircraft, or vessel to which this Act applies; and

(b) it is on or in the sea bed or is the place, or in the immediate vicinity of the place, where the remains were left by the crash, sinking or stranding of that aircraft or vessel;

but no place in international waters shall be a protected place by virtue of its comprising remains of an aircraft or vessel which has crashed, sunk or been stranded while in service with, or while being used for the purposes of, any of the armed forces of a country or territory outside the United Kingdom.

(7) The power to designate any land as, or as part of, a controlled site shall be exercisable in relation to Crown land as it is exercisable in relation to other land.

(8) The Secretary of State may by order made by statutory instrument substitute references to a later date for the reference in subsection (3)(a) above to 4th August 1914 or for any reference to a date which is inserted by an order under this subsection; and a statutory instrument containing an order under this subsection shall be subject to annulment in pursuance of a resolution of either House of Parliament.

Offences in relation to remains and prohibited operations

2.—(1) Subject to the following provisions of this section and to section 3 below, a person shall be guilty of an offence—

(a) if he contravenes subsection (2) below in relation to any remains of an aircraft or vessel which are comprised in a place which is part of a controlled site;

(b) if, believing or having reasonable grounds for suspecting that any place comprises any remains of an aircraft or vessel which has crashed, sunk or been stranded while in military service, he contravenes that subsection in relation to any remains by virtue of which that place is a protected place;

(c) if he knowingly takes part in, or causes or permits any other person to take part in, the carrying out of any excavation or diving or salvage operation which is prohibited by subsection (3) below; or

(d) if he knowingly uses, or causes or permits any other person to use, any equipment in connection with the carrying out of any such excavation or operation.

(2) A person contravenes this subsection in relation to any remains—

(a) if he tampers with, damages, moves, removes or unearths the remains;

(*b*) if he enters any hatch or other opening in any of the remains which enclose any part of the interior of an aircraft or vessel; or

(*c*) if he causes or permits any other person to do anything falling within paragraph (*a*) or (*b*) above.

(3) An excavation or diving or salvage operation is prohibited by this subsection—

(*a*) if it is carried out at a controlled site for the purpose of investigating or recording details of any remains of an aircraft or vessel which are comprised in a place which is part of that site; or

(*b*) if it is carried out for the purpose of doing something that constitutes, or is likely to involve, a contravention of subsection (2) above in relation to any remains of an aircraft or vessel which are comprised in a protected place or in a place which is part of such a site; or

(*c*) in the case of an excavation, if it is carried out for the purpose of discovering whether any place in the United Kingdom or United Kingdom waters comprises any remains of an aircraft or vessel which has crashed, sunk or been stranded while in military service.

(4) In proceedings against any person for an offence under this section, it shall be a defence for that person to show that what he did or, as the case may be, what he caused or permitted to be done was done under and in accordance with a licence under section 4 below.

(5) In proceedings against any person for an offence under this section in respect of anything done at or in relation to a place which is not part of a controlled site it shall be a defence for that person to show that he believed on reasonable grounds that the circumstances were such that (if those had been the circumstances) the place would not have been a protected place.

(6) In proceedings against any person for an offence under this section it shall be a defence for that person to show that what he did or, as the case may be, what he caused or permitted to be done was urgently necessary in the interests of safety or health or to prevent or avoid serious damage to property.

(7) A person who is guilty of an offence under this section shall be liable—

(*a*) on summary conviction, to a fine not exceeding the statutory maximum;

(*b*) on conviction on indictment, to a fine.

(8) Nothing in this section shall be construed as restricting any power to carry out works which is conferred by or under any enactment.

(9) References in this section to any remains which are comprised in a protected place or to any remains which are comprised in a place which is part of a controlled site include references to remains other than those by virtue of which that place is a protected place or, as the case may be, to remains other than those in respect of which that site was or could have been designated.

Extraterritorial jurisdiction

3.—(1) Where a contravention of subsection (2) of section 2 above occurs in international waters or an excavation or operation prohibited by subsection (3) of that section is carried out in international waters, a person shall be guilty of an offence under that section in respect of that contravention, excavation or operation only—

(*a*) if the acts or omissions which constitute the offence are committed in the United Kingdom, in United Kingdom waters or on board a British-controlled ship; or

    (*b*) in a case where those acts or omissions are committed in international waters but not on board a British-controlled ship, if that person is—
        (i) a British citizen, a British Dependent Territories citizen or a British Overseas citizen; or
        (ii) a person who under the British Nationality Act 1981 is a British subject; or
        (iii) a British protected person (within the meaning of that Act); or
        (iv) a company within the meaning of the Companies Act 1985 or the Companies Act (Northern Ireland) 1960.

(2) Subject to subsection (1) above, an offence under section 2 above shall, for the purpose only of conferring jurisdiction on any court, be deemed to have been committed in any place where the offender may for the time being be.

(3) Where subsection (1) above applies in relation to any contravention, excavation or operation, no proceedings for an offence under section 2 above in respect of that contravention, excavation or operation shall be instituted—
    (*a*) in England and Wales, except by or with the consent of the Director of Public Prosecutions;
    (*b*) in Northern Ireland, except by or with the consent of the Director of Public Prosecutions for Northern Ireland.

Licences to carry out prohibited works, operations etc.

4.—(1) The Secretary of State shall have power to grant licences authorising the doing of such things as are described (whether generally or specifically) in the licences for the purpose of enabling those things to be done without the commission of any offence under section 2 above.

(2) A licence under this section shall be capable of being granted to a particular person, to persons of a particular description or to persons generally; and such a licence may be contained in an order designating a controlled site.

(3) The Secretary of State in granting a licence under this section may impose such conditions with respect to the doing of anything authorised by the licence as he may specify in the licence for any purpose connected with protecting or preserving any remains to which the licence relates.

(4) A licence under this section shall continue in force, subject to any amendments made from time to time by the Secretary of State, until the expiration of such period as is specified in the licence or until revoked, whichever is the earlier.

(5) Where a licence (other than a licence contained in an order designating a controlled site) is granted, amended or revoked under this section, the Secretary of State shall, as he thinks fit, either—
    (*a*) send a copy of the licence, amendment or revocation to the licensee; or
    (*b*) publish such a copy in such manner as he considers appropriate for the purpose of bringing it to the attention of persons likely to be affected by the licence, amendment or revocation.

(6) The grant of a licence under this section is without prejudice to the rights of any person (including the Crown)—
    (*a*) as the owner of an interest in any land where any remains of an aircraft or vessel are, or are thought to be, situated; or
    (*b*) as the owner of, or the person entitled (whether under any enactment or rule of law or otherwise) to claim, an interest in any such remains.

Supplemental provision with respect to licence applications

5.—(1) A person shall be guilty of an offence if, for the purpose of obtaining a licence under section 4 above (whether for himself or another or for persons of any description), he—

(*a*) makes a statement, or furnishes a document or information, which he knows to be false in a material particular; or

(*b*) recklessly makes a statement or representation, or furnishes a document or information, which is false in a material particular.

(2) A person who is guilty of an offence under subsection (1) above shall be liable—

(*a*) on summary conviction, to a fine not exceeding the statutory maximum;

(*b*) on conviction on indictment, to a fine.

(3) The Secretary of State may by order made by statutory instrument require an application made to him for a licence under section 4 above to be accompanied, in such circumstances as may be specified in the order, by a fee of an amount so specified.

(4) A statutory instrument containing an order under subsection (3) above shall be subject to annulment in pursuance of a resolution of either House of Parliament.

(5) Any fees received by the Secretary of State by virtue of an order under subsection (3) above shall be paid into the Consolidated Fund.

Powers of boarding by authorised persons

6.—(1) Subject to the following provisions of this section, an authorised person shall be entitled for the purpose of determining whether an offence under this Act is being, has been or is to be committed to board and search—

(*a*) any vessel which is in United Kingdom waters; or

(*b*) any vessel which is in international waters and is a British-controlled ship.

(2) An authorised person shall not board a vessel under this section unless at the time he made his first request to board the vessel he had reasonable grounds for believing—

(*a*) in the case of a vessel other than a British-controlled ship, that an offence under this Act was being committed on board the vessel; or

(*b*) in the case of a British-controlled ship, that such an offence was being, had been or was to be so committed.

(3) An authorised person who has boarded a vessel under this section may seize anything which is on board the vessel if he has reasonable grounds for believing—

(*a*) that it is evidence of an offence under this Act or has been obtained in consequence of the commission of such an offence; and

(*b*) that it is necessary to seize it to prevent its being concealed, lost, altered or destroyed.

(4) An authorised person may use such force as is reasonably necessary for the purpose of exercising any power conferred on him by this section and may do anything else reasonably necessary for that purpose, including ordering a vessel to stop.

(5) A person on whom a power is conferred by this section shall, if required to do so by the master of the vessel, produce his authority before exercising the power.

(6) Any person who intentionally obstructs a person who is exercising any power conferred by this section shall be liable on summary conviction to a fine not exceeding level 3 on the standard scale.

(7) For the purpose only of conferring jurisdiction on any court, an offence under subsection (6) above shall be deemed to have been committed in any place where the offender may for the time being be.

(8) In this section "authorised person" means a person authorised in writing by the Secretary of State to exercise the powers conferred by this section (whether in all cases or only in cases specified or described in the authority) or a person of a description of persons so authorised.

Supplemental provisions with respect to offences

7.—(1) Section 43 of the Powers of Criminal Courts Act 1973 and Article 7 of the Criminal Justice (Northern Ireland) Order 1980 (power to deprive offenders of property used, or intended for use, for purposes of crime) shall have effect in England and Wales and in Northern Ireland respectively as if an offence under section 2 above were an offence punishable on indictment with imprisonment for a term of two years or more.

(2) Where a body corporate is guilty of an offence under this Act and that offence is proved to have been committed with the consent or connivance of, or to be attributable to any neglect on the part of, any director, manager, secretary or other similar officer of the body corporate or any person who was purporting to act in any such capacity he, as well as the body corporate, shall be guilty of that offence and shall be liable to be proceeded against and punished accordingly.

(3) Where the affairs of a body corporate are managed by its members, subsection (2) above shall apply in relation to the acts and defaults of a member in connection with his functions of management as if he were a director of the body corporate.

Administrative expenses

8. There shall be paid out of money provided by Parliament any administrative expenses incurred by the Secretary of State in consequence of the provisions of this Act.

Interpretation

9.—(1) In this Act, except in so far as the context otherwise requires—

"aircraft" includes a hovercraft, glider or balloon;

"British-controlled ship" means a ship registered in the United Kingdom or a ship exempted from such registration under the Merchant Shipping Act 1894;

"controlled site" means any area which is designated as such a site under section 1 above;

"Crown land" has the same meaning as in section 50 of the Ancient Monuments and Archaeological Areas Act 1979;

"international waters" means any part of the sea outside the seaward limits of the territorial waters adjacent to any country or territory;

"military service" shall be construed in accordance with subsection (2) below;

"nautical miles" means international nautical miles of 1,852 metres;

"protected place" shall be construed in accordance with section 1(6) above;

"remains", in relation to, or to part of, an aircraft or vessel which has crashed, sunk or been stranded, includes any cargo, munitions, apparel or personal effects which were on board the aircraft or vessel during its final flight or voyage (including, in the case of a vessel, any aircraft which were on board) and any human remains associated with the aircraft or vessel;

"sea" includes the sea bed and, so far as the tide flows at mean high water springs, any estuary or arm of the sea and the waters of any channel, creek, bay or river;

"sea bed" includes any area submerged at mean high water springs;

"United Kingdom waters" means any part of the sea within the seaward limits of the territorial waters adjacent to the United Kingdom.

(2) For the purposes of this Act an aircraft or vessel shall be regarded as having been in military service at a particular time if at that time it was—

(*a*) in service with, or being used for the purposes of, any of the armed forces of the United Kingdom or any other country or territory; or

(*b*) in the case of an aircraft, being taken from one place to another for delivery into service with any of the armed forces of the United Kingdom.

(3) Where a place comprising the remains of, or of a substantial part of, an aircraft or vessel which has crashed, sunk or been stranded while in military service is situated only partly in United Kingdom waters, that place shall be treated for the purposes of this Act as if the part which is situated in United Kingdom waters and the part which is situated in the United Kingdom or in international waters were separate places each of which comprised the remains of a substantial part of the aircraft or vessel.

Short title, commencement and extent

10.—(1) This Act may be cited as the Protection of Military Remains Act 1986.

(2) This Act shall come into force at the end of the period of two months beginning with the day on which it is passed.

(3) This Act extends to Northern Ireland.

(4) Her Majesty may by Order in Council make provision for extending the provisions of this Act, with such exceptions, adaptations and modifications as may be specified in the Order, to any of the Channel Islands or any colony.

INCEST AND RELATED OFFENCES (SCOTLAND) ACT 1986*

(1986 c. 36)

An Act to make provision for Scotland in respect of incest and related offences. [18th July 1986]

INTRODUCTION AND GENERAL NOTE

Background to the Act

This Act replaces the existing law of incest in Scotland with a new statutory offence of incest. It also creates two new offences of a related nature, and makes certain procedural provisions in relation to incest and the new offences. The Act is based on recommendations contained in the Scottish Law Commission's *Report on the Law of Incest in Scotland* (Scot. Law Com. No. 69; Cmnd. 8422, 1981, hereafter *"Report"* and the draft Bill appended to that report. It is something of a tribute to the thoroughness and sensitivity of that report that the Act embodies those recommendations with few major alterations. Such departures from the draft Bill as are to be found in the Act are due largely to developments occurring after the report and draft Bill were originally presented to Parliament in 1981.

Prior to this Act the law of incest in Scotland was effectively based on the Incest Act 1567, which punished with life imprisonment those "that abusis thair bodies with sik persones in degrie as Goddis word hes expreslie forbiddin in ony tyme cumming, as is contenit in the xviii Cheptour of Leviticus" (in effect verses 6 to 17 inclusive of Chapter 18). It is possible that in addition to the statutory offence the common law prohibited intercourse in circumstances where that intercourse would not have been criminal under the Act of 1567. (See *H.M. Advocate* v. *R. M.*, 1969 J.C. 52, and Mackenzie, *The Laws and Customs of Scotland in Matters Criminal,* I. 15. 2. (1697)). But the scope of the common law of incest and the extent to which it survived the legislation of the Reformation period has never fully been explored, and in practice all charges of incest were brought under the Act.

The deficiencies in the old law were well-recognised and had been so for some time (see, *e.g.* I. F. Grant, "The Law of Incest in Scotland" (1914) 26 J.R. 438; "The Law of Incest in Scotland: A Long Overdue Reform" (1941) 53 J.R. 112.) Quite apart from the obscure and archaic language in which the 1567 Act was expressed, the substance of the law was in many respects out of keeping with the attitudes and needs of modern Scottish society.

In the first place the range of prohibited relationships was very wide, encompassing not only relationships of the full and half blood to the degree of great-grandparents and great-grandchildren, but also a lengthy list of relationships by affinity, extending in the line of ascent and descent to grandparents and grandchildren-in-law. The range of proscribed relationships by affinity was extended greatly by the rule that where affinity presented a bar to intercourse, that bar persisted notwithstanding the termination (by death or divorce) of the marriage upon which it was based. Although these extensive prohibitions were limited by the principle that where parties were free to marry intercourse between them could not be incestuous (Criminal Procedure (Scotland) Act 1938), nevertheless the range of prohibited relationships in Scots law was markedly wider than in other Commonwealth and western European jurisdictions (*Report*, Appendix III).

At the same time, however, there were significant gaps in the law. The 1567 Act took no note of relationships traced through or to a person whose parents were not or had not been married to each other (*H.M. Advocate* v. *R. M.*, above; *H.M. Advocate* v. *J. M. R*, 1985 S.C.C.R. 330), and although there was some authority for the view that intercourse between a woman and her "extra-marital" son was incest at common law (see *H.M. Advocate* v. *R.M.*, above) the general exclusion of such relationships from the law of incest was a significant omission in a community in which an increasing number of children are born outside marriage.

Adoptive relationships were similarly excluded from the ambit of the 1567 Act. For the purposes of the law of incest adoption had no effect on the adopted persons's relationship with his or her "natural" family or adoptive family, with the result that intercourse between adoptive parent and child, or adoptive siblings was not incest. There was, however, a view that adoptive children should for all purposes be assimilated to natural children and that intercourse between adoptive parent and child, at least, ought to be treated as incest. (see *Report*, para. 4.14).

* Annotations by Christopher Gane, Lecturer in Law, University of Lancaster.

The Act in outline

The Act's provisions are discussed in detail below, but it is convenient at this point to set out the major changes in the law. These are effected by inserting four new sections—2A, 2B, 2C and 2D—into the Sexual Offences (Scotland) Act 1976.

1. *Substantive changes*

(a) *The prohibited relationships.* Incest is restricted to sexual intercourse between persons related by consanguinity or adoption. Sexual intercourse between persons related by affinity (including step-parent and step-child) will no longer constitute incest. (S.2A; *Report,* paras. 4.1. to 4.10);

(b) *Relationship by adoption.* The definition of incest is extended to include intercourse between adoptive parent and child and former adoptive parent and child. (S. 2A(1); *Report,* paras. 4.12 to 4.17);

(c) *Illegitimacy.* The term "illegitimacy" is not used in the Act. The Act provides that in determining a relationship by consanguinity no account is to be taken of the fact that the relationship is traced through or to any person whose parents are not or have not been married to one another (*cf.* the Law Reform (Parent and Child) (Scotland) Act 1986). (S. 2A(2)(*b*); *Report,* para. 4.11);

(d) *Step relationship.* Although intercourse between step-parents and step-children and step-grandparents and step-grandchildren (including former step-relationships of these degrees) will no longer constitute incest, sexual intercourse between step-parent and step-child and former step-parent and step-child will still be an offence in certain circumstances (effectively where the parties would not be free to marry under the terms of the Marriage (Prohibited Degrees of Relationship) Act 1986). (S.2B; *Report,* paras. 4.18 to 4.29);

(e) *Sexual abuse of a position of trust or authority.* A new offence is committed by any person of or over the age of 16 years who has sexual intercourse with a child under the age of 16, if he or she is a member of the same household as the child and stands in a position of trust or authority in relation to that child. (S.2C; *Report,* paras. 4.30 to 4.36).

2. *Procedural changes*

(a) *Mode of trial.* Incest will no longer come within the exclusive jurisdiction of the High Court. In common with the other offences created by the Act, incest may now be tried on indictment in the High Court or the sheriff court, and indeed may be tried on summary complaint before the sheriff if the Lord Advocate so directs. (S.2D(1); *Report,* paras. 5.1 to 5.7);

(b) *Penalties.* The maximum penalty following conviction in the High Court of any of the offences contained in the Act is life imprisonment. On conviction on indictment before the sheriff it is two years' imprisonment, and on summary conviction it is three months' imprisonment. (S.2D(5); *Report,* paras. 5.8 to 5.10);

(c) *Background reports.* Before passing sentence on a person convicted of any offence under the Act, the court must obtain background reports on the accused, and in passing sentence must take into account any information before it which is relevant to his character and to his physical and mental condition. (S.2D(6); *Report,* paras. 6.9. to 6.22);

The statutory offences

The offences created by the Act are all clearly related in the sense that each of them prohibits sexual intercourse between parties whose relationship to each other is such that sexual intercourse between them ought not to be permitted. But there is a significant difference between incest on the one hand and the offences created by ss.2B and 2C on the other. The offences under ss.2B and 2C are intended primarily to protect young persons from sexual abuse by adult members of the family or household. Consequently in these cases the offence is committed only by one party—the step-parent or former step-parent in the case of s.2B or the person in a position of trust or authority in the case of s.2C—even if the "victim" is a fully consenting party to the offence.

The "unilateral," protective nature of the offences under ss.2B and 2C is of considerable importance in the light of the decision in *R.* v. *Tyrrell* [1894] 1 Q.B. 710. In that case it was held that where Parliament has created an offence for the protection of the members of a class of persons (in that case girls between the ages of 13 and 16) a member of that class cannot be guilty of inciting, or aiding and abetting an offence against him or herself. If this rule forms part of Scots law (and the matter has not been settled by any decision of a Scottish court, see Gordon, *The Criminal Law of Scotland* (2nd ed.), para. 5–05 *et seq.*), and the offences under ss.2B and 2C are of a kind envisaged by the rule, then it would seem to follow that the consenting "victim" of an offence under either of these sections cannot be art and part guilty of the offence, or guilty of inciting its commission.

This may be acceptable in the case of section 2C, where all potential victims are young persons under 16, and in many cases under section 2B where the victim will be a child or young person. But there may well be cases under section 2B where the victim is an adult who has willingly entered into a sexual relationship with the accused and who is not in any sense "exploited." In such cases the application of the rule in *Tyrell's* case is much less easily defended.

As to whether a person can be guilty art and part of incest when he or she is not within the prohibited degrees and therefore cannot be guilty as a principal offender, see *Vaughan* v. *H.M. Advocate,* 1979 S.L.T. 49. In that case the accused was charged with causing a young boy to have incestuous intercourse with his mother. He was not related to either party, and argued that as he was not within the class of persons referred to in the Incest Act 1567 he could not be convicted on the ground that be assisted in the commission of an offence by persons who were within the degrees referred to in the Act. The High Court held that the essence of the offence was the act of intercourse between two persons within the prohibited degrees, and that a person who abetted such intercourse was guilty art and part, notwithstanding the fact that he or she could not be guilty as actor. There is nothing in this Act which would affect the decision in *Vaughan,* and indeed it would appear to be applicable to the other offences created by the Act.

Special capacities

Ss. 67 and 312(*x*) of the Criminal Procedure (Scotland) Act 1975 provide that "Where an offence is alleged to be committed in any special capacity, as by the holder of a licence, master of a vessel, occupier of a house, or the like, the fact that the accused possesses the qualification necessary to the commission of the offence shall, unless challenged by preliminary objection before his plea is recorded, be held as admitted." In *Smith* v. *Allan,* 1985 S.C.C.R. 190 the High Court held that the words "or the like" in s.312(*x*) were not limited by the application of the *ejusdem generis* rule of construction, and that "any special capacity" means "any capacity which is special to the individual charged which is necessary to the commission of the offence libelled." (*Per* the Lord Justice-Clerk at p.193.)

The question arises as to whether these provisions apply to the offences under this Act. In *H.M. Advocate* v. *J. M. R.* (above) it was held that s.67 did not apply in a case where the accused was charged with a contravention of the Incest Act 1567 by having incestuous intercourse with his step-daughter, described in the indictment as "your lawful step-daughter and the lawful daughter of your wife." No evidence was led to establish that the girl was the lawful daughter of the accused's wife and the Crown sought to rely on s.67. Lord McDonald held that that section had no application to the instant case. The question was not one of any special capacity in which the accused was acting at the time of the offence, but whether the girl was, as was libelled, the lawful daughter of the accused's wife.

Structure of the offences

The offences created by the Act are not easily analysed in terms of *actus reus* and *mens rea.* At first glance, indeed, they appear to be offences of strict liability since none of them require proof by the Crown of a mental element. However, since the accused may avoid conviction by establishing the absence of any mental element, such as knowledge of the relationship between the parties, it is clear that these are not offences of strict liability properly so-called, and it was not the intention of the Scottish Law Commission that they should be strict, (*Report,* paras. 4.37 *et seq.*).

It is perhaps easier to analyse the offences in terms of "offence conditions" and "defence conditions." The onus of proving the former rests on the Crown, but once these have been established the accused will be convicted unless he proves one or other of the "defence conditions." The offence conditions vary from offence to offence, although sexual intercourse is a condition common to all the offences. The defence conditions, on the other hand, are more uniform, and fall into three broad categories:

(*a*) proof that the accused was unaware of an offence condition such as the relationship between the parties;

(*b*) proof that the accused did not consent to intercourse, or intercourse with the other party;

(*c*) proof that the accused was married to the other person at the time of the offence by a marriage entered into outside Scotland and recognised as valid by Scots law.

While offences of this type are not unknown in Scots law, the placing of an exculpatory onus on the accused is sufficiently unusual as to require some clear and particular justification. The Law Commission's reasons for adopting this approach were (a) that they wished to retain a mental element, but (b) they recognised the difficulties which might face the Crown in proving matters which could be peculiarly within the knowledge of the accused—such as knowledge of the relationship between the parties. (c) It was also noted that this approach had already been adopted in some sections of the Sexual Offences (Scotland) Act 1976 and a certain consistency of approach could therefore be achieved (*Report,* paras. 4.37 *et seq.*).

The approach adopted in the Act is, however, open to a number of criticisms. In the first place the argument that the prosecutor should be relieved of proving an element of an offence because it is likely to be peculiarly within the knowledge of the accused, if consistently applied, would relieve the prosecutor of proving *mens rea* in most offences. Such an approach is clearly contrary to modern principles of criminal responsibility, and it is difficult to see why it should be accepted in respect of incest and related offences but not others. Experience in relation to other offences which require proof of knowledge does not suggest that there is an insuperable practical problem. It is perhaps worth noting that in cases of incest under the corresponding English legislation (the Sexual Offences Act 1956) the prosecution is required to prove knowledge of the relationship and this does not seem to have produced serious difficulties.

Secondly, it is possible to distinguish the offences created by the Act and those already contained in the 1976 Act from the point of view of matters of defence. In the 1976 Act the matters of defence, such as ignorance of the girl's age in an offence under ss.4, 8 or 10, may be treated in that manner because they form no part of the definition of the offence. It is accepted that these offences are offences of strict liability so far as concerns the girl's age, and there is no question of the prosecutor having to prove knowledge of the girl's age as a condition of proving the accused's guilt. That, however, is not the case with all of the matters of defence envisaged in these offences. On the contrary, at least so far as concerns knowledge of the relationship between the parties, the Commission themselves accepted that "the guilt of the accused should continue to depend on his knowledge of the facts" (*Report,* para. 4.37). But the Act does not give effect to this view. Guilt under the Act does not depend upon knowledge, since a verdict of guilty may be returned without proof of knowledge if the accused fails to prove ignorance. In other words, an element of the offence, something which it is accepted ought to be established in order to found guilt, has been converted into a matter of defence, the absence of which must be established in order to prove innocence.

PARLIAMENTARY DEBATES
Hansard: H.L. Vol. 468, col. 660; Vol. 469, col. 63; Vol. 470, col. 614; Vol. 471, col. 883; Vol. 472, col. 510; Vol. 478, col. 737; H.C. Vol. 97, col. 1030; Vol. 100, col. 1342.
The Bill was considered by Second Scottish Standing Committee on June 11, 1986.

COMMENCEMENT
The Act received the Royal Assent on July 18, 1986 and comes into effect on a day to be appointed by the Secretary of State under s.3(2).

EXTENT
The Act applies to Scotland only (s.3(4)).

Incest and related offences

1. After section 2 of the Sexual Offences (Scotland) Act 1976 there shall be inserted the following sections—
"**Incest**
2A.—(1) Any male person who has sexual intercourse with a person related to him in a degree specified in column 1 of the Table set out at the end of this subsection, or any female person who has sexual intercourse with a person related to her in a degree specified in column 2 of that Table, shall be guilty of incest, unless the accused proves that he or she—
(a) did not know and had no reason to suspect that the person with whom he or she had sexual intercourse was related in a degree so specified; or
(b) did not consent to have sexual intercourse or to have sexual intercourse with that person; or

(c) was married to that person, at the time when the sexual intercourse took place, by a marriage entered into outside Scotland and recognised as valid by Scots law.

TABLE

DEGREES OF RELATIONSHIP

Column 1	Column 2

1. *Relationships by consanguinity*

Mother	Father
Daughter	Son
Grandmother	Grandfather
Grand-daughter	Grandson
Sister	Brother
Aunt	Uncle
Niece	Nephew
Great grandmother	Great grandfather
Great grand-daughter	Great grandson

2. *Relationships by adoption*

Adoptive mother or former adoptive mother.	Adoptive father or former adoptive father.
Adopted daughter or former adopted daughter.	Adopted son or former adopted son.

(2) For the purpose of this section, a degree of relationship exists in the case of a degree specified in paragraph 1 of the Table—

(a) whether it is of the full blood or the half blood; and

(b) even where traced through or to any person whose parents are not or have not been married to one another.

(3) For the avoidance of doubt sexual intercourse between persons who are not related to each other in a degree referred to in subsection (1) above is not incest.

This section amends the Sexual Offences (Scotland) Act 1976 inserting into it four new sections, 2A, 2B, 2C, and 2D. The provisions of these sections should therefore be read in the light of the rest of the 1976 Act and any judicial decisions construing the provisions of that Act.

GENERAL NOTE TO S.2A

This section creates the new statutory offence of incest, which is now confined to sexual intercourse between persons related by consanguinity or adoption, in the degrees specified in parts 1 and 2 of the Table.

In common with the other offences created by the Act, this offence may be analysed in terms of the "offence conditions" set out in the first paragraph of subs. (1) and the "defence conditions" set out in paras. (a), (b) and (c) of subs. (1).

Subs. (1)
Offence conditions

"*male person . . . female person*": Not surprisingly, no attempt is made to define these terms, although modern medical techniques, and a better understanding of certain psycho-sexual phenomena make the assignment of an individual to one or other of these categories less cut and dried than was formerly the case.

The criteria by reference to which a person is to be characterised as "male" or "female" have never been stated authoritatively in Scots law. In cases of doubt the choice would seem to lie between a test based on biological factors such as chromosomes, gonads and genitalia, and a psychological or social test which has regard not only to biological factors but also to the individual's gender identity. What authority there is in Scots law—*X, Petitioner*, 1957 S.L.T.(Sh.Ct.) 61—suggests the former approach, although the case is of little value as an authority since the issue of sexual identity was not fully considered and did not form part of the *ratio* of the decision. The "biological" test is adopted in English law: *Corbett* v. *Corbett (otherwise Ashley)* [1971] P. 83, *R.* v. *Tan* [1983] 2 All E.R. 12; *White* v. *British Sugar Corporation Ltd.* [1977] I.R.L.R. 121. Authorities favouring the "social" or "psychological" approach may be found in several U.S. jurisdictions: *Re Anonymous,* 57 MISC., 2d 813 (1968) (New York); *M. T.* v. *J. T.,* 140 N.J. Super. 77 (1976) (New Jersey); *Richards* v. *U.S. Tennis Association, et al.,* 93 MISC. 2d 713 (1977) (New York). A similar approach has been adopted in some continental jurisdictions: Tribunal de Grande Instance, Paris, November 24, 1981; (1982) J.C.P. 19792. And see also *Van Oosterwijck* v. *Belgium* (1980) 3 E.H.R.R. 557; *Rees* v. *U.K.* App. 9532/81; (1985) 7 E.H.R.R. 429 (European Commission of Human Rights).

"sexual intercourse": This term is not defined in the Act or in the 1976 Act. Under the previous law incest required sexual intercourse only in the limited sense of penetration of the vagina by the penis, to any degree (*Jas. Simpson* (1870) 1 Coup. 437). It was the Law Commission's view that the offence should continue to be so defined (*Report,* para. 4.5) and no attempt was made in Parliament to extend the offence to include other sexual conduct. It is clear, therefore, that incest is restricted to heterosexual intercourse, and further, that other sexual acts involving penetration (such as oral or anal intercourse) or other sexual acts not involving penetration do not constitute incest.

relationships by consanguinity
    Under the previous law, intercourse between blood relations was prohibited in the line of ascent and descent as far as great grandparents and great grandchildren. In the collateral line it was prohibited between siblings and uncle and niece and aunt and nephew. (See Gordon, *Criminal Law of Scotland* (2nd ed.), para. 35–03; Criminal Procedure (Scotland) Act 1938; Marriage (Scotland) Act 1977 s.2(3) and Sched. 1.) The Act, therefore, does not change the extent of the prohibition on intercourse between persons related by consanguinity.

relationships by adoption
    Under the previous law, adoption had no effect on the range of persons with whom intercourse was prohibited. Where intercourse between the adopted person and his original relations was incestuous prior to his adoption it remained so after it. Where intercourse between the adopted person and a member of his adoptive family was not prohibited prior to adoption, they remained untouched by the law of incest after the adoption. This was so even where the parties, by virtue of adoption, came within the prohibited degrees for the purpose of marriage. (*H.M. Advocate* v. *R. M.,* 1969 J.C. 52; Adoption (Scotland) Act 1978, s.39.)
    So far as concerns the adopted person's original family the position is unchanged under the Act. So far as concerns the adoptive family, part 2 of the Table brings the law of incest into line with that governing the prohibited degrees of marriage by prohibiting intercourse between adoptive parent and child or former adoptive parent and child. It should be noted that no other adoptive relationships are affected. It therefore remains the case, *e.g.* that sexual intercourse between adoptive siblings or adoptive grandparent and grandchild is not incest.

"unless the accused proves": The Law Commission's view was that while it was proper and appropriate to place on the accused the burden of establishing certain defences the standard of proof required of the accused ought not to be the high standard of proof "beyond reasonable doubt" but proof "on a balance of probabilities" (*Report,* para. 4.4). This would accord with the general principle that where a probative burden is placed upon the accused it may be discharged by proof on a balance of probabilities (*cf.,* for example, proof of the special defence of insanity).

Defence conditions
    These are set out in subss. (1)(a) to (c). They are expressed in the alternative so that proof of any one of them will result in acquittal of the accused.

Subs. (1)(a)
    The accused must not only prove that he or she did not know that the person with whom he or she had intercourse was related in one of the specified degrees, but must also show that he or she had no reason to suspect that they were so related. Since the defence is only made out where the accused had no reason to suspect the existence of the relationship, an

accused who simply did not suspect that there was such a relationship, where such suspicion could reasonably have been expected, would appear not to come within this defence.

Subs. (1)(b)

. Two distinct cases are envisaged by this provision. The first is where the accused does not consent to sexual intercourse, as in the case of a woman who is raped, or where a man has intercourse with a sleeping or unconscious woman (which would not be rape in Scots law, notwithstanding the absence of consent; *Charles Sweenie* (1858) 3 Irv. 109; *H.M. Advocate* v. *Logan*, 1936 J.C. 100; *Sweeney and Another* v. *X.,* 1982 S.C.C.R. 509), or possibly where the accused did not understand or was mistaken as to the nature of the act (*cf.* the case of *R.* v. *Williams* [1923] 1 K.B. 340).

The second case is where the accused consents to intercourse, but does not consent to intercourse "with that person." The subsection is intended to deal with the situation where A has intercourse with B (who is related in a prohibited degree) in the belief that he or she is having intercourse with C (who is not so related). Such a belief may arise because of deception by B (*cf. William Fraser* (1847) Ark. 280) or because of an error on A's part (*cf. R.* v. *Collins* [1973] Q.B. 100). Whether it is correct to say in either case that the accused did not consent to intercourse with B is another matter. It is possible to argue that A has consented to intercourse with B, but that consent is given under an error as to identity—an error which is not relevant to the question of consent. (Which was the view adopted by the High Court in *William Fraser's* case.)

An interesting question would arise if A were to have intercourse with B (who is related within a prohibited degree) in the belief that he or she is having intercourse with C (who to A's knowledge is also related within a prohibited degree). In such a case it would seem that A "does not consent" to have intercourse with B in exactly the same way as if A had believed B to be someone not related within a prohibited degree. That being the case A would seem to come within the terms of subs. (1)(*b*). In order, then, to avoid the absurdity of, say, acquitting A on a charge of incest with his mother by allowing him to prove that he thought the woman was his aunt, it is necessary to treat A's belief as a defence only if the facts as he believed them to be were consistent with innocence.

Subs. (1)(c)

This defence protects parties who are related within a prohibited degree for the purpose of the Scots law of incest, but who have entered into a marriage outside Scotland which is recognised as valid by Scots law. Without subs. (1)(*c*) intercourse between such parties would be incest.

The defence places a heavy practical burden on the accused. Proof of the validity of a foreign marriage will involve not only questions of Scots law, but also questions of foreign law as well since the issue of the formal validity of a marriage is, according to Scots law, determined by the *lex loci celebrationis*. On the validity of foreign marriages from the point of view of Scots law see, Clive, *Husband and Wife* (2nd ed.) pp. 144 *et seq., Burke* v. *Burke,* 1983 S.L.T. 331, R. White, "Foreign Marriages: Some Validity and Immigration Issues" (1986) 116 SCOLAG 79, Scottish Law Commission, Consultative Memorandum No. 64, "Private International Law: Choice of Law rules in Marriage" (1985).

Subs. (2)

Relationships of the half blood

Subs. (2)(*b*) applies the rule of the previous law that where intercourse is prohibited because of a blood relationship, the prohibition extends to relationships of the half-blood as well as the full blood, whether consanguinean (*i.e.* where the father is the common relative) or uterine (*i.e.* where the mother is the common relative).

Thus, it is incest for a man and woman who share the same father or mother to have intercourse as it is for a man and a woman who have the same father and mother.

Illegitimacy

The Commission recommended (*Report,* para. 4.11) that the "illegitimate" child should be placed with regard to incest in the same position as the "legitimate" child. The Law Reform (Parent and Child) (Scotland) Act 1986 for most purposes disposes of the notion of illegitimacy in the civil law and this is reflected in the terms of subs. (2)(*b*).

For the future, sexual intercourse between parties within a prohibited degree of relationship by consanguinity is incest notwithstanding the fact that that relationship is traced through or to any person whose parents are not or have not been married to one another.

36–7

Subs. (3)

There were suggestions in the case of *H.M. Advocate* v. *R.M.,* 1969 J.C. 52 that the Act of 1567 did not completely supersede the common law of incest. This subsection is intended to exclude any possibility of a residual common law offence surviving this Act (the Incest Act 1567 is repealed by s.2(2) and Sched. 2 of this Act).

Intercourse with step-child

2B. Any step-parent or former step-parent who has sexual intercourse with his or her step-child or former step-child shall be guilty of an offence if that step-child is either under the age of 21 or has at any time before attaining the age of 18 lived in the same household and been treated as a child of his or her family, unless the accused proves that he or she—

   (*a*) did not know and had no reason to suspect that the person with whom he or she had sexual intercourse was a step-child or former step-child; or

   (*b*) believed on reasonable grounds that that person was of or over the age of 21 years; or

   (*c*) did not consent to have sexual intercourse or to have sexual intercourse with that person; or

   (*d*) was married to that person, at the time when the sexual intercourse took place, by a marriage entered into outside Scotland and recognised as valid by Scots law.

GENERAL NOTE TO S.2B

The removal of relationships by affinity from incest means that without further provision sexual intercourse between step-parents and step-children, or former step-parents and step-children would be regulated only by the general law, so that, for example, consensual sexual intercourse between a man and his 16-year-old step-daughter would not be an offence at all. The Law Commission's view was that incest was not the appropriate remedy to protect young step-children (*Report,* para. 4.21) but that in some respects the present alternative criminal offences were not adequate. In particular, the existing penalties did not reflect the element of breach of trust in such cases (*Report,* para. 4.21).

The Law Commission's solution was to propose a new offence consisting of intercourse with a step-child or former step-child, under the age of 16. A provision to that effect was contained in the draft Bill, and the Bill as introduced into Parliament. During the passage of the Incest and Related Offences (Scotland) Bill through Parliament, the Marriage (Prohibited Degrees of Relationship) Act 1986 was passed. That Act permits marriage between former step-parents or grand-parents and former step-children or grand-children, provided that both parties have reached the age of 21 at the time of the marriage and the younger party has not at any time before attaining the age of 18 lived in the same household as the other party and been treated by the other party as a child of his family.

If the Law Commission's original proposals had been enacted against this background, it would not have been unlawful for a man and his 17-year-old step-daughter, or former step-daughter, to have sexual intercourse albeit that in general there would have been a bar to marriage between them. A number of members of Parliament felt that the law could not tolerate the situation in which parties could lawfully engage in sexual intercourse but could never lawfully marry, and clause 2B was amended at a late stage (third reading) to bring it into line with the provisions of the Marriage (Prohibited Degrees of Relationship) Act 1986. The amendment extends, however, only to the cases of step-parents and children and former step-parents and children. It does not extend to step-grandparents and children or former step-grandparents and children with the result that intercourse between parties who stand in that relationship to each other is not incestuous (albeit that such parties are still within the prohibited degrees of marriage unless they come within the "proviso" to the Marriage (Prohibited Degrees of Relationship) Act 1986).

Offence conditions

"*sexual intercourse*": See note to section 2A(1) above.

"*under the age of 21 . . .*": Subject to the defence conditions, the accused commits an offence if he or she has intercourse with a step-child or former step-child while the latter is under 21. The parties need not have lived in the same household nor need the child have been treated as a child of the accused's family.

"*before attaining the age of 18 . . .*": If before attaining the age of 18 the step-child or former step-child has lived in the same household as the step-parent, and been treated as a child of his or her family, intercourse with the step-child is an offence, even if it takes place after the step-child has left the household, and irrespective of the age of the step-child.

It is not necessary to show that the child considered itself to be a member of the step-parent's family. The test is the objective one of being treated as a member of that family. The Act leaves open the possiblity that a child might be treated as a member of the step-parent's family by persons other than the step-parent. Certainly it does not expressly state that the step-parent should have treated the child as a child of his or her family.

Whether or not a child has been treated as a member of the step-parent's family is presumably a matter of fact and degree, and may well depend upon the age and circumstances of the child at the time when the step-relationship is created. In this respect a dependent ten-year-old may well be regarded differently from a seventeen-year-old student leading a relatively independent life.

"*household*": See note to s.2C(*b*) below.

Defence conditions

Subs. 2B(a)
Cf. note to subs. 2A(1)(*a*).

Subs. 2B(b)
What would constitute "reasonable grounds" for believing that a person is over 21 is essentially a question of fact (*cf. H.M. Advocate* v. *Hoggan* (1893) 1 Adam 1), but it will not normally be sufficient to rely upon a person's appearance. See *H.M. Advocate* v. *Macdonald* (1900) 3 Adam 180; *H.M. Advocate* v. *Hoggan* (above).

Subs. 2B(c)
Cf. note to subs. 2A(1)(*b*).

Subs. 2B(d)
Cf. note to subsection 2A(1)(*c*).

Intercourse of person in position of trust with child under 16

2C.—Any person of or over the age of 16 years who—
    (*a*) has sexual intercourse with a child under the age of 16 years;
    (*b*) is a member of the same household as that child; and
    (*c*) is in a position of trust or authority in relation to that child,
shall be guilty of an offence, unless the accused proves that he or she—
    (i) believed on reasonable grounds that the person with whom he or she had sexual intercourse was of or over the age of 16 years; or
    (ii) did not consent to have sexual intercourse or to have sexual intercourse with that person; or
    (iii) was married to that person, at the time when the sexual intercourse took place, by a marriage entered into outside Scotland and recognised as valid by Scots Law.

GENERAL NOTE TO S.2C
This section arises from the need to protect children from sexual abuse within the family where such children do not fall within the scope of the offence of incest, or the special provisions relating to step-chidren. Clear examples are foster-children, and the child or children of one party to an unmarried relationship.

The major difficulty perceived by the Commission was that of "defining the persons or the relationships to which it should apply" (*Report*, para. 4.32). The solution proposed by the Commission and accepted by Parliament is the offence contained in section 2C.

Offence conditions

"*sexual intercourse*": See note to s.2A(1) above.

"*a member of the same household*": No attempt is made in the Act to define these terms, or to give any guidance as to their meaning. The Law Commission noted the use of this phrase in s.32(2)(*e*) of the Social Work (Scotland) Act 1968 and sections 168 and 364 of the Criminal Procedure (Scotland) Act 1975 (*Report,* para. 4.33). So far as the Commission were aware the use of the phrase in these statutes had not caused any difficulty, and no attempt was made by them to define it, although they did express the view that it would exclude "casual visitors" such as "babysitters and the like who are not members of the household". They also felt that the word "household" would not extend to "institutions such as residential schools or children's homes" (*Report,* para. 4.33).

Unfortunately this phrase, and similar expressions, have proved to be notoriously difficult to construe in other contexts. What, for example, of houses occupied by more than one family, or persons on the margins of a household, such as a lodger or the occupant of a bed-sitter within a family home who shares facilities and occasional meals with the family? And what of the person who has been a member of a household but who is absent? Suppose, for example, that X's boyfriend normally lives with her and her 14-year-old daughter, but has been absent from the household, working away, for the past three months. He returns and on the night of his return has sexual intercourse with the daughter? Would it make any difference that his absence was not voluntary but involuntary, for example due to a prison sentence? Authorities from other areas of the law, and other jurisdictions, suggest the following general guidelines:—

(a) *General definition of "household."* In *McGregor* v. *Haswell,* 1983 S.L.T. 626, Lord Emslie stated that "the word 'household' in section 32 [of the Social Work (Scotland) Act 1968] is plainly intended to connote a family unit or something akin to a family unit—a group of persons, held together by a particular kind of tie who normally live together, even if individual members of the group may be temporarily seperated from it."

(b) *A question of fact.* In *Simmons* v. *Pizzey* [1977] 2 All E.R. 432, the House of Lords held that in the context of s.58(1) of the Housing Act 1969, the word "household" should be given its ordinary natural meaning (*per* Viscount Dilhorne at p. 437) and that the expression "household" and the question of its membership should be treated as a question of fact and degree, there being "no certain indicia the presence or absence of any of which is by itself conclusive" (*per* Lord Hailsham at pp.441–442). See also *England* v. *Secretary of State for Social Services* (1981) 3 F.L.R. 222, *per* Sir John Arnold P.

(c) *Physical presence in the household.* An individual may be a member of a household even though he or she is not physically present in the household (*McGregor* v. *Haswell,* above). Even lengthy absences may not be sufficient to remove a person from the household, at least where these are involuntary. (See, *e.g. Taylor* v. *Supplementary Benefits Officer* [1986] 1 F.L.R. 16: the applicant's husband who had been sentenced to nine months' imprisonment was to be considered as part of her "household" during that period, at least for the purposes of s.1(1) of the Family Income Supplements Act 1970.) *Cf.* R (F.I.S.) 3/83 in which the view was expressed by the Commissioner that enforced temporary absence of four months was not sufficient to justify treating the applicant's husband as no longer being a member of the household for the purposes of determining her entitlement to Family Income Supplement.

On the other hand, it is important to distinguish between those who are members of the household, and those who are merely living in it. In *Wawanesa Mutual Insurance Co.* v. *Bell and Bell* (1957) 8 D.L.R. (2d) 577, Rand J. suggested that a member of the family such as an uncle might not be a member of the household, if he was present merely as a temporary guest of the head of the household. In that case it was held that the younger brother of the head of the household, who had lived with the latter and his wife for about three years, more or less as a lodger, paying for bed and board when able to do so, was not a member of the elder brother's household. Emphasis was placed in that case on the fact that the younger brother was engaged to be married, and planned to leave his brother's house as soon as he was able to do so.

(d) *Withdrawal from the household.* An individual may of course withdraw from a household. Whether such withdrawal means that he or she ceases to be a member of that household may depend more upon the intentions of that person in withdrawing than on the attitudes of the other members of the household towards that withdrawal. Indeed, a person may withdraw effectively from the household without the consent or even the knowledge of the other members—see, *e.g. Calverley* v. *Gore District Mutual Fire Insurance Co.* (1959) 18 D.L.R. (2d) 598.

"*position of trust or authority*": The condition is expressed disjunctively. In other words an accused may be in either a position of trust or a position of authority (or both) as regards the child. Again the Act offers no guidance as to the meaning of this phrase. The Law Commission preferred this phrase "as being less restrictive than custody, charge and care" (*Report,* para. 4.34). The Commission did not attempt to give an exhaustive or comprehensive definition of the phrase, preferring that the words be given their "ordinary meaning" and that "it be left to the court to decide as a matter of fact whether the relationship between the accused and the child can properly be described as being one of authority or trust."

It seems, however, that this cannot entirely be a question of fact. Any person who has custody of the child ought, in principle, to stand in a position of trust or authority towards the child as, indeed, should any natural or adoptive parent, whether or not he or she has custody of the child.

Outside these narrow categories it is possible to envisage a variety of cases in which an individual may be seen as standing in a position of trust or authority. "An adult such as a friend of the child's mother, or a relative by marriage living in the same household might establish a relationship of trust or authority over the child" (*Report,* para. 4.34). There may even be situations in which a parent confers upon another adult some "authority" over the child, and this may even arise in relatively short-term situations—as, for example, where a child is left in the care of a friend or relative for a holiday.

Proceedings and penalties for offences under ss.2A to 2C

2D.—(1) Proceedings in respect of an offence under section 2A, 2B or 2C of this Act may be brought on indictment or, if the Lord Advocate so directs, on a summary complaint before the sheriff.

(2) Summary proceedings in pursuance of this section may be commenced at any time within the period of 6 months from the date on which evidence sufficient in the opinion of the Lord Advocate to justify the proceedings comes to his knowledge.

(3) Subsection (3) of section 331 of the Criminal Procedure (Scotland) Act 1975 (date of commencement of summary proceedings) shall have effect for the purposes of subsection (2) above as it has effect for the purposes of that section.

(4) For the purposes of subsection (2) above, a certificate of the Lord Advocate as to the date on which the evidence in question came to his knowledge is conclusive evidence of the date on which it did so.

(5) Subject to subsection (6) below, a person guilty of an offence under section 2A, 2B or 2C of this Act shall be liable—

(*a*) on conviction on indictment in the High Court of Justiciary, to imprisonment for any term of imprisonment up to and including life imprisonment;

(*b*) on conviction on indictment before the sheriff, to imprisonment for a term not exceeding 2 years; and

(*c*) on summary conviction, to imprisonment for a term not exceeding 3 months.

(6) Before passing sentence on a person convicted of any such offence, the court shall—

(*a*) obtain information about that person's circumstances from an officer of a local authority or otherwise and consider that information; and

(*b*) take into account any information before it which is relevant to his character and to his physical and mental condition.

(7) In subsection (6) above, "local authority" has the meaning assigned to it by section 1(2) of the Social Work (Scotland) Act 1968.".

Subs. (1)
"*proceedings on summary complaint*": Incest, as one of the "Pleas of the Crown" was formerly triable only in the High Court. This subsection permits incest (and the other

offences created by the Act) to be tried on indictment in the Sheriff Court and, indeed, on summary complaint before the sheriff where the Lord Advocate so directs.

Subs. (2)

Summary proceedings in respect of a contravention of any statute must normally be brought within six months of the date of the contravention, although the statute or order in question may specify a different period: Criminal Procedure (Scotland) Act 1975, s.331(1). Subs. (2) is intended to take account of the difficulties encountered in the detection of offences of this nature by permitting proceedings to be brought within a period of six months from the date on which evidence, sufficient in the opinion of the Lord Advocate to justify proceedings, comes to the knowledge of the Lord Advocate. The time limit to summary proceedings for incest and related offences begins to run not from the date of the commission of the offence, but when evidence of the offence becomes available—which of course may be some substantial time after the commission of the offence.

Subs. (3)

S.331(3) of the Criminal Procedure (Scotland) Act 1975 provides that for the purposes of determining when summary proceedings commence summary proceedings are deemed to commence on the date on which a warrant to apprehend or to cite the accused is granted, but only if such warrant is executed without undue delay.

Subs. (5)

The maximum penalty for incest remains at life imprisonment, but this may only be imposed by the High Court.

It is of course competent for the sheriff to remit a case to the High Court for sentence if he consideres his powers under section 2D(5)(*b*) to be inadequate: Criminal Procedure (Scotland) Act 1975, s.104.

Subs. (6)

There is a general obligation on the court under s.42(1) of the Criminal Justice (Scotland) Act 1980 to obtain background reports when considering a first sentence of imprisonment, and under ss.207(4) and 415(4) of the Criminal Procedure (Scotland) Act 1975 when considering imposing a sentence of detention. In both cases the obligation is imposed because of the nature of the sentence under consideration. The requirement under section 2D(6) is not linked to the nature of the sentence but rather to the nature of the offence.

Subs. (7)

The local authorities referred to in s.1(2) of the Social Work (Scotland) Act 1968 are the regional and islands councils.

Consequential amendments and repeals

2.—(1) The enactments specified in Schedule 1 to this Act shall have effect subject to the amendments set out in that Schedule, being amendments consequential on the provisions of this Act.

(2) The enactments specified in Schedule 2 to this Act are hereby repealed to the extent specified in the third column of that Schedule.

Short title, commencement and extent

3.—(1) This Act may be cited as the Incest and Related Offences (Scotland) Act 1986.

(2) This Act shall come into operation on such day as the Secretary of State may appoint by order made by statutory instrument.

(3) An order made under subsection (2) above may contain such transitional provisions and savings as appear to the Secretary of State necessary or expedient in connection with the coming into operation of this Act.

(4) This Act extends to Scotland only.

SCHEDULES

SCHEDULE 1

CONSEQUENTIAL AMENDMENTS

The Criminal Procedure (Scotland) Act 1975 (c.21)

.1. In section 171(3) (presumption and determination of age of child), for the words "(*b*) to" there shall be substituted the words "(*c*) and" and after the word "section" there shall be inserted "2A,".

2. In section 331(2) (statutory offences time limit), after the words "mentioned in" there shall be inserted the words "paragraph (*d*) of".

3. In section 368(3) (presumption and determination of age of child), for the words "(*b*) to" there shall be substituted the words "(*c*) and" and after the word "section" there shall be inserted "2A,".

The Sexual Offences (Scotland) Act 1976 (c.67)

4. At the beginning of section 4(1) (intercourse with girl between 13 and 16), there shall be added the words "Without prejudice to sections 2A to 2D of this Act".

The Adoption (Scotland) Act 1978 (c.28)

5. At the end of section 41(1) (status conferred in Scotland by adoption), there shall be added the words "and incest.".

SCHEDULE 2

ENACTMENTS REPEALED

Session and Chapter	Short title	Extent of repeal
1567 c.15.	The Incest Act 1567.	The whole Act.
1 & 2 Geo. 6. c.48.	The Criminal Procedure (Scotland) Act 1938.	The whole Act.
1975 c.21.	The Criminal Procedure (Scotland) Act 1975.	In Schedule 1, paragraph (*b*).

LATENT DAMAGE ACT 1986*

(1986 c. 37)

An Act to amend the law about limitation of actions in relation to actions for damages for negligence not involving personal injuries; and to provide for a person taking an interest in property to have, in certain circumstances, a cause of action in respect of negligent damage to the property occurring before he takes that interest.   [18th July 1986]

INTRODUCTION AND GENERAL NOTE

The Latent Damage Act is intended, in the words of the Lord Chancellor when moving the Second Reading of the Bill, to "effect an important and valuable change in the limitation law as it affects the tort of negligence." The Act is based upon recommendations in the 24th Report of the Law Reform Committee (1984 Cmnd. 9390). It amends the law of limitation of actions in negligence cases involving latent damage (other than personal injuries). Before outlining the scope of the Act, it is thought to be appropriate to provide a fairly detailed historical background to the Act, as the law in this area is complex and confusing, and it is hoped that such an account will facilitate an understanding of the Act's provisions.

Background

S.2 of the Limitation Act 1980 provides as follows:
    "An action founded on tort shall not be brought after the expiration of six years from the date on which the cause of action accrued."
Negligence is not actionable *per se*, and damage must therefore exist before the cause of action in negligence accrues. Difficulty has been experienced in some cases in determining what damage is, together with the associated question of when it occurred, and the problem of latent damage has posed especial problems. Latent damage has been helpfully defined as "damage which does not manifest itself until some time after the act or omission which 'causes' it" (see annotations to Limitation Act 1980, s.2). Latent damage clearly poses considerable problems to its unhappy victims, who may be held to be time-barred without ever realising that they had a cause of action.

Thus, in *Cartledge* v. *E. Jopling & Sons Ltd.* [1963] A.C. 758 (decided on the basis of s.2(1) of the Limitation Act 1939, which is identical in effect to s.2 of the 1980 Act) it was held, in the words of Lord Reid ([1963] A.C. 758 at 771–2) that: ". . . a cause of action accrues as soon as a wrongful act has caused personal injury beyond what can be regarded as negligible, even when that injury is unknown to and cannot be discovered by the sufferer; and that further injury arising from the same act at a later date does not give rise to a further cause of action." The plaintiffs in that case, who had inhaled noxious dust, causing pneumoconiosis, over a number of years, had suffered substantial injury some time before medical science could have discovered that this was so. Their action was time-barred because they had suffered damage more than six years before the writ was issued. The impossibility of awareness of the existence of damage was irrelevant. The House of Lords expressed their distaste for the conclusion that they felt compelled to reach, and their hopes that the law

* Annotations by David K. Allen, M.A., LL.M., Barrister, Lecturer in Law, University of Leicester.

would be changed were realised by the Limitation Act 1975, s.1 (see now Limitation Act 1980, ss.11–14) whereby in personal injury cases the plaintiff may claim within three years of the date of knowledge, if that is later than the date on which the cause of action accrued.

In the 1970s the problem of latent damage and limitation periods came to the fore in contexts other than that of personal injuries. The type of case in which the problem has presented itself frequently is that where a building has been constructed upon inadequate or defective foundations, and it is not until several years after the damage occurs that it manifests itself in cracking walls, sticking doors, etc., as the building moves. In *Dutton* v. *Bognor Regis Urban District Council* [1972] 1 Q.B. 373, where negligent inspection was alleged against a local authority acting under building byelaws made under the Public Health Act 1936, Lord Denning M.R. stated that the damage was done when the foundations were badly constructed, and consequently the limitation period began to run from the time of construction (see also *Higgins* v. *Arfon Borough Council* [1975] 2 All E.R. 589).

However, in *Sparham-Souter* v. *Town and Country Developments (Essex) Ltd.* [1976] Q.B. 858 (again an action alleging negligence against the local authority), Lord Denning recanted the views he had expressed in *Dutton*, and he and his colleagues held that the limitation period began to run from the time when the owner discovered, or with reasonable diligence ought to have discovered, the defective state of the property.

This clearly afforded considerable protection to the victims of latent damage in such cases, but seriously disadvantaged defendants and their insurers. The matter was further considered not long after *Sparham-Souter* by the House of Lords in *Anns* v. *Merton London Borough Council* [1978] A.C. 728. Lord Wilberforce, who delivered the leading judgment responded as follows to the question "When does the cause of action arise?": "the Court of Appeal was right when, in *Sparham-Souter* (etc.) it abjured the view that the cause of action arose immediately upon delivery, *i.e.* conveyance of the defective house. It can only arise when the state of the building is such that there is present or imminent danger to the health or safety of persons occupying it" ([1978] A.C. 728 at 760). (The notion of health and safety of occupiers derives from the statutory context in which the local authority exercises its powers of inspection.)

It was not clear to what extent, if at all, the *Sparham-Souter* test of "reasonable discoverability" had been approved by the House of Lords in *Anns* and, even if it had, whether it was applicable to defendants other than local authorities. A broad view was taken by Judge Fay Q.C. in *Eames London Estates Ltd.* v. *North Hertfordshire District Council* (1980) 259 E.G. 491. He held, in a case concerning liability in negligence of a developer, a builder, an architect and a local authority, for defective premises, that with defective buildings the limitation period began to run upon the occurrence of whichever was the later of the date the plaintiff first acquired an interest in the property and the date he first learned of the damage.

At around the same time the courts began to recognise that a person whose contractual obligations involved a requirement that he exercise reasonable care could be concurrently liable to his co-contractor (and also to third parties) in negligence. Previously it had been thought that the correct view was as expressed in the decision of Diplock L.J. in *Bagot* v. *Stevens Scanlan & Co. Ltd.* [1966] 1 Q.B. 197, denying that the tortious limitation period was applicable to the defendant architects who were in breach of their contractual duty to exercise reasonable care and skill. However, in a line of cases from the mid 1970s onwards, the courts accepted the existence of concurrent liability (see, *e.g. Esso Petroleum Co. Ltd.* v. *Mardon* [1976] Q.B. 801; *Batty* v. *Metropolitan Property Realisations Ltd.* [1978] Q.B. 554; *Midland Bank Trust Co. Ltd.* v. *Hett, Stubbs and Kemp* [1979] Ch. 384; *Ross* v. *Caunters* [1980] Ch. 297 (liability to third party).

The particular significance of this development as regards limitation periods lies in the fact that the starting point for the limitation periods in contract and tort may be different. S.5 of the Limitation Act 1980 (repeating similar provisions in earlier enactments) states:

"An action founded on simple contract shall not be brought after the expiration of six years from the date at which the cause of action accrued."

The cause of action on a simple contract accrues on breach (*Gould* v. *Johnson* (1702) 2 Salk. 422; *Gibbs* v. *Guild* (1881) 8 Q.B.D. 296, 302 *per* Field J.). The damage resulting from the breach of his contractual duty of care by, for example, an architect or an accountant, may not occur until some time after the breach, and thus it may be extremely beneficial for his client to be able to base his claim on the existence of a concurrent tortious duty. It should be noted however that contractual professional obligations may be held to be continuing in nature, in which case the cause of action can be dated from the last time at which defects in the work could have been remedied, thus narrowing the potential gap that exists between the accrual of the cause of action in contract and in tort (see *Brickfield Properties Ltd.* v. *Newton* [1971] 3 All E.R. 328, but N.B. *Bellway*

(South East) Ltd. v. *Holley* (1984) 28 B.L.R. 139, and s.14(1) of the Supply of Goods and Services Act 1982, whereby a term is to be implied into any contract for the provision of services that a service is to be carried out within a reasonable time.) This may have the effect of limiting the kind of continuing obligation held to exist in a case such as *Midland Bank Co. Ltd.* v. *Hett, Stubbs and Kemp* [1979] Ch. 384.

Law Reform Measures

The Law Reform Committee in its "Twenty First Report, Final Report on Limitation of Actions" (1977 Cmnd. 6923) was concerned, *inter alia*, at the problems raised by the meaning and applicability of the tests propounded in *Sparham-Souter* and in *Anns*, both of which had been decided shortly before the Committee reported. No consensus was reached by the Committee on the problem of latent damage at that time. However, after an initial indication by the Lord Chancellor that the problem was best left to be solved by the courts (*Hansard*, H.L. Vol. 400, col. 1234), in August 1980 he invited the Committee "to consider the law relating to—

(i) the accrual of the cause of action, and
(ii) limitation

in negligence cases involving latent defects (other than latent disease or injury to the person) and to make recommendations."

A Sub-Committee of the Law Reform Committee was set up, and it issued a Consultative Document in July 1981. Most of the responses had been received when the House of Lords delivered its judgment in *Pirelli General Cable Works Ltd.* v. *Oscar Faber and Partners* [1983] A.C. 1, which restored the balance firmly in favour of defendants. The House of Lords overruled *Sparham-Souter*, considering that that decision had not been approved in *Anns*, and held that the cause of action in a claim in tort for negligence in the design or workmanship of a building accrues at the date of the damage, whether that damage is discernible or not. As in *Cartledge*, the House of Lords regretted the judgment which it felt compelled to give, and expressed the view that a legislative solution to the problem would be necessary.

Problems have been found with certain words of Lord Fraser, who delivered the leading judgment in *Pirelli*. He said: ". . . except perhaps where the advice of an architect or a consulting engineer leads to the erection of a building which is so defective as to be doomed from the start, the cause of action accrues only when physical damage occurs to the building" ([1983] 2 A.C. 1 at 18). This potential basing of the cause of action on the defect, not the damage has not, in general, found favour with the courts in subsequent cases (see, *e.g.* *Ketteman* v. *Hansel Properties Ltd.* [1985] 1 All E.R. 352; *Jones* v. *Stroud District Council* (1986) 279 E.G. 213, largely on the basis, as explained by Lawton L.J. in *Ketteman*, that if "doomed from the start" was not applied in *Pirelli* itself, where damage in the form of cracks near the top of the chimney in question must have occurred within about ten months of the building work being finished, it was difficult to see when it would apply. Nevertheless "doomed from the start" remained as a possible trap for the unwary.

Prior to the Latent Damage Act, therefore, the position was that, in an action alleging negligence in the design or workmanship of a building, the cause of action accrued when damage occurred to the building. If the defendant was a local authority, the cause of action accrued when there was a present or imminent threat to the health or safety of persons occupying it (on the nature of the duty owed by the local authority in such cases, see *Peabody Donation Fund (Governors)* v. *Sir Lindsay Parkinson & Co. Ltd.* [1985] A.C. 210; *Investors in Industry Commercial Properties Ltd.* v. *South Bedfordshire District Council* [1986] 1 All E.R. 787. On what is meant by a present or imminent threat to health or safety, see *Percival* v. *Walsall Metropolitan Borough Council* (1986) 279 E.G. 218). If the defendant was a professional person such as a solicitor (see *Forster* v. *Outred & Co.* [1982] 2 All E.R. 753); an accountant (see *Mathew* v. *Maughold Life Assurance Co. Ltd.* (1985) 1 P.N. 142) or a surveyor giving advice (see *Secretary of State for the Environment* v. *Essex Goodman & Suggitt* [1986] 2 All E.R. 69) time began to run when the plaintiff acted to his detriment in reliance on the negligent advice. In all cases discoverability of the existence of damage was irrelevant; it was the occurrence of damage, as determined in those various contexts, that occasioned the accrual of the cause of action. As will be seen from the transitional provisions of the Act (below), these principles will remain applicable in a number of cases for some time to come.

The Law Reform Committee, having pondered over the implications of *Pirelli* for the existing law, and the comments that it had received, presented its 24th Report (Latent Damage: Cmnd. 9390) in November 1984. The Committee identified three principles as being of critical importance in this area of the law:

(i) that plaintiffs must have a fair and sufficient opportunity of pursuing their remedy;

(ii) that defendants are entitled to be protected against stale claims;

(iii) that uncertainty in the law is to be avoided wherever possible.

The Committee's strategy, based upon these principles, was to effect a balance between the hardship of a *Sparham-Souter* test to defendants and their insurers on the one hand and the problems posed to plaintiffs by the *Pirelli* test on the other hand. They proposed that a balance be effected in the following way. There should be no change in the general rule of substantive law whereby a cause of action in negligence accrues at the date of occurrence of the resulting damage. However, in negligence cases involving latent defects, the six-year period should be subject to an extension which would allow a plaintiff three years from the date of discovery or reasonable discoverability of the existence of significant damage. There should, however, be a long stop applicable to all negligence cases involving latent defects (other than personal injuries) which should bar a plaintiff from initiating proceedings more than fifteen years from the defendant's breach of duty, whether damage had yet occurred or not. This strategy commended itself to the Government, and forms the basis of the Latent Damage Act.

S.1 of the Act makes provision for the three-year discoverability period and the fifteen-year long stop.

S.2 provides for the case of a person who is under a disability at the "starting date" (see below) for the purposes of the discoverability provision, and also makes s.1 inapplicable to cases of latent damage involving deliberate concealment.

S.3 allows a subsequent purchaser of property a fresh cause of action in circumstances where damage occurred to the property during the ownership of the previous owner, but did not manifest itself until after a subsequent purchaser acquired his interest in the property. The cause of action is treated as having accrued on the date of damage, but the subsequent purchaser can, of course, benefit from the discoverability provision.

S.4 contains the transitional provisions, and s.5 the short title, interpretation and date of commencement.

PARLIAMENTARY DEBATES

Hansard: H.L. Vol. 472, cols. 307 and 797; Vol. 473, cols. 82 and 97; Vol. 474, cols. 8 and 1039; Vol. 478, col. 906; H.C. Vol. 99, col. 441; Vol. 101, col. 119.

The Bill was considered by Standing Committee E on June 24, 1986.

Time limits for negligence actions in respect of latent damage not involving personal injuries

Time limits for negligence actions in respect of latent damage not involving personal injuries

1. The following sections shall be inserted in the Limitation Act 1980 (referred to below in this Act as the 1980 Act) immediately after section 14 (date of knowledge for purposes of special time limits for actions in respect of personal injuries or death)—

"Actions in respect of latent damage not involving personal injuries

Special time limit for negligence actions where facts relevant to cause of action are not known at date of accrual

14A.—(1) This section applies to any action for damages for negligence, other than one to which section 11 of this Act applies, where the starting date for reckoning the period of limitation under subsection (4)(*b*) below falls after the date on which the cause of action accrued.

(2) Section 2 of this Act shall not apply to an action to which this section applies.

(3) An action to which this section applies shall not be brought after the expiration of the period applicable in accordance with subsection (4) below.

(4) That period is either—

(*a*) six years from the date on which the cause of action accrued; or

(*b*) three years from the starting date as defined by subsection (5) below, if that period expires later than the period mentioned in paragraph (*a*) above.

(5) For the purposes of this section, the starting date for reckoning the period of limitation under subsection (4)(*b*) above is the earliest date on which the plaintiff or any person in whom the cause of action was vested before him first had both the knowledge required for bringing an action for damages in respect of the relevant damage and a right to bring such an action.

(6) In subsection (5) above "the knowledge required for bringing an action for damages in respect of the relevant damage" means knowledge both—

(*a*) of the material facts about the damage in respect of which damages are claimed; and

(*b*) of the other facts relevant to the current action mentioned in subsection (8) below.

(7) For the purposes of subsection (6)(*a*) above, the material facts about the damage are such facts about the damage as would lead a reasonable person who had suffered such damage to consider it sufficiently serious to justify his instituting proceedings for damages against a defendant who did not dispute liability and was able to satisfy a judgment.

(8) The other facts referred to in subsection (6)(*b*) above are—

(*a*) that the damage was attributable in whole or in part to the act or omission which is alleged to constitute negligence; and

(*b*) the identity of the defendant; and

(*c*) if it is alleged that the act or omission was that of a person other than the defendant, the identity of that person and the additional facts supporting the bringing of an action against the defendant.

(9) Knowledge that any acts or omissions did or did not, as a matter of law, involve negligence is irrelevant for the purposes of subsection (5) above.

(10) For the purposes of this section a person's knowledge includes knowledge which he might reasonably have been expected to acquire—

(*a*) from facts observable or ascertainable by him; or

(*b*) from facts ascertainable by him with the help of appropriate expert advice which it is reasonable for him to seek;

but a person shall not be taken by virtue of this subsection to have knowledge of a fact ascertainable only with the help of expert advice so long as he has taken all reasonable steps to obtain (and, where appropriate, to act on) that advice.

Overriding time limit for negligence actions not involving personal injuries

14B.—(1) An action for damages for negligence, other than one to which section 11 of this Act applies, shall not be brought after the expiration of fifteen years from the date (or, if more than one, from the last of the dates) on which there occurred any act or omission—

(*a*) which is alleged to constitute negligence; and

(*b*) to which the damage in respect of which damages are claimed is alleged to be attributable (in whole or in part).

(2) This section bars the right of action in a case to which subsection (1) above applies notwithstanding that—

(*a*) the cause of action has not yet accrued; or

(*b*) where section 14A of this Act applies to the action, the date which is for the purposes of that section the starting date for reckoning the period mentioned in subsection (4)(*b*) of that section has not yet occurred;

before the end of the period of limitation prescribed by this section."

DEFINITION

"action": s.5(2).

GENERAL NOTE

This section inserts a new s.14A and s.14B into the Limitation Act 1980. It is applicable to all cases of latent damage other than personal injuries.

GENERAL NOTE TO S.14A

The effect of s.14A is that where no latent damage is present time will run, as before, for six years from the accrual of the cause of action. Such will also be the case where the three-year period from the "starting date" (see subs. 5), *i.e.* the date of discovery/discoverability, expires prior to the six-year period from the date of accrual of the cause of action. Thus, if damage is immediately patent, time runs for six years from the date such damage occurs. If damage occurs in year one, and becomes discoverable in year two, time runs out not three years from the date of discoverability but six years after the date on which the damage occurs. The value of the section to plaintiffs can be seen in those cases where, for example, the damage occurs in year one but does not become discoverable until year five. Then the primary six-year period is overridden by the three years from discovery secondary period, and such will be the case however long after the occurrence of damage its existence is discovered, subject to the long stop for which provision is made in s.14B (see below). Cases such as *Pirelli, Forster* and *Secretary of State for the Environment* would be decided differently if tried under s.14A.

Subs. (1)

Negligence. The lack of a definition of "negligence" in the Act raises a potential difficulty. The word could be restricted to cases of tortious negligence, or could extend to cases where breach of a statutory duty or breach of contract entails a breach of a duty of reasonable care. The especial significance of this lies in the fact that although, as noted above, for a decade the courts appeared to be content to accept the existence of concurrent liability in contract and tort, together with its implications for limitation periods, some doubt was cast upon the correctness of this approach by Lord Scarman, delivering the advice of the Privy Council in *Tai Hing Cotton Mill Ltd.* v. *Liu Chong Hing Bank Ltd.* [1986] A.C. 80: "Their Lordships do not believe that there is anything to the advantage of the law's development in searching for a liability in tort where the parties are in a contractual relationship" (at 107). Lord Scarman went on to give as a reason for taking this view the need to avoid confusion, since different consequences did follow according to the nature of the cause of action, limitation of actions being an example.

This apparent backpedalling from a state of affairs accepted as recently as the decisions in *Pirelli* (H.L.); *Forster* (C.A.) and *Costa* v. *Georghiou* (1985) 1 P.N. 201 (C.A.) is somewhat surprising. Since the decision in *Tai Hing* the existence of concurrent liability has continued to be accepted in *Thake* v. *Maurice* [1986] 1 All E.R. 497, and in *Forsikringsaktieselskapet Vesta* v. *Butcher* [1986] 2 All E.R. 488, though the matter awaits detailed judicial analysis. It is suggested that it would be unfortunate if a person in privity with the negligent defendant were restricted to a limitation period running for six years from the date of breach (irrespective of discoverability), leaving only those not in a contractual relationship with the defendant to benefit from the provisions of the Latent Damage Act. The Lord Chancellor did not appear to regard this as a problem (H.L. Vol. 473, col. 123 ("the negligence complained of can arise out of the performance of a contract")) and it may be that Lord Scarman's words in *Tai Hing* will not prove to threaten plaintiffs' interests in the manner feared.

Section 11 of this Act, i.e. special time limit for actions in respect of personal injuries.

Cause of action accrued. In the Second Reading of the Latent Damage Bill in the House of Lords, Lord Wilberforce (H.L. Vol. 472, col. 812) made the point that the Bill failed (as the Act does) to clarify what is meant by the accrual of the cause of action. The examples that he employed, taken from the typical building case where foundations inadequate for the site are laid, illustrate this difficulty. Does the cause of action accrue when there is a little subsidence and a plate holding up the building slips a little; or perhaps when weeds come up through a crack in the cement, or perhaps not until there is a crack in the wall?

A further aspect of this problem concerns the type of loss in issue. For example, in *Ketteman* v. *Hansel* it was argued that even if physical damage had occurred during the limitation period, the relevant damage was economic loss which was suffered when the defective foundations were laid. This argument was rejected by Lawton L.J., but it is unlikely that the last has been heard of it. The concept of "doomed from the start" (see General Note), in so far as it still exists, could pose further problems regarding the date of accrual of the cause of action.

These problems will clearly be relevant to cases such as those mentioned above where time continues to run for six years from the date of damage. Further, the three years from discoverability rule only comes into operation if three years from the "starting date" (see subs. 5) elapses after the end of a six-year period from the date of damage. Accordingly it will be necessary to know when the date of damage was, in order to know whether the discoverability rule comes into play. It may be that questions concerning the date of accrual of a cause of action are better dealt with by the courts than by Parliament, but a consequence of the lack of a definition is to add significantly to the complexity of the operation of the Act.

Subs. (5)

The object of this subsection, which includes a Government amendment from the initial draft clause, is, in the words of the Solicitor-General (H.C. Vol. 101, col. 119) to "make it clear that the only person whose knowledge is relevant is any person in whom the plaintiff's cause of action was vested before it came to the plaintiff, and the plaintiff himself." Thus, to use an example given by the Solicitor-General (H.C. Vol. 101, col. 119), where a will has been carelessly drawn, the knowledge of one beneficiary that he has suffered damage will not of itself cause time to begin to run at large against other beneficiaries. Each has his own separate cause of action against the negligent defendant.

Subss. (6)–(10)

These provisions are modelled on s.14 of the Limitation Act 1980, which defines the date of knowledge for the purposes of s.11 (personal injury claims) and s.12 (Fatal Accident claims) of that Act. The intention is to ensure that only the discovery of significant damage will cause the three-year period to begin to run. The test is considerably more elaborate than the "reasonable discoverability" test in *Sparham-Souter*, and it is doubted whether the older authorities will be of particular value in assisting with the application of subss. (6)–(10).

Subs. (7)

This is designed to ensure that a plaintiff should not be regarded as possessing "the knowledge required" simply because, to take a common example, he notices cracks in a wall of his house. Quite how large or numerous the cracks will have to be before a reasonable person would institute proceedings remains to be seen, but the existence of additional symptoms such as sticking doors and windows would no doubt be relevant.

Subs. (8)(c)

This covers cases where the plaintiff alleges that the defendant is vicariously liable for another's acts. The "additional facts" might include, for example, whether an employee was acting within the scope of his employment so as to render his employer vicariously liable.

GENERAL NOTE TO S.14B

S.14B makes provision for the fifteen-year long stop. No action for negligence can be brought (other than for personal injuries) after fifteen years have elapsed since the last date on which any act or omission alleged to constitute negligence occurred. Identification of this date, especially in cases of continuing obligations (see General Note) will be far from easy. This is an absolute bar (subject to s.2(2) below), and operates even if the cause of action has not yet accrued or, if s.14A is applicable, even though the "starting date" (see s.14A(5)) has not yet occurred. This is the first time a long stop provision has been used in English law, though when the Product Liability Directive is enacted it will have a companion.

The R.I.B.A. in their response to the Law Reform Committee employed a fictional example which showed that, in a case of an action against a negligent engineer who claims a contribution from a negligent architect, using the longest possible time limit at each stage, judgment against the architect could, even with the benefits of s.14B, be made 42 years after commission (29 years after the Final Certificate) (Supplement to R.I.B.A. Journal, May

1985). Such a case may not be typical, but it illustrates the potentiality onerous implications of the section for defendants and their insurers, albeit that it was intended to benefit them.

Provisions consequential on section 1

2.—(1) The following section shall be inserted in the 1980 Act immediately after section 28 (extension of limitation period in case of disability on date of accrual of cause of action)—

"Extension for cases where the limitation period is the period under section 14A(4)(b)

28A.—(1) Subject to subsection (2) below, if in the case of any action for which a period of limitation is prescribed by section 14A of this Act—

(a) the period applicable in accordance with subsection (4) of that section is the period mentioned in paragraph (b) of that subsection;

(b) on the date which is for the purposes of that section the starting date for reckoning that period the person by reference to whose knowledge that date fell to be determined under subsection (5) of that section was under a disability; and

(c) section 28 of this Act does not apply to the action;

the action may be brought at any time before the expiration of three years from the date when he ceased to be under a disability or died (whichever first occurred) notwithstanding that the period mentioned above has expired.

(2) An action may not be brought by virtue of subsection (1) above after the end of the period of limitation prescribed by section 14B of this Act."

(2) In section 32 of the 1980 Act (postponement of limitation period in case of fraud, concealment or mistake), at the end there shall be added the following subsection—

"(5) Sections 14A and 14B of this Act shall not apply to any action to which subsection (1)(b) above applies (and accordingly the period of limitation referred to in that subsection, in any case to which either of those sections would otherwise apply, is the period applicable under section 2 of this Act)."

DEFINITIONS
"1980 Act": s.5(2).
"action": s.5(2).

GENERAL NOTE
This section inserts a new s.28A and s.32(5) into the Limitation Act 1980. S.2(1) makes provision for s.28A, and s.2(2) for s.32(5).

GENERAL NOTE TO S.28A
S.28 of the 1980 Act makes provision for extension of the limitation period when the right of action has accrued to a person suffering under a "disability". S.28A ensures that similar provision is made in cases to which s.14A applies where the person is under a disability at the "starting date" (see s.14A(5)). Such an action may not, however, be brought after the end of the long stop period. By s.3(3) of the Latent Damage Act (see below) s.28 is stated to be inapplicable to a cause of action accruing to a subsequent owner of property under s.3.

Subs. (1)(b)
"disability"
A person is under a disability for the purposes of the Limitation Act 1980 while under the age of 18 (*i.e.* an infant; Family Law Reform Act 1969, s.1(1)(2)) or of "unsound mind": Limitation Act 1980, s.38(2). See also s.38(3) and (4) which provide further guidance as to the meaning of "unsound mind"; and annotations to Limitation Act 1980, s.28.
A disability which occurs after the "starting date" (which, by definition, must be a

disability by reason of becoming of unsound mind), will not prevent the limitation period from running (*Purnell* v. *Roche* [1927] 2 Ch. 142; *Owen* v. *De Beauvoi* (1847) 16 M. & W. 547, 567 *per* Parke B.).

Subs. (2)

GENERAL NOTE TO S.32(5)

S.32 of the Limitation Act 1980 makes provision for postponement of the limitation period in cases of fraud, concealment or mistake. The new s.32(5) states that ss.14A and 14B do not apply to cases to which subs. (1)(*b*) of s.32 (deliberate concealment by the defendant of any fact relevant to the plaintiff's right of action) applies. See also s.32(2) for further elaboration of the meaning of "deliberate concealment". Thus, in accordance with the recommendations of the Law Reform Committee, the long stop will not come into play in such cases, nor will the secondary three-year period.

"concealment"

On the meaning of "deliberate concealment" see *Clark* v. *Woor* [1965] 2 All E.R. 353; *London Borough of Lewisham* v. *Leslie & Co. Ltd.* (1979) 12 B.L.R. 22; and annotations to Limitation Act 1980, s.32.

Accrual of cause of action to successive owners in respect of latent damage to property

Accrual of cause of action to successive owners in respect of latent damage to property

3.—(1) Subject to the following provisions of this section, where—
    (*a*) a cause of action ("the original cause of action") has accrued to any person in respect of any negligence to which damage to any property in which he has an interest is attributable (in whole or in part); and
    (*b*) another person acquires an interest in that property after the date on which the original cause of action accrued but before the material facts about the damage have become known to any person who, at the time when he first has knowledge of those facts, has any interest in the property;
a fresh cause of action in respect of that negligence shall accrue to that other person on the date on which he acquires his interest in the property.
    (2) A cause of action accruing to any person by virtue of subsection (1) above—
    (*a*) shall be treated as if based on breach of a duty of care at common law owed to the person to whom it accrues; and
    (*b*) shall be treated for the purposes of section 14A of the 1980 Act (special time limit for negligence actions where facts relevant to cause of action are not known at date of accrual) as having accrued on the date on which the original cause of action accrued.
    (3) Section 28 of the 1980 Act (extension of limitation period in case of disability) shall not apply in relation to any such cause of action.
    (4) Subsection (1) above shall not apply in any case where the person acquiring an interest in the damaged property is either—
    (*a*) a person in whom the original cause of action vests by operation of law; or
    (*b*) a person in whom the interest in that property vests by virtue of any order made by a court under section 538 of the Companies Act 1985 (vesting of company property in liquidator).
    (5) For the purposes of subsection (1)(*b*) above, the material facts about the damage are such facts about the damage as would lead a reasonable person who has an interest in the damaged property at the time when those facts become known to him to consider it sufficiently

serious to justify his instituting proceedings for damages against a defendant who did not dispute liability and was able to satisfy a judgment.

(6) For the purposes of this section a person's knowledge includes knowledge which he might reasonably have been expected to acquire—

(*a*) from facts observable or ascertainable by him; or

(*b*) from facts ascertained by him with the help of appropriate expert advice which it is reasonable for him to seek;

but a person shall not be taken by virtue of this subsection to have knowledge of a fact ascertainable by him only with the help of expert advice so long as he has taken all reasonable steps to obtain (and, where appropriate, to act on) that advice.

(7) This section shall bind the Crown, but as regards the Crown's liability in tort shall not bind the Crown further than the Crown is made liable in tort by the Crown Proceedings Act 1947.

DEFINITION
"1980 Act": s.5(2).
"action": s.5(2).

GENERAL NOTE
This section is designed to deal with the problem of, *inter alios*, the subsequent purchaser who is not the owner of the property when the damage occurs (see *Perry* v. *Tendring District Council* (1984) 30 B.L.R. 118). Previously such a person was unable to claim against the person whose negligence had caused the damage as he had no interest in the property at the date the damage occurred. Henceforth such a person will be able to claim, provided that the "material facts" (see s.3(5)) had not become known, before such a person acquired his interest, to a person who at the time had an interest (*e.g.* the previous owner). For example, A, the owner of Blackacre, sells the property to C, unaware that it has already sustained damage as a result of D's negligence in designing it. Provided that A did not know of the "material facts" before C acquired his interest, C may sue D, his cause of action accruing for the purposes of s.14A on the date on which A's cause of action accrued. The section avoids the risk of a series of limitation periods running in relation to one property by providing that a cause of action accruing to any person is to be treated as based on breach of a duty of care owed to the person to whom it accrues and, for the purposes of s.14A, is to be treated as having accrued on the date on which the original cause of action accrued.

Subs. (1)(b)

"*acquires an interest in that property*"
The section is not limited to persons acquiring a legal estate in land but would, for example, apply to a person acquiring an equitable interest under a long lease.

Subs. (4)(a)
e.g. a trustee in bankruptcy.

Supplementary

Transitional provisions

4.—(1) Nothing in section 1 or 2 of this Act shall—

(*a*) enable any action to be brought which was barred by the 1980 Act or (as the case may be) by the Limitation Act 1939 before this Act comes into force; or

(*b*) affect any action commenced before this Act comes into force.

(2) Subject to subsection (1) above, sections 1 and 2 of this Act shall have effect in relation to causes of action accruing before, as well as in relation to causes of action accruing after, this Act comes into force.

(3) Section 3 of this Act shall only apply in cases where an interest in damaged property is acquired after this Act comes into force but shall so apply, subject to subsection (4) below, irrespective of whether the original cause of action accrued before or after this Act comes into force.

(4) Where—

(*a*) a person acquires an interest in damaged property in circumstances to which section 3 would apart from this subsection apply; but

(*b*) the original cause of action accrued more than six years before this Act comes into force;

a cause of action shall not accrue to that person by virtue of subsection (1) of that section unless section 32(1)(*b*) of the 1980 Act (postponement of limitation period in case of deliberate concealment of relevant facts) would apply to any action founded on the original cause of action.

DEFINITION

"1980 Act": s.5(2).
"action": s.5(2).

Citation, interpretation, commencement and extent

5.—(1) This Act may be cited as the Latent Damage Act 1986.

(2) In this Act—

"the 1980 Act" has the meaning given by section 1; and

"action" includes any proceeding in a court of law, an arbitration and any new claim within the meaning of section 35 of the 1980 Act (new claims in pending actions).

(3) This Act shall come into force at the end of the period of two months beginning with the date on which it is passed.

(4) This Act extends to England and Wales only.

Subs. (3)

The Act received the Royal Assent on July 18, 1986.

OUTER SPACE ACT 1986

(1986 c. 38)

An Act to confer licensing and other powers on the Secretary of State to secure compliance with the international obligations of the United Kingdom with respect to the launching and operation of space objects and the carrying on of other activities in outer space by persons connected with this country.　　　　　　　[18th July 1986]

PARLIAMENTARY DEBATES
Hansard: H.L. Vol. 470, col. 335; Vol. 470, col. 1096; Vol. 471, col. 823; Vol. 472, col. 11; Vol. 478, col. 906; H.C. Vol. 95, col. 135; Vol. 100, col. 1260.
The Bill was considered by Standing Committee H on June 17, 1986.

Application of Act

Activities to which this Act applies

1.—This Act applies to the following activities whether carried on in the United Kingdom or elsewhere—
(*a*) launching or procuring the launch of a space object:
(*b*) operating a space object;
(*c*) any activity in outer space.

Persons to whom this Act applies

2.—(1) This Act applies to United Kingdom nationals, Scottish firms, and bodies incorporated under the law of any part of the United Kingdom.

(2) For this purpose "United Kingdom national" means an individual who is—
  (*a*) a British citizen, a British Dependent Territories citizen, a British National (Overseas), or a British Overseas citizen,
  (*b*) a person who under the British Nationality Act 1981 is a British subject, or
  (*c*) a British protected person within the meaning of that Act.
(3) Her Majesty may by Order in Council extend the application of this Act to bodies incorporated under the law of any of the Channel Islands, the Isle of Man or any dependent territory.

Licensing of activities

Prohibition of unlicensed activities

3.—(1) A person to whom this Act applies shall not, subject to the following provisions, carry on an activity to which this Act applies except under the authority of a licence granted by the Secretary of State.
(2) A licence is not required—
  (*a*) by a person acting as employee or agent of another; or
  (*b*) for activities in respect of which it is certified by Order in Council that arrangements have been made between the United Kingdom and another country to secure compliance with the international obligations of the United Kingdom.
(3) The Secretary of State may by order except other persons or activities from the requirement of a licence if he is satisfied that the requirement is not necessary to secure compliance with the international obligations of the United Kingdom.
(4) An order shall be made by statutory instrument which shall be subject to annulment in pursuance of a resolution of either House of Parliament.

Grant of licence

4.—(1) The Secretary of State may grant a licence if he thinks fit.
(2) He shall not grant a licence unless he is satisfied that the activities authorised by the licence—
  (*a*) will not jeopardise public health or the safety of persons or property,
  (*b*) will be consistent with the international obligations of the United Kingdom, and
  will not impair the national security of the United Kingdom.
(3) The Secretary of State may make regulations—
  (*a*) prescribing the form and contents of applications for licences and other documents to be filed in connection with applications;
  (*b*) regulating the procedure to be followed in connection with applications and authorising the rectification of procedural irregularities;
  (*c*) prescribing time limits for doing anything required to be done in connection with an application and providing for the extension of any period so prescribed;
  (*d*) requiring the payment to the Secretary of State of such fees as may be prescribed.

Terms of licence

5.—(1) A licence shall describe the activities authorised by it and shall be granted for such period, and may be granted subject to such conditions, as the Secretary of State thinks fit.

(2) A licence may in particular contain conditions—

(*a*) permitting inspection by the Secretary of State of the licensee's facilities, and inspection and testing by him of the licensee's equipment;

(*b*) requiring the licensee to provide the Secretary of State as soon as possible with information as to—

    (i) the date and territory or location of launch, and

    (ii) the basic orbital parameters, including nodal period, inclination, apogee and perigee,

and with such other information as the Secretary of State thinks fit concerning the nature, conduct, location and results of the licensee's activities;

(*c*) permitting the Secretary of State to inspect and take copies of documents relating to the information required to be given to him;

(*d*) requiring the licensee to obtain advance approval from the Secretary of State for any intended deviation from the orbital parameters, and to inform the Secretary of State immediately of any unintended deviation;

(*e*) requiring the licensee to conduct his operations in such a way as to—

    (i) prevent the contamination of outer space or adverse changes in the environment of the earth,

    (ii) avoid interference with the activities of others in the peaceful exploration and use of outer space,

    (iii) avoid any breach of the United Kingdom's international obligations, and

    (iv) preserve the national security of the United Kingdom;

(*f*) requiring the licensee to insure himself against liability incurred in respect of damage or loss suffered by third parties, in the United Kingdom or elsewhere, as a result of the activities authorised by the licence;

(*g*) governing the disposal of the payload in outer space on the termination of operations under the licence and requiring the licensee to notify the Secretary of State as soon as practicable of its final disposal; and

(*h*) providing for the termination of the licence on a specified event.

Transfer, variation, suspension or termination of licence

6.—(1) A licence may be transferred with the written consent of the Secretary of State and in such other cases as may be prescribed.

(2) The Secretary of State may revoke, vary or suspend a licence with the consent of the licensee or where it appears to him—

(*a*) that a condition of the licence or any regulation made under this Act has not been complied with, or

(*b*) that revocation, variation or suspension of the licence is required in the interests of public health or national security, or to comply with any international obligation of the United Kingdom.

(3) The suspension, revocation or expiry of a licence does not affect the obligations of the licensee under the conditions of the licence.

Other controls

Register of space objects

7.—(1) The Secretary of State shall maintain a register of space objects.

(2) There shall be entered in the register such particulars of such space objects as the Secretary of State considers appropriate to comply with the international obligations of the United Kingdom.

(3) Any person may inspect a copy of the register on payment of such fee as the Secretary of State may prescribe.

Power to give directions

8.—(1) If it appears to the Secretary of State that an activity is being carried on by a person to whom this Act applies—

(*a*) in contravention of section 3 (licensing requirement), or

(*b*) in contravention of the conditions of a licence,

he may give such directions to that person as appear to him necessary to secure compliance with the international obligations of the United Kingdom or with the conditions of the licence.

(2) He may, in particular, give such directions as appear to him necessary to secure the cessation of the activity or the disposal of any space object.

(3) Compliance with a direction may, without prejudice to other means of enforcement, be enforced on the application of the Secretary of State by injunction or, in Scotland, by interdict or by order under section 91 of the Court of Session Act 1868.

Warrant authorising direct action

9.—(1) If a justice of the peace is satisfied by information on oath that there are reasonable grounds for believing—

(*a*) that an activity is being carried on by a person to whom this Act applies in contravention of section 3 (licensing requirement) or in contravention of the conditions of a licence, and

(*b*) that a direction under section 8 has not been complied with, or a refusal to comply with such a direction is apprehended, or the case is one of urgency,

he may issue a warrant authorising a named person acting on behalf of the Secretary of State to do anything necessary to secure compliance with the international obligations of the United Kingdom or with the conditions of the licence.

(2) The warrant shall specify the action so authorised.

(3) The warrant may authorise entry onto specified premises at any reasonable hour and on production, if so required, of the warrant.

(4) The powers conferred by the warrant include power to use reasonable force, if necessary, and may be exercised by the named person together with other persons.

(5) A warrant remains in force for a period of one month from the date of its issue.

(6) In Scotland the reference in subsection (1) to a justice of the peace shall be construed as a reference to a justice of the peace or a sheriff and the reference to information shall be construed as a reference to evidence.

Obligation to indemnify government against claims

10.—(1) A person to whom this Act applies shall indemnify Her Majesty's government in the United Kingdom against any claims brought against the government in respect of damage or loss arising out of activities carried on by him to which this Act applies.

(2) This section does not apply—

(*a*) to a person acting as employee or agent of another; or

(*b*) to damage or loss resulting from anything done on the instructions of the Secretary of State.

General

Regulations

11.—(1) The Secretary of State may make regulations—

(*a*) prescribing anything required or authorised to be prescribed under this Act, and

(*b*) generally for carrying this Act into effect.

(2) Regulations under this Act shall be made by statutory instrument which shall be subject to annulment in pursuance of a resolution of either House of Parliament.

Offences

12.—(1) A person commits an offence who—

(*a*) carries on an activity in contravention of section 3 (licensing requirement);

(*b*) for the purpose of obtaining a licence (for himself or for another) knowingly or recklessly makes a statement which is false in a material particular;

(*c*) being the holder of a licence, fails to comply with the conditions of the licence;

(*d*) fails to comply with a direction under section 8;

(*e*) intentionally obstructs a person in the exercise of powers conferred by a warrant under section 9; or

(*f*) fails to comply with such of the regulations under this Act as may be prescribed.

(2) A person committing an offence is liable on conviction on indictment to a fine and on summary conviction to a fine not exceeding the statutory maximum.

(3) Where an offence committed by a body corporate is proved to have been committed with the consent or connivance of, or to be attributable to neglect on the part of, a director, secretary or other similar officer of the body corporate, or a person purporting to act in any such capacity, he as well as the body corporate is guilty of the offence and liable to be proceeded against and punished accordingly.

In this subsection "director", in relation to a body corporate whose affairs are managed by its members, means a member of the body corporate.

(4) Proceedings for an offence committed outside the United Kingdom may be taken, and the offence may for incidental purposes be treated as having been committed, in any place in the United Kingdom.

(5) In proceedings for an offence under paragraph (*a*), (*c*), (*d*) or (*f*) of subsection (1) it is a defence for the accused to show that he used all due diligence and took all reasonable precautions to avoid the commission of the offence.

(6) A person other than a person to whom this Act applies is not guilty of an offence under this Act in respect of things done by him outside the United Kingdom, except—

(*a*) an offence of aiding, abetting, counselling or procuring, conspiracy or incitement in relation to the commission of an offence under this Act in the United Kingdom; or

(*b*) an offence under subsection (3) (liability of directors, officers, &c.) in connection with an offence committed by a body corporate which is a person to whom this Act applies.

(7) Section 2 (person to whom this Act applies) shall not be construed as restricting the persons against whom proceedings for an offence may be brought.

Minor definitions

13.—(1) In this Act—

"dependent territory" means—

    (*a*) a colony, or

    (*b*) a country outside Her Majesty's dominions in which Her Majesty has jurisdiction in right of Her Government in the United Kingdom;

"outer space" includes the moon and other celestial bodies; and

"space object" includes the component parts of a space object, its launch vehicle and the component parts of that.

(2) For the purposes of this Act a person carries on an activity if he causes it to occur or is responsible for its continuing.

Index of defined expressions

14. The following Table shows provisions defining or otherwise explaining expressions used in this Act (other than provisions defining or explaining an expression used in the same section):—

activities to which this Act applies	section 1
carrying on an activity	section 13(2)
dependent territory	section 13(1)
outer space	section 13(1)
person to whom this Act applies ..	section 2
prescribed	section 11(1)(*a*)
space object	section 13(1)

Short title, commencement and extent

15.—(1) This Act may be cited as the Outer Space Act 1986.

(2) This Act comes into force on such day as the Secretary of State may appoint by order made by statutory instrument.

(3) The Secretary of State may appoint a later day for the commencement of so much of section 2(2)(*a*) as refers to the status of British National (Overseas).

(4) Activities to which this Act applies begun before the commencement of this Act may be carried on without a licence under section 3 for six months after commencement; but sections 8 and 9 (directions and action to secure compliance with international obligations) apply to such activities as they apply to activities carried on in contravention of that section.

(5) This Act extends to England and Wales, Scotland and Northern Ireland.

(6) Her Majesty may by Order in Council direct that this Act shall apply, subject to such exceptions and modifications as may be specified in the Order, to the Channel Islands, the Isle of Man or any dependent territory.

PATENTS, DESIGNS AND MARKS ACT 1986*

(1986 c. 39)

An Act to amend the enactments relating to the registers of trade marks, designs and patents so as to enable them to be kept otherwise than in documentary form and so as to give the enactments due effect in relation to any portion of a register not kept in documentary form; to make amendments of the Trade Marks Act 1938 in relation to the use of the Royal Arms and other devices, emblems and titles and in relation to the protection of trade marks and service marks for whose protection application has been made overseas; to make other amendments of the Trade Marks Act 1938 in its application to service marks and amendments of other Acts in relation to such marks; and for connected purposes. [18th July 1986]

INTRODUCTION AND GENERAL NOTE

This Act enables the Comptroller General of Patents, Trade Marks and Designs to keep the registers of patents, designs and trade marks on computer thereby making the process of searches and obtaining copies of entries on the register easier, quicker and more cost effective than previously. It is envisaged by the terms of the Act that it will be possible to obtain both certified copies of entries on the various registers and uncertified copies in respect of both of which a fee will be charged. With the introduction of registered service marks and the prospect of the privatisation of the Patent Office, the practicality of computerisation is all too apparent. The other amendments provided for in this Act constitute a "tidying up" exercise in the wake of the Trade Marks (Amendment) Act of 1984, with which this Act should be read. No major changes to the existing law have been introduced in this Act in view of the current discussions surrounding the proposals for re-shaping of the law of intellectual property embodied in the White Paper.

COMMENCEMENT

The Act comes into force on the same day as the Trade Marks (Amendment) Act 1984, namely October 1, 1987. However, the Act does provide that any applications for registration of service marks made prior to the commencement date of both Acts and pursuant to the provisions of the Trade Marks and Service Marks Rules 1986 shall be treated as if the applications had been made immediately after the commencement date. The purpose of this is to enable the Trade Marks Registry to process applications in the interim and thereby to reduce the backlog of outstanding applications as at the date that the Acts come into effect.

---

* Annotations by Fiona Clark, Barrister.

EXTENT

This Act extends to Northern Ireland and to the Isle of Man (subject to any amendments made by Order in Council).

PARLIAMENTARY DEBATES

Hansard: H.L. Vol. 469, col. 1164; H.L. Vol. 470, col. 920; H.L. Vol. 473, cols. 477, 611, 1123; H.L. Vol. 474, col. 139; H.L. Vol. 478, col. 1074; H.C. Vol. 99, col. 871; H.C. Vol. 101, col. 263.

The Bill was considered by Standing Committee D on June 26, 1986.

Registers of trade marks, designs and patents—computerisation etc.

1. The amendments specified in Schedule 1 to this Act (which relate to computerisation of the registers there mentioned and to associated matters) shall have effect.

GENERAL NOTE

Schedule 1, which is brought into force by this section and is printed below, amends section 1 of the Trade Marks Act 1938, section 17 of the Registered Designs Act 1949 and section 32 of the Patents Act 1977 in that it empowers the Comptroller-General to maintain the registers of trade marks, designs and patents other than in documentary form. The wording of the previous sections is otherwise largely adhered to with the exception that in the case of the Trade Marks Register, the previous requirement that the register also should contain the description of the registered proprietor or registered user is dispensed with.

In relation to each of the registers it is provided that both certified and uncertified copies of entries in the registers may be obtained on payment of the requisite fee. Certified copies of or extracts from the Registers are to be admitted in evidence without further proof and a certificate of the Registrar is to be prima facie evidence if the matters so certified. This effects no substantive change in the law (see sections 57 and 58 of the Trade Marks Act 1938, section 35 of the Patents Act 1977 and section 24 of the Registered Designs Act 1949 which are now repealed).

There is also a saving for the effect of sections 69 and 70 of the Police and Criminal Evidence Act 1984. This has the result that if it is required to use any computerised copies of entries in the registers in criminal proceedings, then they will not be admissible in evidence unless it is shown that (a) there are no reasonable grounds for showing that they are inaccurate because of improper use of the computer and (b) that at all material times the computer was operating properly, or if not, was not operating in such a way as to affect the production of the document or the accuracy of its contents.

Service marks etc.

2.—(1) In section 1 of the Trade Marks (Amendment) Act 1984—

(*a*) the following subsections shall be substituted for subsections (1) and (2)—

"(1) Subject to subsection (2) below, the Trade Marks Act 1938 shall have effect with respect to service marks as it has effect with respect to trade marks (references to goods having effect as references to services).

(2) The Act of 1938 shall have effect in relation to service marks as mentioned in Schedule 1 to this Act." and

(*b*) the following subsection shall be substituted for subsection (7)—

"(7) In this Act "service mark" means a mark (including a device, name, signature, word, letter, numeral, or any combination thereof) used or proposed to be used in relation to services for the purpose of indicating, or so as to indicate, that a particular person is connected, in the course of business, with the provision of those services, whether with or without any indication of the identity of that person.".

(2) Subject to any Order made after the passing of this Act by virtue of subsection (1)(*a*) of section 3 of the Northern Ireland Constitution Act 1973, service marks shall not be a transferred matter for the purposes of

that Act but shall for the purposes of subsection (2) of that section be treated as specified in Schedule 3 to that Act.

(3) The enactments mentioned in Schedule 2 to this Act shall have effect subject to the amendments there specified.

GENERAL NOTE

The amendments provided for by this section and Schedule 2 of this Act are largely amendments consequential upon the Trade Marks (Amendment) Act 1984. The previous subsections (1) and (2) of section 1 of that Act are amended to introduce a statutory definition of "service mark" (see section 2(1)(*b*) which had been a noteable omission. "Mark" is defined as including a device, name, signature, word, letter, numeral, or any combination thereof. This is the same as the definition in section 68 of the Trade Marks Act 1938 as amended by the Trade Marks (Amendment) Act 1984. As to what constitutes "use in relation to services" see section 68(2) of the Trade Marks Act 1938 as amended by the Trade Marks (Amendment) Act 1984. The definition of "service mark" includes the words "whether with or without any indication of the identity of" the person connected with the services. However, in order to be registrable, a mark must distinguish or be capable of distinguishing the proprietor of the mark within the meaning of sections 9 and 10 of the Trade Marks Act 1938 and thus the mark itself must in any event either be an indication or be capable of indicating the proprietor.

The Schedule 2 amendments also include the amendment of section 26 of the 1938 Act (as amended by the 1984 Act), which relates to revocation of registered marks on grounds of non-use. The purpose of the amendment, which appears in Schedule 2 at Part III, para. 4, is to remove what had been perceived to be a lacuna, namely, that the proviso to section 26(1) allowed the Registrar to take into account bona fide use of a service mark upon or in relation to goods associated with the provision of the services in respect of which the mark was registered in certain circumstances, but there was no corresponding provision in relation to the bona fide use of a trade mark upon or in relation to associated services.

By virtue of Schedule 2, Part III at para. 11, it is provided that there shall not be Sheffield service marks or cotton service marks. This is because it is envisaged that the Sheffield Register and the Manchester Register will be abolished in the foreseeable future. The Schedule also implements Article 4 of the International Convention for the Protection of Industrial Property by giving priority to applicants for registration who have within the previous six months applied for a registration in a convention country. Damages for infringement run only from the date of the U.K. application and not from the date of the application in the convention country (see the new section 39A(3) of the Trade Marks Act 1938).

The amendments also ensure that licence agreements relating to service marks may also take advantage of exemptions from registration under the Restrictive Trade Practices Act 1976 in similar terms to those which apply in respect of trade marks licence agreements.

Further, this section also brings into effect the provisions of Schedule 2 which amends certain statutes so that where there is a reference to registered trade mark, that also includes registered service mark and ensures that any reference to the Trade Marks Act 1938 will be to that Act as amended by the Trade Marks (Amendment) Act 1938. In addition, the Comptroller is granted the similar rights to suspend enemy service marks as already exist in relation to enemy trade marks under the Patents, Designs, Copyright and Trade Marks (Emergency) Act 1939.

Repeals

3.—(1) The enactments mentioned in Part 1 of Schedule 3 to this Act are repealed to the extent specified in the third column of that Part of that Schedule in consequence of section 1 above and Schedule 1 to this Act.

(2) The enactments mentioned in Part II of Schedule 3 to this Act are repealed to the extent specified in the third column of that Part of that Schedule in consequence of section 2 above and Schedule 2 to this Act.

Short title, extent and commencement

4.—(1) This Act may be cited as the Patents, Designs and Marks Act 1986.

(2) The amendment or repeal of any enactment by this Act has the same extent as that enactment.

(3) Subject to subsection (2) above, this Act extends to Northern Ireland.

(4) The following provisions of this Act shall extend to the Isle of Man, subject to any exceptions, adaptations or modifications contained in an Order made by Her Majesty in Council—

(*a*) section 1 so far is it relates to paragraphs 1 and 2 of Schedule 1;
(*b*) section 2(1);
(*c*) section 2(3) so far as it relates to paragraphs 1(2)(*e*)(i) and (ii), 2(2)(*b*), 3 to 7 and 9 to 12 of Schedule 2;
(*d*) section 3(1) so far as it relates to the Trade Marks Act 1938;
(*e*) section 3(2); and
(*f*) this section.

(5) Her Majesty may by Order in Council make provision for extending to the Isle of Man, with such exceptions, adaptations or modifications as may be specified in the Order, sections 1 and 3(1) above so far as they relate to the Registered Designs Act 1949 and the Patents Act 1977.

(6) Section 1 above (with Schedule 1) and section 3 above, so far as it relates to Part I of Schedule 3, shall come into force on such day as the Secretary of State may by order made by statutory instrument appoint and different days may be appointed in pursuance of this subsection for different provisions or different purposes of the same provision.

(7) Section 2 above (with Schedule 2) and section 3 above, so far as it relates to Part II of Schedule 3, shall come into force on the same day as the Trade Marks (Amendment) Act 1984; but anything done before their commencement which, if it had been done after it, would have constituted an application for the registration of a service mark shall be treated as if it had been done immediately after it.

SCHEDULES

SCHEDULE 1

Computerisation

Trade Marks Act 1938 (c.22)

1. The following section shall be substituted for section 1 of the Trade Marks Act 1938—

"Register of trade marks etc"

1.—(1) The Comptroller-General of Patents, Designs and Trade Marks (in this Act referred to as "the Registrar") shall maintain the register of trade marks, in which shall be entered—

(*a*) all registered trade marks with the names and addresses of their proprietors;
(*b*) notifications of assignments and transmissions;
(*c*) the names and addresses of all registered users;
(*d*) disclaimers, conditions and limitations; and
(*e*) such other matters relating to registered trade marks as may be prescribed.

(2) The register shall continue to be divided into two parts called respectively Part A and Part B.

(3) The register need not be kept in documentary form.

(4) Subject to any rules under this Act, the public shall have a right to inspect the register at the Patent Office at all convenient times.

(5) Any person who applies for a certified copy of an entry in the register or a certified extract from the register shall be entitled to obtain such a copy or extract on payment of a fee prescribed in relation to certified copies and extracts; and the rules may provide that any person who applies for an uncertified copy or extract shall be entitled to such a copy or extract on payment of a fee prescribed in relation to uncertified copies and extracts.

(6) Applications under subsection (5) above or rules made by virtue of that subsection shall be made in such manner as may be prescribed.

(7) In relation to any portion of the register kept otherwise than in documentary form—

(*a*) the right of inspection conferred by subsection (4) above is a right to inspect the material on the register; and

(*b*) the right to a copy or extract conferred by subsection (5) above or the rules is a right to a copy or extract in a form in which it can be taken away and in which it is visible and legible.

(8) A certificate purporting to be signed by the Registrar and certifying that any entry which he is authorised by this Act or rules to make has or has not been made, or that any other thing which he is so authorised to do has or has not been done, shall be prima facie evidence, and in Scotland shall be sufficient evidence, of the matters so certified.

(9) A copy of an entry in the register or an extract from the register which is supplied under subsection (5) above and purports to be a certified copy or certified extract shall, subject to subsection (10) below, be admitted in evidence without further proof and without production of any original; and in Scotland such evidence shall be sufficient evidence.

(10) In the application of this section to England and Wales nothing in it shall be taken as detracting from section 69 or 70 of the Police and Criminal Evidence Act 1984 or any provision made by virtue of either of them.

(11) In this section "certified copy" and "certified extract" mean a copy and extract certified by the Registrar and sealed with the seal of the Patent Office.".

2. The words "name or address" shall be substituted for the words "name, address or description" in subsection (1)(*a*) and (*b*) and subsection (2) of section 34 of that Act (correction of register).

Registered Designs Act 1949 (c.88)

3. The following section shall be substituted for section 17 of the Registered Designs Act 1949–

"Register of designs etc.

17.—(1) The registrar shall maintain the register of designs, in which shall be entered—

(*a*) the names and addresses of proprietors of registered designs;

(*b*) notices of assignments and of transmissions of registered designs; and

(*c*) such other matters as may be prescribed or as the registrar may think fit.

(2) No notice of any trust, whether express, implied or constructive, shall be entered in the register of designs, and the registrar shall not be affected by any such notice.

(3) The register need not be kept in documentary form.

(4) Subject to the provisions of this Act and to rules made by the Secretary of State under it, the public shall have a right to inspect the register at the Patent Office at all convenient times.

(5) Any person who applies for a certified copy of an entry in the register or a certified extract from the register shall be entitled to obtain such a copy or extract on payment of a fee prescribed in relation to certified copies and extracts; and rules made by the Secretary of State under this Act may provide that any person who applies for an uncertified copy or extract shall be entitled to such a copy or extract on payment of a fee prescribed in relation to uncertified copies and extracts.

(6) Applications under subsection (5) above or rules made by virtue of that subsection shall be made in such manner as may be prescribed.

(7) In relation to any portion of the register kept otherwise than in documentary form—

(*a*) the right of inspection conferred by subsection (4) above is a right to inspect the material on the register; and

(*b*) the right to a copy or extract conferred by subsection (5) above or rules is a right to a copy or extract in a form in which it can be taken away and in which it is visible and legible.

(8) Subject to subsection (11) below, the register shall be prima facie evidence of anything required or authorised by this Act to be entered in it and in Scotland shall be sufficient evidence of any such thing.

(9) A certificate purporting to be signed by the registrar and certifying that any entry which he is authorised by or under this Act to make has or has not been made, or that any other thing which he is so authorised to do has or has not been done, shall be

prima facie evidence and in Scotland shall be sufficient evidence, of the matters so certified.

(10) Each of the following—

(*a*) a copy of an entry in the register or an extract from the register which is supplied under subsection (5) above;

(*b*) a copy of any representation, specimen or document kept in the Patent Office or an extract from any such document,

which purports to be a certified copy or certified extract shall, subject to subsection (11) below, be admitted in evidence without further proof and without production of any original; and in Scotland such evidence shall be sufficient evidence.

(11) In the application of this section to England and Wales nothing in it shall be taken as detracting from section 69 or 70 of the Police and Criminal Evidence Act 1984 or any provision made by virtue of either of them.

(12) In this section "certified copy" and "certified extract" mean a copy and extract certified by the registrar and sealed with the seal of the Patent Office.".

Patents Act 1977 (c.37)

4. The following section shall be substituted for section 32 of the Patents Act 1977—

"Register of patents etc.

32.—(1) The comptroller shall maintain register of patents, which shall comply with rules made by virtue of this section and shall be kept in accordance with such rules.

(2) Without prejudice to any other provision of this Act or rules, rules may make provision with respect to the following matters, including provision imposing requirements as to any of those matters—

(*a*) the registration of patents and of published applications for patents;

(*b*) the registration of transactions, instruments or events affecting rights in or under patents and applications;

(*c*) the furnishing to the comptroller of any prescribed documents or description of documents in connection with any matter which is required to be registered;

(*d*) the correction of errors in the register and in any documents filed at the Patent Office in connection with registration; and

(*e*) the publication and advertisement of anything done under this Act or rules in relation to the register.

(3) Notwithstanding anything in subsection (2)(*b*) above, no notice of any trust, whether express, implied or constructive, shall be entered in the register and the comptroller shall not be affected by any such notice.

(4) The register need not be kept in documentary form.

(5) Subject to rules, the public shall have a right to inspect the register at the Patent Office at all convenient times.

(6) Any person who applies for a certified copy of an entry in the register or a certified extract from the register shall be entitled to obtain such a copy or extract on payment of a fee prescribed in relation to certified copies and extracts; and rules may provide that any person who applies for an uncertified copy or extract shall be entitled to such a copy or extract on payment of a fee prescribed in relation to uncertified copies and extracts.

(7) Applications under subsection (6) above or rules made by virtue of that subsection shall be made in such manner as may be prescribed.

(8) In relation to any portion of the register kept otherwise than in documentary form—

(*a*) the right of inspection conferred by subsection (5) above is a right to inspect the material on the register; and

(*b*) the right to a copy or extract conferred by subsection (6) above or rules is a right to a copy or extract in a form in which it can be taken away and in which it is visible and legible.

(9) Subject to subsection (12) below, the register shall be prima facie evidence of anything required or authorised by this Act or rules to be registered and in Scotland shall be sufficient evidence of any such thing.

(10) A certificate purporting to be signed by the comptroller and certifying that any entry which he is authorised by this Act or rules to make has or has not been made, or that any other thing which he is so authorised to do has or has not been done, shall be prima facie evidence, and in Scotland shall be sufficient evidence, of the matters so certified.

(11) Each of the following, that is to say—

(a) a copy of an entry in the register or an extract from the register which is supplied under subsection (6) above;

(b) a copy of any document kept in the Patent Office or an extract from any such document, any specification of a patent or any application for a patent which has been published,

which purports to be a certified copy or a certified extract shall, subject to subsection (12) below, be admitted in evidence without further proof and without production of any original; and in Scotland such evidence shall be sufficient evidence.

(12) In the application of this section to England and Wales nothing in it shall be taken as detracting from section 69 or 70 of the Police and Criminal Evidence Act 1984 or any provision made by virtue of either or them.

(13) In this section "certified copy" and "certified extract" mean a copy and extract certified by the comptroller and sealed with the seal of the Patent Office.

(14) In this Act, except so far as the context otherwise requires—

"register", as a noun, means the register of patents;

"register", as a verb, means, in relation to any thing, to register or register particulars, or enter notice, of that thing in the register and, in relation to a person, means to enter his name in the register;

and cognate expressions shall be construed accordingly.".

SCHEDULE 2

Service Marks etc.

Part I

References to Trade Marks to Include References to Service Marks

1.—(1) Any reference to a trade mark in a provision to which this paragraph applies shall include a reference to a service mark and accordingly any reference to a registered trade mark includes a reference to a registered service mark.

(2) The provisions to which this paragraph applies are—

(a) in the Crown Proceedings Act 1947 (including that Act as it applies in Northern Ireland in relation to the Crown in right of Her Majesty's Government in the United Kingdom and in right of Her Majesty's Government in Northern Ireland), subsections (1) and (3) of section 3 (provisions as to industrial property);

(b) in the Printer's Imprint Act 1961, subsection (1) of section 1 (relaxation of requirements as to printer's imprint etc.);

(c) in the Income and Corporation Taxes Act 1970, section 132 (deduction of fees and expenses);

(d) in the Tribunals and Inquiries Act 1971, paragraph 22 of Schedule 1 (tribunals under general supervision of Council on Tribunals);

(e) in the Patents Act 1977—

(i) subsection (2) of section 19 (general power to amend application for patent before grant);

(ii) subsection (4) of section 27 (general power to amend specification after grant of patent);

(iii) subsection (7) of section 123 (publication of reports of cases);

(f) in the Unfair Contract Terms Act 1977, paragraph 1(c) of Schedule 1 (scope of sections 2 to 4 and 7 of Act);

(g) in the State Immunity Act 1978, section 7 (liability of States as respects proceedings relating to intellectual property etc.);

(h) the definition of "intellectual property" in subsection (5) of section 72 of the Supreme Court Act 1981, subsection (5) of section 15 of the Law Reform (Miscellaneous Provisions) (Scotland) Act 1985 and subsection (5) of section 94A of the Judicature (Northern Ireland) Act 1978 (all relating to the withdrawal of privilege against incrimination of self or spouse in certain proceedings);

(i) in the Supreme Court Act 1981, paragraph 1 of Schedule 1 (causes and matters assigned to Chancery Division);

(j) in the Civil Jurisdiction and Judgments Act 1982, paragraph 2 of Schedule 5 (proceedings excluded from Schedule 4 to that Act) and paragraphs 2(14) and 4(2) of Schedule 8 (rules as to jurisdiction in Scotland);

(*k*) in the Companies Act 1985—
    (i) subsection (1)(*j*) of section 396 and subsection (4)(*c*) of section 410 (charges which have to be registered); and
    (ii) Part I of Schedule 4 and Part I of Schedule 9 (form and content of company accounts and special category accounts); and
(*l*) in the Companies Act (Northern Ireland) 1960, subsection (2)(*i*) of section 93, Part I of Schedule 6 and Part I of Schedule 6A (corresponding provisions for Northern Ireland).

PART II

REFERENCES TO 1938 ACT TO INCLUDE REFERENCES TO ACT AS EXTENDED

2.—(1) Any reference to the Trade Marks Act 1938 in a provision to which this paragraph applies shall include a reference to that Act as it has effect by virtue of section 1 of the Trade Marks (Amendment) Act 1984.

(2) The provisions to which this paragraph applies are—
    (*a*) in the Patents and Designs Act 1907, subsection (1) of section 62 (Patent Office) and subsection (2) of section 63 (officers and clerks);
    (*b*) in the Patents, Designs, Copyright and Trade Marks (Emergency) Act 1939, subsection (1)(*c*) of section 4 (effect of war on registration), subsection (1) of section 6 (power to extend time limits), subsection (1) of section 7 (evidence) and subsection (1) of section 10 (interpretation); and
    (*c*) the entry relating to a person appointed to hear and decide appeals under the Trade Marks Act 1938 in Part III of Schedule 1 to the House of Commons Disqualification Act 1975 (other disqualifying offices).

PART III

OTHER AMENDMENTS

Trade Marks Act 1938 (c.22)

3. In subsection (1) of section 19 of the Trade Marks Act 1938 (registration) after the word "registered", in the second place where it occurs, there shall be inserted the words ", subject to section 39A(2) below,".

4. In the proviso to subsection (1) of section 26 of that Act (removal from register and imposition of limitations on ground of non-use) for the words after "bona fide use" there shall be substituted the words "of the mark by the proprietor thereof for the time being in relation to—
(ii) goods of the same description; or
(ii) services associated with those goods or goods of that description,
being goods or, as the case may be, services in respect of which the mark is registered.".

5. The following section shall be inserted after section 39 of that Act—

"Registration of trade mark following overseas application

39A.—(1) Any person who has applied for protection for any trade mark in a relevant country or his legal representative or assignee shall be entitled on an application for registration made within six months of the application for protection in the relevant country to registration of his mark under this Act in priority to other applicants.

2. A mark registered on an application made under this section shall be registered as of the date of the application in the relevant country and that date shall be deemed for the purposes of this Act to be the date of registration.

(3) Nothing in this section shall entitle the proprietor of the mark to recover damages for infringements happening prior to the date of the application for registration under this Act.

(4) The registration of a mark under this section shall not be invalidated by reason only of the use of the mark in the United Kingdom during the period of 6 months within which the application may be made.

(5) The application for the registration of a mark under this section must be made in the same manner as an ordinary application under this Act.

(6) Where a person has applied for protection for any mark by an application which—
    (*a*) in accordance with the terms of a treaty subsisting between any two or more relevant countries, is equivalent to an application duly made in any one of those countries; or

39–8

(b) in accordance with the law of any relevant country, is equivalent to an application duly made in that country,

he shall be deemed for the purposes of this section to have applied in that country.

(7) Subject to subsection (8) below, Her Majesty may by Order in Council direct that this section shall apply to a country specified in the Order.

(8) If a country is not a dependent territory, an Order in Council under this section may only be made in relation to it with a view to the fulfilment of a treaty, convention, arrangement or engagement.

(9) An Order in Council under this section shall be subject to annulment in pursuance of a resolution of either House of Parliament and may be varied or revoked by a subsequent Order.

(10) In this section—

"country" includes any territory;

"dependent territory" means any of the Channel Islands or a colony;

"relevant country" means a country which was specified in an Order in Council under this section at the time of the application under this section or such other time as may be specified in the Order in Council.".

6. In section 61 of that Act (restraint of use of Royal Arms etc.) for the words "or supplies goods to" there shall be substituted the words "supplies goods to or provides services for".

Patents, Designs, Copyright and Trade Marks (Emergency) Act 1939 (c.107)

7. The Patents, Designs, Copyright and Trade Marks (Emergency) Act 1939 shall have effect with respect to service marks as it has effect with respect to trade marks, except that in the application of that Act to service marks it shall have effect as if the following section were substituted for section 3 (power of comptroller to suspend trade mark rights of an enemy or an enemy subject)—

"Power of comptroller to suspend service mark rights of an enemy or an enemy subject
    3.—(1) Where it is made to appear to the comptroller that it is difficult or impracticable to describe or refer to some activity without the use of a service mark registered in respect of that activity, being a service mark which is registered in the name of an enemy or an enemy subject, whether alone or jointly with another, or which is, or has at any such time as aforesaid been, in the proprietorship of an enemy or an enemy subject, whether alone or jointly with another, the following provisions of this section shall have effect.

    (2) On the application of any person who proposes to provide in the course of business in the United Kingdom or the Isle of Man services including an activity which is or is intended to be the same as or equivalent to or a substitute for the activity in respect of which the service mark is registered, the comptroller may order that the right to the use of the service mark given by the registration thereof shall be suspended—

    (a) so far as regards use thereof by the applicant and any such use thereof by any other person in relation to services connected in the course of business with the applicant as would not be an infringement of the said right if the applicant were the proprietor of the service mark,

    (b) to such extent and for such period as the comptroller may consider necessary for enabling the applicant to render well-known and established some description of, or means of reference to, the activity which he proposes to carry on in the course of business, being a description or means of reference which does not involve the use of the service mark.

    (3) Where an order has been made under the last foregoing subsection, no action for passing of the shall lie on the part of any person interested in the service mark in respect of any use thereof which, by virtue of the order, is not an infringement of the right to the use thereof given by the registration thereof.

    (4) An order under this section may be varied or revoked by a subsequent order made by the comptroller.".

Restrictive Trade Practices Act 1976 (c.34)

8. In paragraph 4(2) of Schedule 3 to the Restrictive Trade Practices Act 1976 (excepted agreements—trade marks)—

    (a) in paragraph (a) after "certification trade mark)" there shall be inserted "or of a service mark"; and

(*b*) in paragraph (*b*)—
    (i) after "6(1)" there shall be inserted "or 11(2)";
    (ii) after "7(1)" there shall be inserted "or 12(2)";
    (iii) after "is to be applied" there shall be inserted "or
        (iii) the kinds of services in relation to which the mark is to be used which are to be made available or supplied; or
        (iv) the form or manner in which services in relation to which the mark is used are to be made available or supplied; or
        (v) the descriptions of goods which are to be produced or supplied in connection with the supply of services in relation to which the mark is to be used; or
        (vi) the process of manufacture to be applied to goods which are to be produced or supplied in connection with the supply of services in relation to which the mark is to be used.".

Trade Marks (Amendment) Act 1984 (c.19)

9. The following subsection shall be inserted after section 2(3) of the Trade Marks (Amendment) Act 1984 (extent)—
"(4) This Act shall extend to the Isle of Man subject to any exceptions, adaptations or modifications contained in an Order made by Her Majesty in Council.".

10. In paragraph 14(2)(*b*) of Schedule 1 to that Act (modifications of Trade Marks Act 1938 in application to service marks) for the words from "the words", in the first place where that phrase occurs, to "in relation to" there shall be substituted the words "paragraphs (i) and (ii) and the words following them there shall be substituted—" ".

11. After paragraph 18 of that Schedule there shall be inserted—

"Section 38

18A. Section 38 and Schedule 2 (Sheffield marks) shall be omitted.

Section 39

18B. Section 39 (trade marks for textile goods) shall be omitted.

Section 39A

18C. In section 39A (registration of trade marks following overseas application)—
(*a*) in subsection (2), for the word "A" there shall be substituted the words "Subject to subsection (2A) below, a";
(*b*) the following subsection shall be inserted after that subsection—
    "(2A) Where an application for protection for a service mark was made in a relevant country before the date on which the Trade Marks (Amendment) Act 1984 came into force, a service mark registered on an application under this section shall be registered as of that date.";
(*c*) the following subsection shall be substituted for subsection (8)—
    "(8) If a country is not a dependent territory, an Order in Council under this section may only be made in relation to it—
        (*a*) with a view to the fulfilment of a treaty, convention, arrangement or engagement; or
        (*b*) if Her Majesty is satisfied that provision has been or will be made under the laws of that country whereby priority for the protection of service marks in respect of which application for registration under this Act has been made will be given on a basis comparable to that for which provision is made by this section in relation to applications for registration made in a relevant country.".".

12. In paragraph 25(3) of Schedule 1 to that Act (modification of Trade Marks Act 1938 in application to service marks) after the last word "services" there shall be inserted the words "or otherwise in relation to services".

Section 3   SCHEDULE 3

Repeals

Part I

Repeals Consequential on Section 1 and Schedule 1

Chapter	Short Title	Extent of repeal
1 & 2 Geo. 6, c.22.	Trade Marks Act 1938.	Sections 57 and 58.
12, 13 & 14 Geo. 6, c.88.	Registered Designs Act 1949.	Section 24.
1977 c. 37.	Patents Act 1977.	Section 35.

Part II

Repeals Consequential on Section 2 and Schedule 2

Chapter	Short Title	Extent of repeal
7 Edw. 7, c.29.	Patents and Designs Act 1907.	Sections 88, 91, and 91A.
4 & 5 Geo. 5, c.18.	Patents and Designs Act 1914.	The whole Act.
18 & 19 Geo. 5, c.3.	Patents and Designs (Convention) Act 1928.	The whole Act.
1 & 2 Geo. 6, c.22.	Trade Marks Act 1938.	In section 19(1), the proviso.
1 & 2 Geo. 6, c.29.	Patents &c. (International Conventions) Act 1938.	The whole Act.
12, 13 & 14 Geo. 6, c.62.	Patents and Designs Act 1949.	The whole Act.
1984 c.19.	Trade Marks (Amendment) Act 1984.	Section 1(3). In section 2(3), the words "and the Isle of Man". In Schedule 1, paragraphs 1 and 21. In Schedule 2, paragraph 5 and the heading preceding it.

EDUCATION ACT 1986

(1986 c. 40)

An Act to provide for the making of grants by the Secretary of State to the Fellowship of Engineering and the Further Education Unit and to make further provision in relation to the arrangements under Part VI of the Local Government, Planning and Land Act 1980 for the pooling of expenditure by local authorities on education and for connected purposes. [18th July 1986]

PARLIAMENTARY DEBATES
Hansard: H.C. Vol. 97, col. 277; H.C. Vol. 99, col. 870; H.C. Vol. 101, col. 136; H.L. Vol. 478, cols. 270, 1076.
The Bill was considered by Standing Committee F on June 26, 1986.

Grants

Payment of grant

1.—(1) The Secretary of State may out of money provided by Parliament make grants to—

(*a*) the body corporate constituted by Royal Charter and known at the passing of this Act as the Fellowship of Engineering; and

(*b*) the company formed and registered under the Companies Act 1948 and known at the passing of this Act as the Further Education Unit;

in respect of expenditure incurred or to be incurred by either of them for the purpose of any of its activities.

(2) In making a grant under this section the Secretary of State may impose conditions for any purpose mentioned in subsection (3) below and may also impose such other conditions as he thinks fit.

(3) Those purposes are—

(*a*) requiring the repayment of the grant in whole or part if any other condition is not complied with;

(*b*) where the grant is made in respect of capital expenditure, requiring the payment to the Secretary of State on the sale of, or of any part of, a grant-aided asset of such sums related to the value of the asset at the time of the sale as he may by notice in writing specify to the recipient of the grant as being in his opinion reasonable having regard to the extent to which the asset has been acquired, provided or improved as a result of the grant; and

(c) requiring the payment of interest in respect of any period during which a sum due to the Secretary of State in accordance with any other condition remains unpaid.

(4) A condition imposed under subsection (3)(*b*) above may require a payment to be made even if the grant has been repaid at the time of the sale; and in that subsection "grant-aided asset", in relation to a grant, means an asset acquired, provided or improved as a result of the expenditure in respect of which the grant is made.

Further provision in relation to the arrangements under Part VI of the Local Government, Planning and Land Act 1980 for pooling expenditure by local authorities on education, etc.

Recovery of negative pooling adjustments

2.—(1) In this section, "shortfall year", in relation to an authority, means any year in which the amount of block grant payable to the authority for that year is less than the amount, or aggregate amount, by which the block grant so payable to them falls to be decreased in accordance with the pooling provisions; and the difference between the amount of block grant so payable to them and the amount of the decrease required is referred to as the authority's pooling deficit for that year.

(2) Where, in consequence of any estimate or calculation made by him for the purposes of the pooling provisions or section 66 of the Local Government, Planning and Land Act 1980 (estimates and calculations of the amount of block grant payable to an authority for any year), it appears to the Secretary of State that any year is, or is likely to be, a shortfall year in relation to an authority, he shall calculate their pooling deficit for that year on the basis of the best information then available to him and notify the authority in writing accordingly.

(3) Where, in consequence of any estimate or calculation made by him for the purposes of those provisions or that section, it appears to the Secretary of State that any calculation he has made for the purposes of this section is no longer accurate, he shall recalculate the pooling deficit of the authority concerned on the basis of the best information then available to him and notify them in writing accordingly or, if it appears to him, on the basis of that information, that the year in question is not, or is not now likely to be, a shortfall year in relation to that authority, he shall give them written notice of that fact.

(4) Where any authority are notified under this section that a year is a shortfall year in relation to them, they shall be liable to pay to the Secretary of State an amount equal to their pooling deficit for that year as so notified to them from time to time.

(5) The Secretary of State may, for the purpose of recovering any amount due to him from an authority under this section—

(a) require them to pay the whole or any part of the amount to him at such time or times as he thinks fit; and

(b) at such time or times as he thinks fit deduct the whole or any part of the amount from—

(i) the domestic rate relief grant payable to them for the year to which the liability relates or any subsequent year; or

(ii) the block grant payable to them for any subsequent year.

(6) Where it appears to the Secretary of State from any recalculation under this section that the year in question is not, or is not now likely to be, a shortfall year in relation to the authority concerned, he shall repay to them any sums already recovered in respect of their pooling deficit for that year.

(7) Where it appears to the Secretary of State from any such recalculation that an authority's pooling deficit is, or is likely to be, less than the amount which he has previously notified to them as their deficit for the year in question, he shall repay to the authority the amount, if any, by which the sums recovered in respect of their pooling deficit for that year exceed his latest calculation of that deficit and may also repay to them such other sums so recovered as he thinks expedient.

(8) Any calculation made for the purpose of determining whether any year is a shortfall year in relation to an authority shall take account of any adjustment which falls to be made under section 62 (adjustment of block grant for the purpose of balancing payments with the amount available for grant in any year) or 63A (adjustment of block grant for rates equalisation contribution) of the Act of 1980.

Payment of positive pooling adjustments

3.—(1) The Secretary of State may, for the purpose of ensuring that the operation of the pooling provisions does not increase the total amount paid in respect of block grant for any year, direct in relation to any authority whose block grant for that year falls to be increased in accordance with those provisions that they shall cease to be entitled either to the whole or such part of that increase as he may direct but shall instead be entitled to a payment under this section ("a substitution payment") equal in amount to the block grant to which they cease to be entitled in pursuance of the direction.

(2) Any direction under this section may be revoked or modified by a later direction.

(3) Where the Secretary of State gives a direction under this section, he may direct that any sum already paid to the authority in respect of—

(*a*) block grant for the year to which the direction relates; or

(*b*) a substitution payment for that year;

including, in either case, any sum treated by virtue of a direction under this section as so paid, shall be treated as paid to them in respect of the substitution payment to which they are entitled in pursuance of the direction or, as the case may be, in respect of block grant for that year.

(4) The Secretary of State shall be liable to pay any amount due to an authority in respect of a substitution payment and shall have, in relation to the payment of any such amount, the same powers as he has in relation to the payment of block grant.

(5) Where the block grant payable to an authority for any year falls to be increased in accordance with the pooling provisions those provisions shall be read as requiring the amount of that increase to be paid to the authority irrespective of whether any block grant is otherwise payable to them for that year.

Application of sections 2 and 3 and supplementary provisions

4.—(1) Sections 2 and 3 of this Act shall have effect only in relation to the year commencing on, and any year commencing after, 1st April 1986.

(2) In those sections—

(*a*) "the pooling provisions" means section 63 of, and Schedule 10 to, the Local Government, Planning and Land Act 1980 and any regulations for the time being in force under that Schedule (provisions relating to the adjustment of block grants in connection with the arrangements for pooling education expenditure of local authorities); and

(*b*) "year" means a year for block grant purposes.

General

Expenses

5. There shall be paid out of money provided by Parliament any expenses incurred by the Secretary of State under this Act and any increase attributable to this Act in the sums payable out of moneys so provided under any other Act.

Short title, commencement and extent

6.—(1) This Act may be cited as the Education Act 1986.

(2) Section 1 of this Act shall come into force at the end of the period of two months beginning with the date on which this Act is passed.

(3) This Act extends to England and Wales only.